Psychology of Pain

Dedication

**In memory of
Bernard Skevington (1907–1988)**

Psychology of Pain

SUZANNE M. SKEVINGTON

University of Bath and
Royal National Hospital for Rheumatic Diseases,
Bath, UK

JOHN WILEY & SONS

Chichester · New York · Brisbane · Toronto · Singapore

Other Wiley Editorial Offices

John Wiley & Sons, Inc., 605 Third Avenue,
New York, NY 10158-0012, USA

Jacaranda Wiley Ltd, 33 Park Road, Milton,
Queensland 4064, Australia

John Wiley & Sons (Canada) Ltd, 22 Worcester Road,
Rexdale, Ontario M9W 1L1, Canada

John Wiley & Sons (SEA) Pte Ltd, 37 Jalan Pemimpin #05-04,
Block B, Union Industrial Building, Singapore 2057

British Library Cataloguing in Publication Data

A catalogue record for this book is available from the British Library

ISBN 0–471–95771–2 (cased)
ISBN 0–471–95773–9 (paper)

Typeset from the author's disks in 10/12 pt Plantin by Pure Tech India Ltd, Pondicherry
Printed and bound in Great Britain by Bookcraft (Bath) Ltd
This book is printed on acid-free paper responsibly manufactured from sustainable forestation,
for which at least two trees are planted for each one used for paper production.

Contents

About the Author

Suzanne Skevington

School of Social Sciences, University of Bath,
Claverton Down, Bath BA2 7AY, UK.

Suzanne Skevington is Senior Lecturer in Psychology at the University of Bath and Honorary Senior Research Fellow at the Royal National Hospital for Rheumatic Diseases, Bath. She has published widely in research journals dealing with social and clinical psychology, psychosomatic medicine, pain and health care, as well as articles which reflect her interest in women's studies. She is the editor of *Understanding Nurses* (John Wiley & Sons, 1984) and has co-authored and contributed to several other books in the area of health psychology. In 1995, she was awarded a Fulbright Scholarship to research and lecture on pain and quality of life in the United States. She is a consultant to the Division of Mental Health at the World Health Organisation in Geneva. She is currently a member of two task forces set up by the International Association for the Study of Pain, to examine pain in the psychology curriculum, and review pain specific to women.

Preface

The first two chapters of this book provide the groundwork for studying pain in a social context. Chapter 1 provides the starting point by reviewing the biological basis of pain. Many books have been written on this subject, and extensive discussion is limited by space. This chapter is intended as an introduction for those who are not familiar with this material and seek a brief overview. Regrettably little is known about how pain signals are processed by the brain as cognitions, emotions and motivations, how they are transmitted in the descending pathways and how they are then translated into action. A variety of methods used to measure pain are evaluated in Chapter 2; those designed to record subjective reports are of particular interest here. The chapter closes with a discussion of how pain language may be assessed.

Chapter 3 starts by examining research on different social groups with a discussion about who has pain and who reports it. Social learning theory, behavioural medicine and recent cognitive applications are examined closely with reference to the assumption that different social groups learn to report pain in different ways. Progress in this field is evaluated and its shortcomings outlined in favour of a more explicitly social approach to the study of pain. Chapter 4 begins to elaborate the research that portrays a social view of the pain sufferer. Here we take a look at the images, commonsense theories and beliefs that people hold about pain and illness and the comparisons they make with others. How pain sufferers explain the origins of their pain and the extent to which they take responsibility for it expands the discussion of beliefs and expectations in Chapter 5. The extent to which they believe they can control pain has implications for the generation of depressogenic thoughts and memories, and this is discussed here.

Chapter 6 outlines the social psychological processes that affect decision making about whether and when to seek relief from pain. As these areas of research have been largely neglected in the study of pain, material from health psychology is applied to look at what advice is available, to understand more about health risks and hazards and to consider conflicts in decision making and rules of thumb that aid decisions. This cognitive material is set against the powerful role of moods and emotions in distress and suffering, outlined in Chapter 7. Here, communicating symptoms is examined as well as the interpersonal processes of the consultation. Helping and being helped are assessed, and the beliefs and behaviour of health professionals are scrutinised as an integral part of the social dynamics of treatment.

Coping with pain is the topic of Chapter 8, and a discussion of how health professionals cope with pain patients concludes this debate. The social features of treatment are addressed in Chapter 9, beginning with the subjects of caring and palliation. Adherence to treatment, placebo effects and alternative/complementary treatments are examined. Broader issues are addressed in the final chapter; these include the ethics of carrying out social investigations of pain, and the development of a policy for managing pain. Pain research is set within the wider context of improving the quality of life for those who suffer. Lastly, in conclusion, a model for a social psychology of pain is offered.

This book has been designed to integrate an expanding body of knowledge on the social psychological aspects of pain, and to generate ideas for future therapeutic departures. It is hoped that it may expand the horizons of thinking for those jaded by psychiatric and behaviourist approaches. The aim is to focus on those processes involved in the social evolution of the chronic pain patient. In debating the viability of these ideas, there is some critique of theories and methods. This book was written with researchers and clinicians in mind. It should be a resource for medical students and other health professionals, primarily nurses, physiotherapists and pharmacists, in the current drive to put more pain into the curriculum (Pilowsky, 1988). It should be useful in postgraduate health psychology and clinical psychology courses, advanced undergraduate options on psychology degrees, and for medical sociology and other social and science courses with a health element.

Acknowledgements

There are many people I need to thank for their contributions to my knowledge, interest and analysis of pain. From my earliest years in psychology I owe a debt of gratitude to my teachers. Many persisting interests go back to the formative years I spent as a postgraduate with the MRC Social Epidemiology and Psychiatry Unit in Penarth and in the Department of Psychology at University College Cardiff, where thoughts on epidemiology, reporting behaviour, stress and anxiety were guided, nurtured and shaped by Jack Ingham, Jim Robinson, Mike Wood and Kenneth Rawnsley.

Without Henri Tajfel's indelible influence, I would have been unable to contemplate developing a social analysis of pain. Henri's enthusiasm for social psychology in general, for intergroup relations in particular, and for life stay with me. It was he who taught me the value of interdisciplinary thinking in the post-doctoral years when I worked with him in Bristol.

I would especially like to thank Kenneth Craig at the University of British Columbia, who gave me space and peace for three months in the early 1980s to write and think about pain. It was from that time that the embryonic ideas for this book emerged.

I am deeply indebted to Norman Sartorius for continuing to inspire me to think globally about illness and suffering. Without him, my own quality of life would have been much poorer.

My gratitude extends to the many colleagues, friends, postgraduates and students at the University of Bath and elsewhere who have discussed pain and illness with me over the years. Special thanks go to Chris Eccleston for discussion of Chapters 2 and 9 and for encouragement, and also to Jim Robinson for reading Chapter 3 and many other writings with such care, skill and diplomacy. Thanks to Rod Brunt for valuable comments on acupuncture practice and for his ability to make me laugh aloud at my own writing style. I am grateful to Marina Crassa for drawing my attention to the work of Politis on the Greek oral folk tradition (in Chapter 5). Thanks also to Caroline Selai for the quotation in Chapter 10 and to the Mizen family for the Zulu words for pain, referred to in Chapter 2. Without the warm-hearted and unstinting secretarial help from Joanne Schol and Debbie Lewis this book would not have been completed.

I extend my heartfelt thanks to the many clinical colleagues, too numerous to mention individually, who have provided patients for research over the years and have stimulated me to develop my thinking on pain, illness and disability. Peter Maddison, Jane Hall, Kate Chapman, Joan Davis, Andrei Calin, Tony Clarke and others at the Royal National Hospital for Rheumatic Diseases, Bath, deserve special mention for their part at different times in facilitating, encouraging, exciting and challenging. Thanks are also due to Rod MacLeod for his support; without him I would not have discovered palliative care. I am grateful to Les Shutt at Bristol Royal Infirmary for activating an early interest in peri-operative pain and for reading Chapter 1. I wish to pay a tribute to the immaculate clinical care that I have personally received from Ruth Gillies and Jeff Watkins in recent years. Unknowingly, they provided validity checks on many passing thoughts.

I am indebted to Wendy Hudlass at John Wiley & Sons for her understanding, personal support and kindness over the years and to Michael Coombs, who started it all. I must also thank the referees for their encouraging and constructive comments on the outline and chapters at different stages of the writing process.

This book is affectionately dedicated to my family and friends, who have given me personal insights into pain and suffering. I owe an incalculable debt to my long-suffering partner and collaborator, Nick Britton, for his support, encouragement and faith in the project when my own faltered; in particular, for all those cups of coffee and hours of child care. I look forward to many more happy years rubbing his bad back to activate the A-deltas, while mathematically modelling the gate control theory. The book was begun at about the time Rachel was conceived, and it has been a long gestation. My hope is that she will never know what chronic pain is, and that, in some small way, this book will contribute to the quality of life and care of her generation. Very special thanks go to Sarah Tate for her unstinting support from the beginning to the end.

Introduction

Pain is a more terrible lord of mankind than even death himself.
(Albert Schweitzer)

Since the publication of Melzack and Wall's (1965) gate control theory of pain, psychology has been accepted as an integral discipline in the study of pain. Although pain research incorporates many disciplines, from the philosophical, ethical, socio-logical and epidemiological aspects of the subject through the spectrum to the "harder" sciences of neurophysiology, anatomy, pharmacology and economics, this book will focus on the many and varied social and psychological influences that affect and are affected by the experience and reporting of pain. It attempts to draw together what is currently known about the social aspects of pain and pain behaviour, and to examine some of the mechanisms that help to explain the ways in which people behave when they are ill. This assessment of the social factors affecting pain sufferers has been carried out within the general framework of the study of illness where pain and illness go hand in hand. The book is orientated around the psychosocial processes and influences that take place in the process of becoming a chronic pain patient, beginning with detecting and interpreting symptoms, and moving on to decisions about whether to consult and when. The consultation itself, the actions and medications prescribed and how they are administered and managed affect the ways in which those with chronic disease approach their treatment, influence pain relief and hold prospects for the longer term.

A considerable proportion of research carried out on the psychological aspects of pain is highly patient-centred. While this work has been valuable, until recently there has been an empirical reluctance to acknowledge that pain and its communication are influenced by a plethora of social encounters and social influences across the life-span. The experience and reporting of pain is a two-way street. Advice about signs and symptoms may be sought from family, friends, workmates and acquaintances well before a sufferer decides to seek formal help. A diverse range of formal and informal sources may be consulted and at different stages of the illness in the search for a remedy that will bring relief from pain (Greenley and Mechanic, 1976). Symptoms and treatments may be compared with those of other people encountered in a variety of social situations; waiting rooms, sitting rooms and bus queues provide the environments for rich qualitative data, yet scant attention has been paid in the literature to these social conditions and how they influence the perception and reporting of painful symptoms. An aim of this volume is to appraise and evaluate knowledge about the social aspects of pain, and indicate where research on the social processes of illness might fruitfully be developed.

AN ALTERNATIVE TO CURRENT PSYCHOLOGICAL MODELS

The "medical" model of disease is geared to identifying underlying pathology to obtain a diagnosis and then treating these symptoms by attacking that pathology, but the success of this model is questionable in treating the most prevalent chronic painful diseases. Fordyce (1976) has argued that this model is both inappropriate and ineffective when dealing with chronic painful diseases, despite its demonstrable historical success in treating many infectious disorders. Psychologists are developing theory and practice in ways that may provide real alternatives to the medical model. Two broad areas of contemporary research in psychology have tended to dominate thinking about pain until recently. The first is personality psychology, which has developed and used diagnostic tools for the assessment of stable personality features. This line of investigation has not directly challenged the assumptions of the medical model. A second line of pursuit was derived from behaviourism and from the social applications of behaviourist principles in the form of social learning theory. It has been applied clinically in the creation and elaboration of behavioural medicine. Both of these lines of research are addressed in further detail below. In view of these two approaches, it might reasonably be asked why pain research needs yet another psychological model. The thesis here is that neither of these areas has lived up to its promise, for different reasons. This provides the rationale for this volume. It may be time for a paradigm shift.

The search for a pain personality has lasted for several decades. This approach is most closely aligned with the medical model, in that it is primarily concerned with labelling through diagnosis. An example is the long-term use of the Minnesota Multiphasic Personality Inventory (MMPI), which provides 566 true/false statements in 10 clinical scales plus several research scales. Scale values for each person are used to create a personality profile, which can then be compared against norms from larger populations to determine degrees of normality. Several profiles have been identified that are claimed to earmark particular types of pain patient. Elevations on certain scales are believed to be related to the degree and chronicity of disability in chronic low back pain, for instance (Love and Peck, 1987). Most noted in the pain literature is the Conversion-V profile, so named because of its shape on the profile form, denoting abnormally high levels on the hysteria and hypochondriasis scales (t-scores of above 70), with a valley for the depression scale (10 points) between these two. However, this is not a particularly reliable finding because it has been reported only in some studies and for women patients (see Wade et al, 1992). Other relevant profiles are for the *typical neurotic*, who scores highly on all of the above three scales, and for the *emotionally overwhelmed*, who has high scores on the same scales as the typical neurotic, but in addition expresses intense anxiety and shows elevations on at least three other scales (Wade et al, 1992). But describing the personality profile of a chronic back pain patient gives little insight into how or why they became that way. Studies showing that $x\%$ of patients with chronic pain also show psychiatric illness purport to demonstrate that there is a problem, and the size of it (e.g. Chaturvedi, 1987; Tyrer et al, 1989). However, they provide little information about how best to develop suitable treatments. For chronic back pain at least, the medical model has failed to live up to its promise either to differentiate between patients or reliably to predict response to specific treatments (Love and Peck, 1987). For low back pain patients – the clinician's *bête noire* – Main (1984) reports that level of disability, current stress and inappropriate illness behaviour are much more important predictors than long-standing personality traits or pain ratings.

However, it has recently become clear that far fewer chronic pain patients fit these psychopathological categories than was originally anticipated. Because the MMPI was designed in the late 1940s, some of the original questions use dated language, while judgements about what is normal have changed in the intervening years. New, contemporary, norms were published in 1984. In one study where MMPI profiles of fibromyalgia and rheumatoid arthritis patients were re-evaluated using these contemporary norms, a sizable proportion of those patients originally labelled as psychologically disturbed, about half changed category, almost all of them in the direction of greater normality (Ahles et al, 1986). Such results demonstrate that, as a result of using this labelling approach, patients have not only been inaccurately labelled — with the accompanying stigmatisation that psychiatric illness brings — but, furthermore, have probably been treated inappropriately because of the label. Continuing with the arthritis example, it is now evident that many of the MMPI items that produced Conversion-V elevations for those with rheumatoid arthritis are also features of the physical disease, and therefore artificially inflate these estimates of unjustified pathology (Pincus et al, 1986).

The reliability of this approach is questionable because it depends on the use of ever-changing social norms about how people behave within their social group and culture, at this time in history and with this ideology. In view of these continually shifting variables, such norms must be monitored constantly to be correct. Without such timely monitoring, judgements made in relation to them must be faulty to some greater or lesser degree. Furthermore, these judgements are inevitably laden with the values of those who designed the scale, reflecting possibly as much about the designers' history, culture, social group and ideology as those of their patients. Experience changes people, and their psychological make-up is constantly under revision. This, therefore, brings into question the assumed nature of the stable personality trait (see Krahé 1992 for an expansion of this debate).

Secondly, many chronic pain patients do not have any psychopathological features. In a recent study of 59 chronic pain patients, Wade et al (1992) found that 44% had profiles within a normal range. They found it difficult to resist the personologist's temptation to label these normal chronic pain patients as denier/copers — that is, people who deny uncomfortable emotions and maintain control over unacceptable impulses. While it is clearly useful to be able to identify with confidence those who need to be offered psychiatric help, for a sizable minority without these disorders, it is questionable whether they should be systematically treated as potential psychiatric "cases", with the stigma that such labels carry. Furthermore, the persistent, widespread and long-term use of personality tests may have been detrimental to the general acceptance of psychological assessment by patients in the pain clinic. In addition, this approach has side-tracked research from more productive lines of investigation. The search for the elusive but irresistible concept of a "rheumatoid personality" provides a suitable example here. This concept attracted more than

90% of all research into the psychological aspects of rheumatoid arthritis until the early 1980s (Achterberg-Lawlis, 1982), despite repeated questioning of its scientific credibility. There is little consistent evidence that chronic pain patients are any more disturbed than other patients with a chronic limiting illness (Gardiner, 1980; Naliboff, Cohen and Yellen, 1982). In another area, undue attention has been paid to investigating the purported deleterious effects of "compensation neurosis", so hampering progress in studying chronic pain. Investigation of the roles of activity and employment in the treatment and rehabilitation of patients would have been more enlightening here (Dworkin et al, 1985).

Unlike studies of personality, behavioural medicine is process-orientated, and looks not at people and their histories, but at the environment in which they live and at how experience and learning have shaped their behaviour as pain sufferers. Fordyce's model (1976) focuses on the treatment of the behaviour of chronic pain patients rather than the relief of pain *per se*. It does this by dealing with the learning that generates and maintains these behaviours (see Chapter 3). While behavioural medicine has adopted a more cognitive style during the past decade in the development of cognitive behaviour therapies, investigations of pain cognitions have largely been restricted to the thoughts of single patients conceptualised in methodologies arising from a style of individual psychology that views people as isolates, rather than as members of social and cultural groups subject to social pressures. It places pain patients under the psychologist's microscope by artificially dissociating them from others around them and minimising the key environmental or contextual factors that are vital to the interpretation of pain behaviour. This contrasts with methodologies currently in use in social psychology, which have so far been under-utilised in the study of pain. These methods were designed to observe and record the many ways in which people are affected by others with whom they come into contact and the multiplicity of social influences that surround them. It attempts to situate people as social beings within their history, culture and ideology. Consequently, the social approach elaborated in this book shares more with the environmentalist view of pain put forward by those working in behavioural medicine than with the more individualistic stance adopted by personologists.

Behavioural medicine is more concerned with finding "objective" measures of observable behaviour than with the broader meanings of pain and illness for those who suffer. The approach presented here explores the interaction between pain sufferers and their social environment. It departs substantially from the limited neo-behaviourist reinforcement view that a patient's behaviour "elicit[s] responses from significant others" (Turk and Rudy, 1986), by incorporating a variety of other known social processes in addition to learning principles. The social learning theory approach to pain is limited in its ability to integrate information about the broader social, cultural and contextual issues that affect the ways in which pain patients behave. Social learning is just one small aspect of the wider range of social thoughts, emotions and motivations to be found in the clinic, and pain researchers have barely begun to assess the broader social milieu in which pain sufferers live.

Much of this contextual information has been devalued, and this attitude may have impeded progress in research. For instance Turk, Meichenbaum and Genest (1983) devoted less than a page to methods of assessing cognitions such as participants' attitudes and their self-confidence, concluding that the methodology for doing this is "difficult". They hinted that self-report diaries, videoed reconstruction and imagery recall about thoughts and feelings might be used in evaluation, and noted that these thoughts and feelings are "filled with treatment implications" (p.104). Much of the research in their otherwise excellent book concerns itself with conventional methods of "objective" evaluation favoured by those working in behavioural medicine. There was an overwhelming preference for physiological indices, supplemented by those one-dimensional subjective variables that could be adapted for use with a 10 cm line. However, by applying the methods of cognitive psychology, pain publications in the late 1980s began to take the measurement of context and meaning much more seriously, and this volume attempts to draw this material together.

The approach presented here is more than just a socio-cognitive model of pain, where the pain sufferer is viewed largely as a "rational" person with some spontaneous errors and biases in thinking (Fiske and Taylor, 1984; Skevington, 1983a). Implicit in this notion of rationality is that social cognitions can somehow be divorced from emotions and motivation. This stance is unrealistic and inappropriate for any comprehensive psychological model of pain. Pain research has consistently identified affective components with evaluative and sensory ones (Melzack, 1975). Nevertheless, theory on social cognition provides a useful departure point from which to begin a social analysis of pain, because it views people as active seekers of information rather than passive recipients. This, of course, is as true for health carers and the families of those in pain as it is for the sufferers themselves. It postulates that the way in which people react to a stimulus, or to a piece of information, depends not solely on the qualities of that stimulus but also on the prior expectations and standards they hold. This enables them to compare new, incoming information with the old. Selected and simplified by the brain in becoming meaningful, this knowledge is ultimately used both as a guide to how people will later behave and in predicting how the world works (Eiser, 1980). While the socio-cognitive model has some application to the social processes seen in chronic pain patients (Skevington, 1983a) and provides a useful alternative model to the medical model, it still provides a restricted view of how people in pain behave, because the social bit of social cognition is only vestigial. Once physiological and anatomical tests are exhausted in the clinic, the language of pain and illness remains one of the major means whereby health carers can elicit information about their clients. Thus, communication must provide vital clues not only to physical and mental well-being but also to attitudes, beliefs, expectations and so on, which affect decision-making processes and behaviour. Language is the main tool whereby pain sufferers engage help from others in the attempt to gain relief from their condition. In looking at this use of language, Sternbach (1978) describes chronic pain patients as "petitioners for aid". It is arguable that if we knew more about the styles of communication used by people in engaging help and how these communications are then interpreted by health carers, this would improve the management of chronic painful illness.

The emphasis of this book pays more attention to the social concepts of illness and sickness and is less concerned with the biological notion of disease. The approach elaborated here is in line with Kleinman's (1988) definition of illness as "the innately human experience of symptoms and suffering ... and how the sick person and the members of the family or wider social network perceive, live with and respond to symptoms and disability" (p.3). Kleinman says that illness has meaning. Illness experiences and events radiate or conceal more than one meaning, and powerful emotions attach to these meanings, as do powerful interests. On the other hand, sickness encompasses broad understandings about a disorder, which are affected by economic, political and institutional forces. Kleinman points out that while we talk about patients adopting a sick role, in fact they spend far more time in the roles of sick family member, sick worker, sick self and so on, than in the role of patient. In this way he invites pain researchers to investigate these different roles in the search for more comprehensive wisdom about who the pain patient truly is. An underlying assumption of this volume is that patients' descriptions of their pain should be acknowledged as a phenomenal truth (Copp, 1974). The writing of this book has been motivated by an awareness of the poverty of existing social approaches in explaining the symptom of pain.

The notion of gestalt is central to social psychology, and this must be so for any application to pain. The Gestaltists of the 1930s believed that the whole was more than just the sum of the parts. Recalling childhood memories of dot-to-dot pictures provides a simple example. On joining the dots together with a pencil, starting at number 1 and ending at 30, the maze of dots turns out to be a rider on horseback. The dots are still in the same places but suddenly their configuration becomes meaningful — it is more than just the sum of 30 dots. Similarly, if you went to Florence to look at Michelangelo's statue of David in the dark and had only a torch to inspect it, you would only be able to consider one feature at a time because of the statue's size. A Gestaltist would argue that, despite the incredible powers of the human brain to piece images together, seeing it in its glorious entirety in daylight would be more than the sum of these parts. This premise holds true, particularly in social situations. Take the example of six patients attending a new social support group who have never met each other before. If each was individually assessed using the most perfect psycho-metrically sound test that psychologists could hypothetically devise, and this information was then pooled, it would still be impossible to predict in advance how this group would behave when they met, purely by summating what is known about the individual participants. This is because there is a unique set of rules or laws about social behaviour that is quite different from those laws that govern the behaviour of individuals alone. A different set of behaviours govern social situations, which deserve separate investigation. It therefore follows that these qualities of interaction between group members — the group dynamics — are not amenable to measurement by those techniques designed to assess individuals, so special and different types of measures, and different theories too, are needed to evaluate the features of social situations. This is the material of social psychology. Similarly, when those with pain talk to others about their suffering; whether they are health professionals, friends, family or people in the bus queue, they share and generate thoughts, emotions and so on about pain and illness that could not be predicted from knowledge about them as individuals. For this reason, social psychology has an important role to play in the understanding and management of pain sufferers.

John Donne eloquently expressed these ideas around 400 years ago:

> No man is an *Island*, entire of itself; every man is a piece of the *Continent*, a part of the *main*; if a *clod* be washed away by the *sea*, *Europe* is the less, as well as if a *promontory* were, as well as if a *manor* of thy *friends* or of *thine own* were; any man's *death* diminishes *me*, because I am involved in *Mankind*; And therefore never send to know for whom the *bell* tolls; It tolls for *thee*.
> (*Devotions upon Emergent Occasions*. Meditation XVII)

Biological Mechanisms of Pain 1

The aim of this chapter is to examine the neurophysiological, anatomical and biochemical evidence for mechanisms that have been implicated in causing pain. This review of basic scientific research provides the groundwork for clinical investigation into the relief of pain, so it is necessary to explain those processes involved in the transmission of pain within the central nervous system (CNS). It is impossible in this limited space to do more than summarise some of the salient features of this very large field; these are presented in greater detail in other volumes. We begin with a definition of pain, then trace the processes of pain transmission from the peripheral nerves into the CNS at a spinal level and up the ascending pathways into the cortex. In the last section, the descending pathways are considered. These transmit information from the brain to the spinal cord, so completing a pain control feedback mechanism. Some of the most influential theories of pain are considered in this chapter, together with their psychological implications.

Pain has been defined as "An unpleasant sensation and emotional experience which is associated with actual or potential tissue damage or is described in terms of such damage" (Merskey et al, 1979). Merskey et al (1979) say that pain is *always* subjective, being an experience associated with actual or potential tissue damage. While pain is "unquestionably" a sensation, it is also always unpleasant and hence is an emotional experience. They make the point that experiences that resemble pain but are not unpleasant should *not* be labelled as pain. Similarly, unpleasant experiences without sensory qualities are not pain either. Subjectively there is no way to distinguish the pain reported by those without tissue damage from that reported by those who have that experience due to tissue damage. In both cases the experience is considered to be pain and is reported in the same way, so both types of report should be accepted as pain. Consequently, in accepting the contribution of a psychological state to pain, the above definition avoids tying pain to the stimulus.

THE PERIPHERAL NERVES

There are many types of nerves but only a few are directly concerned with nociception and the transmission of impulses associated with pain. These nerves transmit information from receptors in the skin, muscles, joints and the viscera. Some carry nociceptive impulses while others carry impulses that directly affect the perception of pain, but do not carry nociceptive information *per se*. Better insulated and larger myelinated nerves surrounded by a thick fatty sheath conduct impulses more quickly than those with less myelin. Three types of neuron seem to be involved in pain discrimination: (i) large, heavily myelinated A-beta fibres, (ii) more thinly myelinated A-delta fibres, and (iii) finer, unmyelinated C fibres. The conducting range of A-deltas is 2.5–35 m s^{-1} whereas that of C fibres is only 0.5–2 m s^{-1}. Stimulated A-beta fibres, which respond to light pressure, evoke pain-free sensations and tend to inhibit the response of spinal cord cells to noxious sensations when injury occurs, but when stimulation is increased so that it affects the adjacent A-delta fibres as well, facilitation overwhelms this inhibition and pain is more likely to be reported. The stimulation of A-betas contributes to the sensation of tenderness, which may be distant from the injury (Wall, 1983).

A-delta and C fibres are the principal transmitters of impulses experienced as pain although there may well be other categories of nociceptive fibres involved (Besson and Chaouch, 1987). Activated A-deltas and Cs tend to overlap in sensitivity and may respond to one type of stimulation or be polymodal, responding to varying degrees of pressure, heat, cold and chemicals. Each has a high or low threshold for any of these modalities. There are several types of fast conducting A-delta fibre and many of these are nociceptive. Damage to these fibres produces prolonged firing, facilitation in the spinal cord and intense pain as a result. Clinicians have documented the immediate sensation resulting from such damage as "first" or acute pain, to distinguish it from a "second" pain, which can supersede it and is largely transmitted by slower conducting C fibres (Bowsher, 1977). Volunteers spontaneously report only the first of these pains but can be trained to focus on the second (Bromm, 1989). C fibres are very numerous, constituting about 70% of all afferent nerves. They produce a "burning" pain on stimulation. When stimulated, two pain sensations are reported, with mean latencies of 420 and 1300 ms, corresponding with microneurographic recordings. (For a review of microneurography see Wall and McMahon, 1985.)

Wall (1983) has questioned Nature's purpose in providing the body with two types of nerve that appear to perform similar functions but at different speeds. It is sometimes not possible to say whether pain is produced by A-deltas, by C fibres, or by both, but the best studies show that it is usually produced by the A-deltas. If this is the case, then what do the C fibres do? (Wall, 1989). Less is known about the C fibres than about the A group because they have been more difficult to study (especially in the spinal cord), despite the discovery of the new enzyme marker horseradish peroxidase (HRP). When injected intracellularly, HRP is taken up by the terminals and transported retrogradely to the cell bodies. It has prompted a widespread re-evaluation of the CNS because it enables physiologists to locate reliably the cells of origin of distant axon terminations (Brown, 1981). C fibres differ from A-deltas because they perform three important functions in the inflammation process following injury. Firstly, the endings of stimulated C fibres in the periphery leak substances that produce vasodilation, neurogenic oedema and the sensitisation of nerve endings as an axon reflex. Secondly, when a volley from certain C fibres arrives in the spinal cord, this appears to cause the secondary tenderness linked to deep tissue damage. Thirdly, through the combined use of nerve impulses and chemical messages, C fibres inform the CNS about the metabolic state and nature of the tissues where they terminate. The body's need to monitor different aspects of tissue chemistry appears to explain why C fibres are so numerous and varied (Wall, 1989). The chemistry of different types of C fibres differs according to which target tissue they serve, and the fibres respond to change if that target tissue changes. Thus, if tissues are damaged or nerves severed, a new chemical message will be transmitted because the nerve fibres are now exposed to a new chemical environment (Wall, 1989). C fibres may contain one or more of a range of peptides and enzymes such as substance P, somatostatin, cholecystokinin and fluoride-resistant acid phosphatase. Some authors have described this as an "inflammatory soup" (Handwerker, 1991). These diverse C fibres are thought to be variously responsible for the three reactions occurring in injured skin — the vasodilatory flare, the neurogenic oedematous weal and increased sensitivity of nerve endings (Lynn, 1977) — as speed is not crucial in establishing an inflammatory response. Substance P produced in the bodies of slow conducting primary afferent fibres appears to be particularly important in neurogenic inflammation (Cuello and Mathews, 1983). Non-neuronal cells also have a role in inflammation, producing chemical mediators that act on nociceptive neurons. Some act directly on receptors, like 5-hydroxytryptamine and histamine, but others, such as bradykinin, act indirectly through receptors linked to a second messenger system that sensitises the neurons (Rang, Bevan and Dray, 1991). Because of this, bradykinin antagonists have recently been earmarked as potentially useful in peripheral action because they show promise in being able to reduce inflammation and oedema in wide-ranging conditions such as arthritis, burns, trauma, peritonitis, sore throat and asthma (Dray, 1991). Wall (1983) suggests that C fibres monitor the changes in the metabolic state of the tissues surrounding an injury and use transported chemicals to communicate them to the CNS, which accounts for plastic changes to the fibres and CNS following injury. Peripheral tissue injury and electrical stimulation of unmyelinated fibres may lead to hyperexcitability and neuronal plasticity in the dorsal horns of the spinal cord. The receptive fields of neurons in the superficial laminae and the neck of the dorsal horns expand under these conditions and this correlates with hyperalgesia, but so far the evidence is not strong enough to explain dorsal horn plasticity (Dubner, 1992).

While this review has concentrated on the processes in the periphery, it is important to note that articular, muscular and visceral afferent fibres also play a role in nociception, although this is currently less well understood because of unsatisfactory methods of stimulation. They connect with nociceptive specific and non-specific cells in the dorsal horns, indicating that both types are involved in referred pain (Besson and Chaouch, 1987). Diseases of the viscera tend to produce dull, achy and poorly localised pain at the outset, but eventually the pain is localised much more, and "referred" to those somatic structures with afferents entering the same spinal segments as afferents from the viscera. Thus, hyperalgesia in the same somatic structures may be associated with visceral pain (see Ness and Gebhart (1990) for a full account). These referred sensations are classified into parasthesias like tingle, itch or numbness, increases in pain intensity, changes in the perceived temperature of particular bodily areas and feelings of pressure or constriction (Katz and Melzack, 1987). As theory about pain strongly influences the ways in which pain is investigated and treated, the pain mechanisms that follow will be discussed with reference to the debates about these theories. Research on the central mechanisms is better understood in the context of these theories.

THEORIES ABOUT PAIN

Anatomical investigations of the skin led 19th century pain theorists to believe that there were special receptors for each type or modality of pain; that Meissner's corpuscles responded exclusively to touch, Pacinian corpuscles to pressure, Ruffini and Krause end-organs to heat and cold, respectively, and free nerve endings to pain. They believed that each receptor was attached to an afferent nerve, and impulses were then transmitted through the lateral spinothalamic tract to a "pain centre" in the brain. Melzack and Wall (1982, 1989) have shown that the assumptions of these specificity theories were oversimplified. Specificity theories assume " a rigid, fixed relationship between a neural structure and a psychological experience" (Melzack and Wall, 1982, p.99). However, there is evidence that free nerve endings and endings surrounding the hair follicles are capable of giving rise to all of the sensory qualities of the skin. While most of the fibres described contribute to the pain process when stimulated, they would need to produce pain and only pain to justify the label of "pain fibres", as claimed by specificity theorists, and physiologists have been largely unable to confirm this exclusivity (e.g. Van Hees and Gybels, 1972).

Pattern theories superseded specificity theory. Their supporters proposed that excessive stimulation of the skin receptors created particular patterns of nerve impulses that were summated in the dorsal horns of the spinal cord and caused pain. These theories have been criticised because they discounted findings that showed physiological specialisation (Wall and Melzack, 1983, p.209). While more complex types of specificity and pattern theories have surfaced for reconsideration in recent years (see Cervero and Iggo, 1980), none has usurped the gate control theory (GCT) as the major working theory about pain. The GCT of pain (Melzack and Wall, 1965) is a type of pattern theory, because it proposes that the balance of the input between large and small fibres is important in pain sensation. It also incorporates a mechanism within the spinal cord for low level decoding of this pattern. Crucially, it was also the first to acknowledge and integrate known psychological mechanisms that affect individual perceptions and interpretations of pain. The claims of specificity theorists remain unsupported by the abundant clinical, physiological and psychological evidence showing many and diverse instances where injury does not produce pain and where pain occurs in the absence of injury (Melzack and Wall, 1982). The relatively common incidence of such cases requires that any viable theory of pain must necessarily incorporate psychological mechanisms; previous theories had not done so. Some of this documented psychological evidence is reviewed below, before the GCT is explained in more detail.

An impressive series of naturalistic observations of casualties rescued from Anzio beach during World War II fuelled an early debate about the contribution of psychology to the experience and reporting of pain. Henry Beecher (1956) reported that of a sample of soldiers seriously wounded in battle, merely a quarter said that they needed an analgesic. It is noteworthy that these soldiers were not shocked, were fully cooperative and were mentally clear (Beecher, 1972). Far more pain was reported by soldiers who had sustained much smaller wounds, and Beecher persuasively explains these findings in social and environmental terms as follows: those with serious wounds saw their injuries in a positive light because they knew they would provide a "ticket to safety", while the slightly injured believed that they would be returned to action, so such injuries were seen to be a disaster. In a related investigation, Beecher (1956) found that the lesser wounds of civilian surgery were associated with more pain than the greater wounds of war, which were painless in some cases. Only 32% of the war wounded wanted narcotics, compared with 83% of civilian surgery patients. Hence, the intensity of the pain depended on the meaning or significance of the wounds. Those wounded in battle who had relatively little pain had escaped from overpowering anxiety and the fear of death, but for the civilians their injuries were a disaster, so indicating how "emotion can dominate the central nervous system" (Beecher, 1965) and block pain perceptions. Beecher's explanation for his findings is based on the social context of these wounds.

These and other studies suggest that there is no direct one-to-one relationship between the number of pain endings stimulated or the intensity of that stimulation and the pain experienced. This is a central assumption of both GCT and the definition provided at the beginning of this chapter. It is still not known why people report little or no pain after some injuries, but Beecher's results have been supported by more recent results from a casualty department where 138 accident patients were asked about their perceptions of pain (Melzack, Wall and Ty, 1982). A substantial 37% said they did not feel pain at the time of injury and these civilian figures are comparable with those of Beecher. Here, embarrassment was the most salient emotion and this negative mood contrasts with the positive emotions recorded by Beecher. While the majority reported that pain began within an hour of injury, in some cases delays of up to 9 hours occurred. (The sample consisted of people between the ages of 16 and 85, who could comprehend English. It excluded the dazed or confused, those on drugs or alcohol and those requiring immediate intervention.) These casualty patients were not in an overall state of analgesia resulting from systemic changes because they complained of minor discomforts from the hospital procedures and from other undamaged parts of the body. However, the results showed that 53% of those with injuries to the skin had a pain-free period compared to 28% of those with deep tissue injuries. This indicates that the type of wound may provide a partial explanation. The powerful results from these studies indicate the importance of the psychosocial context in which pain is experienced, and provides an important theme for this book.

While somewhat culture bound, an edited report from an English newspaper documents a further example:

> An injured motorist was making a good recovery in hospital yesterday after putting the health and safety of his dog conspicuously before his own when his car overturned shattering the windscreen. The disappearance of David M for 90 mins after the accident caused a police search at Guisborough, North Yorkshire. They were anxiously trying to reunite him with an item they found lying on the dashboard of his car. Mr M, still

bleeding more than slightly, had walked a mile to ask Mackinlay Hyde's garage to recover the car. He had taken off his tie and was using it as a lead for his spaniel which had fled from the crash. The garage receptionist asked him what he had been doing since the accident. "Looking for the dog," he explained. While handing him a coffee, the receptionist saw the left side of his face for the first time, and realised he was quite seriously injured. Without being specific about why, she said she would call an ambulance. "Don't worry, I'll go by taxi," said Mr M, but at her insistence and that of a colleague, he waited for the ambulance which took him to Middlesbrough general hospital where surgeons sewed back on the ear retrieved from the car, having kept it packed in ice ready for him.
(*Guardian*, 11th March 1993)

THE GATE CONTROL THEORY OF PAIN

The GCT is concerned with the balance between impulses from the large, fast conductors and those from the small, slow conducting afferents, and with the interpretation of these impulses at the spinal cord level and later during transmission to the brain (Melzack and Wall, 1965, 1982, 1989). It is proposed that activity in the large afferents may inhibit activity in the smaller fibres where both connect in the dorsal horns of the spinal cord. Impulses sent to the brain by postulated central transmission cells or T-cells situated in the dorsal horns of the spinal cord depend on the relative activity of these large and small fibres in the posterior roots of the spinal cord. A predominance of small fibre activity causes presynaptic facilitation, so substantially increasing T-cell activity, which constitutes an "opening of the gate", and the consequent perception of pain as the brain interprets these impulses. Through a preponderance of large fibre activity, the gate is "closed" and pain is not perceived.

Evidence for this gating effect was first published in a small-scale study by Wall and Sweet (1967). By electrically stimulating large fibres (sensory nerves supplying the painful area) for 2 min with a square wave 0.1 ms pulse at 100 cycles per second, they found that intense chronic cutaneous pain was relieved for half an hour in four out of eight patients with diseases of the peripheral nerves. GCT predicts that the stimulation of large fibres might reduce pain because of activity in the small cells of the substantia gelatinosa (SG). If these large fast conductors are proportionately reduced in number, say by damage, the spinal cord receives excessive slow impulses from the smaller fibres, and this mechanism gives rise to pain. Normally impulses from the large fibres inhibit the small fibres, suppressing firing and so inhibiting pain. The GCT refines and expands an earlier fibre dissociation model (Noordenbos, 1959). (For a thorough comparison of these two theories see Sunderland's (1978) discussion of causalgia.)

A revision of the GCT has shown how the cells of the SG have an inhibitory effect on the deeper dorsal horn neurons. Each large and small fibre excites a T-cell and sends a collateral to a suppressor cell in the SG, where large fibres excite the suppressor and small ones inhibit it. Activation of a T-cell by a large fibre is followed by inhibition, as the suppressing SG cell is activated by the collateral, so closing the gate. Small fibres activate the T-cells and this effect is accentuated by the inhibition of the SG. As in the earlier account, the balance between the two is critical to the firing of the T-cells (Melzack and Wall, 1989). Mathematical modelling of available neurophysiological evidence using non-linear equations has shown that the main assumptions of the GCT are consistent with the known facts (Britton and Skevington, 1989).

Nociceptive afferent fibres generally enter the spinal cord via the dorsal roots and have their cell bodies in the dorsal root ganglia. The dorsal horns of the spinal cord are layered, and the first six laminae together with the tenth (which surrounds the central canal) are of greatest interest to pain researchers. Recent evidence shows that these laminae do not have precise borders and do not perform an exclusive function. They contain cells of more than one type, which differ morphologically and chemically (Wall, 1989). Morphologically, laminae I, IIo and IV–VII contain nociceptive specific and non-specific units, but the nociceptive specific neurons are mainly found in the superficial laminae. The recent discovery of many different peptides has caused a debate about whether substance P is truly the most important neurotransmitter released by nociceptive afferents (Besson and Chaouch, 1987). The term "lamina" refers to the position of the cell bodies, but the dendrites ramify into adjacent and distant laminae, making contact with axons from the periphery and other cells. The location of cell bodies is now believed to be less important than the eventual destination of their dendrites (Wall, 1989). Initial studies indicated that A-delta and C fibres terminated in laminae I and IIo (generally held to be the SG), but HRP injection has shown that A nociceptive afferent fibres project to distant areas of the spinal grey matter, and exactly where these C fibres terminate is still unclear (Besson and Chaouch, 1987). Most A-beta afferents terminate in laminae III, IV and V. Because cells from the SG and deeper laminae respond to noxious and innocuous stimulation, they are called wide dynamic range (WDR) neurons. While the functions of these areas are still being investigated, some features deserve particular comment. Firstly, the marginal zone (lamina I) seems to be important in inhibition because it has many cells that respond to noxious stimulation; a multi-receptive and multi-convergent cell has recently been identified here, which appears to contribute to a larger system of cells responsible for inhibition. Secondly, lamina II appears to be specialised; some of these neurons differ from those in other laminae and show marked habituation when the skin is stimulated (Willis, 1985). Particularly numerous in lamina III are conglomerates of synaptic structures referred to as glomeruli. Here, terminals from thick fibres interconnect with those fibres that transmit pain impulses and fibres from supraspinal centres in the brainstem (Ottoson, 1983).

However, such descriptions can be misleading because they create the false impression of a hard-wired system where particular lines may be labelled for pain (Wall, 1989). Wall and others have marshalled sufficient evidence to demonstrate that this is patently not the case: the system is not rigid, but plastic. Neurons can change irreversibly in response to events. Unlike proponents of other theories about the role of the dorsal horns in the perception of pain, Wall (1989) proposes that the system may be classified according to the context. This is because there is no fixed relationship between the afferents and the sensory or behavioural outcome, and no fixed relationship between the input and output of individual dorsal horn cells. However, responding to pain is neither random nor exclusively the result of mental processes. Wall and others show that the afferent barrage arriving in the spinal cord can be processed at one of three different speeds, and, furthermore, the speed of this information processing depends on the context of other information coming in from the periphery and the integration of descending messages from the brain. Information can be either processed rapidly with the gating mechanism, depending on the relative stimulation of large and small fibres, or assimilated more slowly (minutes or hours rather than seconds) to result in a sensitivity control. Here, peptides may be responsible for the slow changes occurring in sites like lamina I. A third possibility is that there may be prolonged action (over days or months), which provides a connectivity control. This has been demonstrated by the cutting of peripheral nerves to produce a "cascade" of slow changes that sweep centrally from a lesion and involve cells on which these afferents terminate, so abolishing their receptive fields (Wall, 1989, p.162). These cells subsequently adopt a new receptive field activated by the nearest intact afferents, which in turn ultimately supply changes in the thalamus and cortex.

Skin stimulation evokes nerve impulses that are received and transmitted by the spinal cord systems. In addition to the cells of the SG, impulses were thought to go to central transmission cells deeper in the dorsal horns, the axons of which formed part of the ascending spinothalamic tract connecting with the brain, and to dorsal column fibres that project into the brain (Melzack and Wall, 1970). This moderation of impulses in the SG before their passage to the T-cells was at one time deemed to represent the gating mechanism. However, to date, the T-cells have not been conclusively identified, even though there is good circumstantial evidence to support their existence in one or more forms. More recently the focus of research appears to have shifted from the identification of T-cells to the "synaptic decision" that appears to be taking place in the dorsal horns and trigeminal nuclei (Melzack and Wall, 1989). This complex mechanism contrasts with an alternative view of the SG as a simpler receiving station and relay nucleus (Cervero and Iggo, 1980).

Research activity investigating how plasticity works has focused on the role of the N-methyl-D-aspartate (NMDA) receptor that prolongs the duration of synaptic potentials, especially in the dorsal horns of the SG. An afferent barrage through unmyelinated C fibres triggers long-lasting changes in excitability, making these complex receptors hyperexcitable. This barrage "winds up" the NMDA receptors, so enhancing, amplifying and extending their responsiveness to noxious stimulation, and has the effect of making rapid and long-term alterations in the membrane and cell chemistry of these dorsal horn cells (Wall, 1991; Woolf, 1991). The details of this mechanism are still being investigated but there is evidence for the following sequence. Firstly, excitatory amino acids (EAAs) arrive at non-NMDA EAA receptors and cause an influx of sodium ions, which depolarises the cell within seconds. This depolarisation removes the magnesium block on NMDA receptors that might be excited by EAAs, causing an influx of sodium and calcium ions. This results in a longer lasting depolarisation, lasting tens of seconds; the cell is now hyperexcitable. Substance P arrives and causes the intracellular production of calcium within a few minutes. This keeps the cell depolarised and the NMDA receptors unblocked. So far, the process is reversible; the irreversible changes associated with plasticity occur when this intracellular calcium induces genes (Wilcox, 1991).

Furthermore, and more importantly, the presence of an opioid appears to prevent the induction of a c-fos proto-oncogene, which allows this changed pattern of enhanced responsiveness of dorsal horn neurons to be genetically encoded (Tolle et al, 1991). The production of this gene in nociceptive neurons appears to be the key to understanding plasticity, and for that reason its discovery may have far-reaching consequences (Dickenson, 1991). While large doses of morphine are required to suppress the hyperexcitability of these neurons post-operatively, there is evidence that small opioid doses given *before* the noxious stimulation of surgery where inflammation would be expected prevents this central hyper-responsiveness from occurring. The pre-emptive administration of opioids may not only reduce nociception but may also be critical in the prevention of neural plasticity, because the NMDA receptor appears to have a crucial role in some deleterious maladaptive pain states. Although the recent focus has been on NMDA as one of the most promising recent findings, the action of NMDA receptors may be only one of several processes that occur when C fibres are sensitised (Dickenson, 1991).

Clinical evidence supporting this gating action was published in 1988 in two key papers on the prevention of post-operative pain. It is argued that by "closing the gate" before surgery begins, the barrage of impulses resulting from tissue damage is largely parried, so that post-operative pain is subsequently reduced or prevented. In the first study, McQuay, Carroll and Moore (1988) looked at the outcome of 929 patients receiving general anaesthetic for elective orthopaedic surgery over a 7-year period. Documenting the time from the end of surgery to the first post-operative analgesia, the timing and type of premedication, whether a nerve block or local anaesthetic (LA) was used, and the use of opiate during anaesthesia, they found that for those receiving no pre-operative medication and no LA block, the median time to first analgesia was 105 minutes ($N = 514$). Those receiving opiate premedication but no LA block lasted significantly longer without analgesic — 328 minutes ($N = 216$). The patients who had an LA block without premedication waited significantly longer than the first two groups (480 minutes; $N = 117$), while for the 82 patients who had both premedication and an LA block, the time exceeded 9 hours. The finding was confirmed when requests for additional analgesics were examined. This has led to a debate about the timing and the practical importance of pre-emptive analgesia, but also has theoretical implications for the GCT. However, prospective randomised longitudinal controlled trials need to be carried out using not only opioids, but also LA through spinal and nerve blocks and infiltration, non-steroidal anti-inflammatory drugs (NSAIDs) and paracetamol as pre-operative interventions (McQuay, 1992). There is also some evidence that the intravenous route is more effective than the epidural route, although the reason for this is unclear (McQuay, 1993).

In the second study, of 25 amputees, the results indicated that patients with painful pre-operative conditions had good post-operative pain relief if they had received a lumbar epidural block during the three days before surgery (Bach, Noreng and Tjellden, 1988). None of those receiving a block had post-operative pain 6 months later, and for the majority pain was relieved for up to a year. Data from these two studies support the GCT because the results indicate that effective pre-operative analgesia "closes the gate" in the spinal cord, so deterring the subsequent pain barrage created by the severing of nerves during surgery from being transmitted up the central nervous system. Wall (1988) points out that pre-emptive pre-operative analgesia has prolonged effects that often outlast the presence of drugs in the body, and that once pain is established, for instance by severing nerves, it is often necessary to use massive doses of narcotics to subsequently suppress the ensuing neuronal hyperexcitability.

CRITIQUE AND RE-EVALUATION

The GCT is a useful conceptual model and a body of evidence supports it as a neurological reality, but, despite this, sceptics still search for more evidence to confirm specificity theory (e.g. Hensel, 1972). Beecher (1972) observed that, "Surgeons have been more loathe to give up the 19th century concept of specificity theory than most other groups of clinicians". It is claimed that some of the evidence cited in support of GCT has neither been reliably substantiated nor is consistent with a gating mechanism. Iggo (1972) points out that it has not been confirmed that continuous afferent activity goes through the dorsal roots of the spinal cord in the absence of intentional stimulation, except for thermal receptors and slow adapting (type II) mechanoreceptors. This would be necessary to set the T-cells in their initial condition. Secondly, C fibres do not appear to be uniformly sensitive to all kinds of stimulation, as the theory implies. Some cells in the SG only receive stimulation from high threshold nociceptors. Thirdly, Iggo suggests that the early arrival of impulses in A fibres may "set the stage" for the central activity of C fibre impulses through interaction between the two. Other critics, such as Nathan and Rudge (1974), reject the idea of a gating mechanism and propose a convergence of afferent nerve impulses in lamina V. While the current widespread clinical practice of electrically stimulating large afferents (transcutaneous electrical nerve stimulation; TENS) arises directly from the gate control model and has established value in relieving pain, some estimates put the success rate at only about a third of chronic cases, so undermining the power of the theory. Several studies have failed to confirm the claim of Mendell and Wall (1964) for the existence of a presynaptic gating mechanism activated by painful stimuli, yet Nathan (1976) concedes that presynaptic inhibition does seem the most likely mechanism.

Despite recent improvements in technique, there are considerable difficulties in staining the numerous closely packed and highly interconnected SG cells. Of relevance to GCT, these investigations have stimulated debates about whether lamina III should be included in the SG. The SG has both excitatory and inhibitory cells and, despite the theory of presynaptic inhibition, it is not yet known whether the mechanism of inhibition is presynaptic, postsynaptic or both. A physiological feature that is crucial to the theory is that hyperpolarisation exists with positive phase in the dorsal root potential. Until this controversy is resolved, the "disbelievers" are unlikely to be convinced (Nathan, 1976). Woolf and Wall (1982) point out that the experimental results argue against postsynaptic inhibition, but conclude that it is "unlikely that afferent mediated inhibition acts solely by presynaptic inhibition". Others have suggested that pain is more directly related to the rate of fibre degeneration than to the selective loss of large or small fibres, and there are recorded cases where pain appears not to have been felt if small fibres are missing (Weisenberg,

1980). Sunderland (1978) says that several features of causalgia (severe burning pain) cannot be accounted for by the theory. Some of these criticisms were tackled in an extensive update of the literature and reformulation of the theory (Melzack and Wall, 1982), but Melzack and Wall have more recently adjusted their original position to say that it is now more useful to restrict the term "gate control" to "the rapidly acting mechanisms which receive and control the transfer of impulses from the input afferent fibres to cells which in turn trigger the various effector systems and which evoke sensation" (Melzack and Wall, 1989, p.27).

THE ASCENDING SYSTEM

The output of pain impulses from the dorsal horns is transmitted to the thalamus by two major ascending systems in the anterolateral quadrant of the spinal cord, although several others have been identified. Most fibres cross to the contralateral side of the spinal cord from their cell bodies before forming the white matter of the spinothalamic and spinoreticular tracts. The majority of cells of origin of the ascending spinothalamic tract carry somatosensory nociceptive information, but there are many nociceptive non-specific neurons present too, indicating other functions. Collaterals partly link this tract to the brainstem reticular formation, and there is a dense projection to the mesencephalon from lamina I in particular (Besson and Chaouch, 1987). More is known about this tract because the cells are not altered during anaesthesia, unlike the less well understood spinoreticular tract, which is thought to be responsible for the sensory discrimination qualities of pain (Willis, 1985). Similarly, little is known about a propriospinal system of short fibres that are distributed throughout the cord in the grey matter and appear to carry some information about pain (Melzack and Wall, 1982).

Furthermore, it has been conventional to emphasise the importance of the spinothalamic tract as a result of the surgical practice of anterolateral cordotomy, which severs this tract and other projection systems (Melzack and Wall, 1989). The enthusiastic use of cordotomy for severe pain (e.g. Noordenbos, 1959) has been largely unsuccessful because, although pain is immediately relieved, it returns within a short period and when it returns it is often worse. The rationale for using cordotomy completely ignores the important role of the thalamocortical systems in the generation of pain (Melzack and Wall, 1989), and this mechanism explains surgical failures to relieve pain by severing those pathways that are known to carry noxious information (Melzack and Wall, 1982). Because pain following surgery is relieved for only 3 months on average, Noordenbos (1959) has suggested that surgical methods should be restricted principally to relieving chronic pain in malignant cancers. He suggests that present surgical methods may be effective largely because of the *size* of the lesion and so can hardly be regarded as specific.

Before reaching the brain, the spinothalamic tract bifurcates into a lateral or neospinothalamic tract and a medial paleospinothalamic tract. Long, unbroken and rapidly conducting fibres form the neospinothalamic tract, which is responsible for the sensory discrimination of the spatial, temporal and magnitude characteristics of pain. Dendrites from these cells project into the major terminus of the ventroposter-iolateral nucleus in the thalamus and impulses are then passed through rod-like cells to the cortical columns of the somatosensory cortex (Willis, 1985). Neocortical and other processes are responsible for evaluating the new information in relation to past experiences. The small pathways of the paleospinothalamic tract carry some noxious information and project into the medial and intralaminar nuclei of the thalamus. Short, multisynaptic, slowly conducting chains of fibres divide to form the two branches of the spinoreticular tract, and project into the reticular formation and the periaqueductal grey (PAG) of the midbrain, where the two systems are reintegrated. Here, pain intensity and the thermal and tactile qualities of pain are perceived. This multisynaptic system enables impulses to be enhanced or suppressed at many stages during transmission.

CENTRAL CONTROL AND THE DESCENDING SYSTEMS

Studies of the cortex show that sensory input is localised, identified in terms of physical properties, evaluated in terms of past experiences and modified before it activates discriminative or motivational systems. The higher centres of the frontal cortex appear to be responsible for the interplay between cognitive and motivational – affective activities, since these are disturbed following frontal lobotomy. Given our definition, it is questionable whether lobotomised patients still truly have pain, as they appear not to suffer. They rarely complain of pain or request medication, even though they may report the sensory qualities of prick or burn (Melzack, 1986). Connections between centres in the brainstem like the reticular formation, the hypothalamus and the limbic system account for strong unpleasant emotions and motivations reported by those in pain. The reticular formation is involved in the aversive drive linked with pain, and stimulation of the nucleus gigantocellularis and central grey matter produces aversive behaviour, while stimulation of the medial and intralaminar nuclei of the thalamus produces fear-like responses (Melzack, 1986). Escape from and avoidance of pain are learned (see Chapter 3), and these centres appear to match new, incoming information with memories of past experiences (Wall and Melzack, 1983). The cortex, in turn, sends impulses to the spinal cord to inhibit T-cell firing through descending systems in the white matter; for example, some pyramidal cells in the cortex are known to affect cells in spinal cord laminae III and VI (Melzack and Wall, 1982).

A central control mechanism in the brainstem is an integral part of the gating process. Many structures in the brain project into the dorsal horns and inhibit the dorsal horn cells from firing, and this correlates well with behavioural analgesia (Melzack and Wall, 1989). The gating model proposes that descending fibres from the PAG and nuclei raphes magnus (NRM) inhibit the transmission from afferent fibres to the T-cells, being mediated by inhibitory neurons in the SG. Hagbarth and Kerr (1954) discovered that by stimulating brainstem structures (including the reticular formation, cerebellum and the cerebral cortex), the responses evoked in the ventrolateral spinal cord virtually abolished pain. They deduced that the brain must inhibit transmission of impulses in the dorsal horns of the spinal cord. The brain site responsible for inducing this analgesia was later identified as being in the PAG in the reticular formation (Reynolds, 1969). Reynolds found that stimulation of the PAG produced abdominal analgesia in rats, but did not affect their consciousness, mobility or reaction to light and sound. This phenomenon is known as stimulation-produced analgesia (SPA); it works by activating endogenous opioids.

The neurons in the PAG, and also those throughout other areas of the CNS (especially the SG and hypothalamus) known to be responsible for pain regulation, have copious enkephalin receptors which bind with morphine and with morphine-like endogenous opioid substances called endorphins and enkephalins. A third class of dynorphins has been identified, but is considered to be less important. Enkephalin forms part of the larger and more stable endorphin molecule and may act as a local transmitter to the endorphins' more general "master role" (Terenius, 1981). Evidence from several lines of electrophysiological and anatomical research supports this view. Strong analgesia can be measured after a few seconds and diminishes within minutes of stimulation, indicating that some pharmacological substance with powerful pain-relieving properties is released into the area to sustain the effect. Limited evidence suggests that intractable pain may be relieved for years by periodically stimulating electrodes permanently implanted in the periventricular and PAG matter, so releasing endorphins and enkephalins (Hosobuchi, Adams and Linchitz, 1977). These chronic pain patients did not report weakness, paraesthesia, seizure, numbness or loss of consciousness, so indicating that a true anaesthesia had been obtained rather than a motor or placebo effect (Fields, 1988).

Supporting evidence emerges from several sources. Firstly, stimulation markedly inhibits cells in lamina V of the dorsal horns and selectively affects noxious inputs rather than all tactile ones. Secondly, serotonin plays "an important but not a unique role in these antinociceptive systems" (Frenk et al, 1986, p.30). Thirdly, some forms of SPA act on the same anatomical sites using the same mechanisms of action as opioid analgesics such as morphine, and many studies have shown that naloxone — an opiate antagonist — can partially block the effects of stimulation (see Frenk et al (1986) for a review). Finally, small amounts of morphine injected directly into the PAG have produced analgesia, so implicating endogenous endorphins and enkephalins in this mechanism (Melzack and Wall, 1989, p.139).

These control centres now appear to be more widespread than formerly envisaged, implicating not only the raphe nuclei and reticular formation, but also the spinal segments, dorsal column nuclei, vestibular nuclei, the olive, trigeminal nuclei, locus coerulus, tectum, red nucleus, hypothalamus and the pyramidal tract. Melzack and Wall (1989) indicate that all of these might contribute to analgesia and changes in sensitivity but their relative importance and the exact conditions in which they become effective are still being investigated. The following discussion focuses on those centres that have received the most research attention to date. As the PAG projects to two centres in the rostral ventromedial medulla (VMM) — the nucleus reticularis gigantocellularis and the paragigantocellularis in the bulbopontine reticular formation — this anatomical evidence, together with that from pharmacological and physiological sources, indicates that the PAG and VMM together may be primarily responsible for the descending transmission of impulses in the pain mechanism. Neurons in this medullary region project to the trigeminal nucleus caudalis and via the dorsolateral funiculus to the dorsal horns of the spinal cord, and this projection is especially dense in those laminae in the dorsal horns (probably I and V) that contain the terminal nociceptive primary afferents (see Fields, 1988). Besson and Chaouch (1987) hypothesise that the PAG and VMM with their spinal projections make up a negative feedback loop activated by nociceptive stimulation and producing an inhibition of the spinal transmission of nociceptive information. They see the VMM as a "turntable", or the final common pathway of this system, because the effects of the PAG are partially exerted through it. Fields' group, on the other hand, have formulated a different theory following identification of two types of cells in rat PAG and VMM, which fire in response to noxious heat applied to the tail. They show how neurons in the PAG project to and excite cells in the rostral VMM, which in turn project to and inhibit nociceptive dorsal horn neurons in laminae I and V (Fields, 1988). These two types of neuron are termed "on" and "off" cells. It is speculated that "off" cells, which are excited by PAG stimulation and have axons projecting to the spinal cord, may inhibit nociceptive transmission, because this is blocked when "off" cells are active, and is allowed when "off" cells pause. The function of "on" cells is so far unclear. Interesting from a psychological viewpoint is the finding that these cells respond in monkeys taught to expect a noxious stimulus cued by a light, long before they receive that stimulus. This finding implicates cognitive control in pain transmission through the descending system, as proposed by GCT.

However, other mechanisms have been documented, which need to be considered here. Diffuse noxious inhibitory controls (DNIC) (Le Bars, Dickenson and Besson, 1979) characterise the activities of dorsal horn and trigeminal nucleus caudalis convergent neurons receiving A and C fibre inputs (Le Bars and Willer, 1988). When noxious stimulation is applied to any part of the body, analgesic effects can be produced at distant sites; this is the result of DNIC. Consequently, DNIC indicates a more non-specific system than GCT suggests (Lewith and Kenyon, 1984). Nociceptive activity is correlated with levels of inhibition in some cells of the dorsal horns and in other neurons at the origins of the ascending pathways, indicating that it is triggered by specific nociceptive afferent pathways and is mediated by ascending and descending loops to and from supraspinal structures (Le Bars and Willer, 1988). "Wide dynamic range" neurons are believed to utilise the signal-to-noise ratio in the CNS (Willis, 1985). DNIC affects neuronal activities in rats and cats, and has been used to explain the higher pain threshold in chronic pain patients (Le Bars and Willer, 1988), although this interpretation has been questioned (Peters et al, 1992). It has also been used to explain the action of counter-irritation in reducing pain (Besson and Chaouch, 1987), such as that created by acupuncture, cupping, cauterisation, scarification and many of the traditional methods of folk medicine designed to fight pain with pain (Melzack, 1983a).

So what triggers the brain's analgesic systems? Evidence indicates that stress severity and duration are critical in determining whether opioid or non-opioid systems are triggered. Following the initial excitement over the discovery of the opioid endorphins, it was found that non-opioids also play a crucial role. As a rule, the opioid system responds to shorter and less severe stress, and non-opioid analgesia is associated with more severe stress of greater duration. Furthermore, experiments using foot shock in rats indicate that there may be a third form of analgesia involving the hypothalamus, pituitary and adrenals — those areas of the autonomic nervous system primarily associated with the emotions. Different results arise from the application of continuous and intermittent shock. When intermittent shock is applied, beta-endorphin is released from the anterior pituitary and enkephalin-like peptides from the adrenals. This release corresponds with behavioural changes associated with despair and learned helplessness. Adrenal opioids have receptors in a lower brainstem centre — the nucleus tractus solitarius — which not only receives fibres from the PAG but is also one of the principal projections of the vagus. Stimulating this centre results in analgesia but also changes blood pressure and so provides some explanation for why autonomic changes and analgesia occur with stress (Frenk et al, 1986).

However, there is little information about the influence of endorphins in acute clinical pain. It has been suggested that some of the variability of these states can be accounted for by the action of the endogenous pain network, although the mechanism whereby this system is activated is not understood (Fields, 1988). A controlled study of rats with chemically induced inflammation similar to arthritis showed that while beta-endorphin, prolactin and growth hormone all occurred in acute stress, when chronic pain developed there was a substantial increase in growth hormone secretion (Calvino et al, 1992). This promising evidence suggests that growth hormone may be an important mediator in understanding the physiological link between pain and stress. The discovery of the naturally occurring pentapeptide enkephalin, although only weakly analgesic, has activated a search to find a marketable pharmacological analogue that has prolonged action and non-addictive analgesic properties (Ottoson, 1983). An additional spin-off from this line of research has been a gradual change in policy and practice among health professionals relating to the administration of opiates to those in pain (see Chapters 7 and 9). Now that it is known that the body makes its own opiates and that some people are deficient, there is less resistance to using these drugs for those who are in real need. Endorphin release is also believed to play a role in placebo analgesia (Terenius, 1981).

Price (1988) has produced one of the best theories to date on how the descending controls operate. He integrates the most recent psychological, physiological and anatomical evidence available and draws upon the framework provided by GCT. Retaining the best elements of Melzack and Casey's (1967) extension to the GCT, Price (1988) proposes that while the sensory-discriminative, arousal and some motor responses associated with pain appear to be activated in parallel, psychological and neurophysiological evidence exists to show that affective emotional states depend on sequential processing using cognitive processes. While nociceptive inputs are likely to be associated with an aversive response, Price observes that the emotional aspects of this response are varied, as with anger, frustration and anxiety, depending on the meaning and cognitive appraisal of these sensations. Such cognitive appraisals may in turn affect the emotions experienced, and, furthermore, are affected by attitudes, memories and aspects of personality. Reports that pain is unpleasant because it hurts, he claims, give support to both anatomical findings and evidence from hypnosis that this pain-related affect is processed at the very last stage. More work is needed on this plausible and attractive model.

CONCLUSION

To summarise, in this chapter attention has been paid to the afferent nerves and receptors and to mechanisms within the spinal cord and connections to, from and within the brain, especially the brainstem, thalamus and cortex. In addition, it has been necessary to consider the influence of the autonomic nervous system, given the importance of the emotions associated with acute and chronic pain. Some space has been given to considering the evolving literature on endorphins and plasticity. Various theories of pain have been reviewed, and although it is evident that the GCT is too general and lacks quantitative specifications about the interactions it proposes (Price, 1988), it is still the most important working model for pain researchers in the 1990s. Evidently, cells exist in the dorsal horns which transmit impulses and are candidates for the title of T-cell, but the range of functional properties of the T-cell remain largely hypothetical and opaque, suggesting that a more accurate answer may need to be sought from investigations of neural networks. This theory emphasises the important role of the higher centres in the interpretation of pain and in the feedback loop of information in the form of impulses that open and close the gate in the spinal cord. The rest of this book focuses on the cognitive, affective, motivational and socio-cultural information that is transmitted through these descending pathways from the brain, and their relative efficacy in forestalling, ameliorating or enhancing pain.

Measuring Painful Sensations

2

The aim of this chapter is to evaluate some of the most popular methods of measuring cognitions in the investigation of human pain in the laboratory and clinic. Cognitive methods necessarily underlie any analysis of the social aspects of pain. It is not intended to be either comprehensive or definitive here — more to give a taste of the different ways in which pain has been measured. Many social methods are examined throughout the remainder of this volume, and the material in this chapter provides the basis for understanding social applications of these cognitive methods, as well as giving contrasts to them. Reflexive behaviours and indicators of voluntary performance studied in animal laboratory research are not reviewed here; neither are human physiological correlates considered in depth, since comprehensive overviews exist elsewhere (Chapman et al, 1985). A distinction between the perception and the reporting of pain is conceptually useful here even though in practice the boundaries are blurred. Because it is not possible to disengage perceptions entirely from reports of pain, measurement methods tend to combine the two in differing proportions. Often, they emphasise the assessment of one of these aspects, sometimes with the intention of excluding the other. For instance, threshold and other psychophysical methods were largely designed to measure pain sensation, while studies on the language of pain focus more on pain reports. An evaluation of sensation provides a starting point for the debate on pain reports, and the social factors that influence them form much of the subject matter of the rest of the book.

AN IDEAL PAIN MEASURE

Some key issues concerning the measurement of pain are addressed in this section. First of all, we must address what might be the characteristics of an ideal measure for assessing a painful stimulus. Beecher (1956) proposes a number of essential characteristics. Pain should be measurable in physical units so that comparisons can be made. A good stimulus must induce a clearly detectable pain sensation without damaging the tissues. It should be easily applied and to a part of the body where there are minimal neurological and histological variations. A pain end-point should be identifiable, and the use of repeated stimulation above the threshold should not interfere with subsequent stimulation. Furthermore, there should be a relationship between the intensity of the stimulus and the intensity of the pain experienced, with the least difference between the two across the intensity range. Gracely (1983) adds that measures should be sensitive to change and bias free. They should also allow for random errors and exaggerations in the reporting of pain, and should provide immediate information about the accuracy and reliability of a person's performance. Furthermore, they should permit the sensory-discriminative properties of pain, such as its intensity, location, duration and many different qualities, to be distinguished from the hedonic properties, which are the motivational and emotional characteristics associated with the unpleasantness of anxiety, fear, aversion and distress. Gracely says that an ideal measure would be sufficiently unspecialised to allow for the measurement of clinical and experimental pain, so that it would be possible to make reliable comparisons between the two. Lastly, it should be an absolute measure, which enables valid intrapersonal and intragroup comparisons to be made over a period of time. This contrasts with existing measures, which either build in relativity between people or between stimuli, or evaluate changes following particular procedures. Such strict criteria provide a yardstick against which to evaluate the measures of pain presented here.

Central to this discussion are views about the relative importance placed on subjective and objective styles of measurement. Wall (1983) says that pain is "*always* subjective", reinforcing Beecher's stance (1960) over three decades ago that:

> many investigators seem grimly determined to establish – indeed, too often there does not seem to have been any question in their mind – that for a given stimulus there must be a given response; that is, for so much stimulation of the nerve endings, so much pain will be experienced, and so on. This fundamental error has led to enormous waste. It is evident in work in our laboratory that there is no simple relationship between stimulus and subjective response.

In a more recent reassessment of the measurement of post-operative pain, the Royal College of Surgeons and College of Anaesthetists (1990) still conclude that there are no objective measures of pain, only subjective ones. Campbell and Lahuerta (1983) have pointed out that the subjective nature of pain is one of the major problems in studying it. Nevertheless, the search for a method that is truly "objective" has taken up considerable research time and energy. While objectivity is frequently claimed, this often means that subjective biases inherent in the method, and the full range of psychometric properties, have not yet been thoroughly researched. For instance, Willer (1983) claims an "objective" method of measuring pain using nociceptive reflexes. He showed a "strong correlation" between a pricking pain and a long latency reflex — the RA-III reflex — recorded from a flexor muscle of the lower limb. This was elicited by percutaneous electrical stimulation of either the ipsilateral sural nerve or the skin in the distal receptive field of this nerve. While Willer (1983) presents several interesting studies to show why he thinks that this method works, how these data tap into the inherently subjective nature of pain is not entirely clear. Williams (1988) believes that there is a spurious distinction between the objective and subjective measures of pain — what are sometimes categorised as "hard" and "soft" measures. His review of the literature leads to the following conclusion: "The truth is that a carefully constructed interview or questionnaire can reach higher levels of reliability and validity than many laboratory tests" (Williams, 1988, p.240). Insightfully, he observes that the argument that the subjective experience of pain cannot be measured begs the question about why we try at all. The real issue is not about how measures are obtained, but about whether they have acceptable levels of reliability and validity. An "even greater fallacy" is that because objective testing is deemed to be more direct, it is therefore believed to be somehow more accurate than self-report. Williams argues that measures are *always* indirect, whether they are performed in the laboratory under artificially controlled conditions or *in situ* using quasi-experimental or statistical controls (Williams, 1988).

The main criticisms that have been levelled at the assessment of verbal report fall into four broad groups (Reading, 1983). Critics believe that their most serious point is that verbal reports can be biased or falsified, and considerable effort has been devoted to showing that verbal pain reports are biased. However, systematic biases can be investigated, monitored and integrated into an assessment. Much slower to emerge has been any serious analysis of whether such biases are deliberate or unintentional, and the investigation of intention must be central to any accurate and comprehensive interpretation of these biases. As intention is integral to legal investigations, some methods might be drawn from this area for future research.

A related criticism is that pain reports are disproportionate to the severity of the noxious input. This view appears to be inconsistent with the acceptance of the gate control theory (GCT) as the working pain model, which was founded on substantial clinical evidence that there is no direct one-to-one relationship between neuronal activity and subjective report (see Chapter 1). If this is correct, then what does it mean to have an appropriate pain report? Is there some agreed metric or norm of appropriateness that can be used to compare individual patients? While some would argue that damage and disease have not yet been identified, Wall and Melzack (1989) say that more modest claims should be made for modern diagnostic tools, because they may not always locate injured tissues. They observe that for 80% of low back pain cases, it is not possible to detect injury and this pertains to many other diverse areas of medicine where the cause of a painful disease is still unknown, even though treatment may be effective. Furthermore, the politics and ideology of pain management are important here. Curiously, pain researchers express far less interest in those who report *less* pain than would seem to be appropriate to the amount of noxious input they appear to be receiving than vice versa. This suggests that investigators have an overriding concern with the issues of exaggeration related to malingering — an interest in bias in one direction only, rather than biases in general.

A third criticism is that pain reports may not be concordant with other indices of pain. The reason for this discrepancy may be more to do with the tendency of many investigators to have viewed pain as a unidimensional rather than a multidimensional phenomenon, than with methodological accuracy itself. One effect of selecting a single measure of, say, pain intensity, in isolation from the many other qualities of pain is that the chosen measure may turn out to have been inappropriate. Consequently, it is not surprising when other measures then fail to correlate highly with it.

Lastly, verbal assessments of pain have been criticised for being potentially reactive, sensitising the patient to that pain and consequently affecting the way in which the pain is ultimately judged. However, this problem is not exclusive to verbal reports of pain.

Many studies in psychophysics depend on the use of laboratory subjects who have "been trained to suppress or neglect their emotional responses, to ignore distraction and to adopt the culture of the experimenter" (Wall, 1979). Results from such studies may mislead because it is assumed that participants are able to detect sensations that are devoid of emotions. As Wall (1979) points out, pain and its associated emotions are two faces of the same coin, but they reflect a single experimental concept, so the results derived must be influenced by affect. While the notion of affect-free sensation is a useful conceptual tool, it bears no relation to the subjective experience of acute or chronic pain. Furthermore, the instructions given and their method of delivery have been viewed as relatively unimportant, as judged by the infrequency with which they are reported in publications. Consequently, different instructions given to participants across a range of studies may account for more of the variation in findings than has been acknowledged hitherto. While investigators will continue to express their personal preferences for particular methods, it is worth bearing in mind a remark once made by the eminent psychophysicist S.S. Stevens (1958) that methodology can easily become "methodolatry". The nature of the problem being tackled should dictate what method is chosen, not vice versa. Furthermore, choosing a particular method reflects the investigator's own ideology. It says as much about how the researcher conceptualises a problem as it does about the reactions obtained from the people studied, although this is rarely acknowledged publicly. For this reason, it is preferable to see the results from a particular method as the product of a two-way social interaction between the investigator and the investigated — not the artificially contrived one-way street. Regrettably, this interaction has rarely been investigated, although it provides a focus of interest to those interested in developing social methodologies for pain research.

TRADITIONAL THRESHOLD APPROACHES

The problem of measuring painful sensations was one that preoccupied the first experimental psychologists. Concerned with the mind–body problem, Fechner wrote equations to describe the functional relationships between psychic or mental events and physical or material events. These methods have become an integral part of psychological technique. Early studies of sensation mapped out the sensitivity of different areas of the skin. Von Frey devised novel tools for measuring touch sensitivity by fastening human and horse hairs of various thicknesses to short sticks with sealing wax. Von Frey hairs had the advantage of applying maximum pressure almost instantaneously and constantly (Osgood, 1953). Such issues are still pertinent to modern studies of experimental pain. Reviews of current methods of pain induction using thermal or radiant heat, and mechanical, chemical and electrical methods are available elsewhere (Beecher, 1956; Campbell and Lahuerta, 1983). Recent evidence shows that these different methods do produce equivalent effects. For instance, Harris and Rollman (1985) introduced students to using cognitive strategies before exposing them to painful electrical stimulation, the cold pressor test or intense pressure. They found that cognitive strategies were equally effective in relieving pain from all three methods.

Variations in pain are often attributed to individual differences in "threshold", but in fact not one, but several, types of threshold have been identified. The *sensation threshold* is the lowest level of intensity at which people report that they feel the most minimal sensations like warmth or tingling. This threshold can only be studied in conscious and cooperative people, and it fluctuates constantly. On its own, it is not a particularly useful measure, because it provides little information about the sensations linked with chronic pain. Reliability is also an issue. When people have been asked to identify a point at which painful and non-painful experience can be separated, reports are unreliable and participants' expectations affect the results (Chapman et al, 1985). Here, subjectivity is seen to mar an ostensibly objective measure. The sensation threshold is sometimes confused with the *pain perception threshold*, or the lowest level at which people report that a sensation is painful, so providing an indicator of minimal pain. The pain perception threshold is identified when pain is detected 50% of the time over a sequence of trials. Stimulus intensity can be increased gradually in an ascending series of discrete units, from not being perceived until it is just perceived. Similarly, the amplitude can be reduced in a descending series, so that where pain just ceases also defines the threshold. There are, however, ethical problems with the latter procedure. Cultural background affects the pain perception threshold, as a study of Nepalese Sherpa has shown. Clark and Clark (1980) found that these porters were more stoical about pain than the Europeans for whom they worked. While both groups were sensitive to changes in electrical shock in the laboratory, the Sherpa needed higher intensities before they would describe them as painful. Cultural differences in levels of stoicism demonstrate that learning plays an important role in the predisposition to report pain. As a result of tradition, norms and imitation, societies set their own rules and expectations about whether and when it is appropriate to express pain, and the acceptable style for doing this. Such studies lay bare the distinction between, on the one hand, how much pain people feel, and, on the other, how much they report. Consequently, these two aspects need to be assessed separately.

While threshold measures are easy and cheap to use, one view is that they are largely insensitive to monitoring changes in analgesic states. Indeed, more seriously, Beecher (1956) claimed that they were unable to distinguish between responses to placebo and to morphine. Despite these findings, there has been a persisting attempt to demonstrate that these methods are sensitive to treatment change, but conclusions remain equivocal because the studies are often flawed. For example, in a clinical trial to treat temporomandibular joint and facial pain patients, those who improved increased their pain threshold, changed their sensitivity to pain and showed an improvement in discriminating between different levels of painful stimulation compared to non-improvers (Malow and Olson, 1981). However, the classification of patients into conveniently equal samples of improved and unimproved groups was performed three weeks following treatment by participating oral surgeons and dentists, rather than by "blind" assessors, so introducing potential for biased *post hoc* judgements and raising questions about the reliability of the results.

A third threshold measure, the *pain tolerance level*, bears some relation to clinical pain because it represents the point at which people withdraw from unbearable pain, so usefully describing its aversive qualities. It is ethical to use it only in an ascending series. One problem with this measure is that although it is defined as how much someone can bear, paradoxically, the amount that a person can bear may change as they become accustomed to it. Furthermore, anxiety may be generated with the pain, depending on which procedure is used, so it is difficult to disaggregate the contribution of these factors to the results. The measures are substantially affected by placebo effects and produce disadvantageously large individual differences (Chapman et al, 1985). Other measures in use include the *pain sensitivity range* (PSR), which is the difference between the pain tolerance level and the pain threshold, and the *drug request point*, which requires participants to consider the level of pain at which they would require a mild analgesic were they actually in pain. Here, the use of a hypothetical judgement makes it difficult to operationalise, so this measure has not been used widely.

How much pain people can tolerate is also culturally determined. Zborowski's (1952) classic study of Anglo-Saxon protestant Old Americans ($N = 26$), Jews ($N = 31$) and Italians ($N = 24$) living in the United States showed different reporting styles in the different cultures. Italians and Jews called for immediate pain relief; the Italians were happy when pain was alleviated, but Jews were sceptical and suspicious of the future. They were concerned with the implications of their pain and continued to complain even after it had been reduced. Old Americans adopted a more phlegmatic attitude towards pain by withdrawing socially and only crying out when alone. Subsequent investigation of the sensation thresholds of these three groups by Sternbach and Tursky (1965) found no differences between the groups in the levels of detectable sensation. This leads to the important conclusion that people are essentially similar in the way in which they detect pain, implying a relatively uniform physiology universally. It also underlines the primacy of culture in determining the style used to report pain and the inclination to do so.

These early psychophysical methods have been adapted in various ways. With *adjustment methods*, participants are presented with a constant standard stimulus and adjust a variable stimulus to the point where the two are perceived to be different. This produces a *just noticeable difference* (JND), which is the smallest step that can be discriminated during stimulation. In devising the Dol scale of JNDs, Hardy, Wolff and Goodell (1952) identified 20 discernible degrees of pain in response to radiant heat between the pain threshold and the most excruciating level. However, more recent work by Wolff (1983) has shown that healthy volunteers can distinguish only 11 steps, which might explain why the Dol scale was never entirely validated at the time of development and fell into disuse. With the *serial exploration method*, the experimenter adjusts the stimulus in small, discrete amounts across a range, until a difference (JND) is detected. While these two methods are probably the best for measuring absolute threshold, Osgood (1953) claims that they are susceptible to "unconscious suggestion and outright malingering". Thus, indirect comparison methods where one stimulus is compared with another are superior where the actual size of the threshold is not important, and are particularly useful for comparing individuals or procedures.

An application of comparison methods is demonstrated by the *tourniquet pain test*. A blood pressure cuff is wrapped tightly around the upper arm before the participant opens and closes the fist at a fixed rate. This procedure produces a deep, slowly increasing, intense pain, analogous to pathological pain. It also creates similar sympathetic nervous system responses, such as tachycardia, pupillary dilation and sweating (Sternbach, 1983a). The amount of time it takes to match the intensity of the subject's own clinical pain level with their endurance of ischaemic pain (maximum pain tolerance) is calculated, and the tourniquet pain score is the ratio of the clinical pain level to maximum pain tolerance. Although this method is reported to be reliable and valid (Sternbach, 1983a), the available evidence indicates that this test is not very sensitive to change (Fox, Steger and Jennison, 1979; Sternbach et al, 1977).

While these methods are still in current use, they are more often used to assess some of the social aspects of pain. For instance, in the study of acute pain, they have been used to look at how a woman's age and her experience of childbirth affect perceptions of pain. Hapidou and De Catanzaro (1992) found that women who had been in labour used this experience as an "anchoring" event against which to judge subsequent painful events. Thus, older parous women (means age 35) reported a higher pain threshold during the cold pressor test than either younger (age 24) or equivalently older nulliparous groups, who did not differ from each other. This study supports gathering evidence that a memorable painful experience directly affects the pain threshold. The results raise interesting questions about whether other previous intensely painful events, such as from a compound fracture or myocardial infarction, might also be used as "anchors", and how this in turn might affect the current predisposition to report pain to a physician. Social factors directly affect the perception of pain beyond the laboratory, and for this reason need to be monitored systematically. An imaginative but less controlled approach has been to study pain perception thresholds in response to naturally occurring painful stimulation in existing pathological conditions. Regular Scandinavian sauna bathers who were being treated for rheumatoid arthritis, central pain or neuropathic pain of peripheral origin were asked to reflect on changes in pain during saunas in the previous year. The hot pain perception threshold is 41–43°C, which is equivalent to the skin temperatures typically reached during some phases of a sauna. The results for the majority of arthritics showed that they had no change in pain on exposure to heat, but more than half had an exacerbation of their condition afterwards (Nurmikko and Hietcharjn, 1992). Although the gathering of retrospective information and the use of self-selected samples compromises the reliability of these results, the approach overcomes some of the contextual problems inherent in laboratory studies.

Results from psychophysical measures have sustained controversy about differences in pain perception between groups within populations, so contributing to the formation of stereotypical judgements about major social groups. An early study by Notermans and Tophoff (1967) supported the existence of significant sex differences. While concluding that thresholds were no different, they reported that men tolerated more pain than women in experimental situations. Testing more than 40 000 adults for tolerance to pressure on the Achilles' tendon, Woodrow et al (1972) confirmed that the mean tolerance for men was 28.7 pounds per square inch and for women only 15.9, indicating a greater tolerance in men for pain. However, conclusions in this area have proved to be more equivocal than they first appeared. Subsequent studies have shown that sex, age and ethnicity have interactive effects. Men tolerate more pain than women in old age, and whites have higher pain tolerance compared with blacks and orientals, but age and race differences are much more marked in men than in women (Woodrow et al, 1972). (For an extensive review of studies of pain threshold in different ethnic groups, see Weisenberg (1977).) There are, however, serious methodological problems associated with some of these studies. For instance, only a few studies used corrections for skin temperature. In addition, the small numbers of subjects and the lack of controls for socio-economic level may also have contributed to equivocal conclusions. The reported changes with age depend upon which technique is being used. With pressure, pain tolerance appears to decrease with age, but if radiant heat or cold is applied, tolerance increases with age, so possibly reflecting changes in different pain perception systems (Woodrow et al, 1972). An example from the literature on pain in children supports this finding. For ethical reasons, few such experimental studies have been carried out, but one study of cold pressor pain in 37 children aged between 6 and 12 years has shown that pain ratings tended to be higher for older children ($p = 0.06$) (Le Baron, Zeltzer and Fanurik, 1989).

An additional and under-researched dimension to this debate is that pain expression is affected by the social context in which it occurs. An early study by Blitz and Dinnerstein (1968) showed how suggestion and various instructions during hypnotism could alter pain threshold, drug request point and quit point. The act of reporting pain, however, is almost always conducted in the immediate or eventual presence of another person, such as in a consultation with a physician. While the focus of research has largely been on the social and cultural differences between patients, there has been little interest either in the impact of the investigator's social characteristics, or in the evaluation of how interpersonal interaction between patient and investigator affect the results. Woodrow et al (1972) mentioned how men were predisposed to impress an attractive female technician, but they go on to dismiss "sex appeal" as an important factor in the higher pain tolerance of men. While these authors were refreshingly self-disclosing about the possible biases in their results, so enabling potential biases to be inspected, many researchers omit records of the sex of the experimenter. Even fewer try to balance the sexes of the investigators when designing their research, or deem it important to assess interactive effects *post hoc*. Age, race and social class factors should also be considered in the same light, and should be reported as a matter of course (Weisenberg, 1980). These equivocal conclusions may be due to the unreliable nature of early techniques of psychophysical measurement, but many social factors involved with the conduct of experiments may also have affected these results. This line of argument provides the conceptual underpinnings for a study by Levine and De Simone (1991), in which 68 undergraduates exposed to the cold pressor test were randomly and equally assigned to male and female experimenters in a balanced design. The results showed that women reported higher pain intensity than men ($p < 0.001$), but more interesting were the results showing that men gave significantly lower pain ratings to a woman experimenter than to a man. However, there was no difference in the way in which women reacted to experimenters of either sex. In line with current thinking on traditional sex roles, Levine and De Simone suggest that men respond to the opposite sex experimenter with a more stoical "macho" image, but the sex of the observer does not appear to significantly affect the way that women behave towards observers of differing sex.

In summary, then, there is evidence that these "hard" psychophysical methods are affected by a wide range of social and cultural factors. These may take the form of expectations, subjective biases, socio-demographic characteristics associated with differential learning patterns, and the social interaction between those who participate in research and those who carry it out. Together these issues are highly problematic for those in search of an objective measure of pain measurement. By their own rules, the assumptions made in this body of work are too simple, philosophically naive and in their use have the potential to be politically and clinically dangerous.

RATIO SCALING, MAGNITUDE ESTIMATION AND CROSS-MODALITY MATCHING

While Fechner thought that it was only possible to measure sensation indirectly, an aim of the proponents of the "new psychophysics" was to seek ways of measuring sensation directly (Stevens, 1957) and to this end, the pioneering technique of magnitude estimation was devised. To carry out this task, data must be collected using an interval scale where the distance between two numbers on a scale is of known size, or from a ratio scale that includes a true zero point as its origin, so that the ratio of any two scale points is independent of the unit of measurement (Siegel, 1956). The ratio method is preferred to interval scaling because in pain measurement these categorical scales are sensitive to bias effects, such as stimulus frequency, range, distribution effects and category-end effects (Gracely, McGrath and Dubner, 1978). For magnitude estimation, an arbitrary number like 100 is assigned to the first stimulus and if the second stimulus is judged to be twice as intense as the first, then it will be 200 and so on. These "direct" methods enabled Stevens to show that the psychophysical function is non-linear, performing to a power law that is deemed to reflect the operation of neural activity. Perhaps the best analogy is with a transducer, and it is proposed that the form taken by this psychophysical function is determined by a sensory transducer. However, sensory transducer theory is problematic because it is debatable whether an unobservable theoretical construct like sensation is really measurable. In addition, it is widely acknowledged that the context of stimulation influences both the way in which the stimulus is represented in the memory stores of the brain, and the way in which it is expressed as a response (McKenna, 1985), so this model is limited. The ways in which pain sensations are influenced by different social factors are central to the thesis presented in this volume.

In recent years comparative studies have been carried out between magnitude estimation and threshold methods, particularly in an attempt to reach closure about alleged socio-demographic differences. For instance, Lautenbacher and Rollman (1993) report an investigation where they found no sex differences in heat pain, and warmth and cold thresholds, but in the electrical detection of pain and tolerance thresholds, women were lower. When they used a magnitude estimation task with thermal stimulation there were no differences between the sexes, but with electrical stimulation women judged the pain as more intense, but only above a certain level (2.5 mA). Although they report significant correlations between the two methods for pain responsiveness, there was no such relationship where non-painful stimuli were concerned. They note previous studies showing that women are more pain sensitive to pressure than men, and draw the conclusion that the statistical evidence for sex differences depends very much on the type of method used.

Magnitude estimation tasks were hailed as a revolutionary new way to measure pain. The technique has since been modified to enable people to compare the intensity of their pain with the intensity of other phenomena, such as sound, light and pressure, in a process known as cross-modality matching (CMM). For example, the same set of words is repeatedly rated using handgrip force, light duration or line length, so responses are expected to be more consistent and less biased than with category rating scales. Exemplifying CMM, Gracely, McGrath and Dubner (1978) report two experiments showing that ratio scales of sensory and affective verbal pain descriptors are reliable, valid and objective. In the first task, 16 subjects gave verbal magnitude estimates for 30 adjectives (15 of each type) using seven line lengths, ranging from 1.3 cm to 33 cm in equal log steps. Then participants used a dynamometer to judge when their handgrip strength was equivalent to their chosen verbal rating. In a second similar task, a digital reaction timer recording was used to compare time duration (ms) with the same verbal descriptors. Gracely and Dubner have used CMM in a variety of ways to cast light on the ways in which people use verbal descriptions of pain. In one study, where they used this ratio measure to examine the relationship of the word "pain" to the descriptions of sensory intensity and unpleasantness, they concluded that the expression "pain" is more than a simple combination of sensory intensity and/or unpleasantness (Gracely and Dubner, 1987). There is a problem of gestalt here, with the whole understanding of pain being more than just the sum of these measurable parts. Despite the conceptual complexities of carrying out this work, Morley and Hassard (1989) have developed a CMM task that can be self-administered. They asked 20 chronic pain patients to self-administer a CMM task, scaling pain intensity and unpleasantness adjectives twice, the second time after two or three weeks. They found success rates of 65% and 70%, respectively, on the two occasions and high overall internal consistency (0.90). However, consistency was low for unpleasantness descriptions (25% and 40%) on both occasions. In an intriguing investigation of individual differences, they found that intelligence was related to a person's ability to scale intensity descriptors. This seems to indicate that this method is unsuitable for use with all volunteer participants. Such findings validate Hall's (1981) criticism that the CMM method presupposes that participants are able to carry out the complex cognitive task of judging ratios.

Hall (1981) has questioned how far the CMM procedure produces bias-free scales that are reliable and objective. In a rejoinder to Hall, Gracely and Dubner (1981) argue that ratio scales impose fewer constraints on users and are therefore less inclined to bias. It also tends to be assumed that this task is carried out both accurately and conscientiously, but boredom from this highly repetitive task is a potential hazard. Accuracy is likely to be compromised when opioids and analgesics are administered.

Furthermore, diazepam (Valium) affects only the affective dimension of pain and fentanyl only the sensory aspects, so the scaling appears to be differentially affected by drugs. The objectivity of the scale has also been questioned because it "most likely resides on the agreement between subjects upon the rank ordering of the adjectives, rather than in agreement on the scale values themselves" (Hall, 1981). These imperfections in themselves do not negate the use of this method, but users need to be aware of them when they measure pain.

One property of an ideal assessment is that it enables reliable comparisons to be made between clinical and experimental pain; Gracely and Dubner (1981) have developed a Descriptor Differential Scale (DDS) with this feature in mind. The DDS requires people to rate their clinical pain and compare it with verbal comparison stimuli using psychophysical principles. It is useful in clinical pain assessment because it enables those already in chronic or acute pain to judge whether the pain they feel is equal to, greater than or less than anchoring descriptors on a 10-point scale. This way their sensations are rated in relation to each word. The reliability of this scale was tested in a study of 91 dental patients who had a molar tooth extracted (Gracely and Kwilosz, 1988). Twelve words like "faint" were placed at the centre of a line (zero) with plus and minus at the extremes. Participants were asked to indicate whether their pain was more than faint or less than faint on the continuum. While the method proved to be fairly reliable over a very short retest interval of 1 to 2 hours, items in the middle of the scale like "moderate" and "barely strong" were more reliable than those at the extremes, such as "extremely intense" and "weak". Nevertheless, the DDS appears to discriminate between different pain dimensions and is sensitive to the effects of different pharmacological agents (see Gracely and Dubner, 1981). Together with its clinical utility, these features represent a cautious step forward in scaling.

More complex psychophysical methods have appeared in recent years, which hold promise for those in search of the ideal measure. The functional measurement (FM) scaling procedure was developed to show that it is possible to scale and average the intensity or unpleasantness of pain sensations induced by noxious stimulation, say to the tooth pulp, and symbolised by a word. As with some other methods, FM sets a testable validity criterion, which has to be satisfied before the resulting scales are acceptable for use in testing. Gracely and Wolskee (1983) asked 20 subjects to rate five sensory intensity or unpleasantness descriptors twice in 50 stimulus pairs using a dynamometer, in log steps from pain threshold to pain tolerance. Separate scales of pain intensity, verbal magnitude and psychophysical ability were produced from this. However, the scale avoids some of the interpretative problems found in signal detection theory analysis (see below), because the verbal magnitude scale controls for changes in response bias. The technique also requires little data.

Gracely et al (1988) find stimulus-dependent methods appealing because the results are expressed in terms of sensory magnitude of stimulus intensity, so assumptions do not need to be made about the psychological units of pain. This unambiguous data is also comprehensible to non-experts. The method enables assessment of the time course of pain sensitivity and is responsive to intravenous narcotic analgesia, monitoring the progress of analgesia at threshold and sub-threshold levels of pain. Because these analgesic manipulations are less obvious to participants, Gracely et al (1988) claim that this reduces their susceptibility to bias.

In search of an even more sophisticated assessment of pain, Gracely and Dubner's groups have piloted the random staircase method, which appears to retain the advantages of stimulus-dependent procedures, while scaling supra-threshold sensations. By modifying the method of limits, the intensity of successive stimuli is based on the response to each trial, so that this response determines the intensity of the next stimulus in the "staircase". Thus, there is a choice of two responses to any stimulus and the response determines how intense the next stimulus will be. Hence, a response of "no pain" will increase the intensity of the next trial, while a response of "mild pain" decreases the intensity of the following stimulus. In this way it is possible to track those responses that contribute to a determination of threshold. However, if this procedure was used exactly as described above, participants would quickly learn that the way in which they responded affected the intensity of the next stimulus. To prevent this association from occurring, stimuli from one of two staircases are randomly presented in a double random staircase, and a computer determines a random alternation between the two. The response to any one stimulus determines the intensity of the next stimulus presented by that staircase when it is randomly selected again, so the relationship between stimulus and response is not at all obvious. It is claimed that the technique can be used to assess compliance because only appropriate responding keeps the two staircases converging on a graph and stops them drifting apart. Similarly, a multiple random staircase method using up to six staircases can be used to track pain sensitivity at different levels of intensity (Gracely, 1989). Gracely (1989) claims that these stimulus-dependent measures are very quick, easy and efficient to use. They also require fewer stimuli and shorter sessions than response-dependent methods, where a series of fixed stimulus intensities are presented and a response to each is recorded separately.

While the important psychometric properties of recent methods are in many cases very good, there is widespread concern about finding a method that maintains secrecy about what is being done with a view to detecting malingerers. The development of such methods is carried out in the search for objectivity, and with the aim of distilling subjectivity out of the assessment. It is questionable whether this attempt at disaggregation is a legitimate or realistic pursuit. Implicit in this approach is the assumption that results from confused or puzzled subjects are superior in psychometric terms to answers obtained from those who understand the methods involved. Indeed, Gracely (1992) goes as far as to suggest that one of the pitfalls of ascending and descending series methods has been that they have *not* been spaced sufficiently close together to create confusion! Here confusing the participant is seen as a major strength of the staircase method. Covering up a procedure is unlikely to prevent participants from trying to guess the experimenter's working hypothesis. Furthermore, it increases the likelihood that they will come up with wild beliefs in the absence of available information. Does this then satisfy a self-fulfilling prophecy? Few severely ill patients and ethically recruited volunteers would deliberately subvert the results where the methods were transparent, even though there are some social systems that appear to encourage this behaviour more than others (see Chapter 10), but in the small proportion of cases where reports are intended to mislead, these actions must convey an important message to the researcher. Understanding and interpreting these messages should be an integral part of good clinical practice, and this subgroup is worthy of further scientific investigation in its own right. However, we may be deflected from the consensually shared aim of assessing pain well in most pain sufferers if we allow the enterprise of developing good methodologies to be driven by the behaviour of small minority of subversives.

SIGNAL DETECTION THEORY

A similar approach to studying pain using ratio scaling arose from the inception of information processing models. Signal detection theory or sensory decision theory (SDT) has been used to look at the effects of experimentally applied painful stimuli in the laboratory and has been useful in the assessment of analgesia. In SDT, the brain is conceptualised as having continuous but variable neural noise arising from constant environmental stimulation and thought processes. The theory considers how people deal with the overlapping effects of internal noise and a signal with noise, and, in its application, helps to explain how pain signals might be detected. Two measures are considered important for SDT analysis. The first is an *index of detection* or *discriminability* called d', which measures a person's accuracy in distinguishing between stimuli of various intensities. It is the difference between the means of two distributions — signal with noise and noise only — when this difference is divided by the standard deviation of the noise only distribution. As the value of d' is deemed to be related to the functioning of the neurosensory system, high values imply that neurosensory input is adequate for decision making, and low values that sensory processes have been interfered with. A second measure, β, estimates a person's willingness or reluctance to use a particular response. This measure is thought to reflect people's attitudes towards their sensory experience. A high criterion implies stoicism and a low one that the person already reports pain (Clark and Yang, 1983).

Participants in SDT experiments report whether they detect a stimulus (a hit) or do not detect it (a blank or false alarm). While it is possible to miss a stimulus or to reject it incorrectly, hits and blanks have been the focus of most SDT research on pain. Hits are plotted against blanks to graph the *receiver operating characteristic* (ROC), which is based on a Gaussian distribution. Comparisons between people can be made using d' to look at their ability to discriminate, to find out how often they report pain and to estimate their stoicism. One strength of the SDT method lies in its ability to separate these sensory elements from affective or attitudinal dimensions in the evaluation of pain, in a way that magnitude estimation tasks and traditional threshold measures are not able to do (Clark and Yang, 1983). As it is a widely held belief that pain reports can be altered by many psychosocial features and processes such as placebos, suggestion, attention, biofeedback and hypnosis (Melzack and Wall, 1989), it is particularly useful to be able to examine these two aspects independently. To exemplify, Clark (1969) gave a placebo to participants who believed that they were receiving a powerful analgesic. After receiving noxious thermal stimulation it was found that their pain threshold had been markedly raised. Applying SDT to this problem showed that this change was due to an increase in the pain report criterion (β), reflecting greater stoicism, not to a decrease in thermal discriminability (d'). So, by deduction, the placebo worked through social demand characteristics, not by altering that person's neurosensory activity (Clark and Yang, 1983).

Like threshold methods, SDT has been used to look at differences between sexes, ages and cultures, and for different personality traits like anxiety (e.g. Malow, 1981). In general, the results tend to confirm that sensation thresholds and the ability to discriminate between stimuli are largely universal. Where differences are consistent, this is usually attributable to variation in socialisation about ways of reporting pain. But is SDT any better in assessing socio-demographic differences than threshold methods? During the 1970s, results from several studies led to the conclusion that men tolerate pain better than women. However, results from SDT subsequently contradicted this, by displaying a wide range of individual differences for both sexes, with highly overlapping distributions for men and women. For example, Harkins and Chapman's (1977) data showed that women did not have a significantly lower threshold than men. Furthermore, their results indicated that group differences were more plausibly attributed to different attitudes than to biological factors (Wolff, 1983). Going on to consider age, Harkins and Chapman (1976, 1977) found that attitude bias can confound sensory threshold determinations. Young and old men (mean ages 21 and 71 years) rated trigeminal pain following noxious stimulation to their teeth, first for 100 practice trials, then for 200 experimental trials. Their age did not affect either absolute detectability or sensation threshold, but the ROC curves and d' changes revealed that elderly men were much more cautious about labelling a faintly perceived stimulus as painful than were those who were young. However, elderly men were less able to discriminate between two noxious stimuli, but higher trait anxiety explained this poorer discrimination. Such changes associated with ageing may be due to alterations in the cutaneous receptors at the periphery, rather than to changes in the central nervous system (CNS).

However, SDT has not confirmed the differences between ethnic groups that were indicated by threshold methods. Chapman et al (1982) used dolorimetry to the central incisor to compare the efficacy of acupuncture in Japanese and Seattle students. In functionally similar laboratories, subjects received acupuncture to the bilateral traditional facial points or a control condition, on two consecutive days and in a counterbalanced design. SDT measures showed a reduction in perceptual capability and an increased bias against reporting stimuli as painful following acupuncture, but no racial or cultural differences were found between the groups in terms of perceptual capability, reporting bias or pain threshold. While caution must be exercised in extrapolating from transient acute to chronic pathological states, these results provide an interesting anchor point for the interpretation of clinical data. Reviewing evidence for ethnic differences in pain, Wolff (1985) reports that little scientific progress has been made since 1968 because anecdotal differences remain the major source of material. He proposes that other neglected socio-cultural factors, such as whether people belong to a minority or a majority group, seem more likely to be the cause of differences than racial variables *per se*. In general, members of minority groups tend to show lower pain response levels than those belonging to majority groups. Wolff (1985) suggests that SDT is too simple to accommodate the many non-sensory factors like emotions and education, which may make noticeable contributions to the ethnic differences reported.

Despite early acclaim, there is growing doubt that SDT is the best method for measuring pain. Criticism comes not just from those who oppose logical positivist methods, on the grounds that the experience of pain cannot be meaningfully reduced to a handful of numbers, but also from psychophysicists who say that the application of SDT to the study of pain has not always been carried out with the care and accuracy that the technique demands (Rollman, 1977). Unfortunately, many of the problems encountered in studying pain cannot be adequately fitted into this detection/discrimination paradigm. Furthermore, interpretation of the results is difficult if d' changes but β does not. The method also precludes the concurrent assessment of both high hit rates and false positives (Chapman, 1977). Rollman (1977) points out that in investigations of pain the signal must not just be present (hit), as required by SDT, but — more than that — it must also be painful. He challenges the notion that a clear distinction can be made between sensory changes and motivational ones, and comments on the limitations of work carried out using a very large number of trials with only a small number of carefully trained subjects and a single optimal frequency value. Here, boredom is only one item in an extensive list of problems. In a major review, Wolff (1983) concludes that many of the deficiencies outlined by Rollman have been corrected in more recent SDT studies, so the debate has served to improve practices in this field.

But how comprehensive is the evaluation of pain using sensory and attitudinal components? While there is a legitimate debate about which aspects of sensation are being assessed by SDT, Coppola and Gracely (1983) say that the more important issue is whether there are key factors unrelated to stimulus painfulness that affect a person's ability to discriminate. While the separation of an attitudinal component from its sensory elements has conceptual appeal, precisely what the attitudinal component measures remains obscure. Some researchers have interpreted values of β as a tendency to respond conservatively or liberally. Others have used SDT to show that social influences like suggestion can raise the withdrawal criteria for pain tolerance, so affecting the decision to withdraw: in one study this occurred without influencing the discrimination of noxious thermal input to produce an anticipated analgesic-like effect (Clark, 1974). Even if we accept that attitudes are being measured here, the term is not operationalised in the way that social psychologists would use it and deserves better definition. Yet the concept is valuable, because, unlike many other psychophysical methods outlined in this chapter, this one incorporates the notion that people make decisions that are influenced by others, and make them within a social context rather than in an asocial vacuum. Such "attitudinal" judgements probably reflect a person's social, emotional, cultural, historical, political and ideological characteristics. Thus, β represents a somewhat rudimentary attempt to assess much broader social issues in a systematic way. It is a step forward, because implicitly the method not only acknowledges that those in pain bring their attitudes to bear on decision making about pain, but it also incorporates an assessment of them, rather than ignoring them, trivialising them or pretending that participants shed them like some psychosocial overcoat at the laboratory door.

So far in this chapter, we have considered several methods that have been designed with the aim of objectively assessing pain, and considered some of the methodological and philosophical deficiencies. Methods that include subjective assessment as part of the package are more likely to be amenable and adaptable to a psychosocial analysis of pain. In the second half of the chapter we go on to examine methods that are entirely subjective in their orientation.

UNIDIMENSIONAL SUBJECTIVE RATING SCALES

Underlying the design of the Visual Analogue Scale (VAS) was the thinking that only patients can assess the intensity or severity of their own pain (Scott and Huskisson, 1976). However, philosophically it is questionable as to whether respondents can truly make a one-to-one judgement between their position on the VAS and the corresponding sensation. Described as a "simple, robust, sensitive and reproducible instrument that enables a patient to express the severity of his pain in such a way that it can be given a numerical value" (Huskisson, 1983), the VAS is usually presented as a plain horizontal 100 mm line, without subdivisions or numbers. It is argued that the superimposition of numbers would result in preferences being expressed that would interfere with the distribution of results (Scott and Huskisson, 1976). Huskisson (1983) claims that its uniformity is the reason why it is very sensitive to change. The length is critical: scales of 10 cm and 15 cm have smaller measurement errors than those of 5 cm or 20 cm (Seymour et al, 1985). For this reason it needs to be reproduced accurately so that the number of millimetres from a predesignated end can be measured reliably. The labels at the poles vary, but their wording should ideally be selected from the vernacular; typically in pain research they read "no pain" to "worst pain ever". While ratio scaling has been hailed as the best available means of obtaining measures of pain, interval scaling still has its adherents, partly because of its simplicity. The VAS is easy to use, involving few instructions for patients and rapid administration and scoring for the assessor. It appears to be universally usable for most people over the age of 5 years, although McQuay (1990) cautions against using it with sleepy post-operative patients or the elderly. It is attractive to many researchers because it correlates highly with many other "objective" methods, such as the Ritchie Articular Index, which is used to measure tenderness in arthritic joints (Gaston-Johansson and Gustafsson, 1990). It can be adapted to create a ratio scale for the purposes of magnitude estimation tasks and is useful in distinguishing the separate properties of pain sensation intensity from pain unpleasantness, being superior in psychometric terms to numerical rating scales (NRSs) in this respect (Price et al, 1994; see below).

Although the scale is adaptable to the measurement of current pain, usual pain, worst pain and so on, there are concerns about how far a single rating of pain intensity is an accurate indicator alone. Two hundred chronic pain patients completed two weeks of hourly pain ratings in a study by Jensen and McFarland (1993). They found that stability of measurement increased as more pain ratings were completed, although the sample could be subdivided into those who reported stable pain over 7 days (33%) and those who reported unsystematic instability (45.5%). Findings about the instability of pain ratings are not unique to pain but form part of a much broader debate about the measurement and stability of a wide range of behaviours (Epstein, 1979). Single measures of pain intensity were shown by Jensen and McFarland (1993) to be less reliable and valid than a measure of average pain using this composite score. They concluded that estimates of pain intensity were adequate after only four measures, regardless of whether this was four from the same day, one from each of four consecutive days, or two from each of two consecutive days. The best method was twice daily ratings over four days. Others who have studied the pain profiles of chronic patients from their hourly intensity ratings have identified two important patterns (Jamison and Brown, 1991): (i) linear profiles (43%) reflecting lower pain in the morning, worsening throughout the day, and (ii) curvilinear profiles (25%) like an inverted U, which was typically described by headache patients.

A main criticism of the VAS is its unidimensional nature: it erroneously portrays pain as a unitary phenomenon, usually in terms of pain intensity. But pain is a highly complex, multidimensional experience, which has many discernible linguistic dimensions, as the McGill Pain Questionnaire shows (Melzack, 1975). The wide-spread use of the pain intensity VAS provides fuel for a debate argues that research into the *quantity* of pain has been performed at the expense of investigating its many *qualities* (Reading, 1983). Taking heed of this criticism, separate VAS scales have been created to distinguish the intensity of sensory pain from the unpleasantness of affective pain. These have been used to evaluate chronic clinical pain, as well as experimentally induced acute pain. For example, D.D. Price et al (1983) applied thermal heat to the forearms of 30 chronic pain patients and 20 healthy volunteers, but found no difference in sensory and affective responses using these scales. But chronic pain patients in general, and cancer patients in particular, tend to give higher ratings on the VAS affective scale than on the sensory dimension, so supporting a body of evidence that shows that affective pain is an overriding phenomenon associated with chronicity. In contrast, women experiencing the acute pain of the first two stages of labour showed less VAS affective pain than sensory pain. However, affective pain, not sensory pain, was significantly reduced when women focused their attention on the birth of the child rather than on their pain *per se* (Price, Harkins and Baker, 1987). These findings show how the emotional aspects of different types of acute clinical pain can be powerfully and selectively affected by psychosocial and contextual factors, as reflected by the sensitivity of these measures. This dichotomy in scaling has also proved useful pharmacologically, as lower doses of morphine sulphate (0.04–0.06 mg kg^{-1}) reduce affective pain but not sensory pain, while higher doses (0.08 mg kg^{-1}) reduce both sensory and affective VAS responses. These results provide "benchmark" data, which enable comparisons to be made with other analgesics (Price et al, 1985). Another application has been to elaborate the dimensions of pain intensity itself by looking at how patients rate different painful areas of the body. In one study, patients with rheumatoid arthritis rated VAS pain intensity while moving and resting their most painful limbs, knees, feet and wrists (Badley and Papageorgiou, 1989). Only weak evidence was found to support the theory that either overall pain might be dominated by the pain of the most powerful joint, or that some groups of joints may contribute more than others to the overall estimate of pain. Perceptively, the authors comment on how little research has been conducted into the ways in which people synthesise multiple pains into a single overall report. They also raise questions about whether various psychosocial, cultural and behavioural factors influence overall pain differently from component pains.

The accuracy of the VAS may depend upon the length of time between ratings. Reville et al (1976) found the VAS to be highly accurate and reliable over 7 days when women estimated acute labour pain following childbirth. However, the accuracy of the VAS may also depend on whether the pain is chronic or acute. For instance, overprediction was recorded for patients with chronic rheumatic disease by Scott and Huskisson (1979), and these patients made fewer incorrect estimates after two weeks than two years later, indicating a cognitive change in the stored memory rather than a change in the use of the method. The accuracy of the VAS may also depend on whether patients are instructed to anticipate their pain or to recall it retrospectively. Rachman and Lopatka (1988) used the VAS to record patients' expectations of arthritis pain prior to physiotherapy. They found that 57% made correct estimates, and there were fewer underpredictions (18%) than overpredictions (25%). Where a correct match was made, 62% of trials showed no change in reported pain, while 21% showed a decrease and 18% an increase. Following the overprediction of pain, there was no change for only 47%, an increase in pain for 25% and a decrease for 27%. This suggests that those who overpredict tend to continue to report more changes in pain, regardless of the direction of that change, so overprediction would be better considered as an index of reporting instability than one-way bias. By way of some explanation, Rachman (1986) suggests that recall in a pain-free state usually means that people will underestimate their pain.

However, the accuracy of the VAS has been questioned when it has been compared to categorical scaling. Linton and Gotesdam (1983) interviewed 15 chronic pain patients (mean age 43) and asked them to indicate their pain level and how much it could be ignored or was disabling, using a categorical Verbal Pain Scale (VPS). The scale categories ranged from 0 = no pain, 1 = pain present but easily ignored, 2 = pain present, cannot be ignored but does not interfere with daily activities, 3 = pain interferes with concentration, 4 = pain interferes with all tasks except taking care of basic needs such as eating and toilet, to 5 = rest or bed rest required. Patients completed the VPS at the same time as a 100 mm VAS labelled from "no pain" to "unbearable pain", daily for four to nine weeks and compliance was high. After treatment they were asked how much pain they recalled having at the first interview. Although it is not entirely clear whether they were measuring the same concept, results from the VAS and VPS were found to be significantly correlated ($r = +0.68$). More discrepancies between baseline and recalled pain occurred for the VAS than for the VPS, which was because VAS baseline pain had been overestimated. As underestimates and overestimates occurred with the VPS, it is deemed to be superior to the VAS. However, categorical scaling erroneously assumes equal intervals between the points of the scale. Furthermore, and in common with many other psychometric measures, it imposes the originator's concepts, language and categories on a respondent who may or may not find them meaningful. Despite these problems, it will be interesting to see whether the VPS gains the same popularity as the VAS in the future. The idea of integrating pain intensity with level of disability to give a comprehensive assessment is attractively pragmatic, and others have also tried to do this using more sophisticated Guttman scaling to provide a hierarchy of responses (Von Korff et al, 1992). However, it is not altogether clear whether these two concepts can be legitimately combined in this way. Many would argue that they are separate dimensions and demand separate assessment.

The Visual Analogue of Pain Relief Scale (VAPRS) is a further variation on the theme, being a comparative scale. "Complete relief" is presented at one extreme and "no relief" at the other, and the scale is divided into equal parts. Its advantages are that the size of response does not depend on initial pain severity, because all patients start from the same baseline. In addition, there is no need to assume linearity. The disadvantages outweigh the advantages, however, when it is compared with the usual VAS scale of pain severity or intensity. The most serious of these is that patients are unable to record an increase in pain, so the ratings are inevitably biased in favour of the treatment being evaluated. Furthermore, individual differences are masked, because the scale gives the erroneous impression that all patients start with the same level of pain (Langley and Sheppard, 1985). Taking the view of a clinician rather than a psychometrician, McQuay (1990) claims that where pain relief needs to be evaluated, there is no reason to prefer the VAS over categorical scales, but where simplicity is required, category scaling is recommended. However, the results may depend on which group of patients is tested. A recent study of 53 Italian chronic cancer patients has shown that, although patients tend to use different styles of rating scale in the same way, the VAS, NRS and verbal rating scale (VRS) are most strongly associated with pain relief (De Conno et al, 1994).

In view of the wide range of relative advantages and disadvantages with each of these scales, studies that have compared a range of measures with reference to acceptable scientific criteria are of great value. In one such study, Jensen, Karoly and Braver (1986) asked 75 chronic pain patients to judge present pain, least pain, most pain and average pain intensity using six types of scale. In addition to the VAS, participants were presented with an NRS of 100 divisions (NRS-101) and an 11-point box scale, where numbers were inserted within boxes and joined together like a row of bricks in a wall. In each of these scales, the extremes were marked "no pain" and "pain as bad as it could be". A six-point categorical behavioural rating scale (similar to the VPS) integrated an assessment of pain and disability. A four-point VRS ranged from "no pain" through "some pain" and "considerable pain" to "that pain which could not be more severe". A five-point VRS ranging from "mild", through "discomforting", "distressing" and "horrible" to "excruciating" was also included. The results showed that the scales were similar in terms of correct usage and predictive validity, but when important psychometric criteria were considered, the NRS-101 was the best. Other studies confirm the superiority of the NRS over the VAS in terms of measurement error (Downie et al, 1978).

The NRS-101 has several practical advantages, being simple to administer and easy to score. It can be used in both verbal and written forms without the problems of reproduction associated with the VAS and has 101 response categories. Usage is not affected by the respondent's age. A Brazilian study showed that a 10-point NRS had superior reliability to the VAS and a 5-point VRS, when the pain intensities of subgroups of literate and non-literate outpatients with rheumatoid arthritis were compared (Ferraz et al, 1990). These results suggest that a simpler version of the NRS may be the most appropriate measure for testing a much broader cross-section of the population in pain research. At the same time, its universal use could facilitate cross-cultural comparisons. The results from these studies thus support a move away from the use of the VAS and towards these improved measures.

Subjective measures of pain report are essential for any comprehensive assessment of clinical and experimental pain where knowing about the intensity or severity of pain is important. For practical reasons of speed and ease, most are likely to remain in use. However, the use of more than one measure seems advisable to control for the various disadvantages of each, nor does this preclude the inclusion of good "objective" measures wherever appropriate. More recent designs appear to show some better psychometric properties than the popular VAS and may be more comprehensible to a broader section of the community. Nevertheless, despite their many values, they are no real substitute for a comprehensive assessment of the many dimensions of painful experience, and for this reason are limited in their use.

THE LANGUAGE OF PAIN

Verbal and non-verbal communications of pain are social behaviours, since they are designed to convey messages of suffering to others. Their measurement is of fundamental importance to any development of a social approach to the investigation of pain, and this is explored in the sections that follow. Some social behaviour is involuntary or only partially controllable, but much of it is under voluntary control. Furthermore, the same behaviours can be expressed at different levels, so crying and groaning are partially controllable, but they may also be under greater voluntary control when used in interjections like "ouch". These interjections are potentially useful for tactical purposes but they may also be employed to engage sympathy or help (Ehrlich, 1985). At a verbal level, Ehrlich says that pain descriptions can be phrases or words, or pain may be told in a narrative or story.

NON-VERBAL AND OBSERVATIONAL PAIN ASSESSMENT

Measuring pain in children provides a number of methodological challenges. Investigations using the perspectives of the child as well as one or more observers more comprehensively assess the social interaction and social context of the pain and related behaviours, but it is mistaken to assume that parents and physicians can provide an adequate or accurate substitute for asking the children themselves: their viewpoints are just different. A valuable study by Manne, Jacobsen and Redd (1992) makes the point. Differences in perspective were demonstrated in a study of children receiving venipuncture, and the parents and nurses engaged in this procedure. Not only were reports from these three types of observer different, but furthermore they had been derived from three diverse sources of information. The nurses' ratings of the child's pain were based on how distressed they perceived the child to be. Parents on the other hand, made their ratings by integrating their subjective perceptions of the child's pain with their personal preconceptions about the procedure and its painfulness. The child's conceptualisations of the event and report depended on chronological age, together with stage of cognitive development.

In other studies the tendency has been to attempt to dodge some of the methodological and philosophical complexities inherent in carrying out this type of research by giving priority to the reports of proxies, principally the views of parents and physicians. McGrath (1987), on the other hand, has made a strong case for subjective reports being treated as the "gold standard" when dealing with children, so that priority is given to what they say. The problems that affect research in this area have also been valuable in advancing thinking about pain measurement in adults. This priority should be afforded to what adults say, too. Using parents to interpret their child's pain carries its own methodological problems because, parents can strongly modify a child's behaviours, particularly when the child has a chronic or life-threatening disease. Parents may have their own difficulties in adjusting to the treatments prescribed, and may consequently pressurise their children into being excessively compliant or coping "like little adults" during invasive procedures (McGrath, 1987, p.156). This means that when distressed, children may suppress verbal and non-verbal emotions. As a result, their reactions are not passive reflections of their pain but are highly dependent on the type of social and emotional context in which that pain occurs (McGrath, 1987).

Three main problems are encountered in studying children's pain language. Firstly, children's verbal fluency and stage of cognitive development may restrict their ability to communicate their pain adequately. Secondly, behaviours observed in children do not necessarily reflect their pain intensity. Thirdly, the meaning of a particular behaviour may vary; crying, for example, has been observed to have three meanings and there may be more. It could be an expression of the child's pain, an expression of fear or anxiety, or it may provide a distraction from the pain (Manne, Jacobsen and Redd, 1992; Van der Does, 1989). However, the second and third points are not exclusive to the study of pain in children; they should be more widely considered with reference to self-report in adults, because this richness of meanings also extends to them. Furthermore, where wide variations in the meaning of adult behaviours has been observed, there has been less inclination to treat such behaviours at face value, as happens in paediatrics. More common has been the tendency to interpret this variation in adult reports as capriciousness, or as an intention to deceive the assessor or to bias the results for other intangible rewards. The latter view seems to be particularly common in clinical contexts where sizable compensation claims are known to be pending. It is because these variations in meaning exist that methods which observe a patient's behaviour without also obtaining meanings as subjective reports must have limited success, because they have only obtained a fraction of the data that would permit a fuller and more meaningful interpretation of that behaviour.

Observational methods have been developed with the explicit aim of providing objective measures of pain. As there are excellent self-report measures available for use with children aged 4 years and over (McGrath, 1990), a major challenge now lies in interpreting observed pain behaviour in babies and infants. There is little consensus about methods here. One approach has been put forward by Levine and Gordon (1982), who recommend that greater attention is paid to pain-induced vocalisation (PIV) in pre-lingual children. PIV is the screaming cry in response to noxious stimulation. Levine and Gordon suggest that a spectrographic analysis of PIV in infants might relate to the differential diagnosis of common childhood disorders such as recurrent abdominal pain. The implications of this work could be instrumental in revising a popular misconception among some surgeons that because children are unable to describe their pain, they are therefore insensitive to it and do not need anaesthetic for simple surgical procedures. This view persists despite the "considerable restraint" sometimes required during surgery (Levine and Gordon, 1982, p.88).

Pain drawings provide an interesting non-verbal self-report method. Claims have been made for their predictive value in assessing personality, but these claims have proved unconvincing where the subscales of the Minnesota Multiphasic Personality Inventory (MMPI) have been investigated (Ransford, Cairns and Mooney, 1976) and gain only limited support with the General Health Questionnaire (GHQ-28), where results have been correlated with the percentage of bodily area involved (Ginzburg, Merskey and Lau, 1988). However, beyond the personality arena, more hopeful results have been obtained. In one study, Margolis, Tait and Krause (1986) asked "blind" raters to evaluate 45 views of painful anatomical areas obtained from 101 chronic low back pain patients by assigning weights to these areas according to the percentage of body surface covered. Spectacular inter-rater reliability was reported (0.99) to support the claim that this bodily surface system is highly reliable. It also correlates well with a four-point penalty system, where penalties were awarded for unreal drawings with poor anatomical localisation, expansion or magnification of pain represented by unrelated symptomatology, over-involvement with pain and endorsement of painful body areas distant from the back. Good test–retest reliability over 71 days has been reported for this method (Margolis, Chibnall and Tait, 1988). Despite its application to the manipulating pain patient, further research needs to be done to establish confidence in using this method.

Observational methods used to study adult pain behaviour fall into three broad types: (i) somatic interventions, such as seeking surgery or medication, (ii) impairments to functioning, such as loss of mobility, deteriorating personal relations or avoidance of occupational commitment and (iii) pain complaints, such as moaning, crying and facial contortions (Chapman et al, 1985). Behavioural measures of activity are widely used as part of the standard assessment of patients in many pain clinics, so they deserve detailed consideration. But how useful are they? In validating an observational method for assessing non-chronic back pain, Jensen, Bradley and Linton (1989) videoed the activities of 61 nurses who had been on the sick-list for back pain during the previous two years. Two trained observers coded the results in accordance with a widely used system developed by Keefe and Block (1982). These activities included sitting, standing, reclining, pacing, shifting, guarding, bracing, grimacing, sighing, and active and passive rubbing. There was high inter-rater reliability between observers for guarding, bracing and sighing, and kappa coefficients ranged from 0.68 for grimacing, to 0.93 for sighing. While significant test–retest correlations were obtained for all activities except bracing, only guarding was significantly correlated with pain intensity and only guarding was related to spinal mobility — one of five additional measures obtained. This leads to the conclusion that from this wide range of activities, only guarding may be used confidently in the assessment of non-chronic back pain. The reliability of measuring these activities in chronic low back pain has been addressed in a study of 71 patients and 40 controls (Follick, Ahern and Aberger, 1985) where participants were videoed performing a sequence of movements like sitting, standing and walking. A 16-category observation system showed "acceptable" reliabilities for guarding, bracing, bodily adjustments or weight distribution, restricted movements, grimacing, limitation statements expressing disability or impairment, and sounds such as moaning, groaning or grunting. Discriminant analysis revealed that partial movement, limitation statements, sounds and position most reliably classified group membership for 94% of patients and 95% of controls in the first analysis, and 89% overall in a second analysis. Thus, the results suggest that for low back pain patients at least, some of these observable activities may provide reliable measures.

Not surprisingly, trained observers perform more reliably than mechanical measuring devices like the actometer and "uptimer", which were designed to measure "up-time", or time spent out of bed walking or standing. These gadgets are unreliable in their measurement of clinical outcome for chronic low back pain patients (Morrell and Keefe, 1988; Sanders, 1983). It seems possible, then, that despite the rigours of training, the subtle interpersonal messages communicated non-verbally between patient and observer are somehow received, translated and coded, creating greater accuracy with this method than any existing mechanical approach provides. This may be because of observers' interpretations when coding. The data support the use of observers as a supplement to, not as a substitute for, the use of subjective reports from patients themselves.

However, one danger is that in the absence of verification of meaning from the patients themselves, the researcher's own opinions may be used to interpret the data. In a study by Gil et al (1987) of the relationship between social support and adjustment to chronic pain syndromes, high satisfaction with social support was found to be associated with more pain behaviours like guarding, rubbing and bracing ($p < 0.06$). The authors believed that this reflected poorer adjustment in those with social support, and their views, rather than reports from chronic pain patients, were used to interpret the observed activities as maladaptive. While guarding was deemed to be adaptive during the acute phase, it was unclear at what point in the progression of the disease a label of "maladaptive" might be applied, and, indeed, no convincing case was made as to why it should be applied at all. Secondly, the authors interpreted their findings to mean that those who were satisfied with their social support were satisfied as a result of positive reinforcements from the environment that were obtained when they engaged in pain behaviour. This conclusion might have been justified had it been backed up by video data of patients engaging socially with their family or friends, but instead it was made following observations of pain patients performing these activities alone. Consequently, any explanations based on the processes of social interaction in the absence of such data must necessarily be speculative. This devalues the so-called "social" approach to the study of pain, by failing to provide data on social interactions to support interpretation. Many studies based on "social" learning theory suffer from the same problem because they have neglected to investigate social interaction directly, as a dynamic process between those who have regular and salient contact with pain patients (see also Chapter 3).

Unless patients are asked why they behave in a particular way, researchers are left to make a partially informed guess, with all the compromises to accuracy that this affords. Without subjective reports to hand, an open-minded atheoretical investigator may not appreciate some of the many meanings that accrue to a particular piece of behaviour. In contrast, the committed theorist may miss plausible alternatives in an attempt to tie the theoretical interpretation to the data. The result of both of these approaches is that, in the process, a certain number of patients will be misunderstood, and this does not bode well for the development of trusting empathic relations between physician and patient and so for treatment outcome. However, this is not a case for abandoning theory. Indeed, there is "nothing so practical as a good theory" (Lewin, 1951), in the field of pain as elsewhere. Instead, this is a plea for the development of more elaborate theories that are able to accommodate the rich spectrum of meanings heard daily in clinics. It works against the "one dose fits all" ideology. Albert Einstein is reputed to have said, "Everything should be made as simple as possible, but not simpler".

Many of these observational methods have been derived by those in search of an "objective" means of measurement. Perhaps one of the biggest advances in this area has been in the development of the Facial Action Coding System (FACS), which is based on 44 movements or action units linked to the musculature of the face (Ekman and Friesen, 1978) (see Chapter 7). Although observers can record which muscles are moving, how much and when, such observational methods used on their own will only lead to increasing speculation about what those muscular movements mean for someone in pain. The only way to discover the meaning with any level of certainty is to record the articulated experience. This avoidance of asking about pain in the pursuit of objectivity may have provided the pain literature with as much information about the researchers' theories while viewing the actions of their pain patients as it has about the ways in which their patients think about their pain.

VERBAL PAIN ASSESSMENT

Similes are used by those in pain to describe their sensations, but these do not necessarily accurately represent the phenomenon described, so embodying an interesting philosophical paradox. Thankfully, few of those who describe their pain as a "stabbing" pain have ever been stabbed, but what does it feel like to be stabbed? On occasions when stab victims have been asked to say how it felt, one person described it a "dull ache" (Miller, 1978). This anecdotal evidence raises questions about whether we employ a "sensation vocabulary"; which is ordered and tidy. Ehrlich's (1985) view is that, because of this paradox, any attempt to demand linguistic precision from a describer will inevitably flounder. However, many others dissent from this view, and expect to find that pain language, precisely used, can give a good indication of diagnosis. The design of the McGill Pain Questionnaire, for instance, was predicated on this assumption. People are readily able to linguistically identify the many qualities of pain, and many different ideas and words are represented cross-culturally. For example, perusal of a Zulu – English dictionary published in 1946 showed that under the word "cut", different words for castration and circumcision were listed, as well as terms for cutting the skin, hair, ears for rings, forehead and nose, a wound in the head and a gash. Similarly, for "pain", there were separate descriptors for the pain before and after labour. There were also three types of throbbing in the wrist and two sorts of throbbing in the side. There was stabbing pain, pain of a wound, pain in the stomach and pain in the chest. Pangs of pain also had their own discrete description (Roberts, 1946).

In a translation of the McGill Pain Questionnaire from English into German, 9 of the 76 original adjectives could not be satisfactorily translated, and 10 new German words needed to be added to complete the lexicon (Radvila et al, 1987). Although the McGill Pain Questionnaire is written in English, it may be regarded as a "sketch of the semantic field of the word 'pain' for Anglophone Canadians" (Harré, 1991), so despite the common language, it would have differed in some ways had the pool of items originated in Britain. The problems of obtaining semantic and conceptual equivalence even between versions of the same scale written in a common language mean that there is only limited agreement about exactly how many pain qualities there may be. Furthermore, different methodologies produce differing results. Early introspection techniques identified only four basic and distinctive qualities of the painful experience. Titchener (1920) called these "quick pain", "clear pain", "ache" and "prick". At about the same period, Dallenbach (1939) listed 44 pain qualities.

In a pioneering article, Melzack and Torgerson (1971) reported 102 English descriptors of pain. A selection of these were later integrated into the McGill Pain Questionnaire (Melzack, 1975). In collating these adjectives, Melzack and Torgerson included Dallenbach's list, supplementing it with others drawn from the clinical literature and a limited number obtained from hospital patients. The McGill Pain Questionnaire was developed as a tool for studying the effects of various styles of pain management. Methodologically it would have been preferable to have surveyed adjectives used by patients to communicate their pain in clinical interviews, sampled from a representative cross-section of diagnostic groups, instead of relying largely on terms published by scientists and clinicians. The use of focus group methodology to obtain a vernacular would have been another way to overcome this problem. It is not surprising, therefore, that some words published in the original version of the McGill Pain Questionnaire are outside the vernacular. For example "lancinating" is incomprehensible to the majority of patients. The poor quality of this initial stage in the scale's development also means that the list is not comprehensive. For example, many arthritis patients use "stiffness" and "pain" almost interchangeably, and it is a key characteristic in confirming the diagnosis, but stiffness is not included in the McGill Pain Questionnaire.

Melzack and Torgerson (1971) divided the adjectives into three classes and thirteen subclasses, ascribing a descriptive label to each division. They concluded, "the final classification then appeared to represent the most parsimonious and meaningful set of subclasses without at the same time losing subclasses that represent important qualitative properties". As patients were not used as judges, it must be assumed that this structure was most parsimonious and meaningful to the researchers, which begs the validity of the exercise. These subclasses were presented to 20 people with university education (14 males and 6 females; mean age 30), who agreed or disagreed with the classification of each word. This procedure had the effect of structuring and pre-empting the exercise by providing a forced-choice task, rather than by giving free choice to decide whether an alternative subclass might be more appropriate. The task should have been performed by a representative sample of pain patients matched for sex, age and socio-economic status. Words gaining less than 65% agreement were presented in a subsequent forced choice task. Consequently, the restrictions of this procedure effectively removed any opportunity to change the nature of the 20 categories designated by the authors, or to add new items to the original list of 102, once the standardisation process had begun. However, some refinements were made using a second group of 20 similar subjects (12 male and 8 females) to assign words to categories. Intensity ratings in subclasses were examined by 140 students, 20 physicians and 20 Canadian patients, who rated them on a seven-point Thurstone scale. These results were then used to make adjustments to improve the discrimination properties of the scale. Melzack and Torgerson have since acknowledged that the procedures they used to assign descriptors to classes were based largely on *a priori* considerations verified using statistical techniques that are inadequate by modern standards. These procedures demonstrate some of the fundamental weaknesses in the design and conceptualisations of this pain scale, which is not only the most quoted scale in pain research today (Melzack, 1983b), but is probably the one most commonly used for research on chronic pain patients (Keefe, 1982). Although most pain researchers view the McGill Pain Questionnaire as an important advance in pain measurement, Harré (1991) comments that what is billed as pain measurement by many studies that use it is "actually an investigation of the lexicon of pain talk, and of efforts to recruit that lexicon to clinical practice" (p.102).

The final scale consisted of 20 subclasses; there are 42 sensory words divided between 10 subclasses, 14 affective or emotion-based words in 5 subclasses, a single subclass of 5 evaluative words and 4 miscellaneous categories of 17 words (Figure 2.1). Respondents choose a single descriptor from each subclass of words. Despite the shortcomings of the design, considerable evidence has been accumulated to show that the dimensions of sensory, affective and evaluative pain represent important properties of pain language and experience, and the scale represents a major breakthrough in the measurement of pain qualities. The original standardisation was based on data from 297 patients with a wide variety of painful conditions, such as arthritis and low back pain (Melzack, 1975). Drawings of the human body have also been incorporated so that the spatial distribution of pain can be recorded. Words describing the temporal properties of pain have been included, like "brief", "continuous" and "intermittent". Respondents are also able to record the intensity

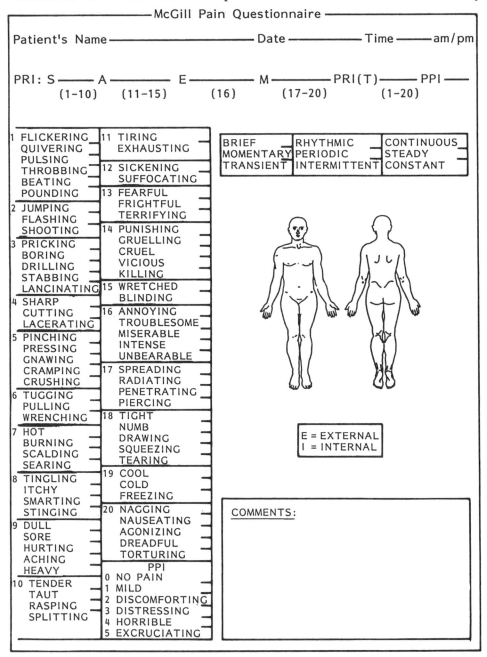

Figure 2.1 The McGill Pain Questionnaire (*Pain*, Vol.1, R. Melzack, *The McGill Pain Questionnaire: major properties and scoring method*, pp. 277–299, 1975, with kind permission from Elsevier Science BV, Amsterdam, The Netherlands)

of their pain using a five-point scale from mild (1) to excruciating (5). These are assumed to be equal intervals, and therefore to act as anchors for overall pain intensity. Keefe (1982) has commented on the disadvantageous use of categorical scaling in the McGill Pain Questionnaire, which yields low level ordinal data and introduces response bias by imposing response constraints. Because of this, he says, it provides qualitative evaluations of pain, but not quantitative ones, as claimed.

A weighting, or value between 1 and 5, has been allocated to each descriptor, and the present pain intensity (PPI) is derived from the number/word combination chosen. Within a subclass, words were ranked as a result of the intensity ratings assigned by doctors, nurses and students (Melzack, 1975), and the rank values are summed to obtain a pain rating index (PRI) or score for each category and to provide a total pain score. The PRI has been used to assess the three components of pain and to make differential diagnoses. The *a priori* structure of the PRI has been tested and subjected to cross-validation (Turk, Rudy and Salovey, 1985). The number of words chosen (NWC) is an additional index, although the instructions limit this choice to a single word from each subgroup. Several other indices have been proposed as additional measures (e.g. Charter and Nehemkis, 1983).

But how often are the adjectives used? Melzack (1975) showed that all of the classes were utilised, but some more frequently than others. Sensory classes were used more often (125 words) than affective ones (86 words), and 95% of patients selected a word from the small evaluative group. Sensory pain is also weighted more heavily than the other dimensions in these indices by virtue of its contribution to 10 classes, and this is problematic. The stated procedure for administering the scale is that patients are not allowed to fill out the questionnaire themselves, because they may "unreliably" choose more than one item from each category or not describe their pain at the time (Melzack, 1975). The list from each subclass is read aloud, so respondents may need to remember up to six words before making a choice. This methodology biases the results, because primacy and recency effects may operate in the recall of these lists (Skevington, 1991). Those who are highly anxious about being assessed at the time of completion and those with memory disorders associated with ageing may be unable to retain the list in the short-term memory long enough to perform the careful comparisons required for accuracy. Furthermore, patients may erroneously conceptualise the activity as a "memory test" rather than a method for obtaining their views about how the pain feels. The assumption underlying this procedure is that the words will be read in a "standard" voice without emphases or biases, so that a free choice is made between all of the words of a subclass, but to what extent such standardisation is practicable is debatable.

Some words may not be meaningful and may need to be defined. Melzack (1975) comments that patients are often "grateful" for being provided with words, because it saves them having to search for words that enable them to communicate with the physician, but conversely it is arguable that this method "puts the words into patients' mouths" rather than eliciting the varied spontaneous language they use in clinical interviews to describe their pain. Their own speech resources must, by definition, be more meaningful to them than words provided by others. At best, the meaning of a word can be defined by the McGill Pain Questionnaire test administrator using a dictionary if required, or in the worst case — and more often, in practice — it is merely guessed at by the participant (or administrator). Pain patients are "petitioners for aid" (Sternbach, 1978), and in this role they are likely to be keen to learn and use "appropriate" language that will gain them the help they need to obtain pain relief. Thus, it is arguable that by supplying lists of pain adjectives, practitioners and researchers are effectively teaching their patients a pain language that not only shapes their thinking about their illness, but also provides a legitimate lexicon that may be recycled in later consultations as the "correct" descriptor to use. By supplying the words and following the prescribed instructions, we blinker ourselves to our patients' ability to describe pain in their own varied language, which in many cases is not reducible to a single word in the English language. For example, a patient with early synovitis who was asked to describe her pain said, "it is like a suit of armour which is too tight". The author is still struggling to translate this into a single descriptor from the McGill Pain Questionnaire.

To investigate issues associated with the administration of the McGill Pain Questionnaire, Klepac et al (1981) compared the interview with paper-and-pencil replies. By exposing 80 student volunteers to the cold pressor test, they found that interviewees gave higher scores — 2.9 words more — than those who completed the paper version on all three subscales. A significant 15 out of 40 interviewees required one or more dictionary definitions, and from a total of 35 queries, 8 of the replies were then selected as the word. The authors caution that a higher word count is not necessarily better, and question whether subtle demands are being placed on interviewees in articulating their replies. Despite these findings, a more recent review by Wilkie et al (1990) looking at 51 published studies noted that the majority (62%) still do not record whether the McGill Pain Questionnaire was presented orally or in written form.

Interactive computer animation has recently been used to improve presentation and extend knowledge about certain words included in the questionnaire. While some words, such as "flickering", do not lend themselves to a simple drawing, others can be well represented using colour computer images (Swanston et al, 1993). For "burning", a black circle was presented with a reddish centre that could be expanded step-wise in 40 gradations to show its intensity. The word "pressure" was represented by a vice squeezing a round balloon into a thin oval shape in 40 steps. The computer-aided technique was preferred by 68% of chronic pain patients who tried it, compared with 18% who preferred the McGill Pain Questionnaire so the technique provides new frontiers for future research.

In addition, it seems possible that different words within any one subclass may describe conceptually different facets of the respondent's experience, so by restricting replies to a single word from each subclass the fullness of a multidimensional description of that person's experience is lost. Given the ostensible qualitative aims of the questionnaire, it seems conceptually unsound to assert that choosing one (or no) descriptor from a series is somehow more "reliable" than choosing a cluster of words that supply different aspects of the dimension of pain experienced. McArthur, Cohen and Schandler (1989) make several interesting related points; the first is that within any subclass the distance between any adjective pair is treated as the same as any other difference between two adjectives. Thus, the difference between "flickering" and "pounding" is treated in the same way as that between "beating" and "pounding". Not only may this be an erroneous assumption about perception, but it is compounded by a second *non sequitur*, that respondents *recognise* that these differences are the same. A second problem concerns parity in subclass scoring because the subclasses do not contain the same number of adjectives. Those who choose the highest of the adjectives in two different subclasses would score 5 only if there were five adjectives in each class, e.g. "killing", but would score only 2 if the subclass contained two adjectives, as with "exhausting". Thirdly, they point out that the "no response" category is only meaningful if the lowest scoring adjectives for each class are identical, and this is not the case.

McArthur, Cohen and Schandler (1989) have outlined a new psychometric approach to the measurement of pain based on a model-fitting procedure, which enables individual responses and/or stimuli (and meaningful subsets) to be compared. Since they claim that this fulfils Gracely and Dubner's exacting criteria for good measures, developments in this area are eagerly awaited. However, the length of time needed to carry out this procedure is problematic, especially when dealing with very sick and distressed patients and in busy clinics. Consequently, a short form of 15 descriptors is available, using a selection of 11 sensory and 4 affective adjectives, which can be administered in less than 10 minutes (Melzack, 1987). Although this appears to be sensitive to clinical change, some important psychometric properties have yet to be established. Other versions have been produced, either to reduce the number of words or to make them more relevant to the samples under investigation. For example, Skevington (1979) selected the adjectives from Melzack and Torgerson's list that were most appropriate to the arthritis and back pain she was studying. The procedure was modified so that patients could use an unlimited number of words to describe their pain (see also Papageorgiou and Badley, 1989). Some painful conditions such as rheumatoid arthritis or myofascial pain dysfunction syndrome are probably most appropriately described by certain subclasses of the McGill Pain Questionnaire (Skevington, 1991), so restricting choice within sub-classes may artificially depress the total pain score.

So what are the psychometric properties of the McGill Pain Questionnaire? Several reviewers confirm support for its basic structure, reliability and validity. Melzack (1975) examined test–retest reliability in 10 patients who received three copies of the questionnaire over 3 to 7 days. Such a short retest interval is unacceptable to many psychologists (Reading, 1983). Although they reported the same PPI level, their consistency in choice of subclass varied enormously from 50% to 100%, suggesting an unreliable test. In a review, Keefe (1982) shows that the McGill Pain Questionnaire has reasonable discriminant and construct validity, but construct validity was also the focus of a paper by Prieto and Geisinger (1983), who concluded that most studies failed to confirm the three subscales of sensory, affective and evaluative pain. They claimed strong evidence for a four-factor model, where two dimensions were sensory and the other two mixed sensory–affective and evaluative–affective items. They identified three other studies where four factors had been extracted; in each case the fourth factor was predominantly affective, mixed with words from the other subscales. Consequently, this work casts serious doubt upon the construct validity of the affective and evaluative scales of the McGill Pain Questionnaire and provides an argument against using the subscales individually and in favour of using a total pain score. In a comparison of five versions of the questionnaire, Wilkie et al (1990) confirmed that it has concurrent and predictive validity for pain qualities and pain intensity. In view of its shortcomings, however, some researchers have suggested that the use of multiple assessments is desirable when investigating pain (Reading, 1980; Turk, Rudy and Salovey, 1985).

While factor analysis has been the statistic of choice for determining the theoretical structure of the McGill Pain Questionnaire (e.g. Lowe, Walker and MacCallum, 1991), more robust multivariate techniques such as multidimensional scaling (MDS) have gained popularity. MDS is particularly useful in examining semantic problems, as in pain, where the relationships between items are unknown and where there are difficulties in measuring the concept directly. Despite the dubious method of assembling the original 102 terms for the questionnaire, Torgerson and Ben Debba (1983) have reused these to model the concept of pain using MDS to map the relationships and distances between pain descriptors after they have been judged to be similar to or different from each other. These psychological distances can be plotted on any number of dimensions (usually two or three) so that meaningful configurations can be examined. An exploratory procedure is used to model the data first, then confirmatory evidence is supplied by the investigator to reorientate it, to produce a configuration and to find out how well the two fit. Adjustments continue until the best fit is achieved.

In a study of cancer patients and healthy volunteers who made similarity judgements of nine pain descriptors, results from MDS showed that pain intensity was the most important dimension, especially for the patients (Clark et al, 1989). Pain intensity was described by them as mild and annoying at one extreme, and as intense and unbearable pain at the other. For the second dimension of emotional quality, the negative affect of sickening and miserable pain was contrasted with the strong affect of burning for patients, while for healthy volunteers it was contrasted with the weaker emotions of mild and annoying pain. A third somatosensory dimension included burning and cramping. Clark, Janal and Carroll (1989) provide a more detailed discussion of the multidimensional scaling of pain.

To inspect the domain of pain, Torgerson and Ben Debba (1983) have presented preliminary data from a very large ongoing study. To reduce the inconceivable task of asking individuals to make more than 5000 judgements, they have constructed a series of interlocking and overlapping studies. Here, 16 people judged about 20 words from the original McGill Pain Questionnaire subclasses of brightness, thermal pain and temporal pain, and made comparisons with the word "jumping". From the results, four ideal types were identified: brightness, a slow, rhythmic, temporal type of pain, thermal pain and a "rapid, almost vibratory and perhaps arhythmic pain", which was a bit like the description "flickering". They believe that their new hypercylindrical model describes the structure and meaning of pain reasonably well; time will tell.

Work by Turk, Wack and Kerns (1985) demonstrates how useful this technique can be in unravelling the range of behaviours that comprise a construct like pain behaviour, where there is limited consensus. Turk, Wack and Kerns (1985) asked pain specialists to rate 63 pain behaviours mentioned in the literature. They selected 20 of those with the greatest consensus to be judged by 50 members of the International Association for the Study of Pain (IASP), half of them psychologists and half physicians. MDS identified two dimensions that both groups agreed were important in determining pain behaviour. The first was visible versus audible pain behaviour; the second was affective versus behavioural aspects. Within these dimensions, four clusters of items were shown. These were (i) facial or audible expressions of distress like sighing and grimacing, (ii) distorted ambulation or posture, including limping and stooping, (iii) avoidance of activity like taking medication and lying down in the middle of the day and (iv) negative affect such as irritability and asking "why me?". Such work seems to make better sense of the various different classifications of pain behaviour published in recent years and gives a framework to interpretation. However, as with factor analysis, the type and quantity of items put into MDS determines the eventual solution. In a similar Dutch study incorporating 78 components of pain behaviour, Vlaeyen et al (1987) confirmed the visible–audible pain behaviours dimension of Turk, Wack and Kerns, but also identified two other dimensions of withdrawal–approach, reflecting degrees of passivity, and high versus low arousal, contrasting restless and nervous styles with guarded and careful walking. While questions about reliability must be raised, these differences in results may reflect cross-cultural variation in the conceptualisations of pain behaviours by health professionals.

Because the concept of pain is so difficult to measure, much interest has been expressed in assessing pain with the aid of structural equation modelling. This enables theorists to work with latent trait concepts like pain and loneliness, which are difficult to measure directly, using a program to examine linear structural relations (LISREL). Rudy (1989) says that this technique is popular because "it provides the researcher with both confirmatory methodology and comprehensive and statistically powerful techniques for assessing and modifying theoretical models, particularly in research situations where experimental manipulations are not possible or feasible" (p.53). The technique offers potential for the future in pain research, particularly in situations where good theory is on hand to guide model revisions in a systematic manner. A recent example is provided by a study that pooled results from 1700 pain patients to examine the PRI structure of the McGill Pain Questionnaire. Between three and seven dimensions have been recorded in the literature. This variation in results might be attributable to patient samples of different sizes with different diagnoses and special problems (Holroyd et al, 1992). Modelling with LISREL was used to confirm that it is possible to replicate respectable evaluative and affective dimensions, but two sensory factors emerged and persisted during cross-validation, so challenging the idea that there is a single sensory class (Holroyd et al, 1992).

It has tended to be assumed that the language of pain is used quite precisely and therefore could be of value in the correct diagnosis of chronic pain patients (Melzack and Wall, 1989). This feature of clinical utility is addressed here. Dubuisson and Melzack (1976) used constellations of pain words to correctly classify 77% of pain patients into eight pain syndromes using discriminant function analysis. The proportion increased to 100% when sex and the location of pain were also entered into the calculations, so leading to the conclusion that patients with similar diseases tend to use the same pain language. The small subsamples mean that the resulting classification structure must be "suggestive rather than definitive" (Torgerson and Ben Debba, 1983, p.49). Claims have been made that patients with and without medical diagnoses, those with and without psychiatric disturbance and those with different medical diagnoses may be identifiable from the language they use (Kremer, Atkinson and Kremer, 1983). Boureau, Doubrere and Lun (1990) found that a reasonable discrimination could be made between neuropathic and non-neuropathic pain patients using a French version of the McGill Pain Questionnaire. However, other studies report difficulty in differentiating between diagnostic groups. For instance, Atkinson, Kremer and Ignelzi (1982) were unable to distinguish between oncology patients with chronic benign pain and patients undergoing haemodialysis for renal failure on the basis of language.

There are also claims that the sensory scale may predict more than just pain, but also important psychosocial aspects of the respondent's lifestyle. Jamison, Vasterling and Parris (1987) gave a sensory checklist to 507 chronic pain patients, and found that those using the most sensory words were not only younger but had also experienced most interference with their work. They had more conflicts at home and more unsatisfactory social activities with a desire for fewer of them, spent more time in bed sleeping less, and with less satisfactory sexual activities. Discriminant function analysis, however, correctly classified only 59% of patients on the basis of these characteristics — little better than by chance — so replication is awaited with interest.

A value of the McGill Pain Questionnaire has been in its ability to reorientate thinking about pain, by highlighting the importance of measuring emotions. This has been especially important in the expression of chronic pain, where there is abundant evidence that the affective distress of suffering is a priority communication (Kremer and Atkinson, 1984). In a study of 85 patients with low back pain and pain-free volunteers exposed to experimental electric shock, Crockett, Prkachin and Craig (1977) factor analysed McGill Pain Questionnaire categories to find that the first two factors reflected emotions. The first factor tapped the immediate anxiety associated with acute experimental pain (22% of the variance), while the second represented strong emotions associated with the perception of harm (23%). This pattern has also been reported in children's pain language (Savendra et al, 1982) where 100 hospitalised children (aged 9 to 12 years) were compared with 114 healthy peers. Open-ended questioning showed that all children used more sensory (58%) than affective (10%) or evaluative (27%) words when describing the worst pain ever, but hospitalised children used more affective words than those who were healthy. However, using the affective subscale of the McGill Pain Questionnaire has a number of drawbacks (Jensen, Karoly and Harris, 1991). It is not distinctive from the other subscales; there are no estimates of stability and internal inconsistency; and when it is administered separately from the other two subscales, its validity is unknown. In an attempt to improve the measurement of affect, Jensen, Karoly and Harris (1991) are developing a Pain Discomfort Scale, which incorporates the McGill Pain Questionnaire affect subscale with other quantitative measures.

More important from a social point of view is the finding that showed that when pain language was rated by nursing and medical students, considerable emphasis was placed on the perceived affective component in pain. Health professionals see it as closely linked to pain intensity and evaluation (Bailey and Davidson, 1976). Bailey and Davidson (1976) concluded that it is most profitable to concentrate on the affective components of experience. Clinicians who pursue the sensory qualities of pain with their patients to the exclusion of affect are likely to miss the intensity of it, even though sensory words may have some value in diagnosis.

The McGill Pain Questionnaire is still one of the better measures of subjective pain available to us. Its psychometric properties have been carefully and extensively researched, and despite its shortcomings it provides pain sufferers with a more comprehensive means of communicating their experience than many other measures considered here. There are, however, many other measures that have been developed with the aim of investigating aspects of pain-related behaviour, disability, treatment outcomes and so on, that have not been covered here but will be referred to throughout the rest of this book.

CONCLUSION

The measurement of cognitions has been seen as particularly important in the investigation of pain in recent years, and the material in this chapter shows how carefully and systematically measurements have been assessed. Many of those considered have been shown to be acceptable in terms of the most important psychometric properties. Where we take issue with the design of many of the measures outlined in the first half of this chapter is in their neglect of subjectivity in the single-minded pursuit of objectivity. The linguistic rating scales and the McGill Pain Questionnaire have been designed to show that subjectivity is a vital, central and integral part of pain measurement. The dichotomy between objectivity and subjectivity is one that divides psychologists (Watts, 1992). Support for subjectivity is derived from the assumption that it is never possible to eliminate a researcher's interpretations and biases. Methods that claim objectivity should be reported so that they are open to critical scrutiny. Only in this way can distorted interpretations be identified and corrected. In establishing these criteria, this raises questions about whether objectivity is wholly achievable (Watts, 1992). For this reason, pain researchers should perhaps consider more seriously their continued pursuit of the Holy Grail, and turn to developing better subjective measures that are capable of having all of the acceptable psychometric properties. While not perfect, subjective assessments like the McGill Pain Questionnaire tap into the painful experience more comprehensively than most other measures so far available to us.

Cognition has represented the mainstream of thinking and methods in psychology over the past 20 years, therefore any "respectable" social psychology of pain must necessarily distil and integrate what is appropriate here; affect has recently emerged to play an increasingly important and complementary role in explaining socio-clinical behaviour. (This theme is developed further in Chapter 7.) With this historical fusion of interests in mind, those methods that assess the socio-cultural, cognitive and affective elements of the pain experience together are likely to do the job most successfully, in terms of both the contribution to the variance and patient satisfaction. Some cognitive methods are not applicable to social investigations, while others have potential that may not have been tapped. A third position argued by some social psychologists is that we need to develop new and appropriate methodologies to examine the completely different types of behaviour that occur in social situations; at this point we have little to draw from these cognitive methods. The methods presented here are just a starting point for a more truly social investigations of pain. However, understanding needs to be grounded in cognitive modes of thinking before it is possible to apply, contrast and appreciate the social concepts and methods that form the material for the rest of the book. For this reason, this second chapter on measurement of cognitions forms one of two foundation stones for the remainder of the volume.

Learning About Pain

3

In this chapter we consider what is known about how pain is learnt. How far is learning about pain influenced by social factors? Does knowledge about the social impact of learning adequately explain the psychology of the chronic pain sufferer? First we consider how different sections of society learn to interpret sensations, and how this in turn affects their predisposition to report pain. It is popularly assumed that those suffering from pain will seek treatment for their symptoms, but in this chapter we begin to understand how social factors can affect visits to a physician. We unravel some of the social mechanisms whereby these differences in reporting illness in general and pain in particular come about. We then go on to look at the principles underlying treatments offered in behavioural medicine and its use of social learning theory techniques, and consider whether it is able to address comprehensively the full range of known social factors relevant to the understanding of illness and treatment.

CONSULTING ABOUT PAIN AND ILLNESS

THE SYMPTOM ICEBERG

Few people feel completely healthy all of the time. At a recent seminar the author asked 20 people to indicate whether or not they were at that moment experiencing any sensation that might be construed as a symptom; only three said they were totally symptom-free. Although not a scientific test, this demonstrates that many people feel unwell periodically but relatively few consult a physician about their symptoms. Estimates of the size of this non-consulting group vary. In a study of 1344 patients registered with a general practice in Glasgow, Hannay (1979) found that although three-quarters of them had symptoms at any one time, only a quarter visited the doctor. He described this feature as a "symptom iceberg". Many medical and social symptoms had already been referred to lay people or were not referred to anyone. Formally reported symptoms were mainly characterised by severe pain and/or disability. Others found their symptoms worrying or inconvenient. About a third of consulters had severe pain and a quarter were severely disabled, but the majority of symptoms reported were not considered to be serious. Indeed, 10% of those interviewed had sought professional advice for a medical symptom even though they were without pain or disability, and even though they knew that the symptom was not serious. The symptom iceberg can be contrasted with "trivia" brought into the consulting room. These are symptoms that are taken "unnecessarily" for professional advice. Some writers have suggested that as many as 40% to 50% of patients are not objectively ill (Shontz, 1975), but much depends on how these figures are collected. For instance, while Hannay calculated that the hidden illness iceberg was more than twice the frequency of possible trivia, he also found that these two were not mutually exclusive: 7% of those in the base of the iceberg also reported trivia, suggesting that some patients at least cannot be classified exclusively as underestimators or overestimators of symptoms. Instead, they should be viewed as people who cannot or do not report their bodily symptoms appropriately (see also Chapter 2).

So how much self-referral behaviour might be explained by symptom severity? Severity seems to be most closely linked to action when physical symptoms are accompanied by acute anxiety or depression (Ingham and Miller, 1979). More specifically, depression affects the predisposition to report pain, as Magni et al (1990) found in a non-random US sample of 3023 people with musculoskeletal and joint pains. However, Ingham and Miller concluded that, in general, symptom severity was a major, but not the sole, determinant of consulting behaviour. Illnesses causing serious disruption may also lead to more consultations. The rate of symptom onset also seems to be important, those with rapid onset being more likely to be seen as requiring urgent medical attention. Contrary to popular belief among health professionals, however, general attitudes, attitudes towards the doctor and attitudes towards particular symptoms alone do not substantially affect consultation rates. Having said that, a visit to the doctor is much more likely if serious symptoms accompany these predisposing attitudes (Sharp, Ross and Cockerham, 1983).

Two other factors, which will be elaborated in later chapters, need to be flagged here. The first is that those without a close friend or intimate relationship were more likely to consult, because they did not have a source of support or advice for their problem. Secondly, the perceived cause of a symptom affects the likelihood of consultation. In one study, patients in primary care were more likely to consult a doctor if they attributed their symptoms to an internal physical cause or if they were unable to work out a cause (Ingham and Miller, 1986). Other studies have shown that working out the cause is just one of a range of reactions to the presence of a symptom. Egan and Beaton (1987) examined 13 common complaints, such as coughing for three days, nausea and vomiting for 24 hours and so on. They identified 11 other types of reaction to symptoms, apart from spending time working out a cause. Some people cut back on social activities, some ignored their symptoms and just carried on, some went to bed earlier and generally took more rest but others worked less and/or stayed at home. Some consumed special foods or liquids, others treated themselves with non-prescription medication. Some informed their relatives and friends so that they could help, but others just continued to work and told their co-workers or boss so that they would understand if their work suffered. Some contacted a physician, some took prescribed drugs and some went to a hospital casualty department or other emergency service. So, people take a variety of actions prior to consultation and these patterns deserve further detailed research. Ingham and Miller (1986) found that high utilisers of health care averaged 16 visits to the doctor each year, compared with a US average of 2.7, while low utilisers had neither received treatment nor taken medication in the 12 months before the study.

So to what extent are these general findings about consultation rates applicable to the study of pain? Such information about a symptom iceberg leads to the deduction that, like others who become patients, those in chronic pain are a highly selected and statistically abnormal group. It seems likely that there are people with serious pain and disability, similar to those who become chronic pain patients, who for some reason are not motivated to seek treatment and hence do not feature in published morbidity statistics. This raises questions about why those at the base of the iceberg do not attend for treatment and about the psychosocial processes that might be at work here. Studies of pain in general practice demonstrate the prevalence of these complaints. Crook, Rideout and Browne (1984) surveyed 372 randomly selected families and found that 36% had one or more members in pain during the two weeks preceding the survey. They estimated that 11% of this subgroup had a persistent pain and 5% a temporary pain. A surprising 66% of those experiencing pain in the previous fortnight had not used the health care system, so supporting the concept of a symptom iceberg. Reviewing other studies, Crook, Rideout and Browne (1984) observed that around 75% of health care is undertaken without professional help. In line with the findings for general illness, they confirmed that usage by pain patients is moderated by factors such as the degree of seriousness of the pain, the frequency and persistence of attacks, knowledge about cause and previous causal explanations and treatment.

The issue of self-care has been successfully addressed through diary studies. A four-week study of health upsets that included the transient and trivial showed that on 396 of the 714 diary days, one or more medical problems was recorded and on 52% of these days some medical action was taken (Freer, 1980). Self-care was practised on more than 80% of days when medical problems were present. Analgesics constituted 48% of all self-medications for pain, compared with 39% of self-medications for colds and 30% for gastric problems. Furthermore, subjects acknowledged a wide range of non-medical actions or events that they knew to be therapeutic, indicating the necessity of assessing self-care in a holistic way. Relevant to a social analysis of pain was the finding that 53% of respondents required the presence of one or more persons to facilitate social non-medical actions, such as spending time with the family or friends, going out for a meal and attending clubs.

But how much pain is there in hospitals, where pain control would be expected to be carefully monitored. Furthermore, to what extent does hospital treatment contribute to the incidence of pain in the non-hospital population? In a study where 2415 randomly selected inpatients were interviewed, 50% reported pain at the time of the interview and 67% had experienced pain in the previous day (Abbott et al, 1992). Patients who had received surgery in the previous seven days reported moderate to severe pain, but 21% of non-surgery patients were also in pain when interviewed. More important here is that around 20% of the 72% re-interviewed had pain six months later, when many of them were no longer in treatment. Furthermore, although impairment of function had not increased with continuing pain, distress levels had risen, demonstrating the developing importance of the affective component of pain as chronicity became established. So, pain can be a by-product of hospital treatment, and such cases make a sizeable contribution to overall estimates of pain in the general population.

THE SOCIAL INFLUENCE OF OTHERS ON REPORTS OF PAIN AND ILLNESS

Interactions between family members and the sick are instrumental in the decision to seek treatment (see also Chapter 6). Therefore the behaviour and attitudes of others, not just the behaviour of the sick themselves, play a role in the decision to become a patient and the contribution to the health statistics that this involves. Social influence has most often been studied in children, where parental influence must necessarily be taken into account, but parents do not instantly stop affecting their children's welfare in adulthood, as one might believe from the shortage of literature in this area. It is easy to lose sight of the fact that they continue to influence decision making about health to varying degrees throughout the life-span. But do parents affect adolescents' decisions about seeking health care? In a study of around 7000 teenagers and their inclination to visit the doctor for 'flu, fatigue and serious symptoms like blood in the urine or lumps, Quadrel and Lau (1990) found that the child's orientation towards physician use was very similar to that of the parents. Health history, intelligence and autonomy proved to be particularly important predictive factors in their model.

Where younger sick children are concerned, parents' perceptions, beliefs, attitudes and expectations interact with the child's physical condition and behaviour (Turk et al, 1985). If urgent treatment is required, then the family history of life-threatening illness, worry about symptoms, situational factors such as a suggestion from another person that a visit to the doctor would be appropriate, and the nuisance of a complaining child, may affect decision making. Turk et al (1985) found that of 100 mothers seeking urgent medical treatment for their child, 96% of appropriate visits were characterised by the presence of fever, the patient being older and the mother's concern about a family history. Turk et al (1985) found that, together with respiratory problems, these features also predicted situations where attendance was delayed for less than a week, the average delay being 6.5 days. In adults, delay in seeking treatment for the pain of a heart attack has been shown to be related not only to the severity of the pain and to the time taken to recognise and label with accuracy the true source of the symptoms, but also to social factors like the role of a second person — usually a family member or friend — in initiating or delaying the decision to seek help (Hackett and Cassem, 1969).

A further explanation for why people consult comes from work on legitimating illness. Research into health behaviour indicates that when people believe that they are ill, they seek legitimation for their symptoms from others. Legitimation is a social process whereby people prove to themselves and others that their sensations and feelings truly represent sickness. This process is directed and shaped by the rules, roles and norms of the society in which the sick person lives. Telles and Pollack (1981) examined health diaries and interview transcripts from a stratified sample of 50 participants controlled for sex, race and socio-economic status, and identified four stages in this legitimation process. Firstly, people tried to verify the presence or absence of an illness by asking friends, family and colleagues for opinions. People compared their symptoms and health status with others, and those they consulted affirmed or denied that the person was ill. These sources then gave feedback about the kinds of states and feelings that could acceptably be labelled as illness, and were able to confirm that the sufferer's symptoms warranted serious attention. By the third stage, a complainant found ways to demonstrate the validity of their feelings. Verifiable symptoms like bleeding, dislocation or a raised temperature might have been accepted as *prima facie* evidence by others, while back pain and symptoms of psychogenic origin were less likely to be acceptable, being invisible. Back pain is a particularly difficult symptom to legitimate, even for experts. At the final stage, others directed the sick person to an official legitimator of the sick role — usually a physician (Telles and Pollack, 1981). The seriousness of a symptom appears to affect the final stage of this process. Although great pain or sudden disability predisposes sick people to seek help from a doctor without a prior lay consultation, other symptoms, representing the majority of cases, can trigger a series of non-expert discussions (Twaddle, 1969).

Three features deserve further comment here. The first is that the rehearsal and revision of symptoms within the community by prospective consulters is likely to be repeated at the consultation, and again if the patient is subsequently passed on to a specialist. Each time this cyclical process occurs, a more "legitimate" version will be shaped up in accordance with the feedback given (Skevington, 1986). A second aspect of this process concerns physician feedback in what is, after all, an interpersonal process. Ingham and Miller (1976) found that once people attended a clinic expecting treatment, doctors were relatively unwilling to admit that treatment was not required. So, implicitly, they legitimated these symptoms. Although Ingham and Miller's research was concerned with psychiatric symptoms, the process may be relevant to the understanding of chronic pain. By taking action, physicians may unwittingly encourage those who seek help to go on doing so inappropriately, and this inadvertent collusion may be at considerable future cost to the patient as well as to the health service. A third point is that the constant search by some sufferers for a health professional who will provide a firm diagnosis to legitimate back pain, for instance, fosters a style of behaviour that may be interpreted by professional observers as hypochondriasis (Skevington, 1986a). "Doctor shopping" is a problem in the management of chronic pain (Keefe and Brown, 1982), and in the void created by a shortage of legitimation from the formal health care system, sufferers may be motivated to turn to alternative sources for advice and treatment as well as for legitimation. Value judgements are made by health professionals about how much and what type of action is appropriate for a patient's particular symptoms. By taking "too much" action, patients signal hypochondria or hysteria, whereas "too little" action may be interpreted as personal negligence. Such judgements utilise a clinical rule-of-thumb because scientific norms are not available (see Chapter 6).

The processes of legitimation may operate in different ways in different sections of the community, and the reasons why people seek legitimation for their symptoms may be driven as much by systemic or socio-economic factors as by psychological ones. Work on minority groups in the United States has shown that black working-class mothers claiming welfare tended to accept the dominant view that being on welfare was the result of a personal failure. They had not been able to work and had justified living on welfare while looking after pre-school children. Once their children had gone to school, they were more likely to perceive failure in getting a job and to feel helpless about getting off welfare, and were therefore more likely to adopt the sick role and seek approval for it. Hence, the sick role may offer a "substitute" status, where illness exempts people from normal role obligations (Cole and Lejeune, 1972). But the conclusions are equivocal, later investigators found that blacks and those with less education have more positive attitudes towards visiting a doctor and are less sceptical than whites (Sharp, Ross and Cockerham, 1983), so it is not clear whether such factors are, in fact, barriers to utilisation. The psychological costs of treatment are as relevant as monetary costs in the decision to consult, but the relative influence of these variables will depend on the type of health care system involved. In addition to the costs already noted, Sanders (1982) lists the time and effort needed to obtain relevant information, the difficulty of disclosing what might be difficult or highly personal information to an authoritative stranger, the pain and discomfort resulting from any treatment prescribed, the distress associated with receiving bad news, recriminations or blame, the commitment involved in being engaged in treatment, the loss to a person's individuality linked with participating in hospital procedures and the self-image changes associated with "becoming" a patient. Many of these factors are perceived to be costs to the sick person's social relationships. Potentially, they all influence consultation rates.

Attendance figures are also affected by who drops out of treatment and who relapses. In a two-year longitudinal study, Skevington (1995) found that at the time of admission to outpatient treatment, early synovitis patients had a relatively normal distribution of educational qualifications, but by the end of the study, those with higher qualifications were more likely to have left treatment than manual and clerical workers. So, those who remained as patients conformed to the traditional view of arthritis patients as being those with lower socio-economic status. Furthermore, reasons for leaving treatment rarely included a complete recovery. Of 25 arthritis patients who left treatment, only four were without pain at the end of the study. The majority stopped attending because the doctor had told them that there was nothing more that could be done for them, or because their professional relationship had dissolved. Furthermore, the pain status of those remaining in treatment was no different from that of those who left, suggesting that social factors rather than level of pain *per se* were the main reasons for leaving. The social interaction between patient and physician and the "atmosphere" of treatment therefore influence who stays in treatment and who leaves. Relapse is also important. Turk and Rudy (1991) point out that although between 30% and 70% of patients in treatment for chronic pain make therapeutic gains over a one- to five-year period, the figures also show a concomitant relapse rate of between 30% and 70% in the same time. Relapse becomes another confirmation of the hopelessness of the sufferer's situation, and further affirmation of their disability. Such figures also raise questions for patients about the failure of the health care system in general and those who treat in particular. Turk and Rudy observe that in the wake of disheartening outcomes, therapists may feel impelled to search for more aggressive and possibly more controversial treatments. This move towards taking more extreme therapeutic action must have knock-on effects, for both the relationship between doctor and patient and the probability of adherence to treatment.

THE CHARACTERISTICS OF CHRONIC PAIN PATIENTS

What are the characteristics of those who become pain patients? The incidence of pain in the general population varies widely when specific pain problems such as back pain, headache, abdominal pain and facial pain are evaluated, but this may be due more to different methods of quantification than to incidence itself (Brattberg, Thorslund and Wikman, 1989). Patients who are studied in pain clinics are selected by a stringent set of criteria, making such samples far from representative of pain patients in general. Those referred tend to report more constant pain, to have work-related injuries, to report higher emotional distress, to be more negative about the future and to have greater functional impairment, as well as being more frequent users of the health care system. Such referrals are usually made at a time when the pain is most severe or distressing (Turk and Rudy, 1990). However, the characteristics of those referred also tell us something about the criteria used by referrers. These outcomes may be more to do with their professional orientation, ideology and personality than with scientific principles. Further sets of selection criteria operate as the patient progresses through the system. Turk and Rudy estimate that only between one-third and two-thirds of those offered treatment and evaluated ever enter pain management programmes. This is not just the result of the operation of self-selection factors but is also due to the action of various "gate-keepers" within the multidisciplinary pain management team who decide on a patient's suitability for inclusion. This analysis lays bare the social interaction between patient and professional in determining outcomes and, ultimately, statistics.

Pain patients tend to be categorised as chronic after six months of continuous pain, but can we then assume that chronic pain patients are homogeneous as a group thereafter? In an attempt to determine heterogeneity and improve predictability, some studies have compared samples of patients with different pain durations. Drawing from a rheumatology department, an osteopathy clinic and a rehabilitation centre in London, Zarkowska and Philips (1986) contrasted three groups of patients with recent pain onset (mean 47 days), and chronic pain of low duration (2.2 years) and high duration (14.3 years). Those with greater chronicity reported more sensory and affective pain on the McGill Pain Questionnaire, and these scores were positively correlated with complaining on the pain behaviour checklist. Although the study did not have a prospective longitudinal design, the evidence suggests that reporting behaviour does change over time. Broadly similar findings have been reported by Swanson and Maruta (1980). In an unusual investigation of patients with "ancient pain" — chronic pain lasting 25 years or more – Swanson, Maruta and Wolff (1986) concluded they were little different from patients with chronic pain lasting only 6 years. Both groups showed a decrease in intellectual efficiency and similar Minnesota Multiphasic Personality Inventory (MMPI) profiles, reflecting their considerable homogeneity as a group. The groups differed only in their use and abuse of medication. Cases of ancient pain are rare, being estimated at 45 in 1000 consecutive admissions, and a large proportion of these patients (40%) reported pain in the head or face. Furthermore, such patients are renowned for their "resistance to treatment, consuming impact of misery and (the) tireless search for relief" (Swanson, Maruta and Wolff, 1986). Here, the combined characteristics of the pain and the patient explain why these sufferers continue to seek treatment and to be included in the statistics.

What are the processes in the transition from acute to chronic pain? There is considerable variation in the ways that people in pain initially react to symptoms and how these responses change as the condition persists. Some clinicians have recorded what appears to be happening to patients as they pass through various developmental stages during this transition, which provides useful heuristics. However, the style of analysis used necessarily reflects their particular theoretical orientation to treatment, as we shall see later in this chapter. For example, within the terms of behavioural medicine, Keefe, Block and Williams (1980) observed that during the acute phase of the first two months of treatment, overt behaviours like a temporary decrease in activity and temporary reliance on medication and help-seeking from professionals tend to occur. Patients believe that their pain is controllable through medication, engage in active coping and display anxiety with other signs of autonomic arousal. Physiologically, they may have muscle spasms. By the pre-chronic phase of 2–6 months, alternating patterns of increasing and decreasing activity occur. Patients may withdraw from or become reliant on medication. They reduce their contact with the doctor and are usually working or trying to work. At this stage patients recognise that their pain is not entirely controllable through medication. They may alternate active and passive coping styles, deny depression and focus on physical symptoms and pain of variable intensity, which is reactive to stress. Their physiological responses are similar to those of the acute phase. As time passes, there is less likelihood of finding organic pathology and by the chronic phase (6–24 months after onset), activities have decreased indefinitely. "Doctor shopping" may result from numerous treatment failures, and addiction to narcotics may have become established. Patients have stopped work and may be receiving disability payments. Pain is now believed to be uncontrollable and depression is common. Passive coping styles have been adopted and there is a strong preoccupation with bodily complaints. The constant intensity of the pain is the result of chronic muscle spasms. Muscle strength and endurance have decreased but other psychophysiological disorders like headaches increase. At this stage there is a reduction in autonomic arousal (Keefe, Block and Williams, 1980). Although these clinical observations provide a detailed patient-centred analysis, the social input from involved health professionals and family members has not been integrated. In particular, it is important to know how their beliefs, attitudes and behaviour contribute to whether a patient stays in treatment or leaves, and how these things affect the outcome of treatment. In summary, several social factors have been identified that tend to affect the predisposition to seek treatment. While pain is just one symptom of illness and consequent illness behaviour, we have seen that it plays a prominent motivating role in this process.

MODELS OF SICK ROLE AND ILLNESS BEHAVIOUR

In investigating the relationship between chronic pain and injury, psychology is challenged to explain the following conditions: (i) where medical findings are ambiguous as in the occurrence of pain in the absence of injury, (ii) where injury and pain are disproportionate to each other and (iii) where there is a disjunction in the temporal relationship between pain and injury as in cases of chronic post-operative pain, dental pain, phantom limb pain and traumatic injury (Rachman, 1986). Psychosocial models of illness behaviour and sick role behaviour have the potential to make valuable contributions to such explanations, and they are considered here.

ILLNESS BEHAVIOUR: A LABELLING PERSPECTIVE

Illness behaviour has been defined as observable actions that are appropriately communicated (to another person) about the person's perception of disturbed health. In contrast, abnormal illness behaviour is maladaptive behaviour that is out of proportion to the underlying physical disease (Waddell, Pilowsky and Bond, 1989). The Illness Behaviour Questionnaire (IBQ) was developed to assess this (Pilowsky and Spence, 1975). It has been widely used in the study of pain, although pain *per se* is not directly assessed by the instrument. Its psychometric properties are still being debated and although some reviewers conclude that its reliability and validity are quite good (Williams, 1988), others have questioned the conceptual structure of the scale (Main and Waddell, 1987). In an attempt to re-examine its construct validity using 200 chronic low back pain patients, Main and Waddell (1987) found that of the original 67 IBQ items, only 33 had significant loadings. Instead of the seven factors that founded the original subscales, the items loaded on only three factors describing dimensions of affective and hypochondriacal disturbance, life disruption and social inhibition, so the scale's construct validity remains uncertain.

In the absence of objective techniques for measuring pain and in view of the widespread clinical disjunctions described by Melzack and Wall, Rachman and others, it is not clear how it is possible to assess with accuracy whether illness behaviour associated with pain is normal or out of proportion. Pilowsky distinguishes those with "normal" illness behaviour from those who are anomalous. He elaborates the latter into three subtypes: (i) abnormal, where illness behaviour is unusual at the time of a tentative diagnosis, (ii) those with an atypical personality or social behaviour rather than psychopathology and (iii) conscious malingering, which is sometimes evident in prison and military populations. Pilowsky (1990) has devised a new taxonomy that distinguishes somatically focused illness behaviour from a psychologically focused variety. Both types are said to have illness affirming or illness denying properties. Such beliefs about the origins of illness have implications for how treatment might be more directly tailored to the pain patient's orientation. In a recent review of 824 pain clinic patients who completed the IBQ over a 10-year period, Pilowsky and Katsikitis (1994) identified patients who rejected the idea that their condition may be linked to psychological problems, and suggested that they might find behavioural and somatic treatments more acceptable than patients who viewed their problem within a psychological and emotional framework. Cognitive therapy is likely to be more acceptable to the latter.

There has been a tendency to focus on illness behaviour as a personality trait, but there is some evidence to indicate that the prevalent view of chronic pain patients may well have been distorted by the atypical selection of pain centre patients who have been included in published studies (Chapman, Sola and Bonica, 1979). Results from Chapman, Sola and Bonica demonstrated that 200 patients participating in pain centre programmes showed strong conviction of disease, intense somatic focus of illness and mild depression. In contrast, 200 similar private patients had lower conviction of disease, less of a somatic focus of attention, lower hypochondriasis and normal levels of depression. Consequently, previous results may have caused general practitioners to weigh psychological factors too heavily in diagnosis. These profiles appear to reflect two styles of reporting behaviour, which may be due more to social and environmental factors than to personality characteristics.

Pain drawings have been used to assess illness behaviour in studies designed within the paradigm of the popular psychiatric model. In one study those judged to have "normal" illness behaviour drew diagrams of localised pain, which could be related to neuro-anatomical structures and which was considered to be proportional to its intensity (Waddell, Pilowsky and Bond, 1989). In contrast, those with "abnormal" illness behaviour made non-anatomical drawings that were regional and magnified. Sensory pain was shown to be associated with normal illness behaviour while affect-ive and evaluative descriptions earmarked abnormal cases: for example, pain and tenderness are normally localised, but in abnormal cases appear to become widespread, superficial and non-anatomical. However, such statements about normality involve value judgements. Furthermore, as we saw in Chapter 2, pain drawings alone are an unreliable method of assessment; their results alone could lead to erroneous decisions about pain management, but when used with measures like the McGill Pain Questionnaire they may be more reliable. However, affective and evaluative pain are reported by the majority of chronic pain patients (see Chapter 2), not just by those who may be exhibiting abnormal illness behaviour, so interpretation using this combined method appears to be confounded. Consequently, the tendency to label all chronic pain patients as having abnormal illness behaviour increases if this classification is adopted, so for these reasons this approach is unsatisfactory.

Unfortunately, many of these ideas about inappropriate symptoms were developed from studies of psychiatric pain patients (e.g. Main and Waddell, 1984). Although estimates of psychopathology vary, questions have been raised about whether any psychiatric cases of illness behaviour occur within the chronic pain patient population. In a careful study of appropriate and inappropriate symptoms in low back pain patients and asymptomatics, looking at the response to physical examination, it was found that physical severity, failure to treat symptoms and, to a lesser extent, distress were the most important features influencing the expression of illness behaviour (Waddell et al, 1984). However, from the results of their study, the authors concluded there was "no evidence of psychiatric illness either from psychological testing or during psychologist's interview, confirming general clinical experience that referral of chronic pain patients to a traditional psychiatrist usually fails to elucidate any psychiatric explanation or help. It may be suggested that the terms hysteria and hypochondriasis in particular, so variously have been used, unused and abused by clinicians that they should be completely banned in the context of chronic pain" (Waddell et al, 1984, p.212).

It is therefore difficult to assess to what extent the tendency to approach illness behaviour in the negative terms of psychopathology has unduly influenced the way in which clinicians view their patients (see Leavitt and Garron, 1979a). Although some chronic pain patients appear to display signs of unusual behaviour, this consensually shared perspective has continued to generate an active search for psychopathology among those who attend for assessment, in a manner that has not been beneficial to the majority of patients. It would be better to describe this phenomenon in more neutral terms as beliefs about the origins of illness, since that appears to be this work's most important contribution to knowledge (Pilowsky and Katsikitis, 1994). The result of the original thrust of this work has been to create defensiveness among patients who, in the absence of organic findings, are highly sensitised to any signal that their therapist suspects them of malingering. Leavitt (1985) says that once suspicion in health professionals is aroused, the patient is at risk because the clinical response is likely to be more selective and judgemental than balanced and objective. As a consequence, the patient's complaint may not receive the attention it deserves. A major problem with this approach is that it provides stereotypes for clinical use, which militate against the likelihood of patients being treated as individuals. This de-individualisation process means that the patient's behaviour is more likely to be isolated from its social context. It is therefore more susceptible to misinterpretation, which, if persisting, may damage the delicate trusting relationship necessary for successful treatment. The use of this concept as formulated thus has major implications for the adequacy and quality of communications between patients and health professionals. Although the measurement of illness behaviour as it stands is questionable, the concept has much to offer a social psychology of pain. Central to its definition is this aspect of communication between the pain patient and the health professionals. At the same time, cognitive and affective components are successfully married within this social analysis, but in a way that gives emphasis to understanding within the terms of psychological disturbance. Consequently, this interesting concept may be in need of reorientation away from the psychiatric model.

Where back pain is concerned, for the majority of patients the real cause of the pain is not known. Furthermore, many chronic low back pain patients have been erroneously treated with therapies designed to diminish acute pain in ways that are dangerous, potentially leading to iatrogenic complications later (Schmidt and Arntz, 1987). It has been claimed that scales like the Low Back Pain Questionnaire (Leavitt and Garron, 1979b) are capable of distinguishing functional from organic pain patients on the basis of their pain language. Leavitt et al (1979) found that patients who were judged to be without organic disease used more words to describe their pain than those with organic disease; in particular, they described sensations of moderate, bright pain. The transparent aim of such methods has activated a search for more opaque measures. Utilising words from the McGill Pain Questionnaire, the Back Pain Classification Scale has been designed explicitly with the aim of not arousing defensiveness in those who complete it (Leavitt, 1983). It is possible to see how this strategy of attempting to outwit the patient is likely to create an interpersonal scenario in the consulting room where both health professional and patient could potentially become mutually engaged in a cyclical pattern of "duping delight" (Ekman, 1985).

Patients who realise that the therapist questions the truth of their pain reports are likely to alter their behaviour in reaction to these perceptions. The fact that there have been changes in a patient's behaviour — whatever the nature of these changes — may serve to reinforce the health professional's negative schema of that patient, regardless of its veracity. Such interpersonal interactions appear to have little value in the successful treatment of chronic pain.

What is the evidence for malingering and how far is such an approach justified? Although this literature abounds with case studies and clinical opinions, there is little hard data. Firstly, this is because malingering is difficult to quantify, although some writers have recently put faith in the notoriously unreliable use of the lie detector (Gale, 1988; Jayson, 1992). The second reason is that true (rather than suspected) malingerers are reluctant to identify themselves for investigation. This hiatus of information provides fertile breeding ground for the development of medical myths and legends. Intriguingly, some researchers have tried to simulate malingering to investigate it more systematically. Pain-free individuals selected from the Chicago telephone book ($N = 277$) were asked to simulate malingering, and their responses were compared with those from 533 low back pain patients. Of the simulating malingerers, 40% had experienced serious back pain in the past, and 33% had seen a doctor for treatment. Using a Low Back Pain Scale of 103 pain words, Leavitt (1985) found that more back pain sufferers than fakes could be identified from their use of few (4–17) or many (18–54) words. The patients who scored in the fake range of the scale reported 21% more pain than those who did not score as fakes. However, because of the identification problem it is not clear how a similar study could be carried out using a group of "genuine malingerers".

An alternative cognitive explanation for "malingering" behaviour is that patients may be re-experiencing pain or remembering it (Rachman, 1986). As we saw earlier, the accuracy of recall will depend on whether or not people are in pain at the time of recall and the length of time from the original estimate. Because both overestimates and underestimates of pain can be explained in this way, this interpretation enables us to plausibly dispense with the concept of malingering. The notion of seeking psychopathology in pain patients and earmarking malingerers is conceptually and methodologically flawed, and other ways of explaining and treating functional pain should be urgently sought. Setting aside the conceptual debate, if all of the relevant organic tests have been applied and have ruled out potential physical treatments, it seems more practical to accept the symptom at face value and to try to relieve it, without further undue concern for whether or not the pain truly reflects injury or disease. Moreover, the patently social aspects of illness behaviour would be better interpreted and investigated through the paradigms of social psychology.

ILLNESS BEHAVIOUR: A SOCIAL PERSPECTIVE

Kleinman (1988) has also questioned whether a labelling approach is appropriate to the understanding of sick role behaviour. Like Szasz (1968), he sees it as the result in part of an interaction between patient and healer. Szasz (1968) claims that physicians dislike patients who refuse to play the sick role. There is a common presumption that everyone who complains of pain must be sick either in mind or in body, but these sensations may impart meaning to a person's life. A shortage of anatomical and physiological information to explain the pain of hypochondriasis, for instance, makes it necessary to turn to psychosocial explanations for elucidation. Chronic intractable or unbearable pain is usually a sign that the person wishes to adopt the sick role, especially in the absence of apparent bodily illness (Szasz, 1968). Making the useful distinction between sick people and patients, Kleinman (1988) notes that the chronically sick "spend more time in the roles of sick family member, sick worker, sick self than in the role of patients ... which leaves an after-image of a compliant, passive object of medical care". Reorientating thinking, Kleinman points out that the sick person is best seen as the active agent of care, because most self-treatment and most decisions about health are made by sick people and their families and not by health professionals, as is commonly assumed.

Supporting this move away from labelling, other researchers have adopted a situational view of illness behaviour by looking at the environmental conditions and everyday behaviour associated with symptoms and illness. Alonzo's (1984) approach analyses the ways in which everyday illness behaviour may be "contained". The thesis here is that deviations of bodily state from normal processes are kept as a side issue, and such side-tracking enables someone who is sick to maintain their identity as a non-sick person by continuing to be involved in their normal routines. In this way, the person's various roles of wife, lover, parent, teacher and so on are unaffected. Painful signs and symptoms such as aches, stiffness, swelling and pain in the joints and muscles, headaches, indigestion, stomach ache, back ache, itching, burns, bruises, cuts and accidental trauma, chest pain, jaw pain and "female complaints" are typically contained. Alonzo (1984) suggests that four kinds of situation have the potential to produce, contain and allow compromised performance of roles. As people progress through these situations, there is a shift from containment without medical assistance to the implied use of medical resources and/or personnel. At the first stage, people routinely adapt in daily situations where participation is not expected to produce symptoms or signs, and where occasional failures or derelictions of duty are acceptable. A second type of situation can potentially or actually produce these signs and symptoms, immediately or in the future. Here participation in activities is likely to affect a person's physical, psychological or social well-being. Examples include athletes who are not at their peak when competing, dizziness in high risk occupations like steeplejacking and regular periods of unexpected excessive demands such as those made on mothers at home with small children. In the third situation a person's social life allows periods of free time that are designed to deal with the difficulties posed by illness. Here time-out is allowed to tend to signs and symptoms by taking medication, rest and so on. Engaging in this third scenario assists in neglecting the first two types of situation, but as the occurrence of this third type increases, people progress towards becoming ill. In a fourth situation, attention is largely focused on the illness, health training or therapeutic difficulties, which are now acknowledged to be uncontainable.

The containment of signs and symptoms is affected by a person's commitment to their situation, how much they value their participation in particular roles, their personal position or power and the use of excuses, disclaimers and personal credit to remain in a particular situation. Being able to sustain containment depends on the sufferer's resources to manage the signs and symptoms. Their meanings may prevent people from responding to them, whatever the type of situation. Thus, adaptable chronically ill people want to avoid those situations that will aggravate their signs and symptoms and emphasise their illness. They also wish to avoid situations that they believe may have contributed to the illness (Alonzo, 1984). This environmentalist framework of social processes provides valuable insights into the processes of becoming a patient, and is a refreshing departure from the learning theory approach that has tended to dominate thinking in this field.

In a contrasting environmentalist view, Mechanic (1986a) says that a crucial premise in the study of illness behaviour is that socio-cultural and socio-psychological factors shape not only who has the disease but also their predisposition to report that pain and illness. He defines illness behaviour as "the manner in which persons monitor their bodies, define and interpret their symptoms, take remedial action and utilise various sources of help as well as the more formal health care system. It is also concerned with how people monitor and respond to symptoms and symptom change over the course of an illness and how this affects behaviour, remedial action taken and response to treatment" (Mechanic, 1986b, p.101). Commenting on the "extra-ordinary" differences between cultures in the way they conceptualise illness, its causes and methods of treatment, he says that "even in modern populations one finds an interesting blend of sophisticated scientific ideas and folk wisdom learned from close peers and through intuitive processes" (Mechanic, 1986a, p.3). However, Mechanic sees the processes whereby these differences come about as much more than just the result of learning and personality. He sees a person's physical and mental state as being strongly aligned with the sectors of society to which they belong. Thus, structural factors appear to have a major bearing on life-style components like diet and housing. Socio-demographic analyses tend to show that middle-aged women consult more frequently than similar men, and, in line with the incidence of health problems, referrals tend to increase with age. Consulters are inclined to be unemployed, to have active religious allegiance, to belong to social classes III and IV and to be owner–occupiers. Geographical factors like the distance from the health centre also play a part, with those living within 10 minutes bus, car, train or taxi ride being more likely to consult (Hannay, 1979). Minority group membership also affects reporting behaviour. Particularly revealing are studies of poverty in Britain, which have shown that in the 15 years following the introduction of largely cost-free care in the National Health Service, the poor still continue to use self-treatment and to delay seeking professional advice. This demonstrates that beliefs, together with other factors, can and do have a major impact on the decision to consult a physician and, in turn, on provision of services (Susser and Watson, 1971).

Despite the many differences reported, however, reviewers have concluded that investigations of the frequency and distribution of illness episodes in different homogeneous populations show reasonably consistent results, regardless of the method of data collection or the type of population being scrutinised (Jones, 1982). Evidence for the major socio-demographic differences is reviewed in the following subsections.

Sex

Consistently and across a wide variety of measures, research studies have shown that women are more inclined than men to report their symptoms to a doctor. Not only do they visit doctors more often, they also seek more help from many other sources, and which sources they consult depend on their image of illness. Greenley and Mechanic (1976) showed that being female was the most important characteristic of those who used the health service and other help-giving resources most frequently. Women reported more symptoms than men, even when pregnancy and other women-specific disorders were excluded. Ostensibly, women have more complicated reproductive systems than men, which take them into the consulting room more often. They menstruate between 300 and 400 times in a lifetime, and are likely to consult doctors about health conditions that do not necessarily represent sickness such as contraception, pregnancy and menopause. They are also more likely to take their children to the clinic for preventative reasons, as well as for treatment and assessment (Bristol Women's Studies Group, 1979). Together, these features account for some part of the greater consultation rate. This sex difference does *not* seem to be explained by attitudes, since women do not hold more positive attitudes towards their doctors than men (Sharp, Ross and Cockerham, 1983).

However, the sexes do respond to sickness in different ways (Mechanic, 1976). Men are more likely to say that they are unable to carry on a major activity, whereas women tend to reduce their efficiency by limiting the amount or kind of important activities they do rather than stopping altogether, which may be due in part to the incessant demands of family life. Others have suggested that gender-specific socialisation results in variations in the willingness to be self-disclosing, the need for social approval, verbal skills, symptom awareness and saliency, as well as a predisposition to take action in response to symptoms and exposure to health risks. Evidence that women have more ready access to medical care is equivocal, because although many have more flexible working hours than men they are often poorer, and this is a particularly important factor in private health care systems. Furthermore, the demands of child-care militate against this flexibility (Kessler, 1986). Nevertheless, there is support for the idea that those in traditional roles are able to give up work more easily if they develop a chronic illness. All of these factors contribute to sex differences in the reporting of symptoms.

Studies of psychiatric help-seeking cast light on the potential processes at work here. Kessler, Brown and Broman (1981) conclude that women have more emotional problems than men. They also have higher levels of "true" psychological distress, which raises questions about whether they have elevated levels of non-pathological emotionality too. These findings appear to be due to the ability of women to translate non-specific feelings of distress more readily than men into the conscious recognition that they have an emotional problem. As help-seeking only occurs once someone has defined their situation as problematic, this helps to explain why women go to psychiatric treatment earlier. Such processes may also apply to the reporting of problematic physical symptoms, especially where anxiety and depression are implicated. However, other work by Watson and Pennebaker (1991) has explored how negative affect draws attention to a range of health problems, and suggests that it may not be as closely tied to illness visits as was once thought. The causal relationship between stable negative affect and health problems is unclear. Does negative affect produce health problems (psychosomatic interpretation), do health problems cause negative affect (disability hypothesis), or do people differ in the ways in which they perceive, respond to and complain about bodily sensations (symptom perception hypothesis)? The latter seems most plausible, as we shall see in later chapters.

Are there sex differences in the treatment of painful symptoms, which affect what is recorded? Verbrugge and Steiner (1984) examined the frequency of GP consultations for headaches, chest and back pain, fatigue and dizziness or vertigo, and found that the sexes received broadly similar services for these symptoms. However, for headaches they found that women tended to be given counselling while men were more likely to receive injections. This may be explained by the findings that men in the study had more serious and acute headaches than women. Female headache patients, who were older, were also requested to return more often. Men with chest or back pain were more likely to be admitted to hospital, so reflecting the higher prevalence of back injuries among men, which prompts more medical attention for them. However, more women with chest and back pain received laboratory tests, while men were sent for electrocardiograms. These sex differences have four main explanations: (i) patients may request more services, (ii) for any particular symptom, some patients will be distressed while others will be calm, and physicians may respond differently to these different atmospheres, (iii) physicians may hold stereotypical views about treating the sexes, rather than responding to an individual's particular problems and (iv) medical factors, which are absent from the model.

In a subsequent study of prescribing, Verbrugge and Steiner (1985) went on to show that women received a consistent 5% to 10% more prescriptions for common complaints than men. This may be because women showed physicians that they were more pleased with their drugs than men, thereby positively reinforcing sex differences in prescribing behaviour. This is particularly likely if they communicated their inability to stand pain more than men. It may also have occurred if physicians believed that women like drugs and want them more. As the women averaged about twice as many visits per year as men between the ages of 17 and 44 and about one-third more between 45 and retirement age, it was not surprising that prescription costs were higher for this group.

Perhaps the emphasis on differences between the sexes has been unwarranted, especially where pain is concerned. Studies of temporomandibular pain support the conclusion that there is gender similarity in response to pain, whether for clinical pain, experimental pain, pain-related illness behaviour or personality (Bush et al, 1993). Thus, the higher rate of women (2:1) seeking treatment for this condition compared to men (9:1) is consistent with the view that there is greater health awareness among women and greater interest in symptoms. In a broader study, Davis (1981) carried out a stratified survey of 6913 people between the ages of 25 and 74, and found only small sex differences in the reporting of three types of chronic joint symptom typical of osteoarthrosis. Here, the conclusion is that women and men are more alike than different in the reporting of chronic joint symptoms, and it may be differences in treatment behaviour — namely, self-treatment or visits to the physician — together with the severity of the disease that form the most important intervening variables.

But could ostensible sex differences in reporting behaviour among chronic pain patients be explained in terms of their psychopathology? In a survey where 283 chronic pain patients were classified using DSM III, although tendencies towards sex differences were found for all personality types, more startling were the findings of widespread *similarities* between the sexes (Fishbain et al, 1986). Regardless of sex, chronic pain patients were more likely than those without pain to be depressed, to have somatosensory conversion disorder, anxiety syndromes, or drug and alcohol abuse problems, and a sizable number had a personality disorder. Psychogenic pain disorders were rare, and schizophrenia was absent among the 156 men and 127 women in this study. Thus, the evidence suggests that too much emphasis may have been placed on the investigation of differences between the sexes at the expense of overlooking substantial similarities.

Age, Social Class and Urbanisation

As we have already seen, the interactive effects of sex and age on reporting behaviour are often difficult to disentangle. Sex differences are already apparent in adolescence, with boys being less likely to seek medical care than girls. Girls see themselves as more vulnerable to illness, place a higher value on health, and accept more responsibility for it than do boys (Quadrel and Lau, 1990). As with adults, consultation frequency is not evenly spread across the population. One study showed that during young adulthood 25% of the sample reported 50% of all illness episodes, and another 10% experienced under 10% of these episodes. Thus, a relatively small proportion of young people seem to have the greatest susceptibility to illness. At the other end of the life-span, Haug (1981) has shown how the over-60s are more likely than those who are younger to suffer from serious complaints, and are more likely than the under 60s to seek preventive health care. In this age group, women are especially likely to "over-utilise" for common non-serious complaints.

These age differences have been explained in terms of vigilance about health and illness (Leventhal, Leventhal and Schaefer, 1988). Older people appear to be more vigilant and responsive to health threats than the young; they also see themselves as being more vulnerable. However, age differences do not seem to reflect large cognitive differences in the ways in which people represent illness (see Chapter 4). Furthermore, when emotions are considered there is evidence to show that the older age group is less emotional or distressed about illness. The literature does, however, show that older people delay visiting a physician for less time when their symptoms are severe and mild. For intermediate symptoms the young delayed seven times longer than older people. These results suggest that older patients are less able to tolerate ambiguity, and seek health care to reduce it. If the symptoms are consciously attributed to ageing, then this slows the vigilant coping responses typically observed in older patients (Leventhal, Leventhal and Schaefer, 1988).

The pattern is further complicated when pain is considered, because it is far from consistent. The NUPRIN report showed that young people are more likely to experience every type of pain more often than the old, with the exception of joint pain. Furthermore, if their parents experienced severe pain then they themselves were more likely to report back pain, muscle pain and joint pain. However, the results of epidemiological studies suggest that certain pains tend to increase with age, most notably headache, abdominal pain and facial pain. Furthermore, all three pains tended to be more prevalent among women (von Korff et al, 1988). Ageing does not present an appealing prospect in this literature: von Korff et al estimate that by the age of 70, 34% of the adult population will have experienced significant facial pain, 40–50% substantial headache, abdominal or chest pain and 85% will have had severe back pain. Mechanic and Angel (1989) studied 6913 adults aged between 25 and 74 years. Of these, 2431 had pain at the time and 937 had experienced pain during the previous month. They found that only 23% of pain patients had two or more physical findings, but those older than 56 were twice as likely as the 25–45 year olds to have these conditions, and three times as likely to have had five or more. More importantly, the over 65s were the least likely to complain. Regressions showed that older people with a greater sense of well-being complained less in comparison to other age groups than might be expected solely on the basis of the physical findings. This was because they attributed the discomforts of back pain more to the ageing process than the young and so seemed more able to "normalise bodily discomforts". This finding supports the idea that pain perceptions depend not just on the social context but also on social comparisons between people. By comparing themselves with other reference groups, people may come to believe that they are doing relatively well (see Chapter 4).

Related to social class is the issue of urbanisation. In an early but careful comparison of US lay beliefs in rural and urban populations, Mabry (1964) found that rural people reported more symptoms but gave fewer explanations for them than urban dwellers. However, the age distribution showed the rural group was older, and this may have contributed to the result. Age did not appear to affect symptom explanations, because the young learnt from the old within their particular subculture. Results from studies of pain and social class are equivocal. In one investigation of 83 Israeli women in childbirth, higher ratings of acute pain and more pain behaviour were associated with lower levels of education (Weisenberg and Caspi, 1989). Studies of improvements in chronic pain patients who attended pain relief clinics are also deemed to be influenced by class. Larson and Marcer (1984) found that while class was not related to pain level prior to treatment, improvements in anxiety and depression tended to be associated with lower social class. They found no evidence to support current clinical beliefs that lower socio-economic groups have a lower tolerance of pain and more neuroticism. However, their use of an invalidated assessment lays their conclusions open to questions of observer judgement bias. The issue of pain and social class needs further work.

Ethnicity

Ethnicity is also regarded as an important socio-demographic factor affecting reporting behaviour. Cultures vary in how far they encourage or discourage displays of pain, with some communities being far more stoical than others. Cultural expectations vary about how painful a procedure will be; circumcision and clitoridectomy provide examples of how they affect response to physically injurious procedures. In an interesting account of pain suppression during these initiation rites among adolescent members of the Nigerian Bariba tribe, Sargent (1984) shows how expressions of pain and discomfort bring shame because they are interpreted as cowardice. (Beliefs are discussed further in Chapter 4.) Zborowski (1952, 1969) has shown the importance of distinguishing the styles of reporting pain in different cultural groups from the pain sensation experienced. Because differences between individuals do not appear to result from genuine and reliable physiological differences between groups, these reported variations in pain expression are more satisfactorily explained by environmental factors than genetic or biological ones. From cross-cultural comparisons, Zola (1966) has made important observations about the ways in which ethnic groups construe sensations. Firstly, when an aberration is widespread it may not be considered symptomatic, unusual or deviant by some groups, just a natural or inevitable part of life. Furthermore, the degree of attention paid by a society to certain signs or symptoms is related to how far these fit with that society's values. Some societies have no anxiety about expressing hallucinations, for instance, and accept them freely. Zola says that neither the sign itself nor the frequency of its occurrence is significant. The key factor here is the *social context* in which the symptom occurs and is perceived and understood. Thus, tiredness is not seen as a cause for concern in western culture, and can be interpreted positively as proof of hard work, whereas in other cultures it could be viewed negatively.

In a major critique, Lipton and Marbach (1984) caution that far too many implications have been drawn from Zborowski's widely quoted findings that are not justified by the data. For instance, his method did not include questionnaires or items that could be analysed statistically. Lipton and Marbach show how previous investigations lack consistency when defining ethnic categories. In some studies diverse social and cultural groups like Japanese, Filipinos and Asians were combined to form a single category for investigation; these heterogeneous samples are unlikely to provide robust conclusions. Cross-cultural studies also suffer problems of linguistic and semantic equivalence. While English has four basic words to describe pain — pain, hurt, sore and ache — the Japanese have three words for pain and Thais only two (Fabrega and Tyma, 1976), so there are difficulties in equating and weighting such linguistic items for research purposes. Lipton and Marbach (1984) lay bare the equivocal findings on ethnicity. They observe that of the five major studies in this field, Zborowski (1952, 1969) and Zola (1966) showed major inter-ethnic differences for reported pain behaviour and attitudes while other studies report few or none (see Lipton and Marbach, 1984, for a good review). Intragroup differentiation within ethnic groups has been less popular as a focus of investigations. With the study of ethnic group homogeneity in mind, Lipton and Marbach (1984) interviewed 250 patients seeking help for facial pain and compared the results of equal numbers of US blacks, Irish, Italians, Jews and Puerto Ricans. Only 34% of the replies showed qualitative differences between the five groups, so 66% of items were similar across the groups, reflecting considerable homogeneity. Furthermore, the differences reported were confined to specific areas of experience such as the description and intensity of pain, and these differences persisted even when social, cultural, psychological symptoms, history and clinical variables were taken into account.

The results of this careful study demonstrate substantial *inter-ethnic* homogeneity for most aspects of the pain experience. It shows that there is far more *intra-ethnic* variation than has hitherto been acknowledged.

Where intergroup differences do exist, several explanations have been put forward to account for them. In a study of 63 Italian and 81 Irish patients attending an ear, nose and throat clinic and matched for diagnosis and sex, Zola (1966) found that more Irish than Italians identified these conditions as painful. However, the styles of reporting in the two cultures were different. The Irish were more likely to deny that pain was a feature of their illness and to avoid answering direct questions about pain. For instance, they made statements like, "[It's] not really pain [but] like sand in my eye". In contrast, Italians were more likely to dramatise their condition to cope with their anxiety by repeatedly over-expressing it and dissipating it. Thus, the Irish tended to understate and limit their difficulties, whereas the Italians extended and generalised them, presenting more symptoms in more bodily locations and with more types of bodily dysfunctions. Qualitative investigations of differences between groups have not often been appreciated but they appear to have value in explaining different styles of reporting, which may be useful clinically. However, one of the dangers in carrying out work on ethnicity is that stereotypes will be generated, elaborated and implemented within the clinical community, to the detriment of patients. Zola (1983) has the last word here:

> I am totally opposed to training anyone in the details of a particular ethnic group, for this will ultimately squeeze people into unreal categories and reify their culture as we have reified diagnoses. What I favour is making practitioners sensitive to the patient's heritage, their own heritage, and what happens when different heritages come together.

Here, the case is made for cultural awareness among health professionals which still sensitively permits the patient's individuality to be expressed and accounted for in the delicate interpersonal balance of creating a successful therapeutic outcome. Individual differences in history, politics and ideology also affect symptom reporting behaviour but, with the notable exception of Lipton and Marbach's study, these factors have attracted little research attention to date.

In this spirit of studying communication, a more social approach has been to investigate how the language of pain might be used to make more profitable cross-cultural comparisons. A content analysis of 150 spontaneous conversations with Thais enabled Diller (1980) to identify 15 words (mainly verbs) that occurred frequently in Thai descriptions of pain or pain-related emotional states. From transcripts he distinguished a continuum of four types of expression: (i) a primary level of cries and moans, (ii) a secondary level of language-specific interjections like "ouch", (iii) descriptions at a tertiary level like "a horrible burning pain" and (iv) a level of expression deemed to reflect "overall increases in input through cutaneous and proprioceptive channels". In line with current cognitive research, Diller proposes that pain experience periodically undergoes cognitive re-sorting, and that the level of report in use is geared to the type of language being applied. More importantly, the degree of importance attributed to each of the four levels varies according to cultural norms and practices, so in making cross-cultural comparisons researchers need to be aware of which levels are obligatory and which are optional for the particular social group they are studying. These interesting ideas deserve further investigation.

Recently published studies of the social interaction between patients and health carers address the dynamics of interpersonal behaviour and ethnicity in the consulting room more directly (Moore, 1990). To what extent do patients from minority groups vary in their perceptions of pain coping? Communications between dentists trained in their country of origin during treatment of patients from their own ethnic group were content-analysed for the types of pain experienced during dental treatment and ways of removing or easing the pain. Of these pains, 60% were located in the face or head. Eight styles of coping with pain emerged. They were categorised as internally applied chemical agents such as pills, externally applied agents such as creams or compresses, changes of bodily function like sleeping, a psychosocial dimension that included being hugged, active pain coping, passive pain coping, ingestion of special foods or drinks, and the use of non-traditional medicines, namely herbs and acupuncture. Major intergroup differences were found between Anglo-Americans, who used internally applied agents, denial and reassurance, and Chinese patients, who applied more external agents and took special foods or drinks. Moore found that the dentists shared many of their patients' perceptions about remedies, regardless of ethnicity, but differed in their choice of remedy, with the patients' choice reflecting an East–West split. This type of research not only emphasises the importance of the social context in a person's experience, reporting of pain and coping with it, but at the same time demonstrates how misunderstandings may readily occur between health professionals and patients from differing cultures. Such misunderstandings have clear implications for the success of treatment.

But is it sufficient to categorise a patient as a member of a particular ethnic group, or is the explanation about how that person reacts to pain linked more to the degree to which a sufferer identifies with the group? Results from a study by Bates, Edwards and Anderson (1993) showed that for 372 patients from six ethnic groups participating in a multidisciplinary pain centre programme, the best predictors of pain intensity were their ethnic group affiliation and their beliefs about controlling events. Hispanics and Italians, with the highest pain levels, tended to have the weakest beliefs about their ability to take control of events, but for Poles, Irish and French Canadians the pattern was reversed (see Chapter 5 on beliefs about control). Social identification was one of the first processes to be investigated in an early attempt to explain intergroup differences in pain tolerance. Buss and Portnoy (1967), extending work by Lambert, showed that identification with an ethnic group could lead people to defend their group even at the expense of additional personal discomfort. They found that Jewish women tolerated significantly more pain when they were told that Jews generally had a lower tolerance for pain than non-Jews. However, the ways in which they reacted and the strength of the effect depended on whether the out-group was specifically identified or left vague. Using a prescribed hierarchy of comparison groups previously ranked for strength of identification, Buss and Portnoy's results confirmed that the more strongly participants identified with a particular group, the more they tolerated pain. As we shall see later, one of the ways in which people decide about their identity is through making comparisons between their group and other groups (see

Chapter 4). These comparisons help to explain intergroup differences as well as intragroup similarities in socio-cultural reactions to pain (Weisenberg, 1977). People use the information obtained from comparisons to judge what reactions are appropriate to pain. Although this literature is limited, an analysis of intergroup relations demonstrates the profoundly social nature of pain reports.

In this section we have considered research that is integral to any socio-psychological approach to pain. A comprehensive social understanding of pain will need to include knowledge about social conditions at three levels. At the first level, it will incorporate information about socially-based individual differences, which have been thoroughly studied already. A second level of knowledge is in the form of interpersonal interactions and intragroup dynamics. To date, relatively little is known about this specifically in pain sufferers, although this is a growing area of recent research activity. But we also need to incorporate a third, higher order level of social analysis so that the effects of intergroup relations on pain can be included. This research area has been substantially neglected in recent years.

Some types of "social" investigation to date appear to have hindered progress, because detailing the various socio-demographic features of age, sex, ethnic group and so on may have predisposed clinical users of this knowledge more to label and categorise pain patients than to concentrate on unravelling the processes whereby such distinctions come about. In the following section we go on to review one of the best understood of these processes to date, which is learning. The remainder of this volume focuses on what is known about other social processes. Furthermore, the persistent search for differences between groups has now turned out to be a mistaken pursuit because studies of similarities demonstrate high levels of heterogeneity within groups. It is also worth noting that some of these category labels represent real groups in the fullest sense of the word; that is, members who share a collective identity from extensive and regular communication with each other. They exist as social or cultural communities. Other so-called groups are in fact nominated clusters of people who have been subsumed under a collective label. Here, the word "group" is perhaps a misnomer, because these individuals do not share a common identity and may have little or no systematic communication with other members with the same designation. Such interaction with other category members may be on a limited scale and on an *ad hoc* basis, such as in waiting rooms or bus queues. Hence, their "groupness" is artificial, designated more by research convenience than by social parameters. More accurately, these subdivisions within the population should be referred to as categories. So far research has tended to explore the pain and pain behaviour of people in categories, paying less attention to level of identification or communality in groups, and this distinction may prove to be central to the formulation of a more "social" social psychology of pain and pain behaviour.

SOCIAL LEARNING PROCESSES OF PAIN: THEORY AND MANAGEMENT

Ideas about how pain and pain behaviour are learned have been elaborated from social learning theories within the area of behavioural medicine. Here, symptoms are viewed as important in their own right, and are believed to be strongly influenced and maintained by conditioning and learning. At the peak of interest in behaviourism, Beecher (1960) observed that conditioning should be carefully investigated as an important component in the psychic reaction to pain. Behavioural medicine tackles problems in observable terms; headaches, for instance, are definable by electro-myography (EMG) recordings and medication intake. The approach assumes that what happens now or has happened recently in a person's environment is likely to affect that person's experience and reporting of pain. It is relatively unconcerned with the distant past through a re-evaluation of childhood or early development (Boudewyns and Keefe, 1982). It begins with the premise that the healing of non-malignant tissue damage may take up to three months, and after that time reports of pain can be classified as pain behaviour. Although this is "real" pain, the pain behaviour pattern is deemed to have been established by learning and reinforcement. Respondent pain associated with an antecedent event like a wound is treated before operant pain can be tackled.

An underlying premise is that any careful examination of the situation in relation to chronic pain will reveal that significant changes in behaviour are needed by patients and their family (Fordyce, 1976). Patients learn to decrease or stop visible beha-viours they may enjoy, and to do things that they previously considered to be unnecessary or undesirable. For many, the negative consequences of failure to perform these actions were previously remote and beyond their experience. Identified current or potential reinforcers include financial compensation, avoidance of responsibilities, medication and care and concern from others. Visible and audible pain behaviours are targets for change by the withdrawal of reinforcement: such behaviours include facial expressions like grimacing, posture, refusal to work, requesting pain medication and seeking other types of attention for the pain. These reinforcements have been taxonomised by Turk and Flor (1987). There is direct positive reinforcement, such as the anxious, solicitous concern of a spouse and attention from health care providers. Indirect positive reinforcement or pain maintenance results from avoidance or escape from unwelcome responsibilities, such as caring for the family. A third category of avoiding or terminating certain activities protects the person from discomfort or ends it, while a fourth class is about the non-reinforcement of well behaviours. Well behaviour is believed to be incompatible with pain, although the data for this is thin because few holistic studies of the many aspects of well-being have been carried out.

A major aim of therapy is to reduce levels of addictive medication through the use of a "cocktail" where the proportion of active analgesic ingredients is steadily reduced with the patient's consent. Recently, Williams et al (1994) compared the efficacy of this staff-controlled cocktail method of analgesic administration with a patient-controlled reduction method. They looked at 108 patients engaged in a pain manage-ment programme (61% with low back pain) and found that at discharge, 89% of those using the cocktail method were abstinent compared with 63% of the patient-controlled group. One month after treatment, however, this advantage disappeared and by six months the rates were the same, with the non-abstinent cocktail patients taking significantly larger opiate doses by this time. Those who opted for the cocktail method had begun treatment at higher levels of morphine. They were also less confident about their ability to cope without pain and saw their everyday activities as being most disrupted by pain.

Another aim is the development of new social skills such as holding conversations without giving any indication of pain, increasing eye contact and smiling. Increasing activity is also a prime aim of treatment. The pacing and quantity of physical activities such as deep knee bends is increased during rehabilitation. This also involves spending less time in bed. Interesting research by Deyo, Diehl and Rosenthal (1986) supports the view that early activation during acute episodes of back pain is more beneficial than conventional advice to take a week's bed rest. They found that those randomly assigned to a condition where they were advised to spend only two days in bed rather than seven had fewer days of absenteeism subsequently. Furthermore, at three months' follow-up, there was no evidence of an increase in absence from work, symptoms, dysfunction or health care use in those who had taken a shorter rest. Adjustments for compliance reconfirmed the findings.

The value of this approach to the study of pain has been its power to reorientate clinical thinking by providing a realistic alternative to the medical model. It helps to explain how and why people become chronic pain patients without needing to label them with a personality problem. Knowing how pain comes about enables the planning of interventions to intercept the progress of such processes. While constitutional factors, such as genes, and personality factors, like motivation and traits, are acknowledged to play some role in the constitution of chronic pain patients, social learning theorists believe that by far the biggest contribution comes from environmental factors in the form of stimuli or consequences, which are directly related to the various processes of learning (Fordyce, 1976). Therapy aims to provide symptom control with stimulus control (Khatami and Rush, 1982).

However, it is not just chronic pain patients who are required to change, but also those who come into contact with them. The attitudes and behaviour of the hospital team must change too, so that they do not positively reinforce pain behaviours. The health care system inadvertently reinforces pain behaviour by legitimating the physical basis of chronic pain problems. Conventional instructions to "let pain be your guide" can lead to iatrogenic complications and deconditioning, and reduced activity, hence predisposing patients to further health consultations (Turk and Flor, 1987). The act of giving pain relief and its timing is an interpersonal activity that is directly within the powers of medical staff in hospital wards, especially when a p.r.n. schedule has been prescribed. Administering pain relieving drugs on a time schedule ensures continuous pain relief without breakthrough pain. At the same time, it reduces levels of dependency and consequently the power gradient in this relationship. However, operant conditioning is very expensive because it requires an extended period of hospital treatment and specially trained staff (Fordyce, Roberts and Sternbach, 1985) so its efficacy needs careful assessment.

Some studies of pain management programmes show how difficult and complex the social interaction between patients and staff can be. Wooley, Blackwell and Winget (1978) described interpersonal interactions associated with illness behaviour in chronic pain patients. These included demands for care and attention by requesting tests, medication or surgery, and displays of helplessness like inactivity and unresponsiveness to suggestion. Other aspects involved excessive compliance by voicing respect and appreciation, veiled hostility, threats to harm or to leave treatment if more is not provided, argumentation about promised treatment or the past, dividing the professional staff by pitting them against each other, and "silliness" in the form of childishness, flirtation or ignoring advice. Wooley, Blackwell and Winget (1978) see all of these behaviours as engaging attention and eliciting help willingly or by coercion. They say that these social behaviours are best managed through the application of reinforcement and other behaviourist principles. However, social processes other than learning may well play an important role in generating and maintaining these behaviours, and this deserves further scrutiny. A study of 50 chronic pain patients undertaking a 28-day programme for substance abuse provides further insight into staff reactions to these problems: "Patients who complain of severe pain engender powerful conflicts in the physicians who treat them. The fear of producing addiction may result in the under treatment of painful medical conditions. If an addiction is recognised, the physician may be reluctant to interrupt or stop the substance use because of uncertainty that the patient can manage otherwise" (Finlayson et al, 1986, p.179).

Patients' interactions with their partners are also important. Partners are required to be engaged in treatment at all stages and are expected to spend time understanding the nature and processes of reinforcement pertinent to the sufferer's condition, and to learn strategies for dealing with them. Weekends at home are monitored to enable the treatment to continue successfully and to maintain gains. The behaviour of "gate-keepers" who administer drugs in the home must be adjusted to keep pace with the hospital programme. Family members may discourage the patient by punishing well behaviour when patients try to engage in normal activities. Commonly a family will entreat the sufferer to "take it easy" or to avoid exercise or activities that they believe may aggravate the pain, unwittingly promoting disuse. Fordyce (1986) sees this behaviour as arising from a confusion among lay people about the distinction between "hurt" and "harm", as well as from erroneous beliefs that the more exercise people do, the more it will hurt. The results of a study by Fordyce et al (1981) showed that the more pain patients exercised when instructed to continue until pain, weakness or fatigue caused them to stop, the fewer pain behaviours or complaints they exhibited.

But are operant procedures successful? From a review of five well-designed studies, Linton (1986) concluded that there was "considerable support" for the continued use of this style of treatment. During the programme decreased medication has been reported, especially for prescription analgesics, hypnotics and muscle relaxants, in addition to increases in physical activity. These conditioning effects may last for up to eight years after the completion of treatment (Turner and Chapman, 1982a). Other outcome criteria commonly used are re-employment rates, rates of subsequent surgery, re-admissions to hospital and clinic visits, as well as not receiving pain compensation. While earlier studies of contingency management produced equivocal findings, this may have been due to the lack of placebo controls and uncertainty about the stability of outcomes (Bradley, 1983). On the state of the art, Linton (1986) concludes, "The question is no longer does it work, but how well does it work, for whom and why?" (p.129). Questions have also been raised about whether operant programmes have cross-cultural acceptability; there is some suggestion that they may not be acceptable even within the western world. Writing about their experience in Britain, Main and Waddell (1982) concluded, "convincing patients and their families to accept an in-patient program of the sort described by Fordyce seems a major problem. Private patients in the US are of course quite a different population."

While the use of medication has economic costs, measures of the personal costs in terms of subjective well-being seem to have been missed from the design of many studies. Fordyce has argued that people who are more engaged in a broad range of life's activities *must* have a better quality of life than in their former sedentary, addicted and socially isolated state. But if we do not ask patients about their well-being or quality of life, how can we know whether or not they suffer less? This information seems to be especially crucial where therapy involves a withdrawal of what is believed to be pain relieving medication. In a study of 131 patients divided into those who did not take addictive medication (30%), those taking narcotics (33%) and those taking narcotics with addictive drugs (37%), Turner et al (1982) found that patients in the latter two conditions had more pain-related surgeries and admissions to hospital than those without addictive medication. The double-drug group were also more physically impaired, were higher on MMPI scores for hysteria and hypochondriasis and spent more on drugs each month than the others. But levels of pain and subjective well-being did not feature in this design, as in many other similar studies and there has been a tendency for changes in subjective well-being to be assumed rather than quantified. So, until quite recently there has been little information about whether operant programmes decrease subjective pain because the reduction of pain has never been seen as the prime goal of rehabilitation. Reviewing the area, Turner and Chapman (1982a) conceded that such studies needed to be done.

The result of this focused use of objective measures is that the methods available are numerous but conceptually narrow, which has hampered progress in the investigation of much broader social features associated with pain and illness behaviour. The limitations are exemplified by an otherwise worthwhile social psychological study implemented to develop a method for assessing non-verbal pain behaviour. The four experiments assessed the reliability of observing rheumatoid arthritis patients performing a series of standard manoeuvres like sitting, walking, standing and reclining. Following an intensive training course, observers recorded passive and active rubbing (holding and massage), rigidity (holding with excessive stiffness), self-stimulation through repetitive movements, guarding, grimacing and so on (McDaniel et al, 1986). Although their method proved to be relatively reliable, valid and "objective", the study explicitly excluded assessment of the patient's thoughts and feelings associated with these actions. In this void of information, interpretation of these behaviours must be speculative. Until recently, this approach has been largely concerned with obtaining what is seen as the "truth" from patients. "Many pain measurement methods have struggled to make the 'say' behaviour more honest and accurate. Instead of struggling to obtain honest or accurate statements from the person in the form of visual analogue, pain ratings etc, perhaps it is better to look at the 'do' behaviour of the person" (Fordyce, 1983, p.47). Main and Waddell (1982) are also concerned with the accuracy of data obtained from patients admitted to operant programmes in Britain. Nevertheless, Fordyce himself has expressed qualms about the ethics of challenging the veracity of patients' statements by using clandestine video recordings to establish size of lawn mowed, number of steps taken and so on (see also Chapter 10). In making the distinction between what people say and what they do, he recommends that clinicians place more reliance on what they do, so his position appears to be one of emphasising objectivity rather than excluding subjective measures.

An adjacent concern with the scientific identification of malingerers has also permeated work in this field, especially in the success of treating chronic low back pain patients (Leavitt, 1985). Like Fordyce, Leavitt argues that financial rewards colour clinical judgement, and those with long-term disability are "always" more suspect when litigation is pending and when laboratory tests fail to reveal pathology or where the findings are paradoxical. Leavitt (1985) says that patients receiving compensation have fewer physical findings to support their claims and their rates of recovery are "considerably less favourable, regardless of outcome measures applied or therapeutic methods attempted". Patients' credibility is brought into question because their participation in treatment programmes is poor. Furthermore, recovery rates appear to "dramatically improve" following settlement of the claim. Fordyce views compensation as rewarding pain behaviour, so increasing the likelihood that maladaptive behaviour will recur. Some behavioural programmes refuse to treat patients involved in litigation for this reason. One criticism of the operant approach is that important contingencies for pain behaviour are difficult or impractical to control because they depend on the progress of litigation and the size of disability payments. But the findings are equivocal: many studies have failed to find any link between compensation-seeking and pain outcome (Kremer, Block and Atkinson, 1983; see also Chapter 10).

Turk and Flor (1987) note that while pain behaviour is poorly articulated and defined, nobody has yet established a baseline rate of pain behaviours in the population of pain patients with known organic origins. For this reason it is still impossible to assess whether those without known pathology show more pain behaviours than those with organic diagnoses. In line with Skevington (1986), they question whether pain behaviours are exaggerated by those without pathology in order to be more convincing to health professionals. This suggests that pain behaviour may be a direct result of the social interaction between those seeking a diagnosis and legitimation for their condition, and those empowered to do the legitimating. That patients change their pain behaviour when they are conscious of being evaluated is reported in a study of rheumatoid arthritis patients, who showed pain behaviours that were different during private physical examination compared to when they knew that they were being videoed (Anderson et al, 1992). However, it is not news that people change their behaviour during observation and evaluation. Social facilitation theory is one of the oldest theories of social psychology. It says that the mere presence of another person affects the way in which people behave (Triplett, 1897), and this applies to pain patients who know that they are being evaluated. Such audience effects represent one of the most fundamental assumptions of social psychology. In the persisting absence of data about what is the norm for those in pain, is it reasonable and ethical to suspect pain patients of malingering and deception because their behaviour changes under these circumstances?

Behavioural pain programmes share the goals "to treat excess disability and expressions of suffering" (Fordyce, Roberts and Sternbach, 1985, p.115). This consensus has directed the humane endeavour of treating disability by encouraging greater activity, less dependence on drugs and making people in pain more able to return to work. But, as the quotation shows, the other therapeutic goal has been to shape verbal behaviour so that the expression of pain is suppressed. A criticism levelled at operant methods is that they do not treat pain *per se*, but train patients to be more stoical about their pain (Schmidt, 1987; Skevington, 1986). Rachlin's (1985) description of the behaviour of a breed of hypothetical stoical super Spartans and super super Spartans, draws out in humorous and exquisite detail the respective philosophical positions of the behaviourist versus the cognitive–physiological camps. Indeed, suppressing reporting behaviour extends not just to the duration of the programme itself but to subsequent utilisation of clinic services. One study has costed the savings at 38% from a decrease in clinic visits following behavioural medicine interventions. Furthermore, Caudill et al (1991) found that those with the greatest number of pre-intervention visits showed the biggest reductions after treatment, but whether this reduction truly reflects a concomitant improvement in quality of life for these patients was not addressed.

The continued use of these programmes is justified in the absence of other, potentially better, models. However, it is debatable how far individual patients and physicians are persuaded of their efficacy. Patients may seek a significant *clinical* reduction in their pain from an intensive programme but are disabused of these expectations from the start. However, their satisfaction with the course is questionable if they continue to see reductions in pain as a prime obstacle to a good quality life. When at the end of treatment they return to the care of their practitioners, they may report that the pain is still the same. Optimistically, the course has taught them to cope with it better but it is arguable that while some suffering may have been relieved, the pain remains. It is therefore debatable how far fastidious and widespread physician and patient education about the goals of behavioural medicine will dispel purchaser dissatisfaction about the inability of these costly programmes to relieve pain, as a primary goal of any medical treatment is consensually agreed to be the relief of pain and suffering. If existing psychological models are more appropriate to the relief of disability and suffering than pain, this raises difficult questions about whether psychologists should be seeking new models to tackle pain *per se*.

Social learning theories are "social", because in order to provide an explanation for a pain patient's behaviour it is essential to know how both observer and actor behaved. Modelling and imitation enable us to begin to understand family dynamics, being visible in the ways in which children learn to express pain by observing their parents (Craig, 1986). A series of signal detection studies by Craig and colleagues has shown how being exposed to intolerant models affects the sensory components of pain and discomfort. When tolerant models convey the message that the stimulus is not painful, sensory experience is not affected and willingness to report distress is reduced (Craig and Coren, 1975). Furthermore, long-term memories of childhood persist into adulthood. Adult pain patients commonly recall the ways in which their parents reacted to pain. There may have been considerable parental concern and readiness to take action when pain and illness occurred. Alternatively, one or both parents may have been reluctant to respond to pain unless it was very severe (Fordyce, 1976). Such observations raise legitimate questions about to what extent adult pain behaviour is a consequence of these early experiences and observations. Social modelling is particularly obvious in some medical conditions where symptoms mimic known physical states; for instance, the behaviour that leads to the performance of an unnecessary appendicectomy. Craig (1986) also questions why seeing others in pain grasps our attention. He observes that while most people say they do not like to view suffering and violence, there is growing evidence that some derive satisfaction from watching it and many feel compelled to pay attention to it, initially at least.

Fordyce's work has provided a radical departure for clinicians by taking explanations for pain beyond the medical model and putting them squarely within a psychological brief. But how "social" is social learning theory? While the two-person scenarios outlined above have been necessarily simplified for investigation purposes, they have limited the scope for studying the rich social interaction between pain sufferers and those around them, although this has changed quite recently as family studies have become the vogue. A concentration on objectivity to the exclusion of subjective measures has acted as a deterrent to the development of new applications and ideas here. Recognition that patients do not behave in a social vacuum represents a more social departure for the interpretation of chronic pain behaviours within this model. Although health carers have been systematically trained and engaged in changing the treatment environment, direct assessment of *their* behaviour has been downplayed. Like other patient-centred models in pain research, this omission implies that staff behave consistently and uniformly, and that any variations in their behaviour are insufficiently important to warrant monitoring; they are a constant in the equation. Finally, the intragroup and intergroup influences on the behaviour of those who suffer has been ignored. This may be because pain researchers have been unaware of methods and theories in social psychology that would have enabled them to examine these features in systematic ways. This dimension deserves further investigation if the pain phenomenon is to be fully understood.

COGNITIVE DEPARTURES

In its original form social learning theory limited its focus on learning to the exclusion of other cognitions as well as emotions and motivation. Consequently, it could only provide a partial answer to the problem it sought to address. However, it has been adapted in recent years to take account of known influential cognitions like the "attitudinal factors (which) may distinguish clinical success from failure" (McArthur et al, 1987), and recent models in cognitive research. So what is the contribution of cognitive factors in the triggering and maintenance of chronic pain? The cognitive–behavioural approach assumes that affect and behaviour are largely determined by cognitive appraisals and the perceived significance of events. Cognitions are based on the essentially social features of attitudes, beliefs, attributions, expectations and assumptions developed from previous experiences with other people and other events. The way in which people learn to master pain problems is by identifying and correcting these distorted thoughts and beliefs, in particular beliefs about expecting attention from others (Turner and Chapman, 1982b). Cognitive behaviour therapy is designed to correct those faulty cognitions that underpin emotional and behavioural disturbance. They may be beliefs, interpretations or attributions about the pain and medical condition, and may include cognitive reactions to, or appraisals about, the impact of pain on life (Turk and Rudy, 1986). Such statements acknowledge that socio-cognitive factors affect the behaviour of chronic pain patients and so advance the case for a social psychology of pain.

But do chronic pain patients do better with an operant or cognitive approach? In a well-controlled study of 81 mildly dysfunctional chronic low back pain patients, Turner and Clancy (1988) randomly assigned them to one of these two therapeutic conditions or to a waiting list control group. They had back pain exceeding 6 months, with an average of 14 years, and were able to participate in aerobic exercises. They were excluded if they needed surgery. Although there is no standard protocol available, manuals were followed closely and patients were treated in small groups, for 2 hours a week, for eight weeks. Cognitive–behaviour therapy included training in systematic progressive relaxation and imagery, supplemented by home practice, identification of negative emotions associated with pain and stressful events, and identification of maladaptive thoughts. Although the groups were equivalent prior to treatment on a wide range of variables, the results showed that the operant group had benefited more than the cognitive–behaviour group at the end of treatment. Those receiving cognitive treatment were no different on any measure to waiting list controls. All treatments showed significant improvements, especially in the reduction of cognitive errors, but neither treatment group reported significantly less pain than the waiting list group at the end of treatment. However, the cognitive group did make considerable improvements 6–12 months after the end of treatment, so that after a year the two treatment groups were no different. Questionnaires completed after treatment showed that the cognitive group were more satisfied and found treatment most helpful. The results here suggest that cognitive–behavioural programmes may have more to offer than the initial but dwindling rewards of operant schemes. Without the inclusion of these subjective measures, the values of cognitive–behavioural programmes would have been lost.

Data from Manchini, Peterson and Maruta (1988) points to the conclusion that cognitive change may in fact mean attitude change. They report that chronic pain patients' perceptions of their illness and psychosocial functioning undergo "dramatic changes" at the time of discharge from behavioural treatments, as reflected by patient and staff ratings of "improved attitude" at this time, as well as medical usage and lowered depression. Such results tend to support the view that, like operant techniques, cognitive–behaviour therapy changes ways of thinking about pain without necessarily affecting the pain itself. These findings raise questions about whether we would be justified in relabelling cognitive–behavioural techniques as a procedure for creating attitude change in the clinic. The attitude change literature in social psychology is able to account for both gradual cognitive change and the more dramatic "Road to Damascus" experience. This could account for the substantial changes found at the end of treatments (e.g. Manchini, Peterson and Maruta, 1988), as well as studies where incremental improvements occurred in the months following treatment. In the latter case patients appear to continue to seek ways of integrating what they have learned into their everyday routines.

Turning to the components of cognitive behavioural programmes, it is clear that relaxation training forms an important part and this is a feature that deserves comment in its own right. There is considerable diversity in the quantity and style of relaxation training carried out and little attempt to report these procedures in detail or to standardise them. Reviewing 26 different procedures in 80 studies, Hillenberg and Collins (1982) concluded that the more sessions attended, the more effective relaxation tends to be. Furthermore, its effectiveness pertains to a variety of problems, not just pain. With the research focus on the better practical management of pain, theories about how relaxation works are largely absent in this area. A notable exception is a review of behavioural relaxation in the specific treatment of myofascial pain by Scott and Gregg (1980), and this needs to be completed for other prevalent painful conditions. However, a more recent study of relaxation in patients with mildly disabling chronic low back pain by Turner and Jensen (1993) showed no evidence to support the idea that patients receiving relaxation would report a greater decrease in pain than those receiving cognitive–behaviour therapy. They concluded that the two were equivalent in terms of reducing pain, which indicates that the less costly treatment of relaxation training might be more profitably used in preference to cognitive therapy. However, the study also showed that none of the three treatment conditions — relaxation, cognitive therapy or the two combined — altered cognitive errors, depression, disability or pain behaviours more than staying on the waiting list. Not only do these findings indicate the need for studies of how particular therapies produce improvement, they also highlight the conclusion that it is time for a new paradigm.

A recent departure has been to apply multi-modal operant and cognitive approaches as a preventative measure to pre-empt the establishment of chronic back pain by disrupting the process of chronicity. As with operant procedures alone, Linton (1987) says that there is no evidence that it is helpful to procrastinate in initiating these interventions. However, the assumptions tend to be the same, namely that by managing pain rather than treating it, sufferers learn to live with their pain in more appropriate ways and "feel better", but seldom return to their pre-pain state of functioning. Relaxation to intercept the pain–tension cycle and relaxation gymnastics to stretch relevant muscles every half hour affect the development of pain and discomfort (Linton, 1987), but although much of this treatment programme has been predicated on increasing physical fitness, there is little conclusive evidence that strong muscles really do protect people from injuries. In an study of 30 chronic back pain patients, Linton (1985) found that patients did *believe* in a connection between pain and their ability to participate in daily activities, but the activities performed were not consistently related to their pain levels. Supporting the use of subjective reports, he concludes that "what people say is just as important as what they do, even though the two do not always correspond" (pp.293–294). Furthermore, he observes that cultural norms derived from health education programmes about the link between fitness and health may well have influenced these results. This is a valuable comment because, to date, there have been few attempts to situate results of change in pain programmes within background information about changing cultural norms, although lip-service is sometimes paid to them. More often, cultural norms have been considered to be a nuisance factor rather than an integral social feature of the chronic pain sufferer's environment and one which is worthy of direct investigation.

EMG has frequently been employed to assist feedback about levels of muscle tension during relaxation training. Keefe et al (1981) found that back pain patients who attended around 10 sessions, with home practice, reported significant reductions in pain, tension and EMG activity at the completion of training, but attempts to distinguish improvers from non-improvers were confounded by different initial levels of pain in the two groups. In a smaller but well-controlled study of chronic rheumatic back pain patients, where EMG biofeedback was compared with two control conditions of "pseudotherapy" and conventional medical treatment, Flor, Haag and Turk (1986) found that patients in the biofeedback group did better and maintained these benefits on cognitive and behavioural measures, but not on global pain. Biofeedback patients saw treatment as more effective than controls. Furthermore, those who improved most said that they had continued to use relaxation to control their pain and tension because it gave them an increased sense of control. In contrast, those who did not improve reported more helplessness, hopelessness and greater feelings of dependency on medical help. High levels of short-term success with EMG and thermal biofeedback for chronic muscle contraction has also been recorded for chronic headaches, and the best results emerge from patients who are younger, more anxious and who do not habitually use drugs (Chapman, 1986).

Comparisons have also been made with social support (see also Chapter 7). In one randomised controlled trial of chronic rheumatoid arthritis patients, cognitive–behaviour therapy in the form of 5 thermal biofeedback sessions and 10 group meetings was compared with 15 sessions of structured social support with family or friends, and a control group who had no additional contact (Bradley et al, 1987). While both groups found the relaxation and imagery very helpful, the cognitive–behaviour group reported a reduction in pain and unpleasantness, as well as showing less rheumatoid activity after treatment. The results of this study do not encourage the continued use of social support with rheumatoid arthritis sufferers, at least. However, there is only poor agreement about the definition of social support; in Bradley et al's study interactive features like learning how others cope, how to deal "more realistically" with feelings and express them and the effect on the family were included, but other aspects like the perceived quality of the support could have been addressed more directly.

This cognitive branch of behaviour therapy has come to acquire a more social flavour through its concern with social cognitions, yet rarely do the methods incorporate any means of evaluating the dynamics of the ongoing interactions between patient and doctor, patient and family members, patient and workmates and so on. They are more often studied piecemeal. Hence, the social information available to clinicians who use this approach is strictly limited. Where such information is known, this tends to be downplayed as interesting background rather than a focus for serious study. Furthermore, where the measurement of beliefs, expectations and so on has been carried out, results from these self-report measures have tended to be discounted where they conflict with those from direct observation methods, on the assumption that "objective" measures are somehow more accurate. Often the argument has been that the inclusion of subjective measures dilutes stronger effects claimed for more "objective" measures (e.g. Keefe et al, 1986).

What is not widely appreciated in pain research is that, over five decades and using a wide variety of different methods, social psychologists have been unable to record strong and consistent correlations between attitudes and behaviour. There is an extensive literature — too large to review here — showing that people do not behave in accordance with their professed beliefs. A cursory comparison of the opinion poll survey and polled voting results for the 1992 British General Election serves to make an anecdotal point. Furthermore, there are good theories in social psychology to explain this disjunction. Work by Fishbein and Ajzen (1974, 1975) shows that the relationship between attitudes and behaviour is improved substantially if specific behavioural *intentions* are examined, so it is better to ask how pain patients feel about mowing the lawn and whether they intend to do it, than to ask what they think about physical activity in general. The point here is that disagreement between these types of measures is more commonly recorded in psychology than agreement. Consequently, this lack of agreement between measures, which is deemed to confound pain research, is one that is far from exclusive to the study of pain. When set within this more general literature, the assumptions and hypotheses that direct research on malingering and deception in chronic pain patients appear far less tenable.

Pither (1989) has usefully summarised the state of the art in the operant treatment of persistent pain. He says that operant programmes do not "cure" the pain, nor do they attempt to do so, so using the reduction of pain as a yardstick is inappropriate. Such programmes aim to restore normal functioning despite the pain, and in 60–70% of US cases they have been successful in doing this. In particular, programmes have shown that they can increase patients' activity, reduce their pain behaviours, reduce their demands for drugs, return them to work and predispose them to use the health care facilities less. This is a particularly strong economic point, since chronic pain patients are undoubtedly "avid" users of health care resources. More speculative outcomes are occasional records of reductions in depression and in pain intensity. These observations are largely supported by a meta-analysis of 65 studies by Flor, Fydrich and Turk (1992), where they confirmed that multidisciplinary treatments for chronic pain are superior to no-treatment waiting lists or unidisciplinary treatments like medical treatment or physiotherapy alone. Unlike Pither, they claimed benefits for pain, as well as for mood and interference, return to work and use of the health care system, and these were stable over time. Despite the 3089 patients included and the 704 dependent variables examined, many studies considered had not supplied basic information about the means and standard deviations of their outcome variables. The samples came largely from pain clinics (85%) and multidisciplinary pain centres (80%), so they tended to include the most severely disabled patients, with high rates of unemployment, large numbers of compensation and litigation cases, and many cases involving previous surgery and high medication use. While the economic advantages are clear and persuasive in terms of continued use, what is not entirely apparent from the limited number of psychological outcome measures in use is whether the humanitarian objectives claimed to have been fulfilled by Pither and others have truly been achieved and measured or just imputed. How far and on what dimensions has the quality of life of these pain centre patients truly been improved?

A SOCIO-COGNITIVE APPROACH: THE FAMILY

Interpersonal dynamics between pain sufferers and those around them have begun to be studied in recent years, and as such provide an example to point the way that pain research in social psychology might go. Turk, Flor and Rudy (1987) have argued that "chronic pain should be viewed in the context of the social network of the patient with the family being of primary importance" (p.4). Between 70% and 90% of all illness episodes are handled outside the formal health care system, and the family provides a substantial part of this informal health care. By the family is meant not only blood relatives and those who live together, but also groups where a range of material and emotional supports are provided by mutual obligation.

There are many conflicting theories about the aetiological role that families play in the condition of chronic pain patients. Are they responsible for initiating and maintaining the problems, and how much does the presence of a sufferer in the family negatively affect its dynamics (Turk, Flor and Rudy, 1987)? Despite the widespread problems of having a chronic pain patient in the family, many families cope "surprisingly well" and there is a tendency to lose sight of this conclusion in the hunt for "problem" families suitable for research (Turk, Flor and Rudy, 1987). But behavioural models indicate that pain behaviours may be controlled by the external contingencies of reinforcement, so that through attention and sympathy from a spouse, expressions of pain and other pain behaviours may be directly and positively reinforced. The model also points to mechanisms whereby undesirable actions like work or sex may be avoided. Also, there may be a lack of reinforcement from other sources so that the pain behaviours become the only means of reinforcement. The family is also important in creating the right "atmosphere" for the transferral of successful treatment skills and beliefs. A problem commonly faced by behaviour therapy programmes carried out in inpatient units has been the extent to which new behaviours learned in that context are then later transferable to home and work situations outside the hospital. New home-based pain management programmes have been piloted recently, with some anecdotal success in terms of life-style changes, decreased pain levels and increased coping abilities (Corey, Etlin and Miller, 1987). This tentatively suggests that the physical environment of the home, the social atmosphere within it, as well as the people who live there, may all make important contributions to the experience and reporting of pain.

But is there any evidence for modelling in families? Do chronic pain patients come from families where other members are also patients? Early studies suggested that the family size of long-term complainers with pain lasting for more than 60 months was larger than for people without pain complaints (Gonda, 1962). More recent research comparing 40 chronic pain patients receiving acupuncture with 50 pain-free chronic disease patients receiving ear, nose or throat treatment showed that 78% of those in pain had one or more family members who were also in pain, compared with 44% of the comparison group ($p < 0.01$) (Violon and Giurgea, 1984). In a study of size of family in 288 college students, Edwards et al (1985) found that the number of family members in pain corresponded to the number of current pains reported. Taking it a stage further, they showed that particular symptoms like headache and menstrual pain were positively correlated with the number of pain sufferers in the family, so supporting theory about modelling. While they did not find any sex differences in the number of available models, pain models had greatest impact on the reporting behaviour of women, which might account in part for the sex differences outlined earlier.

There is some evidence that married patients do better in behavioural treatments than those who are unmarried. This may be because the partner legitimates the patient's pain, encourages them to see the right specialist, shows concern and support and promotes adherence to medication (Keefe and Brown, 1982). Such findings reduce the case for family-blaming by health professionals (Flor, Turk and Rudy, 1987) and provide an antidote to work, suggesting that how partners behave affects the outcome of treatment. In one small-scale study, patients whose spouses were optimistic showed greater treatment gains than patients who lived with pessimists. Particularly important here was the spouses' optimism or pessimism about how much exercise their partner would be able to do on the programme, how the pain would feel and the length of time they would continue to exercise later (Block, Beyer and Silbert, 1985). Block, Kremer and Gaylor (1980) demonstrate something of the social nature of this reinforcement process. Half of their patients were told that their spouse would be observing them through a one-way mirror, while the other half believed they were being watched by a clerk. Patients whose spouses were solicitous towards their complaints reported more intense pain if they believed their spouse was present than in the comparison condition, but for those with non-solicitous spouses the opposite occurred. While these results have been interpreted in reinforcement terms, an alternative explanation is provided by social facilitation theory. Behaviourists have viewed these alterations in behaviour as an intention to deceive, but at present we have no "gold standard" norms describing the behaviour of pain patients in the presence of others against which to judge whether what is recorded for chronic pain patients is normal or abnormal. Where marital disharmony and interpersonal problems emerge in families of pain patients it is difficult to disentangle cause from effect, and longitudinal studies are needed to look at changing family relations from onset. Payne and Norfleet (1986) concluded that chronic pain patients have higher levels of sexual and marital maladjustments, even in long-term stable relationships, but the data available leaves uncertainties about whether maladjustments were the cause of chronic pain or the result of it. Recently, attention has been focused on the well-being of "significant others" in the family. Where spouses were negatively affected by caring for a pain sufferer, symptoms commonly reported included fatigue, nervousness, tiredness and tension. However, dysphoric mood, marital dissatisfaction and poor physical health were found in only a minority of families (Turk, Flor and Rudy, 1987). Not only is the symptom distribution uneven among spouses of chronic pain patients, but some studies have identified spouses who appear to have even more symptoms than the pain patients themselves. This data raises interesting epidemiological questions about why and how a particular individual becomes the identified patient (Flor and Turk, 1985).

One of the reasons why causality has been slow to become established is because, until recently, it has been common to assess the patient and partner separately rather than observing the dynamic interpersonal exchange between them. While patients alone have been most commonly studied, other research has just looked at spouses. Although of limited value, in isolation it is impossible to glean a comprehensive view about what is happening in these relationships. Spouse assessment of 40 patients in a study by Rowat and Knafl (1985) revealed that 38% of spouses were unable to describe their partner's pain and the rest tended to describe it in sensory terms alone. An important theme in this research was the poor mental health of spouses; uncertainty was faced by 60% of partners, while 83% reported some type of health disturbance, and 69% of statements derived from transcripts dealt with the emotional impact of pain — the sadness, depression, fear, nervousness and irritability faced by those with a partner in pain — with 40% reporting how helpless they felt about relieving their partner's pain. Such studies provide rich insights into what it is like to be the partner of someone in pain and the problems that need to be tackled if partners are to be engaged in helping with treatment. Other studies have suggested that it may not be the patient's pain level *per se* that is most appropriate in explaining a spouse's well-being, but the way in which the patient copes with it. Coping style appears to account for the spouse's mood, sense of control over life and level of marital satisfaction (Flor, Turk and Scholtz, 1987).

Research on spouses has also thrown interesting light on the reporting of sex differences. In a study of 185 chronic pain patients where 59% were married, patients and their significant others completed assessments designed to examine perceptions of pain intensity, interference with life, mood, life control, spouse support and pain behaviours. The results showed that the spouses of women patients agreed more with their partner's ratings than spouses of men, although overall agreement was high. They also found that the more solicitous the spouse, the greater the pain impact on the patient (Flor, Turk and Rudy, 1989). Other studies indicate that among partners of chronic pain patients, women are more sensitive to their partner's distress and pain. This may be because they are more accurate observers of non-verbal cues than men, especially those that reflect negative emotions (Romano, Turner and Clancy, 1989).

How do the family dynamics change when the woman in the family is the chronic pain sufferer, in view of her traditional role as home-maker. In an intensive study of 21 families carefully matched for age, race, length of marriage, education, employment status, income and having a child between the ages of 7 and 11, Dura and Beck (1988) looked at pain families, chronic illness families with diabetes and no-illness controls. They found that the mother's disability was significantly associated with depression and with state and trait anxiety. Ratings of videoed interactions showed that families without illness are more cohesive and have less conflict. However, children in all three groups did not differ in terms of social skills, behaviour problems, absence from school, mother's ratings of health and days with illness complaints over the previous fortnight. This suggests that on these measures, at least, as a family they were largely unaffected psychologically by their mother's condition. The methodology of this small-scale but challenging study is noteworthy for its ability to tap the heart of the interaction between patients and their family members; consequently, it provides a model for future research. Other studies have taken a different perspective. Studying healthy husbands of women with rheumatoid arthritis, Manne and Zautra (1990) found that although these sick wives were significantly distressed, their healthy husbands were not distressed. The quality of the couple's interaction, especially unsupportive, negative interactions surrounding the illness, was an important influence on their mental health. However, each partner was found to be more affected by his or her own worries and ability to cope than by the other partner's problems. These results may be partly explained by the unorthodox role of men as carers.

CONCLUSION

In this chapter we have examined some of the social features of those who become patients in general and pain patients in particular. The discussion about who reports pain is central to any interpretation of studies of chronic and acute pain, and a number of social factors are evidently involved in this selection process. The process of learning was singled out as one that demonstrates how useful psychological models can be in interpreting the behaviour of chronic pain patients and treating them. Sternbach (1983b) has questioned the most fundamental assumption of behavioural medicine: "strictly speaking it is not necessary to assume that pain behaviour is learned or acquired in the first place merely because it can be modified subsequently". Others claim that they have failed to find evidence of learning among chronic low back pain patients, a key group whose condition those who adhere to the operant model would wish to explain. In an important review of progress, Schmidt and Arntz (1987) cite evidence to show that the condition of those with chronic low back pain can be adequately explained through a combination of heightened pain perception threshold and lowered maximum pain tolerance. They say that a lowering of maximum pain tolerance could result in more pain behaviour, more pain avoidance behaviour and shorter endurance. Due to this increased psychological sensitisation, it is not surprising that this group then show more illness behaviour in response to physical trauma than those who are healthy. Together with a heightened threshold for pain, this implies that weak pain stimuli are not labelled as pain at all and stronger ones that are not normally intolerable will be labelled unbearable. In this way the range of painful acute stimuli is effectively narrowed, so giving the appearance of behavioural inflexibility. As an alternative, they offer proprioceptive theory, where it is argued that there is a disturbance in the processing of proprioceptive signals that affects not only pain sensations but also other symptoms like fatigue. It is suggested that where proprioceptive signals are strong, those with chronic low back pain will give up earlier. This is due to inaccuracies in the business of labelling bodily sensation, reflecting an imbalance between objective and subjective perceptions (see also Chapter 4). Here, we make the case that the concepts and methods of behavioural medicine, arising as they do from social learning theory, are inadequate to represent the diverse range of social phenomena observed to be associated with the condition of chronic pain and its treatment. While this approach has been adapted in cognitive, and hence more subjective, terms to produce several relatively successful variations of treatment, a more comprehensive approach is needed to take account of beliefs, attitudes and expectations. It will also be necessary to include a social analysis at an intergroup level (see Chapter 4), social factors involved in decision making about treatment (see Chapter 5) and the emotions and interpersonal dynamics of the consultation (see Chapter 6). Such considerations are integral to a social psychological analysis of chronic pain.

Beliefs, Images and Memories of Painful Illness

4

Back in the beginning of time, they trapped illnesses in sachets and buried them in the great walls of the city. Then many years after, during the revolution, the wall fell into pieces. The new people found the sachets, opened them, as they did not know what was in them, and the illnesses fell mercilessly upon everyone. One of those diseases, the worst one, went around each night from house to house and randomly blew her poisonous breath leaving a mark on every house she touched upon, and that mark could not be removed ever, by anyone. Not even to this present day.
(Politis, 1904)

In this chapter we begin to take a look at some of the evidence for a social psychology of pain. In particular, we consider some of the beliefs, images and memories that people hold about pain, injury and illness, and the ways in which these affect the interpretation of sensation. In the first section we examine folk beliefs and commonsense theories that people hold about their bodies and treatments. Naive theories and images provide some pointers to understanding about how potential patients interpret signs and symptoms and utilise them in decision making about whether to seek advice. Images and representations of pain and illness are discussed. We also consider how these memories are affected by emotions. This is followed by an examination of some of the comparisons sick people make with others in evaluating their condition. Beliefs about identity and identification with others in similar conditions puts the study of pain into a more social framework, and this forms a final section.

COMMONSENSE THEORIES ABOUT SICKNESS AND HEALTH

Ideas of pain and illness within western cultures have profoundly changed historically. Discussing changing attitudes to physical pain during the Middle Ages, Duby (1993) reports that early in the period, military people scorned pain, devaluing it as womanly, while religious people saw it as a sign of divine correction. By the 13th century Christ's suffering had become a central theme for all churchgoers, and it was only at this time that the idea emerged that pain was something which *ought* to be alleviated. Herzlich and Pierret (1985) have pointed out that 500 years ago contemporaneous analyses of patients' accounts showed the reality of illness as a way of life; historically, major epidemics were "sicknesses without sick people". To be a patient today is to have a certain status and not just to suffer from some biological condition. It is also involves being "cared for".

There are cross-cultural differences, too, as we began to see in the previous chapter. Beliefs and expectations about health and health care affect the ways in which people respond to illness, to the treatment they subsequently receive and even to their survival. The meaning of events can directly affect a person's biology, and this is powerfully illustrated by studies of "death dips" prior to events of important cultural significance such as presidential elections (Mechanic, 1985). Using surnames, a survey of deaths between 1966 and 1988 by Phillips and King (1988) showed that deaths among Jewish Americans were higher than expected after the Passover and lower just beforehand. This dip–peak phenomenon did not occur in Blacks, those from oriental cultures or Jewish infants. Demonstrating that this is not an exclusively Jewish phenomenon, Phillips and Smith (1990) showed a similar patterning of deaths for Chinese people around the time of the Harvest Moon festival, which did not occur in non-Chinese controls. How this mechanism works is unclear, but people do seem able to briefly postpone death until after a significant occasion.

Another example is voodoo practices, where death may be accelerated. Aborigines commonly believe that illness is due to malevolence; Cannon (1957) recounts the case of a villager who became seriously ill after an incident where a witch doctor pointed a bone at him. A physician was unable to find fever, pain, symptoms or any signs of disease, and the sufferer was only restored to health when the witch doctor visited his bedside and told him that it had all been a mistake: "a mere joke". Cannon records that death from bone-pointing often occurs in the Australian bush in the absence of any apparent illness or lethal injuries, because victims "fret themselves to death". In these circumstances death appears to be caused by a dramatic fall in blood pressure as a result of an exceptional emotional state, dehydration and starvation.

Another departure point for a discussion of the meanings of pain and illness is to consider beliefs and expectations arising from folk wisdom and superstition. Some examples of "old wives' tales" are:

- "A copper bracelet for rheumatism."
- "A bee sting for arthritis."
- "Where God puts a disease He also puts a cure."

Studies of treatment for arthritis show that over 50% of patients believe in quack or unproven treatments, such as bee venom, vitamins, a copper bracelet and special diets (H.J. Price et al, 1983). Of the 134 patients studied by H.J. Price et al, 49% had used one or more unproven remedies; 56% of these recommendations had come from friends. Vitamins were the most popular suggestion of an unproven remedy from a physician. This provides useful information in understanding the inclination to comply with treatment, an issue to which we will return in Chapter 8. While some practices based on folk beliefs may be produced by a placebo effect, there is some scientific support for others. Pharmacopoeias show that people once chewed willow to help their arthritis; we now know that it contains aspirin. With bee stings a peptide releases histamine into the skin, causing an inflammatory response, but you would need to be stung by six bees to receive the quantity necessary to relieve aching joints. By rubbing a bee sting with an onion — another lay belief — the juice combines with the kinins in the bee venom, so reducing the pain, but rubbing itself closes the "gate" in the spinal cord much faster than the effects of this chemical, so the therapeutic necessity for onion juice is debatable.

In addition to using herbs, poultices, chants and prayers, almost every culture appears to have learned to fight pain with pain (Melzack, 1989). This means that brief, moderate pain is produced in the attempt to abolish severe pain. These painful or almost painful methods of stimulation provide hyperstimulation analgesic. For instance, cupping was used in Ancient Greece and Rome to relieve pain and is still in use in modern China. A heated glass cup is inverted over the painful area; cooling creates a partial vacuum, which sucks the skin into the cup, causing bruising and tenderness. This counter-irritation method, like others such as cauterisation, moxibustion with acupuncture, scarification and trepanation are still in use to relieve arthritic pains, headaches and backache in some parts of the world. Suggestion and distraction of attention are integral to most of these procedures, and it is not possible to rule out a placebo effect until well-controlled trials have been performed, but none of these single components can altogether explain the power of the methods used or the length of reported relief (Melzack, 1989). Perhaps the socio-cultural meanings of pain and illness play a bigger part in the spinal gating mechanism than has been envisaged hitherto.

Inevitably, this raises questions about how people conceptualise health and the ways in which they contrast it with illness. This large topic can only be touched on here, but when Blaxter (1983) examined survey results from 9000 people, she identified three main ideas about what it meant to be healthy. Firstly, health was positive fitness — having energy and strength as well as an efficient or athletic body. Secondly, it was seen as a person's ability to perform their various roles normally; that is, performing roles in ways that are counter to an image of illness, and never being ill. This reflects lay beliefs about a *typus robustus* or hardy personality. Thirdly, health was conceptualised in psychological terms. Blaxter found that people tended to play down the notions of physical fitness or lack of disease in favour of a heavier psychological emphasis on health as being unstressed and unworried, coping with life, and being generally happy and "in tune" with the world.

Valuable distinctions between the concepts of disease, illness and sickness (Helman, 1978; Twaddle, 1980) assist understanding here. Disease is taken to mean the biological dimension of non-health. It is an abstract and "objective" phenomenon believed to be directly measurable using laboratory tests, observations and other signs representing an abnormal physiology. This concept is based on the pathological processes of the biomedical model. Disease is seen to be independent of social behaviour or personality characteristics. In contrast, illness is a more subjective or psychological dimension of non-health, based on perceptions not only of self but also of others around. It has social, moral, psychological and physical aspects, and is of immediate concern to those experiencing painful and other worrisome or uncomfortable "symptoms". Illness can affect social functioning or threatens to do so, and here it overlaps with concepts of sickness. Sickness is the social dimension where the condition affects a person's ability to meet the needs of living in a group. It is socially constructed, being defined by others as unhealthy. Failure to meet social obligations is seen by others to be the result of disease or illness.

Kleinman (1988) sees disease as the practitioner's problem and illness as having meanings for the sufferer; it is the "innately human experience of symptoms and suffering". Elaborating this interactionist perspective, he describes some of the social processes associated with illness by asking questions like: how do family members and the wider social network perceive, live with and respond to symptoms and disability? He argues that representations or images of illness can be understood as explanatory models. They are schemata (see later in this chapter) or frameworks held by sufferers that enable them better to understand their illness, their family, and their clinicians and healers. Illness experiences and events radiate or conceal more than one meaning. While some of these meanings are more potential than actual, others become effective only as a disorder progresses. Power is integral to a definition of sickness, embracing economic, political and institutional influences: "powerful emotions attach to these meanings, as do powerful interests" (Kleinman, 1988, p.9). This social view of pain and illness is central to the thesis presented in this volume.

It seems unlikely that people interpret symptoms such as pain without having some sort of informal theory or idea about how their body works. Helman (1985) has shown how models used by lay people to describe their bodily functions are then extrapolated to provide suitable explanations when the body fails to function properly. The "plumbing" model involves an analogy of pipes, tubes and pumps with chambers of fluid; "letting off steam" is an example. The "machine" model links the usage of fuel with the expenditure of energy, an example being the "recharging of batteries" (Furnham, 1988). Mechanical models encourage the consequent use of mechanical breakdown or damage as an analogy for illness. Patients with the pain and stiffness of chronic rheumatoid arthritis, for example, sometimes describe the sensations in their joints as "feeling rusty, needs oiling". These models use quite simple images, which are stored in the memory and utilised when symptoms occur and in the decision about whether or not to consult.

CHILDREN'S BELIEFS ABOUT PAIN AND ILLNESS

What do children believe about pain? A study by Savendra et al (1982) compared reports from 100 hospitalised children aged between 9 and 12 years with those from 114 healthy schoolchildren of the same age. It was found that children in hospital used more affective words to describe their pain than those who were healthy. Categorised answers to open-ended questions showed three broad types of belief about pain. The first group were beliefs that physical pain arises from external sources, such as falls, hits, cuts and crushes. The second category were beliefs that physical pain arises from internal sources, namely aches and pains, diseases, surgery and surgery-related events. Lastly, beliefs about psychological factors were given.

Because of developmental stages in thinking, children have different ways of conceptualising pain and illness at different times in the life-span, and these affect the ways in which they absorb and interpret knowledge about their health. The stages of development in children's conception of illness have been derived by Bibace and Walsh (1979) from Piaget's original ideas.

At the pre-operational stage of thinking commonly expressed by 4-year-olds, they found that illness was explained as a single symptom such as pain, which was thought to arise from outside the body. It was believed to cause illness in a particular part of the body.

During concrete operational thinking, which develops at about the age of 7 years, children are more able to cope with real events but not with hypothetical ones. At this age, they can distinguish between the mind and body. More than one symptom can be accommodated in their thinking. They also see illness as caused by bad behaviour as well as by germs, so contamination is understood. They are more concerned at this stage with how people become ill, e.g. bugs, smoke and dirt, than with what is happening inside the body. At this stage children understand that internal organs like the heart and the stomach are affected, but they are unable to say how these organs work except through the use of analogies like the heart as a pump. Sickness and wellness are now seen to be reversible. By the age of 11 years, they are more capable of construing hypothetical events and understanding physiological and psychophysiological explanations of bodily functions.

Children's beliefs and ideas about the nature of pain and illness affect their reaction to medical procedures. In studying chronically ill children aged between 5 and 11 years, Brewster (1982) identified three stages of thinking in a maturational sequence. At the first stage children viewed the procedures as punishment. Perrin and Gerrity (1981) have also reported that children's beliefs frequently involved punishment, guilt and self-blame. Belief that illness results from the child's own misbehaviour, especially transgressions, is commonly found in surveys of school-age children in pain (Gaffney and Dunne, 1987). At the second stage, Brewster found that children correctly perceived the procedures but believed that staff empathy depended on expressing pain. By the third stage, children were able to infer empathy and intention correctly from the staff. Specific illness, sex and duration of illness did not affect the way in which the children responded.

A direct implication of these findings is the need to frame information about pain and illness in ways that are particularly meaningful to sick children at their particular stage of conceptual development. While age is some guide to stage, it is merely a norm and for this reason cannot be used as a reliable indicator because it fails to accommodate wide variation in intellectual development. Drawings and the interpretation of pictures have been found to be successful ways of obtaining pain and disease information from children and looking at their cognitive capacity. Beales et al (1983) interviewed 75 patients aged between 7 and 17 years about their pain, and the implications of having juvenile chronic arthritis. They classified responses in four ways: first, there were subjective feelings like "my fingers ache"; second, the children used surface appearance, such as "it makes my knee red"; third, loss of motor ability was described, such as "I can't move my neck properly"; and finally, knowledge of internal pathology was used, like "it damages my bones". The results showed that 7–11-year-olds tended to use the first two categories, while two-thirds of the over 11s included more cognitively advanced descriptions of internal pathology and were more inclined to view illness as an unseen process. Although the older age group could better envisage the inside of joints and other bodily structures and processes, at the same time they were more upset, worried, frightened or sad than those who were younger. Because of their differing levels of cognitive development at the same age, Beales et al (1983) recommend that different strategies should be adopted by health professionals when talking to children in these two age ranges. The 7–11s need descriptions with analogies drawn from their own experience; for example, blood vessels are like pipelines. Disease activity can be usefully explained in military terms. However, the 12–17 year olds were more able to understand simplified textbook-style descriptions phrased in abstract causal terms.

There are practical problems about deciding the most appropriate approach for sick children, because they not only vary enormously in their stage of intellectual development at any one age, but are also able to draw on lower stages of developmental thinking. Whether or not they do this depends on the type of cognitive skill required for the particular activity they are attending to. Thus, they may use concrete operations for some activities or situations but might still be using pre-operational thinking where illness is concerned. This may be further complicated if they are in transition between two cognitive developmental stages. Beales et al (1983) recommend that a child's level of cognitive development in relation to their disease should be assessed using pictorial and verbal methods to facilitate the management of the disease.

UNCERTAINTY

As studies of children show, the conceptualisation and expression of beliefs about pain and illness is not purely a cognitive phenomenon, but includes a range of affective components. This is also true of adults. Viney (1983) identified six principal emotions from interviews with 576 adults up to the age of 90 years who were coping with severe illness. They were asked to comment on the good and bad things in life and describe what the illness was like for them. A prevalent image was one of uncertainty. People were often uncertain when they were unable to find a meaning for their illness, and this made them feel more vulnerable. Typical comments included, "There's a lot I don't know about my illness" and "Why has this happened to me?". Anxiety was common, with statements like, "I've been under a lot of stress lately". Denial was present for some, while others described anger as a reaction to the onset of illness. The frustration of injury and illness were seen to be caused directly or indirectly by chronic pain. Typical comments included "I'm fed up with being sick all the time". Helplessness and depression-laden images were identified during treatment and when it stopped; in particular, those with severe difficulties felt trapped, useless, unwanted and deprived. Viney suggests that hospitals may be more responsible for inducing helplessness than the illness itself, and there is growing support for this view (Taylor 1979). Westbrook and Viney (1983) found sex differences in the way that these themes are reported.

Ambiguity, lack of comprehension and uncertainty are strongly related to stressful events like hospital admissions and surgery (Mishel, 1981). But does uncertainty about control over aversive events have significant effects on health? Replicating previous findings, Suls and Mullen (1981) showed that undesirable changes of ambiguous control are most stressful when people have no idea how long a particular discomfort will last, how severe it will become and whether they should take the blame for it. As certainty of control reduces the stressful impact of an undesirable event, it is important for therapeutic purposes to distinguish what is controllable from what is uncontrollable. This theme is elaborated further in Chapter 5.

So what happens if it is not possible to give meaning to abnormal physical and/or mental manifestations? The ambiguous meaning of illness is constantly being negotiated. Consequently, accounts produced by sick people are not static but dynamic. As we have seen, uncertainty is also an important component in dealing with chronic disease. Personal narratives from people with diseases like multiple sclerosis show how those who are chronically afflicted construct meaning in the void of uncertainty. Robinson (1990) identified three key themes in these narratives which reflect beliefs about illness. Tragic narratives described an inverted U shape, showing a dramatic change representing a "death in life". Sad narratives reflected loss of hope in attaining valued goals in life. However, positive optimistic narratives about achieving personal goals were called heroic narratives; they were progressive in dealing with life, while ignoring disease.

From interviews with 21 patients with rheumatoid arthritis, Wiener (1975) concluded that uncertainty accounted for most of the variation in the psychosocial problems of living with this painful disease. This is because there are peaks and troughs where the disease flares and then unpredictably goes into remission. Because of considerable variations in severity, progression and the areas involved, the permutations of outcome are endless. They include reduced mobility but no skill impairment, reduced energy but no reduced mobility, reduced energy one day but renewed energy the next and so on. In the case of the early stages of arthritis there is uncertainty about whether there will be any pain, swelling or stiffness, which area will be involved, the intensity of the disability, whether the onset will be sudden or gradual, how long it will last and how frequently flares will occur. This is common to many inflammatory conditions. Strategies used by rheumatoid arthritis sufferers to tolerate uncertainty include the juggling of hope of relief against the dread of progressive pain, disability and dependency, covering up the disability by concealing it, and keeping up the appearance of a normal life-style by not complaining. In addition, some people paced their activities so that if they took longer to complete them because of difficulty, they did not become an impediment to living (Wiener, 1975).

However, it would be mistaken to view uncertainty as a personality characteristic of individual patients. One interpretation is that it is an outcome of the social interaction between patients and health care professionals (Melville, 1987). It is most likely to occur where symptoms remain unexplained because a valid disease cannot be identified and where there is little confidence about the pathological mechanisms involved. In many ways, uncertainty and ambiguity represent an absence of beliefs. This process, which distinguishes certain from less certain cases, involves legitimating of symptoms, usually by a doctor (see Chapter 3). The uncertainty and ambiguity surrounding what patients present and how this is then interpreted by the consulted physician has been instrumental in fostering the use of labelling to create the unhelpful dichotomy of organic versus psychogenic pain patients. However, this phenomenon may not be as widespread as was once believed. An inspection of 1736 medical records showed that in only 8 of these cases were symptoms truly unexplained (Melville, 1987). This led Melville to deduce that the incidence in hospital was very infrequent indeed, in stark contrast to impressions gained from the pain literature that cases of unexplained symptoms are common and are therefore a major problem.

HEALTH PROFESSIONALS

The use of lay theories is not exclusive to patients — despite rigorous training, health professionals hold them too. Few researchers in this area have acknowledged these interactive aspects; an exception is Helman's (1985) anthropological work. Helman showed that not only do folk models differ from the biomedical model but, furthermore, they influence the way in which practitioners behave. Physicians may themselves hold folk views about illness, although they are trained to be "careful never to give them as scientific evidence" (Engel, 1973), and Helman's view is that GPs collude with the folk model. Fitzpatrick (1983) also cautions against over-emphasising the gap between lay theories and medical concepts. Clinicians frequently harness metaphors and analogies to project accurate scientific principles to their patients, but patients probably influence doctors more than vice versa. The knock-on effect is that this phenomenon may predispose doctors towards prescribing ineffective medicines that are more in line with accepted folklore than medical theory (Fitzpatrick, 1983).

Physicians tend to use biomedical models and multicausal explanations that frequently include emotions, stress, personality and physical weakness. Studying patients with gastrointestinal disorders, Helman (1985) observed that clinicians explained the chronic, unpredictable course of such disease through the use of psychological explanations or "psychologisation". These psychologisations are socially constructed in the clinic and shift the responsibility for aetiology, exacerbations or therapeutic failure to the patient's emotions, personality and life-style. Consequently, this interpretation provides a self-serving bias in favour of the physician. Cultural and individual differences are other impediments to understanding, as we saw in Chapter 3. Commenting on the physician's viewpoint, Engel says:

> all too often they underestimate the significance of the personal and cultural value systems which interfere with the patient's ability to assimilate the instruction or comply with the directions. In such a case a physician is likely to absolve himself by pronouncing the patient stupid. A better appreciation of the patient's guiding framework would have made him a better teacher.
> (Engel, 1973)

Taking this a stage further, Helman (1985) shows that patients respond to their physician's position by reifying pathological emotions, personality traits or malfunctioning bodily parts. This may well have the required effect of generating a consensus between them about the interpretation of the patient's symptoms, their seriousness and the treatment to be given. Studying a system of British folk beliefs about the successful treatment of colds and fevers, Helman (1978) shows that hot, cold, wet and dry symptoms need to be appropriately matched to an acceptable means of expelling germs if treatment is to be seen as appropriate. Mismatches have implications for compliance with treatment.

PAIN BELIEFS AND THEIR USES

While it is impossible to review all beliefs about pain and illness, studies of joint pain provide examples of how beliefs might be studied, and display some of the implications of knowing about them. Patients' beliefs are inevitably embedded in and tend to reflect the more general views held by the society and culture from which they come, so surveys of the general population also provide some pointers.

In a qualitative study of 32 patients consulting a GP with suspected rheumatoid disease, Donovan, Blake and Fleming (1989) found that most described arthritis as an inconvenience but few patients saw themselves as "ill". Although pain, stiffness and burning sensations were all described individually, they found that people did not talk about symptoms in isolation, but instead contexturalised them, by saying what they believed the symptoms prevented them from doing, such as not being able to continue with a favourite hobby. So, patients bind together the meaning of these symptoms with their effects to place the symptoms in their own social context. Clinicians who abstract symptoms from their social meanings therefore effectively ignore the considerable social implications for the patient of having that symptom. A message to be drawn from this study is that being able to function socially without prohibitive functional disability is as important to patients as the discomfort itself.

Of 2389 older people with three or more symptoms of arthritis, Elder (1973) found that morning stiffness, pain and swelling were common and accurate images of the disease. A stratified subsample ($N = 160$) showed that the label "arthritis" was used freely to describe persistent aches, pains and stiffness in the joints. Half had learned this label from their physician, the rest from lay people, from television or from "just knowing" about it. Elder looked at the extent to which beliefs about the cause of symptoms varied in relation to the class structure. Around two-thirds attributed the symptoms to ageing, particularly those in the higher socio-economic classes. The lowest socio-economic group tended to blame the climate, the environment, such as cold, damp, water and exposure, and the weather. A quarter blamed accident or injury and heredity, while psychological explanations were rarely given. Most of these beliefs have been investigated individually in depth; the one about the weather provides an example of how this might be done. While there has been continued scepticism about the scientific credibility of an association between weather and pain, in a systematic study of beliefs about the weather, Shutty, Cundiff and De Good (1992) found that patients could reliably identify meteorological variables that affected their chronic pain. Nearly three-quarters of the patients reported that temperature, humidity, precipitation and sudden weather changes affected their pain. Furthermore, weather-sensitive patients reported more intense pain, greater chronicity of pain problems and more difficulties sleeping than their less sensitive counterparts. Temperature and humidity were consistently reported to affect the pain and stiffness of arthritis, and stormy and wet weather the pain from scar tissue following an accident or surgery. Given the relatively widespread nature of these two conditions alone, a case can be made for analysing these beliefs in relation to their possible organic origins (Shutty, Cundiff and De Good, 1992).

Perhaps beliefs about the seriousness of the illness affect the ways in which people interpret their symptoms. In the case of rheumatoid arthritis, the disease is believed not to be fatal (despite its actual life-shortening properties of around 10 years) or to leave the sufferer completely helpless, but it is known to be a major cause of lost working days. It is believed to be less serious than heart and kidney disease and more serious than bronchitis and migraine (Badley and Wood, 1979). But how much information do people have when forming beliefs about seriousness, and how is this information acquired? In a study of public attitudes to arthritis ($N = 503$), Badley and Wood (1979) found that 16% of respondents had suffered an arthritis attack and another 40% were aware of the problem because they had a relative or friend with the disease. There was consensus that arthritis is a very painful condition and that it is not just another name for normal aches and pains. These data indicate that the public have a "fairly realistic idea about the magnitude of the problem of arthritis, of its nature and associations" (Badley and Wood, 1979), and this social consensus about images of chronic illness may indeed prepare prospective sufferers for the future.

The way in which people explain their illness will be partially related to the ways in which they cope with it. Edwards et al (1992) investigated the beliefs of 100 mixed chronic pain patients and 194 non-patient controls (mainly students). Factor analysis showed that chronic pain patients who believed that their pain had an organic basis tended to deny psychological influences, but non-patients were more likely to believe in psychological factors such as thinking, coping and anxiety. Such beliefs are clearly important where a choice of treatments is available because the greatest success in therapy may be achieved by matching the style of treatment to the individual's beliefs, unless an intervention to try to change beliefs is intended. A study by Shutty, De Good and Tuttle (1990) tested the hypothesis that patients who disagreed with the cognitive behaviour therapy concepts presented in a video would perform less well in treatment than those whose beliefs about pain were consistent with the contents of the video. Data from 100 randomly selected outpatients attending a pain management programme confirmed that those who said they agreed with the clinical philosophy of the video were more satisfied and reported less pain at one-month follow-up, as well as showing small reductions in disability. Patients' attitudes and beliefs about pain were relatively independent of medical and socio-demographic variables, so demonstrating the importance of systematically including them in assessments for pain management programmes.

Addressing the direct implications of pain beliefs on the outcomes of therapy, Williams and Keefe (1991) say that gathering fundamental information about pain beliefs is important for three reasons. Firstly, some pain behaviours cause patients to think that their efforts to cope are ineffective. For instance, those who believe their pain to be a mystery may not be positive about their skills of being able to control this pain. Secondly, understanding patients' beliefs may assist therapists in recommending coping strategies suited to particular individuals. Thirdly, some pain beliefs lead to maladaptive coping; for example, patients who believe that their pain will persist may be passive in their efforts to cope and may consequently fail to make use of appropriate strategies. In a study of beliefs about pain in 55 chronic pain patients and how these beliefs affected long-term adjustment, Jensen, Karoly and Huger (1987) identified five important beliefs:

- that the physician will rid them of their pain.
- that they themselves are not in control of their pain.
- that others are responsible for assisting a person who is in pain, which may result in patients searching for and obtaining reinforcement for their pain behaviour.
- that pain patients are permanently disabled and so may resist obtaining work, continuing to be dependent on their doctor.
- that medication is the best treatment for chronic pain.

From this data, Jensen, Karoly and Huger (1987) have developed a fairly reliable 24-item questionnaire with 5 subscales, known as the Survey of Patient Attitudes (SOPA), for use in pain management clinics. Strong beliefs such as these are likely to be counterproductive to the success of cognitive behaviour therapy. The measure was subsequently used to assess the extent to which such beliefs are related to adjustment to chronic pain (Jensen et al, 1994).

Three styles of belief were identified from interviews with 87 chronic pain patients participating in a pain management programme (Williams and Thorn, 1989). Factor analysis showed that the most important belief was about the temporal stability of the pain or how long the pain would last (45% of variance). Of lesser importance were beliefs about pain as a mysterious and poorly understood experience (34%) and beliefs about self-blame (22%). Those who believed in the long endurance of pain and who saw pain as a mystery were found to be less likely to comply with physical therapy or psychological interventions. This shows that beliefs about pain and illness directly affect treatment outcomes. A recent replication in Germany, however, has indicated that the time dimension could be split into beliefs that pain is constant and enduring (constancy) and beliefs about the long-term chronicity of pain (acceptance) (Herda, Siegeris and Basler, 1994). This bears some relation to the original beliefs structure postulated by Williams and Thorn, and suggests that further replications are desirable.

What are the practical applications of this work? Enrolling 120 patients on a management programme for chronic pain, Williams and Keefe (1991) found that 98% of patients could be correctly identified using two out of three of these pain beliefs. The majority (70%) believed that pain was persistent and mysterious. Smaller subgroups believed that their pain was either persistent and understandable (17.5%) or short-term and understandable (12.5%), but self-blame was an unreliable predictor. They found that those who thought pain was mysterious and enduring had weaker beliefs that they would be able to decrease their pain and catastrophised more often. They were also less likely to reinterpret the pain than others. Those with a good understanding of pain and who thought it would go on, were less likely to use praying and hoping as coping strategies. Williams and Keefe recommend that patients in both of these groups should be taught, even "exhorted", to make greater efforts with coping. They speculated that those who believed that their pain would be short term and understandable might respond best to cognitive therapy, but this needs further investigation.

While the findings about self-blame beliefs are not especially important in this study, they are worth comment because they are not unique to the study of pain. Instead, they contribute to an abundant literature in social psychology that demonstrates a general human tendency to blame somebody or something else when personally victimised — that is, external factors beyond personal control rather than internal ones, which would impute self-blame. Furthermore, when people observe someone else's problem they are more likely to blame that person's personality or constitution (internal factors), rather than blaming others involved, or the situation or circumstances of the mishap. This fundamental error of attribution is called an actor–observer effect (Jones and Nisbett, 1972), and may be due to a lack of empathy with the victim or to a shortage of information about the other person's situation (Fiske and Taylor, 1984). As most health carers do not suffer from chronic pain, this analysis gives insight not only into the attributions that chronic pain patients make about their own pain but also into why observations made by pain-free health professionals about their patients may be discordant due to inherent and automatic biases in attributional style. In the absence of empathy and with insufficient information about the patient, there is much scope here for misinterpretation and lack of understanding in the consulting room.

Other research indicates that not only health professionals but also lay perceivers are concerned with whether reports from victims of illness are credible accounts. Observers may discount organic explanations for a victim's symptoms, such as pain, when plausible psychological explanations are equally available. It is suggested that they use a subtractive algorithm to judge a patient's credibility, so that a negative diagnostic result provides a baseline from which to deduct the contribution of other known factors, like psychosocial problems. This then enables them to make estimates of how much credit they should give to that patient's account (Skelton, 1991). Skelton remarks that, whichever way it is presented, the co-occurrence of non-medical psychosocial problems with symptoms can serve to undermine the patient's credibility. He provides limited data to show that the more non-medical problems they present, and the more psychologically distressed that person is, the lower their credibility. While more work is needed on this subject, the results go some way to explaining the management of patients with certain presentation styles within the health care system.

So, lay beliefs have considerable practical value in understanding how patients present their condition and in predicting their response to advice and their likely compliance with treatment. A sufferer's beliefs about pain are elaborated through the assimilation of new information about diagnosis, symptoms, emotional reactions and so on, with pre-existing meanings and action patterns, as we shall see in the following section on schemata. Central to this analysis is the interaction between the beliefs held by patients and those held by their health carers. More work should be carried out on how doctors respond to the expression of different lay beliefs in the clinic and how it affects their prescribing behaviour and style of advice given to patients. Such information is essential to the appropriate management of painful chronic illness.

MEMORY FOR PAIN

SCHEMATA: BUILDING IMAGES AND LABELLING SENSATIONS

Work on the psychology of physical symptoms shows that there are broad individual differences in the ways in which people label particular sensations and these labels appear to activate specific schemata. A schema is a cognitive structure representing organised knowledge in an abstract form about a particular concept, such as illness, or type of stimulus, such as pain. It contains the features of the concept as well as knowledge about the relationships between those attributes. Schemata are theories that people hold, which guide the ways in which they selectively absorb new knowledge, remember it and make inferences and sense from their experiences. Like heuristics or rules-of-thumb, they are used to give structure to reality and to simplify it (Fiske and Taylor, 1984; see also Chapter 5). Schemata are flexible states, interpreting and mixing past and present experiences:

> They mirror the regularities of experience, providing automatic completion of missing components, automatically generalising from the past but also continually in modification, continually adapting to reflect the current state of affairs.
> (Norman, 1986)

Kleinman provides an exquisite description of the ways in which schematic processes could, and perhaps should, be understood within their socio-cultural context in the clinic:

> The chronically ill become interpreters of good and bad omens. They are archivists researching a disorganized file of past experiences. They are diarists recording the minute ingredients of current difficulties and triumphs. They are cartographers mapping old and new territories. And they are critics of the artifacts of the disease. There is, in this persistent re-examination, the opportunity for considerable self-knowledge. But — as with all of us — denial and illusion are readily at hand to assure that life events are not so threatening and supports seem more durable. Who can say that illusion and myth are not useful to maintain optimism which itself may improve physiological performance ... the meanings of chronic illness are created by the sick person and his or her circle, to make over a wild, disordered natural occurrence into a more or less domesticated, mythologized, ritually controlled, therefore cultural experience.
> (Kleinman, 1988, p.48)

There are different views about what types of schemata are relevant to the understanding of pain and illness. At a very broad level, Shontz (1975) theorises that we hold bodily schemata which contain the primary hedonic distinction between painful and non-painful stimulation. Most of the relevant work in this area has concentrated on looking at schemata for different illnesses, as well as for particular symptoms like pain, and the remainder of this section addresses these areas. Research in cognitive psychology suggests that the sensations of pain are set up in a sensory schema in the memory stores, and that this framework is later utilised to recall those sensations. A schema integrates information about pain, which may be elaborated as a person continues to experience pain. It may also be reduced if the pain ceases as time passes. As a result of elaborations arising from repeated experiences of pain as the illness becomes chronic, the pain schema can come to dominate conscious thought. The illness schema has been conceptualised as a distinct, meaningful and integrated structure. It includes beliefs (accurate or not) about the relationship between mind and body and how it works, a cluster of sensations, symptoms, emotions and physical limitations in line with these beliefs, and naive theory about the mechanisms underlying these relationships. These provide implicit and explicit prescriptions for corrective action (Lacroix, 1991). Lacroix has made progress in developing a scale for health professionals to use in assessing these schemata.

There is some evidence that chronic pain patients hold schemata representing different coping styles for pain and illness, and these may be relevant to the success of cognitive treatments. Ciccone and Grzesiak (1984) identified eight types of schemata in the thinking of chronic pain sufferers. They bear many similarities to known behavioural features of coping with chronic illness and, as such, provide evidence for the validity of that research (see Chapter 8). "Awfulisation" shares similarities with catastrophisation, while over-generalising or a belief that the pain or misfortune will continue indefinitely has affinity with the stable attributions of learned helplessness. External locus of control is included (see Chapter 5). A schema for mislabelling somatic sensation reflects the tendency of chronic pain patients to label all sensations as "pain", rather than making discriminations between many somatic sensations. This style of schema, discussed below, has also been noted by Pennebaker (1982). The schema of cognitive rehearsal is well documented in the cognitive behaviour therapy literature. The tendency for people to believe that their worth depends on how well they perform suggests a schema for self-efficacy (see Chapter 5). Ciccone and Grzesiak (1984) also include a schema for low frustration tolerance or the tendency to give in to short-term comforts and avoid longer term discomforts. They also record self-downing, which is similar to self-blame. Injustice is a schema chronic pain patients hold when they believe that fate has treated them unfairly, and their tolerance of unfairness may be affected by this (Ciccone and Grzesiak, 1984). Schemata formed in childhood about disease and treatment as a punishment for misdemeanours are elaborated in a more complex way for adults who are ill. Such devaluing schemata about states of sickness are generated socially through communications with others. Evidence that these schemata are also used by the healthy when judging the sick comes from an investigation of disease as a form of justice, in which 105 students were asked to judge scenarios of people with indigestion, pneumonia and stomach cancer. The results showed that as the severity of illness increased, the attractiveness of this victim of physical illness decreased, although instances of derogation did not change (Gruman and Sloan, 1983).

Findings such as these raise questions about how it is possible to reshape schemata using socio-cognitive methods. As people make an active search for meaning to attach to their symptoms and sensations, pain schemata are continually being revised and reformed by broad-ranging experiences arising out of social events with friends, family and physicians, and from newly perceived bodily sensations. Because the schemata of chronic pain patients combine together in an idiosyncratic way and are shaped by a multiplicity of processes and events in a patient's history, it makes sense to try to tailor treatment to their schemata about pain and illness. It also may help to explain why a uniform or "one dose fits all" approach to the treatment of chronic pain may have been less successful than promised. Underlying assumptions that they are a homogeneous group may have created treatment strategies that were insufficiently adaptable to the plethora of schemata that patients brought into treatment.

But how do these schemata arise? One theory is that people draw different inferences from information they retain, and these help to generate schemata in chronic pain sufferers. Descriptive inferences enable people to fill in the gaps when information is missing or unavailable. Evaluative inferences, which are warnings of impending threat or being alert to potential benefits, also mobilise emotional responses. Both of these types of inference can, of course, be incorrect, so that misinterpretation or misappraisal occur (Ciccone and Grzesiak, 1984). For example, Hackett and Cassem (1969) looked at the ways in which people inferred meaning from sensory information arising from the chest and abdomen, and found that the pain of a heart attack is frequently misinterpreted as the pain of indigestion and vice versa, often with costly physical, financial and psychological consequences. One explanation for misinterpretations comes from proprioceptive theory (Schmidt, 1987), which draws on findings in cognitive psychology to indicate that pain may result from disturbed proprioceptive processing, which includes not only pain signals but also tiredness, anxiety and tension.

Other writers have taken a labelling approach. Simply the way in which a bodily sensation is labelled can determine whether it is interpreted as painful, particularly if the circumstances are ambiguous. Pertinent to this line of investigation is a study by Anderson and Pennebaker (1980), which looked at how labels affected the encoding of ambiguous sensory information into schemata about pain and pleasure. Forty-nine students placed a finger on a vibrating emery board for one second. Before the test began, all participants signed a consent form but the wording differed for each of three subgroups. One group were told that the procedure would be painful; the consent form said "I understand that I will come into contact with a stimulus which has been found to produce a degree of pain". In the second condition the word "pleasure" was substituted for the word "pain". No interpretation of the sensation was provided for a control condition. Afterwards the students rated their sensation on a 13-point scale from pain to pleasure. The results showed differences between groups, with the pain group largely describing the sensation as painful and the pleasure group as pleasant; the comparison group gave mixed replies. More interesting were the results of interviews after the experiment, which showed that people in both the pain and pleasure groups were adamant that the sensation could not conceivably have been reinterpreted in any alternative way. Sensory information is frequently ambiguous, but expectations appear to affect the ways in which people interpret that sensory input. Furthermore, once expectations have been set, it is difficult to change the way people think about a particular experience. This study demonstrates how the environmental context of ambiguous sensation is vital to the derivation of meanings about it. More important from a therapeutic viewpoint, it shows how schemata about sensations are highly resistant to change once labelled. It also provides a rare empirical basis from which to better understand the phenomenon of masochism (Skelton and Pennebaker, 1982).

Other studies have looked at the labelling process in the context of drug administration. In a study by Nisbett and Schachter (1966) electric shocks were given to some participants who were made highly fearful, and to others who had little fear. Half of each group received a drug. Regardless of whether they received a drug, all those who were fearful attributed their bodily sensations to receiving shocks, but those with little fear who had also received the drug tolerated four times more shock than those without it. The implications of these findings are that the labelling of bodily sensations is somewhat manipulable, and that these variations are directly connected with the individual person's interpretation of their environmental conditions. This has also been shown for other symptoms like insomnia, sleeplessness being a condition that is closely associated with experiencing pain. Storms and Nisbett (1970) gave participants placebos before going to bed. Some were told that the pill would increase their level of arousal and others that it would decrease it. Those who were told that arousal would be increased went to sleep earlier because they were less upset, attributing their sleeplessness to the pill. Sleeplessness in the other group was more upsetting because it could not be attributed to the pill. In demonstrating suggestibility effects, this study shows how instructions can backfire to produce a reverse placebo effect. Such effects may depend upon how introspective people prove to be and their examination of specific symptoms. A study by Gibbons et al (1979) went on to show that self-focused attention reduces the suggestibility of a placebo effect; that is, it increases a person's awareness of their internal bodily state. The findings have direct implications for the way in which instructions are given when doctors prescribe medication. A discussion of causal attributions continues in Chapter 5.

The labelling process is connected with arousal in chronic pain patients, because high levels of arousal can be labelled as either anxiety or pain (Arntz, Dreesen and De Jong, 1994). Other studies show that naturally occurring states of physiological arousal are as manipulable as drug-induced states. Nisbett and Schachter (1966) gave all participants a placebo before they received electric shocks. Half of them were told that the side effects would cause arousal-related symptoms like palpitations and tremors, while the others were given no expectations. The results showed that those who were in an artificial state of arousal did not attribute it to the shock and experienced it as less painful and more tolerable. Those in a low state of fear relabelled their state, so demonstrating the plasticity of explanations in the wake of expectations.

There are not just schemata about symptoms and ways of coping with them, but about illnesses too. Leventhal and Defenbach (1991) say that a disorder is labelled once a person decides that he or she is suffering. This process is carried out by examining the clustering of symptoms, together with the use of a symmetry rule which links these symptom clusters to their illness labels. Once the labelling of a particular diagnosis is established, that person will expect to experience certain symptoms in accordance with the elaboration of the illness schema. Two qualifying rules are thought to affect this process. The first is the stress–illness rule, where observers tend to discount other people's symptoms as signs of illness on days that they believe to have been stressful for them. Such contextual factors also lead sufferers themselves to increase self-medication. Secondly, with the age–illness rule, expectations change about the body and its capabilities. Expectations about athletic ability and energy change between the ages of 30 and 40 years. Expectations about sensory capacities and arthritis-related conditions change between 50 and 60 years. These rules modify the ways in which sufferers and observers make judgements about their illness.

However, the labelling effects of diagnosis may be deleterious and this process can seriously undermine a sense of well-being (Croyle and Jemmott, 1991), as a series of studies have shown. Participants who believed there was a chance that they might have a (fictitious) enzyme deficiency, "thioamine acetylase" (TAA), perceived the results of a subsequent enzyme test to be more serious and more emotionally upsetting if they also thought that the deficiency was rare, namely that relatively few other people had the deficiency (incidence of one in five). If they believed it to be a common disorder, where four out of five people had it, then they were reassured by sharing a similar fate with others. This difference in evaluating prevalence is described as a scarcity heuristic or rule-of-thumb, which predisposes people to evaluate their condition in an even more extreme fashion (see also Chapter 6). These perceptions have consequences for the promptness with which symptoms are reported and treatment is sought. Two people with the same problem but different beliefs about prevalence may also disagree on how life-threatening it might be, could have different emotional reactions to it and might take different action as a result of it (Croyle and Ditto, 1990; Croyle and Jemmott, 1991; Jemmott, Croyle and Ditto, 1988). In a subsequent investigation of how people appraise this TAA deficiency, Ditto, Jemmott and Darley (1988) found that those who learned that the results of their saliva test indicated a defect, minimised the threat of discovery by displaying defensiveness. This was especially true among those who had not been informed about the possibilities for treatment. Ditto, Jemmott and Darley say that people utilise mental representations of illness to appraise their health threats (see the section on "Representations of pain and illness", pp. 118–120). They ask themselves whether the sign of illness — in this case the saliva test — indicates a risk that they have an underlying condition. They say that the perceived threat of illness will depend on the probability that this quiescent condition will result in particular consequences.

Another view of this labelling process comes from work by Bandler, Madaras and Bern (1968), who suggested that people look at how they respond to an aversive situation and then derive conclusions about themselves from what they observe about their own behaviour in this context. So they are self-reflective about their own reactions; that is, they notice whether they escape or endure the discomfort and use these observations about their reactions to interpret their own feelings. Observing themselves wanting to escape enables people to infer that the shocks were intense. In this way, their own reaction plays an integral role in shaping and controlling whether they ultimately conclude that the stimulus was painful or not. It has been suggested that hypnosis might be one way of discouraging people in pain from taking the escape route, the idea being that their perceptions might be reshaped so that they interpret the pain as less, when escape is suppressed (Reading, 1982). The very action of reaching for the pill bottle may encourage sufferers to infer that their pain is more intense than in circumstances when they do not take such action. Such inferences are derived from self-comparisons and self-labelling.

We continue by examining a particular example of an illness schema that is highly resistant to change, as seen in a rare group of patients with Munchausen's syndrome. The prototypical Munchausen pain patient has disease simulation at the centre of their life, and tends to be male with an erratic job history. Non-prototypical patients may have access to medical knowledge, working in medical careers, or could be borderline schizophrenics (Fishbain et al, 1988). How these schemata are established and maintained is not known, and the motives that underlie the simulation and fabrication of illness and the infliction of deliberate self-harm have been widely questioned. One interpretation is that such people need to keep their pain and suffering as a sign of proof of their disability. They feel resentful towards physicians for allowing them to continue suffering, and therefore wish to defeat them (Elton, Stanley and Burrows, 1983). Social learning theorists say that patients have an ulterior motive for fabricating or simulating the symptoms of a "factitious illness" because they see the potential for making practical, financial or social gains from their behaviour. Rejecting this view, Kleinman (1988) says that the only motive for the behaviour seen in Munchausen's syndrome is patienthood, because the behaviour observed is not within the conscious control of the patient. While factitious illness is integral to some psychopathological conditions, it is easy to overlook the perspective that it may also result from culturally prescribed behaviours like ritual scarification. Kleinman observes that social interaction between health professionals and their patients may be dominated by collusion, stereotyping, demoralisation, threats and fear. He articulates a strong case for relocating Munchausen patients within their very complex social context, so that their behaviour may be better understood. They are "suspended in the web of relationships that constitute a life world, including relationships with the health care and disability systems that frequently impede the transition from impaired role back to normal social statuses" (Kleinman, 1988, p.181).

His work raises interesting questions about how pain is managed at its earliest stages, and, in particular, about how health professionals and others provide information to patients about their sensations at the time of acutely painful surgical procedures, which enable them to form schemata about their condition and so make sense of it. It is unclear whether certain cognitive adjustments made to schemata during the periods of anxiety surrounding surgery increase the likelihood that some patients will develop chronically painful conditions later. What *is* now appreciated, however, is that simply informing people that they have inaccurate expectations or false hypotheses about their body is generally insufficient to create substantial and permanent changes in the way in which they conceptualise this information (Hackett and Cassem, 1969). Schemata about the sensory, affective and evaluative properties of pain will be affected by social interaction between pain sufferers, their health professionals, family members and friends. For this reason they are a legitimate area of investigation for a psychosocial analysis of pain.

REMEMBERING THE MOOD OF PAIN

As schemata are structures within the memory, it seems important to set this discussion within the broader context of memory for pain and how this is affected by mood. It is important to understand how the memory for pain works because it is used in diagnosis and treatment, and in assessment following treatment. However, investigations of memory for pain are fraught with philosophical problems, like whether patients recall pain *per se* or pain words (Erskine, Morley and Pearce, 1990). It is also central to good communications and the successful management of therapy that therapists are able to understand some of the normal biases and distortions commonly found in processing and storing information in the memory.

Reports on the accuracy of memories for pain are not always consistent in their conclusions (see also Chapter 2). A widely quoted small-scale study of 16 headache patients by Hunter, Philips and Rachman (1979) showed that recall was surprisingly accurate five days after head pain and did not show evidence of significant decay. Others maintain that *post hoc* evaluations of chronic pain are at best questionable and at worst, significantly exaggerate actual treatment gains (Linton and Melin, 1982). Furthermore, there is some evidence to show that accuracy of recall is not uniform for all bodily sites and conditions. Jamison, Sbrocco and Parris (1989) found that while a small majority of patients in their sample tended to overestimate pain intensity levels (59%), patients with cervical and low back pain were more accurate than those with abdominal pain, facial pain, headache and lower extremity pains. They concluded that overestimating pain was predicted by whether or not the pain was due to an accident, whether standing aggravated the pain most of all, abnormal findings in a medical examination and whether the patient relied on tranquillisers.

Memories recalling chronic continuous conditions may be quite different from those for acutely painful disorders or acute pain caused by clinical procedures, however (Erskine, Morley and Pearce, 1990). Contextual factors are also likely to have a much greater effect on recollections in everyday conditions than pain induced in experimental studies, so caution is needed when conclusions are drawn. The semantic memory is likely to be implicated here because the meanings given to pain affect recall. It seems plausible that patients register the cognitive referents of input signals and not just the properties of the sensory input, as hitherto assumed. The cognitive referents for chronic pain patients might include the experiences of being a pain patient, mood, life-style and the consequences of pain (Erskine, Morley and Pearce, 1990). It therefore seems likely that memories of the social context in which pain occurred may also be key features to the understanding and remembering of that pain. The use of autobiographical memory techniques in the investigation of contextual factors associated with pain would be an asset in investigating this area.

Patients' expectations about pain and treatment are based on memories and emotions related to pain, but does this affect their accuracy? Kent (1985) asked waiting dental patients how much pain they expected from treatment and compared their responses with their reported experiences. While anxious patients expected more acute pain than they subsequently reported, non-anxious patients had very accurate expectations. A postal follow-up three months later showed that the memories of patients who had been anxious were markedly different from those obtained immediately after the appointment. They had reconstructed their memories to become consistent with their existing levels of anxiety. The research demonstrates why schemata about dental treatment are so hard to extinguish. This is because anxious people do not have persisting accurate recall of acute pain induced by clinical procedures. The presence of high anxiety seems to affect how information is attended to, processed, stored and recalled. However, it is not entirely clear whether chronic pain patients with poor recall only have a poor memory for pain or whether their memory is also poor for other personal information. Comparisons of memory for pain in people with acute or chronic pain indicate that the non-sensory or reactive dimensions of pain may be most susceptible to memory decrement (Roche and Gijsbers, 1986).

Other studies show that changes in pain may affect the accuracy of memory in chronic pain patients participating in a pain management programme. A study by Bryant (1993) showed that those who were more anxious and depressed during treatment and afterwards, were much more likely to overestimate their initial pain. Studies of phantom limb pain have also been important in developing understanding about the schematic processing of information about pain. They strongly indicate that emotions are stored in perceptual or schematic memories alongside sensory information. The pain memory stored in relation to the phantom is closely linked to a former emotionally upsetting experience associated with it, such as an accident. Furthermore, recalling these important life events may simultaneously reactivate a phantom that may have been dormant for many years (Leventhal and Mosbach, 1983).

Depression is a negative mood commonly associated with chronic pain which may well affect the way that it is reported. Depressive mood is also associated with a reversal of the normal inclination to remember positive past events, but this tendency does not appear to be due either to depressed people having had more depressing events happen to them during their lives from which to select, or from their being over-inclusive about which events are categorised as negative (Williams and Scott, 1988). Instead, depressed patients over-generalise their memories, particularly for negative events such as anger. Their accounts show that they do not provide specific details about when and where particular autobiographical events occurred. Williams and Scott (1988) concluded that depressed people have problems encoding the information at the time the event occurred, as well as having a retrieval deficit when required to recall it later in therapy. This research has implications for the interpretation of pain recalled by depressed chronic pain patients during therapy and for research where such retrospective information is obtained.

How does mood influence the recall of past pain? Associative network theory indicates that each memory has an emotion node attached to it. Emotions are seen as units within the semantic network that encode memories. These nodes network with other memories of past events when the same emotion was also aroused (Bower, 1981). Physiological and verbal events may activate emotion nodes beyond a threshold, so that the node excites any related memory structures. In this way, the arousal of a particular emotion and its spreading activation makes the recall of connected past events much more likely; they become more readily available. Bower and others have produced evidence to show that depressed or sad people have greater access to negative memories such as painful events. Furthermore, they have difficulty recalling pleasant memories and find it easier to learn material that is negatively orientated. Because memories stored in one mood are best recalled in the same mood, this indicates that the mood or emotion is encoded and stored along with the memory itself (Bower, Gilligan and Monteiro, 1981). This would explain why activation of a memory that contains the negative affect of depression is then able to spread to other related memories. It illustrates how the rekindling of a depressive memory can lead to further depressive memories being activated, resulting in the downward spiral of negative emotion commonly reported in the aetiology of depression.

The association between emotion, pain and depressed mood is not well understood, although its existence is well documented. A high proportion of those in chronic pain have some kind of depressive syndrome (Dellemijn and Fields, 1994). In one longitudinal diary study, mood was found to be associated with the frequency of headaches obtained from 15 undiagnosed "chronic worriers" who reported around two headaches a week (Nutty, Wilkins and Williams, 1987). In another study, depressed patients with chronic low back pain reported more stressful life events — mainly those related to back pain — than those without depressed mood (Atkinson et al, 1988). Applying and extending the above ideas to pain, Pearce et al (1990) have shown that chronic pain patients may overestimate the intensity of past painful episodes, because the mood connected with their current pain is similar to the mood that they experienced at the time the pain first began. This is a mood congruity effect. However, a second laboratory study with pain-free students produced only ambiguous conclusions about whether the emotional state is about being in pain, or about being a pain patient.

When acute pain is present there is evidence that it selectively decreases the encoding of positive words and increases the retrieval of negative ones. Those in pain recalled more negative words whether or not they were in pain during word exposure, so the presence of acute pain appears to reduce the likelihood that positive events will be recalled in the future (Seltzer and Yarczower, 1991). Its presence also increases the chance that past negative events not linked with pain will be recalled during a painful episode. This suggests that acute pain may disrupt the encoding of positive events and facilitate the retrieval of those events that are negative. How far these findings are generalisable to chronic pain conditions still needs to be examined.

Another explanation of this mechanism has arisen from the study of circadian rhythms. These rhythms are an important source of continuous neural activity, and Melzack and Wall (1982) have suggested that pain may be associated with the disruption of the normal pattern of impulses in the nervous system. In a recent review of dysrhythmia, dysphoria and depression, Healy and Williams (1988) have argued that disruptions to these familiar rhythms caused by shift work and jetlag can create a pervasive dysphoria. Thus, the social pressures associated with some modern working practices may well have substantial effects on the experience and expression of pain.

Recall may affect a whole range of behaviours associated with the consultation process, some positively and some negatively. The recall of past disorders may be affected by external cues. Recent stressful events may revive previous memories and, because of this, lead to greater reporting accuracy, while the absence of events may facilitate forgetting (Aneshensel et al, 1987). Receiving professional care seems to affect reporting in four ways: (i) the disorder may be more memorable for those who were treated because it was a more severe and disrupting experience, (ii) it may be remembered better because it was explicitly labelled and identified, (iii) those being treated may view psychiatric disorders such as depression as less stigmatising, and so will more readily disclose them to an interviewer, and (iv) conversations with clinicians may make the symptoms more memorable because they provide an opportunity to rehearse the details of illness. Consequently, treatment may well improve the reliability of self-reports because the disorder was severe and retains its saliency, stigma is reduced and the disclosure of psychiatric disorder is facilitated. Under-reporting is more likely to occur when the episodes are psychiatric conditions, when they are in the distant past and if the survey interviewer is a stranger (Aneshensel et al, 1987). This research has major implications for the study of pain and depression.

IMAGES OF ILLNESS

REPRESENTATIONS OF PAIN AND ILLNESS

The memories that people have about pain and illness are also affected by images. Early psychologists suggested that people are able to see pictures in their "mind's eye", but more recently these images have been conceptualised less as mental photographs and more as models or analogues of the things they represent. Cognitive psychologists argue that people must hold internal representations of the world and how it works, otherwise they would not be able to think about it in the ways they do. For example, representations of spatial images retain information about how objects are positioned in space. They help to explain how people who are going on holiday are able to plan and pack luggage of unusual shapes into the boot of a car and still close it. They may also explain how those in pain are able to locate their physical discomfort and how it is possible for an amputee to describe the position and movements of a phantom limb in space. Representations of linear orderings provide information about a sequence of events. These enable a victim of an accident to explain the events leading up to how they came to be in pain, or someone with a malignant neoplasm to chart the pattern and progression of their disease.

Research on phantom limb pain provides insight into the nature of chronic pain representations. Katz and Melzack (1990) analysed 55 recollections from 29 patients over 5 years, for location and pain qualities. They found that phantom limbs have a tingling feeling and a definite shape, which resembles the bodily part before amputation. These memories are adjusted as the sufferer moves, and alter in shape and size with time. They are often observed in patients who have lost afferent input through amputation, brachial plexus avulsion, spinal cord injury and spinal anaesthesia. Such memories may include painful sensations of ulcers, corns and ingrowing toenails, as well as pain-free sensations like the imprint of a watch strap, finger rings, bandages and shoes. The results showed that pain was crucial to the development of these memories, and stress may also have been implicated. Patients were able to distinguish somatosensory memories of pain prior to healing from former pain from an earlier injury, not presently healed, where a pain-free interval had occurred before surgery. Pain in a limb at or near the time of amputation was highly likely to recur as phantom limb pain, probably because the memory traces had been recently activated. Severe pains from gangrene and ulcers were more likely to be included in the memory than more minor pains.

Vivid "flashbulb" memories of single intensely painful incidents like a motorbike accident often accompanied the somatosensory memory after the amputation. Morley (1993) has carried out experimental work on flashbulb memories of everyday painful and non-painful events in medical students. He found that memories of painful events were more surprising, were charged with negative emotions and had provoked greater changes in activity than their non-painful equivalents, but it is not clear how far these results are applicable to chronic pain patients. Patients in the Katz and Melzack study also reported complex somatosensory memories, which could include visual, tactile and motor components that had accompanied the original experience. In one case, the visual image of a phantom foot wearing a white sock with black patent shoe straps was revived at the same time that the phantom limb pain recurred. Katz and Melzack concluded that these memories were not purely images or cognitive recollections but more "direct experiences of pain (and other sensations) that resemble an earlier pain in location and quality". This experience appeared to be the result of reactivating a neural representation in the brain, which was formed by the sensory qualities of the original painful experience and subsequently strengthened. The representation encoded the spatial and temporal features of the pain produced by the quality, intensity and bodily location of the lesion. Affect, particularly anxiety, is an integral part of this post-traumatic chronic pain syndrome. Furthermore, Katz and Melzack (1990) report that the experience is modulated by the personal meaning of pain and social factors.

Representations of symptoms may or may not be accurate, but regardless of their veracity they do affect how people behave. Leventhal, Meyer and Nerenz (1980) found that many hypertensives erroneously believed that they could monitor their asymptomatic blood pressure changes. Furthermore, the longer people were in treatment for hypertension, the more likely it was that they would search for, and find, a symptom to represent their disorder, suggesting that this search may be a product of having a chronic illness. Six months after treatment, 92% of the newly treated hypertensives in the Leventhal, Meyer and Nerenz study reported a symptom that they believed allowed them to monitor blood pressure changes. Paradoxically, this occurred despite the fact that 80% of these patients also believe that people cannot tell when their blood pressure is raised. This demonstrates how people are quite able to maintain representations and beliefs about their health that appear to have inherent logical contradictions. Such evidence flies in the face of cognitive dissonance theory (Festinger, 1954), a popular theory in social psychology, which suggests that people are unable to tolerate the imbalance of inherent contradictions, and are motivated to correct the imbalance by removing the sources of psychological discomfort. However, there is little robust empirical support for this persisting theory.

A model of adaptation has been offered to explain how representations of illness contribute to the process of becoming a patient (Nerenz and Leventhal, 1983). They suggest that patients hold both concrete (real) and abstract representations of their episode of illness. At the first stage, these representations are created through the reception and interpretation of appropriate information in defining a potential health threat. This is followed by action planning or coping, when alternative responses are assembled, selected, sequenced and performed. During a third phase, appraisal and monitoring processes set the criteria for evaluating the response, or for appraising whatever efforts were made to cope. Two parallel feedback loops regulate this model; one represents the health threat, and regulates danger, while the other regulates subjective feelings and cognitions linked to emotions. There is an appraisal delay between the detection of symptoms, the representation of illness and the ultimate formulation of ideas about cures and consequences.

In contrast to the position that people seek labels to define their bodily status outlined earlier, Leventhal, Meyer and Nerenz (1980) argue that people define abstract bodily status with sensations and symptoms, and in so doing they elaborate their cognitive system. They suggest that when people construct an illness representation of their physical condition it has an identity that includes a disease label and symptoms, a perceived cause of the disease, perceived consequences of the disease and a time-line. In confirming these representations, Lau and Hartman (1983) added the existence of a perceived cure as a fifth item in this list and showed that 42% of patients had matched their representations for cause with cure. This suggests that illness schemata about the cause of a disease can directly influence the path of recovery. People with the same symptoms vary enormously in how they experience and complain about them and this model of representations explains this variable propensity to report, much better than the conventional germ model (Lau and Hartman, 1983). Subsequent evidence confirms that sick people actively search for and construct these illness representations. Furthermore, this process is influenced by prior beliefs about the time-line for the development of their particular disorder (Baumann et al, 1989).

From factor analysis, Turk, Rudy and Salovey (1986) have identified four themes from the reports of chronic pain patients, which bear some resemblance to representations reported by Leventhal and others for the chronically ill. These are (i) the personal responsibility for causing the illness and obtaining a cure, (ii) the controllability of illness by self or others, (iii) seriousness, which includes knowledge about contagion, the difficulty of cure, the need for medical attention and whether the illness is long-lasting, and (iv) knowledge about whether symptoms and other aspects of the disease will change over time. These themes have been used to design an Implicit Models of Illness Questionnaire, but it is difficult to know whether the items comprehensively cover the range of representations used by chronic pain patients. More conceptual work will be needed before consensus can be reached about a definitive and reliable set of representations that are common to the development of painful chronic disease.

DISEASE PROTOTYPES

A related approach has been to look at the use of prototypes, which are a special type of conceptual representation held in the memory stores. Prototypes are formed as a result of assimilating and integrating the most typical examples of what someone knows about an issue. They are composites assembled from many pieces of information and many experiences (Rosch, 1973). In categorising the world, people decide whether or not an item belongs to a particular category by comparing it with a stored prototype. High similarity to the prototype means that it is then included in the category, while dissimilarity results in discarding it or reallocating it to another category.

Patients hold prototypes about different types of health care workers and how they deal with pain. These are generated and elaborated by comparing personal experiences and sharing information with other patients (see the section on "Social comparisons", pp.125–130). Patients' prototypes will be developed through frequent consultations, and with a wide variety of authorities. The habit of "doctor shopping" for a cure for chronic pain provides a relevant example of how prototypical, and possibly stereotypical, information may affect patient behaviour and treatment prospects. Looked at from the patient's point of view, such action represents "the vulnerability of pain and the pain of vulnerability" (Kleinman, 1988). Conversely, health professionals have prototypes about typical patients, which are assembled from repeated experiences of dealing with similar cases during a working lifetime. Some "cases" are seen as more prototypical than others. Prototypes can be used to make accurate and rapid diagnoses, which, at best, lead to the choice of the most effective treatment. But this categorisation process may also involve associated value judgements of categorised people and hence stereotypes may be formed. While stereotypes can be positive as well as negative, they form the "professional biases that underwrite invidious stereotypes of certain categories of chronic patients; for example as 'crocks' or 'trolls' or 'your typical pain patient'" (Kleinman, 1988, p.53). To counteract this all-too-human feature, Kleinman recommends that clinicians and researchers "unpack their own interpretive schemes, which are portmanteaus filled with personal and cultural biases" (p.53).

Some categories are clearly defined while others have "fuzzy" boundaries. Diagnosis typically and implicitly utilises the ideas of prototype theory in the manner in which it is carried out. For instance, in treating rheumatic diseases the sero-negative patient provides fuzzy boundaries to a category where the diagnostic prototype is sero-positive. A further point is that an individual may have several different versions of a particular representation. Expert knowledge, or lack of it, affects not only how these ideas are represented for different people but also the number of versions they may have of the same concept. For example, pain experts may have several representations of pain. This becomes evident as they are utilised for different purposes; use will depend on the context. Different representations may be available for talking to a student, a member of the local back pain association, a newly admitted patient or another pain expert.

Prototypes help to explain how people organise and recall health information. Furthermore, they appear to play a critical role in illness behaviour. People process information about physical symptoms according to preconceived notions about how the symptoms fit together. As they have quite stable representations of symptoms and other features of the disease, these are used as benchmarks against which other symptoms are later matched. To test the idea that it should be easiest to recall symptoms when those symptoms most closely fit a prototype, Bishop and Converse (1986) presented 37 students with 60 symptoms (previously rated on a seven-point scale) and asked them to say which symptoms related to each of 40 diseases, including chicken-pox, 'flu, heart attack, hay fever and stroke. This symptom information was then used to develop case histories of the predicaments of different hypothetical sick people. The results confirmed that more of the highly prototypical descriptions (32%) were positively identified as diseases than were descriptions that had medium (15%) or low (5%) prototypicality, so people retain information about how well or poorly clusters of symptoms represent a particular illness. Symptoms fall into syndromes with specific meanings for lay people as well as for experts, and lay people use this knowledge to help legitimate sickness for themselves and others. Although these meanings may have no validity in biological terms, they do affect coping and emotional responses in important ways, such as responding to an enlarged lymph node, a changing mole, a persistent cough or fatigue (Leventhal, Leventhal and Schaefer, 1988).

New participants in the Bishop and Converse study were then asked to recall symptoms that they had previously allocated to diseases with the help of sets of randomly assigned pictures designed to assist recall. It was found that more symptoms were recalled from highly prototypical sets than from sets with poor prototypicality or random sets. Prototypes for the disease were, of course, most common among those who had the disease. Although the number and range of diseases used in this study was quite limited, the results indicate that people retain prototypes for many diseases, but not for all. These diseases are most likely to be consensual if they are also common. This study shows how these illness prototypes are defined through social interaction and negotiation.

In addition to symptom prototypes, Leventhal, Leventhal and Schaefer (1988) have indicated that there are generic prototypes for acute and chronic illness. There is also evidence of illness-specific prototypes for colds, allergies, cardiac disease etc., which are stored at both abstract and concrete schematic levels. In a study of the prototypicality of the seriousness of symptoms, Bishop et al (1987) found that participants took fewer milliseconds to respond to highly prototypical symptom sets and were more likely to identify these diseases correctly than for random sets or those with poor prototypicality. More of the serious symptom sets were seen to be indicating a disease than groups of less serious symptoms. To investigate the five illness representations confirmed by Lau and Hartman (1983) (outlined earlier), they used a disease story that included a set of symptoms. The results confirmed that 76% of the sample used one or more of the representations; around 25% were able to label the symptoms, 28% listed a cause or reason for their occurrence, 13% gave actions for a cure, 6.8% gave consequences and 2.5% a time-line. More labelling and consequence associations were made for the serious symptoms, while non-serious symptom sets were associated with cause, time-line and cure.

Most interesting from an illness behaviour perspective is the finding that if serious symptoms are in a set, then people are more likely to perceive them as a disease. With non-serious sets, on the other hand, it depends on how prototypical they are as to whether a disease is perceived or not. The most problematic sets were those containing serious symptoms that did not seem to add up to a clear disease picture, so serious random sets caused frustration and uncertainty, and hence are most likely to encourage people to seek help. It appears that information about illness and symptoms is conceptualised as concrete instances like specific diseases rather than as generalised abstractions like illness schema (Rodin and Salovey, 1989). Prototypes for common diseases are fostered by the media. They may provide prototypes for diseases with clear and obvious symptoms, which help people to interpret their bodily changes and to access further information about their condition (Rodin and Salovey, 1989). These findings underline the profoundly social nature of this process.

SOCIAL REPRESENTATIONS

The idea that representations may be socially derived has not been well researched in the health literature, and the various social processes that contribute to their acquisition have not been well explored. A social representation is a structured system of beliefs that is widely shared with others and is constantly changing through discussion. That they are shared with other people distinguishes social representations from the individual cognitive representations described above. The detailed content of these representations is not very important, unlike the more familiar concept of attitudes, where the contents are of prime importance (Fraser and Jaspars, 1986). Social representations are generated by widespread social interaction between groups, individuals and the media. They are representations of a "thinking society" (Moscovici, 1988). They are collective understandings or interpretations, which are internalised by people through communications with their environment. Moscovici (1988) says that the process of creating social representations is analogous to the actions of a committee during the process of collective decision making. On a committee, each person may cast his or her own vote to express a broad range of opinions, knows how the others have voted and can strive to change the mind of opponents with combined effort. But the final decision is a joint effort of the participants and usually expresses the sense of the meeting.

Novel or unfamiliar representations become familiar through large-scale social processes via the media and fundamental psychological mechanisms (Fraser and Jaspars, 1986). A recent health example is the way in which information about AIDS has become increasingly less novel and more familiar, as a result of the publicity campaigns of the 1980s. In this way, social representations of the disease are generated and shaped by social interaction at various levels of the social system. It is therefore possible to envisage that social representations of painful illness and disability are also socially generated and shared by sufferers. Casual observation suggests that they are shared and revised in waiting rooms and clinics, as well as in family gatherings and other social situations. They are also shared through many other channels, such as television, advertising and the newspapers. Some of the earliest work on French health representations by Herzlich (1969) provides prime examples of social representations of illness shared by doctors, paramedics and lay people. Representations of sickness and health are continually being revised. Definitions of who is healthy and who is sick are not fixed; they are "a matter of great inherent ambiguity that is actively negotiated between symptomatic people and other people" (Twaddle, 1980).

Farr and Moscovici (1984) postulate three evolutionary phases whereby representations are produced and reproduced socially and from this description, it is possible to better understand how images of painful illness are generated and maintained. In the first phase, science predominates and a new theory is generated. At the second phase a new idea is disseminated throughout society, and social representations are created. In the final ideological phase the representation is taken over by some social group or institution and is reconstructed, so that the product created by society as a whole can be enforced in the name of science (Jahoda, 1988). Applying these stages to representations of pain, it is clear that, historically, there have always been theories about pain; the main ones were summarised in Chapter 1. The gate control theory of pain is the most plausible of those currently available, and

Figure 4.1 Melzack and Wall on the gate: Australian cartoon copyright © 1990 The International Association for the study of Pain. Reproduced by permission

Melzack and Wall's (1965) seminal paper in *Science* provides the image for the first phase of the most recent cycle of contemporary social representations of pain (Figure 4.1). This is said to be one of the 10 most frequently cited papers in the English language. In the second phase, the spinal mechanism is represented by the powerful image of opening and closing the gate. This key image is immediately accessible to lay people, and hence is readily disseminated in the media. It is also easy to teach in programmes of re-education for chronic pain patients to explain their symptoms and suffering. The third ideological phase of reconstruction is still taking place within the meetings of the International Association for the Study of Pain (IASP) and other pain societies. They provide a forum for debate about whether new representations that challenge the idea of a gating mechanism should be publicised and shared further with other clinicians and researchers (some dissenters were mentioned in Chapter 1).

SOCIAL COMPARISONS AND SOCIAL IDENTITY

Comparisons with others enable those who are sick to evaluate their own condition and make sense of it. Comparisons also play an important role in treating pain where groups of people meet together. Subjective measures of cognitive behaviour therapy outcomes have shown that successful patients reported that "it had been very important to compare themselves to other patients" (Linssen and Zitman, 1984). Comparisons must also form a component of the work in social support groups. Defining who is sick or healthy is arrived at through social intercourse with family, friends and acquaintances, as well as with those who have special knowledge or training in health matters. Part of this negotiation is likely to involve comparisons with other people's condition and with past and future states or stages in one's own life. The formation and retention of beliefs, schemata and representations about pain and illness enable people to make these comparisons.

Festinger (1954) predicted when social comparisons would be most likely to be made in his social comparison theory. He proposed that people were more likely to compare with others when they lacked an objective basis for defining reality. Within this state of factual ambiguity, they turn to a social definition of reality, which is evolved through the mutual sharing of opinions. So in circumstances where there is cause for doubt about the medical reality of a person's condition, everyone becomes entitled to an opinion (Sanders, 1982). Festinger said that people preferred to compare themselves with similar others, because if they compared themselves with those who were different, it prevented them from judging their own abilities precisely. Fillenbaum (1979) found that elderly patients believed they were in good health if they thought they were doing better than similar others, but they were also influenced by whether dissimilar others had superior or inferior health. In other words, they were not so much concerned with good health *per se*, but with qualified good health in relation to their peer group, using statements such as "[My health is good] considering [I am] an elderly male" (Sanders, 1982).

Social comparisons are evaluations that are both persuasive and automatic. There is increasing evidence that these judgements are not unbiased, even though people often try to make them "correct". They have a direct social effect of changing the level of closeness that people feel towards each other. Weisenberg (1977) reminds us that health professionals as well as patients make comparative judgements when observing differences in socio-cultural reactions to pain. For instance, social comparisons are used to judge what emotional expressions are appropriate when people are in pain, and these judgements have implications for management, diagnosis and treatment.

Here, the old adage about "comparisons being odious" is only partly true. Although some conditions of comparison involve self-enhancement, others create negative feelings of failure or inadequacy. Those facing the misfortune of pain and illness can enhance their own feelings by comparing themselves with others who are less advantaged than themselves in a process of *downward comparisons* (Wills, 1981). In addition to the threat to physical well-being, downward comparisons tend to occur when there is chronic low self-esteem. Lateral or same level comparisons also seem more likely to happen under these circumstances. Comparisons of personal outcomes, for instance, can lead to people perceiving themselves to be relatively deprived and leave them feeling resentful (Wood, 1989). *Upward comparisons* tend to occur when somebody encounters another with comparable illness who appears to be functioning effectively. As a general rule, people seem to shift from upwards to downwards comparisons when they feel stressed or threatened (Wills, 1991).

But who do people compare themselves with, and when? A study by Blalock, De Vellis and De Vellis (1989) showed that a substantial proportion of people with rheumatoid arthritis compared themselves not only to other sufferers but also to those without illness. However, the type of comparison made depended very much on the context of those comparisons. The majority of rheumatoid arthritis patients compared themselves to those without the disease when setting performance standards, but where they experienced performance difficulties in writing, tying shoes etc. they compared themselves to other disabled people with rheumatoid arthritis. More investigations are needed into situations in which particular comparisons are made. Blalock, De Vellis and De Vellis (1989) also found a relationship between social comparisons, perceived ability and satisfaction with ability; those people who think their abilities are not very good may still be satisfied with them when comparing themselves with others who are in the same condition or worse. Such comparisons produce a "feel good" factor. Further support for this process has been shown in a qualitative study of how social comparisons are used by rheumatoid arthritis patients to make judgements about their quality of life (Skevington, 1994).

What happens if people have a choice of making upward or downward comparisons? In line with the predictions of downward comparison theory, patients with rheumatoid arthritis who were offered information about other patients preferred to know more about those with more severe illness. Over 90% wanted to know about others whose pain was greater than their own. However, when offered information about patients whose spirits were more often high or more often low, three times as many wanted to known about copers than non-copers, and nine times as many wanted information about those who led active rather than inactive lives. The results showed that for both of these features, upward comparisons were preferred, so whether comparisons are upwards or downwards appears to depend on what aspects of the illness are being assessed. However, in the absence of longitudinal studies, it is difficult to evaluate whether these comparisons represent only the early phase of coping in the development of a painful illness (Blalock, De Vellis and De Vellis, 1989).

Downward social comparisons are frequently made by those with serious medical problems. This may be because they are frequently unable to obtain accurate information about the course of the disease or the best ways to control it. Also, they are faced with potential threats to their self-esteem, especially when they view themselves as victims. Furthermore, any periods of emotional distress may not be alleviated by the various coping strategies already known to them, like taking control and problem solving. Because these three issues cannot be resolved by behavioural action, a search for meaningful comparisons may be instigated, which will enable esteem to be enhanced, reduce feelings of being a victim and foster well-being (Affleck and Tennen, 1991). Self-enhancing comparisons are often used by people with medical problems to combat the psychological effects of perceived victimisation. Jensen and Karoly (1991) looked at whether this effect was moderated by the extent to which people perceived themselves to be in control of their symptoms, illness severity and length of illness. When chronic pain patients ($N = 118$) were asked to say how often they used comparative self-appraisals to cope with their condition, it was found that those who most frequently appraised themselves in relation to other states were less depressed, but only if their painful illness had begun within the past five years. Jensen and Karoly (1991) identified four strategies that were used to make downward comparisons with others who were less fortunate than themselves (a total of 74% of the variance). These were selectively focusing on one's own good personal characteristics, considering the possibility that "it could be worse", and believing that one is coping better than others with the same condition, so confirming earlier work with breast cancer patients (Taylor, Wood and Lichtman, 1983). Finally, patients were more likely to use self-evaluation if they also felt more in control of the pain.

Jensen and Karoly (1991) raise an interesting question about whether these evaluations are coping strategies or merely a habit of optimistic thinking (see also Chapter 5). From studies of rheumatoid arthritis patients, Affleck and Tennen (1991) have concluded that most patients compare themselves favourably with a "typical" patient with their illness, so supporting the idea that prototypes are in use. They see their illness as less severe than the average and believe that they have adjusted to it better than average, when neither of these perceptions is accurate. Those rheumatoid arthritis patients who considered their illness to be less severe than average (a condition that was confirmed to be biologically less active) often attributed this to less disability and less pain. Those who believed that they were better adjusted thought that they had superior abilities to control emotions and thoughts and to maintain an optimistic frame of mind, as well as keeping physically active. Furthermore, they were also seen as better adjusted by their health carers, so such social comparisons seem to have some degree of accuracy.

Comparisons are not only used to evaluate pain but also in other related areas of health such as quality of life. They enable people to deduce norms against which their own performance and self-perceptions may be evaluated. Sartorius (1991) suggests that sickness facilitates comparisons at three levels. At an individual level comparisons may include how a person would ideally like to be, how they were at salient anchor points prior to their illness, and best ever. At an interpersonal level, people may compare themselves with others from the same social groups — those of the same age, sex, social status, ethnic group and other relevant social and cultural categories. They may also compare themselves with others suffering from different diseases, with those at different stages of the same illness and with those who are free from sickness. Comparisons also extend to others in salient social groups like friends and acquaintances, workmates and colleagues. At a third, socio-cultural, level they take stock of the doctor's opinion of how they should be, based on the expert's knowledge about the path of the disease and widespread views of health and sickness. They also take into account society's expectations about how they should be. These different types of comparison enable people to judge how their quality of life is affected by their health, and to derive an identity based on their knowledge of illness and the comparisons they make with others (Skevington, 1994).

Sickness is an identity that must be assumed, acquired and imposed on others; it is a social phenomenon. Sick people have "an identity which is constructed through that sick person's relationship with medicine" (Herzlich and Pierret, 1985, p.147). By making comparisons with other people and other states, pain sufferers use beliefs, schemata and representations to label themselves, and in so doing can develop a sharper image of who they are. In short, they elaborate an identity based on this categorisation of knowledge. Chronic illness often creates identity problems. Despite disruptions and alterations caused by setbacks and flares, complications, disability and impaired functioning, those with chronic conditions are struggling to have valued lives (Charmaz, 1990). The loss of status derived from work, and the attendant losses of income and a social network from the work environment, can have a profound effect on the sick person's identity. Investigating how such changes were handled by sufferers and their "relevant others", Charmaz (1990) found that the identity of chronic sufferers changed as they outlined their plans and assessed the prospects of their developing illness. Their preferred identities were identity goals representing hopes and desires; they represented their vision of the future and the motivation to achieve these plans. In time, a preference hierarchy of identities is developed. At the highest possible level, a supernormal social identity demands extraordinary achievements within conventional limits. At the next level down, the restored self reconstructs pre-illness identities. The third level, the contingent personality identity, contains ideas about what is hypothetically possible, but is uncertain because of illness. At a fourth level, an identity based on the salvaged self retains valued activities and characteristics from the past at the point that physical dependency occurs. When illness continues, this often means reducing identity goals, and a consequence of this reduction is that the sick person will opt for a less preferred identity within the hierarchy (Charmaz, 1990).

In the quest for a more positive social identity, chronically ill people may use the mechanism of trying to distance themselves from their illness by publicising the view that there is more to their identity than just being ill (Herzlich and Pierret, 1987).

Most of the time they report feeling just like everyone else. Reflecting on his own experience of disability, Zola (1977) asks: "Why cannot others see me as someone who has a handicap, rather than someone who is handicapped?". Herzlich and Pierret (1987) observe that the chronically ill are caught between what they have, and what they are, what they would like to be, and the way others see them: "today's sick are concerned not so much with being like everyone else as with living like everyone else" (p.54). In adjusting their identity, they are trying to come to terms with the constraints and limitations of illness.

Beyond the health context, Tajfel (1978) has shown how groups as well as individuals use social comparisons to derive their identity as a group. They do this by comparing the characteristics of their own group (the ingroup) with those of similar comparable groups (outgroups). These comparisons also enable them to maintain their identity and self-esteem as a group. Favourable comparisons with others provide an ingroup with a profound "sense of belonging", known as a positive social identity. This is the collective sense of well-being derived from belonging to a highly valued group. Groups who do not have a positive social identity experience a more negative and diffuse sense of belonging, and often see themselves as less valued. A loss of a positive identity can also involve a lowering of self-esteem (Tajfel, 1978).

While social support in small groups of chronic pain patients has been widely researched (see also Chapter 7), the collective identity of large and heterogeneous groups of people with painful illness has been entirely neglected. The well-being and positive self-esteem that arise from belonging to a valued group with a positive social identity need to be carefully explored for their benefits to those with chronic pain. Whether people with a particular painful illness form an identity as a group or remain a collection of individuals with a shared diagnostic category will depend in part on whether they communicate and organise as a group. The success of communications will also depend on functional features such as the size of the group and its resources. For the many people with arthritis, the Arthritis Care organisation in Britain provides a network through its newspaper and activities. However, it is more difficult for those with less common painful diseases to meet and communicate with each other. They share problems similar to those faced by social minority groups in the evolution of a social consensus. The creation of a positive social identity is more problematic for groups where members are scattered and for smaller groups (Skevington, 1981). An example of successful minority networking in Britain is shown by the National Ankylosing Spondylitis Society (NASS). Ankylosing spondylitis is a relatively uncommon chronic arthritis of the spine and lower back. It affects 0.7% of men and a negligible, but increasing, number of women (Huskisson and Hart, 1978). Through NASS, widely dispersed sufferers are kept in touch with each other and with new medical advances through a regular news bulletin. They appear to have a positive and cohesive social identity as a group within the limitations of their chronic illness. Their high public profile in turn gives them a more positive social identity and vice versa, so enabling them to make a collective stand for limited resources. An analysis of the social identity of chronic illness groups enables us to better understand the broader psychosocial influences that affect people's reporting behaviour, coping patterns and approach to treatment. This continues and expands a discussion about the necessity for three different levels of understanding about the social psychology of pain, begun in Chapter 3. Studies in social identity to date have rarely been applied to health issues, and deserve thorough investigation, not only for groups with particular painful illnesses, but also into the social identity of chronic pain sufferers in general.

CONCLUSION

In this chapter we have begun to consider some of the beliefs, images and representations that people hold about painful illness and how they use them. In the next chapter, we go on to look at beliefs about control, with special application to pain control. We also examine beliefs about causation, and the extent to which these attributions enable people to cope with their daily activities and mood.

Beliefs about Control and Causation Affecting Pain and Illness

5

In the previous chapter we considered some of the broader beliefs, images and representations that people hold about pain and illness. Here we go on to consider how they are used to explain these conditions. What do people believe to be the cause of their condition? Do some explanations make them feel more in control of what is happening to them? To what extent are choice, predictability and freedom influential factors? Do particular styles of explanation help people to cope better with their condition or are they counterproductive to good mental and physical health? How far do these beliefs, attributions and cognitions affect people's perceptions about what they are actually able to do to relieve their pain? Do particular ways of thinking influence whether those in chronic pain will become depressed or not? The themes of belief about control and causation form the main thrust of this chapter and underpin a broader discussion of pain control and relief, which is developed in later chapters.

THE CONCEPT OF CONTROL

Lay people distinguish two separate sets of causes for disease. They believe that diseases either come from endogenous or internal sources or are exogenous, being externally caused. Endogenous explanations can be expressed as resistance to disease, heredity and predispositions, while exogenous explanations might include an evil will, a demon or sorcerer, noxious elements, emanations from the earth or microbes (Stacey, 1988). In the previous chapter we saw how these popular conceptions of the causation of illness and disease were variations on the themes of existing medical theories (Herzlich, 1969). These explanations are generated, modified and maintained by a rich and complex social interaction between the sick person and his or her therapist. But do all sick people discern causes for their pain and illness? There is some evidence that not everyone searches for causal explanations following a major negative life event, such as the onset of a painful illness. In one study, 55 men were asked to explain the cause of their rheumatoid arthritis. A small proportion ($N = 8$) who were unable to think of a cause appeared to have poorer mental health, being more anxious, depressed and hostile than those who had been able to construct a meaningful case (Lowery, Jacobsen and Murphy, 1983). Most sick people appear to actively search for explanations about how their illness and pain were caused; Weiner (1985) has asked why this constant pursuit of "why"? Weiner goes on to say that this search for causal explanations is most likely to occur in situations of great importance, particularly those involving potential loss or stress or where outcomes are unexpected. These are the circumstances surrounding the onset of many painful diseases. Most of the breast cancer patients (95%) studied by Taylor, Lichtman and Wood (1984) had decided on a cause for their cancer around two years after diagnosis. However, the adjustment of those who had and had not formulated a cause was found to be no different, although adjustment was found to be worse for those whose attributions were about a particular stressor and for those who blamed others, usually a physician. So making of attributions in certain circumstances may not necessarily predispose people towards good mental health.

The ways in which people make attributions or causal explanations for events and view the apportioning of responsibility for their health in general and pain in particular has been studied extensively within the concept of the locus of control. In originating this concept, Rotter (1966) distinguished beliefs in personal responsibility for events, or an internal locus of control, from an external locus of control where other people or factors beyond personal control were believed to be responsible. These two aspects were deemed to represent a bipolar personality dimension. Subsequently, the external locus has been subdivided, to distinguish beliefs that "powerful others" are responsible for events from beliefs that events happen as a result of luck, chance or misfortune (Levenson and Miller, 1976). This triadic concept has been usefully applied to health in recent years. Beliefs in chance happenings have become a focus of interest in their own right. In general, people find it difficult to believe that events occur just by chance. They tend to underestimate the extent to which their behaviour is controlled by particular situations or by forces outside their control. Under certain conditions they believe that they can influence chance events and hence have an *illusion of control* (Langer, 1975). To this end, they may sift out information to disconfirm a hypothesis, even in the face of massive contradictory evidence. Searching for disconfirmation has been found to occur even in studies where repeated rewards have been given for accurate observations. Consequently, people fail to process correctional information due to an *illusion of contingency* (Wortman, 1976). An example of the powerful influence of schemata on selective data collection is visible here (see Chapter 4). Control seems to be important even in situations that appear to be governed by chance. While striving to be competent and to master their environment, Langer (1975) says that people often confuse having skills or making an effort with chance happenings. She reports that factors like being in competition, being able to choose, being familiar with the stimulus or response and being involved in a chance situation can all lead people to believe that they might be able to exert some control over chance happenings. Initiating or causing a chance event also seemed to induce this spurious belief that they had greater control, greater choice and more responsibility for what had happened. An anecdotal example is of someone who draws the prize-winning ticket at a raffle and is then seen by those watching to have somehow "caused" the outcome (Wortman, 1976).

Levenson's three dimensions were applied to beliefs about controlling health by Wallston, Wallston and De Vellis (1978) in their Multidimensional Health Locus of Control (MHLC) scale. Chronic illness profoundly affects people's beliefs about health control; it is commonly associated with strong external beliefs about chance happenings, misfortune or fate, and strong beliefs about the powers of others, such as doctors, to control what happens to health (Skevington, 1983b). As it stands, the

MHLC may have limited use in the study of pain. A factor analytic investigation of the MHLC using data from 120 chronic low back pain patients failed to replicate the three subscales (Main and Waddell, 1991), although Skevington (1990) has confirmed these dimensions in developing a specific Beliefs in Pain Control Questionnaire (BPCQ), which bears some conceptual similarities to the MHLC. It has been standardised for use with chronic pain patients with arthritis and cancers of the ovary and breast, as well as for use with those seeking acupuncture and disease-free controls. Trials are currently under way to investigate how these beliefs about pain control affect physical and psychological health, whether they influence response to treatments and whether they reflect different styles of coping.

Beliefs about pain control have already been found to influence behaviour during treatment and the predisposition to seek alternative therapy. Pritchard (1989) gave the BPCQ to 75 patients with chronic arthritis, together with other measures of compliance with orthodox and unorthodox treatments. The results of factor analysis showed that those with weak beliefs that pain was controlled by chance happenings were also in a higher socio-economic group and were unlikely to have visited an acupuncturist or chiropractor. Low chance scores on the BPCQ distinguish those who are satisfied with their medical treatment from those who are not, and Pritchard suggests that these beliefs may reflect the type of relationship patients have with their doctors. Pritchard also found that beliefs that powerful doctors and chance happenings control pain predicted non-compliance; in particular, these beliefs were linked to the non-use of day splints and refusing or dropping out of non-drug treatments, respectively. This may be explained by the finding that non-compliers were likely to be less depressed. However, although Wallston and Wallston (1982) also confirm that strong beliefs in powerful others predict compliance with a medical regimen, their data, unlike that of Pritchard, shows that strong beliefs in the internal control of health are the best predictors. This discrepancy in findings about internal beliefs and compliance may be due to differences in the way in which people answer questions about broad aspects of their health, which may be different to the way they answer specific questions about pain control. Nevertheless, knowledge about pain beliefs appears to have clinical value in the interpretation of treatment behaviour.

In a study lasting 2½ years, which looked at whether therapy received matched patients' beliefs about health control, Harkapaa et al (1991) randomly assigned 476 recurrent back pain patients to inpatient, outpatient and control group programmes. Controlling for age and sex, their regression analysis showed that strong beliefs in an internal health locus of control were related to a reduction in disability and higher frequency of exercise by the end of the course. Also, strong belief in the powers of others was related to low levels of back exercises at follow-up. A high level of psychological distress was also associated with this behaviour. Overall, their results showed that inpatients were most likely to carry out the exercises and do them more often than other groups. Furthermore, those who were most disabled benefited most and practised most. Although Harkapaa et al (1991) used the general health locus of control scale, they conclude that specific behaviours might be better predicted by specific cognitions. This lends support to the future use of specific measures of pain control.

Beliefs about control are also related to coping. A study of chronic pain patients by Crisson and Keefe (1988) confirmed that those with strong beliefs that their health was controlled by chance were more likely to be depressed, anxious and obsessive–compulsive, and to have greater psychological distress than those with weaker beliefs. Beliefs in chance also predicted a greater reliance on the coping strategies of diverting attention, praying and hoping when dealing with pain, and greater helplessness about dealing with problems effectively. These findings about beliefs align with findings about reductions in self-efficacy or feelings of lost self-confidence about being able to perform certain actions successfully (see below). The other side of the coin is that patients with strong internal beliefs report less intense pain and less frequent pain, and show fewer pain-related behaviours than those who have weaker internal beliefs (Toomey et al, 1991). This adds up to the conclusion that internality is good for pain and pain coping strategies, and that beliefs in chance happenings are associated with poorer psychological health and poorer coping, whatever scales are in use.

However, this extensive investigation of locus of control beliefs in health has not led to closure of the problem. As the three dimensions are orthogonal, it is theoretically possible, for example, to hold strong beliefs on all three. Taylor, Lichtman and Wood (1984) reported that their breast cancer patients strongly believed in the powers of others to control their cancer, while simultaneously holding strong beliefs about self-control. Wallston has also examined patterns of these beliefs in combination and permutation in his data from the MHLC, in the search for greater predictive power (Wallston, 1989). Patients who seem most adaptive to chronic illness are typified by strong beliefs about personal (internal) control, with strong beliefs in the powers of others and weak beliefs in chance happenings. Rheumatoid arthritis patients with this pattern of beliefs became less depressed over time, even though many had high levels of disease activity. Those with other combinations of beliefs about control and high disease activity were more depressed, so there is some evidence that this pattern may have a psychological buffering effect (Bucklew et al, 1990). However, the stability of these beliefs over the course of a serious long-term illness, and the effect that recovery may have on these beliefs, is not entirely clear (Marks et al, 1986).

The idea of shared control turns out to be most conducive to the best relations between health professionals and their clients (Wallston, 1989; Wallston and Wallston, 1982). Reid (1984) explains how elderly people with chronic illness can display external beliefs, yet still wish to retain control over events, in what he describes as *participatory control*. He argues that total helplessness normally lasts for only a short period of time, and that participatory control may succeed it. The joint components of participatory control are that people become more external and more cooperative over time, as they concede that others may be better able to care for their physical health. Furthermore, in order to reduce the threatening nature of surrendering control, they want to be instrumental in the decisions being made on their behalf by their carers. Consequently, a team spirit can develop whereby a patient effectively participates in controlling important events in a system that is externally controlled. This model also helps to explain how temporary helplessness is dissipated and hence why all chronically ill patients do not automatically become chronically depressed (see the section on "Cognitive distortion and depression", pp.142–143).

Summarising the alternative positions in control theory, Affleck et al (1987) suggest that surrendering control to others is adaptive if there are no opportunities available for personal control and maintaining such beliefs leads to difficulties. Alternatively, people appear to search for those features in a situation that they are able to control, so that they can selectively control them. Studying interviews with 92 patients with chronic rheumatoid arthritis, they found that those who viewed their illness as most predictable believed not only that they were in personal control of their symptoms, but also that they controlled the course of their disease. However, beliefs about controlling particular symptoms like stiffness and fatigue were more important than beliefs about control over the course of the entire disease. The discovery by some patients that they had more control over their symptoms than their physicians tended to engender more positive moods than for those patients whose physicians were perceived to have the greatest control (Affleck et al, 1987). This supports earlier comments on attributional therapy and indicates that the management of pain may be best served by weaning patients away from seeing their doctors as all-powerful and from expectations of 100% cure from treatment.

However, a cautious and balanced view needs to be taken. While there is considerable evidence that beliefs about internal control are associated with positive physical and mental health in general, Wortman and Dunkel-Schetter (1979) have shown that internal beliefs may be counterproductive in some situations. Highly internal patients may maladaptively waste resources in trying to take futile action against uncontrollable chronic diseases, so that when an intervention is subsequently offered, it may be ineffective because the person concerned does not have the reserves to take advantage of it (Burish et al, 1984). Taylor, Lichtman and Wood (1984) question the value of encouraging patients to assert control over their cancer because of the risks of not being successful. Motivation, behaviour and emotions could be made worse than if no attempt at control had been made. Deci (1980) has commented on the negative effects of being given control and then having it usurped.

Several explanations for these negative reactions to perceived personal control have been put forward. Changes in personal control may result in changes in awareness about self-presentation, or how you believe other people see you. It may also be necessary to avoid attempting personal control when social disapproval about failing seems likely (Burger, 1989). In situations that might plausibly be controlled, some people would rather reduce their level of responsibility. By relinquishing control they protect themselves against failure and decrease their responsibility for what happens, in a self-handicapping strategy (Rodin, Rennert and Solomon, 1980). Sick people may use illness or drugs as a self-handicapping strategy if it seems likely that their attempts at control will fail. This excuses their weakness, and at the same time avoids disappointment in the event of failure (Burger, 1989). Furthermore, there is some evidence that failure hurts. Two experimental studies of acute pain by Levine, Krass and Padawar (1993) found that while difficult tasks can lead to more pain being reported, it is perceived failure in the difficult task that leads to the increase in pain, not the difficulty itself. These results support the view that failure, negative emotions and reporting pain are linked together in a causal sequence, so failure appears to hurt in more ways than one.

How does arousal, such as high anxiety, affect the attributions made by people in pain? Attributional theory suggests that those in chronic pain consciously or unconsciously label arousal as anxiety or as pain, and that once it is labelled as pain it cannot be relabelled as anxiety. Arntz, Dreesen and De Jong (1994), however, found little evidence to support this view, although they did find support for an alternative hypothesis that pain is affected more by the focus of attention than by the attributional process, and this was true irrespective of whether the focus was on a relevant or irrelevant source (see also Chapter 8). Such findings explain more about the factors that mediate the complex relationship between anxiety and pain.

The social context and the environment play a vital role in changing the locus of control. For example, Craig and Best (1977) found that pain perception and evaluation are profoundly affected by how other people around you react to pain (see also Chapter 3). In a study of people observing tolerant and intolerant models, they found that internals were more tolerant of pain than externals, but modelling was not affected by beliefs in locus of control. Furthermore, these modelling effects were durable, and the subsequent disclosure of the modelling role did not change how participants rated their pain. Hospital environments provide a scenario where the situation itself appears to facilitate the development of patients' beliefs about controllability; over time they come to believe that they have little or no control over what happens to them (Taylor, 1979). This finding conflicts with the original idea of locus of control as a stable personality characteristic or trait. The existence of differences between socio-demographic categories implies that social and environmental factors shape perceptions of control. For instance, older pain patients report stronger beliefs that their pain is controlled by powerful doctors than younger ones, which may be the consequence of differing styles of socialisation about illness for the two generations (Skevington, 1990).

There are therapeutic implications of the concept of controllability as a psychological basis for the practice of using patient-controlled analgesia (PCA) machines to relieve acute pain. The pharmacological reason for using this technique is that the PCA machine is more effective than intramuscular opiates for post-operative pain relief. For this method to be effective, though, patients must perform the skilled task of titrating for themselves the required amount of analgesic in response to the amount of pain they experience. Post-operative patients take less analgesic from a machine — usually morphine — than they would receive if it was being administered by a nurse or obtained through continuous infusion (Mackie, Coda and Hill, 1991). In a major report on pain after surgery, the Royal College of Surgeons and College of Anaesthetists (1990) noted the need for further research to consider the bolus dose (the amount delivered when the button is pressed), the lock-out interval during which patient demands are ignored, the background infusion rate where analgesic is delivered independently of patient demand, and the maximum dose. For example, in situations where a continuous infusion of hydromorphone has been compared to epidural administration of an intermittent bolus using a PCA machine (with a lock-out time of 15–30 minutes), the analgesic effects were equivalent during the 48 hours following the operation, and side-effect patterns were similar (Marlowe, Engstrom and White, 1989). As well as improved efficiency, reduced dosage of opioids and earlier discharge compared with intramuscular therapy, the Royal College of Surgeons and College of Anaesthetists (1990) report the major advantage of patient satisfaction. Marlowe, Engstrom and White (1989) also say that "patient acceptance of PCA is extremely high".

One theory about how the mechanism works is that uncertainty and anxiety about obtaining adequate pain relief delivered at the time when it is most needed is replaced by beliefs about the certainty of being in control. Another view of this behaviour is that positive reinforcement in the form of pain relief is available as the result of correct action (Johnson et al, 1989). To test this, the conditioning effects of audible signals at the time of drug delivery by PCA machines have been examined using a controlled trial with different types of pump (Hecker and Albert, 1988). The results show that for successful pain control and reduced anxiety, patients needed to know not only that the machine was ready to administer a pre-set dose but also that the drug had been successfully administered. Machines designed in ways that inadvertently create uncertainty about whether the drug has been administered are doubly damaging. They are counter-productive to generating the well-being and recovery of post-operative patients, and they also diminish the job satisfaction of the health care staff. Furthermore, the way in which PCA machines are used may be related to some types of beliefs about control. In a study of 76 elective abdominal and gynaecology surgery patients, Johnson et al (1989) found that pain was related to strong beliefs in chance happenings and to reduced perceptions of personal control over health. They interpreted this to be indicative of helplessness, but the helplessness concept was not directly measured. Consequently, their results give circumstantial support to the prediction that helpless people might be impaired in the way in which they respond to pain while using the PCA machine and for this reason receive inadequate pain relief. Further work needs to be done to investigate other beliefs about controllability in this area.

CHOICE, CONTROL AND PREDICTABILITY

When talking about pain people often ask, "Will it hurt less if I can control it?" (Thompson, 1981). Control is the belief that it is possible to respond in some way, to influence the aversiveness of an event. Many different type of beliefs about control over an aversive event have been identified; some of the important ones are summarised below (Fiske and Taylor, 1984). When exerting cognitive control, people think differently about an aversive event. This type of control might involve distraction, denial and dissociation, which enables the person to avoid thinking about the pain. Cognitive strategies include focusing on an event to become more sensitive towards it. Informational control involves learning about an aversive experience, such as finding out more about a painful medical procedure in advance of a hospital appointment, or recognising the signs that a "flare" is imminent. This provides a warning, which makes an aversive event more predictable (Thompson, 1981). Secondary control allows people to derive meaning from the situation and to "flow with the current". It is more likely to be used once primary control, or active attempts to change the world, have failed (Rothbaum, Weisz and Snyder, 1982). Retrospective control is when a decision is taken after an event about how it might have been better controlled or forestalled. Neither of the latter two types of control have been well researched for pain.

Making decisions about the timing, type or onset of an aversive event is decisional control. Behavioural control is a belief that performing some concrete action, such as rubbing the painful area or taking a pill, will affect the event. By taking this action, the duration or timing is affected; the aversive occurrence may be ended or made less intense or less likely. In a study of five groups of students given different combinations of types of control over pain from electric shock, Weisenberg et al (1985) compared the use of decisional and behavioural control. The biggest reactions to pain were obtained when people were given decisional control alone, suggesting that this type of control exacerbates pain perceptions. Those given decisional and behavioural control together had the least reaction to pain. This indicates that being able to decide when to take action and exactly what type of action to take may be the most effective form of pain control. Trait anxiety and self-efficacy beliefs (see below) predicted these outcomes, and it may be that the added responsibility of decision making for those who were already anxious might have increased their reaction to pain. As both these types of control appear to be implicated in the use of PCA machines, these results have important implications.

Most of these strategies for coping with aversive situations have been tested for their efficacy in relieving acutely painful procedures like surgery, but it is not clear to what extent each is useful in the relief of chronic pain. Most types of cognitive control have been widely researched, and they appear to control chronic pain in some circumstances (see Chapters 3 and 7). Concurrently, some of them have been harnessed in the service of cognitive behavioural pain management programmes, where such coping strategies are formally taught. Informational control seems to be only a partial solution in the alleviation of acute or chronic pain. Some sorts of behavioural control tend to be viewed negatively by those working in behavioural medicine, but "doing something" about the pain, if only carrying out some superstitious activity, may give some short-term relief, if only placebo effect, from the unpleasant condition of helplessness. Other types of control still await more thorough investigation.

What happens when people are given the opportunity to control their pain? Such studies are ostensibly about behavioural control in that they enable patients to "do" something. Bowers (1968) presented aversive electric shocks to laboratory participants. Some were given the facilities to turn off the shock by button pressing. Less pain was reported by those who were able to turn off the shock, even though in almost all cases they elected not to do so. Early studies like these provide evidence to indicate that beliefs about being able to control the pain could be as important as actually controlling the pain itself. Others have confirmed this link between self-control and tolerating noxious stimulation (Kanfer and Seidner, 1973), and the findings tie in with broader research showing that, in general, people need and want to be self-regulators of their own health (Carver and Scheier, 1982; Hyland, 1987). In a recent (largely) single blind randomised controlled trial of women receiving either epidural PCA or a continuous infusion of bupivacaine, Curry, Pacsoo and Heap (1994) found that PCA use produced equally good analgesic effects, but it also had the advantages of producing greater patient satisfaction and the need for less local anaesthesia too. What is interesting here is that the control group were provided with an ineffective button, which when pressed produced a "beep" but no bolus of analgesic. The clinical impression gleaned by the researchers was that of a placebo effect in the control group; indeed "many [control group patients] commented on how useful it had been". Although beliefs were not measured in this study, such results appear to support in clinical practice the conclusions that may be drawn from experimental studies by Bowers (1968) and others, that believing in being in control is almost as powerful psychologically as the control itself. When real control is supplemented by the induction of an analgesic, then it is not surprising perhaps that 13 patients in the control group required top-up analgesic while only one patient out of 29 in the study group required similar action. There were, however, 17 control group patients who did not need analgesic top-up at all.

Are perceptions of control affected by whether or not people are distressed? Kanfer and Goldfoot (1966) examined self-controlling behaviour while exposing students to the cold pressor test. The results showed that the toleration of aversive stimulation could be affected by providing responses that were perceived to control it. Furthermore, the belief that aversive events can be controlled reduces pain as well as distress (Glass et al, 1973). These psychoanalgesic effects are not solely due to improvements in the ability to predict aversive events, but control is now established as important in its own right (Maier, 1991). Taking this distinction between control and predictability a step further, it has been shown that unpredictable shock is more stressful than predictable shock if it lasts for one or two sessions, but when sessions persist over a number of days, predictable shock becomes most stressful (Abbott, Schoen and Badia, 1984). As the clinical signs of predictable shock include weight loss, gastrointestinal pathology and pituitary adrenal hypertrophy, this research gives insight into why the effects of predictable chronic pain are so debilitating and widespread.

To what extent are these results due to control or to choice? Freedom or feeling in control of one's own behaviour are central to the ability to leave a situation. Contrary to expectations, however, people who believe that they have a high level of personal control (internals) do not perceive themselves to have any more freedom than externals, who characteristically believe that other people or other factors are responsible for what happens to them. However, internality does sensitise people to the degree of choice available, and for this reason it is related to perceptions of freedom (Harvey, 1984). Also related to freedom is the notion of self-determination, which is about the freedom to decide for oneself about whether or not to be in control. Control itself is not essential for self-determination, which involves an element of choice (Deci, 1980; Deci and Ryan, 1987). As these components are closely inter-linked conceptually, their empirical assessment needs careful planning.

Some studies have examined how people's views of themselves are affected as a result of having to make unpleasant choices, and this may be relevant to decision making surrounding pain and illness. A memorable lesson is derived from the work of Comer and Laird (1975), in which participants were told that they had been randomly assigned to an unpleasant worm-eating condition or to a neutral weight task. Reports showed that after this information was given, some designated worm-eaters changed their conceptualisation of themselves and decided to suffer, while others saw themselves in a more positive light as showing greater bravery or altruism; these made up the views of two-thirds of the sample. The remaining third changed their evaluation of the event by reinterpreting worm-eating as being not so bad after all. Ten minutes after being assigned to the task they were told that there had been a mistake, and they would now be given the choice of eating the worm or doing the weight task. The majority of those who had expected to eat the worm either did so, or said that they had no preference about which task they would do, while none of those originally assigned to the weight task chose to eat a worm. It is worth noting that this change in self-perceptions persisted. Furthermore, results from a subsequent experiment showed that those who had changed their views about their bravery on the worm-eating task were much more likely to choose a painful shock task than a neutral task when offered the choice. This switch in beliefs and its enduring effects gives insight into why some people appear to be more tolerant of unpleasant situations than others. It also shows that there are catalytic social factors that affect the interpretations we make in unpleasant or aversive circumstances such as being in pain, and indicates why such circumstances might have long-term psychological consequences.

How does perceived control affect the explanations people give to their sensations? Nisbett and Valins (1971) looked at how some social variables affect explanations for painful sensations. Participants received 30 electric shocks; on 10 of these occasions a light came on, indicating that they could escape from the shock by pressing a button. They were told that if they did not find the shock uncomfortable they need not escape from it, but that the experimenter would prefer that they did escape. Nearly all did so. The results showed that the shocks in the escape condition were viewed as substantially more painful than those in a control reaction-time condition, where participants simply had to turn off the light as quickly as possible, so this escape behaviour was the basis for inferring that the shocks were painful. The results relate to the work of Bandler, Madaras and Bern (1968) noted in Chapter 4. Prior to the last 10 shocks, subjects were told that the experimenter wanted them to endure the shock but that they could avoid it by button pressing. Virtually all of the participants complied with the request and reported that these shocks were no more painful than those in the reaction-time condition, in short they inferred pain from their escape behaviour but not the absence of pain from not escaping. These results tell us something about how people perceive their freedom of action and the subsequent explanations they make in interpreting their sensations. Requests to perform behaviour that went against participants' attitudes were seen to be more controlling than when people were asked to perform behaviours in line with their attitudes, in this case escaping. So under circumstances where people perceive that their behaviour is controlled by others, they may be more reluctant to make inferences from their own behaviour (Nisbett and Valins, 1971). This research has implications for the ways in which doctors handle communications with their pain patients. It shows how subtle messages about control can in some circumstances detract from the processes that patients normally use to review their own behaviour. The curtailment of this self-review process may result in greater dependency on the doctor.

The administration of drugs also affects pain through changes in beliefs and expectations about control. In a typical study of threshold determination, participants endured shocks of increasing intensity, from first detection of pain to intolerable pain (Davison and Valins, 1969). Subjects then took a drug (really a placebo), which they were told might affect the sensitivity of their skin. A subsequent series of shocks showed they were prepared to take more shocks and of greater intensity as a result of the drug. Some participants were thanked and were told that when the drug wore off they would be asked to participate in another experiment. Others were told they had received a placebo, because they had been in a control group. The results showed that those who believed that they had received the drug thought that it had prevented them from feeling more pain (external attribution). However, the placebo group assumed that the shocks had been less painful and therefore they had been more tolerant (internal attribution). In the final phase of this study, which was ostensibly an entirely different experiment, the placebo group who thought that the drug had been withdrawn accepted more shocks than in the first phase, believing themselves to be personally responsible for their improvement. The drug group, however, accepted a level of shock similar to the first occasion, assuming that the drug was responsible for improvement at the second phase. This study shows the impact of beliefs, attitudes and other cognitive information on the interpretation of painful sensations. It powerfully demonstrates how the giving of medication *per se* affects people's beliefs and subsequent behaviour. It also shows that the way in which people think about their medication has implications for pain control.

PERSONAL RESPONSIBILITY AND UNREALISTIC OPTIMISM

In addition to believing that increased control will improve their chances of achieving what they desire, patients undertaking cognitive therapies must also be willing to take personal responsibility for decision making and make a direct effort to control outcomes. But to what extent is this objective of personal responsibility for maintaining health shared universally in our society? Survey data needs to be collected before effective strategies can be reliably implemented, because readiness to accept responsibility depends partly on socio-cultural views about aetiology and illness (Pill and Stott, 1982). Does feeling responsible for events or conditions in life have beneficial or undesirable effects on people's health? There is some evidence that responsibility for failure may cause guilt, self-derogation and loss of self-esteem, so the greatest sense of control may not necessarily be the best. Recent studies show that a certain amount of defensive self-deception may be emotionally healthy. Personal responsibility for bad events may enable people to take a more active part in solving their problems or it may "hobble them with guilt and self-recrimination" (Mirowsky and Ross, 1990). Is this phenomenon personal responsibility or self-justification? Mirowsky and Ross (1990) question whether those who are depressed suffer from a dismal misperception or whether they really know themselves. Is it, perhaps, non-depressed people who deceive themselves? To test this defence theory, they classified

809 telephone contacts according to whether they were instrumentalists, who claimed responsibility for their successes and failures (64%), or fatalists, who denied responsibility (7.5%). Instrumentalists were more likely to be educated, young and wealthy, and were less likely to belong to a minority group. They found that the odds of extreme depression were 4.4 times greater among fatalists than among instrumentalists. Provocatively, they also suggest that the association between attributions and depression may be due to nothing more than common socio-demographic origins.

Taylor and Brown (1988) review a growing body of evidence supporting the view that the mentally healthy have the enviable, enduring, pervasive and systematic capacity to distort reality. This benefits their self-esteem, maintains beliefs in their personal efficacy and promotes an optimistic view of the future. Because they rarely assimilate and process negative information, they are unrealistically optimistic about their future and tend to focus on their strengths and competencies rather than their weaknesses. Consequently, they are more likely to take responsibility for their successes and to deny or excuse their failures. Unrealistic optimism enables people to devote their energies to creative and productive work, to care for others, to develop self-satisfying relationships and to be happy. But it may also predispose them to live dangerously, display risky behaviour and neglect preventive action (Taylor and Brown, 1988). All of these issues have implications for health and well-being.

In contrast, depressed people are likely to see both the positive and negative sides of life. They are much more realistic about themselves, with a more even-handed view, taking more realistic responsibility for outcomes. Evidence supplied in Taylor and Brown's review contradicts one of the major assumptions of cognitive behaviour therapy, which says that emotional and psychological disturbances like those associated with depression are caused by irrational and illogical thinking (Kuiper and MacDonald, 1983). These new findings may give insight into why success rates for the treatment of depressed chronic pain patients in cognitive behaviour therapy have been only partial to date and have shown few significant improvements as techniques have been modified in recent years. Taylor and Brown (1988) conclude that realistic perceptions of personal control are more characteristic of those who are in a negative, not a positive state, while exaggerated perceptions of control are part of the mentally healthy person's illusion.

COGNITIVE DISTORTION AND DEPRESSION

Ideas about cognitive distortions and their relationship to depression have been proposed by Beck and colleagues. They take the view that depressed people make systematic errors in their thinking, which may take the form of making arbitrary inferences or drawing mistaken conclusions in the absence of evidence or when confronted by contradictory evidence. Depressed people tend to magnify or exaggerate the significance of a particular event and minimise or discount pleasant occurrences. They select isolated elements from situations to support their negative and pessimistic outlook. The stable and enduring premises that they use and the dysfunctional schemata of past experiences that they store have commonalities with the rigid thinking associated with stereotyping. This distorted view arises from the use of silent assumptions, the use of formulae and basic equations, and the persistent and indiscriminate use of directives like "should" or "must" in their conversation, as well as constant reiteration of "their needs" as a theme (Kovacs and Beck, 1979).

When pain is involved, depressed chronic low back pain patients endorse more cognitive distortions on the Cognitive Error Questionnaire than those who are not depressed (Lefebvre, 1981). Lefebvre showed that both distorted inferences about situations in general, and specific distortions about low back pain in particular, contributed to depression. Cognitive distortions are also associated with disability (Smith et al, 1986) and with psychological distress (Aberger, Follick and Ahern, 1986). The over-generalised assumption that what happens after one experience will apply to a similar event in the future has been closely linked with disability, but the link between disability and cognitive distortion becomes less important when disease severity is taken into account (Smith et al, 1988). Over-generalisation may unnecessarily curtail activities and at the same time promote disability, because patients falsely assume that their functioning will be similarly limited in the future. This creates a self-exacerbating cycle, which can be problematic in therapy. Self-deprecating statements, which are characteristic of the involuntary, recurrent and intrusive nature of negative automatic thinking are reported more often by depressed chronic low back pain patients than by those who are not depressed or who are pain-free (Ingram et al, 1990). Ingram et al also found that fewer positive thoughts were reported by depressed patients than by the non-depressed. These results indicate that enhancing positive thoughts and reducing negative automatic thinking should be the principal aims and focus of cognitive therapy for depressed chronic pain patients.

Perhaps particular times in the illness might be targeted for such action. Work by Gil et al (1990) showed that negative thinking in chronic pain patients is particularly frequent during the time of a flare when compared to those experiencing intermittent pain secondary to sickle cell disease or rheumatoid arthritis. At the time of scale completion, 43% reported a flare. Contained in their Inventory of Negative Thoughts in Response to Pain were items of negative self-statement like "Other people have to do everything for me" and negative social cognitions like "No one cares about my pain". Such items demonstrate the importance of social factors in the experience and expression of chronic pain and depression. This view that depressed people have distorted cognitions will be contrasted with the learned helplessness/hopelessness model presented later. Research is urgently needed with chronic pain patients to resolve the debate about whether depressed chronic pain patients are being unrealistic or realistic in the way they view the world, because this ideological premise dictates the assumptions and atmosphere within the therapeutic environment. To take the view that depressed chronic pain patients are realistic about their life is likely to be empowering for the patient and may have positive therapeutic value.

SELF-EFFICACY

Even though people may believe that it is possible to control some aspects of pain and distress, do they believe that they have the ability to produce the level of performance necessary to exercise direct control over events that tax them? Wallston (1989) has commented that beliefs about self-efficacy may be even more important than beliefs about locus of control in predicting outcomes of treatment. To what extent do those in pain judge that they can change or influence events, especially in situations that are novel, unpredictable and/or stressful? Unless pain sufferers have a reasonable expectation that if they take a particular course of action they will be able to directly control their pain, they are unlikely to attempt it.

Bandura's (1974) model of self-efficacy provides a framework for understanding some of the pain sufferer's behaviour and its relation to attitudes. Bandura (1977) sees self-efficacy not as a personality trait, but as a set of beliefs that the person will be able to perform certain behaviours within a particular environment. In testing this, Lorig and colleagues have developed a specific self-efficacy measure for use with arthritis patients, which includes a comprehensive range of activities, symptoms and social comparisons with others "like you". The retest reliability results confirmed that self-efficacy is a changeable psychological state, not a permanent personality feature (Lorig et al, 1989a). Self-efficacy expectations are about the degree of confidence people have that they can perform or endure the actions necessary to obtain a desired goal. Self-efficacy is a personal conviction that one can be successful in carrying out certain behaviours in particular conditions (Bandura, 1977). Bandura proposes that three dimensions affect performance. Firstly, people's expectations vary in their level of difficulty or magnitude, so their expectations of success may be limited to simple tasks, to those that are moderately taxing or to extremely difficult performances. Efficacy expectations also vary in their level of generality; some expectations are about mastering specific situations while others extend to a wide range of situations. Lastly, expectations vary in strength; that is, in the level of confidence people have that they are able to perform to their own expectations. Nicholas (1989) has standardised a Pain Self-Efficacy Questionnaire with the intention of measuring the strength and generality of pain sufferers' beliefs that they should be able to perform various activities or functions despite the pain. The scale's psychometric properties look promising, with reasonable test–retest reliability ($r = 0.79$) for 27 chronic pain patients retested over 2–20 weeks, and good internal consistency ($\alpha = 0.92$). Nicholas (1989) provides some evidence of concurrent validity in reporting that increased beliefs in self-efficacy accompanied improvements in chronic pain, and reductions in medication use and depressed mood. However, this measure is disadvantaged by the omission of the third "difficulty" dimension from Bandura's model.

Early evidence that self-efficacy might be important to the understanding of pain came from a study by Neufeld and Thomas (1977). They gave false efficacy feedback to participants who had been asked to relax to relieve the pain of the cold pressor test. Those who received both relaxation training and positive self-efficacy feedback tolerated pain for much longer than other groups. As the actual performance of relaxation in all groups was the same, it therefore appears that self-efficacy does affect a person's ability to cope with acute pain rather than just to manage it. Such results have practical implications for the use of PCA machines to control acute pain, but cannot be generalised to chronic pain. Self-efficacy beliefs have direct implications for the management of acute and chronic pain. Across a number of studies of experimentally-induced acute pain, higher beliefs in self-efficacy were associated with better coping. However, Dolce (1987) usefully draws an important distinction between this milder, briefer pain, and more intense and enduring clinical acute pain, which may last for up to several weeks, and which is not so easily terminated, labour pain being one example. Teaching coping skills is only the first step; this stage then needs to be followed up by providing successful experiences to raise awareness about self-efficacy and to strengthen patients' perceptions that their skills are effective. At a third stage, they may also need to be taught when best to apply these skills. Dolce (1987) considers low efficacy beliefs held by chronic pain patients as disability beliefs. Repeated failures of treatment and lack of success in alleviating pain tend to support the beliefs of sick people that they will never return to normal again. Even though patients may leave a pain management programme with normal physical functioning for their age and sex, they may still believe that there have been no benefits from treatment. Their good physical performance charted visibly on graphs does little to alter their low beliefs in self-efficacy. This mechanism has been explained from the attributions they make. Studies by Dolce and others have shown that those who make physical improvements but do not change their self-efficacy beliefs are more likely to have attributed their success to external sources, like the physiotherapist's help and encouragement, than to internal sources like their own personal efforts and other aspects about themselves (Dolce, Crocker and Doleys, 1986). Consequently, their beliefs are undermined. This interpretation also helps to explain relapse. Dolce (1987) suggests that chronic pain patients with low self-efficacy beliefs should be identified early in the treatment and their covert behaviours targeted for intervention.

Coping efficacy can bring relief from pain in three ways (Bandura, 1991). Those who are confident in their beliefs that they can relieve their pain are more likely to seek out the necessary information and skills to do this, and to keep trying them. In contrast, the inefficacious will give up quickly if they are not immediately successful. Weisenberg (1987) found that pain control that is seen to be inadequate may be worse than not having any control at all, so it is important to avoid giving control under these circumstances. Secondly, feeling self-efficacious reduces distressing expectations that create aversive reactions and the physical tension which aggravates discomfort. Lastly, those who believe that they can control their pain are likely to view unpleasant sensations much more benignly than those who fear that they are unable to control them.

Shortcomings of the self-efficacy concept are that measuring self-efficacy depends upon the person's ability to consciously introspect. Furthermore, if people are able to make these judgements, they may only be capable of doing so under certain conditions. In addition, they may be expressing no more than statements of intention, because people are often unable to tell whether their performance is living up to expectations. This raises questions about the novelty of the self-efficacy concept (Brewin, 1988). A further criticism has been that the predictions of self-efficacy theory contradict those of learned helplessness theory when pain tolerance is considered. The endurance of pain in learned helplessness is related to deficient control over stress but, paradoxically, also with controlling self-efficacy. Describing the pattern of opioid and non-opioid release during different styles of coping,

Bandura (1991) argues that pain endurance is achieved through different mechanisms, but this debate has not yet been resolved. Striving for mastery and control of the environment is a recurring theme in the explanation of depression, and self-efficacy expectations may be crucial in accounting for therapeutic changes in depression (Moe and Zeiss, 1982). In the following section, we consider research that looks at how far special cognitions and attributions that include those of uncontrollability contribute to the generation of helplessness and depression, and consider the implications for those who are depressed about their pain.

ATTRIBUTIONS, HELPLESSNESS AND DEPRESSION

Investigations of controllability, attributions and cognitive distortions have stimulated a rich debate about the application of these concepts to the understanding of depression. Depression is believed to be a common disturbance of mood among chronic pain patients but estimates of incidence vary enormously (Romano and Turner, 1985). Some researchers have suggested that this variability can be explained by the type of measure used in different sorts of studies. For instance, epidemiological investigations using self-report measures obtain estimates that are substantially higher than diagnostic investigations. This is because they tend to have high sensitivity and low specificity, resulting in a high rate of false positive diagnoses (Sullivan et al, 1992).

Learned helplessness was formulated in attributional terms by Abramson, Seligman and Teasdale (1978). It was understood to result from a habitual way of thinking that caused people to interpret events in a way that might predispose some to become helpless and depressed when faced with unpleasant life events. Helplessness affected their motivation to escape from unpleasant situations, interfered with their ability to think and learn, and disrupted their emotions. Similar to depression, symptoms of helplessness also included passivity, low self-esteem, sadness, aggression and a reduction in appetite. These effects are not explicable in the physiological terms of norepinephrine depletion because learned helplessness is much longer lasting. The depletion of brain norepinephrine in the locus ceruleus following shocks to rodents is known to be of great importance in producing depression (Weiss, 1991). Central to the concept of learned helplessness is the notion that helpless people have lost control over unpleasant events that happen to them. The theory predicts that those who become helpless following an aversive event like the onset of pain will be more likely to see it as uncontrollable. Furthermore, those who are helpless and depressed are more likely to make a cluster of other attributions like blaming themselves (internal attribution) rather than others for what happened (external), believing that the event will affect every area of their lives (global attribution) not just one small area (specific), and expecting that their condition will persist (stable attribution) rather than go away completely (unstable). To make uncontrollable, internal, stable and global attributions does not in itself cause depression; depression only occurs when an unpleasant event is experienced, failure being an important characteristic of that event.

As this theory has implications for the management and treatment of chronic pain patients with depression, it seems important to look at how far such claims are justified. Seligman (1984) claims widespread support for this theory from cross-sectional and longitudinal studies, natural and laboratory experiments and case studies. However, Coyne and Gotlib (1983) reviewed 20 studies and concluded that there was little empirical support for the learned helplessness theory. They criticised an over-reliance on student samples and laboratory studies using only a single item measure of unknown reliability. They also noted that few studies had looked at reactions to negative events in real-life situations. A more recent meta-analysis of 104 studies (15 000 participants) has largely supported the relationship between attributional styles and depression (Sweeney, Anderson and Bailey, 1986). However, many of these clinical studies used the Attributional Styles Questionnaire (ASQ) as the only helplessness outcome measure, and as the ASQ was designed for student use it is questionable how appropriate it is to clinical populations. Sweeney, Anderson and Bailey (1986) reported that internal, stable and global attributions were positively and reliably related to depression regardless of the type of participant studied, the type of event about which the attribution was made, and the depression status used. However, global attributions best accounted for the chronicity and severity of depression. Real-life events and hospital populations separately produced stronger global attributions, indicating that these naturalistic investigations provide the most robust predictive evidence within the theory. This also implies that the social context of these attributions may have a larger part to play than has hitherto been acknowledged. However, in re-evaluating the inconsistencies in this area using power analyses, Robins (1988) concluded that the strength of the relationship between attributions and depression was unimpressive and mixed, even for the best results from global and stable attributions, although the results improved when attributional composites of internal, stable and global attributions had been used. Robins observes that the meta-analysis of Sweeney, Anderson and Bailey (1986) used accumulated data that went in the positive direction, even though it may not have been significant, and that meta-analysis is unduly influenced by such bias. Unfortunately, no results from people with physical illnesses were included in this overview, so the relationship needs to be tested further in this area, specifically for those in chronic pain where the concept seems most applicable.

Questions about whether depressive cognitions precede depression, as the theory indicates, or accompany it have been examined in three prospective longitudinal studies of helplessness depression. Two of these studies examined depressive symptoms in the community (Dent and Teasdale, 1988; Lewinsohn et al, 1981), and the third investigated depressive cognitions in relation to the painful condition of early synovitis (rheumatoid arthritis) (Skevington, 1993). All three studies showed little support for the learned helplessness antecedent hypothesis that depressive attributions precede depression, but features related to helplessness such as different types of self-esteem and beliefs about controlling pain at the time of admission did help to explain the presence of depression during the two years following admission to outpatient treatment for those with rheumatoid arthritis (Skevington, 1993). All three studies found stronger evidence for a consequence hypothesis that negative attributions develop concurrently with depression. Skevington (1993) found that global attributions about pain, together with the presence of sensory and affective pain, were major consequences of depression in chronic rheumatoid arthritis patients. Attributions that the pain would be stable and uncontrollable, together with affective pain, were more likely to be consequences of depression at the time of admission and diagnosis. These results have implications for the types of therapy that might be employed and the timing of these procedures.

Beyond the attributional brief, several studies have considered the perplexing relationship between pain and depression. Rudy, Kerns and Turk (1988) examined whether the experience of chronic pain is a sufficient condition for the development of depression. Causal modelling confirmed that the direct link between pain and depression was insignificant. An increase in the severity of pain was only indirectly affected by depression, being mediated by an increase in interference with social life, work life and family life combined, and a lack of perceived self-control. Together, these two factors explained 68% of the variance in depression. So the cognitive–behavioural mediation model proposed by Rudy, Kerns and Turk (1988) shows that depression in chronic pain patients is more accurately explained by these two types of appraisal. More recently, results from a large epidemiological study by Magni et al (1994) has confirmed that chronic pain more powerfully predicts depression than vice versa. This was especially true for those with little education, living in rural areas, who were unemployed and female. They were people who reported pain in the hip, back, neck or knee, or who had experienced significant joint swelling in the previous 12 months.

Brewin (1986) reviewed evidence for five models that could explain the relation-ship between attributions and depression, and concluded that a symptom model provided the most direct challenge to the theory of learned helplessness. This model postulates that depressive attributions are a symptom of the clinical state of depression and have no causal effect on the onset or the course of the disorder. Levels of depression influence the intensity or certainty with which these depressive beliefs are held but causation is not one-way, because attributions can predict recovery from or resistance to depression over quite long periods of time (recovery and coping models). Brewin concludes that an attributional analysis may only be pertinent to certain sub-types of depression: "there is little to suggest that attributions are important because of their relationship to specific events in people's lives ... instead ... they have a more direct relationship to depressed mood and may reflect a positive or negative coping style".

Critics like Barnett and Gotlib (1988) claim that in addition to attributional style, five other important psychosocial constructs differentiate between depressed and non-depressed people. These are dysfunctional attitudes, psychosocial support, marital adjustment, coping style and personality. So, while there is still some limited support for the attributional analysis, there is little agreement about the theory; attributions may turn out to be just one small part of the whole explanation about why people become depressed. To counter the critics, a major revision of the theory has resulted in helplessness being replaced by a theory of hopelessness. Retaining only a few of the original features, it is proposed that those with a "hypothesised depressogenic attributional style" will be more inclined to attribute negative events to stable and global factors and to view these events as very important (Abramson,

Metalsky and Alloy, 1989). Time will tell whether the new hopelessness model improves predictions. In recent revisions the concept of uncontrollability has been played down, but if negative events are not seen as uncontrollable then they might dilute or obscure the ability of causal judgements to predict depression, and may explain why some studies show that attributions for life events only explain a small proportion of depression. Brown and Siegal (1988) have produced evidence to show that the type of attributions made and their relationship to depression depend very much on how (un)controllable these negative events are perceived to be.

Helplessness is widely talked about with reference to pain patients and has been assessed in a number of different ways. The Arthritis Helplessness Index (AHI), based on the locus of control construct, was designed by Wallston's group for use with this diagnostic category but its design is such that it does not directly map conceptually onto the attributional dimensions proposed by Abramson, Seligman and Teasdale (1978). Nevertheless, Fitzpatrick et al (1990) have confirmed that on all laboratory and clinical measures they obtained, including a functional classification, erythro-sedimentation rate, haemoglobin, grip strength, joint tenderness and morning stiffness, the sickest patients expressed greatest helplessness on this scale, more depression, lower internal control, less self-esteem and greater psychosocial limitations. It is noteworthy, however, that helplessness was not significantly related to the duration of arthritis. A more direct test of the theory using 91 chronic low back pain patients was conducted by Love (1988). Depressed patients made more global and stable attributions for negative events on the ASQ, while those who were not depressed expressed more specific and unstable attributions. However, while discriminant function analysis identified 85% of non-depressed patients, it only correctly classified 57% of the depressed group. This poor level of identification of depressed patients may have been due to the liberal method of classifying 37 patients as depressed because their Beck Depression Inventory (BDI) scores exceeded 12, when scores between 12 and 16 are intended only to represent dysphoria. Other tests of the theory have been to compare evidence for personal helplessness, which is central to the learned helplessness hypothesis as indicated by self-blame and lowered self-esteem, with universal helplessness where people are without self-blame or hope that others can help. Studying chronic low back pain sufferers, Skevington (1983b) found no evidence for the presence of personal helplessness. However, there was support for the presence of universal helplessness, as participants expressed relatively normal self-esteem and strong beliefs in chance happenings. Both depression and beliefs in chance happenings were positively correlated with affective pain, so evidence for learned helplessness in pain patients remains limited and qualified.

THERAPEUTIC IMPLICATIONS: ATTRIBUTIONAL RE-TRAINING

Attributions of chronic pain patients have been widely studied, but what are the therapeutic implications of this work? Attributional treatments were indicated by Valins and Nisbett (1972), who suggested that therapists might proceed in two stages. First of all they would need to challenge patients' views that internal and idiosyncratic characteristics like genes and personality were responsible for their behaviour. At the second stage they could offer a reinterpretation of this behaviour in situational or environmental terms. By reorientating patients away from blaming themselves for features of their lives that are unchangeable, this attributional switch has an empowering effect. For example, they might deflect patients from blaming their mother's genes for their depression and direct them to work on aspects of the environment that are potentially changeable like finding a job, taking up a hobby etc. This leads patients to believe that there is something they are able to do to help themselves. In the context of pain treatment, Reading (1982) has applied this by suggesting that clinicians should replace beliefs in external control, such as reliance on medication, by encouraging beliefs in internal or personal control when treating those with chronic pain.

Some studies have attempted to alter attributions to relieve depression. Given that depressive symptoms are commonly associated with chronic pain, this could represent a valuable therapeutic technique. However, not all studies have shown depressed and non-depressed pain patients to be different. An absence of differences between such groups on the ASQ led Ingram et al (1990) to conclude that the therapeutic strategy of changing attributions would be erroneous. However, following a major review of 15 studies of depression without pain, Forsterling (1985) reported that re-attribution programmes had been reasonably successful in altering causal cognitions about stability and controllability. He distinguished misattribution programmes, which tried to alter causal cognitions about internal states such as being aroused, depressed or unable to sleep, from re-attribution programmes, which aimed to alter cognitions about behavioural outcomes, like those associated with success and failure. The aim of these techniques is to remove unpleasant psychological conditions like learned helplessness, with the goal of retraining those who are helpless to think more like those who are not helpless during cognitive therapy; that is, to give credit to their own efforts when explaining their successes and failures.

CONCLUSION

Control has been the main theme of this chapter. It is important because it underpins several therapeutic strategies already in use in cognitive therapy. We have looked at how concepts of control and related issues enable us to better understand how people respond to aversive situations like being in pain. Loss of control also contributes to explanations about why people become depressed; in view of the relatively high incidence of depression among those in chronic pain, this provides a further rationale for considering its features. It therefore seems likely that new interventions that enable people in pain to take more appropriate control over what is happening to them could have widespread benefits in the treatment of chronic pain patients. This need not necessarily mean increasing personal or internal control, as we have seen, but might constitute a combination of more than one style of control or a sequence of different styles as an illness progresses; such features deserve urgent investigation.

Because beliefs and attributions about control and beliefs about self-efficacy are formed and shaped socially, this topic must also be central to any social psychology of pain. Many of these features are affected directly by social phenomena; in the knowledge-base and language that is shared between those in pain, in making comparisons with others and in the ways in which the community influences interpretations of their bodily sensations. In the next chapter we shall consider how this information is used in decision making about whether or not to seek professional help in the search for pain relief.

Taking the Decision

6

In Chapter 3 we considered the rates of consultation in particular social groups, and in Chapters 4 and 5 some of the general and specific beliefs that people have about pain and illness. Having detected signs and symptoms and having decided that these are sufficiently problematic, the next stage is the decision about when and who to consult for help. In this chapter we revisit the theme of consultation and look at how beliefs and other social and psychological factors affect this decision making. Although the "obvious" choice of consultant might appear to be a doctor, there is evidence to show that many different sources are consulted, sometimes serially, sometimes simultaneously. Therefore, the first part of this chapter begins by considering different sources of advice and looks at some of the important personality variables that affect consulting behaviour. We discuss models of rational decision making and show how they apply to those who become pain patients. There are several cognitive models that contribute to understandings about the way in which people make decisions about their health in general and about pain in particular, but we also consider models where emotions have been integrated and social factors are taken into account. Risks and risk taking are central to interpretation here.

SOURCES OF ADVICE AND EXPLANATIONS FOR ADVICE SEEKING

Those who are sick readily identify certain types of people as suitable advice givers (Helman, 1984), many of whom are not formally employed in the health service. The credentials for an informal source are more likely to be experience than that person's status or education. Helman identified several important sources of advice consulted by those who are sick. First of all people seek advice from others who have had prolonged experience of the same illness, like cancer, or have received similar treatment, such as chemotherapy. They talk to those who have had personal experience of particular life events such as childbirth or an endoscopy. They search out paramedical health professionals such as nurses and doctors' receptionists, as well as doctors' spouses. This may be because they see them as caring people (see Chapter 9). In addition, sick people consult representatives from some groups who have no ostensible expertise in health at all. Those who work in the public services and who therefore come into regular contact with the public, such as hairdressers and bank managers, may also be asked to act as counsellors on health matters. "Helping" people such as organisers of self-help groups, cults and members of church organisations and their officials may also be consulted for their advice.

Looking at mental health problems in particular, Greenley and Mechanic (1976) confirm that the sources of help are much more varied than hitherto appreciated. Following up around 1000 student consultations over a two-year period, they found that not only did students seek help from the anticipated psychiatric and university counselling services, but they also consulted clergymen, medical services, schools, psychologists, social workers, women's counselling, T-groups (training groups), Samaritans, VD clinics, family courts, community law offices and university lecturers and administrators; 83% used only one type of service. Greenley and Mechanic concluded that most social and cultural factors operate less in the decision about *whether* to seek help than they do in the decision about *where* to seek help. The data showed that consulters and non-consulters could be distinguished by their attitudes, knowledge and reference groups. Official statistics of illness are examined because they are largely based on formal consultations with doctors working within the public health service. Consequently, Greenley and Mechanic's findings show that these figures represent only a relatively small part of a statistical iceberg of the total number of actual consultations per year, if the notion of consultation is broadened in this way. A more accurate assessment of consultation rates would be obtained by including visits to a wide range of other carers and by including advice received informally from credible individuals such as those earmarked by Helman (1984).

There is some evidence that the most unorthodox symptoms may be taken to alternative sources of advice first. Suchman (1965) found that in 74% of cases, unusual physical symptoms were followed by a lay consultation; a further 16% talked to two or more experts. As a result of these consultations 78% of respondents felt that a clear course of action had been defined for them, and over 70% said that other people's opinions had been highly influential in their decision making, so demonstrating the broad social influences that affect this process. Symptoms that resulted in great pain or sudden disability were more likely to lead to doctors being consulted without prior lay consultations, but other symptoms, which formed the majority of cases, triggered a series of non-expert discussions (Twaddle, 1969). Typically, a person would consult others until such time as professional advice was recommended. Furthermore, Twaddle noted that once people were being formally cared for by a health professional, their reliance on lay consultants substantially diminished. People who seek a lay consultation are more likely to be self-disclosing, to have lower self-esteem and to trust the capabilities and goodwill of others. They tend to be more submissive, so being more needy for the opinions of others. They are also introverted, with smaller friendship networks than more gregarious extraverts (see Sanders, 1982 for a review).

Apart from labelling, there are other personality explanations for this consultation behaviour. One is that when dealing with the unpredictability of a stressful aversive event like being in pain, some people monitor information while others blunt it out (Miller, 1979). Monitors are highly attentive to threatening information and are inclined to constantly select and acquire it about any threatening event. Conversely, blunters distract themselves from threatening information. This cognitive mechanism blunts the presence of physical danger and, in so doing, reduces anxiety and other types of arousal. Blunting strategies include self-relaxation, positive reinterpretation, denial, detachment and intellectualisation. Although much depends on both the timing of stressors and the nature of the stressful event, Miller has proposed that the degree of stress experienced and the level of anxiety it produces can be estimated by knowing whether people prefer stress to be predictable or unpredictable. Monitors prefer the stress of knowing about an event, while blunters prefer unpredictability. This "knowing" aspect of predictability is related to controllability (see Chapter 5) (Miller, 1979; Miller and Grant, 1979). These processes may help to explain the wide range of social and individual differences found in response to the aversiveness of pain.

Evidence for these ideas came from a study of women receiving gynaecological examinations, where some were provided with information in advance. The results showed that, contrary to earlier findings by Johnson and Leventhal (1974), voluminous preparatory information could reduce pain from the procedure, but might also exacerbate patient distress. Those who received information could be more anxious both before and after the procedure than those who did not receive it at all. Monitors were most distressed by the procedure, but this was double-edged because monitors also had the greatest spin-offs in mental and physical health. They reported reductions in pain, hostility and anxiety and were most satisfied by the procedure (Miller, 1979). Thus, the costs of this high-level emotional style appear to be outweighed by the benefits of its overall outcome for those undergoing acutely painful procedures.

More recently, Miller, Brody and Summerton (1988) have reconceptualised monitoring and blunting as independent rather than continuous variables. Results from 118 patients in primary health care showed that those most likely to visit a physician would be high monitors as well as low blunters. However, this group reported levels of discomfort, dysfunction and distress similar to those of high blunters and low monitors, who rarely visited the doctor. During consultations the high monitors/low blunters demanded more tests, more respect, and more information and counselling, but wanted to take a less active role in their own care. Furthermore, during the week after the consultation, high monitors/low blunters also perceived less physical or psychological improvement in their symptoms. An implication of this work is that those who are high monitors/low blunters should be given copious information about peri-operative procedures, and low monitors/high blunters only as much information as they want. Thus, Johnson and Leventhal's (1974) pioneering ideas of giving everyone lots of detailed information pertains only to a carefully selected subgroup of those facing surgery. The implications of these personality styles for the behaviour of chronic pain patients in treatment and their recovery has yet to be determined.

An area of research that casts further light on consultation rates arises from knowledge of the hardy personality, which has some commonalities with the *typus robustus*. Are those who become ill and visit their doctors less "hardy" in some way than those who do not? It has been proposed that a hardy personality might provide a buffer against physical and mental illnesses. Three elements have been identified as comprising the hardy personality: challenge, commitment and control. Everyone experiences stressful events in their lives, and even the best motivated people are unable to avoid every stressful circumstance, but hardy people feel that they have some degree of influence or control over stressful events and their causes and solutions, rather than feeling powerless or helpless. They have a profound sense of being involved with, or committed to, their daily activities rather than feeling alienated. Furthermore, they have the ability to be adaptable to unexpected changes and to view change as a challenge — an opportunity to further their personal growth, not an unexpected and unknown threat (Gentry and Kobasa, 1984; Kobasa, Maddi and Kahn, 1982). Typical of studies performed in this area is one of white, middle-class gynaecology outpatients aged 25–35 years. Those with high stress and fewer psychiatric symptoms of anxiety, depression and obsessions were significantly more committed to their work, family and themselves, had more personal control, and found events more challenging than a comparable group of women with high stress and more symptoms (Kobasa, 1982). The aversive events of a painful illness can be suitably applied here as representing such stressors.

One line of approach has been to investigate whether hardiness is generated or enhanced by a particular social environment. Do hardy people have better social support than others, for instance? Social support is a diverse and difficult concept to define, but it tends to include the components of emotional concern like sympathy and caring, instrumental aid such as giving money or assistance, providing information in the form of advice, suggestions or directions, and appraisal, which involves personal evaluation as well as feedback and social comparisons (see also Chapter 7). The quality of the relationship is a psychological resource, while the network of linkages provides a social resource (Gentry and Kobasa, 1984). Gentry and Kobasa (1984) concluded that social support best mediated illness where there was high stress. Furthermore, it affected health outcomes differently depending on the type of disease. Important here was the presence of not just one, but several, "significant others". Furthermore, certain types of people seemed better equipped to reduce strain than others; for instance, supervisors and managers tend to be the best sources of relief from job strain.

Despite its intuitive appeal, there have been several substantial critiques of the hardiness concept and the methodology used to evaluate it. While the concept of control is well established (see Chapter 5), challenge and commitment have been found wanting, under scrutiny (Hull, Van Treuren and Virnelli, 1987). The reliability of hardiness as a concept is questionable, because results from key studies have not been replicated (Allred and Smith, 1989). In particular, factor analysis has not always confirmed Kobasa's original three dimensions, so it is difficult to know what the concept of hardiness is. Evidence for a buffering effect against stress is light. A further limitation is that it is not accepted as "good" theory because it is possible to explain resistance to stress in terms of underlying aspects of optimism (Scheier and Carver, 1987). Some reviewers have suggested that a lack of hardiness may reflect nothing more specific than general maladjustment or psychopathology (Funk and Houston, 1987). However, investigations into hardiness do seem to support growing consensus about the importance of the relationship between optimism and physical well-being (Scheier and Carver, 1987) introduced in Chapter 5.

HEALTH RISKS

Other factors in the equation that have been investigated in decision taking are perceptions of health risks. Throughout this model of the patient as a decision maker run the themes of risk appraisal, risk reduction and health maintenance. How do people perceive risks and how far are these perceptions rational? Some researchers have seen the study of risk taking behaviour within the wider context of positive health behaviour. Do people who do not take risks on the roads also prepare for health emergencies, not smoke, wear a seat belt, take preventive health care action like visiting a dentist for a check-up and use condoms? Are they more likely to keep themselves in good physical shape with exercise? Mechanic and Cleary (1980) have concluded that poor health behaviours do seem to be part of a general life-style, where people lack the ability to anticipate problems and seem unable to mobilise their resources to cope sufficiently. Not only were they highly distressed, but they also appeared to be more marginalised within the community and less "in tune" with the health care system.

How can risk factors be assessed generally? There are some factors to guide us about who may be at risk so far as general health is concerned. There are gender differences in risk taking, and some of this discussion relates to findings reported in previous chapters. Men take more risks than women. Men drink more, smoke more and have higher job hazards, while women, especially the highly educated, tend to take more preventive health care, are more physically inactive and have higher levels of stress and unemployment (Mechanic and Cleary, 1980; Verbrugge, 1989). Verbrugge (1989) has observed that although psychosocial factors predispose more women to illness and health care, the morbidity gap narrows once important risk factors have been controlled. Once risks are controlled for, men are found to have higher morbidity rates on general and chronic health grounds. Furthermore, sex differences in health reporting behaviour may also be explained by looking at risk factors. Although women attend more often for health care in terms of medical visits, drug use and short- and long-term care for disability, these sex differences are diminished when morbidity levels and risks are taken into account — so much so that the pattern reverses to show men with excess disability and more medical care. While these "unveiled excesses" are not significant, they do show a consistent pattern. Verbrugge (1989) concludes that women's poorer health profile is due to the acquired risks associated with their female role and to stress, and only to a lesser extent to their health attitudes. Consideration of social factors shows that men are disadvantaged, and their greater mortality rates add to this picture. She proposes that women's risks could be reduced by promoting engaging in productive roles, blunting stress, fostering happiness and promoting aerobic activities.

When statistics on pain patients are inspected, the age distribution is found to be similar to that of the general population. However, men from lower socio-economic groups are over-represented in both pain clinics and in workmen's compensation claims in the US, and therefore appear to be at greater risk (Williams, 1988). Certain types of occupational group carry risk factors for pain and health too. Nurses are commonly featured in the back pain statistics (Linton et al, 1989), and many types of manual workers are susceptible to joint disease or soft tissue injuries which may ultimately result in chronic pain. The medical literature documents fish filleter's fingers, bricklayer's hands, cellist's and ticket-clipper's thumb, labourer's spine, porter's neck and puppeteer's elbow, to mention just a few (Huskisson and Hart, 1978). Other risk factors that have been examined include long stays in hospital during childhood, and families where other members have chronic pain (Williams, 1988). A recent review by Gamsa (1994) concludes that although some research has shown that those with chronic pain come from families with many siblings, others have been unable to replicate these findings. Some studies have shown that chronic pain patients are the eldest or the youngest in the family, but others have been unable to confirm these results. Some studies have indicated that factors like parental punishments, neglect and physical and sexual abuse are risk factors for pain, but, once again, such suppositions have not been confirmed (Gamsa, 1994; Williams, 1988). Lack of confirmation may be due to methodological and conceptual limitations in the research, but another plausible explanation might be that conflict in pain families is as great as family conflict in the general population (Gamsa, 1994); this has yet to be thoroughly explored.

Many risk factors have been implicated in the aetiology and maintenance of painful conditions but careful work still needs to be carried out to establish the extent to which beliefs and stereotypes about risks held by health professionals can be substantiated. In migraine and tension headache, for instance, the biggest risk factors are stress and mental tension, but other common precipitants are believed to be alcohol, especially red wine, chocolate, weather changes and the menstrual cycle. However, a large cross-sectional epidemiological study of over 700 people with headache disturbance found no significant relationship between pain and patterns of smoking or intake of coffee, alcohol, chocolate or oral contraceptives (Rasmussen, 1993). Female hormones have been identified as prime candidates in the debate about migraine, because migraine sufferers often appear to obtain some or total relief during pregnancy. Among the women in Rasmussen's study who had been pregnant, 48% of those with migraines and 28% of those with tension headache reported that their pain had disappeared. There was also evidence that women were more likely to experience head pain during the two days before the onset of menstruation than mid-cycle. The premenstrual incidence was much greater for those with tension headache (71%) than those with migraine (24%). A lack of refreshing sleep was commonly reported, and by both sexes, but it is not known whether this is a cause or an effect of pain.

The problem for health professionals is how to deal with those who are "at risk". In contrast with those in a sick role or a well role, the person who is in an "at risk" role is in a problematic situation (Kasl, 1974). Such people are not institutionalised in a hospital or clinic, but they do have duties attached to their role, such as exercise. They also lack privileges like a reduction in social obligations. Furthermore, performing this "at risk" role has an indefinite time-span, so it may be difficult to sustain preventive activities. Such activities, if performed, lack regular reinforcement from health professionals and are short of the internal feedback that would normally be provided by changes in symptomatology and treatment. All of these features mitigate against those who are at risk continuing with the very preventative actions that would maintain a low level of risk. The well role should be the goal of good health, but in defining ourselves as not well, Twaddle (1969) says that we utilise certain signs. He shows that changes in feeling states, in particular the presence of pain and weakness, are central to this decision, but these signs are usually not present at the time when the person is at risk. Furthermore, if pain is associated with the screening of at risk patients, it may act as an aversive deterrent to repeated screening being carried out. Keefe et al (1994) reviewed women's experience of mammography from reports of five studies. Compression of the breast during the procedure produces variable amounts of pain and discomfort, but adequate compression is necessary for good imaging. Around 22% said that the procedure was too painful and a majority reported mild or moderate discomfort. The studies showed that women who expected pain did indeed feel pain; some of these expectations were due to negative experiences with prior mammography. In looking at the factors used in the decision about whether to have mammography, Keefe et al (1994) identified incentives such as the doctor's request and the perceived benefits of the procedure like lowered anxiety. The deterrents included fears about medical interventions, especially pain, and the financial costs of the procedure.

However, conclusions about whether perceptions of mammography as painful is a significant predictor of the decision about whether to attend are only equivocal. A study of 1160 women offered screening in Britain confirmed that while the most important predictor of pain was previous expectations of pain, the discomfort had little effect on the intention to reattend or on satisfaction with the procedure (Rutter et al, 1992). As shown elsewhere in this volume, expectations about pain increased its likelihood; 66% of those who expected discomfort reported it, while only 35% of those who had not expected it reported that pain had occurred. More specifically, where it occurred the pain was most often described as crushing or tender. In agreement with the conclusion of Keefe et al about findings in other studies, Rutter et al (1992) reported that more than two-thirds of the women who participated said that having a tooth drilled, having a smear test and giving blood were more uncomfortable than having a mammogram. From their review, Keefe et al reported that compliers believed that getting a mammogram would be inconvenient, were white, were married, had a history of breast cancer and believed that their doctors thought having the procedure was important for them. That they tended to remember receiving a previous health information package also suggests that they were aware of, and interested in health, although the term "monitors" is not used. Non-compliers, on the other hand, saw mammography as unnecessary in the absence of symptoms, as too time consuming, troublesome and inconvenient, and believed that their doctors had advised them not to have one. One practical solution is to give women control over the speed of breast compression because fast compression, which is technically best, can be more uncomfortable. Other suggestions are to provide more written information about the procedure for those who want it and to persuade women to use established coping methods such as distraction (see Chapter 8) (Keefe et al, 1994).

Perceived risks need to be seen within their social, cultural and historical context; they differ today compared with the prevalent risks 20 years ago. Now we are preoccupied with the risks of coronary heart disease, with the means of travel and with energy sources; to counterbalance this, we see ourselves as less at risk from infectious diseases than in previous times (Williams, 1989). Williams (1989) has commented that social life today is both highly organised and at the same time more precarious. There is much anxiety about public hazards as well as about private risk taking. While personal risk taking is encouraged, paradoxically at the same time it leads to more hazards and is therefore more prohibited. Of particular concern here are the factors weighed by patients who are offered new drugs, particularly where the side effects are unknown or are not public knowledge. In recent years there have been instances where legal proceedings have been taken against drug companies because the side effects incurred turned out to be greater health hazards than originally believed. So it seems increasingly likely that health professionals will need to know about the many ways in which patients evaluate the information they receive about their health, its prognosis and the relative efficacy of treatments. Because something like 80% of treatments currently on offer in medical settings have never been formally evaluated, health professionals' confidence in their replies to such enquiries must necessarily be low, or if confidence is high, their replies must be relatively unreliable, being based on personal experience with individual patients rather than the outcome of power statistics combined with the best experimental designs.

As we saw earlier, giving information does not always have positive effects psychologically, but depriving people of information about risks — a policy which continues in Britain — not only can foreclose the potential for autonomy and empowerment where both may have some therapeutic value, but is also ethically questionable. In research on prenatal diagnosis, there has been careful scrutiny of the reasons why patients should be given information. These guidelines seem broadly applicable to many other medical situations. Green (1989) says that patients should know the purpose of a test and the likelihood that it will detect an abnormality. They should know what the procedure involves, the risks that it entails, what the results mean, the options for further investigations and the risks and limitations involved in those investigations.

Subjective Expected Utility (SEU) theory is favoured by those who believe that decisions are made rationally. It looks at the way in which people make choices within a rational framework, and has clear implications for how people in pain might weigh the factors when deciding, for instance, whether to take a particular drug. A fundamental assumption here is that people's estimates about the probability of an outcome are independent of estimates of the desirability of that outcome. First of all, it should be possible to say whether outcome A or B is preferred; this is the principle of decidability. Secondly, if A is preferred to B and B to C, then by deduction A will be preferred to C; this is the principle of transitivity. Thirdly, if every event that Act 1 produces is an outcome at least as desirable as that of Act 2, then for at least one event the outcome of Act 1 is better than that of Act 2. On logical grounds, you should therefore prefer 1 to 2; this is the principle of dominance. Lastly the "sure thing" principle says that during the process of making a choice, the outcome not related to your choice should not influence your choice (Wright, 1984). "Rational" theories like SEU and game theory have been criticised by Janis (1984) because they do not truly describe what people do. Moreover, they fail to explain what people are actually doing when they make choices. Furthermore, it is unlikely that people's preferences will remain stable. For instance, pain sufferers may make quite different decisions during a bout of severe pain than when pain is bearable. Utility estimates obtained under one condition may therefore not be the same as in other circumstances. For these reasons SEU would be flawed in predicting these decisions. Nevertheless, Janis and Mann (1977) see some value in these prescriptive models because they can be used in making vital decisions about a serious physical defect or illness. They argue that to make a sound decision, it seems necessary to make the best estimates of probability that each of the expected consequences will occur, and to consider the relative importance of each of the anticipated favourable and unfavourable consequences.

In contrast, decision making about health has been addressed by the Health Belief Model (HBM) (Rosenstock, 1966). Within this model, social and cognitive factors have been used to explain why some people take care of their health while others do not. The original components of the model were derived from a national study of health beliefs obtained from 1493 adults over 21 years (Kirscht et al, 1966). Their conceptual organisation provides one of the few working models to help to explain who will seek health care, but evidence for understanding chronic behaviour is limited (Kasl, 1974). The model was originally designed to explain compliance with treatment and for this reason it might usefully be applied to pain patients. The decision making of the HBM hinges on how attractive particular goals will be to patients, and their estimates of the likelihood that they will be able to reach these goals. These ideas share similarities with the newer concept of self-efficacy.

Several factors have been proposed within the model that affect whether people will take action about their health. This state of readiness depends firstly on the extent to which people believe themselves to be *susceptible* to a particular condition or illness. Those who believe that they are more likely to become ill are more likely to act than those who believe they are less susceptible. While there are some positive correlations between perceived susceptibility and compliance connected with preventative health care like screening and immunisation, the findings are not consistent across a wide range of health behaviours. In general, people tend to underestimate their chances of becoming ill, as further work on susceptibility has shown. We observed earlier that mentally healthy people are unrealistically optimistic, and this is particularly true so far as the risks of becoming ill are concerned. Furthermore, the healthy see themselves as particularly "immune" to illness if they have not experienced important negative life events. In contrast, the sick judge that their level of risk is similar to that of their peers, but still believe that they themselves are invulnerable (Rodin and Salovey, 1989). This seems to occur most often in circumstances where a negative event is believed to be controllable. However, experiencing even a minor illness affects these judgements. In one study of student health, experiencing a minor illness was associated with a greater perception of comparative risks for other types of health problem, some quite serious. Ill students saw health problems as being more preventable than healthy students, especially when they considered cancers, tooth decay and VD (Kulik and Mahler, 1987). Furthermore, being in a state of unrealistic optimism is risky because not only is less attention paid to educational messages, but also unrealistic optimists have inhibitions about participating in health protective behaviours (Taylor and Brown, 1988).

Developing this theme of unrealistic optimism and risk, Weinstein (1984) notes that risk campaigns make two fundamental assumptions about the way in which people consider their health. The first is that people often underestimate their susceptibility to illness; the second is that they assume that perceived susceptibility leads to preventive action. In explaining why people think that it will not happen to them, he points out that, while there is some evidence that perceived vulnerability does lead to preventive behaviours, there is also plenty of data to show that people are unrealistically optimistic, viewing their own personal risk as below the average. Furthermore, this optimism is not just an artefact of self-presentation or a pose; he quotes evidence to show that people genuinely believe that their risk standing is better. They give themselves credit for factors that decrease their own risk, but fail to ask themselves whether others may have as many risk factors or more. Weinstein (1983) asked 88 college students to rate 11 health and safety risks. In one condition participants were provided with information about how typical Rutgers students performed and were asked to judge their own risks in relation to similar others. The results showed that students were most unrealistically optimistic about being susceptible to high-risk conditions such as having diabetes, a heart attack, lung cancer and so on, but the provision of typicality information destroyed this optimistic bias. Where students only evaluated their own risk factors, the evidence showed that some discussion of risk factors might actually make people more unrealistic about these risks (Weinstein, 1983). Weinstein offers a social interpretation of these results in concluding that without the benchmarks of the standing of others, people find it impossible to interpret their own position and so tend to assume that they are better off than most. Here he puts risk assessment within the context of social comparisons to explain how people make judgements about risks.

Beliefs about the *severity* of consequences from contracting a particular condition form the second component of the HBM. These tend to be coupled with beliefs about whether the organic and social consequences of a severe illness are likely to be important or not. Beliefs about susceptibility and severity together contribute to the perceived threat of the disease within the model. Rosenstock and Kirscht (1979) found that doctors' ratings of the severity of a condition correlated closely with those of their patients. Indeed, the argument hinges on people's *perceptions* of severity rather than the actual severity of illness itself. Evidence for this aspect of the model is less convincing than that for susceptibility. Rosenstock (1974) has suggested that maladaptive behaviours are more likely at low and high severity levels, but adaptive behaviours are more likely when severity levels are perceived to be moderate. As Croyle and Jemmott's (1991) work on the mythical TAA deficiency showed (see Chapter 4), judgements about severity and related perceptions of risk are considerably affected by how the illness is labelled.

The model also incorporates perceptions about the *efficacy* of treatment. People's beliefs that they are severely ill may not in themselves be sufficient to cause them to seek treatment, if at the same time they believe that there is no effective treatment for their self-diagnosed condition. For instance, the incidence of people with "bad backs" may be substantially underestimated in published statistics because many people with chronic back pain problems believe that there is no cure and deduce from this that a visit to a physician would be worthless. Other factors incorporated into this model include the potential benefits of taking action and whether they are effective in reducing the susceptibility to or severity of the condition. Here, an assessment is made about the financial and psychological costs related to starting and continuing with that action once it has been advocated. The mammography studies reviewed by Keefe et al (1994) provide a recent and relevant example. High expectations about the success of treatment can interact with the costs of and barriers to treatment. For example, if treatment is believed to be painful, like the treatment for severe burns, fears about treatment for pain may themselves inhibit action. Other barriers may be that the recommended treatment is difficult to obtain, say for geographical reasons or due to long waiting lists, as, for example, with low priority hernia repair. The treatment may be expensive (most relevant in systems of private medicine), which acts as a deterrent. Side effects and the complexity and duration of treatment are also important here. Unpleasant side effects and the risk of iatrogenic disorders may be a price to high to pay for pain relief. In a review of a decade of work on the HBM, covering 46 studies, Janz and Becker (1984) concluded that perceived barriers are the most important dimension within the model.

The HBM has been used to predict health behaviours in a wide range of areas, but the predictive value of the model would improve if it also incorporated cues to action, a range of health values and the three dimensions of health locus of control. While applications of the model to illness prevention and screening are of less direct interest to those concerned with the study of pain, the model has been used to look at sickness behaviour, threatening health communications and risky behaviours. Personal habits concerning diet, smoking, exercise, weight, safety practices and the use of alcohol are known to be related to the development of chronic conditions. Kirscht (1988) points out that it is unlikely that health beliefs exert much influence on the flow of habits. He distinguishes the repetitive, automatic and habitual behaviours, which are poorly predicted by the model, from the complex, conscious decision making, which has the best predictions. Health beliefs become much more salient when people are either contemplating changing their behaviour or have decided to make the effort to take part in a systematic programme of change. Here health beliefs not only guide behaviour but are affected by the course of effort (Kirscht, 1988).

The HBM is suited to the study of pain because it focuses on the avoidance of subjective discomfort, but at the same time one of its limitations is that it gives overriding weight to this feature (Janis, 1984), and this must affect the way in which pain is evaluated within the model. Like SEU theory and some other models of rational choice, it is unable to distinguish those conditions where people give priority to avoiding subjective discomfort at the risk of endangering their lives, from conditions where they will seek out and assess medical information about the real consequences of alternative action with a view to maximising their chances of survival (Janis, 1984). Perhaps a more serious criticism concerns the prediction of compliance, because the model neglects to acknowledge that non-conformity can be unintentional. It is unable to explain what motivates people or why they might not be motivated to comply with treatment instructions (Svarstad, 1976). The model forms an attractive package and at first glance appears to offer a comprehensive answer to one of the puzzles of health psychology about why people visit their doctors, but there are many valid criticisms. Kirscht (1974) believes that the operationalisation of health beliefs is a problem in itself, and there is little consensus about how this should be done. The idea is implicit that certain levels of readiness are optimal in stimulating behaviour, but theory and research have yet to define what these levels might be (Rosenstock, 1974). Furthermore, the statistical evidence for this model remains weak (Wallston and Wallston, 1984). Some critics believe that the model has not brought us much closer to understanding either how health beliefs are acquired or how stable they might be over a lifetime.

One response to these disappointing findings has been to add new variables to refine predictions, but in so doing the theory has become so general that it is almost impossible to show how a specific set of beliefs combine to lead to a decision. Like established dimensions, new features have been operationalised in many different ways, so a comparison of results is difficult and consequently reliable conclusions about the viability of the model are almost impossible. Many studies have only scrutinised a single dimension without applying a rigorous overall test, and most treat the HBM as if the features were additive, despite evidence to suggest that they might be interactive or even multiplicative. Several authorities have advocated that this catalogue of variables or "laundry list" approach should be substituted for a sound and more complex predictive model of different levels and statuses (Kirscht, 1974; Wallston and Wallston, 1984). A more serious limitation is that the model has only addressed half of the problem by being narrowly patient-focused. The behaviour and attitudes of the therapist/prescriber have never been built into a model of what is patently an interactive, two-way process. In addition, the social context or environment in which advice and prescriptions are given must also be formally evaluated as an integral part of the process.

Other theories from social psychology are also applicable to the area of predicting and understanding decision making about health. Perhaps most interesting among these is the Theory of Reasoned Action (TRA) (Ajzen and Fishbein, 1980). The emphasis here is on predicting a person's behaviour from attitudes and intentions. Like the HBM, it assumes not only that people are rational and make systematic use of the information available to them, but also that they consider their actions before deciding whether or not to perform a particular behaviour. This model contrasts with other theoretical views of people as having emotions, overpowering desires or unconscious motives, or even as thoughtless, mindless or even capricious individuals. The TRA focuses on a person's intention to behave in a particular way, so the stronger the intention, the more that person is likely to perform a particular behaviour. This intention is the joint result of the person's positive or negative attitudes or judgements towards performing a particular behaviour, together with the social pressures applied by others to encourage that person to conform to norms about the acceptable way to behave. The relative importance of these attitudes and norms will affect a person's intention to behave in a particular way, and how that person will ultimately behave. Thus, whether a person with pain intends to visit the doctor and does so is likely to be influenced by how positively or negatively that person views the consultation and becoming a patient, together with the pressures exerted by family, friends and others about what is the appropriate action for someone in this situation to take.

Attitudes reflect underlying beliefs in this model. For instance, people hold positive attitudes towards those issues that they believe will produce a positive outcome. Because these attitudes are related to what that person does, they are called behavioural beliefs, so attitudes towards the doctor will be related to beliefs about what doctors can do for you. Within this model, beliefs about pain control would be expected to underpin attitudes towards the treatment being offered for pain, and, if positive, would predict success in treatment, as we saw in an earlier chapter. Social norms also reflect underlying normative beliefs, which are about whether people think that they should or should not behave in a particular way; this is related to social approval and other types of social influence. In this way, particular social norms influence decisions about whether or not it is appropriate for a sick person to see a doctor, take medication or complain about suffering. Although Ajzen and Fishbein recognise the importance of socio-demographic variables, authoritarianism, socialisation, kinship roles, intelligence and a host of personality characteristics, these external variables are not incorporated into the theory because, while they are viewed as factors affecting beliefs; exactly how they influence such beliefs and behaviour is not important to the workings of the theory.

More recently, a Theory of Planned Behaviour (TPB) (Ajzen, 1985, 1987) has superseded the TRA. The original model was unable to account for behaviours over which people did not have complete control, so perceived behavioural control has been added, although actual control is of interest here too because it has an impact on intentions and actions. The inclusion of the concept of control means that this revised theory is more applicable to the study of pain because, as we saw in Chapter 5, control is central to psychological interpretations of pain and pain behaviour. In this way, it performs a similar function to the idea of self-efficacy (Ajzen, 1991). It is worth bearing in mind that although neither the TRA nor the TPB was explicitly designed with health issues in mind, they have both been successfully applied in this way (e.g. Ajzen and Timko, 1986). After decades of research in social psychology showing that attitudes do not reliably predict behaviour, this model has, through the incorporation of intentions, substantially improved these predictions. For this reason it needs to be taken seriously in pain research as one of the best models available for examining the relationship. If beliefs about control, self-efficacy and other attitudes towards treatment can be better utilised to predict who will and who will not benefit from treatment, then those chronic pain patients most appropriate for particular treatments might be better targeted.

However, one criticism of both the HBM and the TRA / TPB is that they take little account of those emotions that are an integral part of response to illness and decision making about consultations. Melzack (1975) and others have shown that the sensory aspects of pain are inextricably linked to affective components, and any theory that can successfully explain the decision making of pain sufferers will need to take into account the broad spectrum of affective responses that influence these decisions and their execution. While these theories describe the socio-cognitive components associated with health decisions, a purely rational approach is insufficient to account for decision making in pain sufferers. As we saw in Chapter 3, the autonomic responses of anxiety in acute pain can be replaced by the affective components of depression and helplessness as a painful, chronic illness becomes established. It is therefore artificial to ignore the effects of emotions for reasons of theoretical purity when designing models of health, even though it might be methodologically and theoretically convenient to do so.

CONFLICT AND HEALTH DECISIONS

We have seen that the rational approach derived from cognitive science does not provide the full answer to why and when people seek treatment; many emotional factors affect decision making too. Mechanic (1977) shows that the decision to seek care when similar others do not, or to seek help at one point in time rather than another may often be due to contingencies that have little direct relationship to the symptoms themselves. He cites studies showing that people in psychological distress are more likely to seek care for their symptoms, because illness relieves the tension of pressing social expectations and can be a legitimate way of excusing failure to meet social responsibility. Pain is a prime example of a symptom that not only has an affective component but is also commonly associated with psychological distress, so Mechanic's work has direct implications for the understanding of how and when pain is reported. Furthermore, the application of some of these rational models leads to the view that patients are passive recipients of decisions in the consulting room, rather than being active in taking decisions about their treatment. Janis and Mann (1977) offer the conflict theory model of personal decision making as an alternative to these rational models. They say that many ill-conceived and poorly implemented decisions are connected with decisional conflict, and in particular, with attempts to ward off the stress of having to make difficult choices. They see stress as a major source of errors in decision making. How decision makers cope depends on whether they are aware of any serious risks for the different alternatives, whether they are hopeful that a better alternative might be available, and whether they believe that they have the necessary time to seek out and consider these alternatives before they have to make their decision.

Janis and Mann have identified five stages that enable people to arrive at a *stable* decision. These stages were derived from studies observing people with health problems, people trying to give up smoking or lose weight, or people contemplating a course of medical treatment. At the beginning of this process, people find that their current course of action is being challenged. They need to take an active decision about whether to ignore the challenge or to take it on and change their behaviour; this appraisal and increased awareness results in an arousal of conflict. To progress to the second stage they need to believe that they are taking serious risks if they do not change. If challenged by the pain of a broken leg, for instance, the sufferer should be aware that there may be serious consequences to ignoring that pain by walking around on it. In considering the various alternatives at the third stage, the active decision makers are often hopeful that there is an important and acceptable alternative way to deal with the challenge. Weighing the alternatives, they begin a search for the best one by looking at the varied consequences of each. This enables them to reach a tentative decision about the most appropriate path of action. In deliberating about their commitment to the best alternative, they become increasingly committed to it and so work out the best way to implement the decision. At this fourth stage they also make contingency plans about what to do if the action fails and about how to tell others about their actions. At the last stage new challenges are ignored and adherence to the regime is considered. They take account of the risks for and against changing, and the concomitant feedback involved in attempting to adhere.

Those with a vigilant coping pattern are able to make rational choices, but patterns of defective coping have been identified that interfere with such judgements (Janis and Mann, 1977). These are where sufferers just carry on as normal in a state of unconflicted adherence, and where they uncritically accept what is on offer without having any contingency plans for failure in a state of unconflicted change. They may also try defensive avoidance using techniques like procrastination or shifting the responsibility to others. Alternatively, they may use wishful thinking in order to try to minimise unattractive outcomes. Hypervigilant people may search frenetically for a way out of the dilemma, shifting impulsively between alternatives for any rapid solution that appears to bring relief. In this defective coping style of panic-stricken emotional excitement, important consequences are often overlooked, the memory span shrinks and simplistic ideas emerge. Any of these four defective patterns militates against the correct use of different stages of the judgement process, and hence the ultimate arrival at a stable decision (Janis, 1984). Elements of these embryonic coping styles are reported in a more extreme form in chronic pain patients, as the discussion in Chapter 8 shows.

Janis (1984) has also pointed out how little is known about post-decisional regret, but there has been a revival of interest in this lately. In the rush to give consumers more responsibility for their health by involving them in decision making, there has been little empirical interest in the professional handling of failure, and how to deal with the distress associated with an outcome that is unsuccessful. Wagener and Taylor (1986) interviewed 29 renal transplant patients about their retrospective perceptions of treatment success ($N = 13$) or failure ($N = 16$). They found that patients who considered that their transplant had been a failure consistently reported that the decision was less difficult than those for whom it had been a success. Realistic expectations of success are about 60% in this case. Some failures said, "what else could I have done?", while others said, "I would have done it no matter what the odds were". The results showed that not only do failures see their own contribution to decision making as bigger over time, but they also see other factors as playing a larger role, like pressures, knowledge of side effects and fear of transplant failure. The position that they tended to adopt was that there had been no decision, because there was no choice. In short, dialysis was no longer perceived to be an option. Wagener and Taylor (1986) question whether it might be better for physicians to assume the blame for treatments that either do not affect the patient's health or make it worse. Cognitive research shows how people constantly revise and update their memories of decisions after the event (see Chapter 4). Nevertheless, in policy terms this research tells us that in a society that is inclined to place a high degree of personal responsibility for health outcomes on the patient, it is essential to draw up contingency plans about how it is possible to provide psychological escape routes for patients that will enable them to preserve their self-esteem if their decision turns out to have been the wrong one. This must be as true for choice in pain relief as elsewhere, where failures may be even more aversive, as, for example, in the general case of repeated surgery for back pain.

HAZARDS AND RULES OF THUMB

Summarising research investigating the giving and receiving of medical advice, Leventhal (1975) says that doctors should tell their patients how medical tests and therapeutic procedures will feel, how they will change their bodies and their ability to do things, and what the whole range of implications will be for their future lives. Physicians can provoke fear and suspicion that they are holding back information about risks and unpleasantness, and other bad news. Patients search their facial expressions for clues; smiles, frowns and tone of voice are all monitored closely by those anxious about bad news. Erroneous interpretations of these cues may provoke intense distress at one extreme, or may create expectations of miraculous cures at the other, which, when frustrated, lead to doubt, disappointment and anger (see also Chapter 7).

As we saw in Chapter 5, feelings of personal control, broadly speaking, have positive effects on health and well-being. In the interests of the patient, a primary aim of the health professional should be to provide just as much information to patients as they wish, to enable them to maintain their personal autonomy and to involve them in choices about their health and future. In the role of a non-directive but knowledgeable facilitator, health professionals are in a position to outline the various plausible options and encourage decision making. How this risk information can be most usefully provided in order to give the maximum choice is still a question of debate. Patients who have just been told that their screening test for cervical cancer or for spina bifida in their baby has proved positive are unlikely to be much enlightened in deciding what to do about future treatment by being told how many per thousand per year also show a positive test. Such patients need to know about the likelihood that the test is accurate and, more particularly, how often that test provides a false positive result; in short, they need to know about the test's reliability.

Risk has been defined as the probability that a hazard may be realised at any specified level in a given span of time (Advisory Committee on Major Hazards). Once a hazard is identified, then the risks may be made acceptably low. Harvey (1981) points out that some risks may be unacceptable because they are perceived to be insufficiently controllable, while for other risks controllability is not perceived to be important. He instances those Californians who protest vigorously about nuclear risks and chemical hazards while at the same time living happily on the San Andreas fault. In managing risks it is important to find out what is thought to be a tolerable or reasonable level of risk, because there will usually be a level of residual risk. Risks are not perceived in isolation: there is usually a trade-off between risks and benefits. Someone who is weighing up the pros and cons of flying from Britain to the Continent for a holiday, as opposed to driving their car on congested foreign motorways, may weigh negative factors such as expert statistics on deaths from flying and driving and the costs of travelling with a complaining, car-sick child against positive factors like the convenience of having a car during the holiday and the speed of travelling to that destination by plane (Thomas, 1981). The study of cognitive biases, however, shows that people select and distort those features they attend to in problem solving (Lee, 1981), so risk perceptions about health are neither entirely rational nor free from bias.

The equation between hazard, harm and hurt is one that those in pain consider when contemplating activity, as Fordyce's (1976, 1986) ideas on learning showed (see Chapter 3). Activity is viewed as a hazard by many chronic pain patients because they equate activity with an increase in pain and, therefore, damage. This is because they view pain in pre-gate control theory terms as an experience that reflects a neurophysiological event and damage to the body, rather than as a phenomenon that includes a substantial psychological component. Fordyce points out that hurt and harm are not the same thing, although the families of pain sufferers do not always recognise this (Fordyce, 1986). Thomas (1981) says that we need to look at the substance of what each person takes into account when making a choice; that is, how they define the risk options and how these fit into a wider system of beliefs, because those beliefs may affect how people feel about the two options. This general statement also seems to be pertinent to the behaviour of those being treated for chronic pain. Often, lay people have little statistical evidence on which to make their judgements, so they are obliged to make inferences based on what they remember hearing or observing about the risk in question.

However, it is not only patients who make errors of judgement in decision making. Trained health professionals have the knowledge of experts, yet even with all of this information, Nisbett and Ross (1980) found that medical scientists, like other experts, frequently make errors of inference when they estimate probabilities. Some errors and biases are made due to the use of rules of thumb or *heuristics* (Tversky and Kahneman, 1973, 1974), which are widely used to reduce difficult mental tasks to much simpler ones. They are not always used in circumstances when a slower, more thoughtful approach is appropriate but to speed up the processing of information under more urgent conditions. The use of these rules is valid in some cases but biased in others (Slovic, Fischoff and Lichtenstein, 1981). One bias is that it is easier to imagine events that occur very often than those that occur infrequently; this is the *availability* heuristic. For example, in assessing the risk of dying from lung cancer, smokers making the judgement are likely to recall available instances of lung cancer among friends, acquaintances and those known to their social circle. When examples of an event such as death from cancer are easily brought to mind, it is usually because there are lots of these cases, so use of the availability heuristic may actually produce the correct answer. Biases occur, however, because easily retrieved information seems perceptibly more numerous than information that is less easily remembered, but in fact occurs equally frequently. Searching for one category rather than another may have similar biasing effects. If asked to estimate causes of death, there is a tendency to overestimate dramatic or sensational causes such as accidents, natural disasters and murder, and to underestimate unspectacular causes that claim a single victim at a time, like deaths following vaccination, or as a result of diabetes or stroke.

Anaesthetists are more likely to overestimate the frequency of the more vivid anaesthetic complications occurring in theatre, while complications that occur in the wards are more liable to be underestimated (Wilson and Nerurkar, 1986). To avoid the availability heuristic, Janis (1984) suggests that people should be trained to avoid giving a lot of weight to a single case, irrespective of its vividness. They should be encouraged to give greater weight to findings from larger samples rather than smaller ones, and to unbiased samples rather than biased ones. They might also be encouraged to use the technical definition of the probability of an outcome, and to carry out these simple mathematical calculations before reaching a conclusion.

Availability can be affected by many factors unrelated to frequency. For instance, a recent film or news item can seriously bias the judgements that people make if it is particularly memorable. The influence of easily available information has been shown in an interesting piece of work on *in vitro* fertilisation (Johnston, Shaw and Bird, 1984). Following the extensive and emotional publicity surrounding the birth of Louise Brown, the first "test tube" baby, estimates of the success of *in vitro* fertilisation were dramatically affected. Doctors and prospective patients alike can be influenced to a much greater extent by media reports of the success of such procedures than by their less reported failures. If the news reports are biased towards reporting successes, then resulting public perceptions will be biased. Johnston, Shaw and Bird (1984) studied 25 women waiting for laparoscopic ovum retrieval surgery who had experienced fertility problems for around 9 years and had a high level of anxiety. Despite careful attempts to provide them with accurate statistical information on the likely outcome of the procedure, the majority overestimated the likelihood of an egg being retrieved; only one correctly guessed the actual success rate at that time, which was 8%. As a result, they overestimated the likelihood of becoming pregnant. The profound psychological distress that accompanies failure of this end-of-the-road procedure is made worse by inappropriate prior expectations about risks. However, it does seem possible that women in this situation may exaggerate the success rate to make their anxiety levels more manageable.

Another heuristic that also takes account of availability information is the *simulation* heuristic (Tversky and Kahneman, 1982). It is used to create hypothetical scenarios to enable people to estimate how an event might eventually work out, or might have worked out had it happened. If you fall off a ladder and hurt yourself, but do not break a leg, then you might generate a variety of alternatives about what your partner's reaction to that broken leg might have been. This heuristic is particularly useful in looking at the ways in which people understand "near misses", including the frustration, regret and so on that an event might have produced (Fiske and Taylor, 1984).

The *representativeness* heuristic looks at how representative an item is of a particular category in producing a probability estimate. How likely is it that a particular person or event will be a member of a category? Participants in studies of this heuristic may be told:

> Steve is very shy, withdrawn, invariably helpful, but with little interest in people or in the world of reality. A meek tidy soul, he has a need for order and structure and a passion for detail.

How do people faced with this description estimate the probability that Steve is a physician, a farmer, a salesman, a librarian or an airline pilot? They look at the degree to which Steve is stereotypical of each occupation, often concluding that librarian is the most likely answer. In answering, they consider the extent to which the person or event resembles the category they are examining, so strong similarities result in a judgement of high probability, and a loose resemblance in a low one. Errors of judgement occur because people base their judgements on similarity, and similarity is not a reliable rule to use (Tversky and Kahneman, 1974). In performing this exercise, people frequently ignore base rates, and they do not necessarily appreciate the importance of having a large sample. Activities like simply counting the number of heads in every set of 10 coins tossed illustrates in probability terms how often a long run of heads can occur. To exemplify this heuristic within anaesthesia, Wilson and Nerurkar (1986) take the case of patients who are slow to settle when breathing halothane spontaneously. They point out that if by chance an anaesthetist experiences a run of patients in this condition, this may lead to the erroneous conclusion that failure to settle is due to the new induction agent being used that day. Because of these common errors and biases in judgement, there is little to be gained in trying out a few samples of a new drug when in fact to do so might be grossly misleading. A better strategy would be to seek out a good, published large-scale trial that closely matches personal clinical practice.

Similarly, people commonly fail to appreciate randomness, as demonstrated by an error of judgement known as the gambler's fallacy. Roulette players erroneously expect a black to turn up after a long run of reds, say 10. This expectation presupposes that the roulette ball has a "memory". Chance is commonly viewed as a self-correcting process, so a deviation in one direction is believed to be compensated by a similar deviation the other way (Tversky and Kahneman, 1973). People can be excessively confident in their judgements of representativeness because they see a good fit between the data and the category when in fact it may be illusory, and because they are motivated to exercise control over their environment (Hogarth, 1987). This over-confidence takes various forms, such as "knowing" with an undue degree of certainty, and being excessively precise. It is a particular problem for those who believe themselves to be experts, so this inferential feature should not be overlooked by expert health professionals when making diagnoses and giving advice, because it constitutes a central part of their social interaction with patients.

It is also known that judgements of representativeness are subject to misconceptions about regression to the mean. Tversky and Kahneman (1974) recount the example of the flying instructors who noticed that praise of a smooth landing was often followed by a rough landing the next time, while harsh criticism of a poor landing was often followed by improvement. This led flying instructors to conclude that criticism improved performance, but because there is inherent variability about the mean these random and chance fluctuations would be expected from probability theory. The error of judgement in this example concerns hypotheses about a causal relation between criticism and performance where none actually existed. A clinical example is provided by Whitney and von Korff (1992) to show how interpretations of pain data are susceptible to the effects of regression to the mean. Improvements in pain following entry to a pain management course could well be due to the effects of treatment, but they might also be due to placebo effects (see also Chapter 9) or to a regression towards the mean. This effect is most likely to occur in uncontrolled trials and where people have selected themselves for inclusion by virtue of having a flare. The peak of intolerance to pain is the most likely point at which many people who become pain patients seek medical help. It is therefore inevitable that some will spontaneously and subsequently improve whatever the nature of the intervention, or even if there is no intervention at all. Those seeking treatment for pain tend to have higher levels of pain than those who do not see a doctor (Whitney and von Korff, 1992).

A further heuristic is that of anchoring and adjustment. To cope with an ambiguous situation, people may look for an anchor by estimating an initial value to start with and then making successive adjustments to this reference point later to give a final answer. Anaesthetists may have a preconceived idea about the probability that a drug will have a particular effect; this forms the anchor point. New information subsequently obtained from using the drug with different patients causes them to adjust their original estimate to a new value, but this adjustment is often insufficient. In addition, the final answer may be seriously wrong if the initial anchoring estimate was wrong (Wilson and Nerurkar, 1986). Turk and Rudy (1991) suggest that patients may revise their current estimates based on current pain, so that current pain may anchor recall of previous pain. They point out that the recall of medication use and activity levels may be similarly biased, hence they see any such estimates as jeopardising valid conclusions about adherence. Similarly, health professionals use these processes: estimates are made about other people's personality characteristics based on what we know about our own personal characteristics. We expect other people to behave, think and act like ourselves. Furthermore, it is tempting to classify people as abnormal if their behaviour cannot be adjusted to our own anchor. This heuristic seems to be particularly appropriate for use in social situations because there are very few concrete yardsticks for measuring psychological features (Fiske and Taylor, 1984). The most important error made here is insufficient adjustment. Anchoring not only occurs at the start of a process but also in cases where evidence is incomplete.

Other theories have been designed to tackle decision making in a health context. The probability of an outcome is a feature of most normative and descriptive models, as we have seen above, and the value attached to that outcome is acknowledged to be an integral feature. Prospect theory takes these ideas one step further by indicating that decisions are affected by the ways in which probability information is presented (Kahneman and Tversky, 1979). These different presentations have social implications as well as social consequences. People use a reference point for what they stand to win or lose, and different presentations of factually equivalent information can change this reference point. This elaborates the SEU theory prediction that probability information will be used in the same way, regardless of whether it is framed positively as a gain or negatively as a loss. Marteau (1989) has used prospect theory to predict the reactions of medical students reactions to positively and negatively framed information. Playing the role of GP or patient, they made decisions about how they would behave or how they would advise patients on the basis of limited descriptions of patients about to undergo liver surgery who had been offered amniocentesis and the termination of pregnancy, and haemophilia carriers who had been offered termination as a result of foetal abnormality. The negative frames of dying, carrying an abnormal baby and losing a healthy baby were compared with gains in the positive frames. Marteau found that positively framed options were more likely to be chosen, but that the degree of influence depended on the type of health decision made. Thus, framing barely affected the decisions about haemophilia, but had a greater impact on the other conditions. While it is necessary to be cautious in generalising from simulations, this study does provide interesting pointers to the ways in which doctors take decisions and believe their patients take them. This will be discussed further in Chapter 7.

CONCLUSION

In this chapter we have examined decision making within the clinical context. Many of the theories that are based on purely cognitive premises are inappropriate to the study of pain, where social and emotional factors must be central to any interpretation of behaviour. Models in social and health psychology provide different insights into decision making behaviour about whether to take preventative action or comply with treatment; none provides an entire solution. Information about the sources of advice available and the assessment of risks all contribute to understandings about why those in pain attend for treatment or go elsewhere. We have also considered some of the errors and biases in judgement that people make when making decisions. As decision making about health is a two-sided affair, the use of heuristics is as applicable to health professionals as to their patients. In this way, they contribute to a social psychology of pain.

The Consultation Process

7

> The average patient looks upon the average doctor very much as the non-combatant looks upon the troops fighting on his behalf. The more trained men there are between his body and the enemy, the better.
> (Rudyard Kipling)

Previous chapters have examined the social processes that contribute to the decision to consult and to people becoming patients. In this chapter consideration is given to the pain sufferer as part of a complex social interaction between patient and professional within the dynamics of the consultation. This interaction is of central importance not only to the interpretation of illness but also in understanding readiness to comply with treatment and decisions about whether to return in future. These behaviours have widespread policy implications for the planning of health care. In this chapter particular attention is paid to the emotions that affect decision making and interpersonal interactions. Early cognitive science viewed affect as a "contaminant" and hence a source of experimental error that needed to be controlled for, so that it could be ignored in laboratory investigations of pain cognitions (Craig, 1984). Some models examined in Chapter 6 were criticised for their de-emphasis and even neglect of the relevance of emotions associated with health, illness and treatment in the pursuit of methodologically "pure" cognitions. The patent distress of those in pain cannot be underestimated or ignored (Wall, 1979), so this position is no longer tenable. During consultations about pain many different emotions are visible, arising not only from the distress of pain and disability itself and from any bad news received, but also associated with the challenge of the treatments themselves and the context or atmosphere in which it is carried out. It is because of the powerful emotions that arise within the consultation that emotions are considered at this point in the book. The case is made for a socio-emotional analysis as an integral part of any comprehensive investigation of pain and consultations about it.

PAIN, STRESS AND EMOTIONS

What is the evidence for a relationship between pain, stress and emotion? We may consider answers to this question at three different levels. At a pharmacological level, the discovery of beta-endorphins has raised interesting questions about the extent to which they have an analgesic function and whether this is part of a generalised reaction to stress. Beta-endorphins may be activated during psychological therapy, but their production appears to be unrelated to changes in depressive symptoms and is more likely to be a stress marker than a pain reliever (Beutler et al, 1987). At a clinical level, Melzack and Dennis (1978) have identified steps in the processing of emotions associated with the duration of pain. Brief phasic pain occurs at the time of injury and is commonly associated with fear and avoidance but may also be linked to emotions like guilt, pleasure or sexual excitement. Persisting acute pain is represented by high levels of anxiety and self-concern, especially where distress continues. Normally healing would be completed by this stage, but if pain goes on beyond the point of healing then it becomes chronic. Although wide-ranging individual differences are seen in chronic pain patients, the emotions of depression, fear, somatic preoccupation and intense distress characterise this step; contrary to popular belief, only a small proportion of patients become angry and resentful, manipulative and demanding (Craig, 1983). At a third level — the psychophysiological level — there have been many investigations into whether psychophysiological responses known to be associated with autonomic activity change in chronic pain patients. Flor and Turk (1989) reviewed 47 of these studies and concluded that there was little reliable evidence to support this view. Electromyogram (EMG) levels or vascular changes for chronic recurrent headache had not been permanently affected and there was only inconsistent evidence for changes related to chronic back pain and temporomandibular pain disorders. Electrophysiological recordings of the human brain and magnetic brain activities are also assumed to be correlates of pain, but the causal linkage has yet to be established (Chen, 1993). Despite the consistently low correlations reported between psychophysiological measures and subjective reports in the study of pain and emotions, research endeavours have continued in the hope that improvements in technology and design will eventually provide better answers, for example through the inclusion of controls for medication intake and pain status (Flor and Turk, 1989).

As a departure for this discussion it also seems necessary to consider briefly something of what is known about cognitions, emotions and their relation to immunology. Evidence for a role of the central nervous system (CNS) in the regulation of immunity is well established, and stress appears to influence the functioning of the immune system via the CNS and neuroendocrine mediation (Lloyd, 1989). There is also a psychological relationship between negative life events and infectious diseases. For instance, a decrease in desirable events often occurs four days before the onset of the common cold and is linked to reductions in immunity (Evans, Pitts and Smith, 1988). Others have concluded that the link between stress and illness behaviour is more convincing than the association between stress and infectious pathology (Cohen and Williamson, 1991). As illness behaviour is a salient feature in the context of reporting chronic pain, such findings lend broad support for further investigations of this nature.

The relationship between stress and back pain has been the focus of many studies and has become fertile ground for the discussion of mechanisms. Debating the evidence for two versions of the spasm or tension model of back pain, Dolce and Raczynski (1985) compare the physical stressor model with the psychosocial stressor model. The physical stressor model indicates that some mechanical or organic stress in the form of structural damage or poor body mechanics is present, and this triggers reflexive muscle spasms. Nociception instigates protective spasms, so a pain–spasm–pain cycle results. In contrast, the psychosocial stressor model says that back pain results from an increase in paraspinal muscle activity, but that increases in tension and muscle spasm are the result of not coping effectively with the environment and may be compounded by emotional stress such as anxiety. EMG studies tend to confirm increased muscle tension in painful muscles. However, the evidence favours the physical stressor model, and Dolce and Raczynski (1985) recommended that intensive assessments of the back pain musculature and a thorough medical work-up should be carried out, noting the number of muscular sites and types and extent of autonomic arousal, before commencing neuromuscular retraining.

The perception of pain has been shown to be attenuated or accelerated by emotional processes (Craig, 1983), but Liebeskind (1991) takes this argument one step further. He argues that pain *can* kill. Endorsing Bonica's (1990) statement that pain is *never* benign, he sees pain as a "malefic force", which can devastate people's lives and lead to suicide. Citing animal evidence, he shows that pain and stress inhibit the functioning of the immune system and enhance tumour growth by inhibiting the cytotoxic action of the natural killer cells whose function it is to monitor tumour growth. A second line of evidence from the management of acute post-operative pain indicates that effective pain relief can reduce morbidity and mortality in cancer patients (Cousins, 1991). Morbidity and mortality are profoundly affected by emotions, as some of the cross-cultural examples presented in Chapter 4 showed. Liebeskind concludes that pain of a sufficient magnitude "can directly or indirectly suppress immune mechanisms normally serving to defend the body against tumours and can thereby cause a marked increase in tumour growth". In this case, the relief of cancer pain is an imperative, not a luxury.

The study of stressful life events has a long history in psychosomatic research, but greater interest has recently been focused on how people cope with the more dramatic life events and the more trivial. Findings from such studies improve understanding about pain. Post-traumatic stress disorder (PTSD) is precipitated by an "objective" stressor of life-threatening proportions and is often accompanied by phobia and depression. Pain itself may represent a cause or an effect here; it may be a life-threatening stressor or a response to trauma (Muse, 1985, 1986). While there is much circumstantial evidence, the direction of causation has been difficult to establish. For instance, Sherman estimated that PTSD was prevalent in 35% of those who sustained physical injury during the Vietnam war, compared with only 3.5% of those who were not injured (see Sherman, Sherman and Bruno, 1987, for a review). More recent use of single-case designs has lent support to the conclusion that pain is likely to be the cause of PTSD (Schreiber and Galia-Gat, 1993). However, a daily study of 27 male amputees by Arena et al (1990) found that 74% demonstrated a significant pain–stress relationship, with 63% showing simultaneous onset of pain and stress. Clearer understandings about the causal relationship here may provide insights into new strategies for treatment.

Hassles, in contrast, are the minor ongoing stresses and strains of daily living; they are the irritating, frustrating, distressing demands that tend to characterise everyday transactions with the environment. They may be represented by a quarrel, argument, fuss, a difficult problem or trouble. There is a significant social component to the link between hassles and health, as a study of 75 married couples has shown (De Longis, Folkman and Lazarus, 1988). Those with unsupportive relationships and low self-esteem had more problems of a somatic and psychological nature on the stressful days that followed than did those with good self-esteem and support. Thus, those with poor psychological resources may be more vulnerable to illness and disturbed mood when under stress. Hassles that are deeply important to some people, being central to their lives, may be very minor or peripheral to the lives of others. Furthermore, the severity of central hassles correlates with health status, particularly with psychological symptoms (Lazarus, 1986).

Results from a daily hassles scale used over a 20-day period showed a mean of 1.9 headaches and 3.3 musculoskeletal problems such as backache and shoulder pain. Sternbach (1986) has also investigated the relationship between pain and hassles in 1254 adults surveyed in the USA for the Nuprin report. Some 5% reported stress daily, 38% several days a week and 51% less than once a week. The more stress and hassles over a whole year, the greater the frequency and severity of reported pain. Stress was believed to cause headache, backache, stomach and peri-menstrual pains but not joint, muscle or dental pain. It has been claimed that the careful sampling in this study enables predictions to be made within 2–3% accuracy in generalising to the rest of the population. Thus, from a wide range of different sources, the link between pain, stress and emotions appears to be well established.

SUFFERING AND LOSS

Although suffering is an exceptionally unpleasant emotional response that is frequently associated with pain and distress, it is not entirely clear whether pain and suffering are phenomenologically distinct (Rose and Adams, 1989). Suffering integrates many socio-emotional components associated with pain, as the above definition suggests, and so deserves special mention here. Cassel (1982) observes that suffering occurs when an impending destruction of the person is perceived and continues until the threat has passed or until the person's integrity can be otherwise restored. Events likely to cause this threat include the death or distress of loved ones, powerlessness, helplessness, hopelessness, torture, the loss of a life's work, betrayal, physical agony, isolation, homelessness, memory failure and fear. The greater the pain, the greater the suffering is believed to be. But this depends very much on the meaning of the pain, as a casual comparison of cancer pain and childbirth pain confirms. Cassel points out that suffering not only occurs in those with severe and chronic pain; minor pain can also cause great suffering if its cause is unknown. Suffering is also more likely if the pain is believed to be uncontrollable (see Chapter 5). Suffering is not confined to the physical symptoms of disease but also extends to treatment. It commonly occurs in a wide range of social conditions. It may affect the sufferer's body image and may be connected to the fulfilment of social roles. It can also affect a person's identity (Cassel, 1982) and identification with social groups. This has implications for relationships, such as those with the family.

Health professionals are quite often unable to anticipate what their patients will identify as being a source of suffering. This is not so much due to inadequate training but more because of the wide range of highly individual beliefs and meanings that patients assign to their experiences. The only way to uncover sources of suffering with any certainty is to ask the sufferer. While people may describe some features of their condition as painful, upsetting, uncomfortable or distressing, these features may not necessarily also be the source of suffering, as is commonly assumed by observers. Those who are seen to be in pain may also be believed to be suffering greatly, when in reality this may not be so. Mistaken judgements about suffering may themselves cause intense suffering to family and loved ones who are carrying out the caring. It may affect their mental health and their ability to cope and, in so doing, have widespread consequences for the well-being of the community.

Investigating how much a patient's suffering is apparent to health professionals, Davitz and Pendleton (1969) looked at how nurses from different cultural backgrounds infer suffering in their patients. When Thai, Korean, Puerto Rican, Negro and Caucasian nurses were asked to evaluate the suffering described in vignettes of patients, some cultural differences emerged, but more importantly it was found that younger patients were seen to suffer more than the old and that lower and middle class patients were believed to suffer more than those from upper socio-economic groups. Although the results from judgements of these stereotypes must be treated with caution, they suggest that the treatment patients receive is not entirely determined by their level of suffering but is moderated by a wide range of socio-cultural factors like age and social class. These social factors have a considerable influence on the way in which a patient's suffering is interpreted by others. The relative invisibility of suffering has implications for how health professionals respond to suffering in terms of the style and timing of treatment provided.

Patients are more likely to suffer if they feel socially isolated. Their isolation may occur because the physician cannot legitimate their pain, perhaps implying that it may be psychological or faked, or in conditions where patients feel that they are unable to talk about their distress. Individual differences in the ability to use language to describe emotional experiences and to express emotions are well documented, particularly where negative emotions are concerned (Rodin and Salovey, 1989), and this is directly relevant to expressions of distress and suffering commonly associated with pain. At a practical level, Cassel indicates that where meaning can be derived for threatening events, suffering can often be substantially reduced.

Suffering is a difficult concept to operationalise but it is useful because it integrates a rich mixture of the cognitive components of interpretation with a wide range of affective elements like fear and anxiety. The social and interpersonal context in which it occurs are also powerful influences. Suffering involves the uniquely human quality of being able to anticipate the consequences of events. This power of foresight also enables people to ruminate over their diminished capacities and goals, to anxiously anticipate prolonged distress and to contemplate the possibility of physical disability, disfigurement and death (Craig, 1983). Emotionally driven processes such as disorganised hysterical behaviour, inappropriate avoidance strategies and substantial physiological arousal are conspicuous when renewed or severe pain is anticipated.

This phenomenon is particularly evident in oncology clinics, where anticipation of adverse reactions to treatment is common (Boubjerg et al, 1990).

Where suffering has been investigated it has tended to be conceptualised in terms of the theoretical models of the day. For instance, Fordyce (1988) defines suffering as "an affective or emotional response to the Central Nervous System, triggered by nociception or other aversive events like fear, bereavement or threat". Such social learning theorists observe suffering only indirectly in the sense of a person engaging in some behaviour, which is then attributed to suffering. Such indirect methods raise questions about reliable assessment. Hedging his bets, Fordyce (1988) goes on to define pain behaviours as the things people do when they suffer or are in pain. These behaviours can arise because of nociception but may also occur for other reasons. There is therefore good reason to believe that we are some way from developing an adequate theory to explain the different facets of suffering. While the setting, environment or social context of people's sensations undoubtedly affect the extent to which people believe they are suffering (Twaddle, 1980), a social psychology of pain would also need to include the social and cultural norms that influence this interpretation.

There are interesting parallels to be drawn between social expectations surrounding the treatment of those who suffer from illness and disability and those who suffer psychological losses. Suffering may follow from loss of function, such as the loss of a limb following spinal cord injury, as well as from certain stressful life events like losing a loved one. As part of the sick role, it is expected that those who experience illness or disability must suffer. If suffering fails to occur or is invisible, then it may be imposed or its failure to appear may be rationalised away. This action in turn imposes an even greater burden on the individual through a combination of social forces, and raises questions about whether people suffer because others expect it or, in extreme cases, perhaps even force them to do so. Reviewing the myths of coping with loss, Wortman and Silver (1989) observe how much additional suffering may be endured by those who continue to exhibit a "normal" pattern of behaviour following loss. They may be treated harshly by others because they do not conform to society's expectations about patterns of grieving. Patients may be believed to be suffering unconsciously or to be denying or repressing thoughts and emotions if they appear to be well adjusted. Such reasoning may lead paradoxically to a sufferer being credited with supernormal abilities. Furthermore, the inferior status of sufferers means that they are not only labelled as different, but more as an underclass who are stereotypically helpless and incompetent, with limited choices (Shontz, 1975). These interpersonal processes powerfully underline the social nature of suffering.

In western societies there are widespread expectations about the developmental stages of grieving that people experience following loss. Firstly, distress or depression is expected. Failure to experience and express "necessary" distress may well be seen to reflect pathology. Secondly, it is believed that the experience of loss will be "worked through", and that this will be followed by "recovery" at the final stage. Thus, there is only limited tolerance by observers for the considerable variations in the amount of distress experienced and exhibited. Wortman and Silver (1989) conclude that the best evidence shows that there is no current psychological prescription about the "best" way to grieve. Here a "paradox of relief" is identified; on the one hand a moralistic imperative demands that people should not enjoy suffering and should do all they can to escape from it. On the other hand, there are circumstances such as disasters in which others die, where suffering becomes a mixed blessing obtained from social comparisons for the survivors. Beecher's (1956) study of wounded soldiers from Anzio Beach in Chapter 1 provides an example. Sufferers may experience real difficulties in understanding why the "good" suffer and the "guilty" gain relief and how the healthy can be unhappy (Shontz, 1975) — in other words, in coming to terms with these powerful emotions. These observations go against people's beliefs about the existence of a "just world" where principles of equity demand that people receive their just deserts (Simmons and Lerner, 1968).

Undoubtedly cognitions are important in the expression and experience of pain, but this body of research enables us to conclude that there is evidence that suffering is best explained through the integration of a rich variety of sensory, social, cognitive and emotional factors.

THE BALANCE OF MOODS

Six distinct emotions have been consistently and generally identified: happiness, sadness, anger, disgust, surprise and fear (Di Matteo and Friedman, 1982), but it may be valid to consider as many as 47 distinct and representative emotions (Blank, 1982). Only a handful of these emotions, such as depression and anxiety, have been extensively researched in relation to pain. Others, like fear and sadness, are increasingly of interest, but many emotions have been totally ignored. An exception is a study by Wade et al (1990) of the relationship between the unpleasantness of chronic pain and the negative emotions of depression, anxiety, frustration, anger and fear. When those in chronic pain (half with low back pain) were compared with a group with mixed diagnoses, Wade et al (1990) found that anxiety and frustration best predicted pain unpleasantness after pain intensity was controlled for. They recommended that new therapies for the relief of depression associated with pain might be profitably reorientated by targeting the important and relevant emotions of frustration and anger.

Even for the well-researched emotions of depression and anxiety, though, causal relationships with pain have not been established conclusively. Pessimistic explanatory style associated with depression is a risk factor in physical illness of all types across the life-span, as a study by Peterson, Seligman and Vaillant (1988) showed (see also Chapter 5). Among Harvard graduates from the early 1940s who were reassessed after their 25th birthday, those with the most pessimistic outlook turned out to have much poorer health by the age of 45 than those who explained life's events in more optimistic terms. Furthermore, this explanatory style for negative events remained reasonably stable over 52 years (Burns and Seligman, 1989). These findings imply that a pessimistic explanatory style may not only affect whether people neglect their health, but also their predisposition to seek medical help if their health fails.

There are several issues that are important to an analysis of pain and emotions. Firstly, the causal relationship between pain and emotions remains unclear. Do strong emotions cause pain or are they an outcome of discomfort? For instance, diary evidence from headache patients has indicated weakly that intense headaches and high levels of emotionality tend to coexist on the same day ($p = 0.09$) (Arena, Blanchard and Andrasik, 1984). Gamsa (1990) has reviewed studies of a range of emotional disturbances alleged to predate pain; they included family size, birth order, blue collar families, difficulties such as unmet needs, history of parental punishment, neglect and physical and sexual abuse. She found little evidence to support the hypothesis that significant events occurred prior to pain onset, but pain was found to be associated with current emotional disturbances such as depression or diminished life satisfaction. This suggests that emotional disturbance is more likely to be a consequence of pain than an antecedent to it (also reported in Chapter 5). A third tenable but unconfirmed view is that a significant proportion of the emotional disturbance related to chronic pain is a secondary effect (Merskey and Boyd, 1978).

Secondly, it is difficult to disentangle emotions attributable to pain and illness from the wider distressed reactions to being in hospital that patients report. From 200 interviews with general medical patients, Wilson-Barnett (1976) found that they had negative responses to a wide range of activities, some apparently trivial to an outsider, such as using a bedpan, as well as more expected sources of negativity like anticipating painful medical treatment or diagnostic procedures, being away from their family, leaving work or worry about their condition or illness. An interesting finding here was that there were many more positive emotional reactions to being in hospital than negative ones, so on balance the emotional experience of being ill and hospitalised is fairly tolerable for many people. Although suffering is an intensely negative emotional state, there may be times when even those in chronic pain have positive emotional experiences. In studying pain and suffering the research focus has inevitably been drawn towards negative emotions, so reflecting the problem-orientated culture and ideology that has directed the investigation of psychopathology, when more holistic studies of the emotions in their considerable variety might have been more informative. Such a view facilitates the inclusion of more positive subjective perceptions of well-being as an integral part of the assessment.

More specifically, where mood has been investigated in pain patients using comprehensive measures such as the Mood Adjective Checklist, a wide range of moods has been reported. A study of 70 pain patients with intervertebral disk disease showed that while the patient's severity of pain was better explained by negative moods (21% of the variance), a substantial 16% of the variance could be explained by positive moods (Shacham, Dar and Cleeland, 1984). The mechanism whereby the presence of pain affects positive mood appraisal is not understood, which may be because relatively little attention has so far been paid to the more positive side of life for those in pain. One interesting mechanistic model that has been used to explain this phenomenon is that the "pull" between opposing forces of pleasure and pain explain subjective well-being. In this pleasure–pain model, pleasure from, say, happiness is seen to be intrinsically linked to pain or unhappiness, with one usually preceding the other in a sequence and in contrast (Diener, 1984).

The link between pain and mood is just one part of the story, however, because mood is known to have a direct effect on how people evaluate their health in general. In a study by Croyle and Uretsky (1987), videos were used to induce positive or negative mood, and participants were then invited to imagine an illness-related scenario. It was found that those who had been in a positive mood produced more favourable judgements of their health than those in a negative frame of mind. A subsequent study demonstrated that as negative mood increases, people gain greater access to illness-related memories (see also Chapter 5). It showed that, just as depressed mood may increase illness-focused thinking, so illness-focused thinking may produce or exacerbate emotional distress in a self-regulating process. Pain is just one symptom that might profitably be considered with reference to this broader finding.

In a rather different study of emotions in over 500 hospital patients with mobility handicaps, severe and painful illnesses and who had suffered mutilating accidents, Viney (1986) found that those with high levels of positive emotions were more sociable and tended to be less depressed and helpless than other subgroups. Furthermore, the most positive emotions were expressed by patients who had the most social support from their family and community, regardless of their socio-demographic features. The importance of socio-emotional factors was further underlined by the finding that relationship handicaps were significantly related to the expression of positive emotions, so that where there was less interference emotions were likely to be more positive. Thus, the ability to cope with illness seems to be closely associated with the expression of positive emotions.

Discussion in Chapter 5 points to other valuable interpretations of the relationship between cognitions, emotions and health. Taylor and Brown (1988) suggest that the ability to create certain illusions of unrealistic optimism may help people to maintain their sense of subjective well-being by allowing them to take credit for their successes and deny responsibility for their failures. This mechanism provides a self-serving bias. Furthermore, there is evidence to indicate that illusions of unrealistic optimism enable users to devote their energies to creative and productive work, to care for others, to develop satisfactory relationships and to be happy. Of the three types of illusion identified by Taylor and Brown (1988), the first draws on the locus of control idea that exaggerated misperceptions about being in control or being able to master events positively affects physical and mental health (see Chapter 4). Secondly, the tendency to see oneself as better than others using unrealistic positive self-evaluation is not just an interpersonal process, but also occurs with groups, which tend to compare themselves favourably with other similar groups (Tajfel, 1978). A third illusion represents a corollary of beliefs that what is happening right now and in the present is better than what happened in the past and, moreover, that the future will be better still.

An implication of this work is that the sub-clinical population of non-consulters, who are in pain but who do not attend for treatment, may well hold more of these illusional beliefs or hold them more strongly than those who become patients. This deserves empirical investigation. Such non-pathological illusions establish new paradigms for the provision of psychotherapy for those in pain by indicating ways to enhance and maintain a more positive emotional outlook. This positive action can be contrasted with the current tendency to concentrate on the elimination of negative emotions in therapy.

MODELS OF EMOTIONS WITH COGNITIONS

There are several important models to aid interpretation about how socio-emotional processes affect the ways in which bodily symptoms are explained. Social behaviour in the form of social comparisons can affect physiological responses to symptoms, as Cacioppo, Petty and Tassinary (1989) have shown (see also Chapter 4). Explanations provided by 54 women, who were interviewed 36 hours before treatment, for their gynaecological cancers led Cacioppo, Petty and Tassinary (1989) to suggest that signs and symptoms might be compared, in the same way that people compare their personal abilities and opinions with those of others. Symptoms and signs are evaluated in a variety of ways. They may be seen in relation to a situation that has relevant environmental features, like whether there is a virus epidemic around at the moment, or they may be evaluated with reference to contextual features, such as whether you have taken an aspirin lately. New symptoms and signs are compared with a person's own existing cognitions or thoughts on the subject; in particular with their prototypes about disease in general or particular symptoms like pain or fatigue and conditions like allergies. These comparisons serve to support a positive view of oneself and one's own physiological condition (Cacioppo, Petty and Tassinary, 1989). People seem to be motivated to maintain an explicable physiological condition and these comparisons enable them to conserve their self-esteem. Thus, the interpretation of symptoms is governed partly by rationality and partly by emotions. The rationality stems from decision making about whether the interpretation is logically consistent; that is, in showing the extent to which the symptoms compare with the illness prototype. Interpretation is affected by emotions, because the extent to which symptoms are seen to be innocuous or highly threatening will affect people's motivation to obtain an explanation about their physiological condition. The clinical importance of this model is that it explains how erroneous interpretations can occur in the search for meaning. It artfully combines social, cognitive, affective, clinical and physiological factors in a plausible interactionist package that goes some way towards explaining how people respond to bodily changes. Furthermore, as we saw in Chapter 4, such social comparisons may contribute to the way in which sick people assess their identity as individuals as well as part of a group.

Another important model integrating cognitive and affective components, proposed by Leventhal and Everhart (1979), uses pain as a prime example of the symptoms it seeks to explain. They elaborate Beecher's premise that an emotional or reactive component is added to the primary sensation of pain, once that sensation becomes sufficiently strong. Following the production of a painful experience when the physical stimulus activates the sensory–perceptual system, this sensation is — they suggest — then harnessed to memories of past injuries or illness, which give rise to emotional reactions such as fear. These emotional reactions are part of the visible response to pain and may be expressed as pain reports, cries of distress, facial expressions, autonomic reactions and so on. Leventhal and Everhart's subsequent parallel processing model incorporates orthodoxy in cognitive psychology by proposing that there is an elaboration of the stimulus between leaving the peripheral sensory system and entering the perceptual field. This is thought to take place separately but simultaneously at informational, emotional and motivational levels. Entering the perceptual field, the input is consciously filtered by attention, and from this process a focal awareness develops of the nature of the stimulus itself, the distress of pain *per se* and general distress. However, the degree of overlap between these components is debatable (Leventhal and Everhart, 1979). This parallel processing model enables us to take account of the clinical observation that emotional distress about pain is not dependent on the conscious experience of sensory pain. It implies that much of the processing of pain is preconscious, so incorporating well-established findings from cognitive psychology about how attention filters information to bring material from perception into conscious awareness.

In a perceptual-motor theory of emotion, Leventhal and Mosbach (1983) propose a hierarchical processing system, which has superseded previous versions. Here, it is acknowledged that there is interaction between specific sites of emotion like the limbic system, the thalamus and the cortex, and that emotion depends on activity in specific emotion centres of the CNS. Feedback from structures like facial muscles or skin is important in sustaining this emotion. Emotions associated with pain are assumed to be stored with perceptual schemata (see Chapter 4). This is a valuable model because it proposes a dynamic interaction of multiple factors at several levels of operation, where relations are reciprocal and feedback to subsequent behaviour is integral. It may be contrasted with more popular, but oversimplified, earlier models of unidirectional cause and effect (Bishop, 1991). Self-regulation and information processing are accepted as directly influencing people's response to threats to their health. In this model people are more realistically conceptualised as actively seeking out and processing information about their health and painful symptoms, rather than passively receiving it. Leventhal's most recent model provides an interesting framework for research into the rich interaction of social, cognitive and emotional factors associated with the expression and experience of pain. These ideas appear to have been largely ignored by pain researchers to date. Informed by clinical experience and firmly grounded in established psychological research, these models deserve systematic empirical scrutiny.

THE COMMUNICATION OF PAIN

How are emotions communicated? Pain relief is largely engaged through a variety of verbal and non-verbal signs. Hierarchical categories of vocal behaviour have been identified from observations of pain sufferers (Craig and Prkachin, 1983). At one level, the language of pain includes complaints, demands and exclamations as well as qualitative descriptions and ratings. At a second level, paralinguistic vocalisations such as crying, screaming, moaning and sighing occur. Craig and Prkachin (1983) say that verbal report tends to come into play later in the sequence of events during a painful episode, whereas other expressive channels play a more immediate role in communicating the experience. Although the communication of pain through the use of language is a theme throughout this book, in this section the focus is essentially on the non-verbal features of pain communication and their relationship to the emotions expressed. Non-verbal expressions can be categorised into facial expressions like distortion and grimacing, the non-verbal use of the limbs like the startle response and the withdrawal reflex, locomotor activities and the clutching and rubbing of painful areas. There is postural expression, with guarding and inactivity, and there are observable aspects of autonomic activity, such as blanching, flushing, panting and vomiting (Craig and Prkachin, 1983).

As mentioned in relation to Leventhal and Mosbach's model, a current hypothesis about emotions concerns the feedback from facial muscles. Here, the language and physiology of emotions come together. Are our moods more positive because we deduce from the sensory feedback from our facial muscles that we are smiling? In the case of pain, this hypothesis might explain how painful expressions could affect the sufferer's emotional experience of it. Experimental studies manipulating facial expressions have either used the technique of inducing muscle-by-muscle facial movements or have instructed participants to exaggerate or suppress naturally occurring facial movements. Cacioppo et al (1988) looked at how mild negative emotional imagery and unpleasant sensory stimuli led to more EMG activity over the brow muscle region than mild positive stimuli. This seems to occur even when it is not accompanied by significant changes in visceral activity and general facial EMG. In these conditions participants are better able to categorise their own facial expressions of surprise, disgust, sadness, fear and anger than would be expected by chance, so indicating that some forms of EMG activity could be giving continuous feedback about emotional processes that may be "too subtle or fleeting to evoke expressions observable in social interaction" (Cacioppo et al, 1988). Such findings have important implications for our understanding of the communication of emotions associated with pain.

In an investigation of painful facial expressions, Blackman (1980) is reported to have looked at the holding or hiding of expressions while experiencing acute pain from a tourniquet and to have confirmed the facial feedback hypothesis in showing that hiding painful expressions leads to lower pain than facial expressions of exaggerated pain (see Di Matteo and Friedman, 1982). After 5 minutes, subjects' thoughts about pain and their current situation became an increasingly important influence on the pain experienced. This implies that hiding or covering up pain could be a potentially useful method of pain control, and these results have been widely cited as giving broad support to some of the assumptions of cognitive behaviour therapy as currently practised.

What appears to have been largely forgotten by cognitive therapists, however, in their enthusiasm is the caveat that the method is useful "but only so long as this process is consistent with what a person is thinking about the degree and appropriateness of pain". This may help to explain variable success rates to some degree. However, a recent meta-analysis of research on this hypothesis indicates that in published experiments where facial expressions have been manipulated, their effect on self-reported emotional experience is only modest. Across all studies, facial feedback only accounted for 11.8% of the variance in self-reported mood where facial manipulation procedures had been used (Matsumoto, 1987). Although this analysis did not specifically focus on pain, it is possible to deduce that facial expressions associated with pain may be far less important in influencing emotions associated with pain than has hitherto been believed.

The use of Ekman and Friesen's (1978) Facial Action Coding System (FACS) has radically improved the methodology in this area of research. This enables the identification of individual muscle actions in the face that give rise to particular expressions. However, only 10 of the possible 44 action units described in the FACS appear to be relevant to expressions of pain, as a review of seven studies by Craig, Hyde and Patrick (1991) concluded. All recorded brow-lowering and a tightening of the eyelids to narrow the eyes in response to pain. Most observed raising the cheek, which has eye-narrowing properties, closing the eyes and blinking, raising the upper lip and parting the lips or dropping the jaw as pain-related facial action. These actions tend to be related to the severity of discomfort, the clinical syndrome being investigated and socio-demographic features, such as a person's age and sex (Craig, Hyde and Patrick, 1991). Furthermore, Prkachin (1992) has shown that many of these features persist across a range of studies on acute pain, regardless of whether electric shock, cold, pressure or ischaemia was used as a stimulus. Using factor analysis, Prkachin largely confirmed the results of Craig, Hyde and Patrick in defining a single expression that appears to "signal" the bulk of the information about pain, consisting of brow lowering, tightening and closing the eyelids and nose wrinkling or upper lip raising. Blinking is not part of this cluster, being more related to the sudden onset of pain or its early stages and sharing commonalities with the startle reflex.

Children find out in childhood which emotional reactions are appropriate to a particular occasion and when to use voluntary control to mask, suppress or express emotions. The main clues to the masking of facial expressions of pain in adults is a reduced rate of blinking and marginal lid-tightening, reflecting tension around the eyes. Craig, Hyde and Patrick (1991), however, found that the expressions of 120 low back pain sufferers who were encouraged to fake expressions during movement were no different to the real expressions obtained during orthopaedic examinations. They were almost a caricature, being more exaggerated and intensified, but not different. Faked pain thus has considerable similarities with real pain, except that the actions are greatly intensified. An equally important implication here is that there was no evidence of facial clues to deception (Craig, Hyde and Patrick, 1991). When participants were asked to suppress their facial expressions they did so with only limited success, so demonstrating how non-verbal expressions of pain are only partially under voluntary control. Ekman, Friesen and O'Sullivan (1988) confirmed broadly similar findings for smiling. They showed that smiling while lying was no different to a "truthful" smile in muscular terms, except for those smiles that also included traces of fear, disgust, contempt or sadness.

This line of research does not, then, seem to have lived up to its promise to be able to distinguish "genuine" pain sufferers from their less than truthful counterparts; it is interesting that so much reliance has been placed on these types of observational methods to date. Commenting on the assumed objectivity of these methods, Craig, Hyde and Patrick (1991) say that "People judging the emotional significance of another's action appear to assume that non-verbal behaviour is less amenable to dissimulation than self-report and weight it as more important when self-report and non-verbal behaviour are discordant" (p.162). They go on to say that it is "not necessary to attribute differences between self-report and non-verbal expression to a lack of candour or truthfulness" (p.170). Their research confirms that common reliance on non-verbal expressions is unjustified.

However, the clinical desire to obtain an "objective" measure of pain drives much of the research endeavour in this area (see also Chapter 3). Particular targets are patients with "incongruent" pain, especially in the lower back where confident diagnosis is difficult. In orthopaedic examinations incongruent pain patients showed behaviours that deviated from anatomical principles and non-organic signs. They endorsed "exaggerated" symptoms that did not conform to their anatomy or disease course, and produced exaggerated or non-anatomical drawings to illustrate their pain (Reesor and Craig, 1988). Implicit in such investigations is the argument that if we can find out what the facial expressions of organic pain patients are like, then maybe we can distinguish the malingerers. Reesor and Craig's results, however, showed a whole variety of social and physical factors that were associated with this behaviour and helped to explain it. Not only did incongruent pain patients report less perceived control and less self-efficacy during exposure to pain, they also catastrophised more, reported more affective and evaluative qualities of pain and had more restricted physical functioning. Women displayed more incongruous pain signs and there were sex differences in medication, with more women than men being prescribed diazepam. As a consequence, women were more likely to be picked out as malingering.

The social nature of pain has been particularly well exposed in this area, as we began to see in earlier chapters. Although verbal reports of pain have been shown to be sensitive, reliable and discriminating, other modes of communication are important, especially where judgements of pain by others are concerned (Prkachin, Currie and Craig, 1983). Watching others in pain significantly influences how we respond, as a series of carefully controlled experiments from Craig's laboratory has shown. Craig and Prkachin (1983) note that there is reason to believe that observers, whether formally trained or otherwise, are successful in using non-verbal cues about pain in others, although "the precise nature of the cues and the manner in which they are perceived and interpreted are not understood" (p.175). Prkachin, Currie and Craig (1983) asked 30 people to watch videos of others in pain while experiencing electric shock. One subgroup of videoed people were described as being hypersensitive as a result of having the forearm rubbed with an abrasive, others as having taken an analgesic, while a third subgroup were controls. Observers paired with tolerant models were more likely to accept more intense electric shocks themselves, so demonstrating the strength of these modelling effects, but those receiving low and medium shock intensities showed less conclusive results. It was found that the head provided the most important movement cues for communicating pain, especially movements of the eyes, eyebrows, eyelids, mouth, and forehead, while shoulders, torso and arms provided less information. The orthodox manner of tackling the study of emotions has been to try to label muscle actions in relation to observed expressions.

While Craig's group have been reluctant to attribute labels of emotion to facial actions in the absence of subjective reports, others have been less cautious. In a study of patients with temporomandibular joint disorder syndrome, Le Resche and Dworkin (1988) observed muscle actions like brow-lowering and skin-tightening around the eyes and from these actions inferred particular emotions. Without asking patients what they felt through subjective reports, the conclusion that 14 felt disgust and 9 sadness must remain a "guesstimate". As Craig and Prkachin (1983) observe, decisions about another's painful experiences are subject to recognition errors and systematic biases. For instance, some recorded facial actions do not at all coincide with the consensual view of what a painful expression should be and this could easily distort an observer's decision about whether someone is in pain, and if so which exact emotion that person might be feeling. The induction of pain quite often causes changes in facial expression, such as the pulling of lip corners and raising of the cheek. To a casual observer this might be interpreted as an embarrassed smile. This example serves to demonstrate how unreliable judgements about a patient's emotions can be; the only reliable report is that from the pain sufferer himself.

Nevertheless, it is worth noting that there are groups of people for whom non-verbal behaviours may be the only source of information about pain available to a clinician, as in the case of young children and those with communication problems. There are also people who for personal, social or cultural reasons do not report their pain (Le Resche and Dworkin, 1984). In agreement with Le Resche and Dworkin, it is clear that research in this area has hardly started to address the issues of universality or cultural differences in facial expression, nor has it looked at possibilities for masking and dissimulating expressions or variations in expression related to pain type and chronicity. Some consensus about approach may be necessary before these larger aims are achievable.

Research on how these non-verbal cues are interpreted by health professionals is still in its infancy, but this behaviour is clearly an integral component in the social dynamics of the pain consultation. In one study where videoed interviews of identical verbal content were presented to nurses with differing levels of non-verbal expressiveness, it was found that those taking part in very expressive consultations were judged to have more pain and distress than those seen in less expressive interviews. However, non-verbal expressions of pain appear to influence not only how much distress patients are seen to have, but also how this affects observers in terms of how concerned they become. Thus, not only do these non-verbal cues convey information about the patient's subjective state, they also affect the observer's emotions too, although this concern tends to be dissipated by experience. These ratings were unaffected by how nurturing observers were themselves (von Baeyer, Johnson and McMillan, 1984). More studies like this on the effects of non-verbal communication need to be carried out so that the process can be better understood.

HELPING AND BEING HELPED

Research on the medical consultation has centred on what patients say and do inside and outside the clinic or surgery. The area of compliance or adherence, for instance, is largely concerned with how the dynamics of the consultation affect future behaviours. Patients are vigilant to the cues and messages that they receive from their doctors, and physicians themselves are increasingly aware that the way in which they present themselves in clinical practice is one of the keys to the outcome of the therapeutic process. However, good empirical research that tracks the ebb and flow of discourse between pain patient and doctor, and monitors the outcomes is hard to come by. The tendency to downplay or even neglect the contribution of health professionals in shaping their patients' health beliefs, expectations and behaviour has impeded the development of understandings in pain research. While there are methodological and ethical difficulties in studying physicians and patients together, much of the existing body of patient-centred research has been founded on the erroneous assumption that physicians respond logically, reasonably and consistently at all times, managing all patients in some standard way. This position implies that the only variability in behaviour requiring scrutiny within this interaction is that of the patients themselves. Within this framework, health professionals are treated as though they were impartial observers whose own behaviour and emotions had no direct connection with, or influence on, the events inside the consulting room or the patient's behaviour afterwards. This patient-orientated research fails to take account of the human and necessarily idiosyncratic behaviour of physicians and other staff involved in treatment.

A less common approach is merely to consider the input of the helper in the consultation process. The Checklist for Interpersonal Behaviour (CHIP) provides an example of a scale that is technically competent but conceptually misguided (Vlaeyen et al, 1990). If, as its title implies, the CHIP did evaluate the interpersonal responses of patients and nurses *together*, instead of just the one-sided view of nurses, then it might have provided a more satisfactory instrument. As it stands, it measures the behaviour of only one-half of that vital interaction, and no amount of extra training in patient observation for nurses will compensate for that.

It seems more sensible to treat the consultation as a social process in which both patient and helper play different but complementary roles in health outcomes. We need to study patients and helpers together as a unit to truly make sense of why patients behave in the ways they do. At present the gestalt of the pain consultation has often been lost through mistaken attempts to piece together the separate behaviours of the participants, in the hope of understanding the whole. Different methods need to be developed to tap into the social "chemistry" occurring between people, which can not be adequately predicted by assessing them separately, using methods designed solely for individual use. This demands the more social methods developed by those who study interpersonal relations between two or more people, group dynamics and relations between groups. Studies of the pain consultation have made only limited progress to date due to a lack of awareness of methodological developments in social psychology.

Although the interaction between patient and carer is important, the influence of the health care environment must not be ignored in assessment. An interesting analysis of how the atmosphere created by the beliefs and attitudes of staff interacts with patients' health in hospitals has been provided by Taylor (1979). She proposed that the process of being admitted to hospital and the many hospital procedures and routines affect people's beliefs about being in control of their world. She describes two different emotional profiles of people's reactions to health care in institutions. She points out that passive, compliant and inanimate patients, who are labelled by hospital staff as "good patients", may in fact be exhibiting the debilitating features of learned helplessness. In contrast, the "bad patient", who is angry, demanding, suspicious and critical, could well be showing psychological reactance to loss of control over events. To summarise, "bad" patients may be reacting to lost freedoms by trying to restore them (see Chapter 5). These are not personality types, but changing styles of behaviour linked to the environment they find themselves in. Patients may oscillate between these roles periodically, but in general reactance usually precedes helplessness. The point at which reactance gives way to helplessness is not entirely understood, but there is some evidence to suggest that a period of extra uncontrollability may accelerate this process (Raps et al, 1982). Thus, the context of caring is important (see also Chapter 9).

WHO HELPS AND WHY?

In Chapter 3 we saw that the search for help with pain relief is by no means universal. Studies of help-seeking show that people are more likely to ask for help when they expect to have an opportunity to return it in a reciprocal relationship (Wills, 1992). In deciding whether to seek support people often take into account not only their own costs and rewards but also those of their potential helper, so in studies where helpers' tasks required a high level of involvement, paradoxically less help was sought, because of the perceived imbalance in the social relationship. This behaviour has been partly explained by the results of laboratory studies, in which people who asked for more help reported feeling less comfortable about asking and believed that their helper would view them as less competent as a consequence (De Paulo and Fisher, 1980). Furthermore, contrary to popular belief among health professionals, Bury (1985) found that patients seek only as much help as is compatible with maintaining their self-concept, no more. Intimacy also affects this type of self-disclosure because the most intimate relationships enable problems to be discussed at the right time and for the most appropriate action to be taken by those who care most (Wills, 1992).

Furthermore, help may be refused at any stage of the process by the help-seeker. Refusal of inpatient treatment has been estimated at about 40%, so underlining the concept of patients as active rather than passive participants in this process. Reasons for declining inpatient treatment in the USA include lack of insurance coverage, family opposition to further treatment, unwillingness to be hospitalised and transport difficulties. Acceptance and refusal rates also depend on how the samples were obtained (see Turk and Rudy, 1990). However, help-seekers may also be reacting to the individual helper, the style of helping on offer or the atmosphere in which that help is carried out, although this has not always been scrutinised. In one study those recruited to clinical trials and those who were self-referred were found to have quite different socio-demographic and personality characteristics to those referred to pain clinics by community physicians (Deyo et al, 1988). Patient perceptions of how much help will be given and what form it will take in these different contexts may differentially affect whether particular treatments or styles of treatment are pursued.

Studies of help given by untrained volunteers have looked at their motivation for helping. For the person who offers to help there is a dilemma in caring because providing love, care and support at the same time engenders dependency and neediness in those who receive it (Thompson and Pitts, 1992). This mechanism may demotivate some potential helpers. Studying those who volunteered to help people with AIDS, Snyder and Omoto (1992) recorded several reasons for wanting to help. The reasons why they helped ranged from community concern with a sense of social obligation (51%) and personal humanitarian values (88%), to the need for greater understanding (38%), the challenge of personal development (31%) and for reasons of esteem enhancement (31%). These helpers were highly nurturing and empathic and held strong beliefs in social responsibility. Similar studies might profitably be carried out on those who help pain sufferers informally.

An attributional analysis of helping behaviour assists understanding about the circumstances under which people with pain and disability are most likely to receive help from others and how their helpers explain it. Ickes and Kidd (1976) found that helping is most likely to occur when helpers are asked to do something that they are capable of doing and when they can ascribe any favourable outcomes of helping to their own ability, so they can give themselves credit for it. They also need to believe that the people they are helping are unable to help themselves and that their disadvantage is due to lack of ability, rather than any lack of effort or laziness. In the case of negative events like having pain or being disabled, helping occurs most often in situations where the helper believes that the victim was not responsible for what happened; it was unintended. It is also most likely to occur where it is believed that the situation was beyond the victim's control. Pain resulting from accidents or inherited diseases provide suitable examples. These explanations are a common and persisting feature of social interactions of all sorts. Research findings in this area imply that the level of helping given will crucially depend on the attributions helpers make about those who need help; this is true even among those whose job it is to help. For instance, someone with a painful lung cancer may find their helper less helpful than expected if the helper blames the sufferer for consuming 50 cigarettes a day over a lifetime. Furthermore, the more that ailing people are seen to be in personal control of what happened to them, the less sympathy they are likely to receive, the more feelings of disgust they invoke, and the less likely a potential helper is to judge that help is needed (Weiner, 1980). This is as true for health professionals as it is for others in the sick person's environment. There is also evidence to indicate that when helpers are in a positive mood they are more likely to be helpful in several ways. Help is more likely if the potential helper focuses their attention on their own good fortune. Helping also occurs when pleasant social events affect the helper's sense of community, so heightening their readiness to help a stranger. Happy people help more, possibly because it assists in prolonging their positive mood. Helping also occurs in circumstances where people want to avoid negative emotions, such as the guilt they might feel if they did not help (Carlson, Charlin and Miller, 1988). An implication of these findings is that the working atmosphere in institutions as well as informal health care settings contributes to the generation and maintenance of moods, which may or may not facilitate optimal and appropriate levels of helping.

Structural factors in communities and institutions also affect the predisposition to seek help. Patients tend to assume a subordinate position within the power structure when they enter the health care system by seeking help for the relief of their symptoms, and pain patients are no exception to this. Discussing the politics of pain, Sternbach (1978) compellingly describes chronic pain patients as "petitioners for aid". Waitzkin (1985) takes the view that one person's ignorance is another person's power and suggests that this problem of a power differential is compounded by uncertainty, which — as we have seen — is a common feature of chronic illness (see Chapter 4). The presence of pain appears to have the effect of accentuating any existing power differential. Controlling information may reinforce this stratification, particularly among more diffident patients, and health professionals involved in the consultation process should be trained to take account of this consciously in their dealings with patients. At its best, the consultation should empower the patient by being presented as a negotiation with a health professional about the action that needs to be taken to make that patient better.

While the control of information is a major source of power for physicians, decisions about whether, when and how best to impart information, even with the best will in the world, are far from easy. An analysis of informing cancer patients provides an illustration of some of the problems faced. Newall, Gadd and Priestman (1987) examined 14 different aspects of the knowledge and attitudes of cancer patients and found that patients in the USA and the UK were generally satisfied with the timing of the information they received. However, both looked to the authority of consultants for information in preference to junior doctors, perhaps due to the perceived seriousness of their condition. Ray, Fisher and Lindop (1984) question how much surgeons intend a woman with breast cancer to know about her own condition. They found that the style surgeons used depended on their beliefs about different types of breast cancer patient and their necessarily limited knowledge of the individual woman. Discretion is often used with the intention of protecting her from worry, but this patronising and dishonest strategy could also be misinterpreted as a conspiracy of silence. Telling the truth may unnecessarily distress patients and fails to take account of their vulnerability. Being open with some patients but not with others on the basis of their assumed coping styles involves decisions that doctors are often not sufficiently informed to make. Many surgeons refer to "feeling their way" in an attempt to anticipate a patient's reactions on the basis of their intelligence or personality. For many doctors, a pivotal factor is whether patients ask (Ray, Fisher and Lindop, 1984). Although this provides a useful clinical heuristic, it is not grounded in knowledge about the most productive styles of helping.

THE BEST DOCTORS

For those seeking help for their pain, who are the best health professionals to give that help and under what circumstances are they most able and willing to give it? To give good clinical help it is necessary to have critical levels of skill, social demand and group morale (Rachman, 1979); Kleinman (1988) says that the best doctors are those who are more interested in people than in medicine. While they are technically first-rate, they are also human, finding helping and healing rewarding work. They are able to act, while at the same time dealing with emotions, not just with thoughts. They can tolerate the uncertainty and ambiguity associated with treating chronic states. The consumer confirms that a humane and personal approach is the best. A classic study of 800 consultations in paediatric clinics by Korsch, Gozzi and Francis (1968) showed that the most satisfied patients were those who had received friendliness rather than a business-like manner from their doctor. They had consultations in which the doctor appeared to understand their concerns, seemed able to fulfil their expectations about treatment, was perceived to be a good communicator and provided sufficient information. Subsequent studies confirm the superiority of affiliative styles over dominant or active ones in generating greater satisfaction. Doctors who have good non-verbal skills show high levels of immediacy or closeness to their patients by touching them, giving plenty of eye-contact, using close bodily proximity and orientating themselves towards their patients rather than away from them. They were seen as relaxed by patients, partly because they paid particular attention to relaxing their hands, neck and limbs. They were responsive facially, and were able to adjust non-verbal aspects of speech, such as volume, in a manner appropriate to the occasion (Larsen and Smith, 1981).

What do patients expect from their doctors and are these expectations realistic? An early study of 50 doctor–patient relationships in the US found that only 14% of patients had prior convictions about what was wrong before they visited a doctor, so few had clear expectations. During the 18 months of the study, two-thirds of them developed a firm and accurate idea of their diagnosis, although around half had no accurate comprehension about their condition, beyond a name for it (Reader, Pratt and Mudd, 1957). Two-thirds of patients wanted to know whether their condition was serious, and a good physician was believed to be one who was seen to provide this information, together with knowledge about aetiology, the organs involved and the test results. A good doctor was seen to be one who was kind, understanding, interested, sympathetic and encouraging. Good doctors are also honest, sincere and willing to explain and produce results. They take time without being in a hurry, inspire confidence and tell patients just what to do. These findings have been broadly confirmed with a wide range of diagnostic groups, for example by Feinberg (1988) with arthritis patients.

Reader, Pratt and Mudd (1957) found that all patients expected to be questioned by their doctor but not all doctors know how to do this most effectively. Weinman and Higgins (1975) have suggested that doctors should be trained not so much in how they should give information and advice to people but more in how to get information out of them. Patients may withhold information for a variety of reasons, such as an irrational fear of what might be wrong with them: "a doctor must recognise that even in the end if he is an expert, his patients have (and are entitled to have) their own opinions and theories" (p.52). These opinions will profoundly affect not only what patients say about their complaint but also whether they will follow the doctor's advice. To overcome these obstructions doctors need to establish a personal rapport with their patients, ask open-ended questions so that patients are able to express their symptoms and problems in their own way, and use a more holistic psycho-social approach to examine their patients' problems, their causes and consequences (Weinman and Higgins, 1975).

To what extent does medical training foster these qualities? Observing doctors in training, Conrad (1988) describes the various ways in which medical students are taught to detach themselves from their patients. This dissociation is a coping strategy, which enables them to deal better with their own problematic areas of work like having to ask intimate questions and treat attractive patients. Despite a prevailing "ideology of concern", Conrad recorded a scarcity of humane encounters between doctors and patients. Clinical perspectives often focus more on the disease than on the person, for example referring to "the lymphoma in room 304". Usually there is little training in how to talk to patients; ignoring patients was normative in his study. In exceptional cases patients were viewed as "the enemy", especially when excessively long working hours deprived their carers of sleep. Conrad (1988) questions whether the power to diagnose and cure saps the power to care, and suggests that the way forward is to select a new breed of more humane entrants who are chosen for their caring and nurturing qualities, and who have patient-orientated values.

However, a range of social characteristics affect how patients perceive their physician's communication style. Buller and Buller (1987) found that whatever style was presented by doctors, the severity of illness affected the importance attributed to it, so style is seen to be less important if a terminal illness, for instance, is on the agenda. Secondly, the doctor's age is important; younger doctors with more affiliative styles were most favourably received by their patients. Specialty is also a factor, with obstetricians and gynaecologists being seen in the most favourable light. Lastly, the physician's communication style is most important to those who visit the doctor infrequently, and once again the most affiliative styles scored most highly. An interesting point for policy makers is that the amount of time a doctor spends talking does not in itself improve the favourability of the patient's evaluation (Buller and Buller, 1987). Patients are generally more interested in quality time than in a lengthy consultation.

How much time do doctors actually spend with their patients? In an interesting study of 326 encounters between 34 physicians and 314 patients, Waitzkin's (1985) results showed that the average consultation lasted for 16.5 minutes. However doctors typically spent only 1.3 minutes (9%) giving information and the average amount of time taken up by patients' questions was only 8 seconds (1%), although there were substantial variations in both of these figures. When physicians estimated how much time they believed they had spent giving information, they said 8.9 minutes, so overestimating the actual time by a factor of greater than six. Transmission of information was partially explained by the patient's age and education but a further important finding here was that politically liberal doctors gave more explanations, more levels of explanation and more non-discrepant responses than conservatives, which suggests that a physician's ideology and need for power significantly affect the ways in which they transmit information.

Tuckett, Boulton and Olsen (1985) have criticised studies in this area for their undue focus on the quantity of information transmitted at the expense of examining its content; patients' understandings of the consultation have barely been examined. Earlier studies collected baseline information from unreliable memories of what was said, or less commonly from direct recordings of the consultation. These methods are problematic because what a doctor believes patients to have said is not always what a third party judges them to have said. A second problem is that interpretation is difficult because valuable, relevant and significant information cannot easily be disaggregated from the rest (Tuckett, Boulton and Olsen, 1985). Previous studies estimated that between a third and a half of patients forget what they are told in consultations (Ley, 1988), although this rate appears to improve if the information given is categorised (Ley et al, 1973). Tuckett, Boulton and Olsen (1985) have developed a new qualitative method to dissect the content of consultations and, in doing so, have uncovered a high level of understandings and correctness of interpretation among patients. They found that a mere 10% of patients were un-able to recall the key points conveyed by their doctors, 7% forgot the diagnostic significance of what they were told, only 3% forgot the action or purpose of the treatment and 6% did not recall preventive action. More misinterpretations were made by patients who received diagnoses that implied that their condition could be life-threatening, maiming, stigmatising or chronically inconvenient. Misinterpreta-tions occurred more often for the less well educated, for those who had longer consultations and where an exchange of ideas between doctors and their patients appeared limited. Furthermore, this work sheds light on adherence to treatment. Tuckett, Boulton and Olsen (1985) found that 75% of patients who correctly interpreted their doctor's views were committed to their advice. Uncommitted patients tended to come from minority ethnic backgrounds, were over 60, brought children under 10 for consultation or had a consultation that involved unexplored conflicts or an inhibited exchange of ideas. These results provide a much more positive view of the patient as someone with a far better memory than was formerly appreciated. These findings are also likely to improve clinical confidence that instruc-tions provided are not largely forgotten or mislaid, and hence increase motivation to continue providing such advice in the best possible way.

In practice clinicians sometimes do not know what judgements need to be made or what information they need to obtain to reach a decision. Looking at on-the-job experience and decision making by clinicians in the mental health field, Garb (1989) identified two reasons why doctors may have trouble learning. Firstly, some of the feedback they receive from patients is misleading or flawed, and obtaining accurate information may be beyond their control in some cases. The second point is about the all too human nature of cognitive processing. Clinicians may not test the right hypotheses, they have fallible memories and there is a tendency to use hindsight bias. To improve cognitive processing, Garb suggests that doctors could be trained to be more open to alternative hypotheses and to be more prepared to reverse their initial impressions of patients. It would also be productive to dispel the common professional expectation that with hindsight all of a patient's behaviour should be explicable, because there will inevitably be some frustrating examples where this is not possible.

A full medical training is not the only answer to helping the sick, however. There is growing evidence that para-professionals may achieve clinical outcomes that are equal to, and in some cases significantly better than, those obtained by health care professionals. From a meta-analysis of 154 comparisons of professional and para-professional helpers reported in 39 studies, Hattie, Sharpley and Rogers (1984) concluded that para-professionals were effective additions to the health service, particularly when they are experienced. Health care from the physician extender occupations such as nurse practitioner and physician assistant is seen as an integral, desirable and complementary part of the multidisciplinary team. Interviews with 1621 physicians showed that they believed that the skills of physician extenders were best employed in the limited area of improving access to medical care, particularly for the urban poor (Ferraro and Southerland, 1989). Cross-cultural examples from health care systems in Tanzania, Zimbabwe and China demonstrate how effective well-qualified physician extenders can be and provide inspiration for alternative methods of organisation. There are also qualitative reports suggesting that for patients receiving treatment in Canadian pain centres, the most effective consultations are likely to be those where psychologists agree with the physician about the nature of the condition and style of treatment than where they do not agree. Once again, a parallel rather than a subordinate role between the two appears to be the key to successful outcomes (von Baeyer and Genest, 1985).

HELP THROUGH SOCIAL SUPPORT

So far comments have been confined to obtaining help from designated individuals in formal health care teams, but what contribution can families and other people make? Social support has been defined as any input directly provided by another person or group, which moves recipients towards the goals they desire (Suls, 1982). Support can come from a wide variety of sources; these include a spouse or partner, children, other family members, friends, professional care-givers, social groups, communities and other support groups. It is not only "real" people who are seen to provide this support, but divine and symbolic relationships also positively affect feelings of well-being (Pollner, 1989). Four principal types of social support have been identified. The first is emotional concern or liking, love or empathy, which is sometimes represented by listening and concern. Secondly, social support can take the form of instrumental aid, goods or services like money or labour. Thirdly, it may be informational support, perhaps in the form of advice and often about the environment. Lastly, it may take the form of appraisals, so providing information that better facilitates self-evaluation. This process includes affirmation, feedback and social comparisons (Thompson and Pitts, 1992).

Social networks provide community support, in contrast to the interpersonal forms of social support mentioned above. Networks can engender a greater sense of social integration or community. They serve a different function to qualitative support because they provide the knowledge that in times of stress others are able to help with coping. Social networks provide people with more self-esteem, more positive emotions and greater feelings of control over their environment (Rodin and Salovey, 1989). This community aspect of social support shares something in common with the sense of belonging arising from a shared positive social identity outlined in Chapter 4, and gives further support to the proposal that pain, illness and well-being need serious investigation at this higher order level of social analysis. This idea is captured elegantly in the following position statement on the concept of social support:

> Some have viewed social support as a "magic bullet" of social inoculation without fully appreciating just what ingredients of the gross phenomenon are at work. Support has sometimes been considered a set of connections, the embeddedness of individuals in a network of ties, expectations and responsibilities ... also an exchange of specific advice or of tangibles, such as physical or economic assistance ... has been viewed as a subjective phenomenon, not to be assessed by the number of connections or even by the quality of supportive exchange offered but rather as a belonging or perhaps a general positive orientation to one's network.
> (Pilisuk, Boylan and Acredolo, 1987)

However, the influence of social networks can also be negative, as reflected by personal beliefs that the network is more a source of danger and insecurity than protection and support. An example is feeling "let down" and disappointed by those you trust (Pilisuk, Boylan and Acredolo, 1987).

Although the function of social support is to reduce distress, Taylor et al (1986) say that there is equivocal evidence that support may also reduce the likelihood of serious illness. For instance, quality social support is a good predictor of functioning in women with arthritis and has been shown to have the effect of counteracting their depression (Goodnow, Reisine and Grady, 1990). There has also been debate about whether social support is able to prevent the prolongation and worsening of symptoms, and here conclusions are equivocal. Although there is general consensus that social support relieves psychological distress during a crisis, there are two schools of thought about whether this mechanism works in a direct or an indirect way, as there is some evidence to support each view. The direct effects hypothesis claims that social support is beneficial during non-stressful times, as well as during stressful periods in a person's life. Being able to turn to others for support appears to mitigate the effects of misfortunes and is known to attenuate the links between adversity and the development of psychological disorders, at least (Alloway and Bebbington, 1987). In contrast, the buffering hypothesis suggests that the benefits to mental and physical health are most apparent during periods of high distress, so support acts as a sort of reserve that dulls or blunts the effects of stress, so enabling people to cope better. The buffering model better accounts for the onset of illness. It is not clear whether low social support adds to adversity or whether the two act independently on the rate of the disorder in some multiplicative way. A restricted model of buffering offered by Alloway and Bebbington (1987) suggests that exposure to adversity is more likely to result in a disorder if social support is not forthcoming. The onset and persistence of pain provides a suitable example of such adversity.

The characteristics of the best social support groups are small size, involving face-to-face interaction and where emphasis is placed on personal participation. Attendance needs to be voluntary. There must be an acknowledged purpose in coming together, such as needing to solve a problem or cope with a handicap, pain or a particular illness. Last but not least is the importance of providing emotional support (Katz and Bender, 1976). When patients are recruited to pain management courses they often believe that such courses are the last stop at the end of a long line of treatment and may therefore feel obliged or even coerced by the system into participating. In being accepted onto the programme patients agree to attend all social support groups; this may prove to have been a misguided policy. As the stability of social support is also important to health status (Vinokur, Schul and Caplan, 1987), social support groups concerned with pain control should be encouraged and enabled to continue with regular meetings long after the pain management course is completed.

So who wants to join a social support group? In one study, some cancer patients reported high levels of support from their own social groups following diagnosis, some felt very isolated, often because of rejection, while others who appeared to be receiving support were not obtaining the most appropriate style of support that they might have wished for from their family, friends or medical care-givers (Taylor et al, 1986). This disaggregation enables us to better understand why only some people want and need to join. Taylor, Lichtman and Wood (1984) found that only 10% of breast cancer patients from a private practice in the USA wanted to participate. Those who attended tended to be white and from the higher socio-economic groups. In general, men and those from lower status groups do not wish to attend such groups. Furthermore, attenders tend to be more active in obtaining social support of all kinds than non-attenders. Taylor et al (1986) found that attenders were more likely to have consulted a mental health professional about their cancer or about other problems, to have read books to solve their problems and to have been involved in a previous support group for other reasons. However, attenders were no more psychologically distressed than non-attenders — more the reverse — but they were more concerned about their cancer and cancer-related issues in this study. Provocatively, Taylor et al (1986) question whether social support groups encourage people to make "a mountain out of a molehill" or whether the group is in fact helping them to solve their problems.

One aspect of social support is that it brings people into contact with others who are similar to themselves on some important dimension, like a shared problem or diagnosis. Medvene (1992) has examined this need for contact with similar others by looking at self-help groups, which are relatively homogeneous for problem type. He questions whether "misery loves miserable company". Although similarity among group members commonly leads to attraction and liking, Medvene observes that people may not want to meet those who are experientially similar, if they share a negative stereotype that will further stigmatise them through this contact, like being labelled as disabled. Downward social comparison processes are particularly important in making these judgements, as we saw in Chapter 4. The implications of social psychology for pain management here is that while self-help groups may generate increased well-being for many self-selected chronic pain patients, the terms of setting up the groups need to be considered carefully within their social and cultural context so that fears of stigmatisation can be avoided. Setting up social support groups for cancer patients in Greece, for example, is likely to be highly problematic as a result of the widespread cultural norms of secrecy, fear and stigmatisation surrounding the disease.

How does this type of interaction affect health outcomes, especially where pain is involved? A study carried out during the Yom Kippur War showed that the way in which burns patients reacted to injury when sharing a crisis or problem with others was influenced by a number of contextual factors. These were the history of the trauma, marital status, and their knowledge of what had happened to the rest of the group of soldiers, such as guilt feelings associated with the group's fate (Solnit and Priel, 1975). Consequently, the information shared may not always be beneficial to health outcomes. While Suls (1982) observes that social support may have a possible preventive role in reducing uncertainty and worry, setting a good example, enabling problems to be shared, presenting a calming model and providing distraction, at its most negative and unhelpful, the interaction can increase uncertainty, set bad examples and create new problems. At a coping level, the best social support provides a positive rather than a negative label, gives sympathy rather than irritation and resentment and presents helpful, not misleading, information. In recovery good social support maintains rather than discourages a course of treatment, provides incentives rather than depressants to restore health and fosters the desire to stop being a nuisance rather than creating a power or dependency need.

Not enough is known, however, about social situations that have the most harmful effects or about which helpful behaviours are seen to be the most satisfying. In a study of 103 women with rheumatoid arthritis and their husbands, Manne and Zautra (1989) found that both positive and negative aspects of a patient's relationship with her spouse were important in their adaptation to illness. Positive support from the husband was helpful because it gave assistance with cognitive restructuring and information seeking. Where spouses were critical, on the other hand, this encouraged ineffective and, at worst, harmful coping strategies such as wishful thinking about a cure and fantasising. Dunkel-Schetter et al (1992) have identified two principal types of unhelpful support. Firstly, any advice that conveys the message that the recipient is seen negatively is likely to be counterproductive, such as blaming the sufferer for their condition or viewing them as incompetent or a failure. The second type of unhelpfulness arises from over-involvement with the sufferer. Here intrusive, undue concern and excessively solicitous behaviour were found to be damaging to the recovery of stroke victims. Studies of cancer patients show that where they receive a message that minimises and trivialises the cancer, this has the unhelpful effect of clamping down further communications by causing the topic to be changed and discouraging desired discussion (Dunkel-Schetter et al, 1992).

What is the effect of a chronic problem like pain on the patient's spouse? Because "no man is an island", the well-being of significant others is likely to be affected by the constant and regular care they provide to those with pain and disability. It therefore seems reasonable to assume that through a feedback loop this may, in turn, affect the behaviour and well-being of the patients themselves. The consensus is that spouses of those who are chronically ill experience considerable distress, too (Thompson and Pitts, 1992). More specifically, spouses of low back pain patients often find that their relationship with their partner and the level of interpersonal conflict and distress in the family is markedly affected by the debilitating effects of this chronic illness (Feuerstein, Salt and Houle, 1985). In a longitudinal study of 143 families with a cancer patient, significant others experienced substantial distress up to a year after the diagnosis (Eli et al, 1988). Two vulnerable groups were identified: those who had poor functioning initially and remained that way, and those whose mental status declined over the period. Eli et al (1988) found no evidence to support the hypothesis that the psychological adaptation of significant others would improve over time.

It is frequently reported that spouses of chronic pain patients are depressed; fear about their partner's health, guilt, anger, frustration and resentment are common, and may all contribute to this negative mood. In one study patients' pain intensity, spouses' emotional reaction to it, their anger and their satisfaction with the marital relationship together accounted for 35% of the variation in spouses' depression scores in explaining the relationship between pain and depression (Schwartz et al, 1991). Even patients with moderate pain were found to have spouses with clinically significant depression in this study. This raises questions about how well spouses are able to help their partners within this self-perpetuating cycle of mutual helplessness. It also reinforces the need for more family therapy to dispel this interactive mood of dysphoria.

Having an arthritis patient in a family provides a suitable illustration of a typical pattern of the dynamics of family care for those with a long-term painful disease. Although women provide almost all of the assistance to their disabled husbands, husbands of disabled women tend to share the care with their daughters (Bury, 1985). Sons may make a limited contribution where heavy domestic work is essential. Loss of employment due to illness and disability has profound effects on family life (Yelin, Henke and Epstein, 1987), but disabled homemakers have problems too, only different ones. It may not be possible for them to perform the nurturing and instrumental functions associated with the role of homemaker (Reisine, Goodenow and Grady, 1987). Although there are considerable social and cultural variations in expectations about what homemakers should do, Reisine, Goodenow and Grady found that in general the more responsibility a woman took for the main work of cleaning, shopping and cooking, the more satisfied she was with her role, irrespective of whether she was in paid employment.

How the unaffected partner handles difficult emotional reactions tends to affect the marriage. It is worth considering whether a good marriage can improve if the couple join forces in facing a common crisis, but the evidence for this is so far inconclusive. In some diagnostic groups like myofascial disorder and arthritis, levels of pain have been shown to be directly related to the amount of conflict in the family, but not always in the expected direction. For instance, Faucett and Levine (1991) found that the more conflict reported by families of arthritis patients, the less affective pain they recorded. They speculated that this might be because some spouses gave social support by trying to keep the tension levels down during a "flare" in the belief that it helps to control their partner's pain. The social context in which the support is given therefore appears to be as important to the interpretation of research in this area as the quantity and quality of the support itself.

SOCIO-EMOTIONAL ASPECTS OF PAIN TREATMENT: TWO EXAMPLES

Two areas of treatment throw additional light on the socio-emotional aspects of pain. The first example concerns the treatment of children, while the second examines how treatment is carried out in burns units. In previous sections we considered social interactions between health professionals and their patients. Here many investigations have tended to limit the focus to two people, but the practicalities and ethics of caring for sick children inevitably mean that parents must be involved. This necessity therefore provides the opportunity for a social analysis of the dynamics of pain treatment where more than two people are included. It is easy to forget that the treatment of adults involves more than two people, as key family members and friends may directly or indirectly influence the patient's interpretation of and reaction to advice and treatment. However, in the treatment of children these multiple interactions cannot be ignored, which enables us to consider the person in pain within the inherently complex social environment. The example of the burns unit has been chosen because it provides an example of a situation where strong emotions are often evoked in carers and patients during the course of treatment, which can profoundly affect the well-being of all parties concerned.

The two-way communication of anxiety and distress between parent and child is a highly complex phenomenon and a process that is barely understood in health settings. Investigating this interaction during venipuncture, Jacobsen et al (1990) identified age, venous access and the parent's expectations of cooperation as the most important factors affecting a child's distress. Those children who were most distressed by the procedure were younger, with poor venous access, who also had parents who were expecting uncooperative behaviour. Distractions such as using a party blower were less successful in reducing distress than explanations delivered well in advance of the procedure, at a time when the child was receptive. The type of information provided to the child needs to be accurate and intelligible, involving a simple description of the procedure, why it is being carried out and what happens to the blood collected. Briefly noticeable pain that is not unbearable should be described, with the emphasis on relaxing the arm and cooperation to decrease the pain (Harrison, 1991). The organisation of the clinic also needs to be taken into account. Distressed children who are witnessed leaving the clinic by other waiting children may create poor expectations and generate fear and alarm in the waiting room. Harrison reported that her convenience sample (i.e. not a random sample) of "prepared" children who had a story read to them experienced less pain and fear, according to their parents, than unprepared children. It seems that 40% of her sample had been "threatened" with a visit to the doctor. This unexpected finding provides a warning to researchers about the vital importance of assessing results within their broader social and cultural context.

Results from Jacobsen et al's (1990) study together with those from a prospective survey of 227 children and adolescents (Fradet et al, 1990) underscore the predictive importance of asking parents to say how upsetting or distressing their child will judge needle procedures to be. From this simple social communication, children with the highest risk of responding poorly may be identified in advance for the selective use of a local anaesthetic cream, the Eutectic Mixture of Local Anaesthetic (EMLA) cream, which needs to be applied an hour before the procedure begins. However, it should not be assumed that the most distressed children consistently have the most anxious parents. Positive, non-anxious parents quite often have highly distressed children. At the other extreme there are parents who do not reassure their children; in the worst case, their presence may paradoxically reduce the child's cooperation and control and increase anxiety (Broome and Endsley, 1989). A major challenge for health psychology is to identify more accurately these differing styles of child–parent communication in advance.

High levels of distress and eventual helplessness are often reported in situations where children need to be restrained before treatment can be performed (Beales, 1982). This reaction to a potentially frightening and painful procedure can take an emotional toll, not only on the patients and their parents but also on the nurses who perform these procedures. This response to work stress is reflected in the high turnover of staff in these units. Manne et al (1990) used a behavioural intervention package with 23 children who required restraint for venipuncture. It contained the four components of attentional distraction, substitution of an incompatible positive response for an undesirable behaviour, positive reinforcement and parental involvement. They found significant reductions in the parent's distress and the parent's ratings of the child's distress. Although they also observed less distress in the children, the children's assessment of their own distress and the venipuncturist's ratings were not affected. They suggest that reduced parental anxiety was due to an increased sense of control, which helped parents to overcome some of the emotional aversiveness of the situation. As parents' ratings inevitably involve their own feelings and coping strategies, their ratings are no substitute for the child's own view.

Factors have been identified that tend to increase anxiety, fear and the anticipation of pain among children being treated in a burns unit. Beales (1982) found that expectations of pain may be reduced by correcting a child's erroneous beliefs about the nature of the healing process and the role of therapy. They are also affected by improving understandings about the manner in which treatment and nursing procedures are conducted. Some therapeutic actions seem threatening to children. The over fives often see the pain caused by movement of a limb as interfering with healing and for this reason they are likely to resist it. Because bandages put injury out of sight and out of mind, their removal may be resisted because this obliges the child to confront the damage, which makes the injury seem not only more serious but also more painful. Beales (1982) says that the purpose of all procedures should be explained in advance, not during the procedure when anxiety levels are already high.

Drawing on developmental knowledge about the way in which children view their health, Beales makes some valuable proposals for practice. Below the age of about seven, magical explanations will need to be used: "Burns unit personnel have to be prepared to present themselves as fairy godmothers, the drugs they administer as magic potions and the procedures they administer as magical performances". Furthermore, allowing children to lend a hand during procedures like wound cleansing and applying dressings puts them more in control and involves them. If it proves impossible to use these procedures, then distraction should be used so that preparations are hidden, the damaged site is removed from view and staff conversations are curtailed. Any distraction needs to start well in advance of disturbance of the injury, using music, audiotaped stories and so on.

There seems to be little agreement among researchers about the accuracy with which health professionals are able to assess a patient's pain, and this is also true for children who are patients. One reason why these estimates are so unreliable is because it is difficult to be precise about exactly what many behaviours mean (Van der Does, 1989). Here we run into the same problem confronting those who study facial actions. For instance, there are at least three interpretations of the behaviour of a screaming child during wound cleansing on a burns unit. The most automatic assumption is that it is an expression of severe pain, but screaming could also plausibly be related to the anxiety or fear of pain, or it could serve as an attempt to distract attention away from that pain. With insight, Van der Does (1989) observes that in different patients it is difficult, if not impossible, to distinguish one type of screaming from another.

The burns unit represents *par excellence* a cameo of socio-emotional dynamics, where relations between staff and pain patients can be highly charged. It provides a prime example of the dual and paradoxical role of nurses as providers of pain relief and pain inflictors, although many nursing duties involve both of these features to a lesser extent. The tubbing, dressing changes, debridement, physiotherapy and skin grafts essential for good healing create pain additional to that of the original damage (Fagerhaugh, 1974). Fagerhaugh notes that many burns unit staff take the view that "the staff know what's best". They see the infliction of pain as crucial to a patient's recovery and, because of this, the interpersonal relationship between nurses and their patients can be emotional. This dual role can create a high level of distress and internal conflict for carers. The anxiety, depression and feelings of guilt and helplessness commonly reported by nurses working on burns units must necessarily in turn affect their judgements of a patient's pain and suffering.

These studies demonstrate how an atmosphere that reflects a high level of emotion affects not only staff perceptions but their behaviour in administering pain relief. Emotional burn-out in nursing is well documented (e.g. Llewellyn, 1984). Nurses working with burns patients represent one extreme of a continuum of emotionally-loaded situations faced by all nurses when caring for their patients. This analysis would explain the unreliable results reported earlier where rational judgement is affected by emotional overlay. In a study of staff and patients in a burns unit, Choinière et al (1990) reported significant, though small, correlations between nurse and patient ratings. Nurses correctly estimated the amount of pain in only 30% of cases, and pain was frequently overestimated (27%) or underestimated (30%). The number of years they had worked on the unit was the biggest guide to their behaviour. Relatively inexperienced nurses (less than 6 months) were more likely to overestimate pain than nurses with more than two years' experience, who tended to underestimate it. These estimates subsequently affect their behaviour; Fagerhaugh (1974) and Perry and Heidrich (1982) have commented on the tendency among staff to administer decreasing amounts of narcotics the longer they continued to work with burns patients.

A survey of practice in 151 burns units by Perry and Heidrich (1982) showed that none of the medical and nursing staff believed that procedures like tanking, which were performed in 96% of units, caused excruciating pain. Most thought the pain would be moderate. Those who estimated the pain of tanking as most severe after analgesia gave significantly higher doses of narcotics beforehand. They also found that workers in smaller units tended to use more psychotropic drugs, while those in larger units used more narcotics like morphine, but there were huge variations in the amount and potency of analgesic used. While the vigour of debridement varies too, staff were reluctant to assume that differences in comfort, support and the vigour of the procedure could account for this enormous variation in narcotic use. These findings have interesting implications for staff training.

Inevitably, this situation is the result of a dynamic interaction between the behaviour of the staff and their patients. Burns patients who suffer the most behave stoically, are reluctant to disturb the nurses, are too proud to admit their pain, are afraid of long-term drug addiction and erroneously rely on the nurse's expertise and professionalism to administer an adequate dose. Education for staff and patients, together with the careful and systematic introduction of patient-controlled analgesia (PCA) machines, could overcome the majority of these problems (Choinière et al, 1990).

SOCIAL ASPECTS OF ADMINISTERING PAIN RELIEF

How much does pain need to be relieved and what pain relief do patients obtain? In a study of 454 medical and surgical inpatients by Donovan, Dillon and McGuire (1987), it was found that 79% had experienced pain during their time in hospital. However, less than half of these had a member of the health care team ask about their pain. In only 49% of cases was progress in pain relief charted. Furthermore, the average amount of analgesic given was less than a quarter of the average amount prescribed, even though there was some correlation between drugs that were ordered and those that were administered.

There are many different reasons why patients may not get sufficient pain relief; these can be pharmacological, structural or psychosocial. Pharmacological reasons cover poor prescribing practices and insufficient pharmacological knowledge, especially about narcotics. The drug may not be given often enough or may not last until the next dose. There may be undue concern about the risk of respiratory depression. Structural reasons include insufficient staffing to meet the complete needs of patients on a ward. There may be psychosocial reasons, such as the staff not noticing that a patient is in pain, not caring enough or allowing routine procedures to take precedence over their patients' needs (Macrae, 1991). They may have fears about overuse, abuse and addiction or unrealistic ideas about how much people should suffer for a given amount of trauma. They may lack self-experience with pain and the sequelae (Bingle et al, 1991; Fagerhaugh, 1974). Below, we concentrate on the psychosocial reasons.

One way to begin to understand how this phenomenon happens is to look at the beliefs and behaviour of health professionals. Eminent pain specialists observed the following attitudes among hospital staff in interviews by Winn (1991). Some believed that pain was not important because it is not life-threatening; they were inclined to see pain relief as a luxury and a low priority. Because of their pain, patients may be more reluctant to get out of bed and are therefore more susceptible to deep vein thrombosis. Slow breathing due to pain can increase the likelihood of chest infection, so there are serious consequences to ignoring a person's pain; others were mentioned earlier in this chapter. The second attitude commonly encountered is the authoritative posture of "doctor (or nurse) knows best". As a result, some patients believe that they are being "wimpish" if they ask for relief; others become highly anxious when their request for relief is ignored, and this can have knock-on negative physiological effects on recovery. Under these circumstances they may feel obliged to exaggerate their pain, which in turn makes the nurses think that the pain could not be so bad and increases the likelihood they will withhold relief altogether. The third attitude ignores individual differences in personality and circumstances by assuming that "one dose suits all". As the peak of effectiveness varies widely between 10 and 90 minutes after administration, this accounts for the need for considerable variation in the timing of a subsequent dose. Lastly, there is a widespread belief that a patient who is quiet cannot be in pain, because the physical signs of pain are commonly used to assess its severity. It is easily forgotten that quiet withdrawal is a classic sign of severe pain (Winn, 1991).

Donovan, Dillon and McGuire (1987) provide evidence to challenge common beliefs held by health professionals about pain and pain relief, and these are considered below. Many professionals believe that patients in pain make certain that the staff know they hurt. However, they found that when asked directly, some patients did not admit to pain initially. Indeed, for almost half of these patients, the staff had no evidence that they *were* in pain, so the pain itself and the distress associated with pain is not always communicated to carers. Where distress is visible, how does it affect carers' behaviour towards their patients and any action in supplying pain relief? In a study of 50 registered nurses (90% women) working on surgery, medical and intensive or coronary care wards, Dudley and Holm (1984) found that nurses were more likely to infer distress than pain in their patients. They concluded that this tendency to devalue the pain and to put it down to distress could lead to substantial problems in the efficient management of pain medication. Donovan, Dillon and McGuire also investigated the validity of the belief that patients who sleep do not feel pain. They found that while patients with mild pain sometimes had their sleep interrupted, others with moderate or severe pain did not wake. In fact, only 61% of patients in pain were awakened by their pain or prevented from sleeping. This represents a further aspect of how the complex behaviour of quiescent patients confounds staff beliefs, and further reinforces the need for staff to ask directly and repeatedly about pain rather than trying to infer it from observations. There is also a popular belief that pain is generally well controlled in hospitals, but 58% of patients reported excruciating or horrible pain at some stage during their stay; for 7% this was present at the time they were interviewed (Donovan, Dillon and McGuire, 1987). Furthermore, Winefield et al (1990) found that the complete relief of pain was a goal for only 18% of doctors and 32% of nurses, and doctors were more likely to relieve pain until the patient was "comfortable" than the nurses. Methods of encouraging patients to ask for more and better pain relief are patently needed here.

Set against this need to facilitate patient requests are staff beliefs that patients take too many analgesics. However, Donovan, Dillon and McGuire (1987) showed that the average daily intake of analgesic was not large, being equivalent to 12.4 mg of morphine, with the median dose equivalent to only 6 mg. As we noted in Chapter 4, alert and informed patients take smaller doses of analgesic from a PCA machine than when they obtain relief from a nurse, while remaining comfortable and in control. The use of PCA machines simultaneously improves the service and removes the power differential between patients and staff; loss of control may threaten professional identities and consequently create a major impediment to rapidly implementing changes in the way that post-operative pain relief is provided to patients. But do patients want greater control? It seems that they do. In one study, a substantial 37% reported that they would have liked more control over their own pain relief, and 56% of patients said that they thought patients should decide about when to receive more pain killers (Winefield et al, 1990). There are many doctors and nurses working on surgery wards who would agree with this (Lavies et al, 1992).

Pain relief may also depend on the confidence of the doctor in the treatment being advocated (see also Chapter 9). Research into decisions made by consultants treating pain patients indicates that there is little consensus about the best ways to relieve chronic pain over a wide range of conditions, including the surgical procedures of cordotomy, rhizotomy and neurectomy, sympathetic nerve blocks and psychological therapies (Davies et al, 1991). The diversity of opinion among 181 specialists could not be accounted for either by their years of experience or by how often they saw patients with chronic nerve damage. In terms of social interaction, it seems likely that this lack of confidence and generalised uncertainty about success is transmitted to patients via non-verbal cues during the consultation and treatment period. However, over-confidence is also misplaced because failure to relieve pain in the long term results in patient disillusion and further management problems. More work on successful middle-of-the-road styles of pain patient management are urgently needed.

To what extent do physicians with different specialisms agree about pain? Tearnan and Dar (1986) asked 193 doctors from a wide range of specialties to rate acute and chronic neurogenic, joint, bone and myofascial syndromes. Only weak agreement was reached on the ratings of descriptors within syndromes, but these judgements were unaffected by specialty, experience with pain patients or amount of specialised training in pain. The diagnostic utility of pain descriptors was rated more highly for acutely ill patients than the chronically ill, with acute pain being seen as more intensely painful and having greater interference with mood. Tearman and Dar observe that these judgements may well reflect stereotypes taught in training rather than the reality of pain. If so, this raises questions about how physicians' contact with patients is affected as well as their usage of information and their approach to pain relief.

Other studies have looked at the extent to which doctors' interests affect whether patients receive the most appropriate treatment. In a study in the USA, the treatment of patients from 100 pain clinics was assessed. It was found that the chances of a patient receiving a nerve block were around seven times higher if the clinic was directed by an anaesthetist than a non-anaesthetist. So doctors' specialties predispose them to prescribe those types of treatment with which they are most familiar and, presumably, confident (Khoury and Varga, 1988). It is not surprising that health professionals prescribe treatments learned during their training, but this predilection may not turn out to be the most appropriate treatment for their patients' conditions, so successful outcomes become something of a gamble. Awareness of such personal biases, as well as substantial training in other techniques, and awareness of the skills of an integrated multidisciplinary team need to be built into the continuing education of those who work with pain patients.

Giving analgesic can also be affected by whether health professionals are actively carrying out the procedure or passively observing the patient afterwards. In a study of women in pain from suction and curettage abortion, Belanger, Melzack and Lanzon (1989) reported that nurses underestimated their patients' discomfort during the procedure but were much more accurate afterwards. This indicates that staff need to be aware that when their attention is focused on carrying out unpleasant procedures, their patients may be suffering more than they believe simply because they do not have the spare capacity to carry out careful observations at that time. They need to make appropriate allowance for this in analgesic terms by giving compensating premedication.

In the study of Choinière et al (1990), nurses were found to have overestimated the success of analgesia in 46% of cases, but in a startling 25% of cases no analgesic at all had been given. This is just one of several studies showing that health professionals as a group are poor judges of other people's pain, although there is some individual variation. Hodgkins, Albert and Daltroy (1985) found that prior to a procedure patients were better able to predict the pain of needle aspiration and/or the injection of soft tissue or joints than their physician. However, physicians substantially improved their estimates of pain by observing the procedure. Experienced patients are also better at predicting their own pain level. The prevailing view is that proxies in general tend to under-report not just symptoms but also conditions and the utilisation of services. To some extent, the closer you are to the sufferer, the better the estimates of pain become, but this also needs qualification. A study of the next-of-kin of 42 cancer patients by O'Brien and Francis (1988) showed that while patient and family members largely agreed about whether the patient was in pain, there was far less consensus about the frequency and duration of the pain, and about its qualities. In this situation a high level of emotionality may exaggerate existing discrepancies.

Related to estimates about the efficacy of analgesia are beliefs about different types of analgesic. The view that interventions other than narcotics are effective only for mild pain is widespread, but Donovan, Dillon and McGuire (1987) showed that non-pharmacological treatments were effective in between a third and a half of all patients, and were more likely to be effective for moderate pain than for pain that was mild or severe. There are also different levels of knowledge about analgesic techniques. In the study by Lavies et al (1992), it was found that doctors and nurses had similar experience of alternative analgesic techniques. The figures showed that 93% of interns and registrars in this Australian study of cholecystectomy surgery had experience of intravenous infusions, 63% of epidural local anaesthetic, 34% of epidural opioids, 26% of PCA use and 24% of subcutaneous infusions. Of equal interest was the finding that those who had experience of these alternatives also had greater awareness and understanding about analgesia, as judged from their replies to questionnaires. It was they who believed that patients should be more in control of their own pain relief, saw risk of addiction as less than 1% and so on. Lavies et al (1992) recommend that more education in these alternatives should be provided for hospital staff, with the aim of increasing their awareness about the complexities of providing good analgesic relief.

Lavies et al (1992) point out that the basis for staff concern about addiction is negligible, as the incidence has been estimated at less than 1 in 3000 patients. Children are particularly vulnerable to inadequate pain relief as a result of fears about addiction. Although the prescribing patterns of medical staff are not uniform, Mather and Mackie (1983) estimated that in 40% of paediatric surgery cases the major drugs ordered were not given; this was particularly true for children receiving ear, nose and throat surgery and plastic surgery, when non-narcotics like paracetamol tended to be substituted by nurses. Many of the children they surveyed became withdrawn as a result of the pain. They reported that these attitudes were widespread at all levels of the health care system.

Where babies are concerned, a survey of paediatric anaesthetists' perceptions of neonatal pain by Purcell-Jones, Dormon and Sumner (1988) found that 30% believed that babies under a week old do not feel pain, or said that they did not know. This proportion dropped to 15% for babies between one week and one month old and to 0% after a month. Even though older babies were assumed to feel pain, they were often not given any form of analgesia post-operatively, even following major surgery. Of the anaesthetists who believed that babies *do* feel pain, many were concerned about the use of potent analgesics because of the possibility of respiratory depression. This survey showed that anaesthetists believed that the danger of prescribing opioids far outweighed its possible clinical advantages. Paradoxically, the checking of breath, which is a characteristic non-verbal cue to pain, at the same time interrupts the respiratory pattern and hence is more likely to deter an anaesthetist from giving a potent analgesic to that baby than to encourage them to administer a pain killer. Despite this widespread concern, none of these anaesthetists reported any serious consequences in those to whom they had given opioids, suggesting that such fears were disproportionate to the actual risk. Other studies have shown that nurses, too, are profoundly concerned about this serious complication. Furthermore, their anxiety is increased because staff shortages make the close monitoring of patients necessary to prevent this from happening particularly taxing.

The study showed that anaesthetists sometimes presume that the level of pain they observe does not warrant opioid use, so safer drugs like paracetamol or aspirin may well be substituted. They may also believe that none of the drugs available are effective for the very young. Professional updating to inform health professional about neurophysiological research in neonates and pharmacological advances seems essential in changing attitudes here. Purcell-Jones, Dormon and Sumner (1988) also recommend the greater use of regional anaesthesia, caudal block and simple wound infiltration at the end of an operation.

One of the values of Winefield et al's (1990) study was that it investigated doctors' beliefs together with those of their patients. The study showed that 82% of doctors believed that they had been inadequately trained in pain control; juniors were especially dissatisfied. Only a third of doctors and nurses in this study believed that pain control in hospital was good, contrary to the claim of Donovan, Dormon and Sumner. Therefore, the proposals for pain training published by the International Association for the Study of Pain (Pilowsky, 1988) should be an important vehicle for remedying this omission in the curriculum. An evaluation of medical students prior to participation in a six-hour course on pain over a two-week period showed that they overestimated the number of people with acute and chronic pain problems, the percentage addicted to narcotics and the number of children who would react to painful investigations. Although all of these assessments became more accurate and appropriate after the course, students were able to recall very little of this information with accuracy five months later (Wilson et al, 1992). Such findings draw to our attention the fact that few of those entering medical school have any personal experience of pain or academic knowledge of it, and hence the need for introducing it into the undergraduate curriculum.

Other recent recommendations for changing behaviour have included the introduction of a simple pain measure or scoring system on surgery wards, which could be used by patients and staff alike to keep track of pain relief and ensure its continuity and adequacy (Lavies et al, 1992). There have also been recommendations that academic "detailing" should be carried out to improve clinical decision making. For instance, in Bingle et al's (1991) study, 75 physicians were contacted on three occasions at six-weekly intervals by an authoritative team consisting of the directors of medical education, the pain centre and radiation oncology and a clinical pharmacist, with the aim of reviewing their practice of prescribing common narcotics for post-surgical pain. Educational material like booklets on pain control were distributed with drugs. They were also given pens inscribed with the words "Give a large enough dose". Encouraging results showed significant changes in the physicians' prescribing behaviour when compared with prescriptions in the six months prior to the study. Unfortunately, the study did not monitor how much of this narcotic was actually administered by the nurses. It is not clear whether expectations of regular monitoring would maintain these prescribing practices indefinitely, and the extent to which their introduction has merely a novelty effect.

CONCLUSION

We began this chapter by looking at distress and suffering, before considering how moods and emotions in general affect the experience and reporting of pain. This affective component has an important role in the consultation, and needs to be considered together with cognitive information to provide a more complete picture of pain sufferers and their needs. The socio-emotional and socio-cognitive aspects of the consultation were examined within the context of helping and being helped. Particular attention was focused on who the best doctors are and what patients expect from medicine. Knowledge about who helps and under which circumstances gives broad insights into the rich variety of helpers who might potentially be engaged in providing health care; this huge resource has barely been tapped, and will need to be if the targets of health for all are to be achieved by the year 2000. Schemes such as the Seattle project to train a substantial number of members of the general public to cope with heart attacks in public places within the critical 4 minutes before permanent damage provide classic examples of the success of public campaigns in the service of health care. The intelligent use of social support groups for those who wish to use them also has a major role in informing and in maintaining newly learned patterns of behaviour. Two examples of situations where emotions have a particularly high profile in the provision and acceptance of health care were described as examples where intensive research has been carried out. This was done to emphasise the point that socio-emotional components are involved in consultations and treatment, perhaps at a less intense level; it is possible to see how the social dynamics between the various parties concerned may affect this. Furthermore, it is important to recognise that recovery is the outcome of social influences from many more people than just the two who appear to be directly involved. Lastly, we considered some of the socio-emotional impediments to successful pain relief; not just poor training and insufficient staff but more especially the fears, anxieties and widespread erroneous beliefs that commonly underpin the reasons for not providing enough relief. In Chapter 8 we move on to consider how people cope with pain and what happens if they are unable to cope.

Coping with Pain

8

People in pain have some features in common with others in adversity, and in Chapter 7 we considered the broader nature of distress and suffering as a prelude to this discussion. Coping is the third stage in the reaction to a stressor such as being in pain. The two prior stages were considered earlier: these are perceiving a threat or primary appraisal, and the secondary appraisal of conceptualising a potential response to that threat (Lazarus and Folkman, 1984). In this chapter we consider the nature of coping and signs of inability to cope. If coping is a set of strategies, how best can it be measured? Most research on coping either asks how well or how poorly patients with chronic illness cope, or considers whether a particular intervention enhances patients' ability to cope (Watson and Kendall, 1983). Could coping be enhanced by changing the ways in which people think about their abilities, or by absorbing more information? What can be learned by looking at a common condition like depression as an example of what is seen by some as a failure to cope with pain? Lastly, we consider ways in which doctors cope with treating their pain patients by examining their views, taxonomies and behaviour. Again, these topics are seen through the lens of social psychology.

MEASURING COPING

GENERAL MEASURES OF COPING

Coping is a diverse and multifaceted concept, which has been defined as a "purposeful effort to manage or vitiate the negative impact of stress" (Jensen et al, 1991). Wryly, some have commented that coping may be what is measured by stress and coping questionnaires (Keefe, Salley and Lefebvre, 1992), as many have been devised in recent years. Several scales have been used to assess how sick people cope. The Ways of Coping Questionnaire contained 67 items designed to examine the thinking and behaviour used in coping with stressful events in everyday living. Factor analysis originally identified eight dimensions of coping, labelled as confrontation, distancing, self-control, seeking social support, escape or avoidance, accepting responsibility, rational problem solving and positive reappraisal (Folkman and Lazarus, 1980, 1985). Although subgrouping these dimensions has enabled a distinction to be made between emotion-focused and problem-focused coping (Folkman and Lazarus, 1985), others have argued that this dichotomy is an oversimplification of coping styles.

Such designs remind us that coping is an essentially social activity. Many of the types of coping described in the Ways of Coping Questionnaire arise from social interaction with others. For example, confrontational coping may involve hostile and aggressive methods to try to alter the situation; this situation may be a relationship with a loved one. Accepting responsibility and seeking social support may all involve relationships with others. While the remaining strategies appear to be more individual styles of coping, they are learned and maintained through social learning processes such as imitating others and modelling their behaviour. However, there has been a tendency to see coping very much in individual terms rather than as a product of the sick person's socio-emotional interaction with those with whom they live and work. Acknowledgement that it "takes two to tango" opens up a much greater range of possibilities for devising ways of assisting people to cope better with their illness. Relevant others might be more closely involved in assisting in changing unproductive ways of coping used by sick people, for instance. A further social dimension is the positive or pejorative value attributed to different coping styles by health professionals in assessing their patients. Denial and passive avoidance tend to be seen as dysfunctional because they are correlated with negative health outcomes in the long term, but they may have some positive value in providing well-being at some of the earlier stages in the disease process. There are also cultural and subcultural differences in styles of coping, and what may be labelled as dysfunctional in one group may serve more positive health outcomes in another.

How does this scale help us to understand coping in those who are ill? To find out whether people cope any better with diseases that are more controllable than those where they have less control over their medical condition, Felton, Revenson and Hinrichson (1984) studied 170 patients with a range of disorders. They sampled people with hypertension (a potentially controllable disease, through careful changes to diet and the use of medication), moderately controllable diabetes, and the relatively uncontrollable conditions of cancer and rheumatoid arthritis. An analysis of items from the revised Ways of Coping Checklist showed that the use of cognitive strategies like information-seeking was associated with positive emotions. Negative emotions were related to avoidance, blame and emotional ventilation, as well as to low self-esteem and poor adjustment to illness. However, the type of coping strategy used was minimally explained by medical diagnosis. Although all of the coping strategies made a significant contribution to adjustment, wish fulfilment fantasy was most closely linked to diagnosis when demographic differences were partialled out. Wish fulfilment fantasy is an "indulgence", involving pining and longing for the illness to go away. It is thought to provide a possible escape mechanism. This strategy was used frequently by arthritis patients. Other work by the same group has reaffirmed that information-seeking positively influences adjustment and that wish fulfilment fantasy has a deleterious effect. This seems to be especially true for chronic painful diseases like arthritis and cancer where there is little opportunity for personal control. Where coping with pain is concerned, a review by Jensen et al (1991) also records that across five studies that used this measure, wish fulfilment in particular was related to poorer functioning and to a reduction in positive emotions.

However, a study of 151 osteoarthritis patients by Regan, Lorig and Thorensen (1988) found that only five factors resulted from a factor analysis of items, so raising doubts about the construct validity of this scale when used with chronic painful conditions. It has also been criticised on the grounds that none of the domains has theoretical interest, and some items are unfocused or ambiguous, and because the items were chosen for their empirical (rather than theoretical) qualities. Thus, the theory is loosely linked and was generated *post hoc* (Carver, Scheier and Weintraub, 1989). Carver, Scheier and Weintraub (1989) have designed the COPE, which has 13 scales of active coping, planning, suppression of competing activities, restraint coping, seeking social support for emotional or instrumental reasons, focusing on venting of emotions, behavioural and mental disengagement, positive reinterpretation and growth, denial, acceptance and turning to religion. The comprehensive COPE is reasonably reliable ($\alpha > 0.6$) and stable over about 8 weeks (Carver, Scheier and Weintraub, 1989). Despite its lack of specificity to pain, this scale could be more widely used in pain research.

Others have successfully used the Billings and Moos coping scale (Billings and Moos, 1981) to compare the coping strategies of pain clinic patients and those treated for pain by their general practitioner (Crook et al, 1988). A factor analysis of 33 items showed five clusters of exercising self-control, planned action, mobilising resources, dysphoria control and being adverse. Pain clinic patients were significantly more adverse, for instance, they "prepared for the worst, took it out on others when they felt angry or depressed, or avoided being with people in general". Furthermore, the more pain patients used such adverse strategies, the more depressed and anxious they were likely to be, seeing pain as more serious and less controllable.

MEASURING COPING WITH PAIN

The above assessments were designed to study coping with stress in all types of samples, but several measures have been developed for specific use with those in pain. The Coping Strategy Questionnaire (CSQ) includes seven coping styles used by pain sufferers in controlling their pain. These are diverting attention, reinterpreting pain sensations, ignoring pain sensations, praying and hoping, making coping statements about self, catastrophising and increasing activities (Rosensteil and Keefe, 1983). The ability to decrease pain and to control pain have also been added. Reassessing results from the CSQ, Lawson et al (1990) tried to fit several factor analytic solutions to pooled data from 620 participants in five studies. They concluded that the original 42 items could be reliably reduced to three principal dimensions. Furthermore, the results from these composites remained stable when they were tested across a wide range of important socio-demographic variables, such as age, gender, education, depression, duration of pain and pain location. First was the conscious attempt to cope with pain by making coping statements about self and by ignoring sensations. Self-efficacy was also identified, combining the ability to control and decrease pain. A less stable third factor consisted of diverting attention and praying with hoping, in what is considered to be a pain avoidance strategy. This pattern has been partly replicated using results from chronic low back pain patients (Keefe et al, 1990).

One of the most fundamental criticisms of the CSQ is that the items were originally derived from laboratory studies, so they lack ecological validity. Consequently, they reflect the views of health professionals more than spontaneous cognitions held by chronic pain patients, so any positive cognitions held by patients have been neglected (Boston, Pearce and Richardson, 1990). A second point is that even though ignoring pain and coping self-statements have been identified in 12 studies, they have proved to be unrelated to long-term psychological adjustment (Jensen et al, 1991). Thirdly, the CSQ was designed to measure how often patients used particular skills and behaviours in coping, and the perceived effectiveness of these skills in reducing and controlling pain, but it has been criticised on the grounds that it does not appear to distinguish between coping frequency and coping effectiveness (Keefe, Salley and Lefebvre, 1992).

Other debates surround the nature of the dimensions. Considerable attention has been paid to the strategy of catastrophisation in the pain literature (e.g. Turner, 1991; Turner and Clancy, 1986), and several studies have concluded that it is a maladaptive strategy to use in dealing with the pain of rheumatoid arthritis (e.g. Keefe et al, 1989). However, neither catastrophisation nor behavioural coping consistently loaded on any of the three composite factors identified by Lawson et al (1990). In a backlash, there has been a recent call to return to the original dimensions with the argument that the composites obscure the importance of individual coping strategies (Jensen, Turner and Romano, 1992). This appears to represent an attempt to recover ground lost by the relegation of catastrophisation. Fuel for this debate is provided by a recent study of 126 chronic pain patients with whiplash injuries, where attempts were made to fit meaningful solutions to results containing 2–9 factors (Swartzman et al, 1994). The best solution had five factors: distraction, ignoring pain sensations, reinterpreting pain, catastrophising and praying and hoping. Eighteen pain experts were able to successfully classify these items into categories with 90% accuracy, so confirming their construct validity and supporting the inclusion of catastrophisation. While the concept of being adverse reported by Crook et al (1988) shares some common ground with the notion of catastrophisation, supporting the general need for the inclusion of some similar type of dimension here, further empirical work will be needed to resolve the conceptual ambiguity in this area.

For some time, perceptions of control have been known to be relevant to coping through research on the locus of control construct (Chapter 5), but how far do perceptions about control affect attempts to adjust, and is this related to pain severity? Using the CSQ with a battery of other measures, Jensen and Karoly (1991) found that the more chronic pain patients perceived that they controlled their pain, the better was their level of psychological functioning and this reflected greater satisfaction with life. Appraisals of pain control were related to level of activity, but only in patients with less severe pain. The results raise questions about how these outcomes come about. Do those who believe that they can control their pain feel better because this heightened sense of control directly affects their well-being — an inverted version of the learned helplessness model? Alternatively, do strong beliefs in pain control predispose people to initiate and persist in using strategies that are adaptive through the mechanism described by the self-efficacy model (see later in this chapter)?

How useful is the CSQ clinically, and do changes in coping scores relate to changes in pain, health or psychological state? Parker et al (1989) asked 79 patients with rheumatoid arthritis to complete a battery of psychological and physical tests twice in the course of a year. The two strategies used most often were coping attempts (40%) and pain control with rational thinking (20%). Those who scored highly on both of these items were likely to have less pain, helplessness and psychological distress and lower levels of daily hassles than those with low scores. This broadly confirms similar findings with osteoarthritis patients (Keefe et al, 1987) and rheumatoid arthritis patients undergoing surgery for knee replacement (Keefe et al, 1991). Of greater interest, perhaps, were the findings of Parker et al that changes in coping scores over the year were related to changes in pain intensity, helplessness and physical functioning. Such results provide a strong indication that strategies of pain control and rational thinking are potentially modifiable, although, as with other psychological processes, this takes time. These results are also consistent with self-efficacy theory.

Work on the use of coping strategies by the sexes also casts light on differential patterns of reporting behaviour outlined in earlier chapters. Studying coping in patients with intractable pain in the neck, shoulder or back, Jensen et al (1994) found that women were more likely than men to use the two "dysfunctional" strategies of catastrophisation and increasing their behavioural activity. Women were also less likely to use the adaptive strategies of reinterpreting sensations, using self-statement and ignoring pain sensations. This pattern predicts poorer rehabilitation outcomes in women. Factors like lower educational level, employment in unskilled occupations and perceptions of diffuse intractable spinal pain were closely related to the use of dysfunctional strategies like catastrophisation in women. Such results cast light on the greater predisposition of women to seek consultations.

In general, it would be fair to say that there are considerable similarities between coping measures in the many varied dimensions used. For instance, the Vanderbilt Pain Management Inventory distinguishes active strategies, such as accepting responsibility for pain as in taking more exercise, from passive and "maladaptive" strategies like withdrawing or attributing responsibility to an outside source. Brown and Nicassio (1987) found that active coping was associated with less pain, depression and functional impairment and with higher self-efficacy in 361 classical and definite rheumatoid arthritis patients. Passive coping was linked with more depression, pain and flare-up activity. Although the findings are broadly similar to those reported before, the social mechanism whereby this behaviour comes about start to be elucidated here. Brown and Nicassio observed that health professionals often recommended that patients use passive coping strategies like taking rest and limiting exercise during a flare, and this raises questions about whether such instructions mislead chronic pain patients about how best to cope when the flare subsides. We can only speculate about what level of influence health professionals exert in shaping inappropriate action in chronic pain patients.

In rare instances where researchers have gone back to basics to look at what pain sufferers themselves say about the coping strategies they use before utilising that information to develop their measure, a somewhat different picture emerges. Qualitative interview data obtained from chronic pain patients was used to formulate the 30 items of the Pain Cognitions Questionnaire. From this material, Boston, Pearce and Richardson (1990) identified four main factors: (i) active positive coping, (ii) hopelessness, (iii) helplessness and (iv) support and trust. Of interest here is the finding that positive cognitions were the most common responses to chronic pain. These results contrast with the overwhelmingly negative picture painted by other pain coping measures; some of these did not explicitly use data from consultations with pain patients to generate their items.

Viney and Westbrook (1982) also used a qualitative approach in interviewing 89 chronically ill patients with permanent disability. They found that action rather than passivity was the preferred strategy among their interviewees. It was summed up in statements like "When things get difficult I find out [more information]; take positive action". This strategy was more popular than either controlling feelings and making compromises or blanket optimism that "every cloud has a silver lining". These results underline the conclusion of Boston, Pearce and Richardson that positive cognitions are more prevalent than negative ones where chronic illness is concerned, going counter to the conventional image of passive chronically ill patients. However, achieving rehabilitation goals was best predicted by negative features like the degree of fatalism and use of control strategies, in line with results from the pain coping literature on helplessness and hopelessness (e.g. Spinhoven and Linssen, 1991).

The implications of these two studies is that there may be a long history of misleading research reported in this field due to hasty and ill-conceived groundwork. The imbalance in conceptualisations may also be due to the overriding preference of pain researchers for quantitative rather than qualitative research methods, and disdain for the latter. The need to obtain a more holistic view of the positive as well as the negative aspects of a pain patient's life is a theme to which we will return in Chapter 10. Positive aspects of pain have scarcely been explored, which may be a result of the problem-orientated approach that tends to drive research in the medical model.

COPING MECHANISMS

Noxious medical examinations have enabled systematic investigations to be carried out on coping with the distress associated with acute pain. For example, in a study of 40 gall bladder surgery patients it was found that almost half of the variability in the post-operative relationship between pain, mood and analgesic needs could be predicted by the patient's anxiety, extroversion, depression, educational level, previous chronic pain syndromes and attitude towards the use of medication (Taenzer, Melzack and Jeans, 1986). Other researchers have sought to explain people's reaction to surgery more in environmental terms than as a personality trait, and this new way of looking at coping with surgery has enabled a more practical and interventionist approach to be taken. Johnson and Leventhal's (1974) classic study investigated the response of 48 endoscopy patients to two styles of preparation for surgery. Preparatory messages were either about the sensations patients might feel during the investigation or in the form of procedural information about the sequence of events that would occur, with behavioural instructions to carry out certain coping actions, like rapid mouth breathing and swallowing with mouth open and chin down. Using a four-group design and the dosage of the anxiolytic diazepam as an outcome measure, they found that both types of message reduced perceptions of danger, but the sensory description, either on its own or with behavioural instructions, reduced the emotional reaction to the procedure and so assisted coping.

This work has continued to generate interest, and a meta-analysis of results from 21 studies by Suls and Wan (1989) looking at sensory, procedural, combined preparation or no instruction groups has reconfirmed that a combination of sensory with procedural information provides the greatest and most reliable benefits. Furthermore, there is no evidence to suppose that patients suffer information overload from this approach. Sensory preparation alone has some positive benefits; it makes a more significant impact on self-rated pain than procedural information. It is also more effective in reducing negative affect, pain and other types of distress than controls. However, the results are inconsistent, and socio-demographic features like age and sex affect the results. Furthermore, Suls and Wan found that the effectiveness of pre-operative sensory information might be blocked if it was accompanied by a "magnitude warning" about the extent or intensity of the anticipated pain. Thus, being prepared for the discomfort enables patients to cope better post-operatively providing that it is done in a way that does not alarm them. It can also improve the trusting relationship between patient and health professional, so that those with post-operative pain are less likely to feel that, through sins of omission, they have been deceived about unexpected discomforts.

Do patients' expectations about pain affect the way they respond to surgery? Wallace (1985) took pain and mood assessments from 118 laparoscopy patients before and after surgery, together with a post-operative symptom inventory. Only a weak correlation between expected pain and immediate post-operative pain was found, and this relationship disappeared within two hours. Specific symptoms that patients had expected to occur did not tend to be reported later. However, patients who were most fearful and upset when they returned from surgery had also expected most pain pre-operatively, demonstrating an interesting link between pain and negative emotions. Furthermore, the greater the discrepancy between patients' expectations and their subsequent experience, the more their post-operative distress. These findings lend support to the idea that it is better to create a "good" emotional atmosphere before surgery, by providing accurate preparatory information to shape appropriate expectations, than to try to control the pain and distress afterwards. This message about the importance of creating the right expectations has been further underlined by findings from studies of chronic phantom and stump pain among American war veterans. Sherman, Sherman and Bruno (1987) found profound anxiety among amputees who had not been warned up to the day of the operation that they might have phantom limb sensations afterwards. Post-operative anxiety was significantly lowered to a reasonable level once they were reassured that phantom pains are normal and they were not becoming insane.

Furthermore, expectations affect the social dynamics of treatment, as Lindsay, Wege and Yates (1984) found. Patients were asked to describe experiences immediately after dental conservation procedures. They found that although patients could accurately anticipate the pattern of sensations associated with treatment, even if they had not had them before, in general they expected more intense sensations, greater discomfort and had more apprehension than was realistic. Furthermore, despite many disconfirming experiences, patients' expectations persisted. Lindsay, Wege and Yates (1984) say that cognitive theories about fear do not account for these findings. However, schema theory provides a useful alternative framework here to explain this resistance to change (see Chapter 4). The results also showed that dentists' predictions about the sensations of the procedures were very close to the actual experiences of their patients. This high level of accuracy may be because dentists themselves need dental treatment occasionally. More importantly, these results support the idea that information about the senses operates by reducing uncertainty.

However, not all stressful medical procedures are equivalent. Coping and other outcomes might be better predicted if procedures were classified according to the nature of the stress linked to the procedure, the function of the procedure and in relation to the time-line (Weinman and Johnston, 1987). Some procedures, such as barium X-ray, have a diagnostic or investigative role; others, such as herniorrhaphy, have a treatment function. Still others have more than one function, like the dual functions of endoscopy. Weinman and Johnston (1987) draw a distinction between procedural short-term stressors connected with the unpleasantness of a procedure, and the more long-term outcome stress such as the threat of discovering that you have a serious illness. For outcome stress the persistence of anxiety or concern after the procedure seems to be linked not only to the quality of the information given to patients and the nature of the feedback they receive after the test, but also to cognitive biases such as selective attention being paid to more threatening cues.

ATTENTION AND DISTRACTION

The inquiry into coping mechanisms turns to address the issue of whether it is better to attend to pain, or to be distracted from it, revisiting themes from Chapter 7. In a major review of this literature, Suls and Fletcher (1985) distinguished two groups of strategies used to avoid pain: avoidant strategies, where attention is diverted from the source of the stress, and attentional strategies, where attention is focused directly onto the stress, pain or anxiety, so that it is either reappraised or more information about it is sought. Their meta-analysis of 43 studies showed that avoidant strategies were superior to focusing attention in the short term, that is within three days. An important exception to this conclusion is a single attentional strategy where the sensory (non-emotional) monitoring of noxious stimulation proved to be superior to avoidance, reflecting the findings from a large number of studies on coping with acute pain in stressful medical procedures. After 2–6 weeks, a pattern reversal occurs so that potentially chronic pain, stress and anxiety is better dealt with by paying attention to it, rather than trying to avoid it. This was true for studies that had continued for up to five years. It, therefore takes time for attentional strategies to be used and this may in part reflect a "working through" of serious life crises (Suls and Fletcher, 1985).

However, Holmes and Stevenson (1990) have ventured that choice of strategy depends very much on the circumstances. Taking the view that coping strategies will differ for those with acute and chronic pain, they looked at 140 non-hospitalised adults attending a pain clinic or sports medicine centre. For 70 chronic pain patients whose pain had lasted for more than six months, 63% used avoidant strategies and 37% attentional strategies. Of an equivalent group with recent onset of pain in the previous four weeks, 46% used avoidance and 54% attentional strategies. Further analysis supported Suls and Fletcher's (1985) conclusions, however, in showing that chronic pain patients who most often used attentional strategies such as reinterpretation techniques to focus on their pain were less depressed, less anxious and reported more social activity than chronic avoidant participants. The reverse was true for patients whose onset had occurred recently, in less than four weeks. Here avoidant strategies accompanied better levels of mental health. These studies lead to the conclusion that people may be able to improve their adjustment to pain by using those strategies most appropriate to the length of time they have been suffering from it.

A mechanism explaining how distraction is able to reduce pain has been proposed by McCaul and Malott (1984). They take the position that pain is more than just an automatic expression of sensory inputs, as some sensory models of pain and perception suggest, and that cognitive interpretations are crucial to the degree of distress produced. They use a capacity model of attention to explain that pain perception involves controlled, not automatic, processing. Because of this mechanism, it draws upon a person's limited resources of attention. As distraction tasks consume some of this limited capacity, their performance should result in less distress, so the more attention used in distraction, the greater the reduction in pain predicted. The reason why distraction might be more useful in alleviating mild rather than intense pain, and then only for short periods, could be due to boredom or fatigue. They add, "The processing of painful sensations with non-emotional schemas seems to inhibit the negative emotional coding of those sensations and possibly allows other self-generating pain strategies to work more effectively" (McCaul and Malott, 1984).

IMAGERY

This change in approach has stimulated new research on imagery. Imagery may be important in triggering and maintaining some painful disorders. In one study, images of stressful scenes, relaxing scenes and scenes selected by participants were contemplated for 2 minutes by small samples of migraine patients, muscle-contraction headache patients and matched controls. The results showed that those with muscle-contraction headache had the greatest EMG response to imagined stressors (Thompson and Adams, 1984), indicating that their ability to imagine stressful scenes had contributed to the onset of their disorder.

An early categorisation of coping strategies derived by Turk, Meichenbaum and Genest (1983) found that pain patients use imagery to cope in many different ways. They may use mental imagery in imaginative inattention, like thinking about having a nice day at the beach. They can often imaginatively transform pain, so reinterpreting pain sensations with the aim of minimising or trivialising them; an example would be retranslating pain as tingling or imagining the limb being numb following a Novocain injection. When using an imaginative transformation of context, sufferers might envisage being an injured Olympic athlete who continued to compete. Two further strategies using imagery were subsequently discovered by Fernandez (1986). Incompatible imagery uses images that are incompatible with available sensory or emotional information. For transformative images, the context of images can be transformed, as in imagining that you are a spy shot in the arm; the stimulus can be transformed, like imagining steel bands around the abdomen; or the response can be transformed where relabelling occurs, as in the dissociation of cold from pain during the cold pressor test. The other group of strategies reported by Turk, Meichenbaum and Genest (1983) involved shifts in attention, although formulated in different terms from those outlined earlier. These included focusing attention on the physical aspects of the environment, like counting the tiles on the walls or watching TV. Mental distraction focuses attention on particular thoughts, like repeating a limerick or making plans for a future event. In somatisation, the technique is to focus on the painful area in a detached way, observing one's own body as if preparing to write a report on it.

Although such cognitive strategies were found to be effective in improving people's tolerance to pain when compared with no-treatment controls, no single strategy was found to be consistently superior when evaluated in relation to a wide variety of factors, like pain tolerance, pain threshold, self-report and physiological measures (Turk, Meichenbaum and Genest, 1983). Pearce (1983) tended to agree; she noted that despite "considerable optimism and interest", studies showed only minimal support for the efficacy of pain-directed cognitive methods. However, certain techniques have been useful in assisting pain relief for particular diagnostic groups. In a study where 44 rheumatoid arthritis patients were randomly allocated to one of four conditions designed to assist pain control, Rybstein-Blinchik (1979) discovered that pain was more successfully reduced when patients used the re-interpretation strategy of imaginatively transforming their pain than when they used attention diversion, where they thought about important events in their lives, somatisation, where pain words were replaced with the phrase "a certain feeling", or a control condition, where they had a conversation about their pain problems. It is not known whether this behaviour change generalised beyond the setting.

Meta-analysis has recently been applied to the growing empirical evidence on the utility of cognitive coping strategies in altering pain perception. Fernandez and Turk (1989) reclassified coping strategies used by more than 2000 participants in 51 studies. Comparing the efficacy of each strategy with the results from no-treatment controls and placebo/expectancy conditions, they showed that cognitive strategies using pleasant and neutral imagery were the best ones for relieving pain. Positive expectancy was no better than controls. Around 85% of studies found that cognitive strategies had a positive effect. Although each individual strategy was found to attenuate pain, imagery was most effective, and pain acknowledgement the least. Other strategies tested included an external focus of attention, dramatised coping and rhythmic cognitive activity.

Although the relief of pain from attending to pleasant imagery has been widely reported in the laboratory, Raft, Smith and Warren (1986) found that similar reports for clinical pain were less evident. An ostensibly pleasant image can not only fail to relieve pain for some patients but may, on the contrary, aggravate it. In order to improve results on coping, they considered whether different types of imagery might be matched to people's personal preferences. In this study, chronic and acute pain patients chose five pleasant images that they believed would relieve their pain ($N = 52$). From this list the experimenter and the patient chose one image each, and the patient practised relaxation using both images. The results showed that images selected by the experimenter gave the best sustained pain relief to acute pain patients. However, for those with chronic conditions, their pain returned gradually to baseline levels. Most sustained relief was anecdotally recorded for a subgroup of six patients who selected the same image as the experimenter. Therefore it looks as though patients may benefit from guidance in selecting the best image. This result may be as much to do with patients' beliefs in the authority of experimenters, as with beliefs in their greater skill. This ties in with an earlier discussion about patients' beliefs in the powers of doctors to control pain, which were incorporated into some versions of the locus of control construct (see Chapter 5). However, the criteria available to guide the selection of the most suitable image for each patient are still imprecise. The importance of matching also holds true for children aged around 8 to 10 years. A study looking at healthy children's reactions to acute cold pressor pain found that when the majority who "naturally" used mental distractions were given appropriate imagery, they tolerated pain better, but when they were mismatched with sensory focusing, their pain increased, so reducing their coping abilities (Fanurik et al, 1993). Content-wise, the best distraction from injection pain for children appears to be music, especially if the lyrics are novel and if children are singing (Fowler-Kerry and Lander, 1987).

One problem faced by clinicians in this area is that there are broad individual differences among those who present themselves for coping skills training. Some people are much less capable of generating imagery than others. Rather than being a single generalised skill (Turk, Meichenbaum and Genest, 1983), imagery involves a number of closely related but distinct processes (Kosslyn et al, 1984). Where imagery occurs, the four principal processes have been identified as (i) image generation or creating a representation of all of the parts of an image, (ii) image maintenance, where images are retained in the memory, (iii) image scanning, where attention is shifted so that the overall image can be inspected, and (iv) image rotation, where the image is manipulated in space (Kosslyn, van Kleek and Kirby, 1990). Such imagery activities enable people to work out how to best pack their copious and oddly-shaped holiday luggage into a small car boot and still get the lid closed. This diversity of imaging processes may explain why some strategies appear to be more suited to certain individuals than others, because they lock onto a particular component of imagery in which they are already highly skilled.

Cognitive research on imagery gives insight as to why it is so useful in counteracting pain; many types of coping strategy draw upon imagery. The high levels of cognitive complexity associated with this imagery enable understanding of why pain sufferers find the use of imagery so helpful in coping. The most probable answer is because the sufferer's attention is almost completely pre-occupied by the high demands of these processes, so preventing cognitions about pain from intruding while these processes are in operation. Consequently, an attentional capacity model appears to be highly adaptable in explaining pain problems.

TALKING IT THROUGH

Simple cognitive techniques like thinking aloud help us to understand how people cope in stressful and painful situations. Videos of people taking part in the cold pressor test were shown to participants, who were then asked to recount their thoughts as they themselves went through this experience (Meichenbaum, Henshaw and Himmel, 1982). Although coping self-statements and images were no different for those who had seen others tolerate the full 5 minutes and those who dropped out early, there were anecdotal differences in what these subgroups reported that they said to themselves about how to cope with the stress of pain. The internal dialogue suggested that those who were seen to tolerate the pain longest were viewed as facing a challenge, while for those who had given up before the end, the event was seen as a catastrophe and the person as having been overwhelmed. Such attributions may well be important in the socialisation of coping strategies, and need further careful investigation.

Using a "think-aloud" method with students exposed to the cold pressor test, Heyneman et al (1990) found that verbalised thoughts could be used to distinguish catastrophisers from non-catastrophisers. Those who did not catastrophise immersed their arms for nearly twice as long as those who did catastrophise. When catastrophisers were given self-instruction training they improved more than when given attention diversion strategies, but the reverse was true for those who did not catastrophise. When using their least effective strategy, neither group did better than their respective controls. Both the method used and the results found are of considerable importance in showing how the situation affects the strategy.

Is thinking aloud a stress reliever in its own right? There is evidence to back the idea that public disclosure of information does affect people's ability to cope, so this useful methodology may have inherent therapeutic effects. A review of the literature by Pennebaker and Susman (1988) found that childhood experiences and recent traumatic events that had never been discussed were correlated with current health problems. Pennebaker's (1989) 300 participants disclosed highly personal and often traumatic events by writing them down or talking about them privately using a tape recorder. He found consistent themes of death, the family, interpersonal conflicts, illness or accident, failure and humiliation, academic matters, sexual trauma and psychological or behavioural disorders across four investigations. Those who had strong negative emotions were more likely to disclose deeply personal aspects of themselves within the first 5 minutes; the person who receives this highly personal and often unique disclosure is seen to be privileged.

Furthermore, requiring people to confront their traumatic experiences in this way improves their health through their immune system functioning. Pennebaker, Kiecott-Glaser and Glaser (1988) took blood samples from 50 students during four days of writing about traumata and again six weeks later, and found that immune assays, self-report and physician records reflected improvements in immune functioning, particularly among high disclosers. So "confession" or active self-disclosure helps the trauma to be understood better. This study demonstrates the power of believing that you are communicating with others in relieving distress, and shows how the social nature of this process is central to the relief of suffering as well as to the improvement of physical and mental health. Such findings underpin the origins of psychotherapy and go some way towards explaining high levels of well-being reported to accompany some religious practices. These results also have implications for the treatment of depressed chronic pain patients.

CRITIQUE

One problem with the conceptualisation of coping is that none of these is a purely cognitive approach (Linton, 1986); coping has important socio-emotional components, which have not always been explicitly acknowledged. Systematic incorporation of an assessment of emotions in these packages is overdue, and the involvement of relevant others in helping to change coping strategies should not be underestimated. Furthermore, the extent to which the strategies included in these treatment packages have been standardised is not clear. Although claims for success in teaching coping skills are high, as in the case of many other treatments, it is almost impossible to know what exactly happened, what was included, excluded or delivered, and which items were the most effective in a menu of individual components. Frequently, manuals have not been used and procedural details are often inadequately reported; nor, in many cases, have steps been taken to carry out independent quality control or to prevent "drift" away from the original protocol. These issues of treatment fidelity need to be addressed directly if we are to understand exactly why treatments fail (Turk, Rudy and Sorkin, 1993). These comments are not just relevant to the teaching of coping strategies, but also pertain to the range of cognitive treatments for pain.

   Another problem for therapists is that training in particular coping skills may interfere with preferred modes of coping, as studies of imagery have shown. Those in pain are likely to bring one or more well-rehearsed strategies into the laboratory and may then proceed to use them, especially if allocated to a no-treatment control group. For the same reason, they may not comply with instructions in an experimental group. But perhaps this issue is not as critical as it first appears. Tan (1983) reviewed 27 studies and found that in 15 of these, participants coped better when issued with instructions than when left to devise their own strategies spontaneously; in 12 studies there was no difference. Furthermore, some participants who already have the coping skills they needed to relieve pain have low self-efficacy expectations about carrying them out. This brings into question what procedures should be adopted in managing pain control. It tends to be assumed that treatment should focus on the teaching of coping skills, but a more fundamental question is whether it should focus on activating existing skills by improving perceptions of self-efficacy. Some time ago, Turk, Meichenbaum and Genest (1983) concluded that "It is not the strategy *per se*, but the *subject's attitudes and sense of confidence* about these strategies that may play an important role in the pain situation" (p.102). The topic of self-efficacy and coping is addressed later in this chapter.

Lastly, little is known about patterns of coping style use; individual differences in the use of strategies may be tied to some persisting styles of behaviour. For example, in a study of cardiac patients experiencing the pain of angina pectoris, it was predicted that the more time-urgent and hostile type A patients would differ in the way they coped with the pain from type Bs, who did not display these qualities. Although Keefe, Castell and Blumenthal (1986) found no differences between As and Bs on the dimensions of the McGill Pain Questionnaire, they did find that 40% of As reported chest pain when they were upset, excited or angry, compared with only 16% of Bs. This may be bound up with the attendant finding that the more trait and state anxiety patients have, the more likely they are also to experience chest pain when they are distressed. Most relevant here, though, was the finding that type As used coping strategies significantly less often than Bs. In particular, they were less likely to use diverting attention, reinterpreting pain sensations and praying or hoping. Measuring treadmill performance, Keefe, Castell and Blumenthal (1986) found that type As exercised for longer than Bs, but only 26% of As reported pain during treadmill activity compared with 42% of Bs. This suggests that As may be more inclined to minimise or ignore bodily sensations such as pain, in line with models of symptom detection outlined in Chapter 4. Such findings also indicate that coping may require a much broader definition than is currently in use.

Within the theme of coping or failing to cope, it is possible to identify several related areas of research that warrant separate consideration. In the following section we consider how self-efficacy expectations affect coping. Information as coping is also considered, as well as depression as a failure to cope with chronic pain.

SELF-EFFICACY AND PAIN CONTROL

Self-efficacy is about expectations of successful performance in a problematic situation (Council et al, 1988), as we saw in Chapter 5. Many common problems experienced in the context of pain management might be better explained by scrutinising self-efficacy beliefs. Often, those who appear to be most successful in treatment are those who are most confident about being able to manage their pain; these people are deemed to have high levels of self-efficacy and therefore to be coping better. For these reasons, considerable attention has recently been devoted to this area.

Self-efficacy beliefs affect the ways in which pain patients behave in two ways. Firstly, how people judge their social skills and other behaviour affects the way they perform when trying to meet their goals. Secondly, when coping with pain, self-efficacy seems to influence how people deal with situations that are linked with pain (Council et al, 1988). For those with low self-efficacy, this behaviour might involve avoiding particular behaviours and/or situations that induce pain, or that affect pain medication use. Results from research on 40 low back pain patients has shown that while pain and self-efficacy were correlated with performance, expected pain was not the strongest predictor of functional impairment; instead, it predicted 10 movement limitations (Council et al, 1988). The data supports the conclusion that these self-efficacy scores reflected intentions to behave in a particular way; that is, decisions to act that are the result of expectations, and not expectations as such. Arguing from Ajzen and Fishbein's (1980) model which utilises this distinction (see Chapter 6), it is clear that social models can profitably assist in interpreting behaviour in the clinic.

Strong self-efficacy beliefs appear to have direct and indirect clinical effects on a patient's behaviour in a range of important ways. Self-efficacious pain sufferers are likely to be less anxious. Chronic pain patients who expect to be self-efficacious have a greater tolerance of pain, increased levels of exercise and a reduced need for pain medication (Turk, Meichenbaum and Genest, 1983). Where acute experimental pain is concerned, it has been found that self-efficacy ratings were better predictors of a person's tolerance to pain, than the pain ratings *per se* (Dolce et al, 1986a). Self-efficacy can affect a pain sufferer's cognitive ability to attend to information and imagine it. It also has implications for modelling and perceived control over painful stimulation. Cognitions that moderate the placebo effect are related to self-efficacy; they predispose people to endure more pain if given a placebo. As a rule, the highly self-efficacious are more inclined to attempt and to persist at efforts to control pain by non-medical means, as well as to handle a range of stressors, which goes some way towards explaining non-compliance (O'Leary, 1985). If perceived self-efficacy relies on the receipt of medication and medication is then withdrawn, self-efficacy levels are likely to take a plunge (Bandura et al, 1987). Bandura (1991) raises the intriguing question about whether medication might in certain contexts facilitate skills development.

Efficacy expectations influence the degree of effort a patient will expend, despite the costs of engaging in that action and in the face of chronic pain (Kores et al, 1990). Jensen, Turner and Romano (1991) found no evidence to support their prediction that chronic pain patients would only engage in those coping behaviours in which they believed themselves capable and those that they thought would have a positive outcome. However, their results did show that in the short term, patients believed that rest and drugs would make them better, and that some exercises would make them worse; in the long term, they believed in the effects of rest on pain. In studies of exercise, Dolce et al (1986b) have looked at self-efficacy beliefs about exercise quota systems or goals, and their effect on exercise avoidance. These goals are set within levels of tolerance that a patient can achieve, despite physical discomfort. The steps to goal achievement are graded, changing as treatment progresses. Within the limitations of a single case design and a small sample, their results seem to show that self-efficacy expectations increased during treatment (82%), and worry or concern over exercise was reduced (71%).

If self-efficacy increases as a pain management programme progresses, does this directly affect the relationship between pain and depression, as Turk, Meichenbaum and Genest (1983) suggest? The answer is not simple. A longitudinal study with 101 rheumatoid arthritis patients showed that strong self-efficacy beliefs were associated with less functional disability and greater coping using problem solving a year later (Schiaffino, Revenson and Gibofsky, 1991). However, a direct relationship between pain and subsequent depression was not found. On the contrary, it was discovered that strong self-efficacy beliefs were related to greater depression the following year, when the pain was high. This discrepancy in results may reflect one of the methodological problems in studying self-efficacy, which is the lack of consensus guiding the design and choice of measures. Until standardised criteria are available, it will be difficult to establish definite conclusions.

The relationship between self-efficacy and beliefs about control mentioned in Chapter 5 has been investigated thoroughly and using different levels of analysis. One line of research has been to look at whether self-efficacy expectations are related to opioid activation. Exercising control over a potential stressor may be important in the activation of neuro-transmitters and stress-related hormones, and in changing some cellular actions of immune functioning (Bandura et al, 1988). Drawing on knowledge about the actual and perceived control of stressors, Bandura et al (1988) considered evidence for the hypothesis that stress-induced analgesia is reduced by opiate antagonists like naloxone. During the performance of stressful mathematical tasks by 40 yoked students who were screened for pain tolerance and randomly assigned to one of four groups, they enabled those in the high self-efficacy condition to pace the task themselves, while those in the low self-efficacy condition were presented the problems at a set rate which exceeded their abilities. Half of the participants in each self-efficacy group received an injection of the opioid antagonist naloxone, the others received saline. Pain tolerance to the cold pressor test at 20 °C was recorded 5, 15 and 30 minutes after the injection with other measures of stress and time pressure. The results showed that perceptions of being in control produced substantial changes in perceived self-efficacy. The low self-efficacy group, who were stressed by their inability to perform, predictably showed low tolerance to pain when they had received naloxone, but were more pain tolerant with saline after 15 minutes. However, there was no difference in pain tolerance between the naloxone and saline high self-efficacy groups. The less efficacious reported a decrease in self-efficacy, more strain from time pressure and twice as much stress. They were also more autonomically aroused in terms of heart rate; those with high self-efficacy were calmer. As active control has direct effects on the neurophysiological systems, this data explains why perceived self-efficacy is a better coping strategy than stoical endurance. It also facilitates understanding about how beliefs in efficacy affect people's ability to withstand pain. Bandura et al (1988) concluded that endogenous opioids broadly blunt the aversive effects of stressors: "It is not the physically painful stimulation *per se*, but the psychological stress over its uncontrollability that seems to be the key factor in opioid activation".

How is it possible to alter people's beliefs about self-efficacy if they are so important in pain control? Bandura (1991) has outlined four principal processes, drawing on findings discussed in Chapter 4. Firstly, mastery experiences are vital; people retain information about how they have performed previously, and their subsequent action seems to support the common adage that "there's nothing breeds success, like success". Like most problem solving exercises, strategies geared to obtaining the successful goal of mastering pain relief involve the completion of a series of sub-goals *en route*. Secondly, learning processes like modelling cannot be ignored, and this involves social comparisons with others. Vicarious learning is also implicated; people observe how others cope in similar situations via books, television and other media sources. They are also able to profit from observing the successes and failures of others. A third method uses persuasion to change people's beliefs that they have the necessary capabilities to achieve what they are seeking. Psychosocial research on the power of authority and disinterested parties demonstrates how experts can strongly influence judgements about self-efficacy. People are also inclined to seek consensus for changes in their beliefs in an ongoing process of self-monitoring. Lastly, they make inferences, correct or otherwise, from their physiological state about their strength or stamina, and given the ambiguous nature of bodily sensations it may be possible to train people to reinterpret somatic information in less aversive ways. Performances during emotional arousal provide feedback about self-efficacy. They may have the effect of undermining it as a result of performing poorly in conditions like high anxiety (Brewin, 1988).

Social interaction involves the generation and maintenance of strong self-efficacy beliefs, as demonstrated in an interesting study of communications between cardiac patients and their wives, where Bandura (1991) demonstrates the power of social influence on self-efficacy in rehabilitation. Graded treadmill exercises performed by male cardiac patients often convince them that they are moderately strong, despite the pain, fatigue and shortness of breath that this activity produces. Wives, however, often see their partner as debilitated and unable to stand up to physical and emotional strain. Such beliefs predispose them to discourage their husbands from participating in a full range of activities within their ability — activities that are vital to their immediate recovery. In this study wives not only watched their husbands working on a treadmill, but were also invited to try out the exercises themselves. This experience resulted in wives showing an immediate improvement in their judgements of their husband's capability to withstand physical strain; consequently, they were much more tolerant of medical counselling. What is even more interesting here is that cardiovascular functioning was directly predictable from the wife's beliefs: the higher her expectations about his capabilities, the better the functioning, because she was more likely to encourage him to resume appropriate activities. Bandura's research puts the study of self-efficacy beliefs within its social context. It demonstrates why it is a mistake to study them in isolation by extracting them from their social context for the convenience of the investigation. If the results of Bandura's study are to be relied upon, then clinical progress seems most likely to be made where significant other or close others in families are actively engaged in shaping and maintaining self-efficacy beliefs.

PATIENT EDUCATION

One step in stress inoculation is to provide patients with more education about their condition so that they cope better. In cognitive behaviour therapy programmes this may include talks on pain and its gating mechanism, how emotions affect pain, how to bend when picking up heavy objects, and so on. The potential range of issues that patients might be informed about is enormous and the content still relatively unexplored in any systematic way. As most of this material is presented in packages, it is often difficult to separate the individual active components in published research from the more inert aspects.

In one of the earlier studies in this area, pain control classes were convened with groups of 12–14 patients who met for three hours a week for nine weeks (Herman and Baptiste, 1981). Education, group discussion, autogenic training, relaxation and systematic desensitisation were used at each session. The groups were used to lay the groundwork for attitude change by correcting misperceptions about illness and reducing fear, and to replace self-defeating thinking with more constructive thoughts. They provided a forum for mastery experience and enabled patients to enhance each other's motivation. Patients were committed to changing their personal habits and assumed full responsibility for outcomes. Choice was emphasised and unrealistic expectations were dispelled. Results from 75 patients showed that 71% had some improvement in pain, depression and attitude, and a marginal shift to an internal locus of control. Greatest improvements were among married women who were not expecting to receive financial compensation. Improvements were sustained or increased for 85% of those contacted at follow-up after six months.

Education about arthritis has been widely studied and provides an in-depth example. Reviewing whether patient education was effective in studies published over a 10-year period, Lorig, Konkol and Gonzalez (1987) identified 76 studies reporting an educational intervention. Only 34 reported a change in knowledge, and over 90% of these found that the knowledge accrued was about the disease process and/or about the treatment. Exercise, joint protection and relaxation improved pain, disability, depression and other health indices. Of the 48 measures of behaviour change recorded, which included exercise, relaxation, compliance and sleep, 77% increased practising these desired behaviours. However, the review showed up several problems. It was found that the effectiveness of patient education was little different to that found for some other standard arthritis treatments, like non-steroidal anti-inflammatory drugs. Furthermore, for many studies it tends to be implied that changes in behaviour are related to changes in health status, but this association is rarely tested and in three studies where it *was* carried out, the association was poor. Lastly, while randomised designs are deemed to be optimally sound, they are often an inappropriate methodology for this type of study because of the fluctuating nature of the disease: patients commonly enter a study while ill, but then improve regardless of treatment. Confounding the results, control group participants are apt to find alternative sources of relief during the course of a long trial. Lorig and Holman (1989) recommend that pain control should be a major focus of interventions, and that pain may be best relieved by cognitive techniques and possibly physical exercise. Recent studies suggest that programmes that included and emphasised endurance exercise, coping self-efficacy and problem solving might be more effective than conventional programmes, which taught range of motion exercises and joint protection. Most successful are interactive approaches, which emphasise a daily routine of self-management activities. Self-care programmes managing headaches have also reported success that persisted for 12 months, and these changes are associated with improvements in self-efficacy (Winkler et al, 1989). Clinicians treating headache and migraine patients report that those assigned to a relaxation / biofeedback group or to an ergotamine/compliance group are able to utilise self-care techniques at home with a reasonable degree of success (Holroyd et al, 1988). In this study the ergotamine/ compliance group were trained to improve their skills of taking the drug at the optimal time to pre-empt an attack.

Regular self-management courses are run by Lorig and her colleagues to help arthritis sufferers cope better. Typically, 12–18 people complete a 12-hour course (six 2-hour sessions) in which highly credible lay trainers with personal experience of the disease explain the pathophysiology of arthritis, design individualised exercise and relaxation programmes, provide information on nutrition, medication use, and the appropriate use of joints, tackle patient–physician communications and solve medical problems. Participants are followed-up for 12 months. Lorig and Holman (1989) report that pain, depression and outpatient visits decreased significantly 8 months after the start of the course ($p < 0.01$). This continued for 20 months, so the effects of this intervention were sustained, compared with controls. Reviewing the outcome of 707 participants on 73 of these courses, Lorig et al (1989b) concluded that four months later there is an increase in arthritis self-management knowledge, in the frequency of specific exercises and relaxation methods, and in other activities like cycling and walking; furthermore, none of these changes was related to diagnosis. Increased exercise was related to decreased pain, in line with findings from cognitive behaviour therapy programmes, but was the only activity consistently related to improvement. As with cognitive behaviour therapy and other types of attitude change, it takes time for participants to become accustomed to the idea of making appropriate adjustments to their life-style. There appear to be few reliable short cuts to the maturing of this cognitive process or quick alternative solutions, but once changes are made, the effects appear to be relatively enduring.

Although there are visible increments in quality of life, it has been asked whether these considerable investments in re-training are economically justified. Reviewing the outcomes of their programme, Lorig, Mazonson and Holman (1993) found that four years after treatment, the patient's pain was still 20% less on average than the baseline at the start of treatment. Furthermore, patients visited their physician 40% less often, despite the fact that the physical disability of the group had increased by 9% overall. Based on physician fee rates, they calculated savings of $648 for each rheumatoid arthritis patient treated and $189 for osteo-arthritis, so putting the estimated national health budget savings at several million dollars in the USA. It appears that carefully selected and designed education programmes may provide clinically and statistically noticeable increments in well-being, as well as being cost-effective in the long term. As in the case of cognitive therapies, more research is needed to evaluate the impact of separate components in such packages. Although the use of educational packages alone has been successful, so far as the treatment of rheumatoid arthritis is concerned, Keefe and van Horn (1993) have concluded, following a review, that the most promising outcomes come from studies where educational information has been integrated with cognitive behaviour therapy. Further work is required to find out whether this is the case for other groups of pain patients.

COPING WITH CHRONIC PAIN, MOOD AND DEPRESSION

Not only do chronic pain patients need to cope with pain and disability, but mood may be a further impediment to recovery which demands additional coping skills. What proportion of pain sufferers suffer from depressed mood and is there a need to develop coping skills additional to those needed to control pain, to combat depression *per se*? In a fine-grained analysis of the more general relationship between mood and pain linked with stressful events, Affleck et al (1994) conducted a longitudinal study looking at the co-occurrence of mood fluctuations and pain intensity over 75 days in people with joint pain. They found that those with more active inflammatory disease who had experienced an undesirable daily event had more pain that day and the following day. Those with a history of negative events showed more pain the next day too. But an interesting and unpredicted finding here was that those with no recent major life events and with high levels of social support had lower levels of pain and mood disturbance in the day following an undesirable event. This tends to support the buffering idea that those with good social support have better resources to cope when faced with adversity.

In another report on the same sample of rheumatoid arthritis patients, Affleck et al (1992) found that 40% of patients reported using one or more coping strategies each day. The two strategies most often used were taking direct action to reduce the pain (22.6%) and the use of relaxation (23.6%); those who used most relaxation had less daily pain. The disabled were most likely to seek spiritual comfort (16.3%) in coping. Those who used more coping efforts overall were more likely to show declining pain across the 75 consecutive days of the study. Lower pain was related to positive mood, with mood being much less positive for those with high pain. Perceptions of disability and pain control together accounted for 30% of the variance in the intensity of pain, but when these were controlled for, only relaxation coping accounted for a significant change in pain intensity. This demonstrates the importance of relaxation as a coping strategy in reducing tension and the pain resulting from it in the pain–tension cycle.

Does disability influence mood, illness and the ability to cope, and if so how? For women with chronic rheumatoid arthritis, Revenson and Felton (1989) found that although pain was a problem, disability contributed in a significant but modest way to their acceptance of illness and to the negative emotions associated with it. Furthermore, as disability increased, so the acceptance of illness decreased and more negative emotions occurred. Disability, they concluded, is a bit like a stressor, because it "eats away at well-being". Interpreted in these terms, it is a legitimate topic for this chapter. Their usage of a package of coping strategies explained the presence of positive affect and well-being. The data showed no support for the view that coping acts as a buffer to stress, so concurring with earlier findings (Felton, Revenson and Hinrichson, 1984). Instead, it pointed to the conclusion that coping is more likely to counterbalance stress by affecting emotions.

Some consideration has also been given to whether procedures designed to induce positive mood might prove to be a successful stress-reducing intervention in controlling acute pain. Bruehl, Carlson and McCubbin (1993) allocated healthy males to groups where they either received positive emotion induction, were encouraged to think about a pleasant memory or were allocated to a brief relaxation condition, where they were instructed to reduce their respiration rate as they relaxed. Although receiving only a 60-second pain pressure trial, lower sensory pain was reported in the group induced with positive emotions. Thus, the intervention has potential in creating a cognitive state that alters responses to acute pain, interferes with negative evaluations of life events and may serve as a buffer to stress. However, it is difficult to known the extent to which results of investigations on experimental acute pain can be generalised to clinical and chronic conditions.

Also, coping with pain, stress, mood and disability may not provide the entire picture. Other studies have indicated that coping with fatigue plays an important role in any comprehensive treatment of chronic painful illness too. Feuerstein, Carter and Papciak (1987) found that people with recurrent low back pain had a different pattern of mood fluctuations to asymptomatic healthy controls. Matched patients were significantly more tense, anxious and fatigued, and less vigorous. This prospective design also revealed that fatigue was most likely to occur 24 hours after the pain, and so was secondary to it. Fatigue was also related to the level of pain experienced. Feuerstein, Carter and Papciak (1987) suggest that this fatigue–pain relationship is superimposed upon a constantly raised level of anxiety and tension in chronic low back pain patients, and recommend that pain management should enable patients to cope with fatigue as well as anxiety.

These studies on mood provide a background to how people in pain cope with the particular mood state of depression. Although many studies have investigated the incidence of depression among chronic pain patients, estimates of prevalence vary widely, depending on the type of sample, methodology, the scales and the criteria used in selection. Some are as high as 56–65% (e.g. von Knorring et al, 1983) but others are around 10% (Fordyce, 1986). It would be fair to say that there is evidence for some depression in chronic pain patients, but even higher depression is recorded in some patients who do not have pain (Romano and Turner, 1985). This implies that the importance of depression as a risk factor in chronic pain syndromes may have been overplayed. In a prospective study, von Korff, Le Resche and Dworkin (1993) found that the presence of pain more consistently predicted subsequent risks for developing a new pain over three years, than the severity or chronicity of depressive symptoms.

Many studies have been set up with the assumption that depression in chronic pain patients is like that found in psychiatric patients, but Kleinman (1988) questions whether many of the designated 50% of patients with chronic pain syndrome really qualify as depressed. In-depth interviews with "Howie Harris" showed how his "depression" was really a description of a life demoralised by pain and persistent disturbances of sleep, energy and appetite: "even his guilt, low self-esteem and thoughts about death can be traced directly to his experience of severe pain". This makes it difficult to know whether Harris is truly suffering from a psychiatric dis- order "or more likely, is simply depressed owing to his chronic medical problem" (Kleinman, 1988, p.69). The point here is that Harris' response may be a wholly appropriate and realistic response to his condition, rather than inappropriate psychopathology. Kleinman points out that few clinicians and researchers have addressed the idea of chronic illness as a way of life, preferring instead to use the schema of the "pain patient" or a patient with chronic illness. Implicit in this argument is a plea for a more normal conceptualisation of those with chronic pain.

In a controlled prevalence study of depression and other psychiatric disorders in chronic low back pain patients, Atkinson et al (1991) found that chronic low back pain patients in primary care had higher lifetime rates of major depressive illness than pain-free controls (32% compared to 16%). They also used more alcohol and had more recurring major anxiety disorders than controls matched for age, sex and socio-demographic features. The first episode of depression of 58% of the pain sufferers had occurred after the onset of pain and within the first two years, but before onset the incidence of depression in both groups was no different. Other studies show that a sizable proportion of pain patients are relatively free of psychopathology. Although Doan and Wadden (1989) claimed that 78% of depressed pain patients attending a pain management programme could be identified from combining assessments of sensory pain, loss of ability and evening pain, a closer scrutiny of their depression scores (Beck Depression Inventory; BDI) showed that the sample was relatively free from depression. The mean BDI score was 12.9, representing only dysphoria, and around a third of the 73 patients were not depressed, scoring less than 8, with few showing primary clinical depression (scores greater than 16). Where chronic pain patients do report depression, it is much more common to find it expressed as mild depressive symptoms rather than as a major fully-blown syndrome of primary clinical depression (Romano and Turner, 1985; Skevington, 1993).

It is important here to say something in more detail about the scales used to measure depression, because there are important methodological problems in designating psychopathology, which mar interpretation. Results from popular psychometric measures like the BDI are not altogether reliable, and multiple methods of assessment have been recommended to increase confidence when using it. Although the BDI is a sensitive measure of syndrome depression, it was never intended to be used as a nosological screening device. Consequently, it is unclear what the results mean for differently defined depressed samples, and it is especially problematic when researchers make comparisons between non-depressed and depressed people. Few studies have examined depression in non-patient samples with pain (Romano and Turner, 1985), so interpretation is difficult. The BDI scores are unstable; it is estimated that 50% of those who score above one of the several cut-off criteria change classification when retested a few hours later, and this instability persists over four weeks (Kendall et al, 1987), although it is conceivable that this changeability may be as much to do with the nature of the disorder as the measure *per se*. In a longitudinal study of around 1000 households, Aneshensel et al (1987) found that respondents were often inconsistent in the way they reported symptoms, probably due to recall problems, distress and stigma; consequently, they advise caution in interpreting reports of depression. In view of these findings, Beck, Steer and Garbin (1988) have revised their position to say that the measure only assesses state depression, or the mood on the day when it was completed.

The BDI evaluates dysphoria and somatic complaints, but one criticism is that it exaggerates the nature and level of cognitive and affective disorders in medical patients with chronic pain (Williams and Richardson, 1993). When the triangular relationship between pain, disability and depression is considered, high levels of pain and depression were found to be associated with greater disability in rheumatoid arthritis sufferers. However, there was a closer association between pain and disability than between pain and depression, so disability is far from being a negligible influence here (Newman et al, 1989; Peck et al, 1989). However, evaluations of disability may be affected by the use of the BDI, as the somatic items inflate estimates of the association between depression and disability. Thus, both major dimensions of this scale are responsible for inflating estimates of depression if the chronic pain patient being evaluated is at the same time disabled. Furthermore, some depressive symptoms overlap with those of many painful syndromes. Common to both are appetite loss, sleep disturbance (Skevington, 1993), fatigue and energy loss (Bishop, 1988), weight increase due to reduced levels of activity, psychomotor agitation, diminished concentration, feelings of worthlessness and inability to participate in activities (Turk, Rudy and Stieg, 1987). Consequently, it is empirically difficult to disaggregate effects of depression alone from chronic pain or both combined. In one undocumented test, a third of patients who scored in the depression range on the full test no longer scored as depressed when some of these common items were removed (Turk, Rudy and Stieg, 1987). Hence it is still not possible to conclude whether those in chronic pain are more depressed. Because depression may also turn out to be qualitatively different in medical patients than in psychiatric populations, those in chronic pain urgently require different and more appropriate forms of scalar assessment to be developed for depression.

What is the evidence for a social interpretation of the type of depressive mood seen in those with chronic pain? Supporting this view, some studies have shown that a range of social characteristics strongly influence how people cope with pain and depression. For example, in a community survey of 744 people interviewed four times during one year, Aneshensel, Frerichs and Huba (1984) recorded 1531 illnesses. Most of the acute illnesses were disorders of the respiratory system (33%) like colds, musculoskeletal symptoms (24%) such as pain in the limbs or back, and — less frequently — symptoms of the nervous system (8%), including depression, fatigue, and weight and sleep disturbances. Aneshensel, Frerichs and Huba's model of 30 measures showed that the socio-demographic features of age, sex, socio-economic status and income were strongly and consistently linked either to depression, which was associated with hopelessness, well-being and death, or to illness, which was linked with the number of days disabled and the number of illnesses. Such results underscore the central influence of social structure and socialisation in coping with illness and depression.

Attending to some of these factors more closely, it is clear that sex differences in the incidence, expression and diagnosis of depression have been intensively and widely reported, but convincing data-driven explanations are scarce. While biological, psychoanalytic, sex role and learned helplessness theories of sex differences have all received some empirical support, none provides the definitive explanation, nor do any of these factors account for the *magnitude* of sex differences in depression (Nolen-Hoeksema, 1987). Sex differences have also been attributed to the response bias of subjects, but, as we saw in earlier chapters, women report more symptoms of all types and appear to cope with them differently. This raises questions about whether women really are more depressed than men, as scores on the BDI suggest (Beck, Steer and Garbin, 1988), or whether they are just more willing to admit to depression. The hypothesis that men disclose less in public situations than women but the same amount in private has been tested but with inconclusive results (King and Buchwald, 1982). Sex differences in pain reporting and the relationship with depression were investigated by Haley, Turner and Romano (1985) in chronic pain patients ($N = 63$). For women, depression was related to the severity of their pain, but for men it was more closely linked to whether or not their activities had been impaired. Although there were higher levels of pain in depressed than non-depressed women, there was no difference for men. This suggests that women are socialised to cope differently with intense pain and are more likely to respond to it with depression.

Looking at coping with life events generally, Miller and Ingham (1985) identified six types of life event from interviews with 1060 adults and examined whether they could predict the symptoms of depression. Over three months, two patterns emerged as especially potent: depression most often occurred in situations where there had been choice of an outcome and a personal loss. Another situation included a sense of hopelessness and some threat. They identified a hierarchy of seven symptoms, from backache at the bottom end of the continuum through tiredness and anxiety in the mid-range, to depression at the top. Severe life situations, such as a severe loss, were most often associated with the top of the hierarchy and hence with depression. The interpersonal nature of most of these events provides support for a social approach to treatment where depression is implicated. However, it may be unwise to consider particular life events as having equivalent impact on everyone. Coping with events also appears to change across the life-span. Although surveys show that the frequency of chronic pain increases with age, and age is positively correlated with depressive symptoms (Magni et al, 1993), older people report fewer life events, and those that they do experience appear to be less disruptive than they are for the young (Turner and Noh, 1988).

In a study designed to compare how depressed and not depressed chronic low back pain patients coped with stressors, compared with healthy controls, Weickgenant et al (1993) found that depressed back pain patients reported more passive-avoidant strategies than the two other groups, but coping responses for the depression-free groups were similar. They concluded that back pain sufferers use different coping strategies when managing a painful flare than when dealing with general stressors in life that are not pain-related. Furthermore, not all patients used these strategies on every occasion. It appears to be the combination of depressed mood and chronic low back pain that increases the use of passive-avoidant strategies, not the incidence of back pain alone.

In view of the unconvincing record of anti-depressants in the relief of chronic pain (Feinmann, 1985; Goodkin and Gulho, 1989; Magni, 1987), psychological therapies derived from socio-cognitive approaches provide a challenging alternative. In an important review summarising the empirical evidence for and against a cognitive theory of depression in general, Haagu, Dyck and Ernst (1991) say that non-endogenous, uni-polar depression results from the interaction of three factors: (i) dysfunctional beliefs about the importance of certain types of experience, (ii) placing a high value on the importance of that experience, possibly arising from personality factors, and (iii) the occurrence of an appropriate and important stressor that affects their cognitive vulnerability. This is in line with Beck's earlier position that unpleasant and even extremely adverse life situations do not necessarily produce a depression, unless the affected person is especially sensitive to that particular type of situation as a result of their cognitive organisation (Teasdale, 1983).

Teasdale (1985) notes the diversity of cognitive techniques for reducing depression. These range from correcting negative distorted cognitions, training in behavioural coping skills, social skills or self-control skills, to the promise of aerobic exercise. He concludes that none is more effective than the others. We do not know why depression occurs, but Teasdale provides a mechanism to explain how it works and the factors involved in maintaining the various vicious cycles. Memories, current events and symptoms of depression, together with changes in accessibility, can contribute to an experience like pain being perceived as highly aversive and uncontrollable. These negative experiences prompt depression, which is then fuelled and intensified by more memories, current events and symptoms as the cycle continues. These highly aversive and uncontrollable events can take several forms (Teasdale, 1985). They could be major stressful life events, which would be seen as stressful even by those who are not depressed. They might take the form of minor life difficulties or stressors, like marital arguments or difficulties with child management, which, in the absence of depression, might not be seen to be aversive, but where negative cognitions exist are more likely to be interpreted in this way. These are similar to the hassles described by Lazarus (1984) (see Chapter 7). Thirdly, there are memories that come easily to mind in the form of ruminations if the depressed person's attention is not fully occupied. Lastly, there is the depressed state itself, where people experience depression about the depression that maintains it. Teasdale (1985) points out that many symptoms of depression, such as dysphoric mood, lost pleasure, irritability, loss of energy and fatigue, difficulties in concentration, indecisiveness and guilt, are inherently aversive. As we have already seen, many of these aversive symptoms are also shared with chronic pain syndromes, implying their intensely aversive nature should they co-occur. This visible overlap also supports the case for using a single treatment to tackle these aversive symptoms in depressed chronic pain patients.

Drawing on Bowers' (1968) associative network theory (see Chapter 5), Teasdale (1983) puts forward interesting proposals for the treatment of depression. The aversiveness of depression can be reduced by providing information and guidance, which may help patients to view their symptoms as regular features of a common psychological state, which is a natural reaction to certain circumstances and a familiar experience for many people. Such arguments undermine prevalent interpretations of personal inadequacy. By spelling out the behavioural, affective, cognitive and physiological effects, they can be encouraged to see the varied symptoms as manifestations of the problem. This provides a credible rationale for carrying out certain coping responses, and a highly structured framework within which to do this. Monitoring and feedback are an integral part of recognising and encouraging progress (Teasdale, 1985).

Linked to this line of thinking, Haythornthwaite, Sieber and Kerns (1991) have examined the idea that those with depression might present themselves in a socially undesirable way. Correlations confirmed that depressed pain patients tended to endorse more socially undesirable statements when describing themselves. The 37 patients in the pain management programme who were carefully diagnosed with major depression reported more intense pain, greater interference due to pain and more pain behaviours than the 32 who were not depressed. Depressed people are also more likely to be self-absorbed in what is described as a heightened level of self-focused attention; a feature that they share with other psychopathological conditions. This process has been proposed as a self-regulation cycle, which maintains the depression and from which depressed people find it very difficult to disengage (Ingram, 1990).

Cognitive complexity and how it relates to mood is another line of investigation. One study shows strong support for the idea that stress including pain and depression is best buffered by those who have a highly complex view of themselves. Those with a large number of cognitive self-aspects and who maintained greater distinctions among these different views of themselves were less prone to depression, perceived stress, physical symptoms and the occurrence of other illness like 'flu following highly stressful events (Linville, 1987). Important to understanding the maintenance of depression, there appeared to be fewer cognitive ramifications from disastrous events to other thoughts and feelings for those with high complexity. In particular, they benefited from less extreme affective swings in mood.

SOCIAL INTERPRETATIONS OF PAIN AND DEPRESSION

Few researchers have put forward an integrated model of how others who live and work with depressed people might contribute to their disorder. However, Coates and Wortman (1980) outline a mechanism whereby the reactions of others maintain depression. Well-intentioned people may try to control the depressed person's feelings and behaviours in ways that may at the same time inadvertently serve to complicate and worsen the depression. Controlling mechanisms include others being too kind to the depressed person, so maintaining the depression by reinforcing the symptoms. Some may give out ambivalent discrepant responses, which confuse the depressed person, so impeding adjustment. Loved ones may be hostile and rejecting, or may try to raise the spirits of or distract the patient. Some of these mechanisms have been supported in a study by Flor, Kerns and Turk (1987), who found that positive reinforcements from a solicitous partner were directly related to increased levels of pain. In addition, pain patients with partners who ignored or responded negatively when pain behaviours occurred were more likely to be active. They concluded that the way in which the spouse's style of reinforcement was construed by the person in pain was the best predictor of both the pain experienced and pain behaviours. Although these strategies may have a temporary effect, Coates and Wortman (1980) say that they do not provide a permanent solution. Social support for depressed people is eroded because interaction with them is unpleasant and makes others feel anxious and hostile themselves. They may also feel annoyed or irritated at the continual demands for aid and support, which — if expressed verbally or behaviourally — provide mounting evidence to depressed people that those who care also disapprove of them. Depressed people, in turn, have no means of finding out how to counteract this or how to clarify their feelings.

Recently more attention has been paid to the specific role of the spouse and family in creating and maintaining pain and depression, but the causal relationship is not at all clear. In a study of partners of depressed pain patients moderately disabled with severe rheumatoid arthritis, five themes were identified by Revenson and Majerovitz (1991). These were distress at seeing their partner in pain and feelings of being helpless, frustration with their limitations, negative changes in their mood, a reduction in shared pleasurable activities, ranging from sex and socialising to recreational activities, and, lastly, feelings of fear and uncertainty about their partner's future health and implications for their married life. Well-adjusted marriages had spouses with relatively low and normal levels of depression, but, interestingly, the level of support received by pain patients was not related to their partners' depression. Furthermore, the greatest benefits of good network support are experienced by the spouses of severely ill patients; they had fewer symptoms of depression. When the condition was not severe there was a tendency for less network support to be beneficial.

Using an interesting methodology to study the effect of pain on the "closest other", James and Large (1992) found that such people were most conscious of the limitations in their own lives because of the patient's pain and distress at being unable to share the same activities, and also by the communication pattern initiated by those in pain of *not* discussing their illness. Paradoxically, although the closest others thought that they understood the pain person well, those in pain did not themselves feel well understood at all. Feelings of not being understood are common in pain patients, but they may be particularly intense where there is visible disability associated with the pain, as in the case of stigmatised patients with temporo-mandibular pain and dysfunction syndrome. Perceptions of stigma directly predict the incidence of medical consultations and affect intimate relations, especially in those who are single (Lennon et al, 1989). Joiner (1994) has shown how contagious depression can be socially. Studying pairs of college students housed together where one was depressed, he found a significant increase in depressive symptoms in the more mentally healthy room-mate over a three-week period.

Another view is that there is potential for "maladaptive collusion" between spouse and patient in maintaining the pain problem. Kerns and Turk (1984) found that spouses and patients agreed very well about the pain severity and pain experience of the patient. Others studies have reported that high levels of agreement predict poor outcome in severe illness (Swanson and Maruta, 1980). Kerns and Turk (1984) found that for those who were dissatisfied, mood and marital dissatisfaction were correlated. Depression scores failed to predict pain, but depression did predict degree of marital satisfaction, supporting the view that pain and depression may be socially mediated by the behaviour and attitudes of close family members. One limitation of this study was that only male patients and their wives were investigated. The resolution of these contradictory results may depend on the methodology used, in particular the way in which questions are asked; much more work remains to be done here.

The pervasive effects of depression and other aspects of poor health appear to be communicated between the chronic pain patient and the spouse. Using a small sample of 35 chronic pain patients and their families, Chun, Turner and Romano (1993) found that not only were patients more depressed than matched pain-free controls, but their partners were also significantly more depressed than the partners of those in the control group. Although pain patients were more disabled than controls, so too were their partners. When a nominated child from the family was examined for social competence, the children of male pain patients were perceived to be less competent than when the patient was a woman. Such findings show the direct impact of the father's pain problem on the entire family.

Reorientating the debate, Turner and Noh (1988) place greater emphasis on social support than on life events. They claim that social support is an important and consistent risk factor for depression, along with mastery. They add that strategies to increase social support and mastery may profitably be used as interventions in the treatment of depression. Some empirical support for this view has been shown by Kerns and Haythornthwaite (1988) in a study of 131 chronic low back pain patients taking part in an outpatient rehabilitation programme. It was found that depressed people tended to use less social support than the non-depressed. In the literature, the tendency has been to view social support as the positive emotions associated with caring, tangible assistance and the building of esteem (Revenson and Majerovitz, 1991), but in Chapter 7 we noted that it is also important to consider negative social support, including well-intentioned non-support. Support is problematic when it is neither desired nor needed, or when the type of support on offer fails to match the recipient's needs. In a study of networks in rheumatoid arthritis patients with moderately high depression, Revenson et al (1991) found that problematic support, such as giving upsetting or unhelpful information, becoming annoyed when advice was refused and so on, was not at all common, being most often received from only one of six people in a patient's self-defined intimate network. Positive and problem support were shown to make independent contributions to well-being; furthermore, the problematic aspects of support did not cancel out the positive ones. Depression and problematic support were partially related, but their impact depended very much on the context of the good aspects of the relationship. Together, this body of research demonstrates how social factors may be useful in the treatment of depressive symptoms in chronic pain patients, and at the same time provides a useful antidote to the models of pathology traditionally applied in this area.

HOW DOCTORS COPE WITH PAIN

Although coping with pain tends to be a patient-centred activity, it is necessary to consider how doctors cope with it too if we are to begin to understand this rich social interaction. What schemata do they use when managing pain, and how effective are these schemata in improving the control of pain and predicting outcomes in chronic pain patients? Are some schemata "better" in terms of outcome than others? Here, we examine the recent work on taxonomy of pain patients. A good taxonomy will give those who treat greater control over outcomes, greater confidence in their service and more job satisfaction, which in turn is likely to have positive effects for patients. Such investigations should therefore be viewed as a mechanism for improving the health professional's working life as much as that of the person they are trying to treat.

Another study of 76 primary health care physicians by Rubenstein et al (1989) shows how newly acquired skills and information may not necessarily translate into health improvements for patients. In this study volunteer doctors agreed to be randomly assigned to either an educational programme on functional disability, which included receiving four reports on the functional status of a designated patient during the following year, or a control group where they received nothing. The patients themselves picked their most important functional status problem to provide a target for the intervention and completed health diaries for the duration. The results showed that 43% of physicians in the experimental group used the functional status questions to change the patient's therapy, and 93% of them claimed that the intervention was useful and accurate. However, no differences were found in those treated by experimental group physicians compared with controls at the beginning or end. More especially, there were no differences in functional status or other health outcome measures, nor were there any changes to diet, exercise, visits to health professionals or equipment purchased. Despite chance sampling biases in patients and physicians, the study shows how important it is to evaluate training packages and new "skills", regardless of the health professional's enthusiasm for them, because they may not have a significant impact on the patient's physical condition.

Too often the opinions of primary health care physicians referring patients to pain management programmes have been neglected. A study by Deathe and Helmes (1993) used a retrospective questionnaire to enquire about physicians' opinions on 179 patients referred to a six-week pain management programme at the end of the course and three months later. The overwhelming reason for referral was to establish a management plan (91%), but other important factors were physician frustration (33%), concern about narcotic use (48%) and a need to clarify the diagnosis (28%). Furthermore, Deathe and Helmes (1993) found that physicians have a tendency to lose track of coping and behaviour changes over time. Although marred by demand characteristics, this study provides an unusual model for future research in this area.

Which medical procedures are considered most useful in the treatment of chronic pain? In a study by Rudy, Turk and Brena (1988), a random sample of members of the American Academy of Pain Medicine, 85% of whom had been treating pain for eight or more years, were asked to rate 19 medical and diagnostic procedures. Those procedures considered most useful were neurological examinations (89%), observation of gait or posture (81%), assessing spinal mobility (79%), examining muscle for tone, mass and strength (77%) and soft tissue examination (60%), possibly reflecting the predominance of low back pain patients consulting. Four physicians were then asked to assess 100 consecutive chronic pain patients on each of these procedures. Two carried this out following a full medical examination, while two just used patient records. Multidimensional scaling showed no difference between those with and without patient contact. Furthermore, the rank ordering of procedures was similar in both parts of the study, with soft tissue examination ranked highest, followed by neurolexia, observation of gait and posture, examination of muscular function and assessment of spinal mobility.

The views of specialists are of vital importance to the ways in which patients are managed. In a survey of 179 specialists in the treatment of chronic pain, Davies, Crombie and Macrae (1993) found that of the 11 conditions and 11 treatments that they were asked to rate, there was disagreement on more than 20% of the applications of pain therapies. This lack of consensus is almost the same as the 81% agreement reported by Rudy, Turk and Brena (1988). There was particular disagreement about treating trigeminal neuralgia, amputation stump and phantom limb pain. Although there was little consensus on the use of nerve blocks, it was agreed that antidepressants were appropriate for most conditions, suggesting that these pharmacological products are seen to be a panacea in dealing with most types of chronic pain. There was high consensus that neuro-ablative techniques, nerve infiltration and strong opioids were appropriate for treating cancer, but few specialists saw them as valuable in treating other conditions. Creating consensus across such a diverse group is difficult, but even within specialties, Davies, Crombie and Macrae (1993) found major divisions on the use of some techniques. Anaesthetists were equally divided about the use of sympathetic blocks for trigeminal neuralgia, neurosurgeons were not agreed about whether simple analgesia should be used for causalgia, and neurologists were in debate over the use of strong opioids for postherpetic neuralgia. This indicates that more convincing information about technique use is needed in these areas. Two-thirds of respondents had no opinion about neuro-ablative techniques, indicating widespread lack of confidence in their use. Anaesthetists and neurosurgeons volunteered most opinions in this study. These uncertainties about recommended treatments are likely to interfere with how doctors cope with treatment for chronic pain. Furthermore, hesitation or lack of enthusiasm for a prescribed procedure is likely to be transmitted to monitoring patients through verbal and non-verbal cues; the development of clearer professional lines on what types of treatment are most suitable for which conditions through the learned journals and societies is one way of reducing the undesirable likelihood of doctor shopping, even though the atmosphere of the fashionable free-market economy tends to facilitate such activities.

Which clinical findings are suitable for what purposes, and how much weight should be given to separate procedures and to procedures combined together in the treatment of chronic pain? Using weightings attributed to common medical procedures, Rudy et al (1990) recruited 55 chronic pain patients, 30 of whom were examined by two independent physicians who judged which of 23 procedures were most relevant to their problem and the extent of their abnormality. The other 25 were evaluated directly by one physician, and from records by a second. The results were poor, showing confusion and disagreement at all levels of severity of abnormality about the number of procedures needed to evaluate a specific pain patient. A second part of this study showed that an astonishing average of 10 procedures was judged to be relevant to the treatment of each case of chronic pain.

Many taxonomies have been grounded in psychopathology, as, for example, with the four P-A-I-N profiles derived using the Minnesota Multiphasic Personality Inventory (MMPI) (Costello et al, 1987; Robinson, Swimmer and Ralloff, 1989). Although they are appealing in their simplicity, taxonomies such as these may be too restrictive and too stigmatising. Recent research has begun to show that psychosocial taxonomies are more useful and appropriate in classifying those with pain and disability. The West Haven–Yale Multidimensional Pain Inventory (WHYMPI) was developed as a comprehensive assessment protocol for use with chronic pain patients to examine their evaluation of pain intensity, the distress it causes, its effect on their lives, their perceptions of significant others and their activities (Kerns, Turk and Rudy, 1985). Using WHYMPI cluster analysis results to discriminate between different sorts of pain patients, Turk, Rudy and Stieg (1988) discovered three important profiles. The first cluster was composed of dysfunctional patients who perceived their pain to be severe and found that it interfered with a large proportion of their lives. They were highly distressed about their pain and had low levels of activity. A second cluster were interpersonally distressed; they believed that others close to them were unsupportive and did not understand their predicament. A third group represented patients who were adaptive copers; they saw themselves as having lots of social support, relatively low levels of pain and interference from it, and high levels of activity. Furthermore, from an analysis of 18 common medical procedures used in assessment, significantly more medical–physical findings were reported for the dysfunctional group than for either of the other two. However, this group could be divided bimodally into those who had many medical–physical abnormalities and those who had few; consequently the latter subgroup can be interpreted as a fourth cluster.

Using the WHYPSI, a modification of the WHYMPI, Rudy et al (1989) validated these three main profiles using 150 patients suffering from temporomandibular joint disorders. They found that 46% of patients were dysfunctional, 22% were interpersonally distressed and 32% were adaptive copers. These proportions are similar to those found in other studies. People in these clusters did not differ in age, in the amount of time that they had experienced temporomandibular joint disorders or in their abnormalities, so these robust differences in behavioural and psychological responses could not be explained by differences in the level of structural or functional disorders. Other cross-validation for this taxonomy comes from looking at clinical data. In a study of 100 consecutive chronic pain patients, Turk and Rudy (1988) found that dysfunctional patients displayed more pain behaviours, used medication for pain relief more often, spent more time in bed because of their pain and were more likely to be unemployed than designated patients from the other two clusters, so demonstrating its clinical utility.

A replication with 1367 chronic pain patients has confirmed the three essential dimensions using LISREL, but the results indicate that the proportion of adaptive copers may be higher than that of dysfunctionals. Copers had lower symptoms, used fewer tranquillisers and opiates, and had less sleep disturbance and higher employment rates than patients assigned to either of the other clusters. Cross-validation with a subsample confirmed the relative stability and validity of these patient profiles. The implication is that a relatively large minority of chronic pain patients are coping reasonably well with their persisting illness, contrary to popular belief. Moreover, those who need more care for their dysfunctional and interpersonal problems can now be targeted with greater precision. Patients with inter-personal distress will require a social psychological approach to be taken with their family, so that relatives can be made much more aware of the need to provide appropriate styles and levels of social support. If necessary, they may need to be provided with suitable strategies to do this. A reduction in psychosocial distress for these patients should have a subsequent impact on their experience and reporting of pain and other symptoms.

Another method for coping with uncertainty comes from a taxonomy for dealing with impairment, disability and handicap, which was devised from interviews with chronic low back pain patients (Harper et al, 1992). Some 253 problems were identified by two interviewers and classified by participants in 73 workshops. Primary physical impairments were distinguished from twelve more psycho-social impairments and five types of handicap. These taxonomies are designed by health professionals as an aid to others and are set out in the terms of their consensual schemata. For this reason, users should be wary that they will necessarily constrain and contort some of the rich and varied views expressed by the patients. However, their value is that they do help health professionals to structure and frame information that they obtain about patients, and so help them to cope better with their own complex task. How far they improve the service to patients is a different matter. While such knowledge brings firmer guidelines to those who treat pain, a major disadvantage with the taxonomy is the tendency to slip into stereotyping and the attendant problem of failing to attend to the human idiosyncrasies of patients and their particular needs. Medical training should contain a government health warning here: taxonomies can seriously damage your patient's health. The need to maintain a flexible and adaptable approach to delivering health care to pain patients is of paramount importance.

CONCLUSION

In this chapter we have looked at how people in pain cope with their distress, and the particular strategies that they may employ to do this. However, many different categorisations of strategies are available, and much more consensus is needed in the field to show which ones are most important to those dealing with chronic pain. Positive and negative health outcomes are known to be attached to the various use of strategies, but not enough is known about how the use of strategies changes as a chronic painful illness progresses. This coping process is profoundly affected by mood, but also by disability and other symptoms in a highly complex manner. More importantly, we have looked at how coping has been interpreted as an individual process in research and considered the broad range of social factors and processes that affect it. Particularly well documented is how coping is influenced by the relationship between the patient and the spouse, but much more work is needed on how coping is affected by the other important human relations in a patient's life. In the final section, we looked at how doctors cope with their patients through the use of taxonomies, and saw how uncertainties about many well-known treatments for pain act as impediments to coping with the difficult job of pain relief faced by physicians. This lack of consensus has subsequent effects on the quality of treatment and management of patients, where levels of confidence are readily and subtly communicated and may affect compliance and health outcomes. In the next chapter we go on to consider social factors in the treatment of pain.

The Social Features of Treating Pain

9

The aim of this chapter is to consider important social influences that affect the treatment and management of chronic pain and the social context in which these treatments are administered. The type of treatment, who gives it and the ways in which it is given will affect not only patients' perceptions of their disease and their expectations for the future, but will also influence whether they adhere to the treatments prescribed, so affecting immediate well-being and long-term outcomes. It is not the intention here to review every type of intervention, but to examine some of the most important psychosocial features of treatment. In this chapter we first consider aspects of caring. Principles are drawn largely from the specialty of palliative care. We go on to consider under what circumstances people adhere to prescribed treatment, having taken the trouble to seek it. Explaining why people do not do as their doctors wish is puzzling. Here we consider whether engaging patients in negotiation about their treatment is more likely to be successful than conventional approaches. In looking at the giving and receiving of treatment, we apply knowledge about the social interaction between patients and their doctors to an understanding of the placebo effect. Lastly, the psychosocial features of some alternative therapies are examined.

CARING

Caring is central to a social analysis of treatment for chronic pain. The care of those who are terminally ill is explored in detail here, to demonstrate the issues. While helping was examined in Chapter 7, caring carries much more wide-ranging implications. It is frequently long term, and often carries extensive emotional involvements for both parties, as well as social and cognitive components. Caring should be central to the training and identity of health professionals. Given that the majority of people visit a doctor because they are in pain, the comfort generated by relieving pain should provide a major goal in caring for the sick. It is also easy to forget the army of informal and unwaged care-givers — usually family and friends — who look after those with chronic disorders. The elements of caring are thrown sharply into relief, being easier to identify in situations where caring is necessarily intense, extended or both.

The palliative care movement is committed not only to prolonging life for the incurable, but to improving their quality of life and providing dignity until death. Doyle, Hanks and McDonald (1993) say that palliative care affirms life and views dying as a normal process. It does not hasten or postpone death, providing relief from pain and other distressing symptoms. It integrates the psychological and spiritual aspects of care, offers a support system to help patients to live as actively as possible until they die, and offers support to help the family cope while the patient is ill, and with their own bereavement afterwards. These features of care integrate the psychosocial and physical aspects in a holistic way that not only takes account of the patient's needs and well-being, but also acknowledges the needs of those who are close and helps them as an equal priority. In so doing, it tacitly accepts that the impact of illness and death on the immediate community is of integral importance. Palliative care provides a prime model of how care might be more sensitively and successfully carried out in all other areas of medicine. Ventafridda (1989) comments that such care provides a new way of communicating the truth. Fear is the predominant emotion associated with illness and dying, and most people who enter a hospice know implicitly, if not explicitly, that "cure is only an occasional astonishment" (Saunders, 1983a). Dying patients are afraid of being separated from their loved ones and worry about what will happen to them after their death. They are afraid of being unable to finish a task, and afraid of dependency and of losing control of their faculties. They fear being a nuisance, they fear uncontrollable pain and surgical mutilation; they are also afraid of disgracing themselves. Knowing how to allay these fears should be a prime aim of care (Saunders, 1983b). As we noted earlier, alleviating fear and anxiety directly affect the relief of pain.

THE PATIENTS

It is estimated that between 60% and 90% of adult cancer patients with advanced disease have pain, as well as 50% with metastatic disease and 15% without metastases. Around 25% are thought to die without pain relief (Dalton and Feuerstein, 1988). In a study of 208 ambulatory cancer patients, Ahles, Ruckdeschel and Blanchard (1984) showed that 49% had no pain in the previous week, 34% had pain directly related to their cancer, 7% had pain associated with therapy and 11% had pain that was unrelated to their cancer. This pain may arise from the tumour itself and from other surrounding tissues that are directly involved. The necrosis and inflammation caused by tissue invasion are accompanied by the release of pain-inducing products like bradykinins and histamine, which excite peripheral neurons. Stretching due to tumour growth and the surrounding hyperalgesic zone may also cause pain. The tumour may infiltrate and compress peripheral nerves, plexuses and roots, thereby damaging fibres, which become hypersensitive, giving spontaneous or prolonged discharges. Tumour invasion of the lymphatics and blood vessels can cause oedema and ischaemia. Furthermore, the sympathetic autonomic nervous system becomes hyperactive, so amplifying the pain (Pagni, 1983). Pain may result from the treatment for cancer; sclerotic and fibrotic plastrous from radiotherapy can damage nerves, roots and plexuses, and surgical damage to nerve trunks causes pain. Pain may also be due to unrelated conditions, such as restricted joint mobility or herpes zoster following radiation.

Thanks to growing awareness of the analgesic ladder developed through the World Health Organization (WHO), it has been estimated that pain from cancer can now be reduced to a tolerable level in about 90% of cases (WHO, 1990). At the bottom rung of the ladder is the administration of non-opioid and weak opioid drugs. These are changed in a carefully prescribed sequence up to and including the use of strong opioid drugs such as oral morphine, to treat moderate to severe pain. The increasing use of oral morphine has resulted in a recent sharp decline in the use of nerve destruction techniques like chordotomy and neurolytic blocks in the developed world. Drugs are preferentially given by mouth, by the clock on a regular basis, using the right dose to relieve pain for a reasonable length of time — more than 4 hours. It is given by the ladder if the analgesic proves to be ineffective, and with attention to details such as the various discomforts from side-effects (Takeda, 1991).

Beyond the background of stable bearable pain in those with advanced cancer may be the exacerbation of transient "breakthrough pain", which responds poorly to opioid use. Portenoy and Hagen's (1990) research has shown that breakthrough pain is most likely to occur for those with genito-urinary tumours with metastatic cancer, particularly where opioid consumption had exceeded 100 mg on the previous day. The pain was more likely to be related to the tumour (82%) than the therapy, and movement or a cough were the most commonly cited reasons for bringing it on. Changes in position or movement or a "rescue dose" were usually sufficient to bring relief.

Some of the most common reasons for unrelieved pain in cancer patients are linked to the social behaviour of patients and their families (Twycross and Lack, 1983). If patient and family believe that the pain is inevitable and untreatable, this may result in putting on a brave face and failure to contact a physician. Furthermore, suffering from pain is usually reported when the pain is out of control or overwhelming, when the meaning of pain is dire, or when the pain is chronic (Mount, 1983). Suffering can be relieved in the presence of continued pain by giving information to those concerned about the source of the pain, by changing its meaning, or by demonstrating that it can be controlled and that the end is in sight. These social issues surrounding the control of pain must be an explicit focus of action for those who care.

Then there is the failure to take medication as prescribed because patients do not have faith in the tablets. Non-compliance can also occur because sufferers believe that they should take analgesics only if absolutely necessary. Fears of addiction and about increased tolerance prevent the taking of adequate medication. Such action is grounded in the lay belief that if sufferers take the pills, there will be no relief when the pain "gets really bad". Such metaphors about a reservoir of pain relief that somehow gets used up in a drought need to be challenged by informed health professionals who have themselves shed such fears with conviction. There is growing evidence that such fundamental beliefs can be directly influenced by targeted education for patients in the management of post-operative acute pain (Wilder-Smith and Schuler, 1992), and it seems reasonable to assume that similar procedures might be fruitfully extended to the relief of chronic pain. Patients may also stop taking their medication because of side effects without telling their physician. Where chemotherapy is used to treat cancer, patients can attribute a spectrum of meanings or interpretations to sensations caused by side effects, which directly affect the way in which they behave. Physical changes may be seen as a threat or as a sign of disease progression, as an indicator that the treatment makes them ill, or as benign, the latter being the least distressing option (Nerenz et al, 1984).

An investigation into the reluctance of cancer patients to use medication identified a range of major concerns (Ward et al, 1993). Of the 270 mixed patients, 85% were concerned about the side effects of drugs and 45% believed that "good" patients avoided talking about their pain. Those with the highest levels of concern tended to be less well educated, older and with a low income. When the contribution of eight concerns was regressed against pain intensity, it was found that each independently influenced the reporting of pain in this context. They were concerns about addiction, tolerance and side effects, fears that the pain means disease progression, fatalism, the desire to be a good patient, fear of distracting the physician from treating the disease and fear of injections. When patients were divided into those who had received adequate medication for pain in the previous week and those who were under-medicated, it was found that the latter had more interference from their pain and were substantially more concerned on all dimensions, with the single exception of fear of injections. This important study shows only too bleakly how much poorer the quality of life is for patients who do not get sufficient pain relief.

What do patients themselves do to control their distress, and is this action then seen as effective? In Chapter 5 we saw how feeling in control could alleviate distress, so the empowering role of health carers needs to be fully developed in education and training. Fear is inextricably linked with uncertainty about the future in a life-threatening disease like cancer. This uncertainty is exacerbated by the detection of physical symptoms, where each new sensation may be interpreted as a signal that the disease has spread to a new site, so that pain and anxiety become inextricably linked in what has been described as a rational–imaginative process (Chapman, 1979). Paradoxically, uncertainty arises because patients are unable either to label themselves as cured and healthy, or as a future cancer victim. This hiatus effectively prevents them from planning for the future or preparing for a shortened life and continuing illness (Ray, 1980). Such uncertainty can be aversive in its own right and is an important component of suffering.

THE CARERS

The caring business is a two-way street, and effective caring involves both patient and carer. Outlining the social psychological context in which palliative care should ideally be given, Ajemian (1993) discusses the value of effective teamwork among carers. Worthy of particular attention here are the different roles played by carers, their role expectations and associated conflict, the problems of decision making in multi-disciplinary teams, leadership issues, communication norms and conflict resolution. These social features all need to be attended to in ensuring that the mental health of the team is maintained. Such positive action to support those who care could help to alleviate the considerable stress reported by some professionals when they work long term with chronic and terminally ill pain patients. Isolation may be even more profound further up the hierarchy, where asking for support may be seen as loss of face. MacDonald (1993) notes a "state of two solitudes", where oncology colleagues fail to consult with each other and, in so doing, reinforce their own alienation. For everybody's benefit, the maintenance of good staff relations should be of central rather than peripheral concern in places of health care. The quintessential qualities of giving and helping are put perilously at risk if these psychosocial features of care are neglected.

Health professionals share many of the misconceptions and negative attitudes expressed by the public about the much feared condition of cancer, as Fielding (1984) found in a survey of 30 members of staff who dealt largely with cancer patients. The concerns of these physicians, senior nurses and radiotherapists included when to tell patients that they had cancer, dealing with incorrect information given to patients from different sources and problems arising from patients' beliefs and attitudes. Problems were also caused by fear of the unknown, reluctance to ask questions, ignorance about radiotherapy and difficulties in communicating changes in treatment. As possible solutions, these health professionals collectively suggested the increased distribution of written materials, use of ex-patients as supporters, and training in communications skills and patient management for staff. They recommended improved information to other medical specialties and to the public about cancer and the various therapies available. Such action research makes participating health professionals aware of how they can provide more effective care to their patients, and this empowering role simultaneously diminishes some of the distress associated with caring (Fielding, 1984). Hopefully, this also improves their job satisfaction. Creating a better caring environment must inevitably benefit the patients.

The objectives of therapy in managing cancer pain should be to improve sleep, to soothe static pain and to decrease pain caused by movement, while not compromising performance (Ventafridda, 1989). Twycross and Lack (1983) have identified several factors connected with the behaviour of health care professionals that explain why some cancer patients do not obtain the relief they need; these are additional to those already mentioned in Chapter 7. Doctors and nurses may ignore the pain in the belief that cancer pain is inevitable and intractable. They may not appreciate the intensity of the pain because of the patient's "brave face". They may be unaware that "standard doses", which in many cases have been derived from studies of acute post-operative pain, are not relevant to the management of cancer pain, and may consequently give inadequate instructions for use. Analgesic potency may not be adjusted accordingly, possibly due to failure to monitor the patient's progress sensitively. Inadequate pain control may also result from lack of knowledge about administering co-analgesics. Lastly, they may be unable to provide sufficient emotional support to patients and their families.

Reviewing 150 chronic pain patients from pain management programmes with limited life expectancy, taking narcotic analgesics long term, France, Urban and Keefe (1984) looked at the feasibility of narcotic use and whether patients were able to function adequately on this regime. They found that pain relief was adequate for 75% of patients, and this level of relief allowed them to undertake meaningful activities at home and work, despite the residual pain. Overall, no long-term side effects were reported during the programme or at follow-up, with occasional exceptions of fluid retention, nausea and constipation. More importantly, they found no evidence of addiction, although there was a certain amount of habituation at low doses. Such findings should help to dispel fears about addiction prevalent among health professionals.

Taking a global perspective on policy for dealing with cancer pain, Stjernsward (1993) warns that, despite the success of the WHO analgesic ladder, there will not be freedom from cancer pain until governments draw up and publish policy to ensure that relief from pain is one of the highest priorities. This policy will need to include changes to legislation, making drugs like oral morphine both legitimate and available. On this subject McQuay (1991) comments:

> The political message is that the medical use of opiates does not create street addicts. Medical use may indirectly increase availability to those who are already addicted, but restricting medical use hurts patients.

Medical and public education also needs to be available to provide information about pain relief and to allay fears about dependency (Stjernsward, 1993). Stjernsward points out that the need for palliative care will continue to increase because of the growing proportion of older people in the population, as well as growing subgroups of those with cancers and AIDS.

However, even in the developed world the most recent advances in pain relief are not yet widely known and practised. In a recent survey of the use of the WHO analgesic ladder by Norwegian physicians treating cancer, it was found that only 25% knew about it (Warnche, Breivik and Vainio, 1994). Patients needing Step 2 treatment on the ladder were, in 49% of cases, treated with codeine and paracetamol. Although 86% of doctors were prepared to prescribe strong opioids, many said they would only do so in special cases where they believed such drugs were appropriate. Furthermore, where strong opioids were needed, 50% of physicians forgot to recommend continuation with paracetamol or non-steroidal anti-inflammatory drugs (NSAIDs). Only 13% had correct information about opioid dependence; 44% prescribed doses that were too small, and often preferred giving neuroleptics such as chlorpromazine to increasing the dose. Overall, 97% said that they had trouble in treating cancer pain; the reasons ranged from inefficient pain relief (52%), to the side effects of opioids (32%). Slow-release oral morphine was the Norwegian drug of choice, but many doctors reported that getting the balance right between analgesia and side effects was very difficult. Around 70% thought that their education in the treatment of cancer pain had been insufficient.

THE CARING ENVIRONMENT

The provision of total, intensive and long-term care may not necessarily be a negative and stressful experience, as we saw in Chapter 7, with reference to hospitalised children and critically burned patients. Other studies of these situations provide evidence to show that a negative reaction is neither consistent nor inevitable. Klein and Charlton (1980) coded staff interactions with acute burns patients ($N = 16$) as nurses carried out the painful procedures of tanking and wound dressing changes and performed range of motion exercises on the limbs, twice daily. The results showed a "strikingly high" level of somatic and psychological well-being among patients and staff. They displayed more positive than negative reactions in their verbal and non-verbal behaviours. The importance of the social milieu is also visible in the treatment of hospitalised children, where it has been shown that particular types of hospital environment are more likely than others to produce stress in child surgery patients and their mothers. In a study by Skipper and Leonard (1968), 80 tonsillectomy patients and their mothers were randomly assigned to a condition where intensive staff interaction took place, or to a comparison condition. Interactions with staff who provided information and social support reduced the mother's distress and changed her view of the hospital, and this was reflected in the child's lowered temperature, pulse rate, blood pressure, sleep disturbance and reduced recovery period. By changing the mother's schemata, this reduced the child's distress, and their physiological and psychosocial reactions to surgery and the hospital, so showing how important these communications can be in creating the best climate for recovery.

The caring environment may not always accommodate all those who are deemed to need it. As we saw in Chapter 7, not everyone wants to be helped or cared for in the style or place that is on offer. In a study of 28 untreated patients, Sturgis, Schaefer and Sikora (1984) found that patients who had not participated in their pain centre programme had done so for a variety of reasons. These included lack of interest, lack of insurance to cover payment for treatment, the opposition of their spouse to continuing with it, unwillingness to stay in hospital for further treatment and difficulties in travelling to the centre. So although there are some people who are not interested in treatment, most of the people who do not take up care refuse because it is offered at the wrong time, in the wrong place, or is inhibited by a number of practical, structural or social factors that are beyond the prospective patient's control. Comparing those who had not been treated with the same number randomly selected from 100 patients treated during the same period, no differences were found in a wide range of socio-demographic, medical and psychological factors. These were age, time since referral, marital status, income, type of pain or pain rating, number of professional visits, pain-related expense, current income, employment status, disability payment and litigation history. However, those who received care and treatment did use more active strategies to control their pain and reported a respectable 47% reduction in pain intensity.

In view of this similarity between refusers and participants, and the relative inaccessibility of pain management courses to some potential patients, there is a current vogue for exploring the possibility of the non-institutional management of pain. This arises from current economic thinking about providing a leaner, keener and meaner health service, but may also prove to be a more humane and convenient way of caring for larger numbers of those with appropriate types of pain condition. For example, there has been some success in the long-term treatment of tension and migraine headaches in adolescents (aged 16–18) in school, using relaxation and other techniques. This programme had positive results in reducing headache frequency, particularly with participants who practised regularly between training sessions (Larsson and Melin, 1986). However, comparisons with those receiving clinic-based treatment were not made in this study.

In another study, pain patients receiving field visits two or three times a week, were compared with those receiving standard behavioural medicine treatment in outpatient clinics. The results showed 84% success among those in community care, with fewer drop-outs and greater compliance, compared with 61% for the office-based group. Furthermore, a course of care in the community was cost-effective, being the equivalent of two weeks of inpatient treatment (Cott et al, 1990). For some time now researchers have questioned the extent to which it is possible to transfer the new skills that patients learn during inpatient programmes into the real-life situation. The study by Cott et al is an indication that pain treatment could feasibly be carried out in the community where the unique package of social and psychological factors that make up each pain person's life could be addressed directly and appropriately in care.

In general, people prefer to die at home, and the hospice movement has aimed to encourage (but not oblige) the involvement of families in care wherever possible. However, in some cultures where the terminally ill are keen not to become a burden to their family, they may chose to die in medical settings. A study by Mor and Hiris (1983) identified several factors influencing whether terminally ill cancer patients died at home or in a hospital-based hospice. The presence of inpatient beds in the hospice was four times larger than any other factor in this decision. The most important social factor was the age of the primary care-giver, but other contributory factors included who had referred them, the comprehensiveness of their medical insurance, the patient's support network, the patient's education and the patient's needs for care. Together these characteristics accurately predicted 76% of cases. Thus, despite the choices available to patients, Mor and Hiris (1983) concluded that factors linked to the way in which the system works far outweighed individual decisions. This seems particularly ironic given the hospice philosophy of self-determination.

Even the relatively simple provision of information to patients by phone has been shown to be superior to delivering information in a clinic. For 439 osteo-arthritis patients randomly assigned to one of three conditions, those contacted by phone showed improved physical health and reduced pain, compared with controls who had no contact. The physical health of those contacted in clinics actually worsened (Weinberger et al, 1989). Because several social factors could have confounded these results, more research is needed. However, in a related report about contact with osteo-arthritis patients, Rene et al (1992) looked at the impact of monthly follow-up telephone conversations with lay personnel on the symptoms of those who had participated in their self-care programme in the previous year. Compared with the no-call controls, the phone call condition, who had no changes in anti-rheumatic drugs or physiotherapy during that year, reported a significant reduction in pain on the AIMS health status measure. These results suggest that limited personal contact may be more conducive to good health than outpatient appointments, which can be costly in many senses of the word to patient and service alike.

Something of the mechanism whereby this comes about has been indicated in an investigation using weekly behaviour therapy to treat patients with temporomandibular pain (Funch and Gale, 1986). Of the many socio-demographic, psychological and clinical factors examined, only social factors such as the family's reaction to the pain sufferer ($p = 0.007$) and their general attitude ($p = 0.02$) strongly predicted the completion of treatment. Contrary to assumptions, the families of completing patients were less supportive, being more irritated and upset with the sufferer during painful episodes. They were also likely to believe that the patient was not taking their illness seriously enough or to feel sorry for them when they were ill. Compliance may therefore come at a price; that of a tough-minded environment at home. Perhaps being tough with a chronic pain patient is one style that families use to show that they really care. This Clintonian image of "tough love" clashes with the stereotypical view of the saintly carer who sympathetically endures and indulges the patient's every whim (see Chapter 7). More research into styles of caring is needed to look at the dynamics of caring in the home, hospital and workplace.

For the future, better care will depend not only on the development of more efficient analgesics, but also on attention to the many psychosocial factors that influence how care is given, more extensive and better quality pain education and training for health professionals, and on revisions to health care policy by governments and their commitment to change. Quality of care and quality of life are interlocking issues, to which we will return in Chapter 10.

ADHERING TO TREATMENT

In this section the nature of compliance and adherence is examined. Although this is essentially a practical topic, models and concepts that help to explain this behaviour will also be considered. It is misleading to think of compliance as a unidimensional behaviour, concerned solely with medication intake, although it is often presented as being synonymous with this. Ways of measuring medication compliance typically include pill counts and estimates, recording devices such as a silicon chip in the bottle cap, measuring the concentration of a drug in urine, blood or faeces, or measuring a direct pharmacological effect on the body like pupil size or heart rate. However, compliance also includes such actions as keeping an appointment for prevention, such as for a Pap smear, or for management or cure, as in dental care. It can also be applied to keeping to a diet, and using preventative regimes associated with health and safety in the home, in transit or at work (Sackett and Snow, 1979), such as using condoms, wearing a seat-belt or wearing goggles for eye protection. Clearly, different social methods are needed to measure these life-style changes. Compliance has therefore been defined as the extent to which a person's behaviour in terms of taking medication, following a diet or exercise programme and changing their life-style accords with medical or health advice (Haynes, 1979a). Despite research showing that "objective" medication measures have sources of inaccuracy, they are often assumed to be more reliable than subjective reports (Aronson and Hardman, 1992). Subjective assessments are known to vary from time to time, according to the type of advice given, the number of physician instructions and different levels of medical supervision (Svarstad, 1976). Although a range of factors do affect subjective reports, they are well documented and may be controlled statistically or methodologically.

Compliance has been variously estimated at between 10% and 90%, and non-compliance levels for any individual may vary at different stages in the patient's movement through the health care system. Within this broad variation, 20% of patients fail to collect their drugs within one month of being given a prescription, and typically there is a 15–20% rate of broken appointments at outpatient clinics. Non-cooperation occurs in all types of setting, including private practice. Contrary to popular belief, it is not restricted to those in the lower socio-economic groups and with the least education (Di Matteo and Friedman, 1982). Those least likely to turn up tend to have large families, some marital discord or many visits scheduled. Patients who are critical of their doctor or the clinic also tend to break appointments. Although rain has little effect on attendance, temperature extremes have an impact. Furthermore, there is a status effect; patients are more likely to turn up if an appointment is requested by the clinical staff rather than by a secretary (Kasl, 1974). The presence of concurrent illness does not seem to affect adherence rates (Haynes, 1979b). Moreover, in a review of 537 studies by Haynes, Taylor and Sackett (1979), not one study showed that when symptoms increased in severity, so did compliance; other explanations are therefore urgently needed. Such findings indicate that structural and functional impedimenta prevent people from keeping their appointments, not just psychosocial ones.

A recent reconceptualisation of this area suggests that it may be more accurate to see these behaviours not as non-compliance but as non-adherence to treatment. Compliance implies a passive role for patients, who are expected to do as they are instructed. The term "adherence", however, suggests that patients have choices, and actively participate in decisions about their health, illness and treatment (Turk and Rudy, 1991). Consequently, adherence has recently been defined as the extent to which a person's behaviour coincides with medical or health advice (Haynes and Dantes, 1987). The use of these different terms says as much about the attitudes of health professionals towards their patients as it does about the patients themselves. For this reason, it is rich material in understanding the psychosocial features of pain treatment.

The expectations of both parties underpin understandings about the social interaction that affects adherence. When doctors wonder why patients do not follow instructions, their expectation that the patient wants to get better is not fulfilled. Physicians must frequently feel that they are in a "no win" situation: patients feeling better or well is one of the commonest reason for early defaulting on medication, but feeling worse, lack of improvement and continued sickness have also been offered as reasons for non-compliance. When patients discover that their doctor is unable to deliver the treatment and ultimate cure that they have come to expect, they are disappointed and disillusioned. Kleinman (1988) observes that in the USA there is "a wholly unrealistic popular expectation that all diseases should be treatable and that no medical encounter should lead to a negative outcome" (p.241). Although this is a generalisation, such statements indicate that practitioners face an almost impossible task when trying to treat patients with chronic diseases unless and until they are able to adjust these high expectations to a more realistic level. It is against this backdrop of expectations that we must interpret the findings and research on compliance. What do people expect from those who treat? Are they willing to accept partial relief from symptoms or an improvement in quality of life in place of total and effective relief from their disease, and without fear of recurrence? By considering people within this social context, the inconclusive findings of studies that have attempted to improve adherence to treatment begin to look more acceptable.

The shaping of appropriate expectations should begin in primary care, at the onset of disease, and at the point of entry into the health care system (von Korff, 1994). This is particularly pertinent to the treatment of back pain, but also to other commonly reported chronic painful conditions like headache, abdominal pain, chest pain and neck pain. There are discordant expectations between doctors and patients, with many patients expecting doctors to explain their back pain, cure it and restore function. Consequently, back pain treatment is "fraught with misunderstandings" (von Korff, 1994). Furthermore, Turk and Rudy (1991) point out that often health professionals may take a somatic view, while patients take a more functional view of their condition; this may account for some of the dissatisfaction on both sides.

Much of the research in this area is patient-centred, but it is not just the patients who have got it wrong. Von Korff (1994) lays bare the erroneous beliefs held by many primary care physicians about the nature and treatment of back pain. Firstly, physicians often assume that back pain will be acute rather than recurrent or chronic; there is good data to contradict this belief. Von Korff (1994) found that after a year, 34% of primary health care back pain patients had experienced pain for half of the days in the previous six months and 21% every day. Secondly, the routine care in primary health care settings does not conform to established behavioural guidelines for preserving functioning. This indicates that retraining and updating is urgently required. Providing information and skills appropriate to those with chronic pain is essential to limiting expectations about outcome, so that patients are encouraged to take action to fend off potential disability rather than passively expecting the doctor to provide a cure. Furthermore, it is possible to prescribe bed rest and medication on a more beneficial time-limited basis, rather than it being contingent on the presence of pain. Thirdly, there is contentious evidence to indicate that managing back pain in primary care may cause chronic disability (von Korff, 1994). The potential for precipitating iatrogenic illness in this context deserves thorough and urgent investigation.

Sackett (1979) says that physicians should ensure that the course of treatment is sufficiently vigorous to achieve the treatment goal, if patients are compliant. This is an important point, because much of the research in this area is predicated on the assumption that physicians automatically prescribe this way, and consequently insufficient validity checks on this behaviour are carried out. Another underlying assumption is that if only the patients would take their pills precisely as prescribed, they would get better. Some practitioners take the view that it does not matter what the patients believe, so long as they take the pills (Gordis, 1979). But if we knew why people take their pills, then we might have a better understanding about why they do not; for this reason it is as important to focus on the process as on the outcomes. Such views erroneously reify pharmacology in assuming that the drugs would be totally effective, if only human factors did not interfere. Furthermore, if drugs treatments are assumed to be 100% effective, the concomitant implication is that non-compliant patients are lazy, ignorant or wilfully neglecting their health (Stimson, 1974). Worse still, they are disobedient and uncooperative. In viewing non-adherents as a morally stigmatised deviant population, this places health care professionals in the role of agents of social control. Since social control is conventionally used to produce conformity to social rules and values (Kotarba and Seidel, 1984), those who manage pain might ask themselves whether they see being agents of social control as part of their role as carers.

Even full compliance does not guarantee symptom relief or recovery from illness; there may be other things that sick people need to do before they feel better. Writing on pain treatment, Turk and Rudy (1991) observe, "In many cases we still do not know what is the necessary and sufficient set of self-care behaviours required to produce clinical benefit". It is therefore possible that people sometimes do not comply because in the past, when they had taken all of their pills appropriately or carried out instructions to the letter, they remained unwell because the other self-care behaviours required to complete the package necessary for recovery were unknown, or not communicated to them. This is bad news indeed from a psychological view-point, because if there is no positive reinforcement at times when full compliance takes place, this will negatively affect future predisposition to comply, so increasing the likelihood that subsequent non-compliance will occur. However, investigations of reinforcement and other principles of an updated social learning theory approach have only partial explanatory power here (Turk and Rudy, 1991). Since over 250 variables affecting compliance have been identified, it is not surprising that firm conclusions as to non-compliant personality types cannot be drawn.

Adherence is deemed to be important because "it appears to be a clear barrier to the further decline of morbidity and mortality" (Leventhal, Zimmerman and Gutmann, 1984). For example, in a double-blind randomised trial of preventive therapies for people with coronary heart disease, it was found that men who were non-adherent in the placebo group died at twice the rate of adherents over a five-year period (Turk and Rudy, 1991). Here, as in much of the literature, adherence is viewed as desirable behaviour. However, some writers have cautioned against the effects of too much adherence or malignant compliance. Non-compliance can have a positive side in situations where prescribed drugs may present substantial risks to health, and where the long-term benefits and side effects have not yet been established. An example is the long-term use of DMARD therapy for the treatment of rheumatoid arthritis (Rooney and Buchanan, 1990). Excessive anxiety about complying with instructions can result in an obsessive neurotic concern with obtaining the medication at a precise time (Ley, 1988), which has profoundly negative effects on quality of life.

In an attempt to unravel what compliance to medication means, Hulka (1979) studied 46 physicians prescribing to 357 patients, and distinguished several types of error. There were errors of omission, where 18% of drugs were omitted by patients. With errors of commission, patients took an average of 19% more drugs than the physician realised or intended. There were also physician scheduling errors on 17% of drugs. Together, the combined errors for doctors and patients totalled 54%. However, the rate of scheduling non-compliance by patients was a mere 3% and this is the very behaviour that most researchers would consider to be *true* non-adherence, that is, where patients know the correct schedule, but, for whatever reason, do not take their medication exactly as prescribed. By unpacking these different aspects of medication intake, Hulka's results point to the conclusion that concern about widespread non-compliance with medication may have been erroneously overstated in many published studies. Although it is important to be cautious in generalising these results about medication to other dimensions of adherence behaviour, there are examples from other areas where there is considerable ambiguity about whether patients have complied or not. For instance, many pain patients believe that the pain of exercise increases the damage to their body, so if the doctor tells them to "let pain be your guide", they may well interpret this as an instruction to stop as soon as it hurts. Behaviour resulting from such misunderstandings needs to be carefully disaggregated from assessments of "true" non-adherence.

Models of compliance and adherence have so far failed to predict behaviour because they pay scant attention to social behaviour or to the social context of behaviour; in short, they have been too individualistic in orientation and therefore provide only a partial explanation. As we saw in Chapter 6, despite extensive research, the Health Belief Model has proved to be inadequate to deal with the complexities of reality. For instance, it fails to account for the fact that non-conformity can be quite unintentional (Svarstad, 1976). However, more recent social psychological models go some way towards providing a better answer. In recent years, emphasis has been placed on providing patients with more health information (see Chapter 8), but Leventhal, Zimmerman and Gutmann (1984) point out that having knowledge is just not enough. The imparted information must be acceptable to the receiver to be effective. More permanent acceptance tends to occur when new information is linked to old attitudes through established schemata. This procedure might be used to improve the outcomes of patient education programmes outlined in Chapter 8. It should be noted, however, that Leventhal, Zimmerman and Gutmann's (1984) proposed self-regulation model of risk reduction is geared towards changing and stabilising adherence to prescribed medication, not to creating it.

Drawing on Ajzen and Fishbein's (1980) Theory of Reasoned Action (see Chapter 6), they show how it is necessary to convert established beliefs into action. This movement is dependent on several factors: (i) people's beliefs and their intention to act, (ii) on environmental factors being favourable towards that action, and (iii) the need to have a plan about what to do and how to do it. Confidence about being able to act relates to beliefs about self-efficacy, so patients must believe themselves capable of doing whatever is required. This could be done by looking at how patients perceive risks, whether they are able to acquire the skills for the necessary behaviour changes, and whether they can evaluate their own progress by taking credit for their successes and coping with their failures, and then adjusting their efforts accordingly. Feedback on self-care is vital, so that patients can interpret their experiences accurately. Failures should be interpreted as temporary events, which can be attributed to forgetting, laziness, unpredictable circumstances or incomplete information (Turk, Salovey and Litt, 1986). At the final stage any new habits must necessarily be integrated into patients' life-styles. This model appears to have potential to move the debate forward and deserves systematic examination in the field of pain treatment.

In the section on caring (pp.248–251) we saw that drug side effects may affect adherence. It is important to consider how side effect mechanisms work. Evaluating cancer patients who had experienced side effects following chemotherapy, Carey and Burish (1988) looked at the evidence for four theories about how they work. They found no evidence to show that side effects were due to any negative feelings that patients may have about their treatment. Secondly, while side effects do gain attention and sympathy, the punishing effects of treatment like chemotherapy far outweighed any possible secondary gains. Studies where attention has been removed support this view in showing no evidence for a reduction in non-pharmacological symptoms. Thirdly, they found that side effects for only a very few cancer patients could be explained by the presence of brain metastases or local cancer involvement. The most convincing evidence comes from reviews of studies on hypnosis, distraction, progressive muscle relaxation, biofeedback and systematic desensitisation, which support the theory that conditioned and unconditioned learning account for some of the psychological side effects of nausea and vomiting in chemotherapy. Relaxation and counter-conditioning are proposed as the most useful and appropriate interventions to deal with these debilitating symptoms (Carey and Burish, 1988).

COMBATING NON-ADHERENCE

Is it possible to predict who will default on medication or adherence to instructions? An early warning sign that non-adherence may follow is the failure to make an appointment, or cancellation. Other non-adherers attend for a consultation, but express anger or resentment at being referred, possibly because they feel manipulated or coerced by their physician. Concerns about stigmatisation may be an important reason for non-attendance; for instance, patients are more likely to attend for psychological therapy if the psychologist is seen as an integral part of the healthcare team, and interviews referrals on premises that are not associated with treating psychiatric patients. Understanding the reason for psychological therapy can be a barrier to attendance if patients believe that referral means "(we think) the problems are all in your head". Other patients appear to agree with all that is being proposed as treatment is outlined, but then say "yes, but it's not for me". While these observations require systematic investigation, listening carefully to patients' language and noting their behaviour at early encounters are good indicators of whether adherence is likely (De Good, 1983).

De Good's (1983) recommendations for combating non-adherence are social in orientation, dealing directly with changing beliefs and expectations. His guidelines for clinicians begin with defusing the organic versus functional myth, avoiding premature efforts to "psychologise" the patient's symptoms, and making attempts to shape adequate beliefs rather than challenging misconceptions. Some widespread beliefs are incompatible with self-regulation and other behavioural approaches, as in the case of patients who believe that the elusive cure for their symptoms still awaits a correct diagnosis. Encouraging patients to make a commitment to treatment, and fostering realistic expectations about the unlikelihood of a sudden cure and the chances of a flare, are integral parts of generating those beliefs and expectations compatible with maximum adherence. Seeing the value of social psychology in this area, De Good (1983) concludes that we will need to know much more about patients' knowledge and beliefs before we can successfully cope with their problems.

How the message is generated is also very important. In a classic study of eight full-time physicians prescribing 347 drugs in the treatment of 153 patients (mainly Blacks and Puerto Ricans), Svarstad (1976) found that explicit advice about how long to take a drug was given in only 10% of cases. How regularly the drug should be used was explained in a mere 17% of instances, although often dosage schedules were discussed ambiguously. This was because the prescribing physicians assumed that patients would infer this information. Patients did not always receive written instructions about their drugs, so that of 97 drugs dispensed for symptom relief, only 42 included a note to be "taken as needed". Interviewed later, one physician commented "I don't always write that, but that's what I mean" (p.225). Furthermore, Svarstad found that when medication labels were compared with that on the prescription itself, a sizable 20% of 179 drugs prescribed showed some inconsistency. Sometimes pharmacists omitted or altered statements that physicians wanted them to include. Sometimes drugs were dispensed only with instructions from the makers, but without individualised labels telling the patient to take the drug in a different dose or at a different rate. In 29% of cases, doctors gave no information about the purpose of the drug or its name. However, there were considerable individual differences between doctors, with some being very much more likely to do this than others. They often provided this information by referring to colour, form or size: a typical instruction would be to "continue taking the little white tablets". Thus, where patients do not know exactly what to do and do not understand unambiguously how to do it, it seems less likely that they will be able to adhere to treatment. These results show just how often information is absent, misleading or inaccurate, which raises interesting questions about the true rates of non-compliance.

As noted in Chapter 5, being able to remember instructions is vital to the compliance process. While patients may be motivated to adhere, for reasons such as high anxiety they may not recall what they are supposed to do and why. Consequently, adherence is less likely. Other problems of scheduling associated with compliance may be specific to the features of the condition being treated. For instance, Holroyd's work has shown that in treating migraine headache, patients often forgot to take their medication early enough in the episode. Others forgot to eat before taking ergotamine, which can result in nausea and interferes with medication use (see Turk and Rudy, 1991).

How much instruction is given is also important. Svarstad (1976) used scores from a Physician Instruction Index to divide 131 patients into those who had received high and low levels of instruction. Patients who had been intensively instructed had more accurate perceptions of what was needed (62%) than those with low levels of instruction (40%). Furthermore, patients with more instructions predictably conformed more (52%) than those receiving less (29%). Language problems and unwillingness to ask for clarification impeded clear communication. In giving instructions, health professionals have three sources of power as a resource to motivate their patients. They can use *interpersonal power* to appeal to the patient's desire for social approval. They have *expert power*, where they can appeal to reason, so justifying medication use. Lastly, they may utilise *legitimate power* or *medical authority*, by providing a moral imperative, such as telling patients that they "should" or "ought" to comply (Svarstad, 1976). The type of power used is likely to depend on doctors' personal consultation styles (see Chapter 7) and on the power strategies they may have used to try to persuade that patient to adhere or comply before.

How can clinicians improve low compliance, identify patients who will drop out of treatment and manage those who, despite reasonable treatment, have not reached their goal? In a guide for the busy practitioner, Sackett (1979) recommends that a sequence of stages should be followed with the aim of improving compliance. At the easiest level, patients should receive increased attention and supervision from the physician if they are contacted by letter promptly, by being properly instructed and by using more frequent appointments. Moving up a stage of complexity, acute medical regimens require that explicit verbal and written instructions are given. These can be modified to include injectables. Doses can be simplified so that for instance, ×4 daily becomes twice the dose ×2 daily. This can also be done by tailoring the timing and requirements to people's habits, like requesting that they take their tablets at the time they drink their coffee, or through the use of extended role nursing. Special pill packaging like bubble packs and a calender dispenser provide a valuable *aide-mémoire*, as use of the contraceptive pill has shown. Hulka (1979) found that while errors of omission and commission increased as the number of prescribed drugs increased, the rate of scheduling misconceptions remained stable. She recommended that combination medication compatible with a patient's life-style and habits should be used as a priority to improve adherence. Keeping appointments can be improved by mail and telephone reminders and by keeping an efficient schedule in clinics. Referrals to office personnel, pharmacists, public health units and the employees health service provide valuable help at the next stage of complexity. At the most complex level, where chronic medical regimens are involved, increased supervision and further physician instruction are important. Sackett (1979) notes that the periodic monitoring of drug levels may be needed at this stage if parenteral medication is not in use. Reinforcement and feedback should also be used to modify behaviour. With the exception of verbal admonitions, Turk and Rudy (1991) question how much attention should be given to long-term adherence prior to discharging chronic pain patients from a pain management programme. Should they be advised to attend to and deal with backsliding prior to a substantial relapse or is it counterproductive to draw their attention to it at this stage? How can non-adherence be tackled following discharge? Is enough information provided to patients' families and their physicians? It is debatable as to how these resources might be engaged in reinforcing adherence behaviour, particularly in dealing with problems, setbacks and side effects. Perhaps the most interesting of these issues is whether low motivation might be enhanced to maximise readiness for change. These questions have yet to be answered in a satisfactory way.

What role does relapse play in the psychology of the chronic pain patient? For many patients, relapse provides yet another confirmation that their situation is hopeless. At a personal level it may provide reaffirmation of their disability; at a structural level it represents an additional failure for the health care system. The knock-on effects of these disheartening results for treater and treated alike mean that relapse may provide clinicians with the impetus to search for more aggressive and more controversial treatments (Turk and Rudy, 1991). This may be at the expense of the patient's long-term physical well-being and quality of life. The ultimate point of non-adherence is a patient's decision to terminate the relationship with the clinician. Such decisions more often arise from the patient's displeasure with the physician's interpersonal behaviour than because the patient judges the physician to be technically incompetent (Di Matteo and Friedman, 1982). There can be strong negative emotions on both sides (Kotarba and Seidel, 1984) as both clinicians and patients try to deal with the impact of failure. Failure in treatment affects the quality of life and well-being of all parties concerned. Sternbach (1974) has described how the relationship can deteriorate into a cruel "game" of name-calling, taunts, challenges, lies and threats, so that the pain itself eventually becomes secondary and incidental. In this atmosphere of mutual blame, the joint rejection of both treatment and clinician may ultimately be followed by the search for another doctor who will listen, or an alternative therapist. It may also result in the patient being stereotypically labelled as engaging in "doctor shopping". Thus, in these circumstances, not only are pain patients left with their pain, but the procedures and relationships arising from treatment may leave them with a more negative view of themselves, and cynical about treatment and the healthcare system in general, and are likely to alter their behaviour if they seek future care.

THE PLACEBO EFFECT

Studies of placebos provide evidence of the fundamental social psychological underpinnings of treatment. Historically, placebos were a commonplace procedure or medicine, given more to please, pacify and placate than to benefit or cure the patient (Sartorius, 1985). In the history of medicine most treatments were inadvertent rather than intentional placebos, more often harmful than beneficial (Grunbaum, 1989). However, they have also been part of the charlatan's arsenal and, in this atmosphere of quackery, tend to be dismissed more often than taken seriously (Sartorius, 1985). One reason why health professionals shudder at the thought of placebos is because we trust our senses to reflect an "objective" reality, yet the placebo changes that sensation without affecting our objective reality: "[the placebo] seems to shake our belief in the reliability of our sensory experience" (Wall, 1992). It does this in much the same way as do visual illusions, such as Escher prints. Such observations can foster the erroneous belief that those showing the placebo response have nothing wrong with them in the first place, but suffer from a somatic hallucination. Brody (1985), however, maintains that the placebo has a legitimate place within the practice of healing via the use of the imagination or symbolism. Furthermore, Borkovec (1985) says that the placebo effect demonstrates, on the one hand, how little we know about the relationship of human behaviour to suffering, but, on the other hand — in a more optimistic contrast — what incredible potential may exist in human psychological abilities. It is from this stance that this review is written.

Many definitions of the placebo and its effects have been published (White, Tursky and Schwartz, 1985) but it has been defined classically as "Any therapy or component of therapy that is deliberately used for its non-specific psychological or physical effects, or that is used for its presumed specific effect, but is without specific activity for the condition being treated" (Shapiro and Morris, 1978). The criteria for an effective placebo are, firstly, that it can control or reduce as many confounding variables as possible, and, secondly, that it must match the therapy group in every way, with the exception of the active component being investigated and isolated in therapy (Horvath, 1988). There are many methodological problems in studying placebos, but a basic philosophical dilemma is that the effect must be inferred, because for every person who receives a placebo, there is no way of knowing whether that person would have recovered, stayed the same or deteriorated had they not experienced it. Furthermore, any claim for placebo analgesia needs to be distinguished from the natural tendency of some painful disorders to go into remission, so the research enterprise involves showing that improvement due to the placebo has occurred more rapidly than expected (Fields and Levine, 1981). In addition, regression to the mean has commonly been misattributed to the non-specific or placebo effects of treatment (Whitney and von Korff, 1992).

Placebos can take many forms; they may be chemically inert substances in pill or potion form, such as lactose, starch or saline. Procedures like surgery can also produce placebo effects. Nathan (1985) describes two patients for whom surgical intervention was terminated before lesions to the pathways were carried out, but who reported post-operative relief from chronic pain. He acknowledges that the outcome of these interventions might also be explained by unrecognised lesions of the nervous system, or environmental factors generating pain behaviour. Other examples include internal mammary artery surgery performed in the 1950s in the attempt to relieve angina, which subsequently proved to be futile. Furthermore, the action of placebos is not limited to psychological responses; there are numerous examples of physiological change produced by placebos. For example, Hashish, Feinmann and Harvey (1988) looked at outcomes of pain, trismus (spasm caused by teeth grinding) and swelling in a study where an ultrasound machine was, unknown to the therapist, turned on or off. They found that the placebo condition was highly effective in decreasing pain and reducing swelling following wisdom tooth extraction. Such studies display the powerful interaction between mind and body. Curiously, like other drugs, placebos are also reported to have toxic side effects as well as therapeutic power: they not only alter the illness experience but create side effects too. During several different studies carried out by Beecher (1955) patients reported 35 symptoms following placebo intake. These included dry mouth (9%), nausea (10%), sensations of heaviness (18%), headache (25%), concentration problems (15%), drowsiness (50%), warm glow (8%), relaxation (9%), fatigue (18%) and sleep (10%). Symptoms like diarrhoea sometimes appeared within 10 minutes of taking the pills. Such psychosomatic effects lend considerable support to the idea that there is a powerful affective contribution to the action of placebos.

Some of the most interesting social features of treatment have been demonstrated through the investigation of the placebo effect. Quintessentially, it is a socio-psychological phenomenon, because it integrates the patient's beliefs and expectations about the treatment received with those of the person who administered the treatment and the situation or context in which this exchange took place. Two qualifying points are worth noting: the first is that, contrary to the predominant view in the literature on placebos, these expectations may not necessarily be positive. Hahn (1985) has reviewed a range of culturally fostered expectations, some of which, like those associated with voodoo, can lead to the discordant and noxious *nocebo* effect: "Simply put, belief sickens; belief kills; belief heals" (Hahn, 1985, p.182). The second point is that much of the research in this area has tended to take a patient-centred approach by scrutinising how the patient behaves. It could be argued that the placebo effect is as much about the observer or health professional as it is about the actor or patient. The term "placebo" is used to describe someone else's behaviour, not our own, and the presence of an observer is a necessary component of the placebo effect, because the effect depends upon both the observer's understanding and description of the treatment, and the patient's interpretation (Plotkin, 1985). Consequently, studies that artificially isolate the patient's behaviour provide a narrow and distorted picture of this social dynamic. Research in this area shows that a non-specific increase in attention and contact with other people characterises the majority of placebo interventions (Watson and Kendall, 1983). However, definitions that view placebos as non-specific variables have been criticised by Horvath (1988), who argues that they are very specific, both in their action and their effects. Placebos are more often alternative forms of treatment without the specific mechanism of interest, but with many of the common components working within a different theoretical schema. Grunbaum (1985), too, rejects the term "non-specific factors", preferring "incidental factors" instead. The concept of incidental factors gives greater credence to these important variables than the "waste paper basket" terminology implied by the non-specific label.

Whatever we call them, there is consensus that the following characteristics can be manipulated to have a direct effect on the ways in which people respond to a placebo: (i) the relationship between doctor and patient, (ii) the instructions given, (iii) the way preparations are made and (iv) the environmental milieu in which healing is carried out. Other factors considered are the patient's expectations and needs about getting better, the patient's suggestibility, personality traits and psychological state, and the severity or discomfort of the symptoms (Ross and Buckalew, 1985). However, some light has been shed on how placebos work by looking at somatisation, which is the tendency to experience or report numerous physical symptoms (see also Chapters 3 and 4). Wilson et al (1994) earmarked different subgroups of somatisers among 249 temporomandibular joint patients. They found that high somatisers were three times more likely (45%) than lows (15%) to report having one or more painful placebo sites ($p = 0.005$). This suggests that the newly rejigged view of somatisation as a non-psychiatric concept may be important in explaining the placebo mechanism.

From a review of the effects of 39 psychotherapy studies published between 1964 and 1985, Horvath (1988) was able to categorise those including a placebo, or attention as a placebo, in the following ways. Some placebos were theoretically inert with few specific components. Even for placebo drugs which may be inert, Craig (1984) reminds us that the psychological processes that mediate placebo effects are "active, powerful and amenable to systematic application". Other studies have provided a component control placebo, where some elements of the placebo closely mimicked their therapeutic equivalents, but without the active treatment component. A third group of placebo controls were the least satisfactory; they were alternative therapies, where no attempt was made to equate the elements common to both therapy and placebo. Examples included attention placebos of contemplation, group counselling or discussion where social support was received, and alternative therapies where the placebo contained specific forms of actual therapy or multiple components. This latter type is not only very weak but is also alarmingly common in designs of pain research. One example is a placebo-controlled study of multiple therapeutic components in the treatment of tension headache, which showed that intensive training in progressive muscular relaxation, with and without cognitive behaviour therapy, was superior in relieving pain to either a control group who participated in pseudo-meditation (training in body awareness and mental imagery) or continual headache monitoring (Blanchard et al, 1990).

There is little consistent evidence to support the idea that some people have a placebo responding personality while others are non-reactors. Although this line of thinking has been hotly pursued, when socio-demographic features are taken into account no robust differences are reported. But this conclusion has been known for some considerable time; in an early study of post-operative wound pain, 14% of patients were found to be consistent reactors to placebo, which means that all doses they received were effective. A further 31% were consistent non-reactors, where placebo was never effective. The majority of patients (55%), however, did not fall into either extreme, so exposing the weakness of this typology (Lasagna et al, 1954). Contradictory evidence has also been reported, where other important personality dimensions like introversion/extroversion, neuroticism, hypnotisability and suggestibility have been investigated. As a result, there is much more current support for the idea that placebo reactivity is determined by the situation or context: it is the result of an interaction between personal factors and the person's environment. Summarising this position with reference to suggestibility, Peck (1986) says, "although it was originally assumed that certain patients were more suggestible, and hence more suggestible to placebos, the search for a placebo responder has consistently failed. The general consensus is that any individual may be responsive to placebo effects *under the right circumstances*" (p.258). The placebo effects of hypnosis are known to be due to expectations. Studies looking at the effect of hypnotic analgesic suggestion have reported a significant reduction of pain, even for those people who were incapable of being hypnotised (Evans, 1985).

Another area where the interaction between person and milieu has been confirmed is in the study of anxiety. Anxiety levels alone do not improve predictions about placebo responding, but Gryll and Katahn (1978) found that the heightened anxiety of a drug-taking situation, together with the role and actions of the physician, mobilised the patient's faith in the medical profession, particularly faith in the doctor's competence. This in turn increased hope that recovery was on the way. These mood reactions of anxiety represent situationally relevant changes in response to a placebo. They affect pain tolerance, so that those with high anxiety tolerate pain less well following placebo intake, but tolerate pain longer where anxiety is reduced. In contrast, chronic worriers are calmed by a placebo injection and tolerate pain better (Evans, 1985). While anxiety is clearly implicated in the mechanism, looking at it the other way round, there is little empirical support for the idea that stress from pain and anxiety increases the placebo effect (Beecher, 1955; Miller, 1989). Others have theorised that the mechanism works by generating expectations for pain, which then lead to an appropriate cognitive readjustment of behaviour. Yet other models explain these effects in the terms of classical Pavlovian conditioning, which states that people learn through direct experience. Using a four-group design, Voudouris, Peck and Coleman (1990) compared the effects of expectancy and conditioning, together and separately, with those of a control group. Responses to experimental pain were tested with and without the application of placebo cream (cold cream), which participants were told contained a powerful analgesic. The conditioned group showed a placebo effect of pain relief independently and also where it was combined with verbal expectations. Reviewing the evidence, Wall (1992) concludes that together these cognitive and conditioning theories provide the most plausible current explanation of the placebo mechanism.

Biological and physiological theories have also been used to explain the placebo effect. Peptides associated with narcotic analgesia are concentrated in areas like the brainstem, which contains the pain suppression network, and the opioid–peptide link which modulates pain can be blocked experimentally by administering naloxone (Fields and Levine, 1981). In an investigation by Levine, Gordon and Fields (1978), randomly allocated patients in a double-blind trial believed that they would be injected with naloxone, morphine or a placebo following dental surgery. Two drugs were administered to each patient, the first of them two hours after anaesthesia and the second an hour later in one of three sequences, naloxone–placebo, placebo–naloxone or two placebo doses. When placebo responders, defined as those for whom the pain did not get worse, were given naloxone as the second drug the pain increased significantly more than for any other subgroup of participants. They concluded that the placebo effect was mediated by endorphins. Subsequent failure to replicate this work may be linked to some untested assumptions (Evans, 1985). Weakness in the definition of placebo responders also underlines the need for further investigations in the pursuit of confident conclusions.

Clients bring varied preconceptions and expectations to new therapy; often the novelty factor is of great importance in creating these views. Placebos are only effective for relatively short periods of time, regardless of the origins of the pain. They may work for days, weeks or months at best, but do not relieve chronic pain in the long term (Beecher, 1965). However, this relief rate is little different to that found for many opiate drugs and pain management techniques. There is also a habituation effect; one study showed that the more placebo doses given, the less relief from pain was reported. Patients receiving one dose had 53% relief from a placebo, those taking two doses 40% relief, for three doses it was 40% and for four doses only 15% relief

(Lasagna et al, 1954). The clinical implications of novelty are summed up by Di Matteo and Friedman (1982): "Wise physicians know that they should use new drugs while they are effective".

How much evidence is there for the placebo effect in the relief of pain? Beecher (1959) reviewed 15 placebo studies and noticed that for 1082 pain patients a placebo gave "satisfactory relief" in about 35% of organic cases, but only in about 3% when the pain was "contrived". He suggests that placebos work because they act on the emotional components of suffering:

> The great power of placebos provides one of the strongest supports for the view that drugs are capable of altering subjective responses and symptoms, and do so to an important degree through their effect on the reaction component of suffering. (Beecher, 1955, p.1603)

Wall (1992) reminds us of the variability in Beecher's figures, which ranged from 0% to 100% for placebo responders. This variation has been largely overlooked in the mists of time, and in the need for a clear clinical heuristic. Evans (1985) has reviewed the results from 11 more recent double-blind controlled trials, where a total of 908 patients were included. He concluded that, on average, 36% of patients received at least 50% relief from pain following placebo medication, so confirming Beecher's results.

Beecher also found that placebos were about half as effective as morphine — one of the most potent analgesics available. Evidence from more recent double-blind studies confirms that the placebo efficacy for morphine (56%) is equivalent to that obtained for several other common analgesic drugs: for instance, it is 54% for aspirin and 56% for codeine. So compared to standard doses of analgesics given in blind conditions, the placebo effect is relatively constant (Evans, 1985). Cooper (1995) has recently been developing models that enable researchers to separate out the analgesic effect of standards like aspirin and the potential of new drug treatments from any placebo response. In addition to answering questions about dosage, these formulas would also enable pain relief from different treatments to be compared, and the extent of the placebo effect for each procedure to be known. The best effect that single-dose oral drugs can achieve was put at 80%, but the vast majority of studies typically show results between 50% and 60% (Cooper, 1995).

Peck (1986) says that patients do better when they are told that the drug is powerful; morphine is a good example here. In a double-blind study where tricyclic anti-depressants or placebo was given post-operatively to hip or knee arthroplasty patients, in addition to morphine administered via patient-controlled analgesia (PCA), the results showed that 50 mg of amitriptyline was no different from placebo in altering post-operative pain (Kerrick et al, 1993). Kerrick et al concluded that there was no support for its use as a co-analgesic in this situation. However, by including PCA morphine as ethical back-up for pain relief, a situation was constructed whereby patients' faith in the widely known power of morphine to relieve pain may have negated any existing positive expectations about the weaker power of lesser known co-analgesics like amitriptyline. The status effects of the treatment are important, such as its reputation, expense and impressiveness. In general, placebo injections produce larger effects than pills (Miller, 1989), and higher doses of placebo and placebo injections tend to be more effective than low ones.

A timing effect has also been recorded, which seems to reflect an interesting interaction between pharmacological and placebo effects in some clinical practice. Milligan and Atkinson (1991) noticed that many pain patients attending clinics for repeated local anaesthetic injections reported that their pain had returned "two weeks ago". They set up a single-blind study where 20 patients whose pain had returned in the previous one to three weeks were randomly assigned either to a condition where they were given a new appointment two weeks short of the old appointment interval, or to one where the appointment was two weeks longer than the expected appointment time. They found that 85% of the sample had a "return of pain" interval coinciding with the proximity of their next clinic appointment, while the other 15% reported continuing symptom control at a tolerable level. They say that this "two week syndrome" reflects pain behaviour; it sends a message to the doctor saying "this treatment works, but would be better if it was performed more often". A clinical implication here is that it might be possible to extend the interval gradually for some patients.

The role of belief systems is now recognised as important to the placebo effect because it influences the experience of pain and pain behaviour (Craig, 1984). But what do people believe when they take a placebo? To better understand this internal dialogue, Grunbaum (1985) says that it is helpful to differentiate between intentional placebos and inadvertent placebos, because the dialogue is different in each case. An intentional placebo is where the substance must be *believed* to be a placebo by its dispenser, and must also *be* one. Where patients believe that their placebo has failed them, they may argue that for others with their disorder it can be remedial, but that due to incidental factors it was not effective for them. An inadvertent placebo is when the characteristic treatment factors are not remedial for the disease, but where some sufferers credit them with being therapeutic. Moreover, they are inclined to believe that some factors, at least, are indispensable in relieving their disorder. Patients agree with the view that the substance has remedial value, and believe that other sufferers are aware of this. This complex interaction of beliefs demonstrates the powerful social components of the placebo. Intuitively, the dialogue reported by Grunbaum is not surprising, but it is difficult to obtain such information as "hard" data. For patients to voice suspicion that the physician had deprived them of anything but the most active treatment smacks at best of lost confidence, and at worst of paranoia. Ethical problems also arise because it is not possible to use an intentional placebo without deception. It is, however, possible to use a placebo such as a sugar pill as an effective therapeutic device by disclosing its contents to patients (Brody, 1985). Both types of placebo are capable of having the expected positive effects as well as unintentionally exacerbating an illness.

Interesting work on placebos has been carried out on attributions made by patients who take them (see Chapter 5). As we have seen, Beecher's theory is that placebos work partially by reducing the emotional aspects of pain; that is, they reduce suffering or the reaction component. It is possible to draw further principles here from a classic study by Storms and Nisbett (1970). They investigated the emotional behaviour of insomniacs by looking at the effects of insomniac placebo pills on going to bed and the time of sleeping. The pills were described as "pep" pills, which might increase alertness, heart rate and body temperature, or as "sedatives". Those taking the pep pills reduced their insomnia by 12 minutes each night, while the sedative group increased their insomnia by 15 minutes. Those who reattributed their natural bedtime arousal to the pep pills experienced less emotionality, and for this reason fell asleep more quickly. On the other hand, the sedative group attributed their arousal to feeling emotional as a result of taking a drug, even though the drug was supposed to reduce these symptoms and had no physiological effects. This work shows how people's attributions can affect the ways in which pills work, and demonstrates why the monitoring of such attributions is so important with active drugs. It also shows how attributions about the symptoms of emotional states influence the subsequent intensity of those emotions.

These results can be explained by the fact that each person adopted the self-descriptive label of insomniac. Taking the labelling process one step further, Valins and Nisbett (1972) have suggested that self-attributions of pathology are one of two key elements that maintain insomnia; the other is increased anxiety. Storms and Nisbett (1970) provide insights into the cognitions and attributions that create and maintain these key features. They found that insomniacs generated similar accounts of sleeplessness, regardless of their allocated condition. Typically, they would retire to bed, wonder whether it was going to be a difficult night, and look for tell-tale symptoms of insomnia, such as it being too hot or too noisy. Then their initial worries would be confirmed and they could imagine the consequences of another sleepless night, with fatigue the following day, poor work performance, and so on. This expanded their worries over time and they began to speculate about the meaning of insomnia and whether it underlay some deep neurotic disorder or pathology (Storms and McCaul, 1976).

Unrelieved pain is a principal reason for disturbed sleep (Twycross and Fairfield, 1982), particularly where depression is implicated (see Chapter 5). In a survey of 100 consecutive cancer patients, Twycross and Fairfield (1982) found that 51 patients had a good night's sleep prior to admission, for 15 sleep was fair, but for 34 it was bad. This process may therefore be applicable to the behaviour of some chronic pain patients and helps us to understand their attributions. The clinical implications of this work are that successful therapists should convince sufferers to drop their self-diagnosis, whether it is the label of "insomniac" or "pain patient", and reattribute their symptoms to specific stressors in their environment. When this reattribution process is completed, they will then be able to argue that their symptoms do not indicate that there is something fundamentally and irretrievably wrong with themselves — their genes, their personality and so on — but is more to do with traumatic life events or a high stress life-style. This strategy empowers patients, because by making external attributions they gain the potential to change their life-style and feel more in control of their symptoms. One of the most damaging effects of self-attributions is perceived loss of control. This reattribution process stops the self-feeding emotional cycle and relieves a large part of the anxiety (Storms and McCaul, 1976). Together this combination of social, contextual and personality factors assist in explaining how placebos function.

THE PROVIDER

The attitudes of the provider are of equal importance to those of the patient. Two health professionals giving the same drug in the same amounts may have different effects because of the differing beliefs and expectations of the staff, which are communicated to the patient verbally and non-verbally. Miller (1989) reviewed 25 double-blind trials where the provider believed that the drug was strong or weak. His evidence showed that such beliefs largely corresponded with the waxing and waning of symptoms. Because therapists' attitudes vary from scepticism to enthusiasm, and patients' attitudes range from disbelief to faith in the treatment and its provider, the double-blind procedure is a minimum condition for good work in this area. Ideally, studies should be triple-blind, so that patients do not know to which group they have been assigned, dispensers do not know what they are giving (impossible for surgery or psychotherapy), and outcome assessors do not know whether they are evaluating patients from treatment or control groups (Peck, 1986). This ignorance at all levels forms the basis for a good medical joke. Provider friendliness, interest, sympathy and empathy towards the patient affect the placebo mechanism. Gryll and Katahn (1978) found that a warm "atmosphere" in the dentist's surgery reduced pain, and this occurred irrespective of whether the atmosphere was created by the dentist or by the dental technician. Looking further at status effects, they went on to show that when a technician administered a pill with a message that undersold it, it was more likely to reduce pain than if the pill was undersold by the dentists themselves. Such findings underscore the value of teamwork for health professionals.

The ways in which health providers contribute to the placebo effect is called iatroplacebogenesis. Their attitudes towards their patients, the treatment or the results of therapy are described as direct iatroplacebogenesis. Such behaviour may be interpreted by the patients as the doctor liking them and being confident that the therapy will relieve their discomfort. Indirect iatroplacebogenesis arises from doctors' interest in the disease itself or the particular method of treatment, especially where they are specialists. Doctors themselves are usually quite unaware of this influence. A surgeon's scepticism or enthusiasm for a procedure can influence treatment, as a classic report on ligation of the internal mammary artery to relieve angina pectoris has shown (Beecher, 1961). Only when it was found that a sham operation, which exposed but did not ligate the artery, produced equally good results as the real operation did the enthusiasts abandon the procedure. Following the sham procedure, objective measures such as increased exercise tolerance from 4 to 10 minutes without pain and the non-inversion of T waves in the ECG unambiguously confirmed this improvement. Although these small samples were not matched by age and sex, Beecher (1961) concluded that success in surgery can depend upon the surgeon as well as the patient having an appropriate set of beliefs, so underlining the power of this social interaction in affecting outcome.

Staff attitudes to placebos and the patients who receive them colour the judgements they subsequently make about pain and their readiness to give adequate pain relief. Studying house officers and nurses, Goodwin, Goodwin and Vogel (1979) found that the majority of staff substantially underestimated how many patients could have their pain relieved by being given a placebo. Placebos were most often given to patients whom the staff disliked, who were believed to exaggerate their pain, and for whom pain medication had so far failed. Furthermore, a positive reaction to a placebo was interpreted by doctors as confirmation that the pain was purely psychological. The staff used placebos to find out whether the pain was "real" when patients were using more pain medication than they deemed necessary. They also used placebos with "problem" patients. Even staff who knew that a placebo can relieve organic pain tended to give them to patients with whom they were having a difficult relationship. Patients receiving placebos are therefore unlikely to be viewed positively by ward staff, whatever the outcome. However, overdemanding and complaining patients are less likely to respond to placebos than patients who are well liked by hospital staff (Lasagna et al, 1954), so the very patients who could benefit most from a placebo may not be receiving one as a result of staff beliefs. This suggests that staff may be using their own professionally acceptable style of retribution arising from frustration, or in reaction to a manipulating and unpleasant patient. Their behaviour is not based on scientific or clinical principles, but on their own emotional reactions to the interaction with the patient and possibly a need for greater control over the patient's behaviour and the disease. Beecher (1955) recognised that a legitimate reason for using a placebo was as a resource for a harassed doctor dealing with a "neurotic" patient. Patients and staff alike would benefit if these all-too-human features of personal interaction were frankly and openly discussed in staff support groups rather than denied or neglected.

ALTERNATIVE THERAPY

An area where the presence of a placebo effect is often questioned is where "alternative" or complementary therapies are being evaluated. It is often asked whether they work any better than a placebo, yet it is easy to forget that the majority of consensually accepted interventions in daily use in medicine have never been evaluated using the "gold standard" of a double-blind randomised controlled trial with placebo control. In the previous section we considered the placebo effect of ultrasound for dental surgery (Hashish, Feinmann and Harvey, 1988) and the way in which it relieved discomfort. Other standard physiotherapy procedures apart from attention treatment are beginning to be carefully evaluated in a similar way. In a review of the pain-relieving effects claimed in four studies of laser therapy, Devor (1990) found that relief occurs because of powerful suggestion and other placebo components. He says that helium–neon lasers produce a red light, which has the same radiation impact as that of a small red flashlight. Good double-blind controlled trials have not yet been carried out on laser treatment. While there is no problem in the knowing use of a placebo, he cautions against the purchase of very expensive machinery for this purpose.

The model that underlies the use of acupuncture is concerned with the energy flow around the body and the need to restore the balance of energy within the system. There are believed to be 14 meridians or channels, some of which are associated with organs, as well as some subsidiary channels. Acupuncturists consider medical history, life-style, pulse, tongue, complexion, smell, sleep and appetite. Traditional acupuncture takes a holistic approach, so that there are as many ways to treat a bad back as there are patients, although the design requirements of western medicine have rarely allowed acupuncturists to treat in a totally authentic manner (Vincent and Richardson, 1986).

Melzack (1989) claims that acupuncture analgesia has considerable similarities with other near-painful methods like cupping, cauterisation and other counter-irritation methods. As they work through hyperstimulation analgesia, from a pain point of view it is convenient to consider them together. Suggestion and distraction of attention are observed to be commonly used in many procedures of folk medicine, but Melzack (1989) concludes that neither of these processes wholly explains either the power of the methods or the length of relief produced. The tingling, heaviness and numbness induced by twirling a needle at the point of Hoku for 20 minutes at low stimulus levels may induce distraction and diversion of attention, although such claims have not always been substantiated (Lee, Zaretsky and McMeniman, 1978) and are theoretically implausible. Reported long lasting effects raise questions about whether endorphin release is a sufficient explanation for acupuncture analgesia (Chapman et al, 1980). Lewith and Kenyon (1984) concluded that there was enough data available to support the view that acupuncture does release endorphins, which have an analgesic effect. Limited evidence suggests that acupuncture may modify the activity of the autonomic nervous system.

A major methodological problem in this area is to find adequate controls that satisfy the criteria for a well-controlled trial. It is impossible to adequately "blind" an acupuncturist, for instance. Three types of control have been identified by Vincent and Richardson (1986): (i) no-treatment controls, where little or no specific information is given, (ii) alternative treatments, where the efficacy of the new treatment is evaluated, and (iii) placebos. They concluded that there was good evidence from controlled studies that acupuncture relieves pain in the short term, particularly for low back pain and headache. Although the range is wide, effectiveness generally varies from 50% to 80% for the first two types of study, compared with 30% to 35% for placebo-related factors. An early review of 24 controlled studies comparing placebo with acupuncture analgesia for pain relief produced experimentally, for example by ischaemia or tooth pulp pain, recorded a significant analgesic effect in 17 (Reichmanis and Becker, 1977), so giving reasonable support.

The discovery that there is some coincidence between the siting of relevant nerves and meridians has given the practice of acupuncture greater scientific credibility. However, acupuncturists deny that they simply needle nerve trunks, although it is claimed that meridians do follow lines of high electrical conductance. The bodily distribution of trigger and motor points bears considerable similarities to acupuncture points, and procaine infiltration has demonstrated how afferent transmission is essential to analgesia (Melzack, 1983a). Lynn and Perl (1977) comment that it is impossible to obtain equivalence between anatomically different points in terms of nerve density, proximity to nerve trunks and motor effects. Following careful experimental work to test loci, sensitivity and contact points, they concluded that, in practice, the differences between "real" and "placebo" acupuncture points are small or absent. From a more recent review, Richardson and Vincent (1986) say that the overall significance of point location is unclear but it seems plausible that some points are superior to others. Furthermore, the depth of insertion may make a difference to the results.

Reichmanis and Becker (1977) found that stimulation close to an acupuncture point was more effective than at distant sites, so supporting the physiological theory that underpins practice. "Dramatic relief" from myofascial pain has been observed by simply inserting a hypodermic needle through the skin at an acupuncture point, without injecting. Such dry needling at the point of maximum tenderness is reported to have given continuous relief for many months (Melzack, 1983a). As acupuncture needles are deliberately blunt, the equivalence of these two procedures is debatable. The extent to which sham acupuncture constitutes an adequate control is also questionable: this is the insertion of needles at points that are considered by acupuncturists to be therapeutically ineffective for the condition being treated (Lewith and Machin, 1983). Furthermore, there is an attendant ethical problem of obtaining informed consent (Moore and Berk, 1980).

Transcutaneous electrical nerve stimulation (TENS) is effective and is sometimes preferred to acupuncture because it is non-invasive. It can also be used by a range of health professionals or self-administered, with tuition. There is also some evidence that where dental pain is concerned, TENS and acupuncture both give a small but significant amount of sensory pain relief (Chapman, Wilson and Gehrig, 1976). The constriction of the blood vessels that produce aching and burning pains as a result of ice massage of relevant acupuncture points is reported to be as effective as TENS in reducing chronic low back pain (Melzack et al, 1980). In this study 29 patients received two treatments of each, in random order, and were then able to choose a fifth treatment. Of the nine who chose ice, several said that, despite its greater effectiveness, it was more unpleasant or painful than TENS, which raises questions about its clinical acceptability. More recently subcutaneous nerve stimulation (SCNS) has been used in a small study of pain relief for patients with osteo-arthritis of the hip (Cottingham et al, 1985). Despite the lack of differences between treatment and control groups, significant relief was obtained by all patients after about two weeks. The authors concluded that although there was a strong placebo effect, the outcome compared favourably with TENS, but it is not clear whether, given the choice, the patients would have preferred it.

Questions have been raised about whether certain personality factors might affect the efficacy of TENS. In a retrospective study of 50 patients with chronic musculoskeletal pain in the neck or shoulders, small subsamples of non-responders ($N = 8$) were found to have more anxiety, depression and stronger beliefs in powerful others than those who responded to treatment ($N = 13$) with "substantial" pain relief, over a 2- to 6-month period. In a more convincing double-blind trial, where 30 patients received TENS from electrodes placed at each side of the incision following elective surgery to the upper abdomen, those receiving TENS requested 25% less morphine from nurses post-operatively than placebo patients given non-active stimulators. This difference was insignificant until neuroticism scores from the Eysenck Personality Inventory were taken into account. Moreover, neuroticism was found to explain 80% of the variance, although anxiety did not feature. Thus, there is evidence that some personality factors, such as neuroticism, may play a role in pain relief from this procedure.

Where the machine is not functioning and provides a placebo, "mock" TENS is effective in relieving pain in 30–35% of patients (Lewith and Machin, 1983). However, it is not clear whether this procedure is equivalent to needling without electrical stimulation. Vincent and Richardson (1986) point out that its therapeutic power depends on exactly how it is presented to the patient. This seems to be true for a sizable proportion of these manipulations. In a randomised controlled study, the efficacy of a six-week course of acupuncture analgesia for the relief of migrainous headaches was compared with a placebo procedure of mock TENS, where two electrodes were placed on the skin over the mastoid process but no current was passed (Dowson, Lewith and Machin, 1985). The placebo group reported 33% improvement in pain, but the acupuncture group showed only an extra 20% improvement, when 35% more had been expected. They concluded that headache is very sensitive to placebo therapy. Chronicity may be an important variable in the response of headache patients to acupuncture (Levine, Gormley and Fields, 1976).

In a study of chronic low back pain, Marchand et al (1993) randomly allocated 42 patients to one of three groups. They were included in a TENS condition where high frequency (100 Hz), low intensity current was passed through electrodes applied to a dermatome for 30 minutes, a TENS placebo where no current was passed through electrodes or to a control group without treatment. After 16 treatment sessions it was found that TENS was more efficient in reducing pain intensity but not pain unpleasantness. Furthermore, TENS had an additive effect on intensity as the number of sessions increased, which persisted for a week after treatment. Marchand et al (1993) concluded that the sensory–discriminative qualities of pain were affected by TENS, but that affective–motivational aspects were closely linked to the placebo effect. This is in line with other research, which confirms that the affective aspects of chronic pain are more susceptible to psychological intervention.

Some studies on acupuncture have begun with the assumption that those in pain may be more psychologically disturbed, but in general this has not been confirmed. In a study of 344 people where the majority were seeking acupuncture for arthritis, headache or back pain, Lewis and Nadler (1976) found little evidence of psychopathology in a battery of personality tests, including the Minnesota Multiphasic Personality Inventory (MMPI). However, relief from discomfort corresponded with some improvements in mental health during the year of the study. Similarly, Toomey et al (1977) found that those who responded to acupuncture were less depressed and less passive, and had experienced pain for a shorter length of time, than those who failed to respond to therapy, yet they found no differences between responders and non-responders in the way they described their pain or the noxiousness of the stimulation. Using a beliefs in pain control instrument, Skevington (1990) found that acupuncture patients had stronger beliefs in the powers of doctors to control their pain than other types of chronic pain patients with arthritis and breast cancer. However, strong beliefs in personal pain control and weak beliefs that chance happenings affect their pain closely approximate the pattern of beliefs found in pain-free populations, so supporting the idea that acupuncture patients have a relatively healthy profile.

Enthusiasm for acupuncture has waned in the West as studies have shown that it has not lived up to its early promise — or perhaps unreasonable expectations. However, acupuncture for pain relief has a much shorter history than is popularly assumed; although practised for thousands of years in the treatment of illness, it has only been used specifically for pain relief in China since 1949. In one study, acupuncture was given to patients receiving surgery for impacted molars before or after the operation (Ekblom et al, 1991). Those receiving acupuncture prior to surgery were more tense afterwards, and found the operation more unpleasant, with more intraoperative pain than no-acupuncture controls; 15 out of 24 needed more local anaesthetic. Both acupuncture groups had more post-operative pain than controls. The pre-acupuncture group were found to consume more post-operative analgesics, so detracting from the gate control theory of pain. In addition, more patients in both acupuncture groups suffered the post-operative complication of "dry socket" wound. Observations that pre-operative acupuncture patients were more relaxed may have been counterproductive to outcomes. A social interpretation of these results is that these patients had lower expectations of pain because they believed that the acupuncture would offer them some protection; subsequently, they found that their lay theory was alarmingly disconfirmed by the presence of considerable discomfort.

During the 1970s, the Chinese made startling claims for the analgesic effects of acupuncture analgesia during surgery (Lien-Tsang, 1978), but Melzack (1983a) observed that it was used only rarely, in 5–10% of operations. In common with many other alternative therapies, acupuncture for pain relief during surgery was only used when it was enthusiastically and totally accepted by the patient. These strong beliefs may have accounted for some of the successes claimed (Chaves and Barber, 1976). Consequently, it was only used with carefully selected patients. These preparatory techniques draw explicitly upon social psychology. Training involved strengthening positive beliefs about the efficacy of acupuncture in pain relief. Another aim was to develop a close, supportive, interpersonal relationship between the patient and therapist, to minimise surprise and therefore alarm, which might induce anxiety and hence pain. Role modelling and rehearsal were carried out by talking to patients who had already undergone the procedure, and this formed a central part of the training. Prospective patients would visit the ward and hospital operating theatre, and get to know the hospital staff as much as three months in advance of surgery, so that the environment was familiar. Patients were offered the opportunity to try out the acupuncture needles themselves. This long training, familiarisation and socialisation procedure precluded the use of acupuncture in emergency conditions. Information was given by the surgeon and acupuncturist about what would be done and how, and about what effect the needles would have. Narcotic analgesics, local anaesthetics and sedatives were often used pre-operatively. Substantial doubt has been cast on claims that acupuncture can be reliably used to give pain relief during surgery because patients were often heavily sedated in advance. Some observers reported that drugs were given during the operation, and these failed to control pain in 10% of already highly selected patients. The presence of fear, anxiety and tension was likely to produce failure during skin incision, particularly of the sensitive areas such as the mucous membranes of the mouth, throat, genitalia and rectum. Although incision of the internal organs is relatively painless, distention and traction can cause pain, so these operations were often carried out slowly and carefully (Chaves and Barber, 1976).

To what extent are these procedures different from the preparations made for behavioural non-invasive pain relief techniques claimed in the West? Reviewing approaches used in behavioural multidisciplinary pain management programmes, Keefe, Gil and Rose (1986) discuss the importance of patient preparation in the time prior to entering treatment. This preparation includes patient and family education, consideration of the situation in which treatment is given (because psychiatric settings are often unacceptable), and preparations to prevent patients from feeling that the physician has abandoned them. Too often, the ways in which such psychosocial preparations are carried out and their contents are not publicly available in reports. They tend to be neglected, being seen as incidental and irrelevant features of clinical practice. Despite the flaws, a message we can take from Chinese studies of acupuncture is that more careful and systematic accounts about how these vital schemata are created and maintained could provide greater control over clinical outcomes in the long term.

CONCLUSION

Health knowledge based on social psychology has been used here to explain more about the nature of the care and treatment of those in pain. Looking at the rich and complex interaction between patients and carers, and taking environmental features into account, enables a more comprehensive and holistic assessment to be made in the attempt to explain outcomes such as why some people benefit from health care while others do not. In the final chapter we consider some of the broader conceptual and methodological features affecting the social assessment of health and health care for those in pain, and offer a model for consideration.

The Way Forward

10

In this last chapter we consider some of the broader issues that will need to be attended to in studies concerned with a social psychology of pain. Firstly, the investigation of important social factors that affect individual differences needs to be built into research designs. In addition to this more conventional nod in the direction of studying differences between gender, age groups, racial and other social groups, several other lines of investigation might be productively pursued. These are outlined in the first section, using gender as the example. In the second section we address some of the ethical issues that bedevil social research. Although some of these are relevant to the general conduct of all human investigation, others, with a particularly social flavour, have not been widely considered within pain research. In the third section we take a brief look at some of the ways in which social psychology affects policy making for pain patients. We then move on to consider the quality of life of those in chronic pain and how this might be better investigated. Quality of life as a concept has been largely neglected in pain research until very recently, and pain deserves to be seen within the overall picture of the individual's life. Finally, a social psychological model for the study of pain is offered.

GENDER ISSUES

Studying differences between the genders in the experience and reporting of pain has attracted considerable attention, and thus serves as an example of the ways in which the research enterprise might be diversified. Above all, researchers think of sex differences when they think about this area. Some attention was paid to what is known about sex differences in pain and sensitivity thresholds and the reporting of pain in the first half of this volume, but the many *similarities* between the sexes have been largely ignored. It is therefore impossible to deduce whether reported differences are any more or less important than the similarities; they may turn out to be less important than has been recorded in the history of pain to date. If careful investigation showed that many similarities existed, this knowledge would serve to diffuse some of the prevalent stereotypical views about the ways in which women and men report their pain. Investigations of similarities and differences between social groups should be routinely integrated into pain protocols of all types, and their analysis and report should be seen as a requirement of good pain research.

More attention should be devoted to investigating "normal" pains rather than abnormal pain in both sexes. Where women's pain has been investigated, the tendency has been to focus more on their *problems*. There is great scope for investigations of pain across the life-cycle and its chronobiology (Berkley, 1993). Intermittent periodic pain is potentially a regular life event for half of the population. Where such pains occur, they create schematic markers, being carefully monitored for a host of social and cultural reasons, as well as those connected with health and well-being. Little is known about how young women interpret the early experience of pain at menarche, and how this affects their subsequent expectations about pain. It is not known to what extent menstrual pain and other discomforts associated with premenstrual syndrome influence the experience and reporting behaviour of those who subsequently develop a chronically painful condition resulting from disease or surgery. It seems plausible that regular experience with pain and discomfort systematically shape schemata about what pain is and how best to cope with it. Perceptions of pain resulting from successive accidents to adolescent males might provide a similar, but not equivalent, developmental view.

There is also a case for studying painful events and procedures that are specific to the life-style of each social subgroup, with the aim of developing greater under-standing about their willingness to report pain. Although labour pain has been investigated, relatively little is known about the pain of interventions like episiotomy and its implications for the post-natal period. Pain associated with hysterectomy, miscarriage and abortion are also profoundly influenced by social and cultural factors. Where clitoridectomy and circumcision rites are integral to the practices of particular cultures, they also deserve serious scientific attention. Lastly, types of pain, like headache, that are more closely associated with the behaviour of particular social groups deserve to be looked at more closely. A high proportion of women report headaches, for instance, and we have seen that their incidence is closely associated with the late phase of the menstrual cycle and menopause. While a case can be made for laboratory studies of these pains, this should be carried out in tandem with those employing naturalistic methods, which enable assessment of the psychosocial and cultural context of these symptoms.

The majority of pain measures in this field concentrate on the cognitive processes activated in the reporting of pain (see Chapters 2 to 6); hence, with a few notable exceptions, they neglect the assessment of emotions in the normal ranges. However, it is well established that women are more inclined to express their emotions than men, and this is as true for non-pathological conditions as for pathological ones. Measures like the Illness Behaviour Questionnaire (IBQ), while providing scope for an evaluation of normal levels of emotionality, are largely directed at abnormal-ity. However, they do not focus on the diversity of emotions that constitute the normal range of well-being. Many scales are problem-centred, focusing on the negative rather than the positive emotions. Although the detection of psycho-pathology is important, it only applies to a minority of chronic pain patients. This short-sighted pursuit of psychopathology represents a major impediment to progress in obtaining a comprehensive view of pain in general, not just for social pain research.

However, there are some sex-specific problems that need attention. Any com-prehensive analysis of pain in women would need to consider problems specific to women's biology and their treatment. These include pelvic, uterine and cervical pain, and breast pain. It is also necessary to consider pain in diseases where genetic and/or hormonal factors appear to play an important role. Arthritis provides a good example, because the rheumatic diseases commonly affect three times as many women as men. Furthermore, in rheumatoid arthritis, pain and inflammation may be relieved during pregnancy, strongly indicating that hormonal fluctuations associated with the reproductive cycle may be more important in the inflammatory process than has hitherto been considered. Where the incidence of women in the population for a particular condition approaches zero, this also requires careful scrutiny. Although some portion of analgesic efficacy can be explained by physical and physiological factors like body weight and size, there are sex differences in the ways in which people respond to pain and its relief. A greater part of the variance in response to analgesic might be explained by mediating social and behavioural factors, which so far remain unexplored.

There is an extensive literature to indicate that women are much more adept at expressing their emotions than men, particularly where feelings about their health are concerned. Given the predominance of cognitive methods used for the subjective study of pain, it is clear that many emotions have barely been evaluated in the normal or abnormal ranges. There may be good reasons why pain researchers have not yet tapped into this rich seam of reports. It is arguable that existing methodologies still do not adequately enable many emotions to be reported. One way forward would be in the more widespread use of *qualitative* methodologies. Work using these methods has been substantially under-represented in the leading pain journals to date. Such methods need further consideration as legitimate ways of evaluating the painful experience, and they should become a bona fide part of the armoury needed to investigate fully the many subjective aspects of pain.

Lastly, the social impact of women as prime carers and nurturers of those in pain cannot be underestimated. They are major agents in the shaping of other people's perceptions, attitudes and behaviour related to pain and suffering. Because women are more likely than men to seek health care for themselves and to have contact with health professionals while accompanying others for whom they care, such as children, more health promotion and prevention activities should be targeted at them as a group. This could include advice on how to deal with acute pain in children and administering treatment to them, such as leaflets giving information, advice on coping strategies and support to parents with children who have chronic pain and need regular painful interventions such as lumbar puncture. Women often have to cope with adult complaints of common painful conditions like back pain, headache and trauma in the family. Because of their greater interest in health matters, their opinion is often sought in the decision about whether to seek professional advice. In view of this widespread involvement of women in health care at several different levels, the attitudes, stereotypes and behaviour of health professionals towards women need more careful research; this in turn should have direct implications for how health professionals are trained. Directly and indirectly, women are major consumers of health care, and as such have an important role to play in evaluating the service.

ETHICAL ISSUES

While considerable attention has — rightly — been paid to ethical issues relating to animal experimentation and to the investigation of human pain in the laboratory, issues particularly associated with the conduct of social psychological investigations need to be examined. In advancing knowledge about pain, many investigations have used animals; it is also possible to study social behaviour in this way. Existing guidelines place restraints on what procedures may or may not be undertaken; in many cases, these represent an uneasy compromise between the goals of the scientist and the animal's potential suffering (Casey and Handwerker, 1989). Only conscious animals should be used. Guidelines and safeguards for the investigation of pain in conscious animals have been proposed by Zimmerman (1983) to protect against the use of extreme procedures.

Investigations should be reviewed regularly by ethical committees composed of scientists, health professionals and lay people: this is central to any work on pain in humans. There is a need to justify the proposed procedures continually, so that the benefits of the work are clear. Experimenters must try the pain stimulus on themselves; Davis (1981) has argued that there is "no logical reason for using values that are not moderate". He says experimenters should ask themselves whether they would place their own hand on the shock grid. If the answer is negative, then the shock setting is too high. Unfortunately, this does not entirely take care of the range of individual differences observed in humans. Furthermore, pain tolerance levels differ between the species (Casey and Handwerker, 1989). The extent to which animals deviate from normal, both physiologically and behaviourally, when in pain should be measured and recorded, then reasonable steps should be taken to ensure that the minimum pain necessary for the experiment can be applied. The eminent pain researcher Patrick Wall keeps caged rodents as office companions with this ethical imperative in mind. Animals presumed to be experiencing chronic pain should be permitted to self-administer analgesics if it does not interfere with the experiment. Where a neuromuscular blocking agent is used which masks behavioural responses, then a general anaesthetic or appropriate surgery must also be used to eliminate awareness. Finally, the duration of an experiment must be kept to a minimum.

Many of these guidelines apply to work with people. Sternbach (1983b) says that if the administration of pain is justified then attention should be paid to recruiting the fewest possible participants, using the least intense stimulation and the shortest possible duration of pain. Participants should be informed of the risks of physical and psychological harm and precautions taken to minimise any threat or danger. The use of standard analgesics for pain relief should not be excluded. Lastly, he suggests that monetary rewards are a legitimate source of repayment for participation in laboratory studies, although pain relief may be reward for some patients.

The use of aversive stimulation such as shock raises important issues in human experimentation, where noxious stimulation is often interpreted as punishment. Ethical problems also occur where punishment is expected but witheld, in passive avoidance (Davis, 1981). This can expose participants to physical and psychological stress. In general, Davis argues that the use of aversive stimulation with people in the laboratory does not present a substantial ethical problem. This is because of the prevailing moral climate and the rigorous ethical guidelines set by professional societies. Nor does he see it as a particular issue in the clinic, where, for example, behaviour modification is used as an aversive technique, because it is geared more towards healing than to the advancement of knowledge. He claims that most problems occur, firstly, where there is lack of informed consent from the patient or the next of kin, and, secondly, where a patient does not share the interventionist's wish to change his or her behaviour (Davis, 1981). Others, however, would disagree with his analysis. Some of the reasons why people are left in clinical pain have already been addressed in the previous two chapters; they include the indifference of some health professionals to pain and suffering, the patients' inability to communicate their needs for relief and the operation of negligent systems of health care, such as where the pharmacy is closed when pain relief is needed, or where there is no access to narcotics for the terminally ill due to government control of illicit drugs. Areas where the ethical treatment of those in pain could improve are in developing a type of trust between treater and treated, which is egalitarian and earned, rather than paternalistic, acknowledges human rights, provides respect and dignity for those in pain, and re-orientates clinicians more towards healing than curing (Sommerville, 1994).

Davis and others have utilised recent findings about beliefs in pain control to make experimental tasks more tolerable for participants. Discussion of control beliefs in Chapter 5 showed how anticipating pain, and hence increasing its predictability, can make the pain more bearable. So one procedure that might be used is to build in advanced warnings of discomfort and inconvenience as part of the informed consent. In this way, participants are given a free choice in participation at all stages of the study. Withdrawal from the study at any time should be made acceptable. Those wishing to withdraw may feel pressured into continuing because they cannot withdraw without loss of face or because of guilt about spoiling the experiment. Milgram's classic study (1974) on obedience to authority underscores the message here. It shows how pressure from an authoritative white-coated scientist can dramatically affect the behaviour of the average person, so raising questions about what constitutes an honest refusal.

People living in institutions and those ordered by an employer to take part in a study or treatment constitute clear cases of coercion, but these practices are easier to identify as unethical than the muddied distinctions between coercion and legitimate persuasion, and coercion versus a fair exchange of legitimate rewards and services. Incentives to the disadvantaged might be offered, such as social approval, money or parole. Others may be coerced by appeals for sympathy, or be shamed into participation (Kidder and Judd, 1986). Some groups are particularly vulnerable to requests, such as confused elderly people and children. For children, informed consent from the parents is essential. However, what adults tolerate may be quite unacceptable to children, and, although we need to understand how children experience and report pain, "the ethical acceptability of any research involving children is inextricably linked with the scientific value of a particular study" (McGrath, 1993).

Informed consent is an integral part of treatment, as well as a necessary precondition for investigations about pain. But what does it mean to give informed consent? How much information is required and how should it be presented? Consent must be freely given and with ample understanding, but there is only a loose social consensus about what this means, as shown by variable judgements in the courts. Scarman (1986) is clear about the unethical and clinically inadvisable practice of doctors entering patients into a randomised controlled clinical trial, without their consent. But legal action may be taken over the administration of a pain relieving injection, because the patient believed that they did not fully consent to the procedure (Swerdlow, 1982). Doctors working in the USA are required to inform patients about the risks that are central to the treatment proposed and the highly probable side effects. The "reasonable doctor test" is treatment that any reasonable doctor would think necessary, taking into account its urgency, the patient's mental state and, more problematically, the extent to which the doctor judges that the patient wants to be given details, because not all patients require an explanation. Conversely, the "reasonable patient test" requires doctors to tell their patients whatever a reasonable patient would want to know, while placing emphasis on the patient's right to self-determination. Although the patient has a right to know, it may not be a right that he or she wants to exercise, and it should be recognised that some patients do not want to know, as we saw in an earlier chapter.

In providing information prior to an injection, for instance, doctors in the USA must give patients the fullest possible information about how an injection will work, what sensations to expect, the inevitable risks, the likelihood of complications and how these will be treated if they arise. It is right for them to raise in the patient's mind the possibility of alternatives and to give their judgement of the advantages and disadvantages where needed, and also to respect a patient's request for a second opinion (Scarman, 1986). Consequently, patients in this system are faced with a real choice about whether they wish to continue in pain or to seek relief from it, with the attendant risks that this entails. The psychological consequences of choosing what is perceived in retrospect to be the "wrong" option were discussed in an earlier chapter. Feelings of failure and their implications for a patient's subsequent mental health need to be added to this list of risks. Much better forms of assessment need to be developed to assist doctors and their patients in more accurate decision making here. Scarman (1986) also defends the therapeutic privilege given to doctors to monitor the mental and physical health of their patients, and their duty to take a professional decision about situations where no warning or information should be given. The position is summed up as follows:

> the best policy ... is for a responsible, caring doctor to be flexible, considerate and discrete, never imposing unnecessary "informed consent", yet always ready to discuss anything with patients who wish it. Far from being patronising or arrogant, such a policy enhances the dignity of the patient as a unique individual, with changing moods and a changing ability to cope with fear, doubt and uncertainty.
> (Brewin, 1982)

What are the major ethical conflicts that social researchers face? Some techniques that are regarded as acceptable by researchers may be unacceptable from a human rights point of view, so their application is not generalisable. A study of dishonesty in airport taxi drivers provides an example that in real life might be considered to be the activity of an *agent provocateur*. Secondly, the infliction of pain for interrogation and torture purposes shows how published research findings can be utilised in the abuse of human rights. Torture adds dehumanisation to disidentification and depersonalisation (Sommerville, 1994), so is a legitimate area of social psychological work. The meaning of administered pain can be dramatically changed in different circumstances, so in- vestigators need to take wider social responsibility for their research and its findings.

Thirdly, deception has become a moral issue — and unacceptable — in recent years. It can take many forms: at one end of the continuum information is withheld, while at the other, there is a deliberate attempt to mislead. There are extreme examples of carefully staged experiments, where the preparations for deception have involved elaborate rehearsals, a large "cast" and a variety of props — enough to turn the experiment into a theatrical experience. However, where deception has been employed in social psychology, participants are much more likely to have been partially informed. The most ethical position would be to tell all, but the methodological conundrum here is that where full information has been provided, it is difficult to determine the extent to which it has directly affected the participant's behaviour, and therefore the reliability of the results. Participating pain patients in need of relief may obligingly produce the results that they know the investigator is seeking. In other situations, the procedure but not the hypothesis has been disclosed, and participants have agreed to cooperate in a role-play, with some reported success, but it is questionable how far role-play behaviour accurately reflects the normal behaviour of participants in real life. Sometimes we surprise ourselves by behaving quite differently in a particular situation than we might have expected. One strategy for dealing with any necessary partial deception is to draw up a contract between participant and investigator, agreeing that the participant will be "debriefed" about the true nature of the investigation after the study is completed (Kidder and Judd, 1986), although this half-way house is not consensually acceptable to all social researchers.

The use of deception has been increasingly questioned by social psychologists since the 1970s. Deception undermines the public's trust in the individual professional, as well as damaging the image of the profession as a whole. Setting aside ethical issues for a moment, a deceptive performance or cover story may not be perceived to be authentic; if it fails to convince all participants, this raises serious questions about the reliability of the data obtained. A shortage of ecological validity is a most pertinent criticism where social investigations have been carried out in laboratories rather than in natural settings. This increases the case for using quasi-experimental designs to incorporate the social context or environment of those in pain. Examples would be to study pain patients in their family, at the workplace and during real consultations, rather than in artificial, staged or unfamiliar conditions.

Videotaping or audiotaping behaviour may constitute an invasion of privacy in the study of pain, as elsewhere. Structured observation of inpatient activities on a ward, particularly non-verbal behaviour, in the preparation of baselines for behaviour therapy (see Chapters 3 and 7) provide examples. Obliging participants to answer every item on a questionnaire or asking intrusive personal questions in interviews can often be overlooked as invasions of privacy. Obtaining information from a third party, such as a patient's family and friends, without the participant's consent is also problematic.

Is it possible to find ways of studying pain without the use of painful and stressful procedures? Sternbach (1983b) has suggested that one strategy alternative to inflicting pain could be the use of mathematical modelling. While it is possible to use humans and animals in studies of acute pain, the ethics of experimentation with chronic pain are highly controversial, yet chronic pain is the condition where the most important puzzles still need to be solved. Most of what we know about pain to date comes from experimental studies of acute states, and the best theoretical model available — the gate control theory — has had to be based on this limited knowledge (Wall, 1989). Mathematical modelling enables us to use existing physiological data to test particular phenomena in conditions where experimental studies would be unethical, and therefore impossible to carry out, such as in the administration of chronic pain.

As we saw in Chapter 2, linear relationships between the variables that affect pain can be evaluated statistically using LISREL, and these stochastic models have progressed understanding about pain. However, few natural phenomena behave in linear fashion, so the application of non-linear mathematics is more appropriate to the description of pain. Non-linear equations have been used to model an early version of the gate control theory of pain. Because the precise nature of the gating mechanism is still largely hypothetical — the exact T-cells have yet to be unambiguously identified in the dorsal horns — mathematical modelling of existing micro-electrographic recordings from relevant neurons can be represented in equations and tested to find out whether the gating mechanism is plausible in mathematical terms (Britton and Skevington, 1989). Britton and Skevington (1989) found that their model explained all of the most important observations on acute pain stated by Melzack and Wall in justifying the gating phenomenon. Furthermore, the modelling pointed to some misconceptions that have arisen about the consequences of the gate control theory, namely that stimulation of the large fibres leads ultimately to a reduction in pain. In fact, the theory allows for augmentation or reduction, possibly preceded by transient augmentation of pain, depending on the details of the model and the firing fre- quencies in large and small fibres. Non-linear modelling confirmed that all of these different outcomes were feasible. Secondly, the model was able to explain not only pain intensity but also some pain qualities in a way that had not previously been demonstrated. It showed that rhythmic pain and similar adjectives in the same subclass of the McGill Pain Questionnaire could result from an oscillation of potentials in the T-cells and inhibitory SG cells. One shortcoming of the gate control theory is that, so far, it has not been elaborated to explain differences between the ten subclasses of sensory pain, and, perhaps more importantly, between the three major classes of sensory, affective and evaluative pain. More complex versions of the theory can now be modelled, as well as models of specific chronic pain states, where adequate physiological data exist. Modelling could also be used to understand more about plastic changes in the nervous system (Britton and Skevington, 1989). Consequently, the model has many uses, while enabling researchers to overcome an ethical dilemma.

A POLICY FOR PAIN

Earlier in the book we considered how pain might be managed by individual therapists and teams of health workers. In this section we revisit this theme while taking a broader view about the way in which society deals with pain patients through the policies adopted locally by hospitals and nationally by governments. Legislation plays a big role in this process. These social and organisational factors shape and direct the ways in which health care workers are able to treat and manage pain.

Compensation for back pain has become a focus of concern in recent years. In the USA, someone who is injured at work is highly likely to receive substantial compensation from a Workers Compensation Board within a few weeks of the accident. This is a humanitarian way to deal with someone who loses their income without warning, from an accident. The pay-outs are substantial, often many thousands of dollars, in line with national USA compensation norms for divorce and medical negligence. Claim size is moderated by social consensus through the media. Fordyce (personal communication) argues that the rapid and substantial compensation given to people in the USA who are injured effectively rewards people for behaving in ways that exaggerate their pain and illness. This has resulted in the development of a series of policy and practical problems. From neo-behaviourist principles, he suggests that if patients are able to convince a psychologist that they are a "very bad case" and behave as if they are unlikely to ever work again, then the pay-offs are handsome. Huge rewards, delivered instantly, produce rapid learning and increase the likelihood that the behaviour will be repeated through positive reinforcement.

In the USA, the health care team is involved in assessing injuries and delivering to the courts a professional evaluation of the extent to which the accident will affect the individual's life and future ability to work in an existing job or in another job at a lower grade. Health care professionals who regularly give evidence in court have considerable powers to influence the size of financial rewards received as compensation for pain and disability. Consequently, methods of evaluation that will improve prediction about outcome are highly valued and constantly sought. Because the system of compensation is well advertised, accident victims are likely to be aware at the time of admission to hospital that any assessment may substantially affect how much compensation they will receive; it is argued that this may provide a motive for adjusting their behaviour or reports in order to maximise the pay-off. Consequently, there are concerns within this system that the pain management team may be duped by exaggerated pain reports. Case conferences commonly begin with a discussion of how far litigation has progressed. The patient's behaviour and reported health are then evaluated against this background. To make these professional judgements, therapists also draw upon their experience with previous similar patients using social comparison processes. Questions may be raised about whether the patient's reports of pain and pain behaviour concur with the amount of pain that might be expected from a person with those injuries; to what extent does it tally with known organic damage? In the full knowledge that there will always be a proportion of patients who will have "real" pain without damage, any such exaggerations are very difficult to assess. There are also some good methodological, philosophical and psychological reasons why patients may be unable to deliver reliable and accurate assessments of their own condition; these were addressed earlier in this book.

Many anecdotes have been written about those who seek compensation, but what are the facts? Contrary to popular belief, there is no overall support for the view that those who claim compensation are exaggerating their pain experience (Mendelson, 1986). There is evidence, however, that compensation-seekers may be more disabled than others, so their activities may be more disrupted (Tait, Chibnall and Richardson, 1990), which may influence their motivation to seek financial support. It is therefore important to consider which social and psychological factors may affect this behaviour, and whether the compensation system itself affects the duration of symptoms and the way in which sufferers present their pain and disability (Mendelson, 1992). There is only inconsistent support for the idea that those who have the most severe pain are also most likely to claim compensation. On the contrary, Melzack, Katz and Jeans (1985) found that compensation patients reported less evaluative pain and had fewer visits to health professionals, indicating that the financial security of compensation may reduce their anxiety and so improve their pain.

Furthermore, there is only inconsistent evidence to support the idea that litigating patients are any more psychologically disturbed than those who do not claim (Brena and Chapman, 1983). In a comparison of litigating and non-litigating pain patients participating in a behaviour therapy programme, Trief and Stein (1985) found no evidence of psychopathology among litigants using the Minnesota Multiphasic Personality Inventory (MMPI). However, litigants did have higher K scale scores, indicating that they might be more inclined to admit to personal defects and troubles than those who do not seek compensation. This suggests that litigants differ from non-litigants more in their style of reporting behaviour than in its contents. Others have observed that litigants with chronic pain have a "dramatised" complaining style (Brena and Chapman, 1983), and this has been confirmed empirically (Jamison, Matt and Parris, 1988). Such studies challenge the conventional personality explanation of a "compensation neurosis" by providing social explanations for litigants' behaviour. At the same time they assist in dispelling prevailing beliefs that compensation patients are an abnormal and problematic group in a psychological sense, even though they may remain a political and economic conundrum. Finally, there is an interpersonal explanation that should not be ignored. Melzack, Katz and Jeans (1985) have pointed out that compensation cases are stigmatised and doubly victimised, firstly by their accident, and secondly by others who resent or envy their compensation payments. They define a compensation neurosis as "a state of mind, born out of fear, kept alive by avarice, stimulated by lawyers and cured by a verdict" (Melzack, Katz and Jeans, 1985).

Socio-economic factors such as social class also affect this analysis (Volinn et al, 1988). Those most often injured at work are poorer blue-collar workers in more physically arduous manual jobs. Those in middle-class occupations damage their backs more often in sports injuries, such as while playing squash. For someone with negligible income living within a wealthy society, generous compensation payments may represent the largest single sum of unearned money that they are ever likely to receive, short of winning the lottery. The behaviourist view is that, not only does this actively encourage prolongation of illness behaviour, it might also predispose sufferers towards more accidents in the future. Volinn et al (1988) argue that miserly rewards, delivered late and in an air of uncertainty, reduce the power of association. Therefore, learning is poor and the spin-offs are minimal by comparison. Financial compensation tends to be the prerogative of developed countries; for much of the world's population no such system of rewards exists. Another slant on this debate is that those with higher earnings who successfully complete their course of treatment are likely to receive more compensation accordingly, and this in itself is a salient incentive to return to work (Barnes et al, 1989).

Social factors also affect the way in which employers respond. Merskey's insightful comment about claim rates for workers with back sprain sustains this view:

> We might think that this [claim rate] is due to the attitude of workers, but the response of the employers should also be taken into account. When demand for labour is low, those with a history of back pain will be at most disadvantage and least employable and therefore better able to maintain their claims for benefits.
> (Merskey, 1988)

Here, Merskey shifts the onus of responsibility from the vulnerable individual, who, as we saw in Chapter 5, is most likely to be blamed in much the same way that other victims are, to a socio-economic interpretation, where the employer is viewed an agent of social control. These ideas deserve further investigation.

Comparisons between the USA and other systems of accident compensation cross-nationally provide interesting insights. There are systematic differences in the way that pain policy is handled, as we saw with reference to palliative care in Chapter 9. The British style of dealing with accident victims differs substantially from that found in the USA, for historical and cultural reasons. If British workers are injured at work, they may be unaware that they may be entitled to compensation. If aware, they are unlikely to know about how to set the compensation machinery in motion. Furthermore, from a legal point of view, it is necessary for time to elapse after the injury before assessment can be made about the extent to which they remain disabled, unable to work and in pain, and hence before any compensation claim can be instigated. Compensation claims from an employer take place through the relevant trade union, which provides another bureaucratic barrier to swift implementation. It may be five years before the case is heard by the courts, and final settlements can take much longer as progression through different stages of the legal system is prolonged, ten years being quite common. The pay-offs are small by US standards, and awards are by no means automatic. Claimants often give up pursuing compensation payments, preferring to live with the pain rather than persisting with a long drawn out case in the courts, and with the added deterrent of substantial legal expenses, which they may eventually have to pay if they do not win. Consequently, health professionals evaluating pain in Britain work with a completely different set of social, psychological and legal parameters. During the assessment period, neither health professional nor patient knows with any degree of certainty whether the victim will be seeking compensation. The patients themselves are unlikely to be aware at the time of assessment that the way in which they behave may be used as evidence in a compensation claim, because the prospect of making a claim at this stage is relatively remote. Consequently, there is less concern among pain clinic personnel that the reports of pain obtained are exaggerated with the purpose of increasing financial gain, and hence less likelihood of the devaluation of subjective reports. This scenario of delay, unpredictability and inefficiency works to the benefit of assessing health professionals, and, some may say, also has benefits for the patient!

In terms of overall well-being, however, this type of system is most disadvantageous to the sufferer. Evidence suggests that those awaiting compensation payments are significantly more depressed than those who have settled their claims (Guest and Drummond, 1992). Unemployment itself and the uncertainty generated by dealing with the litigation process become additional sources of distress to that produced by the original injury (Tait, Chibnall and Richardson, 1990). Moreover, pain patients are hesitant to return to work because they fear that the case for a claim, and its size, will be affected by such action (Guest and Drummond, 1992). Consequently, the legal process acts as a drag on successful rehabilitation. Legal changes are necessary to remove such disincentives and facilitate the earliest possible return to work. In addition to these systemic changes, more could be done in pain management programmes to set realistic expectations about returning to employment. Active discussions about returning to work during these programmes can improve outcomes. A study by Catchlove and Cohen (1982) found that more of those patients who knew that returning to work was an integral component of treatment, and were warned that returning after inactivity would be tiring and difficult, actually returned to work (60%) than patients from a comparison group where the issue of return to work was not addressed (25%).

An international empirical analysis of different compensation schemes might enable researchers to partial out some of these confounding factors with a greater level of confidence. However, this is not an easy task on the basis of existing figures. A glance at the US national statistics over the past 20 years for the federal social security disability insurance programme shows an astonishing rise in the award of permanent and total disability payments for back pain. While lung cancer increased by 458% between 1957–1959 and 1980, the corresponding figure for back pain over the same period was 2680%. During the same period the population increase was 126% (Fordyce, personal communication). Unfortunately, it is impossible to make valid comparisons between the USA and the UK on the basis of available statistics for the following reasons. Firstly, the Department of Health and Social Security (DHSS) in Britain has only collected this data since 1971. Secondly, Britons with back pain can claim benefit through one or more of six separate schemes: sickness benefit, invalidity benefit, non-contributory invalidity pension, injury benefit or the workmen's compensation supplementation scheme, so these figures are not exclusive to back pain. Thirdly, while the International Classification of Diseases (ICD) is used to classify sickness and invalidity benefits, back pain can plausibly be included under any one of the following: the musculoskeletal system and connective tissue, arthritis and rheumatism and accidents. So it is impossible to disaggregate the back pain figures from the other cases. The accidents category also includes cases of poisoning and violence. To complicate matters further, the ICD 8 classification was used before 1978/79, and the ICD 9 since 1979/80, but since 1979 the DHSS has excluded back pain patients from the arthritis and rheumatism figures. Lastly, small samples of claimants are contacted for the DHSS survey, from which these estimates are made; the sample size was 2.5% before 1974/75, 2% in 1976 and only 1% thereafter, so lowering confidence in later statistics. Such estimates discount the number of people who do not attempt to claim benefit, either because they are not aware that benefits are available or because they are discouraged from making a claim at some stage in the process of becoming a statistic. In view of this statistical minefield, it seems unlikely that many meaningful comparisons can be drawn between these national figures.

New Zealand provides a third cross-cultural example because it fosters attitudes about wellness in more than the USA or the UK. Compensation is dealt with very quickly, in three to six months, resulting in less personal disruption, but it is requested by fewer people and for shorter periods of time (Carron, De Good and Tait, 1985), in contradiction the behaviourist view that speed rewards. Although Canada, Israel, Sweden, some Australian states and some of the states of the USA have less damaging "no blame" policies, which speed compensation settlements for accidents, New Zealand also accepts the principle that compensation for personal injury is a community responsibility and should not depend on the particular cause of the injury or on proving fault. There is also comprehensive entitlement to compensation whatever the cause of the injury (excluding self-inflicted injury and damage caused by ageing, infection or disease), complete rehabilitation of the victim, and *real* compensation for losses (Hutchinson, 1984). In a comparative study of compensation for chronic low back pain patients in the USA and New Zealand, Carron, De Good and Tait (1985) found that US patients consistently used more medication, had more negative moods and were more disadvantaged socially and in sexual, recreational and vocational terms. While patients from the two countries had equal levels of improvement following pain centre treatment and up to one year later, the initial differences favouring the Australasians persisted until follow-up. Those receiving compensation were less likely to return to work in both cultures, but this tendency was more pronounced in the US sample. This suggests that systemic legal and management factors in the USA may enhance existing trends. More studies are needed.

PAIN AND QUALITY OF LIFE

> Standard of living equals two fridges, two cars, two televisions and one psychiatrist.
> Quality of life is one fridge, one TV, one car and no psychiatrist.
> (Michael Caine, quoted by Caroline Selai at a conference)

Quality of life (QOL) is a particular concern where patients suffer from chronic painful diseases because health authorities intervene to relieve relievable distress resulting from disease and to restore and compensate for disability and handicap, among other aims (Walker, 1992). Many health professionals are concerned about their patients' quality of life but do not assess it formally; clinicians tend to perform such assessments using an assortment of heuristics that are rarely formalised in a systematic way. Some appear to find QOL information useful and informative, but clinical trials have sometimes shown that this additional information does not always greatly influence clinical decision making or short-term changes in health status. One conclusion might be that QOL data are inappropriate to such decision making, but it seems more likely that feedback has been badly timed or that it has not been provided in an acceptable and useful manner (Fitzpatrick et al, 1992).

Agreement about a definition of quality of life is difficult to find, and lack of consensus has resulted in the use of extraordinarily diverse outcome indicators in the name of quality of life measures. Because of this, research has often focused more on performance indicators such as rates of absenteeism from work and medication intake than on quality of life itself. For instance, Linton et al (1989) looked at "bad backs" as an important cause of absenteeism among nurses. Being away from work for three consecutive months reduces a person's chances of returning to work to around zero, so health professionals have a role to play in devising a means of pre-empting subsequent bouts of back pain, which might become chronic with permanent disability and redundancy. Swedish nurses who had been absent with back pain in the previous two years were each randomly assigned to a five-week instruction course or to a waiting list period. The spinal mobility of the two groups was equivalent. Grounded in the assumption that a passive life-style leads to disused muscles, the intervention included exercises to strengthen the muscles, a "back school" to teach ergonomics and self-care methods, relaxation, and life-style management to help participants cope with high-risk situations. Improvements were shown from reductions in pain, tiredness and anxiety. Nurses in the intervention group also reported better sleeping and greater satisfaction with their daily activities and their marriages. Although there was no significant reduction in the rate of absenteeism in the six months after the end of the course or in medication intake — two politically sensitive indicators — Linton et al (1989) found that they had designed a programme that improved QOL for those with episodes of back pain and this finding should not be undervalued. The package holds promise, and employers might consider whether the investment of five weeks' salary on a preventative back programme such as this is valuable in the long-term because it keeps expensive, highly trained staff for a working lifetime.

Many definitions of QOL that exist have been derived from the content of research instruments rather than from a conceptual basis or theoretical model (Hunt and McKenna, 1992). Methods of evaluation embrace the qualitative approach of semi-structured interviews, but the quantitative method using a standardised question-naire is more popular. This is particularly true where good reliability, validity and sensitivity have been established and they are quick and simple to administer and analyse. The clinical gold standard that drives the research enterprise has been to find a measure that can be completed and scored within one minute. Such demands hamper the progress and development of multidimensional scales and hinder the inclusion of a broad and comprehensive spectrum of dimensions that may contribute to the individual's QOL, health and health care. The useful but lengthy Sickness Impact Profile provides a suitable example. It assesses the subjective distress and suffering associated with illness on a wide range of dimensions, many of which are directly relevant to people with painful diseases. These include depression and reaction to illness, mutilation, amputation and disfigurement, an assessment of pain tolerance and an evaluation of pain threshold or sensitivity. Assessments of QOL are likely to change as a disease progresses; the impact of a confirmed diagnosis may be substantial on a person's overall QOL, particularly if the diagnosis is of life-threatening proportions and of a potentially painful disease like cancer (Ray and Baum, 1985). The stigma accompanying some diagnoses can also be problematic (Scambler, 1991). Following initial coping and adjustment, the effects of illness on a person's QOL may be better conceptualised and articulated when the disease is moderately progressed. At the later stages of the disease the implications for QOL can be overwhelming (Sartorius, 1991).

However, a prevailing approach to studying QOL has been to use health professionals as judges instead of tapping into patients' own views about their lives. Whether doctors' or patients' views should be given priority has been widely debated (Selai, 1991). One approach, developed principally by health economics, is geared towards assessing social worth; it uses Quality Adjusted Life Years (QALYs). Here, quality of life is assessed by doctors for particular diagnostic groups or conditions and this information is then traded off against survival or mortality rates for these states. In developing QALYs, dimensions of disability and distress were used to represent quality of life. Disability ratings on an eight-point categorical scale ranged from no disability (I), to confined to bed (VII) and unconscious (VIII). Distress from pain and mental disturbance was assessed from none (A) to severe (D). The results were placed on the two axes of a grid, and a value for each slot in the grid was provided by a valuation matrix. The published values were based on replies from a small sample of 70, composed of trained psychiatric and general nurses (20), healthy volunteers (20), doctors (10) and inpatients from psychiatric (10) and medical (10) wards (Kind, Rosser and Williams, 1982). These distress/disability ratings ranged from perfectly healthy (1) to dead (0). After allocating each patient in a particular disease sample to a slot on the grid, based on what was known about their distress and disability, each frequency was multiplied by the published values, then added to obtain the total quality of what was known about life for that sample. Consequently, an average QOL score for sampled patients can be calculated.

It is possible to estimate QOL before and after a particular operation for clinical use; similarly, QALYs for different disorders can be compared. Discounting is used where future benefits are being evaluated; 5% is deducted on the principle that future benefits are evaluated less highly than immediate benefits. For example, someone scoring 0.68 would be confined to a wheelchair or chair, and would report being in moderate pain. So 18 months in that condition is viewed as having the same economic "utility" as one year completely free from disability and distress. The implication here is that people prefer shorter healthier lives to longer ones accompanied by distress and discomfort. However, this assumption may not universally concur with patients' views, which are not directly assessed. Someone with a painful, severely handicapping disorder may see their state as being equally valuable to them as another person's healthy state, perhaps because they have a highly satisfying job, a happier family life or a better standard of living compared with their peers, for instance (Smith, 1985). Generalisations about patients' views can be considerably at odds with the reality of highly diverse patient perceptions of well-being, and what they might say if they were involved in the decision making process. This apparent discrepancy between policy makers' views and those of their clients is underscored by results from a study that showed how in QALY evaluations doctors emphasised distress, while patients viewed disability to be far more serious (Gudex, 1986). These economic utility methods suffer similar disadvantages to those we noted when considering the use of Subjective Expected Utility (SEU) theory in Chapter 6. There are also ethical concerns about making decisions on whether it is kind to patients to prolong their lives with a disease that has a very poor prognosis, particularly if patients themselves are not included in these discussions.

QALYs have been considered for use in making policy decisions in many districts in the National Health Service, even though the method was not originated with such widespread use in mind. Dealing with waiting list priorities is a potential use for QALYs; for example, it is possible to devise protocols for various surgery specialities using available QALY data to ensure that surgical capability is used to best QALY effect (Walker, 1992). Walker claims that, despite considerable interest in the technique, at a conscious level no decisions have been reached by health authorities from looking at QALYs. The reasons for this are threefold: firstly, they could not get the necessary data, secondly, those taking the decisions did not trust the methods and, thirdly, there was some self-interested resistance to using them. Ideology also influences research on the QOL although ideological assumptions are rarely declared. So the "endemic diseases" of what Grimley-Evans (1992) wittily describes as "crypto-popery" and "crypto-Marxism" have been replaced more recently by "crypto-grocery".

There is now a considerable literature on the shortcomings of the QALY, which can only be briefly addressed here (see Buxton, 1992), and new methods of assessment are being sought. A serious criticism about QALYs and more recent variations, like the QALY toolkit and Euroqol measures, is that their content is arbitrary, as a result of conceptual confusion. Some items are not applicable to some respondents and, more specifically, the content does not take account of the capacity of chronic pain and other patients to adapt their lives to their condition (Hunt and McKenna, 1992). In response, Rosser (1987) is developing a more elaborate global index of health-related quality of life (IHQL), for use principally with the chronically ill. It uses a multi-stage category rating technique to evaluate more than 100 descriptors. The original dimensions of disability and discomfort are retained in modified form, but the physical and emotional components of distress are now distinguished. More relevant to the study of pain, a third dimension of discomfort has been added, which refers to physical discomfort (Rosser et al, 1992).

It has been argued by those who support the continued use of QALYs in the distribution of health care resources that such a system is explicit, and therefore open to public scrutiny. However, QALYs are considered to be of equal value regardless of who receives them, and these principles of public equity are only commendable if society agrees that, as a priority, the same respect, concern and protection should be given to every citizen (Harris, 1992). A main criticism of QALYs is that they do not value people; they value a lifetime, not people's lives. It is also argued that they value cheap treatments and badly treated conditions, so potentially they could be open to abuse. They encourage ageism, by giving priority treatment to younger people, and sexism, in favouring the treatment of longer-lived women more than men (Harris, 1992). They also favour the rich over the poor, because poorer people have "conspicuously worse intrinsic health" (Black, 1992). One way around this problem would be to create QALYs for different socio-demographic groups in the community and not solely for disease states and conditions, so, for example, a hernia repair for a 35-year-old is comparable with the same operation for someone of 65 (Walker, 1992).

Ethical issues involved in QOL measurement are concerned with whether it is possible to put a value on life, and what it means to do this. Afflicted individuals and their families are likely to have a very different view from society in general about who should be kept alive on a respirator and for how long. Others might take a moral stance, where life-sentence prisoners, for instance, are denied an equal chance as others in the same physical condition, of receiving life-saving coronary by-pass surgery. As we saw in Chapter 5, the attributions we make about the behaviour of others are often quite different from the well-informed attributions we make about ourselves, and these affect the ways in which decisions are made. Given this inherent feature of attributions and social decision making, it begs the question about whether the outcome would be any different if people other than physicians made these QOL judgements: elected representatives of society, religious leaders and philosophers are among those who have been considered (Williams and Kind, 1992).

Black (1992) maintains that it is ethically desirable that assessments of QOL are made by sufferers with a particular state in preference to "vicarious estimates"; the patient is the expert, not the doctor or nurse. In their plea for the development and use of good patient-orientated measures, Hunt and McKenna (1992) comment succinctly on this health economic approach:

> The introduction of quality adjusted life years (QALYs) ... exemplifies the adoption of particular methods of evaluation which rest upon a medical model of human health and an economic approach to the assessment of interventions. This has created an uneasy alliance which has given birth to some strange offspring. The medical model assumes that individual treatment pursued on a biochemical–surgical basis is the best way to tackle health problems. In this model, the doctor (as professional) is the best judge of both treatment and outcome. The discipline of health economics on the other hand is concerned with individuals and is more orientated towards a macro view of group phenomena in society at large. These two extremes leave little room for the personal preferences of the patient, the social construction of illness or the contextual aspects of recovery. QALYs imply a mechanistic view of human existence and cannot encompass the fact that the content of health services is not solely that patients are treated, but the way they are treated, by whom, in what circumstances, in what surroundings and with what sequelae.
> (Hunt and McKenna, 1992, pp.63–64)

Although health economic measures of QOL have begun to address more directly some issues that are relevant to the study of pain patients, they are still problematic. There are also good methodological and philosophical reasons for wanting to design sound psychometric patient-orientated measures that assess the broad spectrum of the dimensions that are affected when people are afflicted with a painful condition. The WHOQOL is a new self-administered subjective assessment, which is being developed for cross-cultural use. Pain and discomfort are evaluated as one of its many comprehensive facets. It is designed for use not only with those afflicted with chronic diseases but also for people with communication problems, those in high-stress situations, such as migrants and refugees, and other needy and neglected sub-groups whose health states are little investigated, such as informal care-givers of the elderly, disabled, and so on (WHOQOL Group, 1993). This provides a new departure in the assessment of QOL for sick and well people, and has a multiplicity of uses.

A MODEL FOR A SOCIAL PSYCHOLOGY OF PAIN

The ideas and data reviewed in this book show how psychosocial factors strongly affect the expression, reporting and treatment of painful conditions. However, few social psychological models are available to assist understanding, with three notable exceptions. Litt (1986) sets out a hierarchy of six important processes involved in the mediation of successful outcome in the non-medical treatment of headache. These define the scope and purpose of different styles of investigation into the pain problem. At a microscopic level of analysis he identifies biochemical processes, then reactions at specific vascular and general autonomic levels. Cognitive, affective and behavioural processing at midway levels are followed by dyadic interactions. Social processes constitute a macroscopic level of analysis at the top of the hierarchy. The social psychological model for chronic painful conditions outlined in this book is largely concerned with processing at the upper three macroscopic levels.

An interesting ethno-cultural model has been proposed in an unpublished thesis by Bates (see Bates, Edwards and Anderson, 1993) and this shares some elements with the model outlined below. Bates seeks to show how the social aspects of learning, comparisons, attitudes, prior experience and attention all affect the descending inhibitory controls, nociception and eventual pain behaviour of those in chronic pain. In outlining a bio-behavioural profile, Dalton et al (1994) acknowledge the various contributions of environmental influences to health and health care, and the importance of losing control, bound up with the helplessness, low self-esteem and the uncertainty that chronic patients experience. They also list as important health care avoidance, past and current experiences, physiological responsivity and thoughts of disease progression as extensions to the simple model proposed by Rosensteil and Keefe (1983). Nevertheless, there is still room in the literature for a more comprehensive social psychological model within which studies of chronic pain might be developed.

The new model presented here is about the many psychosocial influences that affect the workings of the cognitive controls described in the gate control theory of pain. All the models share the consensual view that these will affect the operation of descending inhibitory controls in the central nervous system, and therefore whether sensations are perceived to be noxious or benign. Such interpretations would be expected to affect people's pain behaviour, particularly their predisposition to act, cope and seek help, and their long-term sick role, illness and well behaviours. This model is concerned with the sick person's subjective views and how other people and other situations modify them (Figure 10.1).

Although it is acknowledged that there are many psychological, biological and physiological processes that affect a pain sufferer's health, the intention here is to focus on processes known to have been directly and indirectly affected by the behaviour of other people. Consequently, explanations based on genetics, personality

Level 1

Individual behaviours affected by
social processes

Perceived bodily sensation
Pain threshold
Pain tolerance and other symptoms

Perceived severity of symptom(s)
Illness and disability

Lifetime personal and social schemata
about pain, illness and disability

Lifetime personal and social emotions
and mood states associated with pain, illness and disability

Lifetime personal representations
(Images) of pain, illness and disability

Personal motivation
or needs for diagnosis, relief of suffering, reduction of disability, and to obtain a cure. Satisfaction about regaining health and reducing anxiety

Level 2

Interpersonal
behaviours

Beliefs about:
1. The *nature of pain*, illness and disability
2. *Causation of pain*, illness and disability (attributions)
3. The *efficacy of* particular *interventions* in treating pain, illness or disability
4. *Self-efficacy* in carrying out the treatment/action advocated
5. *Pain control*: choices and predictable

Current and future expectations
about pain, illness, treatments and a "cure"

Context of encounters/social atmosphere		
Interpersonal encounters:		
Family and close others	Friends, acquaintances and workmates	Health professionals and alternative practitioners

Social motivation
Social support
Need to obtain approval from significant others for action
To utilise social resources, i.e. family, friends and workmates
To utilise health care resources in formal system
Seek help from alternative practitioners

Level 3	Level 4
Group and intergroup behaviour	Higher order factors affecting socio-psychological processing

Social representations
of pain, illness and coping

Group beliefs
Shared consensus and opinions about pain, illness and disability

Group experiences/influence
Peer pressure
Group status and power, etc.

Media influences

Health culture
Health history
Health ideology
Health politics
Quality of life
Economic beliefs about health

Personal and social categorisation(s)
Labelling of condition by self and others, e.g. health professionals, using diagnosis, age, etc.
Personal and social comparisons
Self at other times, states, etc.
Others similar and dissimilar, e.g. fit
Upwards/lateral/downward comparisons
Social identifications
Sense of belonging to, or social isolation from groups. Identification with groups on relevant dimensions, e.g. age, class, cultural, ideological, historical factors affecting health and health care

Figure 10.1 Model of the psychosocial processes and social factors implicated in the generation and maintenance of a chronically painful illness

and intelligence, for instance, have not been included. In this model, the psychosocial processes implicated in the experience and expression of chronically painful disease are conveniently addressed at four levels.

At the lowest level of the hierarchy, it is important to consider how the cognitions, emotions and behaviour of those in chronic pain affect and are affected by the social environment in which they live. Bodily sensations and tolerance for them are affected by a range of socio-cultural factors. Coupled with socially generated perceptions of severity, these influence beliefs and represent a most important impetus to seeking professional help, and its timing. Schemata in the memory stores are central to most of the socio-cognitive mechanisms in this model. They provide a framework for stored events, and are intimately tied to relevant emotion(s). They are constantly being shaped and reshaped by discourse and experience, and are formative in generating expectations and eventual beliefs about pain, illness and disability. Personal images of pain, illness and disability are powerful in assisting with understandings about disease and treatments. They appear to be central to the success of treating chronic pain, especially when shared with others, and backed up by the media as social representations (see the third level, below). Finally, there is the personal drive or motivation to obtain a diagnosis or understand how the body works and why it is malfunctioning, to seek treatment in the form of pain relief and the removal of suffering, and possibly to obtain a cure. There is also intrinsic satisfaction from attempting to regain health and reducing anxiety.

At a second level of explanation are thoughts, emotions, motives and behaviours resulting from communications between those in pain and those with whom they come into contact. Different styles of communication with significant others, inside the family as well as outside, influence pain sufferers' interpretations of their health state and their decisions about seeking health care. Dyadic relationships with friends and acquaintances are also included. Interpersonal encounters with doctors and other health care workers also shape a variety of beliefs and expectations about self, disability, the disease and the treatment, as well as the nature of pain and its control. The social context in which these communications about care take place is an integral part of this analysis, so the family atmosphere, working and leisure environments, and the affective and physical environment of salient health care settings need to be included in assessment. The motivation to obtain approval from others for health care action is central to decision making surrounding the timing of consultations with formal and alternative practitioners. The need to seek social support from others and to utilise other resources available within the family and social network require a variety of skilled interpersonal behaviours, which may suffer attrition as chronicity encroaches.

Pain behaviours and cognitions are affected by group dynamics as well as by relations between groups, where one group may be seen to be getting a different style or quantity of health care to another. Ethnic groups provide a suitable example here. So the third level of analysis is concerned with intragroup dynamics and intergroup behaviour, where the identity of the pain sufferer is formed and maintained through social categorisation, social comparisons and identification processes. Collective beliefs and representations (images) held by groups about pain, illness and treatments and how they work affect the ways in which individuals envisage they may cope with them, irrespective of their verity. These beliefs are fed by the group's past collective experience with the health service and with particular types of professionals on the one hand, and by the influence of the media on the other. Intense suspicion by the Black community of the actions and motives of (largely white) health professionals in the author's home town provides an anecdotal example.

A fourth layer of broader influences must be included to complete any psychosocial analysis of health and illness. They affect all of the processes of the other three layers. The World Health Organization (WHO) defines health as "a state of complete physical, mental and social well-being", and we have seen throughout this book how these three aspects are variously affected by culture, society and the social environment. Mechanic goes as far as to say that these influences are so powerful that "it is mostly at the margins that medical care services have their primary impact" (Mechanic, 1989, p.243). He says that physical illness and psychological discomfort arise "in no small way" from conditions in the family, at work, and in the community more generally, so the biology and psychology of health are inextricably interconnected.

New methods of measurement need to be developed so that the society's health culture, health history, health ideology and politics, quality of life and economic beliefs about health can be taken into account. A much broader assessment of the impact of these features on pain sufferers' experience could give greater insight into why they respond to physicians, treatments and the health care system in the ways they do. Furthermore, it is insufficient to carry out this analysis in isolation from personal, interpersonal, group and intergroup factors; it should be built in, as an integral and comprehensive part of assessment. This approach demands a scientific and clinical reorientation, to see pain sufferers as members of their society in the fullest sense of the word, rather than as operating in a socially sterile and artificial apolitical, acultural, non-ideological black box, as has commonly been the case. Only when we collect this full data will we begin to see the statue of David in anything like its glorious entirety.

References

Abbott, B.B., Schoen, L.S. and Badia, P. (1984) Predictable and unpredictable shock behavioural measures of aversion and physiological measures of stress. *Psychology Bulletin*, **96**(1), 45–71.

Abbott, F.V., Gray-Donald, K., Sewitch, M.J., Johnston, C.C., Edgar, L. and Jeans, M.E. (1992) The prevalence of pain in hospitalised patients and resolution over six months. *Pain*, **50**, 15–28.

Aberger, E.W., Follick, M.J. and Ahern, D.K. (1986) Cognitive distortion and psychological distress in chronic low back pain. *Journal of Consulting and Clinical Psychology*, **54**(4), 573–575.

Abramson, L.J., Metalsky, G.I. and Alloy, L.A. (1989) Hopelessness depression – a theory based subtype of depression. *Psychological Review*, **96**(2), 358–372.

Abramson, L.J., Seligman, M.E.P. and Teasdale, J.D. (1978) Learned helplessness in humans; critique and reformulation. *Journal of Abnormal Psychology*, **87**, 49.

Achterberg-Lawlis, J. (1982) The psychological dimension of arthritis. *Journal of Consulting and Clinical Psychology*, **50**(6), 984–992.

Affleck, G. and Tennen, H. (1991) Social comparison and coping with major medical problems. In J. Suls and T. A. Wills (Eds), *Social Comparison: Contemporary Theory and Research*, Lawrence Erlbaum, Hillsdale, New Jersey.

Affleck, G., Tennen, H., Pfeiffer, C. and Fifield, J. (1987) Appraisals of control and predictability in adapting to a chronic disease. *Journal of Personality and Social Psychology*, **53**(2), 273–279.

Affleck, G., Urrows, S., Tennen, H. and Higgins, P. (1992) Daily coping with pain from rheumatoid arthritis. *Pain*, **51**, 221–229.

Affleck, G., Tennen, H., Urrows, S. and Higgins, P. (1994) Personal and contextual features of daily stress reactivity: individual differences in relations of undesirable daily events with mood disturbance and chronic pain intensity. *Journal of Personality and Social Psychology*, **66**, 329–340.

Ahles, T.A., Ruckdeschel, J.C. and Blanchard, E.B. (1984) Cancer-related pain — I: Prevalence in an outpatient setting as a function of stage of disease and type of cancer. *Journal of Psychosomatic Research*, **28**(2), 115–119.

Ahles, T.A., Yunus, M.B., Gaulier, B., Riley, S.D. and Masi, A.T. (1986) The use of contemporary MMPI norms in the study of chronic pain patients. *Pain*, **24**, 159–163.

Ajemian, I. (1993) The interdisciplinary team. In D. Doyle, G.W.C. Hanks and N. MacDonald (Eds), *Oxford Textbook of Palliative Medicine*, Oxford University Press, Oxford, pp.17–28.

Ajzen, I. (1985) From intentions to actions: a theory of planned behaviour. In J. Kuhl and J. Beckmann (Eds), *Action-Control: From Cognition to Behaviour*, Springer-Verlag, Heidelberg, pp.11–39.

Ajzen, I. (1987) Attitudes, traits and actions: dispositional prediction of behaviour in personality and social psychology. In L. Berkowitz (Ed.), *Advances in Experimental Social Psychology*, Vol. 20, Academic Press, New York, pp.1–63.

Ajzen, I. (1991) The theory of planned behaviour. *Organisational Behaviour and Human Decision Processes*, **50**, 179–211.

Ajzen, I. and Fishbein, M. (1980) *Understanding Attitudes and Predicting Social Behaviour*, Prentice Hall, Englewood Cliffs, New Jersey.

Ajzen, I. and Timko, L. (1986) Correspondence between health attitudes and behaviour. *Basic and Applied Social Psychology*, 7(4), 259–276.

Alloway, R. and Bebbington, P. (1987) The buffer theory of social support – a review of the literature. *Psychological Medicine*, 17, 91–108.

Allred, K.D. and Smith, T.W. (1989) The hardy personality: cognitive and physiological responses to evaluative threat. *Journal of Personality and Social Psychology*, 56, (2), 257–266.

Alonzo, A.A. (1984) An illness behaviour paradigm: a conceptual exploration of a situational-adaptive perspective. *Social Science and Medicine*, 19(5), 499–510.

Anderson, A.D. and Pennebaker, J.W. (1980) Pain and pleasure: an alternative interpretation for identical stimulation. *European Journal of Social Psychology*, 10(2), 207–212.

Anderson, K.O., Bradley, L.A., Turner, R.A., Agudelo, C.A., Pisko, E.J., Salley, A.N. and Fletcher, K.E. (1992) Observation of pain behaviour in rheumatoid arthritis patients during physical examination: relationship to disease activity and psychological variables. *Arthritis Care and Research*, 5(1), 49–56.

Aneshensel, C.S., Frerichs, R.R. and Huba, G.J. (1984) Depression and physical illness – a multiwave nonrecursive causal model. *Journal of Health and Social Behaviour*, 25, 350–371.

Aneshensel, C.S., Estrada, A.L., Hansell, M.J. and Clark, V.A. (1987) Social psychological aspects of reporting behaviour: lifetime depressive episode reports. *Journal of Health and Social Behaviour*, 28, 232–246.

Arena, J.G., Blanchard, E.B. and Andrasik, F. (1984) The role of affect in the etiology of chronic headache. *Journal of Psychosomatic Research*, 28(1), 79–86.

Arena, J.G., Sherman, R.A., Bruno, G.M. and Smith, J.D. (1990) The relationship between situational stress and phantom limb pain: cross-lagged correlational data from 6 month pain logs. *Journal of Psychosomatic Research*, 34(1), 71–77.

Arntz, A., Dreesen, L. and De Jong, P. (1994) The influence of anxiety on pain: attentional and attributional mediators. *Pain*, 56, 307–314.

Aronson, J.K. and Hardman, M. (1992) ABC of monitoring drug therapy: patient compliance. *British Medical Journal*, 305(6860), 1009–1011.

Atkinson, J.H., Kremer, E.F. and Ignelzi, R.J. (1982) Diffusion of pain language with affective disturbance confounds differential diagnosis. *Pain*, 12, 375–384.

Atkinson, J.H., Slater, M.A., Grant, I., Patterson, T.L. and Garfin, S.R. (1988) Depressed mood in chronic low back pain: relationship with stressful life events. *Pain*, 35, 47–55.

Atkinson, J.H., Slater, M.A., Patterson, T.L., Grant, I. and Garfin, S.R. (1991) Prevalence, onset and risk of psychiatric disorders in men with chronic low back pain: a controlled study. *Pain*, 45, 111–121.

Bach, S., Noreng, M.F. and Tjellden, N.U. (1988) Phantom limb pain in amputees during the first 12 months following limb amputation after preoperative lumbar epidural blockade. *Pain*, 33, 297–301.

Badley, E.M. and Papageorgiou, A.C. (1989) Visual analogue scales as a measure of pain in arthritis: a study of overall pain and pain in individual joints at rest and on movement. *Journal of Rheumatology*, 16(1), 102.

Badley, E.M. and Wood, P.H.N. (1979) Attitudes of the public to arthritis. *Annals of the Rheumatic Diseases*, 38, 97–100.

Bailey, C.A. and Davidson, P.O. (1976) The language of pain: intensity. *Pain*, 2, 319–324.

Bandler, R.J., Madaras, G.R. and Bern, D.J. (1968) Self-observation as a source of pain perception. *Journal of Personality and Social Psychology*, 9(3), 205–209.

Bandura, A. (1974) Behaviour theory and models of man. *American Psychologist*, 29(12), 859–869.

Bandura, A. (1977) Self-efficacy: towards a unifying theory of behaviour change. *Psychological Review*, 84(2), 191–215.

Bandura, A. (1991) Self-efficacy mechanisms in physiological activation and health promoting behaviour. In J. Madden (Ed.), *Neurobiology of Learning, Emotion and Affect*, Raven Press, New York, pp.229–269.

Bandura, A., O'Leary, A., Barr Taylor, C., Gauthier, J. and Gossard, D. (1987) Perceived self-efficacy and pain control: opioid and non-opioid mechanisms. *Journal of Personality and Social Psychology*, 53(3), 563–571.

Bandura, A., Cioffi, D., Barr Taylor, C. and Brouillard, M.E. (1988) Perceived self-efficacy in coping with cognitive stressors and opioid activation. *Journal of Personality and Social Psychology*, 55, 479–488.

Barnes, D., Smith, D., Gatchel, R.J. and Mayer, T.G. (1989) Psychosocioeconomic predictors of treatment success/failure in chronic low back pain patients. *Spine*, 14(4), 427–430.

Barnett, P.A. and Gotlib, I.H. (1988) Psychosocial functioning and depression: distinguishing among antecedents, concomitants and consequences. *Psychology Bulletin*, 104(1), 97–126.

Bates, M.S., Edwards, W.T. and Anderson, K.O. (1993) Ethnocultural influences on variation in chronic pain perception. *Pain*, 52, 101–112.

Baumann, L.J., Cameron, L.T., Zimmerman, R.S. and Leventhal, H. (1989) Illness representations and matching labels with symptoms. *Health Psychology*, 8(4), 449–469.

Beales, J.G. (1982) Factors influencing the expectation of pain among patients in a children's burns unit. *Burns*, 9(3), 187–192.

Beales, J.G., Lennox-Holt, P.J., Keen, J.H. and Mellor, V.P. (1983) Children with juvenile chronic arthritis – their beliefs about their illness and therapy. *Annals of the Rheumatic Diseases*, 42, 481–486.

Beck, A.T., Steer, R.A. and Garbin, M.G. (1988) Psychometric properties of the Beck Depression Inventory: twenty-five years of evaluation. *Clinical Psychology Review*, 8, 77–100.

Beecher, H.K. (1955) The powerful placebo. *Journal of the American Medical Association*, 159(17), 1602–1606.

Beecher, H.K. (1956) Relationship of significance of wound to pain experienced. *Journal of the American Medical Association*, 161(17), 1609–1613.

Beecher, H.K. (1959) *The Measurement of Subjective Responses – Quantitative Measurement of Drugs*, Oxford University Press, Oxford.

Beecher, H.K. (1960) Increased stress and effectiveness of placebos and activity drugs. *Science*, 132, 91–92.

Beecher, H.K. (1961) Surgery as placebo – a quantitative study of bias. *Journal of the American Medical Association*, 176(13), 1102–1107.

Beecher, H.K. (1965) Qualification of the subjective pain experience. In P.H. Hoch and J. Zubin (Eds), *Psychopathology of Perception*, Grune & Stratton, New York, pp.111–128.

Beecher, H.K. (1972) The placebo effect as a non-specific force surrounding disease. In R. Janzen, W.D. Keidel, A. Herz, C. Steichele, J.R. Payne and R.A.P. Burt (Eds), *Pain: Basic Principles – Pharmacology Therapy*, Churchill Livingstone, Edinburgh, pp.175–180.

Belanger, E., Melzack, R. and Lanzon, P. (1989) Pain of first-trimester abortion: a study of psychological and medical predictors. *Pain*, 36, 339–350.

Berkley, K. (1993) Sex and chronobiology: opportunities for a focus on the positive. *IASP Newsletter*, Jan/Feb, 2–5.

Besson, J.M. and Chaouch, A. (1987) Peripheral and spinal mechanisms of nociception. *Physiological Review*, 67(1), 67–186.

Beutler, L.E., Daldrup, R.J., Engle, D., Oro-Beutler, M.E., Meredith, K. and Boyer, J.T. (1987) Effects of therapeutically induced affect arousal on depressive symptoms, pain and beta-endorphin among rheumatoid arthritis patients. *Pain*, 29, 325–334.

Bibace, R. and Walsh, M.E. (1979) Developmental stages in children's conceptions of illness. In G. Stone, F. Cohen and N. Adler (Eds), *Health Psychology*, Jossey-Bass, San Francisco, California, p.285.

Billings, A.G. and Moos, R.H. (1981) The role of coping responses and social resources in alternating the stress of life events. *Journal of Behavioural Medicine*, 4(2), 139.

Bingle, G.J., O'Connor, T.P., Evans, W.O. and Delamore, S. (1991) The effect of "detailing" on physicians' prescribing behaviour for postsurgical narcotic analgesia. *Pain*, 45, 171–173.

Bishop, D.S. (1988) Depression and rheumatoid arthritis. *Journal of Rheumatology*, 15(6), 888–889.

Bishop, G.D. (1991) Understanding the understanding of illness: lay disease representations. In J.A. Skelton and R.T. Croyle (Eds), *Mental Representations of Health and Illness*, Springer-Verlag, New York, pp.32–59.

Bishop, G.D. and Converse, S.A. (1986) Illness representations: a prototype approach. *Health Psychology*, 5(2), 95–114.

Bishop, G.D., Briede, C., Cavazos, L., Grotzinger, R. and McMahon, S. (1987) Processing illness information: the role of disease prototypes. *Basic and Applied Social Psychology*, 8, 21–43.

Black, D. (1992) Ethical issues arising from measures of the quality of life. In A.H. Hopkins (Ed.), *Measures of the Quality of Life and the Uses to which Such Measures May Be Put*, Royal College of Physicians, London, p.121.

Blackman, S.L. (1980) The effects of non-verbal expression and cognition on the perception of pain. *Dissertation Abstracts International*, 41(5-B), 1887–1888.

Blalock, S.J., De Vellis, B.McG. and De Vellis, R.F. (1989) Social comparisons among individuals with rheumatoid arthritis. *Journal of Applied Social Psychology*, 19(8), 665–680.

Blanchard, E.B., Appelbaum, K.A., Radnitz, C.L., Michultka, D., Morritt, B., Kirsch, C., Hillhouse, J., Evans, D.D., Guarnieri, P., Attenagio, V., Andrasik, F., Jaccard, J. and Dentinger, M.P. (1990) Placebo-controlled evaluation of abbreviated progressive muscle relaxation combined with cognitive therapy in the treatment of tension headache. *Journal of Consulting and Clinical Psychology*, 58(2), 210–215.

Blank, T.O. (1982) *The Social Psychology of Developing Adults*, John Wiley and Sons, New York.

Blaxter, M. (1983) The causes of disease: women talking. *Social Science and Medicine*, 17(8), 59–69.

Blitz, B. and Dinnerstein, A.J. (1968) Effects of different types of instructions on pain parameters. *Journal of Abnormal Psychology*, 73(3), 276–280.

Block, A.R., Boyer, S.L. and Silbert, R.K. (1985) Spouses' perception of the chronic pain patient: estimates of exercise tolerance. In H.L. Fields, R. Dubner and F. Cervero (Eds), *Advances in Pain Research and Therapy*, Vol. 9, Raven Press, New York, pp.897–890.

Block, A.R., Kremer, E.F. and Gaylor, M. (1980) Behavioural treatment of chronic pain: the spouse as a discriminative cue for pain. *Pain*, 9(2), 243–252.

Bonica, J.J. (1990) Definitions and taxonomy of pain. In J.J. Bonica (ed) *The Management of Pain*. Second edition. Lee and Febinger, Philadelphia, P.A. pp.18–27.

Borkovec, T.D. (1985) Placebo: defining the unknown. In L. White, B. Tursky and G.E. Schwartz (Eds), *Placebo: Theory, Uses and Mechanisms*, Guilford Press, New York, pp.59–66.

Boston, K., Pearce, S.A. and Richardson, P.H. (1990) The Pain Cognitions Questionnaire. *Journal of Psychosomatic Research*, 34(1), 103–109.

Boubjerg, D.H., Redd, W.H., Maier, L.A., Holland, J.C., Lesko, L.M., Niedzweicki, D., Rubin, R.C. and Hakes, T.B. (1990) Anticipatory immune suppression and nausea in women receiving cyclical chemotherapy for ovarian cancer. *Journal of Consulting and Clinical Psychology*, 58(2), 153–157.

Boudewyns, P.A. and Keefe, F.J. (Eds) (1982) *Behavioural Medicine in General Medical Practice*, Addison-Wesley, Menlo Park, California.

Boureau, F., Doubrere, J.F. and Lun, M. (1990) Study of verbal description in neuropathic pain. *Pain*, 42, 145–152.

Bower, G.H. (1981) Mood and memory. *American Psychologist*, 36, 129–148.

Bower, G.H., Gilligan, S.G. and Monteiro, K.P. (1981) Selectivity of learning caused by affective states. *Journal of Experimental Psychology*, **110**(4), 45.

Bowers, K. (1968) Pain, anxiety and perceived control. *Journal of Consulting and Clinical Psychology*, **32**, 596–602.

Bowsher, D. (1977) The anatomo-physiology of pain. In S. Lipton (Ed.), *The Persistent Pain – Modern Methods of Treatment*, Vol. 1, Academic Press, London, pp.1–20.

Bradley, L.A. (1983) Coping with chronic pain. In T.G. Burish and L.A. Bradley (Eds), *Coping with Chronic Disease: Research and Applications*, Academic Press, New York, pp.339–380.

Bradley, L.A., Young, L.D., Anderson, K.O., Turner, R.A., Agudelo, C.A., McDaniel, L.K., Pisko, E.J., Semble, E.L. and Morgan, T.M. (1987) Effects of psychological therapy on pain behaviour of rheumatoid arthritis patients: treatment outcome and six-month follow-up. *Arthritis and Rheumatism*, **30**(10), 1105.

Brattberg, G., Thorslund, M. and Wikman, A. (1989) The prevalence of pain in a general population. The results of a postal survey in a county of Sweden. *Pain*, **37**, 215–222.

Brena, S.F. and Chapman, S.C. (1983) Pain and litigation. In P.D. Wall and R. Melzack (Eds), *Textbook of Pain*, 1st edn, Churchill Livingstone, Edinburgh, pp.832–839.

Brewin, C. (1986) Depression and causal attributions: What is their relationship? *Psychological Bulletin*, **50**(5), 1013–1020.

Brewin, C. (1988) *Cognitive Foundations of Clinical Psychology*, Lawrence Erlbaum, London.

Brewin, T. (1982) Consent to randomised treatment. *Lancet*, **ii**, 919–921.

Brewster, A.B. (1982) Chronically ill hospitalised children's concepts of their illness. *Pediatrics*, **69**(3), 355–362.

Bristol Women's Studies Group (Eds) (1979) *Half the Sky: An Introduction to Women's Studies*, Virago Press, London.

Britton, N.F.B and Skevington, S.M. (1989) A mathematical model of the gate control theory of pain. *Journal of Theoretical Biology*, **137**, 91–105.

Brody, H. (1985) Placebo effect: an examination of Grunbaums definition. In L. White, B. Tursky and G.E. Schwartz (Eds), *Placebo: Theory, Uses and Mechanisms*, Guilford Press, New York, pp.37–58.

Bromm, B. (1989) Laboratory animals and human volunteers in the assessment of analgesic efficiency. In C.R. Chapman and J.D. Loeser (Eds), *Issues in Pain Measurement*, Raven Press, New York, pp.117–143.

Broome, M.E. and Endsley, R. (1989) Parent and child behaviour during immunisation. *Pain*, **37**, 85–92.

Brown, A.G. (1981) *Organisation in the Spinal Cord – The Anatomy and Physiology of Identified Neurones*, Springer-Verlag, Berlin.

Brown, G.K. and Nicassio, P.M. (1987) Development of a questionnaire for the assessment of active and passive coping strategies in chronic pain patients. *Pain*, **31**(1), 53–64.

Brown, J.D. and Siegal, J.M. (1988) Attributions for negative life events. *Journal of Personality and Social Psychology*, **54**(2), 316–322.

Bruehl, S., Carlson, C.R. and McCubbin, J.A. (1993) Two brief interventions for acute pain. *Pain*, **54**, 29–36.

Bryant, R.A. (1993) Memory for pain and affect in chronic pain patients. *Pain*, **54**, 347–351.

Bucklew, S.P., Shutty, M.S., Hewitt, J., Landon, T., Morrow, K. and Frank, R.G. (1990) Health locus of control, gender differences and adjustment to persistent pain. *Pain*, **42**, 287–294.

Buller, M.K. and Buller, D.B. (1987) Physician communication style and patient satisfaction. *Journal of Health and Social Behaviour*, **28**, 375–388.

Burger, J.M. (1989) Negative reactions to increases in perceived personal control. *Journal of Personality and Social Psychology*, **56**(2), 246–256.

Burish, T.G., Carey, M.P., Wallston, K.A., Stein, H.J., Jamison, R.N. and Lyles, J.N. (1984) Health locus of control and chronic disease: an external orientation may be advantageous. *Journal of Social and Clinical Psychology*, **2**(4), 326–332.

Burns, M.O. and Seligman, M.E.P. (1989) Explanatory style across the lifespan: evidence for stability over 52 years. *Journal of Personality and Social Psychology*, **56**(3), 471–477.

Bury, M.R. (1985) Arthritis in the family: problems in adaptation and self care. In N.M. Hadler and D.B. Gillings (Eds), *Arthritis and Society*, Butterworths, London.

Bush, F.M., Harkins, S.W., Harrington, W.G. and Price, D.D. (1993) Analysis of gender effects on pain perception and symptom presentation in temporomandibular pain. *Pain*, **53**, 73–90.

Buss, A.H. and Portnoy, N.W. (1967) Pain tolerance and group identification. *Journal of Personality and Social Psychology*, **1**, 106–108.

Buxton, M. (1992) Are we satisfied with QALYs? What are the conceptual and empirical uncertainties and what must we do to make them more generally useful? In A.H. Hopkins (Ed.), *Measures of the Quality of Life and the Uses to which Such Measures May Be Put*, Royal College of Physicians, London, pp.41–51.

Cacioppo, J.T., Petty, R.E. and Tassinary, L.G. (1989) Social psychophysiology: a new look. *Advances in Experimental Social Psychology*, **22**, 39.

Cacioppo, J.T., Martzke, J.S., Petty, R.E. and Tassinary, L.G. (1988) Specific forms of facial EMG response index emotions during an interview: from Darwin to the continuous flow hypothesis of affect laden information processing. *Journal of Personality and Social Psychology*, **54**(4), 592–604.

Calvino, B., Besson, J.M., Mounier, F., Kordon, C. and Bluet-Pajot, M.-T. (1992) Chronic pain induces a paradoxical increase in growth hormone secretion without affecting other hormones related to acute stress in the rat. *Pain*, **49**, 27–32.

Campbell, J.A. and Lahuerta, J. (1983) Physical methods used in pain measurements – a review. *Journal of the Royal Society of Medicine*, **76**, 409–414.

Cannon, W.B. (1957) Voodoo death. *Psychosomatic Medicine*, **XIX**(3), 182–190.

Carey, M.P. and Burish, T.G. (1988) Etiology and treatment of the psychological side-effects associated with cancer chemotherapy: a critical review and discussion. *Psychological Bulletin*, **104**(3), 307–325.

Carlson, M., Charlin, V. and Miller, N. (1988) Positive mood and helping behaviour: a test of six hypotheses. *Journal of Personality and Social Psychology*, **55**(2), 211–229.

Carron, H., De Good, D.E. and Tait, R. (1985) A comparison of low back pain patients in the United States and New Zealand: psychosocial and economic factors affecting severity of disability. *Pain*, **21**, 77–89.

Carver, C.S. and Scheier, M.F. (1982) Control theory – a useful conceptual framework for personality, social, clinical and health psychology. *Psychological Bulletin*, **92**(1), 111–135.

Carver, C.S., Scheier, M.F. and Weintraub, J.K. (1989) Assessing coping strategies: a theoretically based approach. *Journal of Personality and Social Psychology*, **56**(2), 267–283.

Casey, K.L. and Handwerker, H.O. (1989) Ethical constraints in the use of animals for pain measurement. In C.R. Chapman and J.D. Loeser (Eds), *Issues in Pain Measurement*, Raven Press, New York, pp.159–167.

Cassel, E.J. (1982) The nature of suffering and the goals of medicine. *New England Journal of Medicine*, **306**(11), 639–645.

Catchlove, R. and Cohen, K. (1982) Effects of a directive return to work approach in the treatment of workmen's compensation patients with chronic pain. *Pain*, **14**, 181–191.

Caudill, M., Schnable, R., Zuttermeister, P., Benson, H. and Friedman, R. (1991) Decreased clinic utilisation by chronic pain patients after behavioural medicine intervention. *Pain*, **45**, 334–335.

Cervero, F. and Iggo, A. (1980) The substantia gelatinosa of the spinal cord – a critical review. *Brain*, **103**, 717–772.

Chapman, C.R. (1977) Sensory decision theory methods in pain research – a reply to Rollman. *Pain*, **3**, 295–305.

Chapman, C.R. (1979) Psychologic and behavioural aspects of cancer pain. *Advances in Pain Research and Therapy*, **2**, 45–55.

Chapman, C.R., Sola, A.E. and Bonica, J.J. (1979) Illness behaviour and depression compared in pain centre and private practice patients. *Pain*, **6**, 1–7.

Chapman, C.R., Wilson, M.E. and Gehrig, J.D. (1976) Comparative effects of acupuncture and transcutaneous stimulation on the perception of painful dental stimuli. *Pain*, **2**, 265–283.

Chapman, C.R., Colpitts, Y.M., Benedetti, C., Kitaeff, R. and Gehrig, J.D. (1980) Evoked potential assessment of acupunctural analgesia: attempted reversal with naloxone. *Pain*, **9**, 183–197.

Chapman, C.R., Sato, T., Martin, R.W., Tanaka, A., Okazaki, N., Colpitts, Y.M., Mayeno, J.K. and Gagliardi, G.J. (1982) Comparative effects of acupuncture in Japan and USA on dental pain perception. *Pain*, **12**, 319–328.

Chapman, C.R., Casey, K.L., Dubner, R., Foley, K.M., Gracely, R.H. and Reading, A.E. (1985) Pain measurement: an overview. *Pain*, **22**, 1–31.

Chapman, S.L. (1986) A review and clinical perspective on the use of EMG and thermal biofeedback for chronic headaches. *Pain*, **27**, 1–43.

Charmaz, K. (1990) "Discovering" chronic illness – using grounded theory. *Social Science and Medicine*, **30**(11), 1161–1172.

Charter, R.A. and Nehemkis, A.M. (1983) The language of pain intensity and complexity: new methods of scoring the McGill Pain Questionnaire. *Perceptual and Motor Skills*, **56**, 519–537.

Chaturvedi, S.K. (1987) Prevalence of chronic pain in psychiatric patients. *Pain*, **29**(2), 231–237.

Chaves, J.F. and Barber, T.X. (1976) Hypnotic procedures and surgery: a critical analysis with applications to acupuncture analgesia. *American Journal of Clinical Hypnosis*, **18**(4), 217–236.

Chen, A.N. (1993) Human brain measures of clinical pain: a review of topographical mappings. *Pain*, **54**, 115–132.

Choinière, M., Melzack, R., Girard, N., Rondeau, J. and Paquin, M.J. (1990) Comparisons between patients' and nurses' assessment of pain and medication efficacy in severe burn injuries. *Pain*, **40**, 143–152.

Chun, D.J., Turner, J.A. and Romano, J.M. (1993) Children of chronic pain patients: risk factors for maladjustment. *Pain*, **52**, 311–317.

Ciccone, D.S. and Grzesiak, R.C. (1984) Cognitive dimensions of chronic pain. *Social Science and Medicine*, **19**(12), 1339–1345.

Clark, W.C. (1969) Sensory decision theory analysis of the placebo effect – on the criterion for pain and thermal sensitivity. *Journal of Abnormal Psychology*, **74**(3), 363–371.

Clark, W.C. (1974) Pain sensitivity and the report of pain: an introduction to sensory decision theory. *Anaesthesiology*, **40**(3), 272–287.

Clark, W.C. and Clark, S.B. (1980) Pain responses in Nepalese porters. *Science*, **209**, 410–412.

Clark, W.C. and Yang, J.C. (1983) Applications of sensory decision theory to problems in laboratory and clinical pain. In R. Melzack (Ed.), *Pain Measurement and Assessment*, Raven Press, New York, pp.15–25.

Clark, W.C., Janal, M.N. and Carroll, J.D. (1989) Multidimensional pain requires multidimensional scaling. In C.R. Chapman and J.D. Loeser (Eds), *Issues in Pain Measurement*, Raven Press, New York, pp.285–326.

Clark, W.C., Ferrer-Brecher T., Janal, M.N., Carroll, J.D and Yang, J.C. (1989) The dimensions of pain: a multidisciplinary scaling comparison of cancer patients and healthy volunteers. *Pain*, **37**, 23–32.

Coates, D. and Wortman, C.B. (1980) Depression maintenance and interpersonal control. In A. Baum and J.E. Singer (Eds), *Advances in Environmental Psychology: Applications of Personal Control*, Vol. 2, Lawrence Erlbaum, Hillsdale, New Jersey, pp.149–182.

Cohen, S. and Williamson, G.M. (1991) Stress and infectious disease in humans. *Psychology Bulletin*, **109**(1), 5–24.

Cole, S. and Lejeune, R. (1972) Illness and the legitimation of failure. *American Sociological Review*, **37**, 347–356.

Comer, R. and Laird, J.D. (1975) Choosing to suffer as a consequence of expecting to suffer: why do people do it? *Journal of Personality and Social Psychology*, **32**(1), 92–101.

Conrad, P. (1988) Learning to doctor: reflections on recent accounts of the medical school years. *Journal of Health and Social Behaviour*, **29**, 323–332.

Cooper, S.A. (1992) Innovation in the Design of Analgesic Trials, In *Advances in Pain Research and Therapy: the design of analgesic clinical trials*, Vol. 18, M.B. Max, R.K. Portenoy and E.M. Laska. (eds) pp.117–124. Raven Press, New York.

Copp, L.A. (1974) The spectrum of suffering. *American Journal of Nursing*, **74**(3), 491–485.

Coppola, R. and Gracely, R.H. (1983) Where is the noise in SDT pain assessment? *Pain*, **17**, 257–266.

Corey, D.T., Etlin, D. and Miller, P.C. (1987) A home-based pain management and rehabilitation programme: an evaluation. *Pain*, **29**, 218–229.

Costello, R.M., Hulsey, T.L., Schoenfeld, L.S. and Ramamurthy, S. (1987) P-A-I-N: a four cluster MMPI typology for chronic pain. *Pain*, **30**, 199–209.

Cott, A., Anchel, H., Goldberg, W.M., Fabich, M. and Parkinson, W. (1990) Non-institutional treatment of chronic pain by field management: an outcome study with comparison group. *Pain*, **40**, 183–194.

Cottingham, B., Phillips, P.D., Davies, G.K. and Getty, G.J.H. (1985) The effect of subcutaneous nerve stimulation (SCNS) on pain associated with osteoarthritis of the hip. *Pain*, **22**, 243–248.

Council, J.R., Ahern, D.K., Follick, M.J. and Kline, C.L. (1988) Expectancies and functional impairment in chronic low back pain. *Pain*, **33**, 323–331.

Cousins, M.J. (1991) Prevention of post-operative pain. In M.R. Bond, J.E. Charlton and C.J. Woolf (Eds), *Proceedings of the VIth World Congress on Pain*, Elsevier, Amsterdam, pp.41–52.

Coyne, J.C. and Gotlib, I.H. (1983) The role of cognition in depression – a critical appraisal. *Psychological Bulletin*, **94**, 472–505.

Craig, K.D. (1983) Emotional aspects of pain. In P.D. Wall and R. Melzack (Eds), *Textbook of Pain*, 1st edn, Churchill Livingstone, Edinburgh, pp.153–161.

Craig, K.D. (1984) Psychology of pain. *Postgraduate Medical Journal*, **60**, 835–840.

Craig, K.D. (1986) Social modelling influences: pain in context. In R.A. Sternbach (Ed.), *The Psychology of Pain*, 2nd edn, Raven Press, New York, pp.67–96.

Craig, K.D. and Best, J.A. (1977) Perceived control over pain: individual differences and situational determinants. *Pain*, **3**, 127–135.

Craig, K.D. and Coren, S. (1975) Signal detection analyses of social modelling influences on pain expressions. *Journal of Psychosomatic Research*, **19**, 105–112.

Craig, K.D. and Prkachin, K.M. (1983) Non-verbal measures of pain. In R. Melzack (Ed.), *Pain Measurement and Assessment*, Raven Press, New York, pp.173–182.

Craig, K.D., Hyde, S.A. and Patrick, C.J. (1991) Genuine, suppressed and fake facial behaviour during exacerbation of chronic low back pain. *Pain*, **46**, 161–171.

Crisson, J.E. and Keefe, F.J. (1988) The relationship of locus of control to pain coping strategies and psychological distress in chronic pain patients. *Pain*, **35**, 147–154.

Crockett D.J., Prkachin, K.M. and Craig, K.D. (1977) Four factors of the language of pain in patient and volunteer groups. *Pain*, **4**, 175–182.

Crook, J., Rideout, E. and Browne, G. (1984) The prevalence of pain complaints in a general population. *Pain*, **18**, 299–314.

Crook, J., Tunks, E., Kalaher, S. and Roberts, J. (1988) Coping with persistent pain: a comparison of persistent pain sufferers in a speciality pain clinic and a family practice clinic. *Pain*, **34**, 175–184.

Croyle, R.T. and Ditto, P.H. (1990) Illness cognition and behaviour: an experimental approach. *Journal of Behavioural Medicine*, **13**(1), 31–52.

Croyle, R.T. and Jemmott, J.B. (1991) Psychological reactions to risk factor testing. In J.A. Skelton and R.T. Croyle (Eds), *Mental Representations of Health and Illness*, Springer-Verlag, New York, pp.85–107.

Croyle, R.T. and Uretsky, M.B. (1987) Effects of mood on self-appraisal of health status. *Health Psychology*, **6**(3), 238–253.

Cuello, A.E. and Mathews, M.R. (1983) Peptides in peripheral sensory nerve fibres. In P.D. Wall and R. Melzack (Eds), *Textbook of Pain*, 1st edn, Churchill Livingstone, Edinburgh, p.65.

Curry, P.D., Pacsoo, C. and Heap, D.G. (1994) Patient controlled epidural analgesia in obstetric anaesthetic practice. *Pain*, **57**, 125–128.

Dallenbach, K.M. (1939) Somesthesis. In E.G. Boring, H.S. Langfeld and H.P. Weld (Eds), *Introduction to Psychology*, John Wiley and Sons, New York, pp.608–625.

Dalton, J.A. and Feuerstein, M. (1988) Biobehavioural factors in cancer pain. *Pain*, **33**, 137–147.

Dalton, J.A., Feuerstein, M., Carlson, J. and Roghman, K.R. (1994) Biobehavioural pain profile: development and psychometric properties. *Pain*, **57**, 95–107.

Davies, H.T.O., Crombie, I.K. and Macrae, W.A. (1993) Polarised views on treating neurogenic pain. *Pain*, **54**, 341–346.

Davies, H.T.O., Crombie, I.K., Lonsdale, M. and Macrae, W.A. (1991) Consensus and contention in the treatment of chronic nerve damage pain. *Pain*, **47**, 191–196.

Davis, M.A. (1981) Sex differences in reporting osteoarthritic symptoms: a socio-medical approach. *Journal of Health and Social Behaviour*, **22**, 298–310.

Davison, G.C. and Valins, S. (1969) Maintenance of self-attributed and drug attributed behaviour change. *Journal of Personality and Social Psychology*, **11**, 25–33.

Davitz, L.J. and Pendleton, S.H. (1969) Nurses' inferences of suffering. *Nursing Research*, **18**(2), 100–107.

De Conno, F., Caraceni, A., Gamba, A., Mariani, L., Abbattista, A., Brunelli, C., La Mura, A. and Ventafridda, V. (1994) Pain measurement in cancer patients: a comparison of six methods. *Pain*, **57**, 161–166.

De Good, D.E. (1983) Reducing medical patients' reluctance to participate in psychological therapies: the initial session. *Professional Psychology: Research and Practice*, **14**(5), 570–579.

De Longis, A., Folkman, S. and Lazarus, R.S. (1988) The impact of daily stress on health and mood: psychological and social resources as mediators. *Journal of Personality and Social Psychology*, **54**, 486–495.

De Paulo, B.M. and Fisher, J.D. (1980) The costs of asking for help. *Basic and Applied Social Psychology*, **1**(1), 23–35.

Deathe, A.B. and Helmes, E. (1993) Evaluation of a chronic pain programme by referring physicians. *Pain*, **52**, 113–121.

Deci, E.L. (1980) *The Psychology of Self Determination*, Lexington Books, Toronto.

Deci, E.L. and Ryan, R.M. (1987) The support of autonomy and the control of behaviour. *Journal of Personality and Social Psychology*, **53**(6), 1024–1037.

Dellemijn, P.L.I. and Fields, H.L. (1994) Do benzodiazapines have a role in chronic pain management? *Pain*, **57**, 137–152.

Demjen, S. and Bakal, D. (1986) Subjective distress accompanying headache attacks: evidence for a cognitive shift. *Pain*, **25**, 187–194.

Dent, J. and Teasdale, J.D. (1988) Negative cognition and the persistence of depression. *Journal of Abnormal Psychology*, **97**(1), 29–34.

Devor, M. (1990) What's in a laser beam for pain therapy? *Pain*, **43**, 139.

Deyo, R.A., Diehl, A.K. and Rosenthal, M. (1986) How many days of bedrest for acute low back pain? A randomised clinical trial. *New England Journal of Medicine*, **315**(17), 1064–1070.

Deyo, R.A., Bass, J.E., Walsh, N.E., Schoenfeld, L.S. and Ramamurthy, S. (1988) Prognostic variability among chronic pain patients: implications for study design, interpretation and reporting. *Archives of Physical Medicine and Rehabilitation*, **69**, 174.

Di Matteo, M.R. and Friedman, H.S. (1982) *Social Psychology and Medicine*, Oetgeschlager, Gunn and Hain, Cambridge, Massachusetts.

Dickenson, A.H. (1991) Mechanisms of the analgesic actions of opiates and opioids. In J.C.D. Wells and C.J. Woolf (Eds), *Pain Mechanisms and Management*, Churchill Livingstone, Edinburgh, pp.690–702.

Diener, E. (1984) Subjective well-being. *Psychological Bulletin*, **95**(3), 542–575.

Diller, A. (1980) Cross-cultural pain semantics. *Pain*, **9**, 9–26.

Ditto, P.H., Jemmott, J.B. and Darley, J.M. (1988) Appraising the threat of illness: a mental representational approach. *Health Psychology*, **7**(2), 183–201.

Doan, B.D. and Wadden, N.P. (1989) Relationships between depressive symptoms and descriptions of chronic pain. *Pain*, **36**(1), 75–84.

Dolce, J.J. (1987) Self efficacy and disability beliefs in behavioural treatment of pain. *Behaviour Research and Therapy*, **25**(4), 289–299.

Dolce, J.J. and Raczynski, J.M. (1985) Neuromuscular activity and electromyography in painful backs: psychological and biomechanical models in assessment and treatment. *Psychological Bulletin*, **97**(3), 502–520.

Dolce, J.J., Crocker, M.F and Doleys, D.M. (1986) Prediction of outcome among chronic pain patients. *Behaviour Research and Therapy*, **24**(3), 313–319.

Dolce, J.J., Doleys, D.M., Raczynski, J.M., Lossie, J., Poole, L. and Smith, M. (1986a) The role of self efficacy expectancies in the prediction of pain tolerance. *Pain*, **27**, 261–272.

Dolce, J.J., Crocker, M.F., Moletteire, C. and Doleys, D.M. (1986b) Exercise quotas, anticipatory concern and self efficacy expectancies in chronic pain: a preliminary report. *Pain*, **24**, 365–372.

Donovan, J.L., Blake, D.R. and Fleming, W.G. (1989) The patient is not a blank sheet: lay beliefs and their relevance to patient education. *British Journal of Rheumatology*, **28**, 58–61.

Donovan, M., Dillon, P. and McGuire, L. (1987) Incidence and characteristics of pain in a sample of medical–surgical inpatients. *Pain*, **30**, 69–78.

Downie, W.W., Leatham, P.A., Rhind, V.M., Wright, V., Branco, J.A. and Anderson, J.A. (1978) Studies with pain rating scales. *Annals of the Rheumatic Diseases*, **37**, 378–381.

Dowson, D.I., Lewith, G.T. and Machin, D. (1985) The effects of acupuncture vs placebo in the treatment of headache. *Pain*, **21**, 35–42.

Doyle, D., Hanks, G.W.C. and MacDonald, N. (1993) What is palliative medicine? In D. Doyle, G.W.C. Hanks and N. MacDonald (Eds), *Oxford Textbook of Palliative Medicine*, Oxford University Press, Oxford, pp.3–8.

Dray, A. (1991) The pharmacology of pain control. Paper presented to the Edinburgh International Science Festival, Royal College of Surgeons, Edinburgh.

Dubner, R. (1992) Hyperalgesia and expanded receptive fields. *Pain*, **48**, 3–4.

Dubuisson, D. and Melzack, R. (1976) Classification of clinical pain descriptions by multiple group discriminant analysis. *Experimental Neurology*, **51**, 480–487.

Duby, G. (1993) *Love and Marriage in the Middle Ages*. Polity Press, London.

Dudley, S.R. and Holm, K. (1984) Assessment of the pain experience in relation to selected nursing characteristics. *Pain*, **18**, 179–186.

Dunkel-Schetter, C., Blasband, D.E., Feinstein, L.G. and Herbert, T.B. (1992) Elements of supportive interactions: when are attempts to help effective? In S. Spacapan and S. Oskamp (Eds), *Helping and Being Helped: Naturalistic Studies*, Sage, Newbury Park, California, p.83.

Dura, J.R. and Beck, S.J. (1988) A comparison of family functioning when mothers have chronic pain. *Pain*, **35**, 79–89.

Dworkin, R.H., Handlin D.S., Richlin, D.M., Brand, L. and Vannucci, C. (1985) Unravelling the effects of compensation, litigation and employment on treatment response in chronic pain. *Pain*, **23**, 49–59.

Dworkin, R.H., Richlin, D.M., Handlin, D.S. and Brand, L. (1986) Predicting treatment response in depressed and non-depressed chronic pain patients. *Pain*, **24**, 343–353.

Edwards, L., Pearce, S.A., Turner-Stokes, L. and Jones, A. (1992) The pain beliefs questionnaire: an investigation of beliefs in the causes and consequences of pain. *Pain*, **51**, 267–272.

Edwards, P.W., Zeichner, A., Kuczmierczyk, A.R. and Boczkowski, J. (1985) Familial pain models: the relationship between family history of pain and current pain experience. *Pain*, **21**(4), 379–384.

Egan, K.J. and Beaton, R. (1987) Responses to symptoms in healthy low utilisers of the health care system. *Journal of Psychosomatic Research*, **31**(1), 11–21.

Ehrlich, K. (1985) The language of pain. *Theoretical Medicine*, **6**, 177–187.

Eiser, J.R. (1980) *Cognitive Social Psychology: A Guidebook to Theory and Research*, McGraw-Hill, Maidenhead.

Ekblom, A., Hansson, P., Thomsson, M. and Thomas, M. (1991) Increased postoperative pain and consumption of analgesics following acupuncture. *Pain*, **44**, 241–247.

Ekman, P. (1985) *Telling Lies: Clues to Deceit in the Market Place, Politics and Marriage*, Norton, London.

Ekman, P. and Friesen, W.V. (1978) *Facial Action Coding System*, Consulting Psychologists Press, Palo Alto, California.

Ekman, P., Friesen, W.V. and O'Sullivan, M. (1988) Smiles while lying. *Journal of Personality and Social Psychology*, **54**(3), 414–420.

Elder, R.G. (1973) Social class and lay explanations of the etiology of arthritis. *Journal of Health and Social Behaviour*, **14**, 28–38.

Eli, K., Nishimoto, R., Mantell, J. and Hamovitch, M. (1988) Longitudinal analysis of psychological adaptation among family members of patients with cancer. *Journal of Psychosomatic Research*, **32**(4/5), 429–438.

Elton, D., Stanley, G. and Burrows, G. (1983) *Psychological Control of Pain*, Grune & Stratton, Sydney.

Engel, G. (1973) Personal theories of disease as determinants of patient–physician relationships. *Psychosomatic Medicine*, **35**, 3.

Epstein, S. (1979) The stability of behaviour: on predicting most of the people much of the time. *Journal of Personality and Social Psychology*, **37**, 1097.

Erskine, A., Morley, S. and Pearce, S. (1990) Memory for pain: a review. *Pain*, **41**, 255–265.

Evans, F.J. (1985) Expectancy, therapeutic instructions and the placebo response. In L. White, B. Tursky and G.E. Schwartz (Eds), *Placebo: Theory, Uses and Mechanisms*, Guilford Press, New York, pp.215–228.

Evans, P.D., Pitts, M.K. and Smith, K. (1988) Minor infection, minor life events and the four day desirability dip. *Journal of Psychosomatic Research*, **32**(4/5), 533–539.

Fabrega, H. and Tyma, S. (1976) Culture, language and the shaping of illness: an illustration based on pain. *Journal of Psychosomatic Research*, **20**(4), 323–337.

Fagerhaugh, S.Y. (1974) Pain expression and control on a burns care unit. *Nursing Outlook*, **22**(10), 645–650.

Fanurik, D., Zeltzer, L.K., Roberts, M.C. and Blount, R.L. (1993) The relationship between children's coping styles and psychological interventions for cold pressor pain. *Pain*, **53**, 213–222.

Farr, R. and Moscovici, S. (1984) *Social Representations*, Cambridge University Press, Cambridge.

Faucett, J.A. and Levine, J.D. (1991) The contributions of interpersonal conflict to chronic pain in the presence or absence of organic pathology. *Pain*, **44**, 35–43.

Feinberg, J. (1988) The effect of patient–practitioner interaction on compliance: a review of the literature and application in rheumatoid arthritis. *Patient Education and Counselling*, **11**, 171–187.

Feinmann, C. (1985) Pain relief by antidepressant: possible modes of action. *Pain*, **23**, 1–8.

Felton, B.J., Revenson, T.A. and Hinrichson, G.A. (1984) Stress and coping in the explanation of psychological adjustment among chronically ill adults. *Social Science and Medicine*, **18**(10), 889–898.

Fernandez, E. (1986) A classification system of cognitive coping strategies for pain. *Pain*, **26**, 141–151.

Fernandez, E. and Turk, D.C. (1989) The utility of cognitive coping strategies for altering pain perception: a meta-analysis. *Pain*, **38**(2), 123–136.

Ferraro, K.F. and Southerland, T. (1989) Domains of medical practice: physicians' assessment of the role of physician extenders. *Journal of Health and Social Behaviour*, **30**, 192–205.

Ferraz, M.B., Quaresma, M.R., Aquino, L.R.L., Atra, E., Tugwell, P. and Goldsmith, C.H. (1990) Reliability of pain scales in the assessment of literate and illiterate patients with rheumatoid arthritis. *Journal of Rheumatology*, **17**(8), 1022.

Festinger, L. (1954) A theory of social comparison processes. *Human Relations*, **7**, 117–140.

Feuerstein, M., Carter, R.L. and Papciak, A.S. (1987) A prospective analysis of stress and fatigue in recurrent low back pain. *Pain*, **31**, 333–344.

Feuerstein, M., Salt, S. and Houle, M. (1985) Environmental stressors and chronic low back pain: life events, family and work environment. *Pain*, **22**, 295–307.

Fielding, G. (1984) Professional problems of caring for the cancer patient. *International Review of Applied Psychology*, **33**(4), 145–154.

Fields, H.L. (1988) Sources of variability in the sensation of pain. *Pain*, **33**, 195–200.

Fields, H.L. and Levine, J.D. (1981) Biology of placebo analgesia. *American Journal of Medicine*, **70**(4), 745–746.

Fillenbaum, G. (1979) Social context and self assessments of health among the elderly. *Journal of Health and Social Behaviour*, **20**, 45–51.

Finlayson, R.E., Marutu, T., Morse, R.M. and Martin, M.A. (1986) Substance dependence and chronic pain: experience with treatment and follow-up results. *Pain*, **26**, 175–180.

Fishbain, D.A., Goldberg, M., Meagher, R.B., Steele, R. and Rosomoff, H. (1986) Male and female chronic pain patients categorised by DSM III psychiatric diagnostic criteria. *Pain*, **26**, 181–197.

Fishbain, D.A., Goldberg, M., Steele, R. and Rosomoff, H.L. (1988) Munchausen syndrome presenting with chronic pain: case report. *Pain*, **35**, 91–94.

Fishbein, M. and Ajzen, I. (1974) Attitudes towards objects as predictors of single and multiple behavioural criteria. *Psychological Review*, **81**, 59–74.

Fishbein, M. and Ajzen, I. (1975) *Belief, Attitude, Intention and Behaviour: An Introduction to Theory and Research*, Addison-Wesley, Reading, Massachusetts.

Fiske, S.T. and Taylor, S.E. (1984) *Social Cognition*, Addison-Wesley, Wokingham.

Fitzpatrick, R. (1983) The social dimensions of health. *Social Science and Medicine*, **17**(8), 501–510.

Fitzpatrick, R., Newman, S.P., Lamb, R. and Shipley, M. (1990) Helplessness and control in rheumatoid arthritis. *International Journal of Health Science*, **1**(1), 17.

Fitzpatrick, R., Fletcher, A., Gore, S., Jones, D., Spiegelhalter, D. and Cox, D. (1992) Quality of life measures in health care: applications and issues in assessments. *British Medical Journal*, **305**, 1074–1077.

Flor, H. and Turk, D.C. (1985) Chronic illness in an adult family member–pain as a prototype. In D.C. Turk and R.D. Kerns (Eds), *Health, Illness and Families–A Lifespan Perspective*, John Wiley and Sons, Chichester, p.255.

Flor, H. and Turk, D.C. (1989) Psychophysiology of chronic pain: do chronic pain patients exhibit symptom-specific psychophysiological responses? *Psychological Bulletin*, **105**(2), 215–259.

Flor, H., Fydrich, T. and Turk, D.C. (1992) Efficacy of multidisciplinary pain treatment centres: a metaanalytic review. *Pain*, **49**, 221–230.

Flor, H., Haag, G. and Turk, D.C. (1986) Long-term efficacy of EMG biofeedback for chronic rheumatic back pain. *Pain*, **27**, 195–202.

Flor, H., Kerns, R.D. and Turk, D.C. (1987) The role of spouse reinforcement, perceived pain and activity levels of chronic pain patients. *Journal of Psychosomatic Research*, **31**(2), 251–259.

Flor, H., Turk, D.C. and Rudy, T.E. (1987) Pain and families – II: Assessment and treatment. *Pain*, **30**, 29–45.

Flor, H., Turk, D.C. and Rudy, T.E. (1989) Relationship of pain impact and significant other reinforcement of pain behaviours: the mediating role of gender, marital status and marital satisfaction. *Pain*, **38**, 45–50.

Flor, H., Turk, D.C. and Scholtz, O.B. (1987) Impact of chronic pain on the spouse: marital, emotional and physical consequences. *Journal of Psychosomatic Research*, **31**(1), 63–71.

Folkman, S. and Lazarus, R.S. (1980) An analysis of coping in a middle-aged community sample. *Journal of Health and Social Behaviour*, **21**, 219–239.

Folkman, S. and Lazarus, R.S. (1985) If it changes, it must be a process: study of emotion and coping during three stages of a college examination. *Journal of Personality and Social Psychology*, **48**, 150–170.

Follick, M.J., Ahern, D.K. and Aberger, E.W. (1985) Development of an audiovisual taxonomy of pain behaviour: reliability and discriminant validity. *Health Psychology*, **4**(6), 555–568.

Fordyce, W.E. (1976) *Behavioural Methods for Chronic Pain and Illness*, Mosby, St Louis.

Fordyce, W.E. (1983) The validity of pain behaviour measurement. In R. Melzack (Ed.), *Pain Measurement and Assessment*, Raven Press, New York, pp.145–153.

Fordyce, W.E. (1986) Learning processes in pain. In R.A. Sternbach (Ed.), *The Psychology of Pain*, 2nd edn, Raven Press, New York, pp.49–72.

Fordyce, W.E. (1988) Pain and suffering: a reappraisal. *American Psychologist*, **43**(4), 276–283.

Fordyce, W.E., Roberts, A.H. and Sternbach, R.A. (1985) A behavioural management of chronic pain: a response to critics. *Pain*, **22**, 113–125.

Fordyce, W.E., McMahon, R., Rainwater, G., Jackins, S., Questad, K., Murphy, T. and DeLateur, B.J. (1981) Pain complaint–exercise performance relationship in chronic pain. *Pain*, **10**, 311–321.

Forsterling, F. (1985) Attributional retraining: a review. *Psychological Bulletin*, **98**(3), 495–512.

Fowler-Kerry, S. and Lander, J.R. (1987) Management of injection pain in children. *Pain*, **30**, 167–175.

Fox, C.D., Steger, H.G. and Jennison, J.J. (1979) Ratio scaling of pain perception with the submaximum effort tourniquet technique. *Pain*, **7**, 21–29.

Fradet, C., McGrath, P.J., Kay, J., Adams, S. and Luke, B. (1990) A prospective survey of reactions to blood tests by children and adolescents. *Pain*, **40**, 53–60.

France, R.D., Urban, B.J. and Keefe, F.J. (1984) Long-term use of narcotic analgesics in chronic pain. *Social Science and Medicine*, **19**(12), 1379–1382.

Fraser, C. and Jaspars, J. (1986) Social representations and social attitudes. Paper presented to the Annual Conference of the British Psychological Society.

Freer, C.B. (1980) Self care: a health diary study. *Medical Care*, **8**, 853–861.

Frenk, H., Cannon, J.T., Lewis, J.W. and Liebeskind, J.C. (1986) Neural and neuro-chemical mechanisms of pain inhibition. In R.A. Sternbach (Ed.), *The Psychology of Pain*, 2nd edn, Raven Press, New York, pp.25–47.

Funch, D.P. and Gale, E.N. (1986) Predicting treatment completion in a behavioural therapy program for chronic temporomandibular pain. *Journal of Psychosomatic Research*, **30**(1), 57–62.

Funk, S.C. and Houston, B.K. (1987) A critical analysis of the hardiness scale's validity and utility. *Journal of Personality and Social Psychology*, **53**(3), 572–578.

Furnham, A. (1988) *Lay Theories*, Pergamon Press, Oxford.

Gaffney, A. and Dunne, E.A. (1987) Children's understanding of the causality of pain. *Pain*, **29**, 91–104.

Gale, A. (Ed.) (1988) *The Polygraph Test: Lies, Truth and Science*, Sage, London.

Gamsa, A. (1990) Is emotional disturbance a precipitator or a consequence of chronic pain? *Pain*, **42**, 183–195.

Gamsa, A. (1994) The role of psychological factors in chronic pain – I: A half century of study. *Pain*, **57**(1), 5–16.

Garb, H.N. (1989) Clinical judgement, clinical training and professional experience. *Psychological Bulletin*, **105**(3), 387–396.

Gardiner, B.M. (1980) Psychological aspects of rheumatoid arthritis. *Psychological Medicine*, **10**, 159–163.

Gaston-Johansson, F. and Gustafsson, M. (1990) Rheumatoid arthritis: determination of pain characteristics and comparison of RAI and VAS in its measurement. *Pain*, **41**, 35–40.

Gentry, W.D. and Kobasa, S.C. (1984) Social and psychological resources mediating stress – illness relationships in humans. In W.D. Gentry (Ed.), *Handbook of Behavioral Medicine*, Guilford Press, New York, pp.87–116.

Gibbons, F.X., Carver, C.S., Scheier, M.F. and Hormuth, S.E. (1979) Self focussed attention and the placebo effect: fooling some of the people some of the time. *Journal of Experimental Social Psychology*, **15**, 263–274.

Gil, K.M., Keefe, F.J., Crisson, J.E. and Van Delfsen, P.J. (1987) Social support and pain behaviour. *Pain*, **29**, 209–217.

Gil, K.M., Williams, D.A., Keefe, F.J. and Beckham, J.C. (1990) The relationship of negative thoughts to pain and psychological distress. *Behaviour Therapy*, **21**, 349–362.

Ginzburg, B.M., Merskey, H. and Lau, C.L. (1988) The relationship between pain drawings and the psychological state. *Pain*, **35**, 141–146.

Glass, D.C., Singer, J.E., Skipton Leonard, H., Krantz, D. and Cummings, H. (1973) Perceived control of aversive stimulation and the reduction of stress responses. *Journal of Personality*, **41**, 577–595.

Gonda, T.A. (1962) The relation between complaints of persistent pain and family size. *Journal of Neurology, Neurosurgery and Psychiatry*, **25**, 277–281.

Goodkin, K. and Gulho, C.M. (1989) Antidepressants for the relief of chronic pain: do they work? *The Society of Behavioural Medicine*, 83.

Goodnow, C., Reisine, S.T. and Grady, K.E. (1990) Quality of social support and associated social and psychological functioning in women with rheumatoid arthritis. *Health Psychology*, **9**(3), 226–284.

Goodwin, J.S., Goodwin, J.M. and Vogel, A.V. (1979) Knowledge and use of placebos by house officers and nurses. *Annals of Internal Medicine*, **91**, 106–110.

Gordis, L. (1979) Conceptual and methodological problems in measuring patient compliance. In R.B. Haynes, D.W. Taylor and D.L. Sackett (Eds), *Compliance in Health Care*, Johns Hopkins University Press, Baltimore, Maryland, p.23.

Gracely, R.H. (1983) Pain language and ideal pain assessment. In R. Melzack (Ed.), *Pain Measurement and Assessment*, Raven Press, New York, pp.71–78.

Gracely, R.H. (1989) Pain psychophysics. In C.R. Chapman and J.D. Loeser (Eds), *Issues in Pain Measurement*, Raven Press, New York, pp.211–229.

Gracely, R.H. (1992) Experimental pain models in initial screening for analgesic efficacy. In M.B. Max, R.K. Portenoy, and E.M. Laska (eds), *Advances in Pain Research and Therapy: The Design of Analgesic Clinical Trials*. Vol. 18, Raven Press, New York, pp.33–48.

Gracely, R.H. and Dubner, R. (1981) Pain assessment in humans – a reply to Hall. *Pain*, **11**, 109–120.

Gracely, R.H. and Dubner, R. (1987) Reliability and validity of verbal descriptor scales of painfulness. *Pain*, **29**, 175–185.

Gracely, R.H. and Kwilosz, D.M. (1988) The Descriptor Differential Scale: applying psychophysical principles to clinical pain assessment. *Pain*, **35**, 279–288.

Gracely, R.H. and Wolskee, P.J. (1983) Semantic functional measurement of pain integrating perception and language. *Pain*, **15**, 389–398.

Gracely, R.H., McGrath, P. and Dubner, R. (1978) Ratio scales of sensory and affective verbal pain descriptors. *Pain*, **5**, 5–18.

Gracely, R.H., Lota, L., Walter, D.J. and Dubner, R. (1988) A multiple random staircase method of psychophysical pain assessment. *Pain*, **32**, 55–63.

Green, J. (1989) Foetal diagnosis: problems in communicating with parents. In *Forum on Medical Communication*, Royal College of Physicians, London.

Greenley, J.R. and Mechanic, D. (1976) Social selection in seeking help for psychological problems. *Journal of Health and Social Behaviour*, **17**, 249–262.

Grimley-Evans, J. (1992) Quality of life assessments and elderly people. In A.H. Hopkins (Ed.), *Measures of the Quality of Life and the Uses to which Such Measures May Be Put*, Royal College of Physicians, London, p.107.

Gruman, J.C. and Sloan, R.P. (1983) Disease as justice: perceptions of the victims of physical illness. *Basic and Applied Social Psychology*, **4**(1), 39–46.

Grunbaum, A. (1985) Explication and implications of the placebo concept. In L. White, B. Tursky and G.E. Schwartz (Eds), *Placebo: Theory, Uses and Mechanisms*, Guilford Press, New York, pp.9–36.

Grunbaum, A. (1989) The placebo concept in medicine and psychiatry. In M. Shepherd and N. Sartorius (Eds), *Non-Specific Aspects of Treatment*, Huber, Toronto, pp.7–38.

Gryll, S.L. and Katahn, M. (1978) Situational factors contributing to the placebo effect. *Pharmacology*, **57**, 253–261.

Gudex, C. (1986) QALYS and their use by the Health Service, Paper 20, Centre for Health Economics, University of York.

Guest, G.H. and Drummond, P.D. (1992) Effect of compensation on emotional state and disability in chronic back pain. *Pain*, **48**, 125–130.

Haagu, D.A.F., Dyck, M.J. and Ernst, D. (1991) Empirical status of cognitive theory of depression. *Psychological Bulletin*, **110**(2), 215–236.

Hackett, T.P. and Cassem, N.H. (1969) Factors contributing to delay in responding to the signs and symptoms of acute myocardial infarction. *American Journal of Cardiology*, **24**, 651–658.

Hagbarth, K.E. and Kerr, D.I.B. (1954) Central influences on spinal afferent conduction. *Journal of Neurophysiology*, **17**, 295–307.

Hahn, R.A. (1985) A socio-cultural model of illness and healing. In L. White, B. Tursky and G.E. Schwartz (Eds), *Placebo: Theory, Uses and Mechanisms*, Guilford Press, New York, pp.167–195.

Haley, W.E., Turner, J.A. and Romano, J.M. (1985) Depression in chronic pain patients: relation to pain, activity and sex differences. *Pain*, **23**, 337–343.

Hall, W. (1981) On ratio scales of sensory and affective verbal pain descriptors. *Pain*, **11**, 101–107.

Handwerker, H.O. (1991) What peripheral mechanisms contribute to nociceptive transmission and hyperalgesia? In A.I. Basbaum and J.M. Besson (Eds), *Towards a New Pharmaco-Therapy of Pain*, John Wiley and Sons, Chichester, pp.5–20.

Hannay, D.R. (1979) *The Symptom Iceberg: A Study of Community Health*, Routledge and Kegan Paul, London.

Hapidou, E.G. and De Catanzaro, D. (1992) Responsiveness to laboratory pain in women as a function of age and childbirth pain experience. *Pain*, **48**, 177–181.

Hardy, J.D., Wolff, H.G. and Goodell, H. (1952) *Pain Sensations and Reactions*, Williams and Wilkins, Baltimore, Maryland.

Harkapaa, K., Jarvikoski, A., Mellin, G. and Hurri, H. and Luomai, J. (1991) Health locus of control beliefs and psychological distress as predictors for treatment outcome in low back pain patients: results of a 3-month follow-up of a controlled intervention study. *Pain*, **46**, 35–41.

Harkins, S.W. and Chapman, C.R. (1976) Detection and decision factors in pain perception in young and elderly men. *Pain*, **2**, 253–264.

Harkins, S.W. and Chapman, C.R. (1977) Age and sex differences in pain perception. In D.J. Anderson and B. Matthews (Eds), *Pain in the Trigeminal Region*, Elsevier, Amsterdam, p.435.

Harper, A.C., Harper, D.A., Lambert, L.J., Andrews, H.B., Kai Lo, S., Ross, F.M. and Straker, L.M. (1992) Symptoms of impairment, disability and handicap in low back pain: a taxonomy. *Pain*, **50**, 189–195.

Harré, R. (1991) *Physical Being: A Theory for a Corporeal Psychology*, Blackwell, Oxford.

Harris, J. (1992) Ethical issues in studying quality of life. Paper to the Royal Society of Medicine conference Quality of Life, Nov. London.

Harris, G. and Rollman, G.B. (1985) Cognitive techniques for controlling pain: generality and individual differences. In H.L. Fields, R. Dubner and F. Cervero (Eds), *Advances in Pain Research and Therapy*, Vol. 9, Raven Press, New York, pp. 847–852.

Harrison, A. (1991) Preparing children for venous blood sampling. *Pain*, **45**, 299–306.

Harvey, J.H. (1984) Attribution of freedom. In J.H. Harvey, W.J. Ickes and R.F. Kidd (Eds), *New Directions in Attribution Research*, Lawrence Erlbaum, Hillsdale, New Jersey, pp.73–96.

Harvey, P.G. (1981) An industrialist's attitude to risk. In *Proceedings of the Royal Society of London, A*, **376**, 193–197.

Hashish, I., Feinmann, C. and Harvey, W. (1988) Reduction of post-operative pain and swelling by ultrasound: a placebo effect. *Pain*, **83**, 303–311.

Hattie, J.A., Sharpley, C.F. and Rogers, H.J. (1984) Comparative effectiveness of professional and paraprofessional helpers. *Psychological Bulletin*, **95**(3), 534–541.

Haug, M.R. (1981) Age and medical care utilisation patterns. *Journal of Gerontology*, **36**(1), 103–111.

Haynes, R.B. (1979a) Introduction. In R.B. Haynes, D.W. Taylor and D.L. Sackett (Eds), *Compliance in Health Care*, Johns Hopkins University Press, Baltimore, Maryland, pp.1–7.

Haynes, R.B. (1979b) Determinants of compliance – the disease and the mechanisms of treatment. In R.B. Haynes, D.W. Taylor and D.L. Sackett (Eds), *Compliance in Health Care*, Johns Hopkins University Press, Baltimore, Maryland, p.49.

Haynes, R.B. and Dantes, R. (1987) Patient compliance and the conduct and interpretation of therapeutic trials. *Controlled Clinical Trials*, **8**, 12–19.

Haynes, R.B., Taylor, D.W. and Sackett, D.L. (Eds) (1979) *Compliance in Health Care*, Johns Hopkins University Press, Baltimore, Maryland.

Haythornthwaite, J.A., Sieber, W.J. and Kerns, R.D. (1991) Depression and the chronic pain experience. *Pain*, **46**, 177–184.

Healy, D. and Williams, J.M.G. (1988) Dysrhythmia, dysphoria and depression: the interaction of learned helplessness and circadian dysrhythmia in the pathogenesis of depression. *Psychological Bulletin*, **103**(2), 163–178.

Hecker, B.R. and Albert, L. (1988) Patient controlled analgesia: a randomised, prospective comparison between two commercially available PCA pumps and conventional analgesic therapy for postoperative pain. *Pain*, **35**(1), 115–120.

Helman, C.G. (1978) "Feed a cold, starve a fever" – folk models of infection in an English suburban community and their relation to medical treatment. *Culture, Medicine and Psychiatry*, **2**, 107–137.

Helman, C.G. (1984) *Culture, Health and Illness: An Introduction for Health Professionals*, Wright, Bristol.

Helman, C.G. (1985) Psyche, soma and society: the social construction of psychosomatic disorders. *Culture, Medicine and Psychiatry*, **9**, 1–26.

Hensel, H. (1972) Pain and the concept of specificity. In R. Janzen, W.D. Keidel, A. Herz, C. Steichele, J.R. Payne and R.A.P. Burt (Eds), *Pain: Basic Principles – Pharmacology Therapy*, Churchill Livingstone, Edinburgh, pp.53–59.

Herda, C.A., Siegeris, K. and Basler, H.D. (1994) The Pain Beliefs and Perceptions Inventory: further evidence for a four-factor structure. *Pain*, **57**, 85–90.

Herman, E. and Baptiste, S. (1981) Pain control: mastery through group experience, *Pain*, **10**, 79–86.

Herzlich, C. (1969) *Sante et Maladie: Analyse d'une Representation Sociale*, Mouton, Paris. (Published in English in 1973 as *Health and Illness: A Social Psychological Analysis*, translated by D. Graham, Academic Press, London.)

Herzlich, L. and Pierret, J. (1985) The social construction of the patient: patients and illnesses in other ages. *Social Science and Medicine*, **2**(2), 145–151.

Herzlich, C. and Pierret, J. (1987) *Illness, Self and Society*, translated by E. Forster, Johns Hopkins University Press, Baltimore, Maryland.

Heyneman, N.E., Fremoun, W.J., Gano, D., Kirkland, F. and Heiden, L. (1990) Individual differences and the effectiveness of different coping strategies for pain. *Cognitive Therapy and Research*, **14**(1), 63–77.

Hillenberg, J.B. and Collins, F.L. (1982) A procedural analysis and review of relaxation training research. *Behavioural Research and Therapy*, **20**, 251–260.

Hodgkins, M., Albert, D. and Daltroy, L. (1985) Comparing patients' and their physicians' assessments of pain. *Pain*, **23**, 273–277.

Hogarth, R.M. (1987) *Judgement and Choice: The Psychology of Decision Making*, 2nd edn, John Wiley and Sons, Chichester.

Holmes, J.A. and Stevenson, C.A.Z. (1990) Differential effects of avoidant and attentional coping strategies on adaptation to chronic and recent onset pain. *Health Psychology*, **9**(5), 577–584.

Holroyd, K.A., Holm, J.E., Hursey, K.G., Penzien, D.B., Cordingley, G.E., Theofanous, A.G., Richardson, S.C. and Tobin, D.L. (1988) Recurrent vascular headache: home-based behavioural treatment versus abortive pharmacological treatment. *Journal of Consulting and Clinical Psychology*, **56**(2), 218–233.

Holroyd, K.A., Holm, J.E., Keefe, F.J., Turner, J.A., Bradley, L.A., Murphy, W.D., Johnson, D., Anderson, K.O., Hinkle, A.L. and OMalley, W.B. (1992) A multicentre evaluation of the McGill Pain Questionnaire: results from more than 1,700 chronic pain patients. *Pain*, **48**, 301–311.

Horvath, P. (1988) Placebos and common factors in two decades of psychotherapy research. *Psychological Bulletin*, **104**(2), 214–255.

Hosobuchi, Y., Adams, J.E. and Linchitz, R. (1977) Pain relief by electrical stimulation of the central gray matter in humans and its reversal by naloxone, *Science*, **197**, 183–186.

Hulka, B.S. (1979) Patient–clinician interactions and compliance. In R.B. Haynes, D.W. Taylor and D.L. Sackett (Eds), *Compliance in Health Care*, Johns Hopkins University Press, Baltimore, Maryland, p.63.

Hull, J.G., Van Treuren, R.R. and Virnelli, S. (1987) Hardiness and health – a critique and alternative approach. *Journal of Personality and Social Psychology*, **53**(3), 518–530.

Hunt, S. and McKenna, S. (1992) Do we need measures other than QALYs? In A.H. Hopkins (Ed.), *Measures of the Quality of Life and the Uses to which Such Measures May Be Put*, Royal College of Physicians, London.

Hunter, M., Philips, C. and Rachman, S. (1979) Memory for pain. *Pain*, **6**(1), 35–46.

Huskisson, E.C. (1983) Visual analogue scales. In R. Melzack (Ed.), *Pain Measurement and Assessment*, Raven Press, New York, pp.33–37.

Huskisson, E.C. and Hart, D.F. (1978) *Joint Disease: All the Arthropathies*, 3rd edn, J. Wright, Bristol.

Hutchinson, D.B. (1984) Accidental compensation: New Zealand shows the way, inaugural lecture, no. 99, University of Cape Town.

Hyland, M. (1987) Control theory interpretation of psychological mechanisms of depression: comparison and integration of several theories. *Psychological Bulletin*, **102**(1), 109–121.

Ickes, W.J. and Kidd, R.F. (1976) An attributional analysis of helping behaviour. In J.H. Harvey, W.J. Ickes and R.F. Kidd (Eds), *New Directions in Attribution Research*, Vol. 1, Laurence Erlbaum, Hillsdale, New Jersey, pp.311–334.

Iggo, A. (1972) Critical remark on the gate control theory. In R. Janzen, W.D. Keidel, A. Herz, C. Steichele, J.R. Payne and R.A.P. Burt (Eds), *Pain: Basic Principles – Pharmacology Therapy*, Churchill Livingstone, Edinburgh, pp.127–128.

Ingham, J.G. and Miller, P.M. (1976) The concept of prevalence applied to psychiatric disorders and symptoms. *Psychological Medicine*, **6**, 217–225.

Ingham, J.G. and Miller, P.M. (1979) Symptom prevalence and severity in a general practice population. *Journal of Epidemiology and Community Medicine*, **33**(3), 191–198.

Ingham, J.G. and Miller, P.M. (1986) Self-referral to primary care: symptoms and social factors. *Journal of Psychosomatic Research*, **30**(1), 49–56.

Ingram, R.E. (1990) Self focussed attention in clinical disorders: review and a conceptual model. *Psychological Bulletin*, **107**(2), 156–176.

Ingram, R.E., Atkinson, J.H., Slater, M.A., Saccuzzo, D.P. and Garfin, S.R. (1990) Negative and positive cognition in depressed and non-depressed chronic pain patients. *Health Psychology*, **9**(3), 300–314.

Jacobsen, P.B., Manne, S.L., Gorfinkle, K. and Schorr, O. (1990) Analysis of child and parent behaviour during painful medical procedures. *Health Psychology*, **9**(5), 559–576.

Jahoda, G. (1988) Critical notes and reflections on social representations. *European Journal of Social Psychology*, **18**, 195–209.

James, F.R. and Large, R.G. (1992) Chronic pain relationships and illness self construct. *Pain*, **50**, 263–271.

Jamison, R.N. and Brown, G.K. (1991) Validation of hourly pain intensity profiles with chronic pain patients. *Pain*, **45**, 123–128.

Jamison, R.N., Matt, D.A. and Parris, W.C.V. (1988) Effects of time-limited or unlimited compensation on pain behaviour and treatment outcome in low back pain patients. *Journal of Psychosomatic Research*, **32**(3), 277–283.

Jamison, R.N., Sbrocco, T. and Parris, W.C.V. (1989) The influence of physical and psychosocial factors on accuracy of memory for pain in chronic pain patients. *Pain*, **37**, 289–294.

Jamison, R.N., Vasterling, J.J. and Parris, W.C.V. (1987) Use of sensory description in assessing chronic pain patients. *Journal of Psychosomatic Research*, 31(5), 647–652.

Janis, I.L. (1984) The patient as decision maker. In W.D. Gentry (Ed.), *Handbook of Behavioral Medicine*, Guilford Press, New York, pp.326–368.

Janis, I.L. and Mann, L. (1977) *Decision Making: A Psychological Analysis of Conflict, Choice and Commitment*, Free Press, New York.

Janz, N.K. and Becker, M.H. (1984) The Health Belief Model: a decade later. *Health Education Quarterly*, 11(1), 1–47.

Jayson, M.V. (1992) Trauma, backpain, malingering and compensation. *British Medical Journal*, 305(6844), 7–8.

Jemmott, J.B., Croyle, R.T. and Ditto, P.H. (1988) Commonsense epidemiology: self based judgements from lay persons and physicians. *Health Psychology*, 7(1), 55–73.

Jensen, I., Nygren, A., Gamberale, F., Goldie, I. and Westerholm, P. (1994) Coping with long-term musculoskeletal pain and its consequences: is gender a factor? *Pain*, 57, 167–172.

Jensen, M.P. and Karoly, P. (1991) Control beliefs, coping efforts and adjustment to chronic pain. *Journal of Consulting and Clinical Psychology*, 59(3), 431–438.

Jensen, M.P. and McFarland, C.A. (1993) Increasing the reliability and validity of pain intensity measurement in chronic pain patients. *Pain*, 55, 195–203.

Jensen, M.P., Bradley, L.A. and Linton, S.J. (1989) Validation of an observation method of pain assessment in non-chronic back pain. *Pain*, 39, 267–274.

Jensen, M.P., Karoly, P. and Braver, S. (1986) The measurement of clinical pain intensity: a comparison of six methods. *Pain*, 27, 117–126.

Jensen, M.P., Karoly, P. and Harris, P. (1991) Assessing the affective component of chronic pain development of the pain discomfort scale. *Journal of Psychosomatic Research*, 35(2/3), 149–154.

Jensen, M.P., Karoly, P. and Huger, R. (1987) The development and preliminary validation of an instrument to assess patients' attitudes toward pain. *Journal of Psychosomatic Research*, 31(3), 393–400.

Jensen, M.P., Turner, J.A. and Romano, J.M. (1991) Self-efficacy and outcome expectancies relationship to chronic pain coping strategies and adjustment. *Pain*, 44, 263–269.

Jensen, M.P., Turner, J.A. and Romano, J.M. (1992) Chronic pain coping measures: individual vs composite scores. *Pain*, 51, 273–280.

Jensen, M.P., Turner, J.A., Romano, J.M. and Karoly, P. (1991) Coping with chronic pain: a critical review of the literature. *Pain*, 47, 249–283.

Jensen, M.P., Turner, J.A., Romano, J.M. and Lawler, B.K. (1994) Relationship of pain-specific beliefs to chronic pain adjustment. *Pain*, 57, 301–309.

Johnson, J.E. and Leventhal, H. (1974) Effects of accurate expectations and behavioural instructions on reactions during a noxious medical examination. *Journal of Personality and Social Psychology*, 29(5), 710–718.

Johnson, L.R., Magnani, B., Chan, V. and Ferrante, F.M. (1989) Modifiers of patient-controlled analgesia efficacy — I: Locus of control. *Pain*, 39, 17–22.

Johnston, M., Shaw, R. and Bird, D. (1984) Test tube baby procedures: stress and judgements under uncertainty. *Psychology and Health*, 1, 25–39.

Joiner, T.E. (1994) Contagious depression: existence, specificity to depressed symptoms and the role of reassurance seekings. *Journal of Personality and Social Psychology*, 67(2), 287–296.

Jones, E.E. and Nisbett, R.R. (1972) The actor and the observer: divergent perceptions of the causes of behaviour. In E.E. Jones, D.E. Kanouse, H.H. Kelley, R.E. Nisbett, S. Valins and B. Weiner (Eds), *Attribution: Perceiving the Causes of Behaviour*, General Learning Press, Morristown, New Jersey.

Jones, R.A. (1982) Expectations and illness. In H.S. Friedman and M.R. Di Matteo (Eds), *Interpersonal Issues in Health Care*, Academic Press, New York, pp.145–167.

Kahneman, D. and Tversky, A. (1979) On the interpretation of intuitive probability: a reply to Jonathon Cohen. *Cognition*, 7(1), 409–411.

Kanfer, F.H. and Goldfoot, D.A. (1966) Self-control and tolerance of noxious stimulation. *Psychological Reports*, **18**, 79–85.

Kanfer, F.H. and Seidner, M.L. (1973) Self-control – factors enhancing tolerance of noxious stimulation. *Journal of Personality and Social Psychology*, **25**(3), 381–389.

Kasl, S.V. (1974) The health belief model and behaviour related to chronic illness. *Health Education Monographs*, **2**(4), 433–454.

Katz, A.H. and Bender, E.I. (1976) Self-help groups in western society: history and prospects. *Journal of Applied Behavioural Science*, **12**(3), 265–282.

Katz, J. and Melzack, R. (1987) Referred sensations in chronic pain patients. *Pain*, **28**, 51–59.

Katz, J. and Melzack, R. (1990) Pain "memories" in phantom limbs: review and clinical observations. *Pain*, **43**, 319–336.

Keefe, F.J. (1982) Behavioural assessment and treatment of chronic pain: current status and future directions. *Journal of Consulting and Clinical Psychology*, **50**(16), 896–911.

Keefe, F.J. and Block, A.R. (1982) Development of an observation method for assessing pain behaviour in chronic low back pain patients. *Behaviour Therapy*, **13**, 363–375.

Keefe, F.J. and Brown, C.J. (1982) Behavioural treatment of chronic pain syndrome. In P.A. Boudewyns and F.J. Keefe (Eds), *Behavioural Medicine in General Medical Practice*, Addison-Wesley, Menlo Park, California, pp.19–41.

Keefe, F.J. and van Horn, J. (1993) Cognitive behavioural treatment of rheumatoid arthritis pain. *Arthritis Care and Research*, **6**(4), 213–222.

Keefe, F.J., Block, A.R. and Williams, R.B. (1980) Behavioural treatments of the prechronic vs chronic pain patient. In F.J. Keefe and J.A. Blumenthal (Eds), *Assessment Strategies in Behavioural Medicine*, Grune & Stratton, New York, Chapter 11.

Keefe, F.J., Castell, P.J. and Blumenthal, J.A. (1986) Angina pectoris in type A and type B cardiac patients. *Pain*, **27**, 211–218.

Keefe, F.J., Gil, K.M. and Rose, S.C. (1986) Behavioural approaches in the multidisciplinary management of chronic pain: programs and issues. *Clinical Psychology Review*, **6**, 87–113.

Keefe, F.J., Salley, A.N. and Lefebvre, J.C. (1992) Coping with pain: conceptual concerns and future directions. *Pain*, **51**, 131–134.

Keefe, F.J., Block, A.R., Williams, R.B. and Surwit, R.S. (1981) Behavioural treatment of chronic low back pain: clinical outcome and individual differences in pain relief. *Pain*, **11**, 221–231.

Keefe, F.J., Crisson, J.E., Maltbie, A., Bradley, L.A. and Gil, K.M. (1986) Illness behaviour as a predictor of pain and overt behaviour patterns in chronic low back pain. *Journal of Psychosomatic Research*, **30**(5), 543–551.

Keefe, F.J., Caldwell, D.S., Queen, K., Gil, K.M., Martinez, S., Crisson, J.E., Ogden, W. and Nunley, J. (1987) Osteoarthritic knee pain: a behavioural analysis. *Pain*, **28**, 309–321.

Keefe, F.J., Brown, G.K., Wallston, K.A. and Caldwell, D.S. (1989) Coping with rheumatoid arthritis pain: catastrophizing as a maladaptive strategy. *Pain*, **37**, 51–56.

Keefe, F.J., Crisson, J., Urban, B.J. and Williams, D.A. (1990) Analysing chronic low back pain: the relative contribution of pain coping strategies. *Pain*, **40**, 293–301.

Keefe, F.J., Caldwell, D.S., Martinez, S., Nunley, J., Beckman, J. and Williams, D.A. (1991) Analysing pain in rheumatoid arthritis patients. Pain copying strategies in patients who have had knee replacement surgery. *Pain*, **46**, 153–160.

Keefe, F.J., Hauck, E.R., Egbert, J., Rimer, B. and Kornguth, P. (1994) Mammography pain and discomfort: a cognitive behavioural perspective. *Pain*, **56**, 247–260.

Kendall, P.L., Hollon, S.D., Beck, A.T., Hammen, C.L. and Ingram, R.E. (1987) Issues and recommendations regarding use of the Beck Depression Inventory. *Cognitive Therapy and Research*, **11**(3), 289–299.

Kent, G. (1985) Memory of dental pain. *Pain*, **21**, 187–194.

Kerns, R.D. and Haythornthwaite, J.A. (1988) Depression among chronic pain patients — cognitive behavioural analysis and effect on rehabilitation outcome. *Journal of Consulting and Clinical Psychology*, **56**(6), 870–876.

Kerns, R.D. and Turk, D.C. (1984) Depression and chronic pain: the mediating role of the spouse. *Journal of Marriage and the Family*, November, 845.

Kerns, R.D., Turk, D.C. and Rudy, T.E. (1985) The West Haven–Yale Multidimensional Pain Inventory (WHYMPI). *Pain*, **23**, 345–356.

Kerrick, J.M., Fine, P.G., Lipman, A.G. and Love, G. (1993) Low dose amitriptyline as an adjunct to opioids for postoperative orthopedic pain: a placebo controlled trial. *Pain*, **52**, 325–330.

Kessler, R.C. (1986) Sex differences in the use of health services. In S. McHugh and T. Vallis (Eds), *Illness Behaviour: A Multidisciplinary Model*, Plenum Press, New York, pp.135–148.

Kessler, R.C., Brown, R.L. and Broman, C.L. (1981) Sex differences in psychiatric help-seeking: evidence from four large-scale surveys. *Journal of Health and Social Behaviour*, **22**, 49–64.

Khatami, M. and Rush, A.J. (1982) A one-year follow up of the multimodal treatment for chronic pain. *Pain*, **14**, 45–52.

Khoury, G. and Varga, E.A. (1988) Does the frequency of utilisation of nerve blocks in pain clinics vary with the speciality of the director? *Pain*, **33**, 265.

Kidder, L.H. and Judd, C.N. (1986) *Research Methods in Social Relations*, Holt, Reinhart and Winston, New York.

Kind, P., Rosser, R.M. and Williams, A. (1982) Valuation of quality of life: some psychometric evidence. In M.W. Jones-Lee (Ed.), *The Value of Life and Safety*, North Holland, Amsterdam, pp.159–170.

King, D.A. and Buchwald, A.M. (1982) Sex differences in subclinical depression: administration of the BDI in public and private self disclosure situation. *Journal of Personality and Social Psychology*, **42**(5), 963–969.

Kirscht, J.P. (1974) The health belief model and illness behaviour. *Health Education Monographs*, **2**(4), 387–408.

Kirscht, J.P. (1988) The health belief model and predictions of health actions. In D.S. Gochman (Ed.), *Health Behaviour – Emerging Health Perspectives*, Plenum Press, New York, pp.27–41.

Kirscht, J.P., Haefner, D.P., Kegeles, S.S. and Rosenstock, I.M. (1966) A national study of health beliefs. *Journal of Health and Human Behaviour*, **7**, 248–254.

Klein, R.M. and Charlton, J.E. (1980) Behavioural observation and analysis of pain behaviour in critically burned patients. *Pain*, **9**, 27–40.

Kleinman, A.R. (1988) *The Illness Narratives: Suffering, Healing and the Human Condition*, Basic Books, New York.

Klepac, R.K., Dowling, J., Rokke, P., Dodge, L. and Schafer, L. (1981) Interview vs pencil and paper administration of the McGill Pain Questionnaire. *Pain*, **11**, 241–246.

Kobasa, S.C. (1982) The hardy personality – towards a social psychology of stress and health. In G.S. Sanders and J. Suls (Eds), *The Social Psychology of Health and Illness*, Laurence Erlbaum, Hillsdale, New Jersey, pp.3–32.

Kobasa, S.C., Maddi, S.R. and Kahn, S. (1982) Hardiness and health – a prospective study. *Journal of Personality and Social Psychology*, **42**(1), 168–177.

Kores, R.C., Murphy, W.D., Rosenthal, T.L., Elias, D.B. and North, W.C. (1990) Predicting outcomes of chronic pain treatment via a modified self-efficacy scale. *Behaviour Research and Therapy*, **28**(2), 165–169.

Korsch, B.M., Gozzi, E.K. and Francis, V. (1968) Gaps in doctor–patient communication. *Paediatrics*, **42**, 855–871.

Kosslyn, S.M., van Kleek, M.H. and Kirby, K.N. (1990) A neurologically plausible model of individual differences in visual mental imagery. In P.J. Hampson, D.F. Marks and J.T.E. Richardson (Eds), *Imagery: Current Developments*, Routledge, London, pp.39–77.

Kosslyn, S.M., Brunn, J., Cave, K.R. and Wallach, R.W. (1984) Individual differences in mental imagery ability: a computational analysis. *Cognition*, **34**, 203–277.

Kotarba, J.A. and Seidel, J.V. (1984) Managing the problem pain patient: compliance or social control? *Social Science and Medicine*, **19**(12), 1393–1400.

Kovacs, M. and Beck, A. (1979) Cognitive affective processes in depression. In C.A. Izard (Ed.), *Emotions in Personality and Psychopathology*, Plenum Press, London, pp.415–439.

Krahé, B. (1992) *Personality and Social Psychology: Towards a Synthesis*, Sage, London.

Kremer, E.F. and Atkinson, J.H. (1984) Pain language: affect. *Journal of Psychosomatic Research*, **28**(2), 125–132.

Kremer, E.F., Atkinson, J.H. and Kremer, A.M. (1983) The language of pain: affective descriptors of pain are a better predictor of psychological disturbance than patterns of sensory and affective descriptors. *Pain*, **16**, 185–192.

Kremer, E.F., Block, A.R. and Atkinson, J.H. (1983) Assessment of pain behaviour: factors that distort self-report. In R. Melzack (Ed.), *Pain Measurement and Assessment*, Raven Press, New York, pp.165–171.

Kuiper, N.A. and MacDonald, M.R. (1983) Reason, emotion and cognitive therapy. *Clinical Psychology Review*, **3**, 297–316.

Kulik, J.A. and Mahler, H.I.M. (1987) Health status, perceptions of risk and prevention interest for health and non-health problems. *Health Psychology*, **6**(1), 15–27.

Lacroix, J.M. (1991) Assessing illness schemata in patient populations. In J.A. Skelton and R.T. Croyle (Eds), *Mental Representations of Health and Illness*, Springer-Verlag, New York, pp.193–219.

Langer, E.J. (1975) The illusion of control. *Journal of Personality and Social Psychology*, **32**, 120–155.

Langley, G.B. and Sheppard, H. (1985) The visual analogue scale: its use in pain measurement. *Rheumatology International*, **5**, 145–148.

Larsen, K. and Smith, C.K. (1981) Assessment of non-verbal communication in the patient–physician interview. *Journal of Family Practice*, **12**, 481–488.

Larson, A.G. and Marcer, D. (1984) The who and why of pain: analysis by social class. *British Medical Journal*, **228**(6421), 883–886.

Larsson, B. and Melin, L. (1986) Chronic headaches in adolescents: treatment in a school setting with relaxation training as compared with information contact and self registration. *Pain*, **25**, 325–336.

Lasagna, L., Mosteller, F., von Felsinger, J.M. and Beecher, H. K. (1954) A study of the placebo response. *American Journal of Medicine*, **16**, 770–779.

Lau, R.R. and Hartman, K.A. (1983) Commonsense representations of common illness. *Health Psychology*, **2**(2), 167–185.

Lautenbacher, S. and Rollman, G.B. (1993) Sex differences in responsiveness to painful and non-painful stimuli are dependent upon the stimulation method. *Pain*, **53**, 255–264.

Lavies, N., Hart, L.M, Rounsefell, B.F. and Runciman, W. (1992) Identification of patient, medical and nursing staff attitudes to postoperative analgesia: stage D of a longitudinal study of postoperative analgesia. *Pain*, **48**, 313–319.

Lawson, K., Reesor, K.A., Keefe, F.J. and Turner, J.A. (1990) Dimensions of pain-related cognitive coping: cross-validation of the factor structure of the Coping Strategy Questionnaire. *Pain*, **43**, 195–204.

Lazarus, R.S. (1984) Puzzles in the study of daily hassles. *Journal of Behaviour Medicine*, **7**(4), 375–389.

Lazarus, R.S. (1986) Coping strategies. In S. McHugh and T. Vallis (Eds), *Illness Behaviour: A Multidisciplinary Model*, Plenum Press, New York, pp.303–308.

Lazarus, R.S. and Folkman, S. (1984) Coping with adaptation. In W.D. Gentry (Ed.), *Handbook of Behavioral Medicine*, Guilford Press, New York, pp.282–325.

Le Baron, S., Zeltzer L.K. and Fanurik, D. (1989) An investigation of cold pressor pain in children. *Pain*, 37, 161–171.

Le Bars, D. and Willer, J.C. (1988) Letter to the editor. *Pain*, 32, 259–260.

Le Bars, D., Dickenson, A.H. and Besson, J.C. (1979) Diffuse noxious inhibitory controls (DNIC) – I: Effects on dorsal horn convergence neurons in the rat. *Pain*, 6, 283–304.

Le Resche, L. and Dworkin, S.F. (1984) Facial expression accompanying pain. *Social Science and Medicine*, 19(12), 1325–1330.

Le Resche, L. and Dworkin, S.F. (1988) Facial expressions of pain and emotions in chronic TMD patients. *Pain*, 35, 71–78.

Leavitt, F. (1983) Detecting psychological disturbance using verbal pain measurement: the Back Pain Classification Scale. In R. Melzack (Ed.), *Pain Measurement and Assessment*, Raven Press, New York, pp.79–84.

Leavitt, F. (1985) Pain and deception: use of verbal pain measurement as a diagnostic aid in differentiating between clinical and simulated low back pain. *Journal of Psychosomatic Research*, 29(5), 495–505.

Leavitt, F. and Garron, D.C. (1979a) Validity of Back Pain Classification Scale among patients with low back pain not associated with demonstrable organic disease. *Journal of Psychosomatic Research*, 23, 301–306.

Leavitt, F. and Garron, D.C. (1979b) The detection of psychological disturbance in patients with low back pain. *Journal of Psychosomatic Research*, 23, 149–154.

Leavitt, F., Garron, D.C., Angelo, D. and McNeil, T.W. (1979) Low back pain in patients with and without demonstrable organic disease. *Pain*, 6, 191–200.

Lee, M.H.M., Zaretsky, H.H. and McMeniman, M. (1978) Acupuncture analgesia – assessment using toothpulp stimulation – a brief report. *New York State Journal of Medicine*, 78(11), 1687–1690.

Lee, T. (1981) Perception of risk. *Proceedings of the Royal Society of London, A*, 376, 5–16.

Lefebvre, M.F. (1981) Cognitive distortion and cognitive errors in depressed psychiatric and low back pain patients. *Journal of Consulting and Clinical Psychology*, 49(4), 517–525.

Lennon, M.C., Link, B.G., Marbach, J.J. and Dohrenwend, B.P.D. (1989) The stigma of chronic facial pain and its impact on social relationships. *Social Problems*, 36(2), 117–133.

Levenson, H. and Miller, J. (1976) Multidimensional locus of control in socio-political activists of conservative and liberal ideologies. *Journal of Personality and Social Psychology*, 33, 199–208.

Leventhal, H. (1975) The consequences of depersonalisation during illness and treatment – an information processing model. In J. Howard and A. Strauss (Eds), *Humanising Health Care*, Wiley Interscience, New York, 119–126.

Leventhal, H. and Defenbach, J. (1991) The active side of illness cognition. In J.A. Skelton and R.T. Croyle (Eds), *Mental Representations of Health and Illness*, Springer-Verlag, New York, p.247.

Leventhal, H. and Everhart, D. (1979) Emotion, pain and physical illness. In C.A. Izard (Ed.), *Emotions in Personality and Psychopathology*, Plenum Press, London, Chapter 9, pp.263–299.

Leventhal, H. and Mosbach, P.A. (1983) The perceptual-motor theory of emotion. In J.T. Cacioppo and R.E. Petty (Eds), *Social Psychophysiology – A Sourcebook*, Guilford Press, New York, pp.353–388.

Leventhal, H., Leventhal, E.A. and Schaefer, P. (1988) Vigilant coping and health behaviour: a lifespan problem. Unpublished manuscript.

Leventhal, H., Meyer, D. and Nerenz, D.R. (1980) The commonsense representation of illness danger. In S.J. Rachman (Ed.), *Contributions to Medical Psychology*, Vol. 2, Pergamon Press, Oxford, pp.17–30.

Leventhal, H., Zimmerman, R.S. and Gutmann, M. (1984) Compliance – a self-regulation perspective. In W.D. Gentry (Ed.), *Handbook of Behavioral Medicine*, Guilford Press, New York, pp.369–436.

Levine, F.M. and De Simone, L.L. (1991) The effects of experimenter gender on pain report in male and female subjects. *Pain*, **44**, 69–72.

Levine, F.M., Krass, S.M. and Padawar, W.J. (1993) Failure hurts: the effects of stress due to difficult tasks and failure feedback on pain report. *Pain*, **54**, 335–340.

Levine, J.D. and Gordon, N.C. (1982) Pain in prelingual children and its evaluation by pain-induced vocalisation. *Pain*, **14**, 85–93.

Levine, J.D., Gordon, N.C. and Fields, H.L. (1978) The mechanism of placebo analgesia. *Lancet*, **ii**(8091), 654–657.

Levine, J.D., Gormley, J. and Fields, H.L. (1976) Observations on the analgesic effect of needle puncture (acupuncture). *Pain*, **2**, 149–159.

Lewin, K. (1951) *Field Theory in Social Science*, Harper, New York.

Lewinsohn, P.M., Steinmetz, J.L., Larson, D.W. and Franklin, J. (1981) Depression-related cognitions: an antecedent or consequence? *Journal of Abnormal Psychology*, **90**, 213–219.

Lewis, C.E. and Nadler, M.A. (1976) The recipients and results of acupuncture. *Medical Care*, **VXIV**, 3.

Lewith, G.T. and Kenyon, J.N. (1984) Physiological and psychological explanations for the mechanism of acupuncture as a treatment for chronic pain. *Social Science and Medicine*, **19**(12), 1367–1378.

Lewith, G.T. and Machin, D. (1983) On the evaluation of the clinical effects of acupuncture. *Pain*, **16**, 111–127.

Ley, P. (1988) *Communicating with Patients: Improving Communication, Satisfaction and Compliance*, Psychology and Medicine Series, Croom Helm, London.

Ley, P., Bradshaw, P.W., Eaves, D. and Walker, L.M. (1973) A method for increasing patients' recall of information presented by doctors. *Psychological Medicine*, **3**, 217–220.

Liebeskind, J.C. (1991) Pain *can* kill. *Pain*, **44**, 3–4.

Lien-Tsang, H. (1978) Some people's psychological investigation in the People's Republic of China. *Australian Psychologist*, **13**, 3.

Lindsay, S.J.E., Wege, P. and Yates, J. (1984) Expectations of sensations, discomforts and fear in dental treatment. *Behavioural Research and Therapy*, **22**(2), 99–108.

Linssen, A.C.G. and Zitman, F.G. (1984) Patient evaluation of a cognitive behavioural group program for patients with chronic low back pain. *Social Science and Medicine*, **19**(12), 1361–1365.

Linton, S.J. (1985) The relationship between activity and chronic back pain. *Pain*, **21**, 289–294.

Linton, S.J. (1986) Behavioural remediation of chronic pain: a status report. *Pain*, **24**, 125–141.

Linton, S.J. (1987) Chronic pain: the case for prevention. *Behaviour Research and Therapy*, **25**(4), 313–317.

Linton, S.J. and Gotesdam, K.G. (1983) A clinical comparison of two pain scales: correlation, remembering chronic pain and a measure of compliance. *Pain*, **17**, 57–65.

Linton, S.J. and Melin, L. (1982) The accuracy of remembering chronic pain. *Pain*, **13**, 281–285.

Linton, S.J., Bradley, L.A., Jensen, I., Spangforth, E. and Sundell, L. (1989) The secondary prevention of low back pain: a controlled study with follow-up. *Pain*, **36**(2), 197–207.

Linville, P.W. (1987) Self complexity as a cognitive buffer against stress-related illness and depression. *Journal of Personality and Social Psychology*, **52**(4), 663–676.

Lipton, J.A. and Marbach, J.J. (1984) Ethnicity and the pain experience. *Social Science and Medicine*, **19**(12), 1279–1298.

Litt, M.D. (1986) Mediating factors in non-medical treatment for migraine headache: toward an interactional model. *Journal of Psychosomatic Research*, **30**(4), 505–519.

Llewellyn, S. (1984) The cost of giving: emotional growth and emotional stress. In S.M. Skevington (Ed.), *Understanding Nurses: The Social Psychology of Nursing*, John Wiley and Sons, Chichester, pp.49–66.

Lloyd, R. (1989) *Explorations in Psychoneurology*, Grune & Stratton, New York.

Lorig, K. and Holman, H.R. (1989) Long-term outcomes of an arthritis self-management study: effects of reinforcement efforts. *Social Science and Medicine*, **29**(2), 221–224.

Lorig, K., Konkol, L. and Gonzalez, V. (1987) Arthritis patient education: a review of the literature. *Patient Education and Counselling*, **10**, 207–252.

Lorig, K., Mazonson, P.D. and Holman, H.R. (1993) Evidence suggesting that health education for self management in patients with chronic arthritis has sustained health benefits while reducing health care costs. *Arthritis and Rheumatism*, **36**(4), 439–446.

Lorig, K., Chastain, R.L., Ung, E., Shoor, S. and Holman, H.R. (1989a) Development and evaluation of a scale to measure perceived self-efficacy in people with arthritis. *Arthritis and Rheumatism*, **32**(1), 37–44.

Lorig, K., Seleznick, M., Lubeck, D., Ung, E., Chastain, R.L. and Holman, H.R. (1989b) The beneficial outcome of the arthritis self-management course are not adequately explained by behaviour change. *Arthritis and Rheumatism*, **32**(1), 91–95.

Love, A.W. (1988) Attributional style of depressed chronic low back pain patients. *Journal of Clinical Psychology*, **44**, 317–321.

Love, A.W. and Peck, C.L. (1987) The MMPI and psychological factors in chronic low back pain: a review. *Pain*, **28**, 1–12.

Lowe, N.K., Walker, S.N. and MacCallum, R.C. (1991) Confirming the theoretical structure of the McGill Pain Questionnaire in acute clinical pain. *Pain*, **46**, 53–60.

Lowery, B.J., Jacobsen, B.S. and Murphy, B.B. (1983) An exploratory investigation of causal thinking of arthritics. *Nursing Research*, **32**(3), 157–162.

Lynn, B. (1977) Cutaneous hyperalgesia. *British Medical Bulletin*, **33**, 103–108.

Lynn, B. and Perl, E.R. (1977) Failure of acupuncture to produce localised analgesia. *Pain*, **3**, 339–351.

Mabry, J.H. (1964) Lay concepts of etiology. *Journal of Chronic Disease*, **17**, 371–386.

MacDonald, N. (1993) The interface between oncology and palliative medicine. In D. Doyle, G.W.C. Hanks and N. MacDonald (Eds), *Oxford Textbook of Palliative Medicine*, Oxford University Press, Oxford, pp.11–16.

Mackie, A.M., Coda, B.C. and Hill, H.F. (1991) Adolescents use patient-controlled analgesia effectively for relief from prolonged oropharyngeal mucositis pain. *Pain*, **46**, 265–269.

Macrae, W.A. (1991) Why is pain treated so badly? Paper presented to the Edinburgh International Science Festival, Royal College of Surgeons, Edinburgh.

Magni, G. (1987) On the relationship between chronic pain and depression when there is no organic lesion. *Pain*, **31**, 1–21.

Magni, G., Caldieron, C., Rigatti-Luchini, S. and Merskey, H. (1990) Chronic musculo-skeletal pain and depressive symptoms in the general population. An analysis of the First National Health and Nutrition Examination Survey data. *Pain*, **43**, 299–307.

Magni, G., Marchetti, M., Moreschi, C., Merskey, H and Rigatti-Luchini, S. (1993) Chronic musculoskeletal pain and depressive symptoms in the National Health and Nutritional Examination. *Pain*, **53**, 163–168.

Magni, G., Moreschi, C., Rigatti-Luchini, S. and Merskey, H. (1994) Prospective study on the relationship between depressive symptoms and chronic musculoskeletal pain. *Pain*, **56**, 284–297.

Maier, S.F. (1991) Stressor controllability, cognition and fear. In J. Madden (Ed.), *Neurobiology of Learning, Emotion and Affect*, Raven Press, New York, p.55.

Main, C.J. (1984) Must we play the MMPI game? or is the MMPI the only game in town? Paper presented to the Pain Interest Group.

Main, C.J. and Waddell, G. (1982) Chronic pain, distress and illness behaviour. In C.J. Main (Ed.), *Clinical Psychology and Medicine – A Behavioural Perspective*, Plenum Press, London, 1–52.

Main, C.J. and Waddell, G. (1984) The detection of psychological abnormality in chronic low back pain using four simple scales. *Current Concepts in Pain*, 2(1), 204–208.

Main, C.J. and Waddell, G. (1987) Psychometric construction and validity of the Illness Behaviour Questionnaire in British patients with chronic low back pain. *Pain*, 28, 13–25.

Main, C.J. and Waddell, G. (1991) A comparison of cognitive measures in low back pain: statistical structure and clinical validity at initial assessment. *Pain*, 46, 287–298.

Malow, R.M. (1981) The effects of induced anxiety on pain perception: a signal detection analysis. *Pain*, 11, 397–405.

Malow, R.M. and Olson, R.E. (1981) Changes in pain perception after treatment for chronic pain. *Pain*, 11, 65–72.

Manchini, V.S., Peterson, R.A. and Maruta, T. (1988) Changes in perception of illness and psychosocial adjustment – findings of a pain management program. *Clinical Journal of Pain*, 4, 249–256.

Manne, S.L. and Zautra, A.J. (1989) Spouse criticism and support: their association with coping and psychological adjustment among women with rheumatoid arthritis. *Journal of Personality and Social Psychology*, 56(4), 608–617.

Manne, S.L. and Zautra, A.J. (1990) Couples coping with chronic illness: women with rheumatoid arthritis and their healthy husbands. *Journal of Behavioural Medicine*, 13, 327–342.

Manne, S.L., Jacobsen, P.B. and Redd, W.H. (1992) Assessment of acute pediatric pain: do child self report, parent ratings and nurse ratings measure the same phenomenon? *Pain*, 48, 45–52.

Manne, S.L., Redd, W.H., Jacobsen, P.B., Gorfinkle, K., Schorr, O. and Rapkin, B. (1990) Behavioural intervention to reduce child and parent distress during venipuncture. *Journal of Consulting and Clinical Psychology*, 58(5), 565–572.

Marchand, S., Charest, J., Chenard, J.R., Lavignolle, B. and Laurencelle, L. (1993) Is TENs purely a placebo effect? A controlled study on chronic low back pain. *Pain*, 54, 99–106.

Margolis, R.B., Chibnall, J.T. and Tait, R.C. (1988) Test–retest reliability of the pain drawing instrument. *Pain*, 33, 49–51.

Margolis, R.B., Tait, R.C. and Krause, S.J. (1986) A rating system for use with patient pain drawings. *Pain*, 24, 57–65.

Marks, G., Richardson, J.L., Graham, J.W. and Levine, A. (1986) Role of health locus of control beliefs and expectations of treatment efficacy and adjustment to cancer. *Journal of Personality and Social Psychology*, 51(2), 443–450.

Marlowe S., Engstrom, R. and White, P.F. (1989) Epidural patient controlled analgesia (PCA): an alternative to continuous epidural infusions. *Pain*, 37, 97–101.

Marteau, T.M. (1989) Framing of information: its influence upon decisions of doctors and patients. *British Journal of Social Psychology*, 28, 89–94.

Mather, L. and Mackie, J. (1983) The incidence of postoperative pain in children. *Pain*, 15, 271–282.

Matsumoto, D. (1987) The role of facial feedback in the experience of emotion: more methodological problems and a meta-analysis. *Journal of Personality and Social Psychology*, 52(4), 769–774.

McArthur, D.L., Cohen, M.J. and Schandler, S.L. (1989) A philosophy for the measurement of pain. In C.R. Chapman and J.D. Loeser (Eds), *Issues in Pain Measurement*, Raven Press, New York, pp.37–49.

McArthur, D.L., Cohen, M.J., Gottlieb, H.J., Naliboff, B.D. and Schandler, S.L. (1987) Treating chronic low back pain – I: admissions to initial follow up. *Pain*, **29**(1), 1–22.

McCaul, K.D. and Malott, J.M. (1984) Distraction and coping with pain. *Psychological Bulletin*, **95**(3), 516–533.

McDaniel, L.K., Anderson, K.O., Bradley, L.A., Young, L.D., Turner, R.A., Agudelo, C.A. and Keefe, F.J. (1986) Development of an observation method for assessing pain behaviour in rheumatoid arthritis patients. *Pain*, **24**, 165–184.

McGrath, P.A. (1987) An assessment of children's pain: a review of behavioural, psychological and direct scaling techniques. *Pain*, **31**, 147–176.

McGrath, P.A. (1993) Inducing pain in children – a controversial issue. *Pain*, **52**, 255–257.

McGrath, P.J. (1990) Paediatric pain: a good start. *Pain*, **41**, 253–254.

McKenna, F.P. (1985) Another look at the "new psycho-physics". *British Journal of Psychology*, **76**, 97–109.

McQuay, H.J. (1990) Assessment of pain and effectiveness of treatment. In A.H. Hopkins and D.A. Costain (Eds), *Measuring the Outcomes of Medical Care*, Royal College of Physicians, London.

McQuay, H.J. (1991) Opioid clinical pharmacology and routes of administration. *British Medical Bulletin*, **47**(3), 703–717.

McQuay, H.J. (1992) Pre-emptive analgesia. *British Journal of Anaesthesia*, **69**(1), 1–3.

McQuay, H.J. (1993) Does preemptive treatment provide better pain control? Paper presented to the VIIth World Congress on Pain, Paris.

McQuay, H.J., Carroll, D. and Moore, R.A. (1988) Postoperative orthopaedic pain – the effect of opiate pre-medication and local anaesthetic blocks. *Pain*, **33**(3), 291–295.

Mechanic, D. (1976) Sex, illness, illness behaviour and the use of health services. *Journal of Human Stress*, December, 29–40.

Mechanic, D. (1977) Illness behaviour, social adaptation and the management of illness. *Journal of Nervous and Mental Diseases*, **165**(2), 79–87.

Mechanic, D. (1985) Health and behaviour: perspectives on risk prevention. In J.C. Rosen and L.J. Solomon (Eds), *Prevention in Health Psychology*, University Press of New England (reprinted in D. Mechanic (Ed.) (1989) *Painful Choices*, Transaction Publishers, New Brunswick, pp.70–81).

Mechanic, D. (1986a) The concept of illness behaviour: culture, situation and personal predisposition. *Psychological Medicine*, **16**, 1–7.

Mechanic, D. (1986b) Illness behaviour: an overview. In S. McHugh and T. Vallis (Eds), *Illness Behaviour: A Multidisciplinary Model*, Plenum Press, New York, pp.101–110.

Mechanic, D. (1989) The doctor–patient relationship: traditions, transitions and tension. In D. Mechanic (Ed.), *Painful Choices*, Transaction Publishers, New Brunswick, pp.236–241.

Mechanic, D. and Angel, R.J. (1989) Some factors associated with the report and evaluation of back pain. In D. Mechanic (Ed.), *Painful Choices*, Transaction Publishers, New Brunswick, pp.167–182.

Mechanic, D. and Cleary, P.D. (1980) Factors associated with the maintenance of positive health behaviour. *Preventative Medicine*, **9**(6), 805–814.

Medvene, L. (1992) Self-help groups, peer helping and social comparison. In S. Spacapan and S. Oskamp (Eds), *Helping and Being Helped: Naturalistic Studies*, Sage, Newbury Park, California, p.49.

Meichenbaum, D., Henshaw, D. and Himmel, N. (1982) Coping with stress as a problem-solving process. In H. W. Kohne and L. Laux (Eds), *Achievement, Stress and Anxiety*, Hemisphere, McGraw, New York, p.127.

Melville, D.I. (1987) Descriptive clinical research and medically unexplained physical symptoms. *Journal of Psychosomatic Research*, **31**(3), 359–365.

Melzack, R. (1975) The McGill Pain Questionnaire: major properties and scoring method. *Pain*, **1**, 277–299.

Melzack, R. (1983a) Acupuncture and related forms of folk medicine. In P.D. Wall and R. Melzack (Eds), *Textbook of Pain*, 1st edn, Churchill Livingstone, Edinburgh, pp.691–700.

Melzack, R. (1983b) The McGill Pain Questionnaire. In R. Melzack (Ed.), *Pain Measurement and Assessment*, Raven Press, New York, pp.41–47.

Melzack, R. (1986) Neurophysiological foundations of pain. In R.A. Sternbach (Ed.), *The Psychology of Pain*, 2nd edn, Raven Press, New York, pp.1–24.

Melzack, R. (1987) The Short-Form McGill Pain Questionnaire. *Pain*, **36**, 191–197.

Melzack, R. (1989) Folk medicine and the sensory modulation of pain. In P.D. Wall and R. Melzack (Eds), *Textbook of Pain*, 2nd edn, Churchill Livingstone, Edinburgh, pp.897–905.

Melzack, R. and Casey, K.L. (1967) Sensory, motivational and sensory control determinants of pain: a new conceptual model. In D. Kenshalo (Ed.), *The Skin Senses*, Charles C. Thomas, Springfield, Illinois, pp.423–438.

Melzack, R. and Dennis, S.G. (1978) Neurophysiological foundations of pain. In R.A. Sternbach (Ed.), *The Psychology of Pain*, 1st edn, Raven Press, New York, pp.1–26.

Melzack, R. and Torgerson, W.S. (1971) On the language of pain. *Anaesthesiology*, **3**(4), 50–59.

Melzack, R. and Wall, P.D. (1965) Pain mechanisms – a new theory. *Science*, **150**, 971–979.

Melzack, R. and Wall, P.D. (1970) Psychophysiology of pain. *International Anaesthesiology Clinics*, **8**, 3–34.

Melzack, R. and Wall, P.D. (1982) *The Challenge of Pain*, 1st edn, Penguin, Harmondsworth.

Melzack, R. and Wall, P.D. (Eds) (1989) *The Challenge of Pain*, 2nd edn, Penguin, Harmondsworth.

Melzack, R., Katz, J. and Jeans, M.E. (1985) The role of compensation in chronic pain: analysis using a new method of scoring the McGill Pain Questionnaire. *Pain*, **23**, 101–112.

Melzack, R., Wall, P.D. and Ty, T.C. (1982) Acute pain in an emergency clinic: latency of onset and descriptor patterns related to different injuries. *Pain*, **14**, 33–42.

Melzack, R., Jeans, M.E., Stratford, J.G. and Monks, R.C. (1980) Ice massage and transcutaneous electrical stimulation comparison of treatment for low back pain. *Pain*, **9**, 209–217.

Mendell, L.M. and Wall, P.D. (1964) Presynaptic hyperpolarisation – a role for fine afferent fibres. *Journal of Physiology*, **172**, 274–294.

Mendelson, G. (1986) Chronic pain and compensation: a review. *Journal of Pain and Symptom Management*, **1**(3), 135.

Mendelson, G. (1992) Compensation and chronic pain. *Pain*, **48**, 121–123.

Merskey, H. (1988) Back pain and disability. *Pain*, **34**, 213.

Merskey, H. and Boyd, D. (1978) Emotional adjustment and chronic pain. *Pain*, **5**, 173–178.

Merskey, H., Albe-Fessard, D.G., Bonica, J.J. Carmen, A., Dubner, R., Kerr, F.W.L., Lindblom, U., Mumford, J.M., Nathan, P.W., Noordenbos, W., Pagni, C.A., Renaer, M.J., Sternbach, R.A., and Sunderland, S. (1979) IASP sub-committee on taxonomy. *Pain*, **6**(3), 249–252.

Milgram, S. (1974) *Obedience to Authority: An Experimental View*, Harper & Row, New York.

Miller, J. (1978) *The Body in Question*, Cape, London.

Miller, N.E. (1989) Placebo factors in treatment: views of a psychologist. In M. Shepherd and N. Sartorius (Eds), *Non-Specific Aspects of Treatment*, Huber, Toronto, pp.39–56.

Miller, P.M. and Ingham, J.G. (1985) Dimensions of experience and symptomatology. *Journal of Psychosomatic Research*, **29**(5), 475–488.

Miller, S.M. (1979) When is a little information a dangerous thing? Coping with stressful events by monitoring vs blunting. In S. Levine and H. Ursine (Eds), *Coping and Health*, Plenum Press, New York, pp.145–169.

Miller, S.M. and Grant, R.P. (1979) The blunting hypothesis – a view of predictability and stress. In P.O. Sjoden, S. Bates and W.S. Dockens (Eds), *Trends in Behaviour Therapy*, Academic Press, New York, pp.135–151.

Miller, S.M., Brody, D.S. and Summerton, J. (1988) Styles of coping with threat: implications for health. *Journal of Personality and Social Psychology*, 54(1), 142–148.

Milligan, K.A. and Atkinson, R.E. (1991) The "two week" syndrome associated with injection treatment for chronic pain – fact or fiction? *Pain*, 44, 165–166.

Mirowsky, J. and Ross, C.E. (1990) Control or defense? Depression and the sense of control over good and bad outcomes. *Journal of Health and Social Behaviour*, 31, 71–86.

Mishel, M.H. (1981) The measurement of uncertainty in illness. *Nursing Research*, 30(5), 258–263.

Moe, K.O. and Zeiss, A.M. (1982) Measuring self efficacy expectations for social skills: a methodological enquiry. *Cognitive Therapy and Research*, 6(2), 191–205.

Moore, M.E. and Berk, S.N. (1980) Ethical considerations encountered in a study of acupuncture – a reappraisal. *Clinical Research*, 28(4), 334–342.

Moore, R.A. (1990) Ethnographic assessment of pain coping perceptions. *Psychosomatic Medicine*, 52, 171–181.

Mor, J. and Hiris, J. (1983) Determinants of site of death among hospice cancer patients. *Journal of Health and Social Behaviour*, 24, 375–385.

Morley, S. (1993) Vivid memory for "everyday" pains. *Pain*, 55, 55–62.

Morley, S. and Hassard, A. (1989) The development of a self administered psychophysical scaling method: internal consistency and temporal stability in chronic pain patients. *Pain*, 37, 33–39.

Morrell, E.M. and Keefe, F.J. (1988) The actometer: an evaluation of instrument applicability for chronic pain patients. *Pain*, 32, 265–270.

Moscovici, S. (1988) Notes towards a description of social representations. *European Journal of Social Psychology*, 18, 211–250.

Mount, B.M. (1983) Psychological and social aspects of cancer pain. In P.D. Wall and R. Melzack (Eds), *Textbook of Pain*, 1st edn, Churchill Livingstone, Edinburgh, p.460.

Muse, M. (1985) Stress-related, posttraumatic chronic pain syndrome: criteria for diagnosis and preliminary report on prevalence. *Pain*, 23, 295–300.

Muse, M. (1986) Stress-related, posttraumatic chronic pain syndrome: behavioural treatment approach. *Pain*, 25, 389–394.

Naliboff, B.D., Cohen, M.J. and Yellen, A.J. (1982) Does the MMPI differentiate chronic illness from chronic pain? *Pain*, 13, 333–341.

Nathan, P.W. (1976) The gate control theory of pain: a critical review. *Brain*, 99, 123–158.

Nathan, P.W. (1985) Success in surgery may not require cutting the tracts. *Pain*, 22, 317–319.

Nathan, P.W. and Rudge, P. (1974) Testing the gate-control theory of pain in man. *Journal of Neurology, Neurosurgery and Psychiatry*, 37, 1366–1372.

Nerenz, D.R. and Leventhal, H. (1983) Self-regulation theory in chronic illness. In T.G. Burish and L.A. Bradley (Eds), *Coping with Chronic Disease: Research and Applications*, Academic Press, New York, pp.13–38.

Nerenz, D.R., Leventhal, H., Love, R.R. and Ringer, K.E. (1984) Psychological aspects of cancer chemotherapy. *International Review of Applied Psychology*, 33(4), 521.

Ness, T.J. and Gebhart, G.F. (1990) Visceral pain: a review of experimental studies. *Pain*, 41(2), 167–234.

Neufeld, R.W. and Thomas, P. (1977) Effects of perceived efficacy of a prophylactic controlling mechanism on self-control under pain stimulation. *Canadian Journal of Behavioral Science*, 9(3), 224–232.

Newall, D.J., Gadd, E.M. and Priestman, T.J. (1987) Presentation of information to cancer patients: a comparison of two centres in the UK and USA. *British Journal of Medical Psychology*, **60**, 127–131.

Newman, S.P., Fitzpatrick, R., Lamb, R. and Shipley, M. (1989) The origins of depressed mood in rheumatoid arthritis. *Journal of Rheumatology*, **16**(6), 740–744.

Nicholas, M.K. (1989) Self-efficacy and chronic pain. Paper presented to the British Psychological Society Annual Conference.

Nisbett, R.E. and Ross, L. (1980) *Human Interference: Strategies and Shortcomings of Social Judgement*, Prentice Hall, Englewood Cliffs, New Jersey.

Nisbett, R.E. and Schachter, S. (1966) Cognitive manipulation of pain. *Journal of Experimental Social Psychology*, **2**, 227–236.

Nisbett, R.E. and Valins, S. (1971) *Perceiving the Causes of Ones's Own Behaviour*, General Learning Press, Morristown, New Jersey.

Nolen-Hoeksema, S. (1987) Sex differences in unipolar depression: evidence and theory. *Psychological Bulletin*, **101**(2), 259–282.

Noordenbos, W. (1959) *Pain – Problems Pertaining to the Transmission of Nerve Impulses which Give Rise to Pain: Preliminary Statement*, Elsevier, Amsterdam.

Norman, D.A. (1986) Reflections on cognition and parallel distributed processing. In J.L. McClelland, D.E. Rumelhart and the PDP research group (Eds), *Parallel Distributed Processing: Psychological and Biological Models*, MIT Press, Cambridge, Massachusetts, p.531.

Notermans, S.L.H. and Tophoff, M.M.W.A. (1967) Sex differences in pain tolerance and pain apperception. *Psychiatrica, Neurologica, Neurochirurgia*, **70**, 23–29.

Nurmikko, T. and Hietcharjn, A. (1992) Effect of exposure to sauna heat on neuropathic and rheumatoid pain. *Pain*, **49**, 43–51.

Nutty, D.D., Wilkins, A.J. and Williams, J.M.G. (1987) Mood, pattern sensitivity and headache: a longitudinal study. *Psychosomatic Medicine*, **17**, 705–713.

O'Brien, J. and Francis, A. (1988) The use of next-of-kin to estimate pain in cancer patients. *Pain*, **35**, 171–178.

O'Leary, A. (1985) Self-efficacy and health. *Behaviour Research and Therapy*, **23**(4), 437–451.

Osgood, C.E. (1953) *Method and Theory in Experimental Psychology*, Oxford University Press, New York.

Ottoson, D. (1983) *Physiology of the Nervous System*, Macmillan, London.

Pagni, C.A. (1983) Why is cancer pain treatment so difficult? In S. Ischia, S. Lipton and G.F. Maffezzoli (Eds), *Pain Treatments: Pituitary Neuroadenolysis in the Treatment of Cancer Pain and Hormone-Dependent Tumours*, Cortina International, Verona and Raven Press, New York, pp.1–10.

Papageorgiou, A.C. and Badley, E.M. (1989) The quality of pain in arthritis: the words patients use to describe overall pain and pain in individual joints at rest and on movement. *Journal of Rheumatology*, **16**(1), 106.

Parker, J.C., Smarr, K.L., Buescher, K.L., Phillips, L.R., Frank, R.G., Beck, N.C., Anderson, S.K. and Walker, S.E. (1989) Pain control and rational thinking: implications for rheumatoid arthritis. *Arthritis and Rheumatism*, **32**(8), 984–990.

Payne, B. and Norfleet, M.A. (1986) Chronic pain and the family: a review. *Pain*, **26**, 1–12.

Pearce, S. (1983) A review of cognitive–behavioural methods for the treatment of chronic pain. *Journal of Psychosomatic Research*, **27**(5), 431–440.

Pearce, S.A., Isherwood, S., Hrouda, D., Richardson, P.H., Erskine, A. and Skinner, J. (1990) Memory and pain: test of mood congruity and state dependent learning in experimentally induced and clinical pain. *Pain*, **43**, 187–193.

Peck, C.L. (1986) Psychological factors in acute pain management. In M.J. Cousins and G.D. Phillips (Eds), *Acute Pain Management*, Churchill Livingstone, Edinburgh, pp.257–274.

Peck, J.R., Smith, T.W., Ward, J. and Milano, R.A. (1989) Disability and depression in rheumatoid arthritis: a multitrait multimethod investigation. *Arthritis and Rheumatism,* **32**(9), 1100–1106.

Pennebaker, J.W. (1982) *The Psychology of Physical Symptoms,* Springer-Verlag, New York.

Pennebaker, J.W. (1989) Confession, inhibition and disease. *Advances in Experimental Social Psychology,* **22**, 211.

Pennebaker, J.W. and Susman, J.R. (1988) Disclosure of traumas and psychosomatic processes. *Social Science and Medicine,* **26**(3), 327–323.

Pennebaker, J.W., Kiecolt-Glaser, J.K. and Glaser, R. (1988) Confronting traumatic experience and immunocompetence: a reply to Neale, Cox, Valdimarsdottir and Stone. *Journal of Consulting and Clinical Psychology,* **56**(4), 638–639.

Perrin, E.C. and Gerrity, P.S. (1981) There's a demon in your belly: children's understanding of illness. *Pediatrics,* **67**(6), 841–849.

Perry, S. and Heidrich, G. (1982) Management of pain during debridement. *Pain,* **13**, 267–280.

Peters, M.L., Schmidt, A.J.M., Van den Hout, M.A., Koopmans, R. and Sluijter, M.E. (1992) Chronic back pain, acute postoperative pain and the activation of diffuse noxious inhibitory controls (DNIC). *Pain,* **50**, 177–187.

Peterson, C., Seligman, M.E.P. and Vaillant, G.E. (1988) Pessimistic explanatory style is a risk factor for physical illness – a 35-year longitudinal study. *Journal of Personality and Social Psychology,* **55**(1), 23–27.

Phillips, D.P. and King, E.W. (1988) Death takes a holiday: mortality surrounding major social occasions. *Lancet,* 8613, 728–732.

Phillips, D.P. and Smith, D.G. (1990) Postponement of death until symbolically meaningful occasions. *Journal of the American Medical Association,* **263**(14), 1947–1951.

Pilisuk, M., Boylan, R. and Acredolo, C. (1987) Support, life stress and subsequent medical care utilisation. *Health Psychology,* **6**, 272–288.

Pill, R. and Stott, N. (1982) Concepts of illness causation and responsibility: some preliminary data from a sample of working class mothers. *Social Science and Medicine,* **16**, 43–52.

Pilowsky, I. (1988) An outline curriculum on pain for medical schools. *Pain,* **33**, 1–2.

Pilowsky, I. (1990) The concept of abnormal illness behaviour. *Psychosomatics,* **31**(2), 207–213.

Pilowsky, I. and Katsikitis, M. (1994) A classification of illness behaviour in pain clinic patients. *Pain,* **57**, 91–94.

Pilowsky, I. and Spence, N.D. (1975) Patterns of illness behaviour in patients with intractable pain. *Journal of Psychosomatic Research,* **19**, 279–287.

Pincus, T., Callaghan, L.F., Bradley, L.A., Vaughn, W.K. and Wolfe, F. (1986) Elevated MMPI scores for hypochondriasis, depression and hysteria in patients with rheumatoid arthritis reflect disease rather than psychological status. *Arthritis and Rheumatology,* **29**(12), 1456–1466.

Pither, C.E. (1989) Treatment of persistent pain. *British Medical Journal,* **229**, 12.

Plotkin, W.B. (1985) A psychological approach to placebo: the role of faith in therapy and treatment. In L. White, B. Tursky and G.E. Schwartz (Eds), *Placebo: Theory, Uses and Mechanisms,* Guilford Press, New York, pp.237–254.

Politis, N. (1904) *Studies on the Life and Language of the Greek People,* Vol. II, *Traditions,* Historical Research Publications, Athens, p.553.

Pollner, M. (1989) Divine relations, social relations and well-being. *Journal of Health and Social Behaviour,* **30**, 92–104.

Portenoy, R.K. and Hagen, N.A. (1990) Breakthrough pain: definitions, prevalence and characteristics. *Pain,* **41**, 273–281.

Price, D.D. (1988) *Psychological and Neurological Mechanisms of Pain,* Raven Press, New York.

Price, D.D., Harkins, S.W. and Baker, C. (1987) Sensory–affective relationships among different types of clinical and experimental pain. *Pain,* **28**, 297–307.

Price, D.D., McGrath, P.A., Rafii, A. and Buckingham, B. (1983) The validation of visual analogue scales as ratio scale measures for clinical and experimental pain. *Pain*, 17, 45–56.

Price, D.D., Von der Gruen, A., Miller, J., Rafii, A. and Price, C. (1985) A psychophysical analysis of morphine analgesia. *Pain*, 22, 261–269.

Price, D.D., Bush, F.M., Long, S. and Harkins, S.W. (1994) A comparison of pain measurement characteristics of mechanical visual analogue and simple numerical rating scales. *Pain*, 56, 217–226.

Price, H.J., Hillman, K.S., Toralt, M.E. and Newell, S. (1983) The public's perceptions and misperceptions of arthritis. *Arthritis and Rheumatism*, 26(8), 1023–1028.

Prieto, E.J. and Geisinger, K.F. (1983) Factor analytic studies of the McGill Pain Questionnaire. In R. Melzack (Ed.), *Pain Measurement and Assessment*, Raven Press, New York, pp.63–70.

Pritchard, M.L. (1989) *Psychological Aspects of Rheumatoid Arthritis*, Springer-Verlag, London.

Prkachin, K.M. (1992) The consistency of facial expressions of pain: a comparison across modalities. *Pain*, 51, 297–306.

Prkachin, K.M., Currie, N.A. and Craig, K.D. (1983) Judging non-verbal expressions of pain. *Canadian Journal of Behavioral Science*, 15(4), 408–420.

Purcell-Jones, G., Dormon, F. and Sumner, E. (1988) Paediatric anaesthetists' perceptions of neonatal and infant pain. *Pain*, 33, 181–187.

Quadrel, M.J. and Lau, R.R. (1990) A multivariate analysis of adolescents' orientations toward physician use. *Health Psychology*, 9(6), 750–773.

Rachlin, H. (1985) Pain and behaviour. *The Behavioural and Brain Sciences*, 8, 43–83.

Rachman, S. (1979) The concept of required helpfulness. *Behaviour Research and Therapy*, 17, 1–6.

Rachman, S. (1986) Advances in chronic pain and discomfort. Paper presented to the British Psychological Society Annual Conference.

Rachman, S. and Lopatka, C. (1988) Accurate and inaccurate predictions of pain. *Behaviour Research and Therapy*, 26(4), 291–296.

Radvila, A., Adler, R.H., Galeazzi, R.L. and Vorkauf, H. (1987) The development of a German language (Berne) pain questionnaire and its application in a situation causing acute pain. *Pain*, 28, 185–195.

Raft, D., Smith, R.H. and Warren, N. (1986) Selection of imagery in the relief of chronic and acute clinical pain. *Journal of Psychosomatic Research*, 30(4), 481–488.

Rang, H.P., Bevan, S. and Dray, A. (1991) Chemical activation of nociceptive peripheral neurones. In J.C.D. Wells and C.J. Woolf (Eds), *Pain Mechanisms and Management*, Churchill Livingstone, Edinburgh, pp.534–548.

Ransford, A.O., Cairns, D. and Mooney, V. (1976) The pain drawing as an aid to the psychologic evaluation of patients with low back pain. *Spine*, 1(2), 127.

Raps, C.S., Peterson, C., Jonas, M. and Seligman, M.E.P. (1982) Patient behaviour in hospitals: helplessness, reactance or both. *Journal of Personality and Social Psychology*, 42(6), 1036–1041.

Rasmussen, B.K. (1993) Migraine and tension type headache in a general population: precipitating factors, female hormones, sleep pattern and relation to lifestyle. *Pain*, 53, 65–72.

Ray, C. (1980) Psychological aspects of early breast cancer and its treatment. In S.J. Rachman (Ed.), *Contributions to Medical Psychology*, Vol. 2, Pergamon Press, Oxford, p.153.

Ray, C. and Baum, M. (1985) *Psychological Aspects of Early Breast Cancer*, Springer-Verlag, New York.

Ray, C., Fisher, J. and Lindop, J. (1984) The surgeon–patient relationship in the context of breast cancer. *International Review of Applied Psychology*, 33(4), 531–543.

Reader, G.G., Pratt, L. and Mudd, M.C. (1957) What patients expect from their doctors. *The Modern Hospital*, **89**(1), 88.

Reading, A.E. (1980) A comparison of pain rating scales. *Journal of Psychosomatic Research*, **24**, 119–124.

Reading, A.E. (1982) Attribution and the management of the pain patient. In C. Antaki and C.R. Brewin (Eds), *Attributions and Psychological Change – Applications of Attributional Theory to Clinical and Educational Practice*, Academic Press, London, pp.157–174.

Reading, A.E. (1983) The McGill Pain Questionnaire – an appraisal. In R. Melzack (Ed.), *Pain Measurement and Assessment*, Raven Press, New York, pp.55–62.

Reesor, K. and Craig, K.D. (1988) Medically incongruent chronic back pain: physical limitations, suffering and ineffective coping. *Pain*, **32**, 35–40.

Regan, C.A., Lorig, K. and Thorensen, C.E. (1988) Arthritis appraisal and ways of coping – scale development. *Arthritis Care and Research*, **3**, 139–150.

Reichmanis, M. and Becker, R.O. (1977) Relief of experimentally induced pain by stimulation at acupuncture loci. *Comparative Medicine East and West*, **5**, 281–288.

Reid, D.W. (1984) Participatory control and the chronic illness adjustment process. In H. Lefcourt (Ed.), *Research with the Locus of Control Construct*, Vol. 3, Academic Press, New York, p.361.

Reisine, S.T., Goodenow, C. and Grady, K.E. (1987) The impact of rheumatoid arthritis on the homemaker. *Social Science and Medicine*, **25**(1), 89–95.

Rene, J., Weinberger, M., Mazzuca, S.A., Brandt, K.D. and Katz, B.P. (1992) Reduction of joint pain in patients with knee osteoarthritis who have received monthly telephone calls from lay personnel and whose medical treatment regimens have remained stable. *Arthritis and Rheumatism*, **35**(5), 511.

Revenson, T.A. and Felton, B.T. (1989) Disability and coping as predictors of psychological adjustment to rheumatoid arthritis. *Journal of Consulting and Clinical Psychology*, **57**(3), 344–348.

Revenson, T.A. and Majerovitz, S.D. (1991) The effects of chronic illness on the spouse: social resources as stress buffers. *Arthritis Care and Research*, **4**(2), 63–72.

Revenson, T.A., Schiaffino, K.M., Majerovitz, S.D. and Gibofsky, A. (1991) Social support as a double-edged sword: the relation of positive and problematic support to depression among rheumatoid arthritis patients. *Social Science and Medicine*, **33**(7), 807–813.

Reville, S.F., Robinson, J.O., Rosen, M., and Hogg, M.I.J. (1976) The reliability of the linear analogue scale for evaluating pain. *Anaesthesia*, **31**, 1191–1198.

Reynolds, D.V. (1969) Surgery in the rat during electrical analgesia by focal brain stimulation. *Science*, **164**, 444–445.

Richardson, P.H. and Vincent, C.A. (1986) Acupuncture for the treatment of pain: a review of evaluative research. *Pain*, **24**, 15–40.

Roberts, C. (1946) *An English–Zulu Dictionary*, Routledge and Kegan Paul, London.

Robins, C.J. (1988) Attributions and depression: why is the literature so inconsistent? *Journal of Personality and Social Psychology*, **54**(5), 880–889.

Robinson, H.E., Swimmer, G.I. and Ralloff, D. (1989) The P-A-I-N MMPI classification system: a critical review. *Pain*, **37**, 211–214.

Robinson, I. (1990) Personal narratives, social careers and medical courses: analysing life trajectories in autobiographies of people with multiple sclerosis. *Social Science and Medicine*, **30**(11), 1173–1186.

Roche, P.A. and Gijsbers, K. (1986) A comparison of memory for induced ischaemic pain and chronic rheumatoid pain. *Pain*, **25**, 337–343.

Rodin, J. and Salovey, P. (1989) Health psychology. *Annual Review of Psychology*, **40**(5), 533–579.

Rodin, J., Rennert, K. and Solomon, S.K. (1980) Intrinsic motivation for control – fact or fiction? In A. Baum and J.E. Singer (Eds), *Advances in Environmental*

Psychology: Applications of Personal Control, Vol. 2, Lawrence Erlbaum, Hillsdale, New Jersey, pp.131–148.

Rollman, G. B. (1977) Signal detection theory measurement of pain: a critical review. *Pain*, 3, 187–211.

Romano, J.M. and Turner, J.A. (1985) Chronic pain and depression – does the evidence support a relationship? *Psychological Bulletin*, 97(1), 18–34.

Romano, J.M., Turner, J.A. and Clancy, S.L. (1989) Sex differences in the relationship of pain patient dysfunction to spouse adjustment. *Pain*, 39, 289–295.

Rooney, P.J. and Buchanan, W.W. (1990) In rheumatoid arthritis is compliance in physicians more of a problem than compliance in patients? *Clinical Rheumatology*, 9(3), 315–318.

Rosch, E.H. (1973) Natural categories. *Cognitive Psychology*, 4, 328–350.

Rose, M. and Adams, D. (1989) Evidence for pain and suffering in other animals. In G. Langley (Ed.), *Animal Experimentation: The Consensus Change*, MacMillan, New York, Chapter 3.

Rosensteil, A.K. and Keefe, F.J. (1983) The use of coping strategies in chronic low back pain patients. *Pain*, 17, 33–44.

Rosenstock, I.M. (1966) Why people use health services. *Milbank Memorial Fund Quarterly*, 44, 94.

Rosenstock, I.M. (1974) The health belief model and preventive health behaviour. *Health Education Monographs*, 2(4), 354–386.

Rosenstock, I.M. and Kirscht, J.P. (1979) Why people seek health care. In G. Stone, F. Cohen and N. Adler (Eds), *Health Psychology*, Jossey-Bass, San Francisco, California, pp.161–188.

Ross, S. and Buckalew, L.W. (1985) Placebo agentry: assessment of drugs and placebo effects. In L. White, B. Tursky and G.E. Schwartz (Eds), *Placebo: Theory, Uses and Mechanisms*, Guilford Press, New York, pp.67–82.

Rosser, R.M. (1987) A health index and output measure. In S.R. Walker and R.M. Rosser (Eds), *Quality of Life: Assessment and Application*. Kleuwer, Dordrecht, pp.133–160.

Rosser, R.M., Cottee, M., Rabin, R. and Selai, C. (1992) Index of Health Related Quality of Life. In A.H. Hopkins (Ed.), *Measures of the Quality of Life and the Uses to which Such Measures May Be Put*, Royal College of Physicians, London, pp.297–304.

Rothbaum, F., Weisz, J.R. and Snyder, S.S. (1982) Changing the world and changing the self – a two-process model of perceived control. *Journal of Personality and Social Psychology*, 42, 5.

Rotter, J.B. (1966) Generalised expectancies for internal versus external locus of control. *Psychological Monographs*, 80, 1–28.

Rowat, K.M. and Knafl, K.A. (1985) Living with chronic pain: the spouse's perspective. *Pain*, 23, 259–271.

Royal College of Surgeons and College of Anaesthetists (1990) Commission on the Provision of Surgical Services. Report of the Working Party on Pain After Surgery, September.

Rubenstein, L.V., Calkins, R.T., McCleary, P.D., Fink, A., Kosecoff, J., Jette, A.M., Davis, A.R., Delbanco, T.L. and Brook, R.H. (1989) Improving patient function: a randomised trial of functional disability screening. *Annals of Internal Medicine*, 111, 836–842.

Rudy, T.E. (1989) Innovations in pain psychometrics. In C.R. Chapman and J.D. Loeser (Eds), *Issues in Pain Measurement*, Raven Press, New York, pp.51–61.

Rudy, T.E., Kerns, R.D. and Turk, D.C. (1988) Chronic pain and depression: towards a cognitive behavioural mediation model. *Pain*, 35(2), 129–140.

Rudy, T.E., Turk, D.C. and Brena, S.F. (1988) Differential utility of medical procedures in the assessment of chronic pain patients. *Pain*, 34, 53–60.

Rudy, T.E., Turk, D.C., Zaki, H.S. and Curtin, H.D. (1989) An empirical taxometric alternative to traditional classification of temporomandibular disorders. *Pain*, 36, 311–320.

Rudy, T.E., Turk, D.C., Brena, S.F., Stieg, R.L. and Brody, M.C. (1990) Quantification of biomedical findings of chronic pain patients: development of an index of pathology. *Pain*, 42, 167–182.

Rutter, D.R., Calnan, M., Vaile, M.S.B., Field, S. and Wade, K.A. (1992) Discomfort and pain during mammography: description, prediction and prevention. *British Medical Journal*, **305**, 443–445.

Rybstein-Blinchik, E. (1979) Effects of different cognitive strategies on chronic pain experience. *Journal of Behavioural Medicine*, **2**, 93–101.

Sackett, D.L. (1979) A compliance practicum for the busy practitioner. In R.B. Haynes, D.W. Taylor and D.L. Sackett (Eds), *Compliance in Health Care*, Johns Hopkins University Press, Baltimore, Maryland, pp.286–296.

Sackett, D.L. and Snow, J.C. (1979) The magnitude of compliance and non-compliance. In R.B. Haynes, D.W. Taylor and D.L. Sackett (Eds), *Compliance in Health Care*, Johns Hopkins University Press, Baltimore, Maryland, pp.11–22.

Sanders, G.S. (1982) Social comparison and perceptions of health and illness. In G.S. Sanders and J. Suls (Eds), *The Social Psychology of Health and Illness*, Laurence Erlbaum, Hillsdale, New Jersey, Chapter 5.

Sanders, S.H. (1983) Automated vs self monitoring of "uptime" in chronic low back pain patients: a comparative study. *Pain*, **15**, 399–405.

Sargent, C. (1984) Between death and shame: dimensions of pain in Bariba culture. *Social Sciences and Medicine*, **19**(12), 1299–1304.

Sartorius, N. (1985) Foreword. In L. White, B. Tursky and G.E. Schwartz (Eds), *Placebo: Theory, Uses and Mechanisms*, Guilford Press, New York.

Sartorius, N. (1991) Kvaliteta zivota (quality of life). In B. Vrhovac, I. Bakran, M. Granic, B. Jaksic, B. Lanar and B. Vucelic (Eds), *Interna Medicina*, Vol. 1, Naprijed, Zagreb (in Croatian) p.10.

Saunders, C. (1983a) Pain control in terminal illness. *Journal of Psychosomatic Research*, **27**(5), 441–442.

Saunders, C. (1983b) Pain and impending death. In P.D. Wall and R. Melzack (Eds), *Textbook of Pain*, 1st edn, Churchill Livingstone, Edinburgh, p.472.

Savendra, M.C., Gibbons, P., Tesler, M.D., Ward, J. and Wegner, C. (1982) How do children describe pain? A tentative assessment. *Pain*, **14**, 95–104.

Scambler, G. (1991) Epilepsy. Paper presented to the Conference on Measures of the Quality of Life, Royal College of Physicians, London.

Scarman, Lord (1986) Consent, communication and responsibility. *Journal of the Royal Society of Medicine*, **79**, 697–700.

Scheier, M.F. and Carver, C.S. (1987) Dispositional optimism and physical well-being: the importance of generalised outcome expectancies on health. *Journal of Personality*, **55**(2), 169–210.

Schiaffino, K.M., Revenson, T.A. and Gibofsky, A. (1991) Assessing the impact of self-efficacy beliefs on adaptation to rheumatoid arthritis. *Arthritis Care and Research*, **4**(4), 150–157.

Schmidt, A.J.M. (1987) The behavioural management of pain: a criticism of a response. *Pain*, **30**, 285–291.

Schmidt, A.J.M. and Arntz, A. (1987) Psychological research and chronic low back pain: a standstill or breakthrough? *Social Science and Medicine*, **25**(10), 1095–1104.

Schreiber, S. and Galia-Gat, T. (1993) Uncontrolled pain following physical injury as the core-trauma in post-traumatic stress disorder. *Pain*, **54**, 107–110.

Schwartz, L., Slater, M.A., Birchler, G.R. and Atkinson, J.H. (1991) Depression in spouses of chronic pain patients: the role of patient pain and anger and marital satisfaction. *Pain*, **44**, 61–67.

Scott, D.S. and Gregg, J.M. (1980) Myofascial pain of the temporomandibular joint: a review of the behavioural – relaxation therapies. *Pain*, **9**, 231–241.

Scott, J. and Huskisson, E.C. (1976) Graphic representation of pain. *Pain*, **2**, 175–184.

Scott, J. and Huskisson, E.C. (1979) Accuracy of subjective measurements made with or without previous scores – an important source of error in social measurement of subjective states. *Annals of the Rheumatic Diseases*, **38**, 558–559.

Selai, C. (1991) Some methodological issues. Paper presented to the Royal Society of Medicine Conference on Quality of Life, London.

Seligman, M.E.P. (1984) Helplessness and depression. Paper presented to the British Psychological Society Annual Conference, Warwick.

Seltzer, S.F. and Yarczower, M. (1991) Selective encoding and retrieval of affective words during exposure to aversive stimulation. *Pain*, **47**, 47–51.

Seymour, R.A., Simpson, J.M., Charlton, J.E. and Phillips, M.E. (1985) An evaluation of length and end phase of visual analogue scales in dental pain. *Pain*, **21**, 177–185.

Shacham, S., Dar, R. and Cleeland, C.S. (1984) The relationship of mood state to the severity of clinical pain. *Pain*, **18**, 187–197.

Shapiro, A.K. and Morris, L.A. (1978) The placebo effect in medical and psychological therapies. In S.L. Garfield and A.E. Bergin (Eds), *Handbook of Psychotherapy and Behaviour Change*, John Wiley and Sons, New York, pp.369–410.

Sharp, K., Ross, C.E. and Cockerham, W.C. (1983) Symptoms, beliefs and the use of physician services among the disadvantaged. *Journal of Health and Social Behaviour*, **24**, 255–263.

Sherman, R.A., Sherman, C.J. and Bruno, G.M. (1987) Psychological factors influencing chronic phantom limb pain: an analysis of the literature. *Pain*, **28**, 285–295.

Shontz, F.C. (1975) *The Psychological Aspects of Physical Illness and Disability*, Collier-Macmillan, London.

Shutty, M.S., Cundiff, G. and De Good, D.E. (1992) Pain complaint and the weather: weather sensitivity and symptom complaints in chronic pain patients. *Pain*, **49**, 199–204.

Shutty, M.S., De Good, D.E. and Tuttle, D.H. (1990) Chronic pain patients' beliefs about their pain and treatment outcomes. *Archives of Physical Medicine and Rehabilitation*, **71**, 128–132.

Siegel, S., (1956) *Non-Parametric Statistics for the Behavioural Sciences*, McGraw-Hill, New York.

Simmons, C.H. and Lerner, M.J. (1968) Altruism as a search for justice. *Journal of Personality and Social Psychology*, **9**(3), 216–225.

Skelton, J.A. (1991) Lay persons' judgements of patient credibility and the study of illness representations. In J.A. Skelton and R.T. Croyle (Eds), *Mental Representations of Health and Illness*, Springer-Verlag, New York, pp.108–131.

Skelton, J.A. and Pennebaker, J.W. (1982) The psychology of physical symptoms and sensations. In G.S. Sanders and J. Suls (Eds), *The Social Psychology of Health and Illness*, Laurence Erlbaum, Hillsdale, New Jersey, 99–128.

Skevington, S.M. (1979) Pain and locus of control – a social approach. In D.J. Oborne, M.M. Gruneberg and J.R. Eiser (Eds), *Research in Psychology and Medicine*, Vol. 1, Academic Press, London, pp.61–69.

Skevington, S.M. (1981) Intergroup relations and nursing. *European Journal of Social Psychology*, **11**, 43–59.

Skevington, S.M. (1983a) Social cognitions, personality and chronic pain. *Journal of Psychosomatic Research*, **27**(5), 421–428.

Skevington, S.M. (1983b) Chronic pain and depression: universal or personal helplessness. *Pain*, **15**, 309–317.

Skevington, S.M. (1986) Psychological aspects of pain in rheumatoid arthritis: a review. *Social Science and Medicine*, **23**(6), 567–575.

Skevington, S.M. (1990) A standardised scale to measure beliefs about controlling pain (BPCQ): a preliminary study. *Psychology and Health*, **4**, 221–232.

Skevington, S.M. (1991) Pain control and mechanisms for the measurement of pain. *Journal of Psychopharmacology*, **5**(4), 360–363.

Skevington, S.M. (1993) Depression and causal attributions in the early stages of a chronic painful disease: a longitudinal study of early synovitis. *Psychology and Health*, **8**, 51–64.

Skevington, S.M. (1994) Social comparisons in cross-cultural quality of life assessment. *International Journal of Mental Health*, **23**(2), 29–47.

Skevington, S.M. (1995) Predicting chronic pain patients: a prospective study of illness behaviour in early rheumatic disease. In review.

Skipper, J.K. and Leonard, R.C. (1968) Children, stress and hospitalisation: a field experiment. *Journal of Health and Social Behaviour*, **9**(4), 275–287.

Slovic, P., Fischoff, B. and Lichtenstein, S. (1981) Perceived risk: psychological factors and social implications. *Proceedings of the Royal Society of London*, A, **376**, 17–34.

Smith, G.T. (1985) *Measurement of Health*, Office of Health Economics, London.

Smith, T.W., Follick, M.J., Ahern, D.K. and Adams, A. (1986) Cognitive distortion and disability. *Cognitive Therapy and Research*, **10**(2), 201–210.

Smith, T.W., Peck, J.R., Milano, R.A. and Ward, J. (1988) Cognitive distortion in rheumatoid arthritis: relation to depression and disability. *Journal of Consulting and Clinical Psychology*, **56**(3), 412–416.

Snyder, M. and Omoto, A.M. (1992) Who helps and why? The psychology of AIDS volunteerism. In S. Spacapan and S. Oskamp (Eds), *Helping and Being Helped: Naturalistic Studies*, Sage, Newbury Park, California, pp.213–239.

Solnit, A.J. and Priel, B. (1975) Scared and scarred – psychological aspects in the treatment of soldiers with burns. *Israeli Annals of Psychiatry and Related Disciplines*, **13**(3), 213–220.

Sommerville, M.A. (1994) Death of pain: pain, suffering and ethics. In G.F. Gebhart, D.L. Hammond and T.S. Jensen (Eds), *Proceedings of the VII World Congress on Pain: Progress in Pain Research Management*, Vol. 2, IASP Press, Seattle, pp.41–58.

Spinhoven, P. and Linssen, A.C.G. (1991) Behavioural treatment of chronic low back pain: one relation of coping strategy use to outcome. *Pain*, **45**, 29–34.

Stacey, M. (1988) Lay concepts of health and illness. In M. Stacey (Ed.), *The Sociology of Health and Healing: A Textbook*, Unwin Hyman, London, Chapter 10.

Sternbach, R.A. (1974) Varieties of pain games. In J. Bonica (Ed.), *Advances in Neurology*, Vol. 4, Raven Press, New York, pp.423–430.

Sternbach, R.A. (1978) Clinical aspects of pain. In R.A. Sternbach (Ed.), *The Psychology of Pain*, 1st edn, Raven Press, New York, pp.241–264.

Sternbach, R.A. (1983a) The tourniquet pain test. In R. Melzack (Ed.), *Pain Measurement and Assessment*, Raven Press, New York, pp.27–31.

Sternbach, R.A. (1983b) Ethical considerations in pain research in man. In R. Melzack (Ed.), *Pain Measurement and Assessment*, Raven Press, New York, p.259.

Sternbach, R.A. (1986) Pain and hassles in the United States: findings of the Nuprin Pain Report. *Pain*, **27**, 69–80.

Sternbach, R.A. and Tursky, B. (1965) Ethnic differences among housewives in psycho-physiological and skin potential responses to electric shock. *Psychophysiology*, **1**(3), 217–218.

Sternbach, R.A., Deems, L.M., Timmermans, G. and Huey, L.Y. (1977) On the sensitivity of the tourniquet pain test. *Pain*, **3**, 105–110.

Stevens, S.S. (1957) On the psychophysical law. *Psychological Review*, **64**, 153–181.

Stevens, S.S. (1958) Problems and methods of psychophysics. *Psychological Bulletin*, **55**, 177–196.

Stimson, G.V. (1974) Obeying doctors' orders: a view from the other side. *Social Science and Medicine*, **8**(2), 97–104.

Stjernsward, J. (1993) Palliative medicine – a global perspective. In D. Doyle, G.W.C. Hanks and N. MacDonald (Eds), *Oxford Textbook of Palliative Medicine*, Oxford University Press, Oxford, pp.803–816.

Storms, M.D. and McCaul, K.D. (1976) Attribution processes and emotional exacerbation of dysfunctional behaviour. In J.H. Harvey, W.J. Ickes and R.F. Kidd (Eds), *New Directions in Attribution Research*, Laurence Erlbaum, Hillsdale, New Jersey, pp.143–164.

Storms, M.D. and Nisbett, R.E. (1970) Insomnia and the attribution process. *Journal of Personality and Social Psychology*, **16**, 319–328.

Sturgis, E.T., Schaefer, C.A. and Sikora, T.L. (1984) Pain centre follow-up study of treated and untreated patients. *Archives of Physical Medicine and Rehabilitation*, **65**, 303.

Suchman, E.A. (1965) Stages of illness and medical care. *Journal of Health and Social Behaviour*, **6**, 114–128.

Sullivan, M.J.L., Reesor, K., Mikhail, S. and Fisher, R. (1992) The treatment of depression in chronic low back pain: review and recommendations. *Pain*, **50**, 5–13.

Suls, J. (1982) Social support, interpersonal relations and health – benefits and liabilities. In G.S. Sanders and J. Suls (Eds), *The Social Psychology of Health and Illness*, Laurence Erlbaum, Hillsdale, New Jersey, Chapter 9, p.255.

Suls, J. and Fletcher, B. (1985) The relative efficacy of avoidant and non-avoidant coping strategies: a meta-analysis. *Health Psychology*, **4**(3), 249–288.

Suls, J. and Mullen, B. (1981) Life events, perceived control and illness: the role of uncertainty. *Journal of Human Stress*, **7**, 30–34.

Suls, J. and Wan, C.K. (1989) Effects of sensory and procedural information on coping with stressful medical procedures and pain: a meta-analysis. *Journal of Consulting and Clinical Psychology*, **57**(3), 372–379.

Sunderland, S. (1978) The painful sequelae of injuries to peripheral nerves. In S. Sunderland (Ed.), *Nerves and Nerve Injuries*, 2nd edn, Churchill Livingstone, Edinburgh, Chapter 34.

Susser, M.W. and Watson, W. (1971) *Sociology in Medicine*, 2nd edn, Oxford Medical Publications, Oxford.

Svarstad, B.L. (1976) Physician–patient communication and patient conformity with medical advice. In D. Mechanic (Ed.), *The Growth of Bureaucratic Medicine*, John Wiley and Sons, New York, pp.220–238.

Swanson, D.W. and Maruta, T. (1980) Patients complaining of extreme pain. *Mayo Clinic Proceedings*, **55**, 563–566.

Swanson, D.W., Maruta, T. and Wolff, V.A. (1986) Ancient pain. *Pain*, **25**, 383–387.

Swanston, M., Abraham, C., Macrae, W.A., Walker, A., Rushmer, R., Elder, L. and Methuen, H. (1993) Pain assessment with interactive computer animation. *Pain*, **53**, 347–351.

Swartzman, L.C., Gwadry, F.G., Shapiro, A.P. and Teasell, R.W. (1994) The factor structure of the Coping Strategies Questionnaire. *Pain*, **57**, 311–316.

Sweeney, P.D., Anderson, K.O. and Bailey, S. (1986) Attributional style in depression: a meta-analytic review. *Journal of Personality and Social Psychology*, **50**(5), 974–991.

Swerdlow, M. (1982) Medico-legal aspects of complications following pain relieving blocks. *Pain*, **13**, 321–331.

Szasz, T. (1968) The psychology of persistent pain – a portrait of *l'homme douloureux*. In A. Soulairac, J. Cahn and J. Charpentier (Eds), *Pain*, Academic Press, New York, pp.93–111.

Taenzer, P., Melzack, R. and Jeans, M.E. (1986) Influence of psychological factors on postoperative pain, mood and analgesic requirements. *Pain*, **24**, 331–342.

Tait, R.C., Chibnall, J.T. and Richardson, W.D. (1990) Litigation and employment status: effects on patients with chronic pain. *Pain*, **43**, 37–46.

Tajfel, H. (1978) *Differentiation between Social Groups: Studies in the Social Psychology of Intergroup Relations*, Academic Press, London.

Takeda, F. (1991) WHO cancer pain relief programme. In M.R. Bond, J.E. Charlton and C.J. Woolf (Eds), *Proceedings of the VIth World Congress on Pain*, Elsevier, Amsterdam, pp.467–474.

Tan, S.Y. (1983) Cognitive and cognitive–behavioural methods for pain control: a selective review. *Pain*, **12**(3), 201–228.

Taylor, S.E. (1979) Hospital patient behaviour: reactance, helplessness or control? *Journal of Social Issues*, **35**, 156–184.

Taylor, S.E. and Brown, J.D. (1988) Illusion and well-being: a social psychology perspective on mental health. *Psychological Bulletin*, **103**(2), 193–210.

Taylor, S.E., Lichtman, R.R. and Wood, J.V. (1984) Attributions, beliefs about control and adjustment to breast cancer. *Journal of Personality and Social Psychology*, **46**(3), 489–502.

Taylor, S.E., Wood, J.V. and Lichtman, R.R. (1983) It could be worse: selective evaluation as a response to victimisation. *Journal of Social Issues*, **39**, 19–40.

Taylor, S.E., Falke, R.L., Shoptaw, S.J. and Lichtman, R.R. (1986) Social support, support groups and the cancer patient. *Journal of Consulting and Clinical Psychology*, **54**(5), 608–615.

Tearnan, B.H. and Dar, R. (1986) Physician ratings of pain descriptors: potential diagnostic utility. *Pain*, **26**(1), 45–51.

Teasdale, J.D. (1983) Negative thinking in depression: cause, effect or reciprocal relationship? *Advanced Behaviour Research and Therapy*, **5**, 3–25.

Teasdale, J.D. (1985) Psychological treatments for depression – how do they work? *Behaviour Research and Therapy*, **23**(2), 157–165.

Telles, J.L. and Pollack, M.H. (1981) Feeling sick – the experience and legitimation of illness. *Social Science and Medicine*, **15A**, 243–251.

Terenius, L. (1981) Endorphins and pain. *Frontiers of Hormone Research*, **8**, 162–177.

Thomas, K. (1981) Comparative risk perception: how the public perceives the risks and benefits of energy systems. *Proceedings of the Royal Society of London, A*, **376**, 35–60.

Thompson, J.K. and Adams, H.E. (1984) Psychophysiological characteristics of headache patients. *Pain*, **18**, 41–52.

Thompson, S.C. (1981) Will it hurt less if I can control it? A complex answer to a simple question. *Psychological Bulletin*, **90**(1), 89–101.

Thompson, S.C. and Pitts, J.S. (1992) In sickness and in health: chronic illness, marriage and spousal caregiving. In S. Spacapan and S. Oskamp (Eds), *Helping and Being Helped: Naturalistic Studies*, Sage, Newbury Park, California, p.115.

Titchener, E.B. (1920) Notes from the psychology laboratory at Cornell University. *American Journal of Psychology*, **31**(4), 212.

Tolle, T.R., Castro-Lopez, J.M., Evan, G. and Zieglgansberger, W. (1991) C-fos induction in the spinal cord following noxious stimulations: prevention by opiates but not by NMDA antagonists. In M.R. Bond, J.E. Charlton and C.J. Woolf (Eds), *Proceedings of the VIth World Congress on Pain*, Elsevier, Amsterdam, pp.299–305.

Toomey, T.C., Ghia, J.N., Mao, W. and Gregg, J.W. (1977) Acupuncture and chronic pain mechanisms: the moderating effects of affect, personality and stress on response to treatment. *Pain*, **3**(2), 137–145.

Toomey, T.C., Mann, J.D., Abashian, S and Thompson-Pope, S. (1991) Relationship between perceived self-control of pain, pain description and functioning. *Pain*, **45**, 129–133.

Torgerson, W.S. and Ben Debba, M. (1983) The structure of pain descriptors. In R. Melzack (Ed.), *Pain Measurement and Assessment*, Raven Press, New York, pp.49–54.

Trief, P. and Stein, N. (1985) Pending litigation and rehabilitation outcome of chronic back pain. *Archives of Physical Medicine and Rehabilitation*, **66**, 95–99.

Triplett, N. (1897) The dynamogenic factors in pacemaking and competition. *American Journal of Psychology*, **9**, 507–633.

Tuckett, D.A., Boulton, M. and Olsen, C. (1985) A new approach to the measurement of patients' understanding of what they are told in medical consultations. *Journal of Health and Social Behaviour*, **26**, 27–38.

Turk, D.C. and Flor, H. (1987) Pain behaviours: the utility and limitations of the pain behaviour construct. *Pain*, **31**, 277–295.

Turk, D.C. and Rudy, T.E. (1986) Assessment of cognitive factors in chronic pain: a worthwhile enterprise. *Journal of Consulting and Clinical Psychology*, **54**(6), 760–768.

Turk, D.C. and Rudy, T.E. (1988) Towards an empirically derived taxonomy of chronic pain patients: integration of psychological assessment data. *Journal of Consulting and Clinical Psychology*, **56**(2), 233–238.

Turk, D.C. and Rudy, T.E. (1990) Neglected factors in chronic pain treatment outcome studies – referral patterns, failure to enter treatment and attrition. *Pain*, **43**(1), 7–25.

Turk, D.C. and Rudy, T.E. (1991) Neglected factors in the treatment of chronic pain patients – relapse, non-compliance and adherence enhancement. *Pain*, **44**, 5–28.

Turk, D.C., Flor, H. and Rudy, T.E. (1987) Pain and families – I: etiology, maintenance and psychosocial impact. *Pain*, **30**, 3–27.

Turk, D.C., Meichenbaum, D. and Genest, M. (1983) *Pain and Behavioral Medicine: A Cognitive–Behavioural Perspective*, Guilford Press, New York.

Turk, D.C., Rudy, T.E. and Salovey, P. (1985) The McGill Pain Questionnaire reconsidered: confirming the factor structure and examining appropriate uses. *Pain*, **21**, 385–397.

Turk, D.C., Rudy, T.E. and Salovey, P. (1986) Implicit models of illness. *Journal of Behavioral Medicine*, **9**(5), 453–475.

Turk, D.C., Rudy, T.E., and Sorkin, B.S. (1993) Neglected topics in chronic pain treatment outcome studies: determination of success. *Pain*, **53**, 9–16.

Turk, D.C., Rudy, T.E. and Stieg, R.L. (1987) Chronic pain and depression. *Pain Management*, **1**, 17–25.

Turk, D.C., Rudy, T.E. and Stieg, R.L. (1988) The disability determination dilemma: toward a multiaxial solution. *Pain*, **34**, 217–229.

Turk, D.C., Salovey, P. and Litt, M.D. (1986) Adherence: a cognitive–behavioural perspective. In K.E. Gerber and A.M. Nehemkis (Eds), *Compliance – The Dilemma of the Chronically Ill*, Springer-Verlag, New York, 44–72.

Turk, D.C., Wack, J.T. and Kerns, R.D. (1985) An empirical examination of the pain behaviour construct. *Journal of Behavioral Medicine*, **8**(2), 119–130.

Turk, D.C., Litt, M.D., Salovey, P. and Walker, J. (1985) Seeking urgent paediatric treatment: factors contributing to frequency, delay and appropriateness. *Health Psychology*, **4**(1), 43–59.

Turner, J.A. (1991) Coping and chronic pain. In M.R. Bond, J.E. Charlton and C.J. Woolf (Eds), *Proceedings of the VIth World Congress on Pain*, Elsevier, Amsterdam, pp.219–227.

Turner, J.A. and Chapman, C.R. (1982a) Psychological interventions for chronic pain: a critical review – II: Operant conditioning, hypnosis and cognitive behavioural therapy. *Pain*, **12**, 23–46.

Turner, J.A. and Chapman, C.R. (1982b) Psychological interventions for chronic pain: a critical review – I: Relaxation training and biofeedback. *Pain*, **12**, 1–22.

Turner, J.A. and Clancy, S.L. (1986) Strategies for coping with chronic low back pain: relationship to pain and disability. *Pain*, **24**, 355–364.

Turner, J.A. and Clancy, S.L. (1988) Comparison of operant behavioural and cognitive–behavioural group treatment for chronic low back pain. *Journal of Consulting and Clinical Psychology*, **56**(2), 261–266.

Turner, J.A. and Jensen, M.P. (1993) Efficacy of cognitive therapy for chronic low back pain. *Pain*, **52**, 169–177.

Turner, J.A., Calsyn, D.A., Fordyce, W.E. and Ready, L.B. (1982) Drug utilisation patterns in chronic pain patients. *Pain*, **12**, 357–363.

Turner, R.J. and Noh, S. (1988) Physical disability and depression: a longitudinal analysis. *Journal of Health and Social Behaviour*, **29**, 23–37.

Tversky, A. and Kahneman, D. (1973) Availability: a heuristic for judging frequency and probability. *Cognitive Psychology*, 5, 207–232.

Tversky, A. and Kahneman, D. (1974) Judgement under uncertainty: heuristics and biases. *Science*, 185, 1124–1131.

Tversky, A. and Kahneman, D. (1982) Judgements of and by representativeness. In D. Kahneman, P. Slovic and A. Tversky (Eds), *Judgements under Uncertainty: Heuristics and Biases*, Cambridge University Press, New York, 84–98.

Twaddle, A.C. (1969) Health decisions and sick role variations: an exploration. *Journal of Health and Social Behaviour*, 10, 105–114.

Twaddle, A.C. (1980) Sickness and the sickness career: some implications. In L. Eisenberg and A. Kleinman (Eds), *The Relevance of Social Science for Medicine*. Reidel Publications, Place, pp.111–133.

Twycross, R.G. and Fairfield, S. (1982) Pain in far advanced cancer. *Pain*, 14, 303–310.

Twycross, R.G. and Lack, S.A. (1983) *Symptom Control in Far Advanced Cancer – Pain Relief*, Pitman, Bath.

Tyrer, S.P., Capon, M., Peterson, D.M., Charlton, J.E. and Thompson, J.W. (1989) The detection of psychiatric illness and psychological handicaps in a British pain population. *Pain*, 36, 63–74.

Valins, S. and Nisbett, R.E. (1972) Attribution processes in the development and treatment of emotional disorders. In E.E. Jones, D.E. Kanouse, H.H. Kelley, R.E. Nisbett, S. Valins and B. Weiner (Eds), *Attribution: Perceiving the Causes of Behaviour*. General Learning Press, Morristown, New Jersey, 119–134.

Van der Does, A.J.W. (1989) Patients' and nurses' ratings of pain and anxiety during burn wound care. *Pain*, 39, 95–101.

Van Hees, J. and Gybels, J.M. (1972) Pain related to single afferent C-fibres from human skin. *Brain Research*, 48, 397–400.

Ventafridda, V. (1989) Continuing care: a major issue in cancer pain management. *Pain*, 36, 137–143.

Verbrugge, L.M. (1989) The twain meet: empirical explanations of sex differences in health and mortality. *Journal of Health and Social Behaviour*, 30, 282–304.

Verbrugge, L.M. and Steiner, R.P. (1984) Another look at physicians' treatment of men and women with common complaints. *Sex Roles*, II, 11–12.

Verbrugge, L.M. and Steiner, R.P. (1985) Prescribing drugs to men and women. *Health Psychology*, 4(1), 79–98.

Vincent, C.A. and Richardson, P.H. (1986) The evaluation of therapeutic acupuncture: concepts and methods. *Pain*, 24, 1–13.

Viney, L.L. (1983) *Images of Illness*, Krieger, Malabar, Florida.

Viney, L.L. (1986) Expression of positive emotion by people who are physically ill: is it evidence of defending or coping? *Journal of Psychosomatic Research*, 30(1), 27–34.

Viney, L.L. and Westbrook, M.T. (1982) Coping with chronic illness: the mediating role of biographic and illness-related factors. *Journal of Psychosomatic Research*, 26(6), 595–605.

Vinokur, A., Schul, J. and Caplan, R.D. (1987) Determinants of perceived social support: interpersonal transactions, personal outlook and transient affective states. *Journal of Personality and Social Psychology*, 53(6), 1137–1145.

Violon, A. and Giurgea, D. (1984) Familial models for chronic pain. *Pain*, 18, 199–203.

Vlaeyen, J.W.S., Van Eek, H., Groenman, N.H. and Schuerman, J.A. (1987) Dimensions and components of observed chronic pain behaviour. *Pain*, 31, 65–75.

Vlaeyen, J.W.S., Pernot, D.F.M., Kole-Snijders, A.M.J., Schuerman J.A., Van Eek, H. and Groenman, N.H. (1990) Assessment of the components of observed chronic pain behaviour: the Checklist for Interpersonal Pain Behaviour (CHIP). *Pain*, 43, 337–347.

Volinn, E., Lai, D., McKinney, S. and Loeser, J.D. (1988) When back pain becomes disabling: a regional analysis. *Pain*, **33**, 33–39.

von Baeyer, C.L. and Genest, M. (1985) Role of psychologists in Canadian pain centres. *Canadian Psychology*, **26**(2), 140–147.

von Baeyer, C.L., Johnson, M.E. and McMillan, M.J. (1984) Consequences of non-verbal expression of pain: patient distress and observer concern. *Social Science and Medicine*, **19**(12), 1319–1324.

von Knorring, L., Perris, C., Eisemann, M., Eriksson, U. and Perris, H. (1983) Pain as a symptom in depressive disorders – I: Relationship to diagnostic subgroup and depressive symptomatology. *Pain*, **15**, 19–26.

von Korff, M. (1994) Perspectives on management of back pain in primary care. In G.F. Gebhart, D.L. Hammond and T.S. Jensen (Eds), *Proceedings of the VII World Congress on Pain: Progress in Pain Research Management*, Vol. 2, IASP Press, Seattle.

von Korff, M., Le Resche, L. and Dworkin, S.F. (1993) First onset of common pain symptoms: a prospective study of depression as a risk factor. *Pain*, **55**, 251–258.

von Korff, M., Dworkin, S.F., Le Resche, L. and Kruger, A. (1988) An epidemiological comparison of pain complaints. *Pain*, **32**, 173–183.

von Korff, M., Ormel, J., Keefe, F.J. and Dworkin, S.F. (1992) Grading the severity of chronic pain. *Pain*, **50**, 133–149.

Voudouris, N.J., Peck, C.L. and Coleman, G. (1990) The role of conditioning and verbal expectancy in the placebo response. *Pain*, **43**, 121–128.

Waddell, G., Pilowsky, I. and Bond, M.R. (1989) Clinical assessment and interpretation of abnormal illness behaviour in low back pain. *Pain*, **39**, 41–53.

Waddell, G., Main, C.J., Morris, E.W., di Paola, M. and Gray, I.C.M. (1984) Chronic low back pain, psychologic distress and illness behaviour. *Spine*, **9**(2), 209–213.

Wade, J.B., Price, D.D., Hamer, R.M., Schwartz, S.M. and Hart, R.P. (1990) An emotional component analysis of chronic pain. *Pain*, **40**, 303–310.

Wade, J.B., Dougherty, L.M., Hart, R.P. and Cook, D.B. (1992) Patterns of normal personality structure among chronic pain patients. *Pain*, **48**, 37–43.

Wagener, J.J. and Taylor, S.E. (1986) What else could I have done? Patients' responses to failed treatment decisions. *Health Psychology*, **5**(5), 481–496.

Waitzkin, H. (1985) Information giving in medical care. *Journal of Health and Social Behaviour*, **26**, 81–101.

Walker, P. (1992) Are QALYs going to be useful to me, a purchaser of health services. In A.H. Hopkins (Ed.), *Measures of the Quality of Life and the Uses to which Such Measures May Be Put*, Royal College of Physicians, London, Chapter 5.

Wall, P.D. (1979) On the relation of injury to pain. *Pain*, **6**, 253–264.

Wall, P.D. (1983) Introduction. In P.D. Wall and R. Melzack (Eds), *Textbook of Pain*, 1st edn, Churchill Livingstone, Edinburgh.

Wall, P.D. (1988) The prevention of post-operative pain. *Pain*, **33**, 289–290.

Wall, P.D. (1989) Introduction. In P.D. Wall and R. Melzack (Eds), *Textbook of Pain*, 2nd edn, Churchill Livingstone, Edinburgh.

Wall, P.D. (1991) Neurogenic pain syndromes and their management. In J.C.D. Wells and C.J. Woolf (Eds), *Pain Mechanisms and Management*, Churchill Livingstone, Edinburgh, pp.631–643.

Wall, P.D. (1992) The placebo effect: an unpopular topic. *Pain*, **51**, 1–3.

Wall, P.D. and McMahon, S.B. (1985) Microneurography and its relation to perceived sensation: a critical review. *Pain*, **21**, 209–229.

Wall, P.D. and Melzack, R. (Eds) (1983) *Textbook of Pain*, 1st edn, Churchill Livingstone, Edinburgh.

Wall, P.D. and Melzack, R. (1989) Why the definition of pain is crucial. In P.D. Wall and R. Melzack (Eds), *Textbook of Pain*, 2nd edn, Churchill Livingstone, Edinburgh, pp.11–38.

Wall, P.D. and Sweet, W.H. (1967) Temporary abolition of pain in man. *Science*, 155, 108–109.

Wallace, L. (1985) Surgical patients' expectations of pain and discomfort: does accuracy of expectations minimise post-surgical pain and distress? *Pain*, 22, 363–373.

Wallston, B.S. and Wallston, K.A. (1984) Social psychological models of health behaviour: an examination and integration. In A. Baum, E. Taylor and J.E. Singer (Eds), *Handbook of Psychology and Health*, Vol. 4, *Social Psychological Aspects of Health*, Laurence Erlbaum, Hillsdale, New Jersey.

Wallston, K.A. (1989) Control in chronic illness. Paper presented to the International Conference on Health Psychology, Cardiff.

Wallston, K.A. and Wallston, B.S. (1982) Who is responsible for your health? The construct of health locus of control. In G.S. Sanders and J. Suls (Eds), *The Social Psychology of Health and Illness*, Laurence Erlbaum, Hillsdale, New Jersey, p.65.

Wallston, K.A., Wallston, B.S. and De Vellis, R. (1978) Development of the Multidimensional Health Locus of Control (MHLC) scales. *Health Education Monographs*, 6, 161–170.

Ward, S.E., Goldberg, N., McCauley, V.M., Mueller, C., Nolan, A., Plank, D.P., Robbins, A., Stormoen, D. and Weissman, D.E. (1993) Pain related barriers to management of cancer pain. *Pain*, 52, 319–324.

Warnche, T., Breivik, H. and Vainio, A. (1994) Treatment of cancer pain in Norway: a questionnaire study. *Pain*, 57, 109–116.

Watson, D. and Kendall, P.C. (1983) Methodological issues in research on coping with chronic disease. In T.G. Burish and L.A. Bradley (Eds), *Coping with Chronic Disease: Research and Applications*, Academic Press, New York, pp.39–84.

Watson, D. and Pennebaker, J.W. (1991) Situational, dispositional and genetic bases of symptom reporting. In J.A. Skelton and R.T. Croyle (Eds), *Mental Representations of Health and Illness*, Springer-Verlag, New York, pp.60–84.

Watts, F.N. (1992) Is psychology falling apart? *The Psychologist*, 5(11), 489–494.

Weickgenant, A.L., Slater, M.A., Patterson, T.L., Atkinson, J.H., Grant, I. and Garfin, S.R. (1993) Coping activities in chronic low back pain: relationship with depression. *Pain*, 53, 95–103.

Weinberger, M., Tierney, W.M., Booker, P. and Katz, B.P. (1989) Can the provision of information to patients with osteoarthritis improve functional status? A randomised controlled trial. *Arthritis and Rheumatism*, 32(12), 1577.

Weiner, B. (1980) A cognitive (attribution)–emotion–action model of motivated behaviour – an analysis of judgements of help-giving. *Journal of Personality and Social Psychology*, 39(2), 186–200.

Weiner, B. (1985) An attributional theory of achievement, motivation and emotion. *Psychological Review*, 92(4), 548–575.

Weinman, J. and Higgins, P. (1975) How doctors try their patients. *Psychology Today*, 3, 49–54.

Weinman, J. and Johnston, M. (1987) Stressful medical procedures: on analysis of the effect of psychological interventions and the stressfulness of the procedures. In S. Maes, C. Spielberger, P. Defares and I.G. Sarason (Eds), *Topics in Health Psychology*, John Wiley and Sons, Chichester, pp.205–217.

Weinstein, N.D. (1983) Reducing unrealistic optimism about illness susceptibility. *Health Psychology*, 2(1), 11–20.

Weinstein, N.D. (1984) Why it won't happen to me: perceptions of risk factors and susceptibility. *Health Psychology*, 3(5), 431–457.

Weisenberg, M. (1977) Pain and pain control. *Psychological Bulletin*, 84, 1008–1044.

Weisenberg, M. (1980) Understanding pain phenomena. In S.J. Rachman (Ed.), *Contributions to Medical Psychology*, Vol. 2, Pergamon Press, Oxford, pp.77–109.

Weisenberg, M. (1987) Psychological intervention for the control of pain. *Behavioural Research and Therapy*, 25(4), 301–312.

Weisenberg, M. and Caspi, Z. (1989) Cultural and educational influences on pain of childbirth. *Journal of Pain and Symptom Management*, **4**(1), 13–19.

Weisenberg, M., Wolf, J., Mittwoch, T., Mikulincer, M. and Aviram, O. (1985) Subject vs experimenter control in the reaction to pain. *Pain*, **23**, 187–200.

Weiss, J.M. (1991) Stress-induced depression: critical neurochemical and electro-physiological changes. In J. Madden (Ed.), *Neurobiology of Learning, Emotion and Affect*, Raven Press, New York, pp.123–154.

Westbrook, M.T. and Viney, L.L. (1983) Age and sex differences in patients' reactions to illness. *Journal of Health and Social Behaviour*, **4**, 313–324.

White, L., Tursky, B. and Schwartz, G.E. (1985) Proposed synthesis of placebo models. In L. White, B. Tursky and G.E. Schwartz (Eds), *Placebo: Theory, Uses and Mechanisms*, Guilford Press, New York, pp.431–449.

Whitney, C.W. and von Korff, M. (1992) Regression to the mean in treated vs untreated chronic pain. *Pain*, **50**, 281–285.

WHO (1990) Cancer pain relief and palliative care: report of a WHO Expert Committee. Technical report series 804, World Health Organization, Geneva.

WHOQOL Group (1993) Study protocol for the World Health Organization project to develop a quality of life assessment instrument (WHOQOL), *Quality of Life Research*, **2**, 153–159.

Wiener, C. (1975) The burden of rheumatoid arthritis: tolerating the uncertainty. *Social Science and Medicine*, **9**, 97–104.

Wilcox, G.L. (1991) Excitatory neurotransmitters and pain. In M.R. Bond, J.E. Charlton and C.J. Woolf (Eds), *Proceedings of the VIth World Congress on Pain*, Elsevier, Amsterdam, pp.97–118.

Wilder-Smith, C.H. and Schuler, L. (1992) Postoperative analgesia: pain by choice? The influence of patient attitudes and patient education. *Pain*, **50**, 257–262.

Wilkie, D.J., Savendra, M.C., Holzemer, W.L., Tesler, M.D. and Paul, S.M. (1990) Use of the McGill Pain Questionnaire to measure pain: a meta-analysis. *Nursing Research*, **39**(1), 36.

Willer, J.C. (1983) Nociceptive flexion reflexes as a tool for pain research in man. In J.E. Desmedt (Ed.), *Motor Control Mechanisms in Health and Diseases*, Raven Press, New York, pp.809–827.

Williams, A.C. and Kind, P. (1992) The present state of play about QALYs. In A.H. Hopkins (Ed.), *Measures of the Quality of Life and the Uses to which Such Measures May Be Put*, Royal College of Physicians, London, pp.21–39.

Williams, A.C. and Richardson, P.H. (1993) What does the BDI measure in chronic pain? *Pain*, **55**, 259–266.

Williams, A.C., Nicholas, M.K., Richardson, P.H., Pither, C.E., Justins, D.M., Chamberlain, J.H., Harding, V.R., Rideout, K.L., Ralphs, J.A. and Diendorne, I. (1994) Inpatient vs outpatient pain management: results of a randomised controlled trial. In G.F. Gebhart, D.L. Hammond and T.S. Jensen (Eds), *Proceedings of the VII World Congress on Pain: Progress in Pain Research Management*, IASP Press, Seattle, p.138.

Williams, D.A. and Keefe, F.J. (1991) Pain beliefs and the use of cognitive–behavioural coping strategies. *Pain*, **46**, 185–190.

Williams, D.A. and Thorn, B.E. (1989) An empirical assessment of pain beliefs. *Pain*, **36**, 351–358.

Williams, J.M.G. and Scott, J. (1988) Autobiographical memory in depression. *Psychological Medicine*, **18**, 689–695.

Williams, R.C. (1988) Towards a set of reliable and valid measures for chronic pain assessment and outcome research. *Pain*, **35**, 239–251.

Williams, R.C. (1989) Perceptions of risk: the social consequences for the patient with chronic arthritis. Paper presented to the Forum on Medical Communication, Royal Society of Medicine, London.

Willis, W.D. (1985) *The Pain System – The Neural Basis of Nonceptive Transmission in the Mammalian Nervous System*, Karger Press, Basel.

Wills, T.A. (1981) Downward comparison principles in social psychology. *Psychological Bulletin*, **90**, 245–271.

Wills, T.A. (1991) Similarity and self esteem in downward comparison. In J. Suls and T.A. Wills (Eds), *Social Comparison: Contemporary Theory and Research*, Laurence Erlbaum, Hillsdale, New Jersey, pp.51–78.

Wills, T.A. (1992) The helping process in the context of personal relationships. In S. Spacapan and S. Oskamp (Eds), *Helping and Being Helped: Naturalistic Studies*, Sage, Newbury Park, California, p.17.

Wilson, J.F., Broclropp, G.W., Kryst, S., Steger, H. and Witt, W.O. (1992) Medical students' attitudes towards pain before and after a brief course on pain. *Pain*, **50**, 251–256.

Wilson, L., Dworkin, S.F., Whitney, C. and Le Resche, L. (1994) Somatization and pain dispersion in chronic temporomandibular disorder pain. *Pain*, **57**, 55–61.

Wilson, M.E. and Nerurkar, I.D.J. (1986) Flying kites – believing in a new drug. *Anaesthesia Points West*, **19**(1), 17–19.

Wilson-Barnett, J. (1976) Patients' emotional reactions to hospitalisation: an exploratory study. *Journal of Advanced Nursing*, **1**, 351–358.

Winefield, H.R., Katsikitis, M., Hart, L.M. and Rounsefell, B.F. (1990) Postoperative pain experiences: relevant patient and staff attitudes. *Journal of Psychosomatic Research*, **34**(5), 543–552.

Winkler, R., Underwood, D., Fatovich, B., James, R. and Gray, D. (1989) A clinical trial of a self-care approach to the management of chronic headache in general practice. *Social Science and Medicine*, **29**(2), 213–219.

Winn, D. (1991) Interview with A. Spence and C. Pither on pain. *Nursing Times*, 24 February.

Wolff, B.B. (1983) Methods of testing pain mechanisms in normal men. In P.D. Wall and R. Melzack (Eds), *Textbook of Pain*, 1st edn, Churchill Livingstone, Edinburgh, pp.186–194.

Wolff, B.B. (1985) Ethnocultural factors influencing pain and illness behaviour. *Clinical Journal of Pain*, **1**, 23–30.

Wood, J.V. (1989) Theory and research concerning social comparisons of personal attributes. *Psychological Bulletin*, **106**, 231–248.

Woodrow, R.M., Friedman, G.D., Siegelaub, A.B. and Collen, M.F. (1972) Pain tolerance: differences according to age, sex and race. *Psychosomatic Medicine*, **34**, 548–556.

Wooley, S.C., Blackwell, B. and Winget, C. (1978) A learning theory model of chronic illness behaviour: theory, treatment and research. *Psychosomatic Medicine*, **40**(5), 379–401.

Woolf, C.J. (1991) Central mechanisms of acute pain. In M.R. Bond, J.E. Charlton and C.J. Woolf (Eds), *Proceedings of the VIth World Congress on Pain*, Elsevier, Amsterdam, pp.25–34.

Woolf, C.J. and Wall, P.D. (1982) Chronic peripheral nerve section diminishes the primary afferent A-fibre mediated inhibition of rat dorsal horn neurones. *Brain Research*, **242**, 77–85.

Wortman, C.B. (1976) Causal attributions and personal control. In J.H. Harvey, W.J. Ickes and R.F. Kidd (Eds), *New Directions in Attribution Research*, Laurence Erlbaum, Hillsdale, New Jersey, pp.23–52.

Wortman, C.B. and Dunkel-Schetter, C. (1979) Interpersonal relationships and cancer: a theoretical analysis. *Journal of Social Issues*, **35**, 120–155.

Wortman, C.B. and Silver, R.C. (1989) The myths of coping with loss. *Journal of Consulting and Clinical Psychology*, **57**(3), 349–357.

Wright, G. (1984) *Behavioural Decision Theory – An Introduction*, Penguin, Harmondsworth.

Yelin, E., Henke, C. and Epstein, W. (1987) The work dynamics of the person with rheumatoid arthritis. *Arthritis and Rheumatism*, **30**(5), 507–512.

Zarkowska, E. and Philips, H.C. (1986) Recent onset vs persistent pain: evidence for a distinction. *Pain*, **25**, 365–372.

Zborowski, M (1952) Cultural components in responses to pain. *Journal of Social Issues*, **8**, 16–30.

Zborowski, M. (1969) *People in Pain*. Jossey-Bass, San Francisco, California.

Zimmerman, M. (1983) Ethical guidelines for investigations of experimental pain in conscious animals. *Pain*, **16**, 109–110.

Zola, I.K. (1966) Culture and symptoms – an analysis of patients presenting complaints. *American Sociological Review*, **31**, 615–630.

Zola, I.K. (1977) Healthism and disabling medicalization. In I. Illich I.K. Zola, J. McKnight, J. Caplan and H. Shaker (Eds), *Disabling Professions*, Marion Boyers, London, pp.41–67.

Zola, I.K. (1983) *Some Medical Inquiries: Recollections, Reflections and Reconsiderations*, Temple University Press, Philadelphia, Pennsylvania.

Index

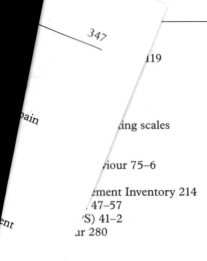